SAMUEL JOHNSON

Books by W. Jackson Bate

BIOGRAPHIES

The Achievement of Samuel Johnson (1955)
John Keats (1963)
Coleridge (1968)

STUDIES IN STYLE

The Stylistic Development of Keats (1945)

WORKS ON LITERARY THEORY AND
THE HISTORY OF IDEAS

From Classic to Romantic (1946)
Criticism: the Major Texts (1952)
Prefaces to Criticism (1959)
The Burden of the Past and the English Poet (1970)

EDITOR

Yale Edition of Johnson
(Vols. II, III, IV, and V)
Edmund Burke

Johnson at sixty

An etching by Mary Palgrave Turner
based on the portrait by Ozias Humphry

Samuel Johnson

W. Jackson Bate

COUNTERPOINT

WASHINGTON, D.C.

LIBRARY OF CONGRESS CATALOGING-IN-PUBLICATIONS DATA

Bate, Walter Jackson. 1918 –
    Samuel Johnson / W. Jackson Bate. — 1st Counterpoint pbk. ed
    (   )
    "Originally published in 1975 by Harcourt Brace Jovanovich, New York and
London"— T.p. verso.
    Includes bibliographical references and index.
    1. Johnson, Samuel. 1709–1784. 2. Great Britian — Intellectual life — 18th
century. 3. Authors, English — 18th century — Bibliography. 4. Lexicographers —
Great Britian — Biography.   I. Title
PR3533.B334 1998
828'.609—dc21
[B]   97-47734

ISBN 1-887178-76-7 (alk. paper)

Cover design by Wesley B. Tanner/Passim Editions

Printed in the United States of America on acid-free paper that meets the
American National Standards Institute Z39-48 Standard.

COUNTERPOINT
P.O. Box 65793
Washington, D.C. 20035-5793
Counterpoint is a member of the Perseus Books Group.

10 9 8 7 6 5 4 3 2 1

FIRST PRINTING

To
the memory of my friend
GEOFFREY TILLOTSON,
forever associated with the years
when I began to love Johnson

What is your warrant for valuing any part of my experience and rejecting the rest? . . . If I had done so, you would never have heard my name.

—Pythagoras

Contents

Contents

Illustrations

Johnson in his late thirties
(*mezzotint by George Zobel after the Reynolds painting*)

Frank Barber   (*Richard Cosway*)

Inner Temple Lane   (*E. Findlay*)

Boswell at twenty-five   (*George Willison*)

Imagined scene of The Club at Reynolds's house
(*James Doyle*)

Johnson's house in Johnson's Court

Hester Thrale   (*Richard Cosway*)

Henry Thrale   (*Sir Joshua Reynolds*)

The Thrale Brewery, Southwark   (*Dean Wolstenholme*)

Mrs. Thrale and her daughter Hester (Queeney)
(*Sir Joshua Reynolds*)

Streatham Park   (*William Ellis*)

Johnson's house in Bolt Court

John Taylor

Johnson in his seventies   (*John Opie*)

Ashbourne Hall

Reynolds's last portrait of Johnson

Death mask of Johnson

Acknowledgments

Thanks are due to the following: Mary Hyde for illustrations from the Hyde Collection of paintings (1, 9, 25, 26, 27), copies of paintings (16, 17), prints or engravings (3, 5, 7, 10, 11, 12, 14, 29, 31), and photographs (2, 6, 8, 13, 15, 18, 21, 23, 24); Arthur Houghton (20, 30); the Metropolitan Museum (4); Haverford College (34); the National Portrait Gallery (35); the Johnson Birthplace (32, 33); the Johnson House, Gough Square (19); the Scottish National Portrait Gallery (22); and the Beaverbrook Art Gallery in Fredericton, New Brunswick (28).

Preface to the 1998 Edition

I am grateful to Counterpoint, and more especially to its publisher Frank Pearl and its editor Jack Shoemaker, for selecting this book to join the distinguished list of works it has published.

I was introduced to Samuel Johnson as a freshman in a writing course, when a teacher read aloud some paragraphs from the great *Preface to Shakespeare* as an example of superb English style. Ever since, Johnson has meant more to me than any other writer; but the reasons have changed. In college and for many years afterward I was in love with generalizations, general truths, which clarified and commanded the confusion of lived experience. I saw that Johnson liked them too, partly for similar reasons; and to me his mind and also his use of his mind were exemplary and inspiring–his coming back to human moral need, his bedrock essentialism. I was not then aware of the chaos of personal emotion and existential struggle from which Johnson's generalizations emerged like lighthouses above the sea–illness, extreme poverty, severe psychological threats, multitudinous unhappy experience. As I became more sensitive to this, I valued Johnson also for his heroic personal battle and–as I see it–his precarious but triumphant victory against immense odds, a victory that is meaningful for all of us since it fosters hope, and fascinating because it is also intertwined with his enormous gift for humor and wit. That Johnson's wisdom was hard won in experience is what makes it so deeply felt and practical, and it is still applicable after two centuries, serving as a prototype of what was the original Latin meaning for our very word *experience* (*ex periculo*: something wrung from peril, danger, and actual trial).

The present book is written as a product of my admiration of Johnson. Without being less of an intellectual inspiration, he has also become a great moral one. While I admire Johnson as Plutarch did the subjects of his biographies, I have come to prize Johnson as an allegory of human life itself–the largest, most varied, engaging, but also appalling and unpredictable example of it that I have encountered.

June 1998

Preface

Johnson loved biography before every other kind of writing. It gives us, he said, "what comes near to us, what we can turn to use." He believed that hardly a single life had passed from which we could not learn something, if only it were told with complete honesty. He was thinking how isolated and compartmentalized all of us really are, and how much we all need—all the more as we reach middle age, and increasingly begin to face the fact of our disappearance—to touch hands with others, to learn from each other's experience and to get whatever encouragement we can.

He was especially concerned to find out how those whom we consider great experiencing natures ever managed to become what they were—what they had to struggle against, and, above all, what they had to struggle against in themselves. As he said to Edmond Malone, the Shakespearean scholar, in talking about "the uses of biography":

> If nothing but the bright side of characters should be shewn, we should sit down in despondency, and think it utterly impossible to imitate them in *anything*. The sacred writers (he observed) related the vicious as well as the virtuous actions of men; which had this moral effect, that it kept mankind from *despair*.

But if we want to know frankly and concretely the difficulties they faced, we also want to know how they surmounted them. There is "no substitute," as Alfred North Whitehead said, for direct perception of concrete achievement "in its actuality . . . with a high light thrown on what is relevant to its preciousness." This is what biography, as Johnson believed, can do for us as nothing else can.

Johnson's own conception of the "uses" of biography changed the whole course of biography for the modern world. One by-product was the most famous single work of biographical art in the whole of literature, Boswell's *Life of Johnson*, and there were many other memoirs and biographies of a similar kind written on Johnson after his death. This is why Johnson quickly became a household name, and has remained so ever since. But this would never have happened if Johnson had not been what he was—a heroic, intensely honest, and articulate pilgrim in the strange adventure of human life.

The biographer of Johnson has immense advantages. Yet there are special difficulties also, and two of them should be mentioned at the start, for they account for some of the characteristics of this book.

For no one else so famous is there such a disparity in sheer bulk of materials between what is known of the first forty or fifty years of his life and what can be known of his remaining years. I have often thought of the shape of these materials as resembling an Eskimo igloo: a long, low entrance down to the age of forty or so, and then a slowly rising dome, reaching its height in Johnson's sixties. Boswell's *Life of Johnson* reflects this. A small fraction of it takes Johnson to his fifties. Then the amount of detail—less in biographical fact than in the treasury of conversations Boswell heard and transcribed—begins to increase. The task of the modern biographer in dealing with the first forty to fifty years is the reverse of what he faces later. During the first two-thirds of Johnson's life, the closest scrutiny of every discoverable detail is necessary in order to fill out the picture. Thereafter the biographer faces a veritable mountain of material—not only in information about Johnson's personal life but also in the publications and, above all, the recorded conversations—and his major problem here is to select and distill as honestly as he can.

A second problem for the biographer of any writer is created by the radical split, which began in the 1930's and 1940's, between "literary biography" and "literary criticism." This polarization is still with us, especially in the English-speaking world. Throughout this time it has been taken for granted that a biographer of Lincoln will deal with the political context and the American Civil War; a biographer of Newton will try to look closely at Newton's actual work; or a biographer of Handel or Mozart will dwell in detail on the music they wrote. This, after all, is the reason they are great. Only with writers was it assumed that there should be a division of labor: that the "biographer" should stay clear of critical discussion of the writer's works, and that the "critic" should tiptoe around biography and history, and focus only on the text before him without the rich but embarrassing complexities of what it meant to be a living person. If we are to find our way into the inner life of a great writer, we must try to heal this split between "biography" and "criticism," and remember that a very large part of the "inner life" of a writer—what deeply preoccupied him, and made him a great writer—was his concern and effort, his hope and fear, in what he wrote. Hence a fair portion of this biography concentrates on Johnson's writing, especially at important moments of his work, though I cannot hope to offer the kind of distilled discussion of Johnson's writings that would be possible if this book considered nothing else.

This book would have been impossible without the authoritative writings and often the direct help and encouragement of many eminent Johnsonians and scholars of eighteenth-century literature during the past thirty years. Several of them are personal friends, and with some of them I have also had the good fortune to collaborate in editing the Yale Edition of Johnson: Mary Hyde, James Clifford, Gwin Kolb, Bertrand Bronson, Robert Halsband, W. R. Keast, H. W. Liebert, Jean Hagstrum, Donald Greene, Allen Hazen, Arthur Sherbo, John Middendorf, Leopold Damrosch, and Albrecht Strauss. To this list I should add six other Johnsonians who befriended and encouraged me but are no longer alive: L. F. Powell, Donald Hyde, Sir Sydney Roberts, George Sherburn, W. K. Wimsatt, and F. W. Hilles, the last two of whom had expected to go over the final version of this book but died just before it was completed. Acknowledgment and thanks for the use of illustrations, most of them from the Hyde Collection, are printed at the end of the List of Illustrations.

My debt to Mary Hyde is particularly large as well as long-standing. For years the famous Hyde Collection of Johnson has been made generously available to me. Moreover, from the time I began this book, Mrs. Hyde has helped me at every stage of the work, reading and criticizing in detail each chapter as it was written. Among others who read the manuscript, criticized it closely, and preserved me from blunders, I should mention especially Douglas Bush, David Perkins, and James Engell.

I have dedicated this book to the memory of Geoffrey Tillotson, who died in 1969. When I first met him in London just after the close of the war, he was already, in his early forties, one of the greatest scholars of eighteenth-century literature. I had not thought it possible for so eminent a man to be so kind to a comparative beginner who was also a stranger. But so he was during that summer of 1947, and again when he came to Harvard a few months later in order to teach there for a term. It was to him that I first confided my hope to write a life of Johnson, though only after I had tried my hand at other biographical writing. From 1947 until the winter of 1968, when I last saw him, I never arrived in London without immediately telephoning him. Then within an hour we would meet and begin talking, almost every afternoon for two or three weeks, of the eighteenth-century England he so loved and of Johnson in particular. Forever, when I think of London, Geoffrey will be walking across Russell Square from Birkbeck College, and I shall be hurrying to meet him.

W. J. B.

Harvard University
Cambridge, Massachusetts

Part I

THE FORMATIVE YEARS

Chapter 1

Birth and Family; Early Illness

Samuel Johnson has fascinated more people than any other writer except Shakespeare. Statesmen, lawyers, and physicians quote him, as do writers and scientists, philosophers and farmers, manufacturers and leaders of labor unions. For generations people have been discovering new details about him and re-examining and correcting old ones. Interest in Johnson is by no means confined to the English-speaking world, though naturally it is strongest there. In Asia, Africa, and South America, groups of Johnsonians meet every year to talk about every aspect of him. The reason why Johnson has always fascinated so many people of different kinds is not simply that Johnson is so vividly picturesque and quotable, though these are the qualities that first catch our attention. The deeper secret of his hypnotic attraction, especially during our own generation, lies in the immense reassurance he gives to human nature, which needs—and quickly begins to value—every friend it can get.

To begin with, there is the moving parable of his own life. "Example," says the proverb, "is the greatest of teachers." As in the archetypal stories in folklore, we have a hero who starts out with everything against him, including painful liabilities of personal temperament—a turbulent imagination, acute anxiety, aggressive pride, extreme impatience, radical self-division and self-conflict. He is compelled to wage long and desperate struggles, at two crucial times of his life, against what he feared was the onset of insanity. Yet step by step, often in the hardest possible way, he wins through to the triumph of honesty to experience that all of us prize in our hearts. This is why, as we get to know him better, we begin to think of him as almost an allegorical figure, like "Valiant-for-truth" in the *Pilgrim's Progress*. The greatest writers, as Keats remarked about Shakespeare, lead "a life of Allegory": their "works are the comments on it." But their lives become allegorical for us because the writers are so deeply akin to us. "His soul," said Mrs. Thrale of Johnson, "was not different than that of another person"; it was simply "greater."

One of the first effects he has on us is that we find ourselves catching, by contagion, something of his courage. As Aristotle said, courage is first among the human virtues because without it we are not very likely to practice the other virtues. Johnson, time and again, walks up to almost every anxiety and fear the human heart can feel. As he puts his hands directly upon it and looks at it closely, the lion's skin falls off, and we often find beneath it only a donkey, maybe only a frame of wood. This is why we so often find ourselves laughing as we read what he has to say. We laugh partly through sheer relief. His honesty to human experience cuts through the "cant," the loose talk and pretense, with which all of us get seduced into needlessly complicating life for both ourselves and other people. We laugh also at the unpredictability and novelty of Johnson's way of putting things. Constantly, as he expresses himself, we have the sense of a living originality—of the genuine personality of an experiencing nature—operating upon all the facts of life. This is why, in collections of famous quotations, Johnson so often ranks next to Shakespeare. As a friend of Johnson's once remarked, he "said even the commonest things in the newest manner."

But what continues to give such resonance to this honesty and courage is the combination of three other qualities rarely found together. One is Johnson's profound moral sincerity, which gives a powerful centrality and sense of purpose to all his thinking. The second is his practicality. He is unable to rest content with mere theory, however magnificently he can express it. Instead, in a way that no other writer on human life has ever equaled, he at once begins to think of the practical problems of What to do? and How to live? The third is his unrivaled range, whether he is talking about common domestic experiences—childhood and education, single life versus marriage, sickness, and death—or about the pursuit of money, or the hunger of the heart for importance, fame, or social standing. To no one since Shakespeare could we more truthfully apply what the ancient Greek epigram said of Plato: "In whatever direction we go, we meet him on his way back." What Coleridge called the "high road" of Shakespeare is, in all the greatest writers, the road home. Whatever we experience, we find Johnson has been there before us, and is meeting and returning home with us.

2

He was born at four o'clock in the afternoon of Wednesday, September 18, 1709,[1] in the town of Lichfield, Staffordshire, which then had a population of about three thousand. He was the first of two sons of a bookseller, Michael Johnson, and his wife, Sarah, who were both much older than parents usually are at the birth of their first child. Michael— a self-made man, large-framed and gaunt, conscientious, prone to melancholy—was by now fifty-two. Sarah, who prided herself that her family connections were socially superior to those of her husband, was forty. They had been married a little more than three years (June 19, 1706). Samuel's birth took place in the bedroom above Michael's shop, in their house, which still stands across from St. Mary's Church and overlooks the Market Square.

Owing to the age of Sarah Johnson, the birth was precarious. What we know of it comes from Johnson himself, who fifty-five years later, at a time of deep mental distress, was trying to steady his mind by getting a firm grasp on the facts of his own life. He started by writing down what he could remember, or remember being told, of his first years:[2] "My mother had a very difficult and dangerous labour, and was assisted by George Hector, a man-midwife of great reputation. I was born almost dead, and could not cry for some time." Hector, obviously worried as he picked up the silent child, tried to reassure the mother, saying, "Here is a brave boy." But the parents feared lest the child might not live, and arranged for him to be christened that same evening in the room where he was born.

Sarah, always conscious of her own family, wished the boy to be named after her older brother, Samuel Ford, just as she was later to ask that her second son be named after her younger brother, Nathaniel. Johnson's two godfathers were selected with the thought that they were men of some local prominence. One of them, who was to continue for a while to have a part in Johnson's life, was Dr. Samuel Swynfen, a physician of about thirty and a graduate of Pembroke College, Oxford. Though he lived on the ancestral estate outside Lichfield, he had taken supplementary lodgings in Michael Johnson's house in order to be nearer his medical practice. That Swynfen's own name was Samuel may have helped Michael to agree more easily in his wife's choice of the boy's name. The other godfather was Richard Wakefield, a lawyer, who had for nine years been serving as Coroner and Town Clerk of Lichfield. A widower without children, described as a "diligent antiquary" fond of books and of comfortable means, he seems to have been a frequent visitor at Michael's bookshop.

Michael had been elected Sheriff of Lichfield back in July. The day following the boy's birth was the one on which the Sheriff, by ancient custom, conducted the annual "Riding," as it was called—a ride of sixteen miles along the circumference of the city in order to make an official check of the city boundaries. A large number of citizens would accompany the Sheriff, who traditionally provided refreshments on the way, followed by a light meal at the Guildhall. Sarah, probably worried about the expense, asked her husband whom he would invite to the "Riding." With generous cheer, Michael answered, "All the town now." The next day, as the son remembered hearing, he "feasted the citizens with uncommon magnificence, and was the last but one that maintained the splendour of the Riding."

3

A decision was then made, with the best intention, that was to have disastrous results. Eager that the frail baby should be as well nourished as possible, Michael urged that they employ a strong and healthy wet nurse. Sarah, who may have doubted her own ability to nurse the child adequately, agreed. They selected the wife of a bricklayer, John Marklew. She had formerly been a servant in the household of a neighbor, William Robinson, and may also have worked at one time in the Johnsons' house. She seemed vigorous, was in her early thirties, and had been nursing her own first child for a full eighteen months—a fact that may have reaffirmed the impression that she had a robust constitution.

What the Johnsons could not know was that the milk of the wet nurse was tubercular. Meanwhile, despite a reasonable confidence that the baby in a few weeks would return home in healthy condition, his mother could not refrain from visiting him daily in order to be sure that there was no neglect, however small. So at least she said, probably not wishing to confess that it was simple fondness drawing her. It may tell us more about Sarah than her neighbors that she was afraid these daily visits would expose her to ridicule. Hence she would deliberately vary the quarter-mile route to George Lane, where the Marklews lived. And, lest Mrs. Marklew think her foolish, she would often, said Johnson, leave "her fan or glove behind her, that she might have a pretence to come back unexpected."

It was soon found that the baby's eyes were becoming infected. With the thought of draining the infection, an "issue" was cut in his left arm (it was not allowed to heal but was kept open—presumably with threads—until he was about six years old). As his condition grew worse and sores appeared, it was realized that he had the tubercular infection of the lymph glands known as scrofula or the "King's Evil." It had spread to both the optic and auditory nerves, leaving him almost blind in the left eye, while also impairing vision in the right, and deaf in the left ear. Some scar tissue remained on his face because of the scrofula. A later operation on the lymph glands left further scars on the lower part of the face and on the neck. Done without anesthetic, it was obviously a traumatic experience for the infant. Sarah, unwilling to admit that an action of the parents could have been even indirectly responsible, preferred to think that the boy inherited the disease, and pathetically cited a small inflammation discovered on his buttock that had appeared before he was sent to Mrs. Marklew. But this minor complaint had completely and quickly healed. Dr. Swynfen was certainly correct in telling Johnson afterward that he had caught the disease from the nurse, "whose son had the same distemper, and was likewise short-sighted, but both in less degree." It tells us something about the severity of Johnson's case that his foster brother, John Marklew, should have been considered to have it "in less degree," and yet, as we now know, was so incapacitated by its later effects that by his middle years, if not before, he was unable to earn his living.[3]

After ten weeks, said Johnson, "I was taken home, a poor, diseased infant, almost blind." In the notes he wrote fifty-five years later, he immediately added something else. His aunt, Mrs. Nathaniel Ford, told him bluntly when he was still very young that "she would not have picked such a poor creature up in the street." With more kindness, "Dr. Swynfen used to say, that he never knew any child reared with so much difficulty."

4

Given a situation so appalling, we are naturally tempted to speculate on the psychological results. We cannot do the subject justice until we come to Johnson at the age of twenty, when he was afflicted with so distressing a breakdown of will, hope, and the ability to "manage" himself that he feared the onset of insanity. But we can at least notice now, and for the next few years, something beyond the general interplay of shame and pride, of frustration and effort, that we should expect. One of the most deeply rooted qualities of Johnson, from his late adolescence on, is a powerful sense of self-demand, a feeling of complete personal responsibility. If it is closely related to some of his virtues, it was also to prove a source of deep psychological distress. This self-demand was later to create a radical self-conflict (with a resulting sense of guilt) in his approach to religion, operating as it inevitably did against religious trust and the capacity for Christian self-surrender.

What is of special interest to us now is how quickly as a small child—in discovering the physical differences between himself and others—he began groping his way to the independence and defiant disregard of his physical limitations that he was always to maintain. The remark by his aunt—that "she would not have picked such a poor creature up in the street"—has a corollary. When someone finally did seem ready to "pick him up" in the street in order to help him, he fought back. This was a kindly widow, Dame Oliver, who had started a little school for infants to which Johnson was sent. Because he was so young (perhaps three or four), and because his parents were afraid he could not see well enough to find his way, someone—probably a maid in the Johnson household—usually took him to Dame Oliver's school and then called for him. One day his escort did not arrive in time, and he began to return home by himself. At a gutter (or "kennel," as it was called) that crossed the street, he got down on all fours, crawling and peering closely as he prepared to make his way over it. Dame Oliver, fearing that a cart might run over him or that he might come to harm some other way, had discreetly followed him. Suddenly aware of her, the child rose and beat her away.[4]

In his attempt to push through and deny his physical infirmities, we can also notice a form of repression and transference that shows the extent to which self-responsibility was already being internalized. For example, the "issue" cut in his arm as a baby was a painful experience, and almost as obviously—since the child was no more than two or three months old at the time—would not be consciously remembered in later years. But Johnson *thought* he remembered it. And he thought he had remembered it because, from what he later heard, he had reacted to the operation with the kind of indifference he would like to have shown. Of this operation, he says, "I took no great notice, as I *think* my mother has told me, having my little hand in a custard." With typical scrupulosity, he wondered whether he really could have remembered the incident: "It is observable, that, having been told of this operation, I always imagined that I remembered it, but I laid the scene in the wrong house [presumably in the Johnson house rather than Mrs. Marklew's]." Yet if he thought for a long time—certainly throughout childhood—that he could distinctly remember the operation, of which he "took no great notice" while it was going on, his recollection becomes curiously vaguer about the results. The "issue," if it was kept open to the age of six, was something other children would be quick to notice; and it continued to an age that conscious memory could easily recall. But what we know of it—for he never mentioned it to others—is only from a short note added as though it were a casual afterthought to the remark about the operation: "How long this issue was continued I *do not remember*. I *believe* it was suffered to dry when I was about six years old." No allusion at all is made, in the "Annals" from which we are quoting, to the later operation, certainly a traumatic experience, on the lymph glands of the neck. It and the impact on him of its aftereffects seem almost blotted from memory. We know of it only because Arthur Murphy in some way discovered it.[5] Nor should we ever have known that he also had smallpox as a child, though some people later might have inferred it from the scars, if the fact had not slipped out in the diary he kept of a trip to northern Wales when he was sixty-four. (He mentions stopping with the Thrales at West Chester, where "my Father went to the fair, when I had the small-pox.")[6]

5

All his life Johnson was to be alertly suspicious of the self-indulgence that he was afraid illness could produce. "Disease," he wrote after suffering a stroke near the end of his life, "produces much selfishness. A man in pain is *looking after ease*." And Mrs. Thrale quotes a remark he would make frequently: "It is so *very* difficult (said he, always), for a sick man not to be a scoundrel." So warmly compassionate in other ways, quicker to find excuses for human nature than almost any other major moralist, he might well seem to his friends surprisingly less compassionate in this one way—at least as a kind of stock response, before he had time to reflect. He was projecting, of course, from his own struggle, starting in early childhood, to stay above the surface and to "manage" himself. What he really feared was not so much pain or inconvenience as the paralysis, the insidious dissolving of effort and will, that could result from indulging or dwelling in imagination on one's own physical ills. It was a rare moment when he let himself admit to Sir John Hawkins that "he knew not what it was to be totally free from pain." In general, at least up through his middle years, he told himself that most of the physical ills of which we make so much are grossly exaggerated by self-centeredness filling the vacuum of boredom and idleness; that a really demanding or rough life, with no opportunity for leisure, would soon shake us out of this; that "labouring men" who are forced to "work hard, and live sparingly" are free from many of the ailments of which others petulantly complain—the products (to cite a phrase that he uses in another context) of "imagination operating on luxury."[7]

At the same time, as if in compensation, Johnson—at least in his adult years—curiously exaggerated the family poverty during his childhood. Mrs. Thrale, though he confided so much to her, found him reluctant to talk about his family and his early life—"one has (says he) *so* little pleasure in reciting the anecdotes of beggary." But though he was certainly to experience poverty—indeed, drastic poverty—in his twenties and thirties, his family during his childhood was far from being in a situation of "beggary." In minimizing, almost repressing, remembrance of physical pain while exaggerating the family's poverty, he was transferring the focus of inner protest to something far less serious. This had some obvious psychological advantages. It is always a help to have an object to blame. For his health as a child, there was no one in particular who could be fairly blamed. The responsibility for getting out of it, or disregarding it, had to be his own. But for anything resembling "poverty" at home, he certainly could not be responsible. That was owing to the temperament and mistakes of others, notably his unbusinesslike father. At the same time, to exaggerate their poverty enabled him to feel more charity for his father. The need to feel that charity must have begun very early, if only as a counterbalance to less affectionate feelings. For insofar as he identified with either of his parents and their respective families, at least until the age of fifteen, he overwhelmingly identified with his brooding father and to some extent his father's family—of such "mean extraction" that, as he once said, with a hint of boastfulness, "I can hardly tell who was my grandfather."

6

A few words should be said about the families and general background of the two parents. When Johnson said, "I can hardly tell who was my grandfather," the man to whom he referred was not his maternal grandfather, Cornelius Ford. Johnson as a child heard a great deal from his mother about that particular grandfather and about "the ancient family of Ford" generally. He referred instead to his paternal grandfather, William Johnson, who was admittedly of humble background. Hoping to better his circumstances, he had moved, in the 1660's, from the tiny agricultural village of Cubley, Derbyshire, to Lichfield, twenty miles away, bringing with him his wife, Catherine, and his four (possibly five) small children. Michael, his eldest son, born in 1657, was then about seven or eight years old. Presumably—for later he had a fair knowledge of Latin—he attended, along with his brother, the excellent grammar school at Lichfield.

A few years later, in 1672, shortly before Michael was to become fifteen, William died. Local charities gave some help to the family. Through one of these charities Michael, when he was sixteen, was apprenticed for eight years to a London stationer, Richard Simpson. Though bookish, Michael, like his son after him, was tall and powerfully built. Still more powerful physically was Michael's younger brother, Andrew. He later tried to follow his brother's example by keeping a bookshop in Birmingham. When Mrs. Thrale long afterward tried to find out more about Johnson's family, and the conversation turned to uncles, Johnson started to oblige her ("Here now are uncles for you, Mistress, if that's the way to your heart"). And he told her about Andrew, who "kept the ring in Smithfield (where they wrestled and boxed) for a whole year, and never was thrown or conquered." It was from this uncle that Samuel, despite his nearsightedness, learned to box so well that he could walk at night without fear through the most dangerous streets of London. One night when four men attacked him, he "kept them all at bay till the watch came up, and carried both him and them to the Roundhouse."[8]

Whatever Michael's business troubles in later years, he began well. Though he was only twenty-four when he returned home to Lichfield after his apprenticeship and lacked capital of his own, he started business within three months as a bookseller, bookbinder, and stationer. People began to feel confidence in the large, reserved, devout, hardworking man. They elected him to town offices. He became a churchwarden at St. Mary's Church (he was a High-churchman and a Tory), took in his widowed mother, opened up branch bookstalls on market days in neighboring towns, and even started to do some publishing. Then something occurred that plainly unsettled him for a long time to come. He became engaged, when he was twenty-nine, to Mary Neild, the daughter of a well-established tradesman at Derby, and confidently got a license for their marriage later in the year. But she changed her mind before the wedding could take place, and within two years married another man, James Warner.[9] The bruised Michael kept the experience to himself. His wife and children almost certainly never learned of it. But it discouraged him from marriage for another twenty years. It also increased—in fact may have helped to bring to the surface—the deep vein of melancholy that his son describes and believed that he himself inherited.

Michael continued to work steadily, and snatched opportunities to travel about on horseback for his business, convinced that activity and exercise helped him to control anxiety and depression.* By the time he was forty, he had begun to supplement his business, which included the sale of vellum and parchment, by setting up a small parchment factory a third of a mile from his shop. Various tanners worked for him—his son was to surprise people years later by knowing "the whole process of tanning"—and Michael welcomed the chance to travel even more, riding around the countryside to buy skins for the business. The parchment factory is remembered because of a short account Johnson gave Mrs. Thrale. When the building had half fallen down for lack of money to repair it, his father was still painstaking and diligent about locking the door every night, even though he was aware that

anybody might walk in at the back part . . . "*This* (says his son) was madness, you may see, and would have been discoverable in other instances of the prevalence of imagination, but that poverty prevented it from playing such tricks as riches and leisure encourage."[10]

---

* Boswell, who did not know of Mary Neild, includes a story told by Anna Seward, since shown to be so improbable as to be almost certainly false, of a serving-woman, Elizabeth Blaney, who became infatuated with Michael when he was an apprentice, and followed him to Lichfield. Eventually Michael, moved by pity, was willing to marry her, but she died.

But this was some years later, when Michael was about seventy and his son in his late teens. The debts Michael incurred when he started business at twenty-four tended to increase. However steady, even methodical in some ways, he was negligent in keeping accounts; and in time things simply became too much for him. Now, however, and up through his marriage, when he was forty-nine, he seemed to be staying abreast. A new house he built just after his marriage indicates hope or determination, if not confidence. In this house, which had far more rooms (fifteen) than the family ever needed, Johnson was born.

7

The large house may also have been a gesture of intention and reassurance to Michael's father-in-law, Cornelius Ford, a yeoman of some property whose family was connected by marriage with the gentry. The Ford family had intellectual interests. An older brother, Henry, had been a prominent London barrister. Cornelius's eldest son, Joseph, who had gone to Cambridge, was by now a well-known physician at Stourbridge. Cornelius himself had a small private library. Though his youngest daughter, Sarah, had at thirty-seven been past the usual age of marriage and Ford realized he could not be too querulous, he made a strangely complicated arrangement about her dowry. In brief, the dowry was to remain in trust. Michael was expected, within nine months of the marriage, to contribute about a quarter as much more to the trust, and then, if there were children, to make still further provision, while also undertaking that his estate be worth not less than £500 by the time of death.[11] The arrangement could be considered somewhat humiliating to Michael as well as a financial burden. Nor was his self-respect helped by his inability to live up to the agreement. Ironically, part of his trouble had been his attempt to fulfill the agreement as soon as possible. Within three months of marriage, he had overextended himself in buying the complete library of the late Earl of Derby, which included over twenty-nine hundred volumes. To do this he had to borrow heavily, and seems never to have recouped the entire expense.[12]

Sarah, already convinced she had married beneath her, felt events confirmed her attitude. In compensation she dwelt on her own background, and would particularly mention her rich widowed cousin, Elizabeth Harriotts, who lived in a manor house twenty miles away and occasionally came to visit. More of a trial to Michael than Sarah's talk about her family were her nagging and suspicious complaints about details of his business. "My father and mother," said Johnson sadly, "had not much happiness from each other":

> They seldom conversed; for my father could not bear to talk of his [business] affairs; and my mother, being unacquainted with books, cared not to talk of anything else. Had my mother been more literate, they had been better companions. She might have sometimes introduced her unwelcome topick with more success, if she could have diversified her conversation. Of business she had no distinct conceptions; and therefore her discourse was composed only of complaint, fear, and suspicion.[13]

Becoming worried about expenses, Michael would suggest economies in the household. One that rankled in Sarah was his suggestion that she reduce visits to and from neighbors because of the cost of tea. (The price was indeed high; tea could sell for as much as thirty-five shillings a pound—a sum that should be multiplied by at least fifteen for the present-day equivalent.) "She lived to say," wrote Johnson, "many years after, that, if the time were to pass again, she would not comply with such unsocial injunctions."[14] But it is not clear that she did comply with these "unsocial injunctions," or that Michael, who was by no means ungenerous, made a serious point of the matter.

8

The condition of the baby's eyes began to worry the parents more as his poor vision became increasingly obvious. Lichfield had no oculist, but Mrs. Harriotts, Sarah's rich cousin, offered to help. When Johnson was in his second year, she asked Sarah to bring him to her place, and arranged for Dr. Thomas Attwood, a prominent oculist from Worcester, to examine him. Nothing could be done, since it was not the lens but the optic nerve that was affected. The following spring, when he was two and a half, his mother took him to London to be "touched" by Queen Anne. Scrofula had for generations been called the "King's Evil" because of the legend that it could be cured by the royal touch. Belief in the cure was waning, and the custom was not continued after the death of Anne, two years later. But Johnson's parents were eager to try anything to help the child and a distinguished Lichfield physician, Sir John Floyer, whose book *The Touchstone of Medicines* Michael had published in 1698, had advised them to try the "royal touch."

It may have been only his mother who was persuaded. For she was already pregnant with her second child; and Johnson, in the "Annals," states that she "concealed her pregnancy, that she might not be hindered from the journey." (He is repeating what she later told him, of course; and the inference is that she may not have wished Michael to know lest he deter her from the trip.) The trip was a difficult one, at least for Sarah, for at that time it took three days in the stagecoach.

Johnson in later years could remember that "we were troublesome to the passengers" in the coach; "I was sick; one woman fondled me, the other was disgusted." In London Sarah stayed at the home of a friend of Michael's, a bookseller named John Nicholson, who lived over his shop in Little Britain, off Aldersgate Street. Johnson remembered "a little dark room behind the kitchen, where the jack-weight [which turned the spit at the fire] fell through a hole in the floor, into which I once slipped my leg." He also mentions "a cat with a white collar, and a dog, called Chops, that leaped over a stick; but I know not whether I remember the thing, or the talk of it." Credentials for the ceremony of the "touching" were strictly required since a special gold piece was given after the "touch." Even so, about two hundred showed up the day Sarah took the child to St. James's Palace. Johnson remembered seeing another boy crying. A religious service was held including prayers, responses, and readings from the Bible. The sick were brought forward one by one. As they knelt, the Queen would lay her hands on them, and then present the amulet—a thin piece of gold, hung from a white ribbon, with St. Michael the archangel on one side, and a ship under sail on the other. Johnson was attached to the memento, and wore it around his neck for most of his life. But of the ceremony itself he could tell Mrs. Thrale only that "he thought he had some confused Remembrance of a Lady in a black Hood."

Before leaving London Sarah bought the boy a small silver cup and a spoon. They were marked "Sam. I.," she said, because if they were marked "S. I.," which were her own initials, they might possibly, on her death, be taken from him. She also "bought me a speckled linen frock, which I knew afterwards by the name of my London frock." Thirty years later, in a period of financial distress, Johnson's wife sold the cup, together with other pieces. The spoon was kept. In addition to these presents for the boy, his mother, said Johnson, bought herself "two teaspoons, and till my manhood had no more." Having spent money in this way, Sarah decided to economize on the trip home, and they took the cheap stage wagon instead of the coach. These huge wagons carried freight as well as up to thirty passengers. Sarah's excuse was that the child's constant coughing—he apparently had a bad cold—would have disturbed the more refined passengers in the stage-coach. Fearing lest she be robbed in the comparatively rough company of the wagon, Sarah sewed two guineas in her petticoat so that she would not be penniless.[15]

9

Two other incidents in Johnson's third year can be mentioned. One, well known, is probably apocryphal. It is cited by Boswell as "curiously characteristick" of what he liked to think of as "the infant Hercules of Toryism." A Miss Mary Adye of Lichfield sent Boswell the story, which has to do with Johnson's absorbed fascination with the noted Tory preacher Henry Sacheverell:

> When Dr. Sacheverell was at Lichfield, Johnson was not quite three years old. My grandfather Hammond observed him at the cathedral perched upon his father's shoulders, listening and gaping at the much celebrated preacher. Mr. Hammond asked Mr. Johnson how he could possibly think of bringing such an infant to church, and in the midst of so great a croud. He answered, because it was impossible to keep him at home; for, young as he was, he believed he had caught the publick spirit and zeal for Sacheverell, and would have staid for ever in the church, satisfied with beholding him.

There are problems in accepting the story. Sacheverell's only recorded visit to Lichfield was when Johnson was nine months old. Moreover, he was under a three-year interdict from preaching at that time and until March 1713. But people have been reluctant to surrender the story.[16]

The other incident, which is related by Johnson himself, is of more interest, particularly because of the way in which it breaks off. At some time during this year, presumably returning from London, he "was first informed of a future state." His mother told him of two places to which "inhabitants of this world were received after death; one a fine place filled with happiness called Heaven; the other a *sad* place, called Hell. That this account much affected my imagination, I do not remember." In order to fix it better in his memory, his mother sent him down from the bedroom to repeat what he had learned to their manservant, Thomas Jackson.[17] At this point in the "Annals"

16

there is a gap of thirty-eight pages. The surviving account does not resume until he is mentioning the course of study at the Lichfield Grammar School some years later. These missing pages were torn out and destroyed by Johnson a few days before he died. To conjecture his reason for getting out of bed, ill as he was, and impulsively destroying these pages is irresistible, if hopeless. The context suggests that there were remarks, even some discussion, about his early resistance to religion. But there could easily have been other matters he did not wish anyone to read. Mrs. Thrale tells a curious incident about him, when her small son was setting off for school. Johnson, fond of the boy (who was to die at the age of nine), made a prayer for him. Then he turned to her and

said to me suddenly, "Make your boy tell you his dreams: the first corruption that entered into my heart was communicated in a dream." "What was it, Sir?" said I. "*Do* not ask me," replied he with much violence, and walked away in apparent agitation. I never durst make any further enquiries.[18]

Chapter 2

First Years at School

Early in October 1712, shortly after Johnson's third birthday, his brother, Nathaniel, was born. For the christening (October 14), he told Mrs. Thrale that his mother "taught him to spell and pronounce the words *little Natty*, syllable by syllable, making him say it over in the evening to her husband and his guests." This sort of thing, she says, and the general habit of parents in showing off "newly acquired accomplishments" in young children, "disgusted Mr. Johnson beyond expression."

He was particularly annoyed by the story of an epitaph he wrote at the age of three for a duck. His stepdaughter, Miss Porter, had heard it from Johnson's mother, and in 1776 told it to Boswell in Johnson's presence. The infant Johnson, still in petticoats, was walking with his father when they came upon several ducks in their path. Not seeing well, the child accidentally stepped on a baby duck. With heavy humor the father said the duckling now had to be buried, and Samuel "must make an epitaph for it." Thereupon the three-year-old Samuel "made these lines":

> Under this stone lyes Mr. Duck
> Whom Samuel Johnson trod on;
> He might have liv'd if he had luck,
> But then he'd been an odd one.

Not wishing to contradict Miss Porter entirely, Johnson simply said that "his father made one half of this epitaph," and added that "he was a foolish old man, that is to say was foolish in talking of his children." Later, when the assiduous Boswell brought up the subject again, Johnson said his father had made up the verses as a whole and "wished to pass them for his child's." Mrs. Thrale, like others, got hold of the story, and mentions that he was generally "mortified at the recollection of the *bustle* his parents made with his wit." The word "bustle" is a favorite of Johnson's, indicating foolish and ill-directed activity carried on for no other purpose than to relieve tedium or "fill up the vacuities of life." (He once defined it as "getting on horseback in a ship.")[1]

In time he came to "loathe" his father's caresses, he told Mrs. Thrale, "because he knew they were sure to precede some unpleasing display of his early abilities." When neighbors came to visit, he would run off and climb a nearby tree so that he "might not be found and exhibited":

"That (said he to me one day) is the great misery of late marriages, the unhappy produce of them becomes the plaything of dotage: an old man's child (continued he) leads much such a life, I think, as a little boy's dog, teized with awkward fondness, and forced, perhaps to sit up and beg . . . to divert a company, who at last go away complaining of their disagreeable entertainment."

In later life he would sometimes offend acquaintances by refusing to hear their children recite verses or sing songs. And when a friend wanted his two sons to recite to him Gray's *Elegy*, one after the other, so that he could judge who did it better, Johnson said, "Let the dears both speak it at once; more noise will by that means be made, and the noise will be sooner over."[2]

The strong language and irritability ("foolish old man," "loathed his father's caresses," "the plaything of dotage") are of special interest. For when we come later to the periods of lassitude, of almost pathological indolence with which Johnson had to wrestle all his life, it is impossible not to notice how much a product these were of internalized self-demand. Long before Freud, Johnson himself was aware of the paralytic effects that can result from the crushing demands of what Freud called the "super-ego." This insight, like so many others in Johnson, came from his own personal experience—the experience of a nature so richly varied and multifaceted that it subsumed most of the quirks, fears, and hopes of others, and, as Mrs. Thrale said, did not at all "differ" from the nature of other people but was simply more so, and "greater." Especially after he got through the poverty of his twenties and thirties and no longer had an external scapegoat to blame, he had an immense psychic struggle with these demands. That he succeeded as he did is one of the reasons why he remains a guide and help to the human spirit.

But his internal self-demand was already so strong that it did not respond happily to the claims of others, especially when these claims seem trivially motivated. Because he identified so much with his father, Michael's expectations and requests fused all the more with his own and intensified them. As a result, he became even more restive under them than he would otherwise have been. On the other hand, for our own picture of what went on in the house, we should see all this in perspective. Michael's attempts to show off the boy were not something that was going on all the time, however vivid the incidents of it remained in Samuel's memory. Though touchingly proud and hopeful of the son about whom he had worried ever since the boy's birth, Michael had much else to occupy him. In fact, to avoid quarreling with Sarah, for whom he rarely had a ready answer, Michael would often contrive to be away from home. "My father," said Johnson to Mrs. Thrale, "could always take his horse and ride away for orders when things went badly."

Nothing approaching the testy impatience with which he would speak of his father ever appeared in his remarks about his mother. "Poor people's children," he once told Mrs. Thrale, "never respect them: I did not respect my own mother, though I loved her: and one day, when in anger she called me a puppy, I asked her if she knew what they called a puppy's mother." If the remark shows a quick wit, it also indicates the extent to which he was an indulged child and allowed to be disrespectful. Another remark, sometimes quoted as expressing disapproval of his mother, actually shows only how secure he felt with her: "My mother was always telling me that I did not *behave* properly; that I should learn *behavior*, and such cant; but when I replied, that she ought to tell me what to do, and what to avoid, her admonitions were commonly, for that time at least, at an end." But as he grew older he began to think more of her good sense; her mind seemed "much enlarged." His love for her, despite her habit of nagging, was genuine if not intense. He even admitted to Mrs. Thrale, in one of his rare references to his brother, that he and Nathaniel quickly became "rivals for the mother's fondness." Moments when she spoiled him with loving indulgence always remained in his memory and moved him deeply. Reflecting on one, he told Mrs. Thrale he thought he would "never have so loved his mother, when a man, had she not given him coffee she could ill afford, to gratify his appetite when a boy."[3]

2

When he was only three, or at most four, his mother began to teach him to read. Another story, besides that of the duck, was told Boswell in Johnson's presence by Miss Porter, who got it from Sarah Johnson. His mother, when he was still "a child in petticoats," put in his hands the Book of Common Prayer, and asked him to go over the Collect for the day until he got it by heart. She then started to go up the stairs. "But by the time she had reached the second floor, she heard him following her. 'What's the matter?' said she. 'I can say it,' he replied; and repeated it distinctly, though he could not have read it over more than twice."[4]

His imagination was especially caught up by fairy tales; and he remembered sitting in the lap of the maid while she told him the story of St. George and the Dragon. He was later fond of maintaining, quite sensibly, that the reading of fairy stories and traditional adventure tales was far better for children—far more likely to arouse imagination and curiosity, and thus induce them to read voluntarily and habitually— than the insipid stories about children included in the eighteenth-century ancestors of our twentieth-century school readers. Talking to Mrs. Thrale about the books she would give her children, "Babies," he said, "do not want to hear about babies; they like to be told about giants and castles, and of somewhat which can stretch and stimulate their little minds." She would then point out "the numerous editions and quick sale of Tommy Prudent or Goody Two Shoes: 'Remember always (said he) that the parents *buy* the books, and that the children never read them.' "[5]

When he was about four, he was sent to the infant school, already mentioned, conducted by Dame Anne Oliver on Dam Street. In his own biographies he was eager to find out what he could about the teachers of those whose lives he was writing, especially if they were themselves writers. "Not to name the school or the masters of men illustrious for literature is a kind of historical fraud, by which honest fame is injuriously diminished." He always remembered Dame Oliver with affection. And he was deeply touched when she came to say good-bye to him as he left Lichfield to enter Oxford, and brought him as a present, "in the simplicity of her kindness," some gingerbread she had made, telling him "he was the best scholar she ever had." Boswell says that Johnson "delighted in mentioning this early compliment," and would add with a smile that "this was as high a proof of his merit as he could conceive." Within another two years he was sent to a school for slightly older children, conducted by Thomas Browne, of whom Johnson told Boswell that he "published a spelling-book, and dedicated it to the UNIVERSE; but I fear, no copy of it can now be had." A little more has since been learned about Browne. A man of around sixty, he had formerly been a shoemaker like Dame Oliver's late husband, Peter Oliver. He had long known the Olivers, and there was probably an arrangement whereby he would take pupils after a certain age from Dame Oliver's school. He was unwell the year he taught Johnson and died a few months later. The schoolroom, Aleyn Reade discovered, was bare of furniture except for a table and chair used by the teacher, while the pupils sat on the floor.[6]

3

At seven and a half (January 1717), Johnson entered the Lichfield Grammar School, where he stayed through the age of fifteen. Here, in the Lower School, he began his study under a gentle, overworked teacher named Humphrey Hawkins. Because he lacked a university degree, Hawkins—then a man of about fifty—never rose above the position of usher or undermaster. With an increasing family, he was paid so little (£5 and later £10 a year) that he supplemented his salary by adding other work: taking students for private instruction, keeping St. Mary's churchwarden accounts, and even washing for the church the surplices and other linen. He was patient and kind to his students and quick to notice Johnson's unusual talents. Johnson remembered with pleasure the time he studied under Hawkins, adding that "I was indulged and caressed by my master." And he wept when he had to leave Hawkins, after two years and four months, and was promoted to the Upper School and another master. The school, both Lower and Upper, was reputed to be unusually good, and had some distinguished alumni.* The building, in St. John Street, across from the Hart's

---

* Among them were Elias Ashmole, who founded the museum named after him at Oxford, the philosopher William Wollaston, Bishop George Smalridge, and especially Joseph Addison. Shortly before Johnson's time it was attended by three pupils who were to become prominent judges (Sir John Willes, Sir Thomas Parker, and William Noel).

Horn Inn, consisted of one large, oak-paneled room, according to Reade, "with massive oak desks for the boys and lofty eyries in the end for the masters."[7]

At the school he found a good friend in Edmund Hector, a nephew of George Hector, the "man-midwife" who had attended Sarah Johnson at her son's birth. But except for Hector, who later provided intimate accounts of Johnson's childhood, Johnson made most of his school friends a little later. With at least two boys, however, who were brothers, he was well enough acquainted to be taken to their home. According to an old history of Lichfield, he was thought to have had "the appearance of idiocy, and the sons of a gentleman in the town were reprimanded for bringing home with them that disagreeable driveller." Within another two or three years, when the boy had become less shy, at least one other Lichfield parent expressed himself very differently. William Butt, overhearing his children speak contemptuously of the large, rawboned youth as "the great boy," said, "You call him the great boy, but take my word for it, he will one day prove a great man."[8]

4

For us today, the particular psychological interest of Johnson's experience during the first two years under Hawkins lies in his vivid, grateful memory of "the multitude of novelties which it supplied." For he appears to be speaking, if not exclusively, at least mainly, of the school curriculum, which consisted almost entirely of Latin, and in particular of intensive drill in Latin grammar. It is this, more than anything else, that he has been closely describing in the boyhood "Annals" from which we have been quoting; and he then goes on to describe almost as specifically the work done when he first enters the Upper School (after which the account breaks off at the age of ten). The psychological interest, to which we should turn in a moment, is that this formidable curriculum seemed—by contrast with his earlier years—something of a relief.

There is no need to repeat in detail the rules and passages memorized, or the parts of grammar books stressed, or the calendar of drill and examination. The account is not only readily available but also well annotated.[9] In brief, the principal book was William Lily's *Grammar*, which had been used, with revisions, as a basic text in English schools since the 1540's.* The rules of Latin grammar were expected to be memorized thoroughly before the actual reading began. The more important sections of Lily's *Grammar*—the rules being put into jingles to help memorization—were traditionally known by the opening words (*e.g.*, that on nouns was *Propria quae Maribus*, and that on verbs *As in Praesenti*); and this is the way that Johnson refers to them. Though he was hardly eight, he responded at once to the first large challenge—memorizing the 141 lines of *Propria quae Maribus*, which, with examples, covered sixteen pages. To stamp it in mind, he would repeat it aloud to his mother and his cousin, Tom Johnson (the son of Andrew, who was currently living with them). So aroused was he by the challenge that in a dream at the time, he remembered going through it "as far as the middle of the paragraph, 'Mascula dicuntur monosyllaba' "—a passage of sixty-four lines. With verbs he had more trouble. The student was expected to go "through the same person in all the Moods and Tenses":

I was once very anxious about the next day, when this exercise was to be performed, in which I had failed till I was discouraged. My mother encouraged me, and I proceeded better. When I told her of my good escape, "We often," said she, dear mother! "come off best, when we are most afraid." She [later] told me, that, when she asked me about forming verbs, I said, "I did not form them in an ugly shape." "You could not," said she, "speak plain; and I was proud that I had a boy who was forming verbs."

Touched by the memory, Johnson adds, "These little memorials soothe my mind."

From Monday to Wednesday each week, time was spent principally on grammatical exercise and drill. Thursday saw a complete re-examination of what had been covered the previous three days. Johnson, like the brighter students generally, found Thursdays a respite. The questions usually repeated what had already been done several times in

---

* Supplementing it later were John Garretson's *Exercises* (for translating from English into Latin), William Willymott's *English Particles . . . for Latin Exercises*, and William Walker's *Treatise of English Particles*, mainly concerned with adverbs and prepositions, and providing examples in both English and Latin. When in his fifties Johnson out of curiosity looked through these last three books, he found "few sentences that I should have recollected if I had [not] found them in any other books,"[10] and added, "That which is read without pleasure is not often recollected nor infixed by conversation, and therefore in a great measure drops from the memory. Thus it happens that those who are taken early from school, commonly lose all that they have learned."

drill. On Thursday nights the pupils read and memorized selections from a Latin version of Aesop's *Fables* and a well-known textbook, *School Colloquies* by Mathurin Cordier (originally in French and adapted for English students by Charles Hoole), which contained dialogues in parallel columns of Latin and English. On Friday mornings the pupils would repeat these passages; the afternoon was devoted again to grammar; and on Saturday there was another examination to close off or finish up the week.

5

The pros and cons of both the subject matter and even of the approach can be debated—and more open-mindedly than is thought possible by the twentieth century theorist of education, who is appalled by the confined focus of the subject and even more by the reliance on memorization and mechanical drill. The historian can reply that both the curriculum and to some extent the procedure (sanctioned by the great Renaissance Humanists) had been in effect for a long time and were to last, in gradually modified form, for almost another two hundred years, and that this system of education at least coincides and cooperates with—if it does not usher in—a long, brilliant culture, off the accumulated capital of which, in almost every way except the natural sciences and technology, we have since been living. Hence, if empirical results rather than mere theory are the real test of educational systems, the system under question has something to be said for it. The usual rebuttal made to this has a point, though it is not a complete answer: that outstanding talent will find a way to emerge and grow whatever the subject matter and possibly (though less certainly) whatever the approach.

But even the warmest advocates of the system did not associate it with pleasure, at least during the first years of drill and memorization. They took it for granted, as did Johnson, that physical punishment— whipping or beating—was necessary as an incentive to learn. True, pedagogues have been known to speak of the satisfaction, even delight, that they themselves felt as children in a course of study like that described. But Johnson was not temperamentally one of them. Probably no man of comparable learning in modern times has been less of a pedant by nature, less docile, and more imaginatively and emotionally restive. An important (and endearing) side of Johnson, and one that continues throughout his life, is revealed in Bishop Percy's remark that

when a boy he was immoderately fond of reading romances of chivalry, and he retained his fondness for them through life; so that . . . spending part of a summer at my parsonage-house in the country [this was when Johnson was fifty-four] he chose for his regular reading the old Spanish romance of FELIXMARTE OF HIRCANIA, in folio, which he read through. Yet I have heard him attribute to these extravagant fictions, that unsettled turn of mind which prevented his ever fixing in any profession.[11]

And he read with vivid empathy. In one of the familiar stories about his childhood, he read *Hamlet* alone in the kitchen at home, at the age of about nine. "He kept on steadily enough, till coming to the Ghost scene, he suddenly hurried up stairs to the street door"—the kitchen was in the basement several steps below the front door—"that he might see people about him."[12] It was an experience he remembered long afterward when he wrote, in his *Observations on Macbeth*, "He that peruses Shakespeare looks round alarmed, and starts to find himself alone."

The real explanation for his grateful sense of a "multitude of novelties," and his feeling that a new world was being discovered, has to do with the interplay of two things already deeply implanted in him. One is the immediately successful outlet it suddenly gave to a temperament so competitive and aggressive that he had to devote considerable effort, in later years, to controlling and if possible redirecting it. Thus far, at home and also at the two infant schools, Dame Oliver's and Thomas Browne's, the active competition had been almost entirely with himself and his own self-demand (competition at that time with his father—hopeless because of the disparity of age—was naturally repressed and took other forms). All his life competition with himself and against the paralyzing grip of self-expectation was what pressed most heavily on him. By contrast, active competition with others came as a relief, arousing attention and effort while freeing him from the burden of self-reproach and amounting—in psychological effect—very closely to what we ordinarily mean by "play." Here, during his first two years at the Lichfield Grammar School, the "pleasure" he remembers is not only because of the encouragement of the master, Humphrey Hawkins, but because he thought that he "really excelled the rest."

But there is something else already interrelating with this that is later of fundamental importance for our understanding of Johnson, of his thought, his values, and much of his personal life: the almost desperate clutch outward to fact and objective reality of any sort in order to cleanse and free the dark subjective self—with all its frantic fears, and all its blind and destructive treacheries, including self-treachery—and to pull it, in self-preservation, up from the serpent pit of subjective isolation into sanity, light, and stability. So deeply is this effort a part of Johnson, so completely coalesced with every aspect of his thought, values, and the cleansing power of expression he was later to achieve, that it is impossible not to see it coming from his total experience. What was to permit its magnificent range is another matter, of course: the unwavering allegiance to the ideal of objective "truth" in its amplest sense. This was to be developed or acquired only gradually. But at least the beginning motivation, the strong sense of the contrast of "external," objective truth with the dark, bewildered prison house of the isolated subjective self, dates back—in however rudimentary a form—to the experience of the half-blind and half-deaf child, with the running "issue" in his arm, who fought to make his own way back from Dame Oliver's school, and who then—thrown into competition at the grammar school—found he could "excel," and discovered, in doing so, a new stability: a stability attained by reaching out, with tenacious grip, to the external challenge of objective fact. The daily drill in Latin grammar could hardly be more than the slightest morning shadow of what he meant when he said years later—in the *Preface to Shakespeare*, writing in the midst of so deep a despair that he feared the loss of his sanity—that "the mind can only repose upon the stability of truth." But it was a start.

Chapter 3

The Lichfield
Upper Grammar School

While Johnson was still only nine (May 1719), the eleven students who made up his class were suddenly promoted from the Lower to the Upper School, presided over by the formidable headmaster John Hunter—the one to whom Johnson referred when he said, "My master whipt me very well."

This sudden promotion was unexpected, and it came earlier than had been the custom. The reason behind it is that Hunter had been given a formal reproof by the Town Clerk for neglecting boys from the town and leaving them to an assistant in the Lower School while he himself concentrated on boarders, who brought extra money. It was a common practice for a school master to increase his income this way. Salaries were small. For students from outside the town, additional fees could be charged. If they were sons of the gentry, the profit from board as well as tuition could be considerable. Hunter was especially adroit in taking advantage of this. An energetic man of about forty-five, who had graduated from University College, Oxford, he drew in students from all over Staffordshire and even adjoining counties. According to Jane Hackett, the daughter of the sacrist of Lichfield Cathedral, Hunter "had often times 99 and near 100 boarders. . . . He was obliged to incorporate several neighbouring houses, and join them to his school-habitation."[1] Parents in the town did not object to Hunter's effort to add boarders. But they did object to his leaving the Lichfield students to Humphrey Hawkins in the Lower School while he did so.

28

When Hunter was reproved by the Town Clerk (who at the time was Richard Wakefield, one of Johnson's two godfathers), he abruptly reached down below the normal age and lifted the entire class of which Johnson was a member, placing them for the time under the immediate supervision of his twenty-four-year-old assistant, Edward Holbrooke, whom Johnson remembered as "a peevish and ill-tempered man." Meanwhile, poor Hawkins, who was powerless, lost half his income when the entire class was removed from him. In doing his first exercise for Holbrooke, Johnson started with resolution. His remark about it has some psychological interest. For it shows how foreign to his general experience is a *steady* attention (as distinct from a powerful attention, working by fits and starts and then withdrawing). The significance is that an experience so commonplace, in which one scarcely notices what is going on aside from one's work, should for him seem so unusual:

In making, I think, the first exercise under Holbrooke, I perceived the power of continuity of attention, of application not suffered to wander or to pause. I was writing at the kitchen windows, as I thought, alone, and turning my head saw Sally dancing. I went on without notice, and had finished almost without perceiving that any time had elapsed. This close attention I have seldom in my whole life obtained.[2]

The "Sally" whom he saw dancing was Sally Ford, a cousin of seventeen, who kept house for their widowed uncle, John Harrison, a saddler in Birmingham.

Sally had come to Lichfield in order to escort the two Johnson boys, Samuel and the six-year-old Natty, who were being sent to Birmingham during the Whitsuntide vacation, at the end of May, for two weeks. "Why such boys were sent to trouble other houses," said Johnson, "I cannot tell. My mother had some opinion that much improvement was to be had by changing the mode of life." The improvement she had in mind was doubtless one that would come less from mere change of scene than from exposure to her own relatives. Part of the time they spent with John Harrison, whose dead wife had been a sister of Sarah Johnson's. But it turned out that Harrison, said Johnson, "did not much like us, nor did we like him. He was a very mean and vulgar man, drunk every night, but drunk with little drink, very peevish, very proud, very ostentatious, but, luckily, not rich." Across from Harrison, on the High Street, was the bookshop of Michael Johnson's brother, Andrew, the former boxer, now in financial straits. Adding to

Andrew's troubles, his third wife, Sarah White, who seems to have been something of a hypochondriac, had incurred before marriage a sizable bill for medicines bought from Thomas Shepperd, an apothecary. Shepperd, who referred to her as an "Ungrateful Slut," was now trying to get both her and Andrew arrested for debt.[3]

Most of the vacation was spent, and more pleasantly, at the home of one of Mrs. Johnson's brothers. This could possibly have been Samuel Ford, who may have been living in Birmingham at the time. More probably it was Nathaniel Ford, then forty-two, a clothier who lived at Sutton Coldfield, seven miles from town. It was Nathaniel's outspoken wife who had once frankly told Johnson that when he was a baby she "would not have picked such a poor creature up in the street." The "Aunt Ford" he now describes sounds much the same: "a good-natured, coarse woman, easy of converse, but willing to find something to censure in the absent." While at his aunt's he ate "so much of a boiled leg of mutton, that she used to talk about it." His mother, "who had lived in a narrow sphere, and was then affected by little things," was worried when she heard his aunt talk of it. She had been eager for her sons to make a good impression, and "told me seriously that it would hardly ever be forgotten. Her mind, I think was afterward much enlarged, or greater evils wore out the care of less." Asserting his maturity on this first trip without his parents, he stayed until a few days after the vacation, writing home that the horses should be sent to pick up him and Natty on "Thursday of the first school week [school would have begun on Monday]; and then, and not till then, they should be welcome." He and Natty would then return, presumably alone. In preparation he had bought or been given "a rattle to my whip," with which he was "much pleased." However, his father showed up with the horses. With heavy good humor, Michael inadvertently irritated the boy both by a mistake of fact and by implying that the children were helpless without him. "He told the ostler, that he had twelve miles home [actually sixteen], and two boys under his care. This offended me."

2

When he returned to Lichfield, the effect of the transition from the Lower to the Upper School, hardly noticed in the short time he had had before the vacation, became pronounced. A different picture now emerges from the one we have of him at the Lower School during the previous two and a half years. There was, of course, the change of masters. Holbrooke was not only "peevish and ill-tempered," but was also, Johnson implies, rather shaky as a Latinist. The class was soon plunged into Phaedrus. Twice they were sent up to Hunter, the headmaster, "to be punished. The second time we complained that we could not get the passage. Being told we should ask, we informed him we had asked, and that the assistant would not tell us," presumably out of ignorance. But then one could imagine Johnson easily able, in time, to pick holes in the learning of the kindly Humphrey Hawkins; and his school friend John Taylor wrote something of a tribute later to Holbrooke's learning.

The change from Hawkins to Holbrooke does not wholly explain the difference Johnson was to show at school. Nor does the incursion now, in the story of Johnson's early years, of the other master he encountered. This was the headmaster, John Hunter, of whom Johnson sometimes spoke as though he were a bugaboo. Long afterward he told the Reverend Mr. Parker that Hunter never really "*taught* a boy in his life"—he simply "whipped and they learned."* He added that Hunter's granddaughter, Anna Seward, later known as "the Swan of Lichfield," looked so much like Hunter that he "could tremble at the sight" of her. (When he said this he was laughing at Anna Seward, who was herself always trying to appear formidable, and who, as he knew, did not like him very much. The remark has been taken too seriously.) Certainly Hunter, whatever his merits, was a pompous man, never entering the school, says Parker, "without his gown and cassock, and his wig full dressed." And he was severe—"very severe," Johnson said to Boswell, "and wrong-headedly severe." He would ask out-of-the-way questions, such as the Latin word for candlestick, and then beat the child without making a distinction, said Johnson, between the child not knowing what he was expected to know and what he had no opportunity of even imagining that he should know. Wielding the rod "unmercifully," as the boy leaned over the three-legged flogging stool, Hunter would say, "And this I do to save you from the gallows." Nevertheless, Mrs. Thrale said Johnson admitted Hunter's "scholarship

---

* Johnson was fond of saying that if he knew Latin as well as he did, it was only because Hunter "whipt me very well. Without that, Sir, I should have done nothing." But actually, according to Edmund Hector, Hunter never punished him for the quality of his own work but merely "for talking and diverting other boys from their business."4

to be very great." "Abating his brutality," he said to Boswell, "he was a very good master." And the Reverend William Shaw wrote that to Hunter's "elegant and correct method of teaching" Johnson "often acknowledged the highest obligations." Lastly, some of Hunter's best students—and he had several who were to become eminent—thought well of him, or at least of his results. Certainly he was not brutal for the sake of brutality. His quick automatic recourse to punishment seems the result of what he himself regarded as businesslike dispatch: a resolve to push through as many students as possible in such a way as to do credit both to himself and to them. He could be temporarily diverted from his resolve by other interests. Thomas Davies, in a biography of David Garrick (he got the details of Garrick's early years at Lichfield from Johnson and is probably quoting Johnson here), says that Hunter fancied himself a sportsman and "a great setter of game. Happy was the boy who could slily inform his offended master where a covey of partridges was to be found: this notice was a certain pledge of his pardon."[5]

What had really happened to make the Upper School such a contrast with the Lower was not the change of masters so much as the fact that Johnson himself was changing, not in essential character but in objects of interest and in the emergence of qualities thus far held in suspension. Back in the Lower School, under Humphrey Hawkins, so preoccupied was he at first with the unfamiliar and formidable challenge of grammatical exercise that, in comparison, the actual reading they did—and memorized—on Thursday nights later dropped from memory. This, even more than the dream in which he went through sixty-four lines of *Propria quae Maribus*, is a measure of his preoccupation. For Johnson all his life could often repeat entire pages that he had only lightly skimmed. So tenacious was his memory that there seemed to be something desperate about it, as though it could itself become a form of self-preservation, of attempted steadiness, against the fluctuating chaos of life. But the reading done on Thursday nights was memorized without attention (which Johnson rightly said was the true secret of memory). His real attention and involvement, during these five years, was elsewhere.

The only passage in this reading that he could later recall distinctly, because it struck home to him, has significance if one looks ahead to the mature Johnson. It was a passage "where it is said of some man, that, when he hated another, he made him rich." As soon as he read this, he repeated it to his mother, "who could never conceive that riches could bring any evil. She remarked [on] it, as I expected."[6]

32

Something close to this idea, in general premise and far more broadly applied, was to be one of the most pervasive themes in Johnson's moral writing, starting with *The Vanity of Human Wishes*. That he should have got the point of the passage at the age of only eight is interesting. It could hardly have been grasped—it would certainly not impress— without some prior sense of the way in which possessions, like attainments, not only pall but bring with them new burdens of anxiety, while also depriving us of a scapegoat to blame for our dissatisfactions; or, if not some prior sense, it involved an imagination already operating so habitually upon experience that it can quickly penetrate to the point through analogy.

But after two and a half years, the novelty of the challenge provided in the grammar school, with its premium on exact grammatical exercise, began to evaporate. Competitiveness, with others, however strong it might be potentially, also declined as a steady (as distinct from a sporadic or occasional) motive when he found himself able to handle the assigned work so much more easily than others did. As his school friend Edmund Hector said, "He seemed to learn by intuition the contents of any book," and "His memory was so tenacious, that he never forgot anything that he either heard or read." Hector recalled having once recited to him "eighteen verses, which, after a little pause, he repeated *verbatim*, varying only one epithet, by which he improved the line." Soon Johnson was at a point where, as he said in retrospect, "They never thought to praise me by comparing me with anyone; they never said, Johnson is as good a scholar as such a one; but such a one is as good a scholar as Johnson." And only one boy was ever compared in this way—Theophilus Lowe, a year and a half older, who was the son of a Lichfield plumber, and who went on to Cambridge and became a clergyman; and Johnson could honestly say, "I do not think he was as good a scholar." So much did his "uncommon abilities for learning" exceed those of the others, said Hector, that they all "endeavoured by every boyish piece of flattery" to get him to help them. One "piece of flattery" for a while was that "three of us, by turns, used to call on him in a morning, on one of whose backs, supported by the other two, he rode triumphantly to school."[7]

3

As both the novelty and the sense of competition began to subside as all-sufficient incentives, two interrelated qualities emerged that were to characterize him the rest of his life. One of them is the extraordinary, almost pathological "indolence" (to use his own word) into which he could increasingly fall—a subject of fundamental importance for understanding him psychologically. More accurately described, it was a powerful inner resistance, even protest, against the unceasing pressure of strong self-demand. This at least was its primary element, before it became complicated by the further self-conflicts it engendered. If it is not yet present in the marked degree we see later, it is on the way. In trying to overcome these rebellious lapses into indolence, he could work with extraordinary bursts of speed, which—in their result—would more than compensate for the delay. (Compensate, that is, in the eyes of others, not in his own; for he himself, judging these bursts of effort by motive rather than result, realized that they were primarily the product of impatience to get a thing over with and out of the way.) This was always to be true of him. One of the finest short discussions in English of idleness and procrastination (*Rambler* 134) was rapidly written in Sir Joshua Reynolds's parlor while the printer's boy, who had come to pick up copy of a new essay for the periodical, waited at the door. "Whatever work he did," said Mrs. Thrale, "seemed so much below his powers of performance, that he appeared the idlest of all human beings." When he was only nine, his mother was becoming aware of this. He had been assigned a series of exercises, and he did one of them quickly. But the task as a whole "being long upon me," she said, "though you could make an exercise in so short a time, I thought you would find it difficult to make them all as soon as you should." Despite his "ambition to excel," said Hector,

his application to books, as far as it appeared, was very trifling. I could not oblige him more than by sauntering away every vacation, that occurred, in the fields, during which time he was more engaged in talking to himself than his companion. Verses or themes he would dictate to his favorites, but he would never be at the trouble of writing them. His dislike to business was so great, that he would procrastinate his exercises to the last hour.

And Hector adds that after a long vacation, during which they had been given a large assignment, Johnson would simply show up at school an hour earlier, the day after the vacation, "and begin one of his exercises, in which he purposely left some faults [which would use up the master's time in correcting] in order to gain time to finish the rest."[8]

Another quality was to prove valuable in the highest degree. His equivalent of a library was, of course, his father's bookshop. Balked by the school procedure from reading either for substance or even for style in any genuine sense, his immense curiosity found outlet in independent dipping into books and skimming them. And his habit of instantly "relating" one thing to another, which Mrs. Thrale rightly thought one of the secrets of his mental superiority, enabled him to get a point quickly, to see its ramifications, and to anchor it to a growing corpus of general thought that was imaginatively and fertilely alive. Here, in this kind of reading, simply because it was done without deliberate purpose, and not confined within a conscious program or demand, the inner protest and instinctive mulishness declined, though it did not completely disappear. For this sort of reading could be viewed as a kind of escape. It could hardly be called "work." Even so, a certain mulishness remained, which we cannot yet discuss fully, since it is more relevant later. This appears, for example, in his growing habit of not finishing books. Later, as if to make a virtue of necessity (since the habit was to become thoroughly ingrained in him), he enjoyed startling others—particularly pedestrian and solemn scholars (just as he enjoyed startling snobbery of any kind)—by flaunting his inability to "read books through." Time and again we come across remarks like the following:

Mr. Elphinstone talked of a new book that was much admired, and asked Dr. Johnson if he had read it. JOHNSON. "I have looked into it." "What (said Elphinstone), have you not read it through?"—Johnson, offended at being thus pressed, and so obliged to own his own cursory mode of reading, answered tartly, "No, Sir; do *you* read books *through?*"

"Alas," as he said to Mrs. Thrale, "how few books are there of which one ever can possibly arrive at the *last* page!" Or, most startling of all, there is the remark to the bookish, literal-minded, and gently overrespectful William Bowles (Boswell amusingly omitted it when he used the account of Johnson that Bowles wrote for him): "I have read few books through; they are generally so repulsive that I cannot." It is delightful to read such remarks by one of the supreme critics of literature, whose range of *verbatim* knowledge, held in ready memory, is possibly unexcelled, and of whom Adam Smith—a grudging critic, who did not like Johnson—could say that he "knew more books than any man alive." What is refreshing is the union of blunt honesty with unpredictability, at once reassuring to human nature while pulling the rug from beneath the pretense and affectation with which writing, like everything else, is so often surrounded.[9]

4

Though Johnson's account of his early life and particularly of his schooling stops at the age of ten, there is every reason to assume that the curriculum was conventional. In the remaining time he spent at the Lichfield Grammar School (six years), the students would have gone through Ovid and Cicero, then Horace and Virgil. Some attention would have been given Erasmus and Renaissance Latin writers (though Johnson's wide reading—or extensive dipping—in the Renaissance Humanists began mainly in his father's bookshop). The curriculum may also have included some Juvenal. By the time he was fourteen, if not before, Johnson would have begun on Greek grammar, starting first with the New Testament in Greek and then turning to Xenophon, Hesiod, and probably some of the Greek Anthology.

Of his schoolfellows, four in particular were and continued later to be important as friends. Edmund Hector, who became a physician in Birmingham, knew him longest at school. Though he was a year and a half older than Johnson, they were in the same class. Hector's account of Johnson's school years, which we have been citing, shows a strong underlying affection. In a note Johnson wrote near the end of his life, he mentions Hector as "the only companion of my childhood that passed through the School with me. We have always loved one another." Two other friends were somewhat older than Johnson. One was the endearing if lax Robert James, four years his senior, who became well known as a physician. For though he was said to have been drunk every day for twenty years, he brought out a large *Medicinal Dictionary* (1743) in three volumes, to which Johnson contributed some articles. James also invented some "fever powders" of dubious value, which were widely sold (they were prescribed for George III, for a while, during his first mental breakdown). Isaac Hawkins Browne, almost five years older than Johnson, went on to Westminster, then to Cambridge, and acquired a small reputation as a minor poet. He sat in Parliament, where, said Johnson, he "never opened his mouth." He spoke only when primed with liquor. Mrs. Mary Cholmondeley said that during the first hour of his company "he was so dull there was no bearing him; the second he was so witty there was no bearing him; the third he was so drunk there was no bearing him." Johnson, stubbornly loyal, spoke of him "as one of the first wits of this country," and told Mrs. Thrale that his talk (he was by now dead) was "at once so artless, so pure, and so pleasing" that Browne was "of all conversers . . . the most delightful with whom he was ever in company."[10]

Lastly there was John Taylor, a year and a half younger than Johnson, who came from Ashbourne, in Derbyshire (where his father was an attorney), and was one of John Hunter's boarders. The relationship, which was to continue the rest of Johnson's life, seems at first a curious one. Taylor epitomized a certain kind of eighteenth-century clergyman who in character was at opposite poles from Johnson. He was genial but heavy and somewhat sluggish in temperament, practical, shrewd, and even worldly. As much because of as despite their differences, they had a firm confidence in each other. There were personal matters Johnson felt freer to confide to the stolid and worldly Taylor than to others who were emotionally or imaginatively more like himself.

Other schoolmates included J. E. Wilmot, already mentioned, who became Chief Justice of the Common Pleas, and Theophilus Lowe, the "rival" scholar who was jealous of Johnson. Lowe offended him by refusing to help him one day (the boys would often take turns doing a lesson and then teaching it to the others), with the result that Johnson henceforth resolved to be independent. With two others Johnson tried to keep some contact in later life. One was Charles Congreve, who rose in the Church, said Johnson, with "considerable preferment," and who, whatever he was as a youth, later showed "great coldness of mind," becoming a complete valetudinarian and a semialcoholic. Johnson told Taylor (March 1776) an amusing story of calling on Congreve, who sat half-comatose in a small room, ten feet square, fearing that in any other room he would catch cold. His talk consisted of a few monosyllables. At last Johnson, giving up on him, asked "the time, which gave him hopes of being delivered from me, and enabled him to bounce up with great alacrity and inspect his watch." Johnson was more successful with Harry Jackson, whom Boswell, on a trip with Johnson to Lichfield (1776), describes: Johnson, quick to pity and completely free of snobbery, treated him "with much kindness, though he seemed to be a low man, dull and untaught. He had a coarse grey coat, black waistcoat, greasy leather breeches, and a yellow uncurled wig." His face was red from drinking ale. Having failed as a cutler, he was now very poor, and was trying to develop "some scheme of dressing leather in a better manner than common." Though Jackson's account of this scheme was "indistinct," Johnson, hoping to be of some help, "listened with patient attention."[11]

His eyesight naturally limited the sports in which he could participate, and he once remarked to Boswell "how wonderfully well he had contrived to be idle without them." In later life, when so much more is known about him, the effort to compensate for his defective vision is so plain (noticing details, rather showing off about it, and instinctively tempted to correct others) that it is impossible not to believe that it began early, even if we lacked the story of his attempt when he was about four to find his way home independently from Dame Oliver's. But there were limits. Sports where he would have to see a ball, or see others clearly at some distance, and do so with speed, were out of the question. When he first entered the grammar school, he gave up the hope of joining in games except in winter, when Stowe Pool was frozen, and the others would be out on the ice. Then, says Boswell, "he took a pleasure in being drawn upon the ice by a boy barefooted, who pulled him along by a garter fixed round him; no very easy operation, as his size was remarkably large."*

Increasingly he turned to swimming, leaping, and climbing, where sharpness of sight was less important. His father had taught him to swim at an early age in a stream that led from Stowe Pool. A Latin poem he wrote long afterward speaks of that spot, which he remembers with tenderness, and of his father teaching him "with gentle voice." He was still good at swimming in his late fifties, though he had little chance to swim for over thirty years. At Brighton in 1766 he surprised a "dipper"—a sort of lifeguard who dipped people in the sea,

---

* The phrasing, in Boswell's separate versions of what he learned from Hector, is open to different interpretations (closely analyzed by Waingrow, pp. 85–86). For example, the other boy could have been wearing what were called "barefoot-clogs," that is, "clogs without irons" (this is Mr. Pottle's suggestion), which means he would have been pulling Johnson, in this way, who would meanwhile have been either on skates or in his shoes ("sliding," which is something we know he liked to do later). Or, if the other boy was actually in bare feet, which would have been extremely unpleasant, Johnson could well appear to have been bullying him (in assertive pride and general revenge against the other for his own frustration because he could not see to skate, as the others were doing). The question is not as minor as it might at first seem. If Johnson, in frustration at the sports of others, was a bully, we should like to know. It would be one more example of something he would have had to overcome in himself. I myself cannot help feeling that bullying in this quasi-sadistic way would have been unlike Johnson, even at this age. His aggressive nature sprang into action only when he was attacked, or when beliefs with which he was personally identified would be attacked.

holding on to them lest they drown—by swimming so well. "Why Sir," said the dipper, "you must have been a stout-hearted gentleman forty years ago." After not having swum for several years, said Hawkins, "he went into the river at Oxford, and swam away to a part of it that he had been told of as a dangerous place, and where some one had been drowned."[12]

His mother, always ready to talk of her family, had doubtless already told him the story about his uncle, Cornelius Ford, that he later told Mrs. Thrale when she said she liked to hear about "uncles and cousins" of her friends. On a trip Ford passed a stone set up in honor of a man who had made a celebrated leap at that spot. "Why now, says my uncle, I could leap it in my boots; and he did leap it in his boots." Jumping over stiles and fences as well as climbing trees became a favorite pastime. The pride he took in his ability to do both is shown by the way in which it persisted. According to a story of Isaac Reed's, when Johnson revisited Lichfield in his seventies, three years before he died, a friend met him returning from Levett's Field, used by the students as a playground. Explaining, he said—"in a transport of joy"— that he had been

in search of a rail that he used to jump over when a boy. . . . "I have been so fortunate as to find it. I stood," said he, "gazing upon it some time with a degree of rapture, for it brought to my mind all my juvenile sports and pastimes, and at length I determined to try my skill and dexterity; I laid aside my hat and wig, pulled off my coat, and leapt over it twice."

Of the stories of his climbing as an older man, one can be cited at the moment. When a dinner, said the Reverend Mr. Parker, was being held for him at Stowe Hill (a hill adjoining Lichfield),

Johnson appeared at the great gate; he stood for some time in deep contemplation, and at length began to climb it, and, having succeeded in clearing it, advanced with hasty strides towards the house. On his arrival Mrs. Gastrel asked him, "if he had forgotten that there was a small gate for foot passengers by the side of the carriage entrance." "No, my dear lady, by no means," replied the Doctor; "but I had a mind to try whether I could climb a gate now as I used to do when I was a lad."[13]

5

Finally, he stopped attending church for most of the time he was at the Upper School.

This is a subject of great interest, or could be if only we knew more about it. The place of religion in Johnson's later life, and the desperation of his self-struggles about religion, cannot be overestimated.* His early skepticism about religious belief and his resistance to it—when viewed in the context of his whole life—would therefore be of compelling interest simultaneously to the theologian, the moralist, the psychologist, and the humanist generally—to the humanist concerned (as Johnson himself was) with how and why people become what they are and attain or care for the values they do. His brave honesty to that larger context was to weigh increasingly on his conscience from his twenties into his fifties, giving somber strength and dimension to all his thinking. This is ultimately why he is as great as he is, though it also created as a by-product some of the most painful psychological problems (operating as they did on his personal nature and history) that he was to face.

But we can piece together only a few things. Those missing thirty-eight pages in the "Annals," which he tore out before his death, would almost certainly have thrown light on the subject. Long afterward he let himself tell something about it to Boswell, though only in very general terms:

> I fell into an inattention to religion, or an indifference about it, in my ninth year. The church at Lichfield, in which we had a seat, wanted reparation, so I was to go and find a seat in other churches; and having bad eyes, and being awkward about this, I used to go and read in the fields on Sunday. This habit continued till my fourteenth year; and still I find a great reluctance to go to church. I then became a sort of lax *talker* against religion, for I did not much *think* against it.[14]

On Easter Sunday (April 1) of 1716, when Johnson was six and a half, some stones and mortar fell from the steeple of St. Mary's Church, which the Johnsons attended, onto the roof. The congregation, which already knew that the steeple was in bad shape, was now afraid that it might fall at any time. Within a month the church was closed for rebuilding. The spire was to be removed permanently, and its stones used to repair other parts of the church. The seats and pews were meanwhile taken to the chapel of St. John's Hospital, about a fourth of a mile distant, which the parishioners attended until St. Mary's was reopened some years later (December 30, 1721). But according to his own account, his "inattention to religion" begins in his ninth year, not in his seventh—the year when St. Mary's was closed. He presumably continued to attend the chapel at St. John's for two

---

* See below, pp. 448–60.

years before he secured his parents' permission not to continue going there with them.

The fact that his parents granted him this permission may therefore indicate that a strong, even militant, stand was taken by the boy. The permission may have come only after some acrimony, and could have served as a bone of contention for some time. The parents were not only devout but conventional. Combined with their disapproval, perhaps even distress for religious reasons, there would have been an understandable anxiety about what others would think. The town was small. The father had held positions in both the church and the town. The boy was still quite young. The parents would not have been impressed by an argument that going to a different church created embarrassment for their son because of his poor sight. He had been getting all around Lichfield and the adjoining countryside easily enough. The chapel was near. A seat could be found there as easily as at school. His parents would have been accompanying him anyway. And in any case, as we have noticed, he had already been going to the chapel for some time. Nor did he, according to his own account, go back to St. Mary's until a couple of years after it reopened. One feels, in the statement Boswell quotes, that the remark about the closing of St. Mary's—though this may have had something to do with the situation—was a way of detouring around details, including details of possible contention with the parents, that disturbed him to recall and that he felt were neither Boswell's business nor a helpful example to someone of Boswell's temperament.

On this as on other personal matters he talked more openly to Mrs. Thrale. But even then it was not so much about his indifference or opposition to religion, except in the most general terms, and certainly not about any stand that he took against his parents, which would naturally have revealed (perhaps in retrospect he could honestly believe would have exaggerated) how strongly he had felt. Instead it was about his attempt to overcome those feelings, and to do so entirely on his own. "At the age of ten"—presumably a year after he had stopped going to church—"his mind was disturbed by scruples of infidelity, which preyed upon his spirits, and made him very uneasy." This uneasiness, he said, he revealed to no one, but set about looking for "evidences of the truth of revelation." Remembering a book he had seen in his father's bookshop, Grotius's *De Veritate Religionis*, "he began to think himself highly culpable for neglecting such a means of information, and took himself severely to task for this sin, adding many acts of voluntary, and to others unknown, penance." When he got hold of the book, he started to read it. But finding his knowledge of Latin insufficient, he "set his heart at rest; and, not thinking to enquire whether there were any English books written on the subject, followed his usual amusements, and considered his conscience as lightened of a crime," believing it enough that he was increasing his diligence to "learn the language that contained the information." Meanwhile, in a kind of juvenile anticipation of Kant's argument that conscience is groundless without the existence of the moral law and immortality of some sort, "from the pain which guilt had given him, he now began to adduce the soul's immortality, which was the point that belief first stopped at" (*i.e.*, the first obstacle that belief encountered for him).[15]

There are three interests especially in this account, brief as it is, that are pertinent when we come to his religious attitudes generally. One is the extraordinary reticence with which this otherwise gregarious human being always preserved his religious struggles. Even this little story was something to be kept to himself. "When he had told me," said Mrs. Thrale, "this odd anecdote of his childhood; I cannot imagine (said he) what makes me talk of myself to you so, for I really never mentioned this foolish story to any body except Dr. Taylor"—the stolid John Taylor, his friend from boyhood, in whom he could confide knowing nothing would ever be said (Taylor, he told Mrs. Thrale on another occasion, "is better acquainted with my *heart* than any man or woman now alive"). A second interest is the early association of "guilt" with "immortality" and consequently religious faith generally. Often, in the later Johnson, we sense his deep reluctance to let go of the feeling of guilt and an unconscious attempt at times to strengthen it. This, when noticed, has been superficially associated with almost everything except what it really was associated with: a form not only of self-punishment but of habitual self-prodding. Finally there is the independence with which he set about trying to inform himself, without speaking to others. He could be confident only if he got it through his own effort. No other alternative presented itself. The burden of responsibility was his own.

6

Meanwhile Michael Johnson's financial problems were beginning to accumulate. By 1725, when his son was approaching sixteen, Michael was already four years behind in his taxes. The Commissioners of Excise were taking a sharp look at him. They noted that he seemed impossible to convict in the local courts. People in Lichfield thought too well of him. Back in 1717 he had been indicted for "using the Trade of a Tanner"—this would have been because of the parchment factory—without having served the seven-year apprenticeship required by law. It did not matter that he himself was doing the physical work of tanning. He was apparently acquitted (the court records are lost), and his fellow citizens showed their loyalty by electing him Junior Bailiff of the town (1718). Now, in his latest difficulties, the Commissioners of Excise wanted to be sure they could catch him. They wrote their local officer (July 27, 1725) that, since the Lichfield courts "would not give judgment against Mr. Michael Johnson, the tanner, notwithstanding the facts were fairly against him," the officer should not take the matter to the local courts "the next time he offends," but should instead send them an affidavit so that "he may be prosecuted in the Exchequer." While this was going on, his fellow citizens again rallied to his support, and persuaded the Bishop—who made the appointment from names given him by the Corporation—to choose Michael as Senior Bailiff, an annual position similar to that of Mayor.

However heartening the good opinion of his neighbors and the citizens generally, Michael could hardly fail to see the handwriting on the wall. The excise tax was particularly hard on an elderly man who had always been casual about business details. The family sentiment doubtless survives in Johnson's description (*Idler* 65) of a Commissioner of Excise as one of the "lowest of all human beings," and the definition of "excise" in the *Dictionary* as a "hateful tax" collected by "wretches hired by those to whom Excise is paid." In any case Michael was even less able now than he had been to pay the £100 he had agreed to pay in the complicated marriage settlement made back in 1706 with his wife's father, old Cornelius Ford. That £100, added to what Ford paid, was to have been put in trust, and more was to be added by both of them if there were children. The trust was handled by old Cornelius's son, Dr. Joseph Ford, the Stourbridge physician, who had not pressed Michael at all, but in return had not gone ahead with the Ford side of the agreement.[16]

Then, after Dr. Ford's death (1721) and that of his widow a year later, the matter was transferred to their son, young Cornelius, then a Fellow at Peterhouse, Cambridge. At first nothing was done. The good-natured Cornelius had much else on his mind. Then a generous settlement was worked out that was quite to Michael's advantage. The Lichfield house, valued at £200, was put in trust for the Johnson family generally. This liquidated Michael's debt, while providing only that he could not himself sell the house for his own purposes. In addition, the Ford estate—from the £200 they still owed to the old trust—gave Michael outright £100 in cash, half the value of the house, while continuing to owe the trust another £100 plus annual interest.

Cornelius came to Lichfield to complete the matter and sign the agreement on September 16, 1725. It was then that he met for the first time his young cousin, the bookseller's son, who that same month became sixteen.

Chapter 4

A Second Beginning:
Cornelius Ford and the Year at
Stourbridge

Cornelius Ford, now thirty-one, was perceptive as well as convivial. A former Cambridge don who had recently become a clergyman, he admired talent. So impressed was he by the intelligence of this large, rawboned youth of sixteen that he invited him to come back to Stourbridge for a visit. The parents, already grateful for his generosity, could hardly avoid being attracted, probably even dazzled, by a quality in Cornelius that was at once winning and remarkably rare: the union of genuine sophistication with good nature, impulsive kindness, and a refreshing lack of pretense. We can assume that Sarah was especially pleased by the invitation. Everything about Cornelius confirmed her family pride. Nor was Cornelius lessened in her own mind by having recently married into a family of some social standing.

For the boy, who had never seen anyone like Cornelius, it was a turning point in his life. Cornelius—or "Neely" as Johnson came to call him—was the first of two men who were to have a profound effect on him during these crucial years of the late teens when one is searching for the encouragement that comes from examples or models that are out of the ordinary; and the formative effect on him was to last indirectly throughout the rest of his life. Before turning to what that effect was, a little should be said about Cornelius himself.

2

The boy's rakish and brilliant cousin was now staying temporarily at his family home at Pedmore, just outside Stourbridge, passing the time until something came up.

After twelve years at Cambridge, first as a student at St. John's and then as a Fellow at Peterhouse, he had found university life too placid for his tastes, resigned his fellowship when he was thirty, and married Judith Crowley, who was forty-three, a member of a prosperous Quaker family. His father, Dr. Joseph Ford, had set a precedent for this, having himself married a somewhat older woman—the widow of Gregory Hickman, whose own family was well established at Stourbridge. Similarly Cornelius might in turn be said to have set a precedent for his young cousin when the time came for him to marry, except that Johnson's bride was to be even older as well as less plentifully endowed with worldly goods, and the initial motives were different. We put it more accurately if we say that at least the example of the admired Cornelius would have helped to smooth over any inhibitions Johnson might have had about a marriage that, because of the disparity of age, could and did seem strange to others. Judith's half brother, Sir Ambrose Crowley, was the iron manufacturer to whom William Penn turned for advice on developing the iron resources of Pennsylvania. Crowley was already acquiring so much money in organizing the iron industry, particularly in the north, that daughters in the family had begun marrying into the aristocracy.[1]

Judith herself did not share in the large fortune of Sir Ambrose. But she had inherited a comfortable amount from her father (he was said to have been so generous that he died a "poor man," but this was only in comparison with his relatives). What she had helped Cornelius pay off debts he had run up in Cambridge. Her lateness in marrying was not because she was unattractive. She had been wooed and had come close to marrying three times.* Even Cornelius had to court her for at

---

* One of her suitors (the second) was James Logan, Penn's secretary in Pennsylvania, later Chief Justice of the Colony, who eagerly wooed her while he was visiting England (1709–11). But her family did not want her to emigrate, and in any case wished her to marry another Quaker—a widower and old family friend, John Pemberton, whom she viewed with distaste and to whom, because of family pressure, she was briefly engaged. Before Cornelius, she does not seem to have been strongly interested in any man. Even James Logan, the man of whom she was

least five years before their marriage in 1724 (three ardent letters to her, written back in 1719, still survive in the possession of the Lloyd family). That she finally agreed is a tribute to Cornelius's capacity to charm. For it was against the wishes of her family, who preferred that she marry a Quaker. Moreover, Cornelius was already known to be fond of gambling. Even so, Judith finally decided not only to go ahead with the marriage, but also (since Cornelius was now an Anglican clergyman and would confront problems with a Quaker wife) to allow herself to be baptized in the Church of England.

Cornelius did not plan to stay in Stourbridge any longer than neces- sary, and was hoping to live pleasantly in London. The prospects were by no means impossible. Among his college friends at Cambridge were Charles Cornwallis, father of the Lord Cornwallis associated with the American Revolution; William Broome, Ford's roommate, who helped Pope with his translation of Homer—Ford was also to become ac- quainted with Pope; and, most important of all, Philip Stanhope, later the famous Earl of Chesterfield, to whom Ford—and thus Johnson— was about to become related by marriage. (Sir Ambrose Crowley's granddaughter, Mary Crowley, married Sir William Stanhope, Philip's younger brother.) About the time Ford met the young Johnson, Stan- hope's father became so seriously ill that it was plain he could not survive, and that the son would soon become Earl. That happened a few months later (February 1726). Chesterfield lost no time in becom- ing a patron of his college friend, giving him a position as one of his chaplains, and also (January 1727) presenting him with a rectory in Rutland. It was thus quite natural for Johnson, following his cousin's example in this as in some other ways, to have turned instinctively to Chesterfield years later when he hoped to find a sympathetic patron for his work on the *Dictionary;* and his bitterness when he was disap- pointed—Ford himself had by then been dead for several years—is a measure of the confidence he had felt.

After getting the rectory Ford contented himself—as was common at the time—with being an absentee, and settled in London in the Covent Garden area. What is almost certainly a portrait of him at the time survives in Hogarth's print *Midnight Modern Conversation,* where, as the central figure, he sits before the punch bowl with a pipe

---

fondest among the earlier suitors and who addresses her in a letter as "My dearest life," is in turn addressed by her merely as "Respected J. L." For discussion of Judith and her suitors, see M. L. Flinn, *Journal of the Friends Historical Society,* XLVII (1955), 71–77.

in one hand and a ladle in the other. He was said to have been able to hold any amount of liquor without showing it (which is something that Johnson, though he abstained from drinking much of his life, liked to think he also could do). Part of the point of Hogarth's picture is just that. The plump, smiling parson, alone among the company, seems to have all his wits, while most of the others sit comatose or totter in stunned disarray. His reputation for licentiousness has been misinterpreted. It existed primarily because he was a clergyman, and his convivial habits would have passed with less notice had this not been so. An informative account of him discovered by Aleyn Reade, and written just after Ford's death,[2] confirms the impression that "what Faults he had might be more properly Excrescencies of good Qualities, than Oppositions to them." Among those "good Qualities" were gregariousness or amiability—"he could not resist the Attractives of pleasing Conversation"; good-natured tolerance of frailties in others; and a complete lack of hypocrisy, the last of which is illustrated by an anecdote told by Colley Cibber. Within a couple of years after he became Earl, Lord Chesterfield was appointed Ambassador to The Hague (1728). Ford then tried to get Chesterfield to take him along to Holland. But Chesterfield knew that his merry and profligate friend was too open-natured to be capable of disguise, and he did not want to risk any chance of scandal with a member of his staff. "You should go," said Chesterfield, "if to your many vices you would add one more." "Pray, my Lord, what is that?" asked Ford. "Hypocrisy, my dear doctor."[3]

3

When Cornelius invited the boy for a visit, the thought was that he would stay for only a few days. But the weeks began to pass. The visit was to last almost nine months. The explanation usually given is that of Sir John Hawkins: that Cornelius, struck by the "uncommon" abilities of the youth, "was unwilling to let him return, and to make up for the loss he might sustain by his absence from school, became his instructor in the classics, and further assisted him in his studies."[4] But it is impossible not to believe that the boy himself, entranced by this very different world, at once so challenging and novel and yet so reassuring, expressed his own reluctance to leave. So meaningful was the experience, and in such essential as well as deeply needed ways, that a few years later—even when all it represented as a release and an open door appeared hopelessly lost—it was to seem to him not only one of the really memorable events in his life but something almost like a second birth.*

Of course he spoke to Cornelius, though the weeks were passing, of his unwillingness to return just yet. And of course Cornelius, confronted with such gratitude and seeing what the visit was accomplishing, was willing to help so gifted a youth—and one so surprisingly different from what even an experienced man like Cornelius had encountered. He had seen too much of the world to be put off by the appearance and manner of his cousin, nearsighted and quasi-rustic in speech ("shuperior" for "superior," "woonce" for "once," "poonsh" for "punch," "there" as though it rhymed with "near"). Cornelius would have had the perception to see that the youth's tenacious memory transcended what is usually meant when we speak of good memory, and that it was instead one part, one aspect, of a general tenacity of mind that, while penetrating to essentials, digests rather than discards detail. In turn, Cornelius's own learning, though he wore it lightly, went far beyond that of the formidable Hunter, not to mention Holbrooke or poor Humphrey Hawkins, as well as that of the kindly William Jorden, Johnson's tutor when he went to Oxford. Already as a student at Cambridge, "his mastery of the classics, and elegant *Latin* and *English* style was conspicuous"; and with his election to a fellowship at Peterhouse, a promising career at Cambridge had lain ahead for him if he had wished to remain in academic life. Whatever the instruction in particular texts that he gave Johnson, there was almost certainly little exercise in drill. Johnson would not have needed it anyway; and Ford, who would have found it tedious, would probably not have agreed to tutor the boy if he had felt that it was still needed. Ford's library at Pedmore was sizable. Most of the formal instruction probably consisted of assigning, perhaps often merely suggesting, texts to be read, and then going over the boy's translations while also discussing the works with him.

But there was plenty of informal instruction as well. Ford's familiarity with literature of the time—that of the late Restoration, the short Queen Anne period, and just afterward—was such that he could "transfuse the Quintessence of them," said John Henley, "into our Society, as smoothly as you rack off a Bottle into a Decanter." In addition, he knew actual writers, had seen at first hand something of

* See below, p. 55.

the literary life of London, and was familiar with the world of affairs. The debonair and casual informality of that imagined world of Cambridge and then London—itself so new to Johnson at sixteen—became still more attractive, even endearing, as it combined with Ford's own good sense and tolerant generosity. Some notions of social behavior were picked up, associated with that magical world, which meant enough to him symbolically to remain with him, as a part of his inner life, during all the years of poverty, from his early twenties to his forties. Then, when he began to enter a world similar to Ford's, they were brought out of cold storage, as it were, ready for use, and sometimes carried to an amusing, at times grotesque, extreme.* A small example would be the kind of nickname that was much more common in the quasi-aristocratic world of Johnson's boyhood than it was forty years later. Cornelius's friends had called him "Neely." Johnson, in later life, was to sprinkle nicknames like "Neely" among his friends: Goldsmith, for example, became "Goldy" ("I have often," said the exasperated Goldsmith, "desired him not to call me *Goldy*"); Langton, "Lanky"; Boswell, "Bozzy"; Cumberland, "Cumbey"; Dodsley, "Doddy"; and Lord Monboddo, "Monny." Old Mr. Sheridan became "She. ry," and later "Sherry-derry."

4

Above all, Ford had values that the boy quickly began to share and appropriate. All his life Johnson was to prize, in works of literature as in thinking generally, knowledge of what, in a favorite phrase, he liked to call "the living world." So Shakespeare, for example, disregarding arbitrary and narrow literary conventions, turns directly, when he is at his greatest, said Johnson, to "the living world," presenting "to his readers a faithful mirror of manners and of life." This is one of those eighteenth-century phrases—"manners and life"—that are charged with meaning and value for Johnson. And his first encounter with all that it signified was Cornelius, of whom, said Mrs. Thrale, he spoke "always with tenderness, praising his acquaintance with life and manners." Along with this was the premium Ford placed on generality and range of knowledge as contrasted with the parochial specialism to which the timid are always tempted to retreat. Johnson would quote from him, said Mrs. Thrale,

* See below, pp. 512–13.

one piece of advice that no man surely ever followed more exactly: "Obtain (says Ford) some general principles of every science; he who can talk only on one subject, or act only in one department, is seldom wanted, and perhaps never wished for; while the man of general knowledge can often benefit and always please."

To the end of his life, Johnson could justly pride himself in having taken this to heart. Nor was it only coverage or range that Ford had in mind, but the grasp of leading principles. This is the point of another maxim of Ford's, which Johnson would quote and which Mrs. Thrale wrote down but for some reason did not publish in her *Anecdotes:*

Mr. Johnson has a great notion of general knowledge being necessary to a complete Character. . . . The Knowledge of Books says he will never do without looking on life likewise with an observant Eye. . . . Nealy Ford . . . was he told me the Man who advised him to study the Principles of every thing, that a general Acquaintance with Life might be the Consequence of his Enquiries—Learn said he the leading Precognita of all things—no need per[haps] to turn over leaf by leaf; but grasp the Trunk hard only, and you will shake all the Branches.[5]

Then there was the emphasis Ford placed on the art of conversation, and the example he himself offered. He prized activity of mind, a constant and ready exercise of the imagination in applying range of knowledge while simultaneously drawing upon acquaintance with "the living world," and he believed that these qualities were best formed in the energetic give-and-take of conversation. To a mind like Johnson's, so quick to acquire verbatim knowledge, the pedantry to which so many laboriously toil would have been tempting, if only because it could have provided some easy victories, like the easy victories at the upper grammar school. But Cornelius's scorn of it, and the value placed on range and imaginative readiness, remained with Johnson. Over sixty years later, when he was writing the *Lives of the Poets,* he quoted Ford when he came to the life of William Broome—the poet who had helped Pope with his translation of the *Odyssey.* (At Cambridge, with his single-minded "addiction" to versifying, Broome had complacently rejoiced in the nickname his companions gave him—namely, "Poet.") Ford, who had for a time been a roommate of Broome's at college, described him as "a contracted scholar and a mere versifier, unacquainted with life, and unskilfull in conversation." The words are those habitual with Johnson—"contracted," "mere," "unacquainted with life," and "unskilfull in conversation." Later, when Broome began

51

"mingling with mankind, he cleared himself, as Ford likewise owned, from great part of his *scholastic rust.*"[6]

What Johnson got, in incorporating from Ford this ideal of the art and uses of conversation, came at so crucial and formative a time that it was to become a way of life—as it was for Ford himself. If there were enormous advantages (he was, after all, to become one of the supreme talkers of history, and conversation was the most lasting single pleasure he had), there were some unforeseen disadvantages from relying too heavily on it. It reinforced, for example, his later inability to be alone. Meanwhile, at sixteen, he threw himself into it with gusto. So much so that Cornelius felt it necessary to give him some gentle but ironic advice that Johnson would quote long afterward but found difficult himself to follow except fitfully: "You will make your way the more easily in the world, I see, as you [*i.e.,* to the extent that you] are contented to dispute no man's claim to conversation excellence; they will, therefore, more willingly allow your pretensions as a writer." (So gently worded was the irony that Mrs. Thrale, looking over her record of conversations when she was preparing her *Anecdotes,* and forgetting the context, interpreted it as a compliment paid by Cornelius to Johnson—a compliment, she thought, that may have been true at the time but was certainly not true of the later Johnson.) Johnson may also have begun the practice, which he said that he had as a boy, of choosing "the wrong side of a debate, because most ingenious, that is to say, most new things, could be said upon it."[7]

But, in any case, the habit of speaking well on a variety of subjects was developing so quickly that Ford's relatives and friends began to take an interest in the Lichfield boy. A part of the context, in this whole experience for Johnson, was the social position of Cornelius at Stourbridge, partly through the Ford family itself, but more through the Hickmans, by way of Cornelius's mother, and through the relatives of his wife, Judith Crowley. Bishop Percy, who grew up a few years later at nearby Bridgenorth, and knew some of the people involved, said that

> At Stourbridge Johnson's genius was so distinguished that, although little better than a school-boy, he was admitted into the best company of the place, and had no common attention paid to his conversation; of which remarkable instances were long remembered there.[8]

He even got to know George, afterwards Lord Lyttelton, with whom, said Percy, he had "some colloquial disputes." (Lyttelton, though a student at Eton, returned for vacations to the Lyttelton family seat at Hagley, a mile from Cornelius's house.) However radical Johnson's incapacity for snobbery of any sort, the discovery that he could himself be accepted and could move in a more sophisticated portion of "the living world" was tonic and reassuring. The gain in this was permanent even though his own life was to prove so different from his early twenties until his forties. Moreover, he could justly feel that his ability to mix with the sort of company Percy describes was partly owing to himself and his own efforts.

On the other hand, what such a company would have prized is also a tribute to Ford and his example. It would not have been what Johnson, except potentially, had brought with him from the upper grammar school and his father's bookshop, or from the combined examples of Michael, Sarah, Hunter, fellow students, and the relatives at Birmingham. It would not have been the ability to recite grammatical exercises at length, or to quote long passages verbatim after having quickly glanced at them, or to cite out-of-the-way reading done in his father's bookshop—unless it was both directly and quickly pertinent. Instead it involved another use of mind, or rather other uses of mind, operating on general knowledge through and by means of exactly those qualities that John Henley was to praise in Ford himself, who seemed to Henley a "Genius of Wit and good Humour": that is, a *"ready* Understanding"—readiness to get a point, which presupposes not only something of an internal fund of knowledge already there, but openness of interest and freedom from self-absorbed querulousness—together with "good Judgment, and lively Imagination." The direct result of these qualities, working in combination, was the interplay of good humor, wit, and knowledge that Johnson—though he himself was to excel more easily in the last two than the first—was henceforth to value so highly.

5

To have learned from Ford to the extent that he did, and to have incorporated so completely the values and habits mentioned, naturally—as in all profound influence, especially at such an impressionable age—involved a strong identification with him as a new and, for Johnson especially, a liberating "role model."

This identification is of the deepest significance for our understanding not only of Johnson's development but also of the character of his thought in his mature years. We can approach the larger implications of this only gradually, as they intermesh or conflict with other considerations. For the moment—for Johnson at sixteen—Ford embodied much that he had unconsciously, gropingly, been looking for, and brought it into clearer focus. This came at a time in his life when children, even those who would be considered fortunately placed, generally identify with models outside the home that provide a lifted horizon. But for Johnson the situation was intensified. To begin with, Cornelius really could be said to represent a higher sphere of existence (we are speaking of Cornelius not as he was entirely, least of all as what he was soon to become, but as he seemed to Johnson at this time and was forever remembered as being). In comparison, Michael Johnson was already becoming—and now, after Cornelius, would increasingly become—a "negative image," associated with melancholy, a narrow world, and, for Johnson, a rather sour smell of failure, or at least of blundering helplessness before life. Moreover, a "negative image" does not mean that we are free of it—or are in the process of rejecting it in any way other than intention. It can be only too actively present. The need in Johnson for something that would really counterbalance and if possible overbalance it was especially acute if only because it could not be easily shed.

Given the circumstances—Michael's own character and the son's growing fear that he shared it, the more than fifty years' difference in age, the general situation at home—the boy's natural, inevitable identification with his father would have unavoidably been one that confined rather than liberated, even if Johnson could have carried it more lightly than he did. But he could not have carried it lightly. His assimilative nature, of which his tenacious memory was one aspect and his strong internalization of demand was another, was such that once a thing was incorporated, it remained; and any battles with it henceforth were condemned to be battles with himself. What Cornelius represented, as the young Johnson now began to internalize it with such eagerness and hope, was nothing less than a means, desperately needed, of freeing and even saving him from a part of himself.

Later, when he was twenty-five and in the midst of deep depression, he was to begin a new diary or journal (written in Latin and headed with the Latin term "*Annales*"), prefacing it with the principal events of his life thus far.[9] Before the age of twenty, there are only three brief entries. They are simple records of fact. The first is the date of his birth in 1709. The second entry is his visit with Cornelius Ford, sixteen years later. Coming as it does, in this sparse list of the major events of his life, and following only the mention of his birth, it is like the record of a second birth. Such indeed it was. (The third item is his entrance to Oxford three years later, which for one short year was in its way a continuation—an extension or next step—into or at least toward the world Cornelius had represented.) The brevity and reserve of the entry about the visit betray a poignance little short of tragic for Johnson when he wrote it at the age of twenty-five. For the brilliant and warmhearted Cornelius, to whom he owed so much and to whom he might possibly have turned when he felt so lost, had by then been dead for three years. In any case, that world was now completely closed to Johnson. He was back where he had been, and to what he had been before he had learned, at sixteen, that there was such a world.

6

In early June 1726, almost nine months after Johnson had left home, he returned to Lichfield, expecting to enroll again in the grammar school. But John Hunter was offended by a truancy that could seem not only excessively long but rather cavalier. From Hunter's point of view, the boy—presumably away for only a few days' visit to relatives—had, without permission, simply let the months go by until he had missed a full two terms, and had not even attended another school while he was gone. He refused to take the boy back.

The parents were naturally distressed. Johnson in a few months would be seventeen. The chances of his going to a university were admittedly uncertain, perhaps remote. But if it were possible, he must first finish his schooling. And even if a university were out of the question, to finish up at a grammar school—which would involve another term or two—was a helpful if not absolutely necessary step to any kind of work that would begin to use his talents. With the Lichfield Grammar School closed to him, considerably more money than Michael could now spare would be needed for tuition and board charges if his son went elsewhere. For Michael's financial difficulties were growing. He hoped that the boy could get a position as a sort of part-time student teacher, and in return get a reduction in the costs. Apparently with the help of one of his relatives, Charles Skrymsher, who lived near the Newport School, in Shropshire, Michael tried to get his son admitted there as both a scholar and teacher's assistant. This was an ambitious hope on Michael's part. The school was excellent, and Samuel Lea, though he had only recently come there as headmaster, was already acquiring a deservedly high reputation. But Lea was understandably reluctant. He did not know the boy. He could hardly have avoided learning that Johnson had been refused even as a student at his local grammar school; and what was now being asked—a teacher's assistantship that would defray expenses—was exceptional. Years later, after the rejected pupil assistant had become famous, Lea "mentioned it as one of the most memorable events in his life, that 'he was *very near* having that great man as his scholar.' "[10]

Cornelius, learning of the situation, quickly stepped in to help. He could hardly avoid considering himself as partly responsible for the problem. He was doubtless planning to leave home soon, since his friend Chesterfield, who had become Earl in February, was now in a position to help him, and had probably already offered him a situation as one of his chaplains as well as promised him the first good living, as rector, that became available. But before he left, he could at least, with the help of his relatives the Hickmans, who had influence at the Stourbridge Grammar School, get the boy entered there in the way Michael had in mind, as a sort of student assistant. According to the rules, no "stranger" could qualify for admission until it was clear that the local children had been provided for satisfactorily; and even then the consent of one of the governors of the school was needed. Cornelius's half brother, Gregory Hickman, had been a governor, and Gregory's brother-in-law, Daniel Scott, was a governor now.[11] The matter was almost immediately arranged, and Johnson was at the school by the end of the Whitsuntide vacation, in July.

The headmaster, John Wentworth, may not have enjoyed the abruptness with which this was done. and it is possible that Johnson was not made an actual assistant but a sort of monitor. But, in any case, there was apparently no financial problem. If the position did not pay all of his expenses, Cornelius may have helped with the remainder. Like other boarders, as distinguished from the local "day students," Johnson presumably lived at the headmaster's house. Wentworth, an Oxford graduate, who was now about forty-eight or forty-nine, had been appointed headmaster when he was only twenty-seven. He had been considered then an able man, and he was still able. But after over twenty years, he seems to have found the job tedious, and to have begun to extend vacations. He was finally discharged six years later (1732) "for being too long absent from school and giving too long a holiday during Whitsuntide."[12]

Relations between Johnson and the headmaster were strained, but primarily, it would seem, because of Johnson's own attitude. He had become a little spoiled. He had been moving for some months in what he could consider a select circle, which had been paying him an appreciative attention he had never received before. After this, and after the stimulating conversations and easy informality with Neely, who had seemed to accept him as an equal, almost any teacher, or any school where he was one of many, could now seem to him an anticlimax. A master would probably have had to excel or at least match Neely—in wit, conversation, learning, knowledge of the world, and, above all, personal attention—in order to receive full approval. Hence Johnson's divided, in some ways contradictory, reactions to Wentworth. On the one hand, there is Mrs. Thrale's statement that "his next master [after John Hunter] he despised, as knowing less than himself." On the other hand, in contrasting the Lichfield and Stourbridge schools, he told Bishop Percy that under Hunter, he had learned "nothing from the master but a good deal in his school," while under Wentworth, he learned "a great deal from the master but nothing in his school."[13]

The explanation is probably found in the opening sentence of his involved, almost defensive, remark to Boswell—that Wentworth

was a very able man, but an idle man, and to me very severe; but I cannot blame him much. I was then a big boy; he saw I did not reverence him; and that he should get no honour by me. I had brought enough with me to carry me through; and all I should get at his school would be ascribed to my own labour, or to my former master. Yet he taught me a great deal.[14]

That Wentworth was "very able" was to his credit. That he was "idle" should not have bothered Johnson too much. Frankly admitting his own idleness, Johnson tended for most of his life to be tolerant of it in others. In any case, Wentworth spent time with Johnson—"he taught me a great deal"—and must have gone over some of Johnson's verse exercises in translation with him in detail. For he thought well enough of them to keep them, which is something a teacher rarely does unless he has real expectations of a pupil. (After his death, in 1741, they passed to a nephew from whom years later William Bowles acquired them and passed them along to Boswell; and, according to Bowles, there was only one other student among Johnson's contemporaries whose exercises Wentworth preserved.)[15] The real trouble, then, was that implied in the words *"to me* very severe." The severity probably did not involve corporal punishment (if only because of Johnson's physical size). It was obviously an affront to his dignity, though even here Johnson could not "blame him much" since "he saw I did not reverence him." Johnson also added (Boswell decided not to include the remark) that he himself was "idle, mischievous, and stole."[16] What he "stole" was probably quite limited in both size and value if only because the boys at Wentworth's house had to live in so open a way. It may have been a book or two from the excellent library that one of the Hickmans had given the school.

7

Meanwhile the social life at Stourbridge to which Cornelius had introduced him continued to be available to him, though to an inevitably more restricted degree. It is more than possible that Cornelius, with the opportunities now open to him and restive to get to London, left while the summer term at the school was under way (he had almost certainly left by the end of the summer; otherwise arrangements would probably have been made for Johnson to stay a while longer; or at least Johnson would have been less willing himself to leave). But even if Cornelius had gone, the doors of the Hickmans' and of their relatives and friends remained open. It is to this summer as much as to the preceding months that Bishop Percy refers in saying that Johnson, "although little better than a school-boy . . . was admitted to the best company of the place," and had some acquaintance with the family of Sir Thomas Lyttelton. Encouraged by the social atmosphere, he may even have tried to learn to dance during his year at Stourbridge. Asked whether he had ever gone to a dancing master, said Thomas Campbell (1775), "Aye, and a dancing mistress too," replied Johnson, "but I own to you I never took a lesson but one or two, my blind eyes showed me I could never make a proficiency." This would have been less likely to occur at home before he went to Stourbridge, or in the years immediately afterward, and even more unlikely when he was later living in such poverty in London during his twenties and thirties. However lacking in grace and defective in vision, he at least got the point. Mrs. Thrale remembered his pleasing "my daughter's dancing-master with a long argument about *his* art; which the man protested, at the close of the discourse, the Doctor knew more of than himself," even though he seemed "a person little likely" to know about it.[17]

Finally, "when at Stourbridge school," said Boswell, "he was much enamoured of Olivia Lloyd, a young Quaker, to whom he wrote a copy of verses, which I have not been able to recover."[18] (Somewhat earlier he had been in love with Ann Hector, Edmund's sister, but that "dropped out of my head imperceptibly.")[19] This is of some interest not only in its own right but in illustrating once again Johnson's eager emotional response to the new world to which Cornelius had introduced him. For Olivia was the niece of Judith Crowley, Cornelius's wife; and, in her situation if not her own personality, she could almost seem a younger version of Judith. Two years older than Johnson, a Quaker as her aunt had been before she married Cornelius, Olivia came from a family that was both cultivated and well-to-do, and on her father's side as well as that of her mother, Mary Crowley, Judith's sister. Her father, recently dead, was Sampson Lloyd, the Birmingham Quaker, who, like Ambrose Crowley, was a wealthy ironmaster. It was his grandson—the third Sampson Lloyd, Olivia's nephew—who was later to found Lloyd's Bank in London, and who entertained Johnson when he came to Birmingham in 1776. From another nephew we have a testimony to her love of literature and her ability to teach it. This was Charles Lloyd (1748–1828), the well-known philanthropist. It was through his aunt, Olivia, when he was a child, that he acquired his lifelong interest in the Latin and Greek classics.* In addition to her other attractions, Olivia was very good-looking, and was later described, in an account of the time, as "the pretty Birmingham quakeress."[20]

Nothing, of course, came of the attachment. Probably nothing could have come of it, given the circumstances, even if they had loved each other for a few years. In any case, the close of this magical year at Stourbridge, which was to come not long after the close of summer itself, meant the abrupt end of direct contact with most of the people he had known there. He was returning to a very different life, whatever new hopes for the future he was now beginning to have. Not that Olivia was forgotten. In some ways she was to serve as a kind of

---

* This is the Charles Lloyd whose son—of the same name—studied with Coleridge at Nether Stowey and became a minor poet, and whose daughter, named Olivia after her great-aunt, Charles Lamb found so attractive. For discussion of the elder Charles Lloyd's translations of Homer and Horace, and the respect with which they were regarded by Coleridge, Wordsworth, and Lamb, see E. V. Lucas, *Charles Lamb and the Lloyds* (London, 1898), pp. 174-235.

prototype of those beautiful and cultivated women—when he was at last in a position to meet them again—whose company delighted and exhilarated him, even though he would unconsciously assert his independence by his readiness to argue with them. Curiously, in his sixties, he was to meet someone not unlike Olivia in a common friend he had with the Lloyd family itself, and to become at once attracted to her. This was the beautiful and learned Quakeress, Mrs. Mary Knowles. His religious disputes with her, as recorded by Boswell, are what we usually remember when we think of her. But the affection and admiration beneath the surface are obvious. In fact, at their first meeting, when she and Johnson were looking at a print of a beautiful woman, while John Wilkes was pointing out features of the picture in detail, Wilkes said that Johnson "all the time" was betraying quite as much interest if not more—indeed "fervent admiration"—for "the corresponding charms of the fair Quaker."[21]

Chapter 5

Poems at Stourbridge

During his visit to Stourbridge, Johnson wrote several poems. About a dozen of them, mostly verse translations, survive.

These early poems—surprisingly good, and almost unknown until recently—deserve some discussion even in a general biography of Johnson. Juvenile works always have a special psychological fascination for us that minor works written later in life do not. In the poems Johnson wrote at Stourbridge, there are two further interests. We are not used to thinking of Johnson as primarily a poet. Yet most of these poems, though they started as mere school exercises, are as good as the verse written by any major poet at the same age (fifteen and sixteen). Even Keats did not succeed in writing better poetry until he had reached twenty. Equally interesting is the way in which these poems—unlike most juvenile verse—anticipate the writer's mature expression. Already, though he is only sixteen, they reflect his assimilative, meditative grip on experience. When he is translating a Latin poet, he is incapable of being light and airy, even if the original tends that way. Instead he often adds a new thoughtful and emotional poignance; and we also sense, beneath the classical surface, the restless turbulence, however severely controlled, that is so much a part of him.

2

Before turning to the Stourbridge poems, we should glance, if only for contrast, to the first poem Johnson is known to have written—some lines that he wrote about a year before, when he was fourteen or fifteen. When we think of the later Johnson, the very title is hilarious: "On a Daffodil, the First Flower the Author Had Seen That Year." (For that matter, one of his first compositions, he once said, had been a Latin poem on the "glow-worm," no copy of which is known.) The "Daffodil" survives because Edmund Hector obtained a copy, and passed the verses along to Boswell, after Johnson's death, saying that since "it was not characteristick of the Flower," Johnson "never much lik'd it." There is admittedly nothing distinctive to the daffodil, as contrasted with other flowers. Years later, when he and Sir Joshua Reynolds were visiting a country house in Devonshire, their host escorted him about the garden and suddenly asked, "Are you a botanist, Dr. Johnson?" Johnson replied he was not, and then, alluding to his nearsightedness, added, "Should I wish to become a botanist, I must first turn myself into a reptile."[1] The style of the poem follows one of the conventional lyric modes of the time—that associated with the lyrics of Matthew Prior. A quick sense of that idiom can be had by contrasting it with the fine condensed poem on the same subject by Robert Herrick, written the century before, which Johnson obviously knew. It is at once more stylized—almost frozenly so—sedate, self-conscious, semi-Latinate, and yet redundant (almost every noun has its adjective).

Of more interest is the general conception of the poem. For the flower is intellectually conceived—not seen concretely—in its relation to process and time (as Johnson's mature thought is always conceiving of life in the context of process and change): it heralds the coming year, but will fade like all earthly things, including "the poet and his theme." In the innumerable poems on this theme, from run-of-the-mill verse to a great poem like Keats's ode "On Melancholy," the conclusion is the theme of *carpe diem*. But already in Johnson an inner moral censorship prevents this. Finally a detail of minor interest deserves mention. In the great moral writing of Johnson, no human weakness is more searchingly exposed than that of "the cold malignity of envy." The subject of envy is constantly coming up in all of its ramifications.

Its unexpected appearance in this first poem is amusingly prophetic. In wishing the daffodil well, during its brief moment, he includes the hope that beautiful virgins looking at it will view its charms "with no *malignant* eye."

3

During the next year at Stourbridge, when he was sixteen, the advance is remarkable. A rather touching "Ode on Friendship," if it dates from this time, as Edmund Hector seemed to imply,[2] was almost certainly a tribute to the new friendship for Cornelius and perhaps the Stourbridge circle generally. The line "when virtues kindred virtues meet" reaffirms this inference. It was in Cornelius that, for the first time, he met someone with qualities that he hoped rather than feared he himself possessed.

Of the three original poems (as distinct from translations) that he wrote this year, the two best—this ode and a school exercise called *Festina Lente* ("Make Haste Slowly")—have one thing in common that helps to explain their immediate superiority over the "Daffodil." They are on moral subjects. And in Johnson, throughout life, the power of expression rises when he storms the main gate of direct moral reflection, cherishing rather than avoiding the obvious, disdaining what Bacon calls the "winding stair." The little "Friendship" ode is gentle and sedate, which is doubtless why Johnson was willing in later years to have it published. But in *Festina Lente* we get something close to the real Johnsonian note that, when it appears, sets him apart from other poets of the time. John Wentworth probably assigned the subject of "make haste slowly" to his impetuous pupil. But the exercise became more than a mere exercise because it was written both with self-knowledge and with that effort to realize "known truths" that is central to his greatness. And it is partly from the self-struggle involved that his best phrasing suddenly springs alive. So even here, in this short early exercise. It could almost remind us of moments in *The Vanity of Human Wishes:* the panorama there (where "*nations sink,* by darling schemes oppress'd, / When Vengeance listens to the fool's request")* is here anticipated in miniature by showing how, through rash impetuosity, entire "cities burn" and "*whole nations fall*"; or crowding num-

---

* All italics in quotations, from here to the end of the chapter, are mine.

bers are seen as "hurry'd" toward "death"; or how—in a strong couplet typical of his mature style—

> Orestes plung'd his vengefull dart
> Into his supplicating mother's heart.

The image of "cliffs" has a strong symbolic association with danger for Johnson (as we see, for example, in the portrait of Wolsey in *The Vanity of Human Wishes*, building on weak foundations "near the *steeps* of fate" and then falling to the "gulfs below"); and he even manages to insert this image twice, as we shall notice in a moment, in two poems he translates from Horace at about this time. So, in *Festina Lente*, in contrast with the use of reason to "calm" the "ruffled soul," we have the dangers of passion in the couplet

> Nor down steep cliffs precipitately move
> Urg'd headlong on by hatred or by love.*

4

It is the translations, among the school exercises preserved by John Wentworth, to which we must especially turn if we wish to look closely into the juvenile poems. They fall into four categories, the first two of less importance, and the latter two of more. First, there are two translations from Virgil's *Eclogues* (I and V), which are competent as verse and reasonably faithful in nuance of language to the original. But these obviously did not much excite him, and they contain much that he himself was later to scorn in the "pastoral" as a poetic form. Second,

---

* A third poem or "exercise" ("Upon the Feast of St. Simon and St. Jude") is of less interest except for its versification. It has been singled out from the poems of the Stourbridge year and given brief praise for no other apparent reason than that it is not in the couplet or one of the other more common forms of the time but in stanzas (the stanza form later used by Christopher Smart in *A Song to David*). From this it is inferred to be unconventional, and therefore "romantic" (and hence by definition "emotional"). A phrase used in the poem is occasionally cited ("extatick fury") as though it characterized the poem itself rather than serving as a rhetorical flourish of intention. The poem starts rather well, but it is overlong, and ends lamely, in a padded series of assertive gestures. Long afterward he was to repeat emphatically that "all religious verses were cold and feeble, and unworthy of the subject." It was a settled conviction throughout most of his mature life, and the experience of realizing it may have begun early. Yet the readiness with which the poem was written (for the feast day of St. Simon and St. Jude on October 28, 1726), and in a complicated stanza for a poet of his age, make it worthy of mention.

there is a translation of the dialogue between Hector and Andromache in the *Iliad*, VI, 390–502. A main interest here is that it is a *domestic* scene that he has chosen. One inevitably thinks ahead to those remarks repeated so often and with settled conviction, that "the passions rise higher at *domestic* than at imperial tragedies," or that a play like Rowe's *Fair Penitent* is "*domestick*, and assimilated to common life."[3] Third, there are the translations of Horace; and, fourth, the translation—almost startling in spots—of Joseph Addison's rather trivial mock-heroic poem, called "The Battle of the Cranes and Pigmies," which Addison had written in Latin as a student at Oxford.

Horace's odes, he later said, were in his early years "the compositions in which he took most delight."[4] They were brief, compressed, and pervaded by a sophisticated and reflective experience of life. Johnson was in time to learn not only brevity but remarkable compression. But the kind of sophistication that Horace represented—certainly the calm, ironic detachment—was remote from his own character, for which immediate, even passionate, involvement was the norm, and for which detachment was possible only through self-struggle. An example of the radical difference in temperament (it has nothing to do with the difference in age—it would have been the same at any time in Johnson's life) appears in his first surviving prose composition, written about the same time (it is dated 1725, when he was sixteen) as his first translation of Horace into verse. It was a fragment from a theme presumably based on a couple of lines by Horace (*Odes*, I, ii). The few words of Horace—self-contained, reflective, somewhat bitter-sweet—become the occasion for a vigorous attack by Johnson on the commercial avarice of imperialism.[5]

In short, an essential part of the appeal of Horace was his expression of what one side of Johnson—otherwise so different—valued as a corrective to his own heady and impulsive nature. Horace's odes could seem, by contrast, like oases of self-control, of cool and urbane wisdom. A good deal of care went into his first verse translation, that of the "*Integer vitae*" ode (I, xxii), which he apparently wrote before he was enrolled at Wentworth's school (since it was not among the exercises Wentworth preserved). And he liked it well enough to revise and print it several years later. It sets the tone for the three translations of Horace's odes that he wrote at Stourbridge for Wentworth (II, ix, xiv, and xx). In all of them he tries to keep the same number of lines as the original. This is always a problem in translating Latin, which is so much more compressed than English. Johnson succeeds in this as well as have most verse translators of Horace; and if in the process he has had to omit what would in English give a richness of nuance corresponding to the original, so have others. But of just as much interest as what these translations are, and what they succeed in doing, is what they are not, which tells us something about the later short poems. For the first thing that strikes the reader familiar with the writing for which Johnson is so widely remembered, valued, and quoted is how untypical of him they seem to be: untypical in their academic tameness, their timid conventionality, and lack of vigorous phrase. To remind ourselves of the age at which they were written is not a complete explanation. Not all juvenilia are academically cautious and mild. In fact, some of Johnson's is quite the opposite. More important, when we look ahead to the short poems written much later, we notice the same thing about many of them. Was Johnson in some way frozen, at an early age, into a style in writing short poems that was really at odds with what he himself most valued in the language of poetry? Behind his abrupt dismissal of Akenside's odes are values that had been lifelong: what makes them "dull" for Johnson is that they do not have "force, nature, or novelty." So in his own shorter poems, with exceptions: there may be some "nature" but there is surprisingly little "force" and still less of "novelty" in his language. For someone who possessed an unrivaled ability, as Thomas Tyers said, to put "the commonest things in the newest manner," even in casual remarks, they read as though the larger part of him was suddenly anesthetized or censored from unwelcome intrusion. The explanation, in the case of the Horatian odes, is the inhibition that inevitably arises when we are consciously trying to imitate something we highly respect that is fundamentally different from ourselves not in degree but in kind.

Significantly, in the two *Epodes* he translated from Horace at this time (II and XI)—a form Horace conceived as less meditated and distilled—Johnson could feel less respectful and hence freer. With the gate of inhibition partly opened, we have the sudden intrusion, particularly in *Epode* II, of unrestrained energy, and a briskness, almost bustle, of movement. At the start Horace is speaking of the happiness of the man who can live in the country, working his ancestral acres "like the pristine race of mortals." The simple Latin phrase is turned at once by Johnson into an exaggerated "metaphysical" conceit: "Like the first race in Saturn's reign, / *When floods of nectar stained the main.*" The man in the country, "free from all money-lending," becomes one "Whom no *contracted* debts molest, / no *griping* creditors

infest." He "does not dread the angry sea" becomes "He sees no boisterous tempests *sweep* / The surface of the *boiling* deep." It is amusing
to find, thirty years before the famous letter to Chesterfield, the word
"patron" already weighted, for the sixteen-year-old Johnson, with
associations of insult and indignity. Horace simply says that the man
retired to the county now "avoids the Forum and the proud thresholds
of more powerful citizens." For Johnson he becomes one who "ne'er
with *forc'd submission* waits / *Obsequious*, at his *patron's* gates." The
vigorous language continues, as he translates Horace's comparatively
gentle description of the activities of the retired man. Johnson is just as
compressed, and by no means distorts the prose sense. But with verbs
bristling in every line (one of the marked characteristics of his mature
prose style is the high proportion of verbs)* and the resulting rapid
movement from one image to another, one begins to feel that rural life
for the retired soul could be fatiguing. A few lines will illustrate.
Around the "lofty poplar trees" he

> *twines*
> With artful hand the *teeming* vines,
> Or *prunes* the barren boughs away;
> Or *sees* from far his bullocks *play*
> Or *drains* the labour of the bees,
> Or *sheers* the lambkins' snowy fleece . . .

Despite his respectful caution in translating the odes, there had been a
minor change of some interest in the first translation he had made (the
"*Integer vitae*" ode). Where Horace says, "Whether his way be
through the inhospitable Caucasus," Johnson writes, "Though
Scythia's *icy cliffs* he treads." We noticed, in discussing the early
Festina Lente, that there is some symbolic association for Johnson of
the image of a "cliff" with "danger." So with "torrent," as in the fine
couplet in *The Vanity of Human Wishes*: "Must helpless man, in
ignorance sedate, / Roll darkling down the *torrent* of his fate?" Similarly, in this picture of supposed rural delights and peace, Horace's
"But when the winter-season of thundering Jove brings rain and
snow" becomes

> But when increas'd by winter shours
> Down *cliffs* the roaring *torrent* pours. . . .

And in the "pleasures" that the winter brings—hunting animals and
snaring birds—the mild irony of Horace becomes more ominous in

* See below, p. 544.

Johnson, suggesting cruelty and pain for the victims and, in the word "secret," something deliberately plotted. Horace says, "He catches in the noose the timid hare and in the trap the migrating crane." Johnson writes that "he sets his nets, employs his skill," and with "secret" traps "ensnares / The *screaming* cranes and fearfull hares."

5

The sudden incursion of energy, when there is no taboo of respect to suppress or censor it, appears even more in the translation—only in our generation published in full—of Addison's Latin mock-heroic poem, "The Battle of the Pigmies and Cranes."[6] It was not simply that Addison was not Horace. But nothing we know of Johnson in his mature years suggests that he would like, or would ever have liked, this form of humor handled in the way Addison handles it. As he said of Gray's "Ode on the Death of a Favourite Cat," it is "a trifle; but it is not a happy trifle." It is overlong for what it tries, as an effort of "fancy," to do ("No poem should be long of which the purpose is only to strike the fancy"); and it also—inevitably, given its subject, a battle—involves suffering that is treated lightly, which is something that always instinctively repelled Johnson, and could even arouse his anger. (It was probably not selected by Johnson himself but assigned or suggested to him by Wentworth, as a recent Latin poem that he might now try as a challenge or change.)

Accordingly, more than in any of the other translations, we have an anticipation of what is typically his own in the use of poetic language. The surprise is to find it so early. For it is a mark not only of his mature style but of what can only be called a "mature" style generally. Fundamentally it is assimilative or incorporative—which is one of the essential characteristics we have been noting in Johnson's psychology, and also the source of his greatest strength as a thinker and writer. Here, at sixteen, it appears in phrases, sometimes entire lines, that suddenly go far beyond the original poetic value and impact.

What is being assimilated and compressed are three things in particular. One is a concrete vigor (even latent violence) not found in Addison. Another is the moral poignance that comes with direct involvement (in contrast with Addison's ironic detachment and mock-heroic stance). A third is the headlong storming of the main gate of the cliché or the commonplace that Christopher Ricks, in a brilliant essay on this poem, rightly describes as one of the most distinctive aspects of Johnson's poetic style.[7] Johnson not merely accepts a cliché or commonplace (as one of those "known truths" that the writer should seek to renovate) but goes out of his way to welcome additional ones, when opportunity offers, as a form of "the stability of truth"—of "known" truth to be incorporated for sanity of mind and heart. In the process of assimilating it into felt and known experience, what is usually thought of as cliché or as "dead metaphor" becomes alive, potentially even turbulent, while still contained within the "objective," the "familiar," the "known." We can quickly see this by comparing a few lines in Johnson's version with those of some other eighteenth-century translations of Addison's poem. Thus, at the start of the battle, Addison, in mock-heroic vein, says that he is going to sing of "these tiny pugilists," the pigmies, and of "their enemy [the cranes] rushing down from black clouds" (*"nigrisque ruentem e nubibus hostem"*). Picking up from that last clause, Thomas Newcombe, in his translation, writes, "Dark through the air, while hovering nations flow, / And from the clouds descends the feathered foe." James Beattie writes, "The small shrill trump, and chiefs of little size, / And armies rushing down the darkened skies." In contrast is Johnson's strong, concentrated phrasing: "from heaven's black concave, like a cloud, / Fresh foes descending glut their swords with blood." He here deliberately incorporates, and then through the context, as Mr. Ricks says, "invigorates the old metaphor which sees a multitude of birds or insects as a cloud" by also seeing them as so many that "they actually darken the air" ("black concave").

Serving the same function as that of the reawakened cliché, a Latin word (again as in Johnson's mature style) may be used in such a way that the context revives its traditional and "known" associations. On the battlefield a dying pigmy is described for five diluted lines by Thomas Newcombe (beginning "There, gently streaming from the hero's veins, / A pigmy's gore the purple field distains; / Deep murmurs from his heaving heart resound . . ."). William Warburton takes four lines and Beattie five. This is condensed by Johnson in a couplet at once concretely and sympathetically imagined. Its superb second line anticipates a quality in the language of *The Vanity of Human Wishes* in which Johnson is unrivaled in his century. Through its compressed, vivid context, the verb "involv'd," while retaining its full abstract implications, rescues back into imaginative conception its original concrete meaning of "wrapped," "shrouded," or "rolled about with":

> There a stout warriour fainting *gasps* for breath
> *And grasps the bloody sand involv'd with death.*

We may cite one final passage because it is different in kind, and yet typical in another way of the mature Johnson. This comes in a few lines near the close where we have, in Addison, not a "moral" (which is what it is to become in Johnson) but the mock-heroic suggestion of one—a sort of finger-wagging admonition that applies great things (the limits of empires) to small ones (the fall of the pigmy state) for what is assumed to be comic or ironic effect. Addison, translated almost literally, writes, "Surely there remains ultimately for every empire a definite conclusion. At length there are certain bounds beyond which it is not right and proper to cross. Thus once the empire of Assyria fell. Thus that of great Persia was toppled into the lowest position; and the Roman Empire, greater than both." It would be tedious to go through the other translations, though the cumulative effect of doing so—in these writers so much older and more experienced than Johnson—would point up still more, by contrast, the kind of imagination and sensibility already present in this youth of sixteen. What in Addison is given merely an ironic bow—the destiny of man, and the inevitable limit of all things human—has touched home to Johnson's more capacious and brooding nature, young as he is. At once the vigor of conception sharpens and the resonance deepens. Persia does not "topple," but "feels the force of Grecian steel," while Rome at its height is seen as suddenly powerless before the inevitable. The rhythm becomes steadier and more urgent as the panoramic sweep widens; and the strong rhyme-words, with their weight of meaning, serve as a sounding board (*ordain / in vain; awe / law*):

> To ev'ry empire bounds the gods ordain
> The limits fix'd they strive to pass in vain;
> So by their great decree Assyria fell
> And Persia felt the force of Grecian steel,
> Not Rome itself that held the world in awe
> Could cancell their irrevocable law.

Chapter 6

Back at Lichfield; a Further Model: Gilbert Walmesley

During the autumn of 1726, probably in early November, Johnson returned to Lichfield after having spent a little more than a year at Stourbridge. He was now seventeen, and he was to stay in Lichfield for another two years.

With Cornelius almost certainly gone—at the very least about to leave—the situation at Stourbridge had inevitably changed. The doors of other houses still remained open to him, but it was Cornelius who had been his particular aid and mentor, and who had felt a special obligation to help him. John Wentworth, however highly he thought of Johnson's abilities, was probably far from eager to continue an arrangement at the Stourbridge school in which the assistant who had been thrust on him—and who openly showed that he "did not reverence" his superior—was able to avoid paying any fees. Not that Wentworth felt free to discharge him. But he could have begun to show a lack of "reverence" in return, and the proud youth could be quick to note it, and, with Cornelius departing or having departed, feel it time to leave. There may have been some point to Edmund Hector's remark that he left after a dispute with Wentworth over the "purity of a phrase" in one of his written exercises.[1] The dispute would hardly in itself serve as a "cause." But it could have been used as a departing occasion or gesture, indicating that the real explanation had to do with his pride generally and his sensitiveness to the situation in which he was now placed.

In any case, he had gone about as far as one usually could in school, and was at an age when one either went to a university or turned to other things. He was only too aware of this. Shortly before his birthday, he either bought, or was given as a present, a Latin dictionary.[2] Throughout his later life he was constantly making resolves, particularly on his birthday or at the first of the year, to make a fresh start without delay. Another habit that was to grow on him was to resort to arithmetic—to numbers and computation—as a way of steadying his mind generally, or steadying his resolve (for example, in facing a large task, to emphasize what was now finished, and what yet had to be done). It was a way of breaking things down into manageable units, of getting perspective. Something of all this, in a mild way, appears already in this dictionary (itself an object that expresses resolve about his future work). For besides his name and the date (August 27, 1726) at the front of the dictionary, he wrote his name a second time at the end of the book, and the date of his birthday: "Sam: Johnson, Septr. 7th, 1726." Then—as if to drive in the passing of time, the finality with which this period of his life was now over, and the need to get started on the next—he subtracted the year of his birth, 1709, from 1726, and put down his age: seventeen.

2

By contrast, the circumstances at home could seem depressing, especially as the months began to pass. Michael, now seventy, was financially so pressed that he was soon forced to borrow from a friend, Richard Rider (later Chancellor of the Diocese). Any thought of a university career for the boy, remote enough before, faded still further, at least as an immediate possibility. There were, of course, relatives on the mother's side who could have helped. But Cornelius was now plunging into a different world. To Johnson, the shame in attaching oneself to him again, as a sort of perpetual dependent and after he had already done so much, would have been painful. The others almost certainly—and probably even Cornelius himself—did not know how badly off Michael really was. Johnson himself, while at Stourbridge, would hardly have advertised this to them. They would have had to be deliberately approached. We can only assume that pride prevented this.

Meanwhile Johnson began to work in his father's bookshop, and with the assumption on his father's part if not his own that, since there appeared no likely alternative, he would begin to learn the trade of a bookseller. This included learning how to bind books. Johnson never lost the art of doing it. He may have found it one of the most attractive duties of his work in the bookshop, and certainly preferable to waiting on the customers. Manual work of any kind he was always to find therapeutic. It got him out of himself; it focused attention and helped to pull the self into unity; and one could see progress in what one was making or doing. But to wait while a customer dawdled about the shop, hesitating between this book or that, prevented him from reading, while at the same time it failed to "fill the mind" (to use a favorite phrase) with any other interest than that of mere "traffic." When he was rebuked, said the Reverend William Shaw, for being so absorbed in a book that he neglected to wait on "some of the best of his father's customers," he replied that "to supersede the pleasures of reading, by the attentions of traffic, was a task he never could master."[3]

3

Naturally his sense of justice was stung when he saw one youth after another, possessing a fraction of his talent and qualification, going on to a university—as a mere matter of course, without apparent effort or anxiety—and doing so with the expectation, taken for granted, of entering one of the professions.

But one of the most striking things about Johnson's whole psychic nature is the severe rein he kept on any temptation (and it could naturally be very strong)· to project outward and to blame external conditions. Instead his whole procedure, as we have been noticing, was to meet a thing head on, as courageously and honestly as he could, and then internalize and contain it. The result—whatever the moral advantages—was time and again a pattern of self-conflict rather than of projection. Often, as we shall see, there is in this a strong element of compensation, a forceful bending over backward. This was to appear most plainly in political and social attitudes that were to develop now and in the next few years. By his early twenties he was to emerge—and remain—a radically uneasy though in some respects firmly genuine defender of established order. The subject is complex, and must be deferred until it can be discussed as something of a unit.* But whatever else is involved, included with it is a powerful inner censorship of

* For general discussion of his political attitudes, see below, pp. 190–203; for discussion of envy in the moral writings, see pp. 306–11.

whatever smacks of political and social envy, a proud disdain and contempt for every aspect of it.

So with personal envy. No writer has been more aware of the frightening potentiality of envy in the human heart, its readiness to spring alive, and the range of emotions and rationalization it can immediately, and self-deceptively, twist to its purpose. His experience, not only now but also, more importantly, throughout the next twenty years, provided as strong a temptation to chronic and even bitter envy as most people are ever forced to undergo. And yet, despite his aggressive nature, there are very few individuals—among those whose life we know well and whose experience has been even remotely comparable —who have been so completely free of any of the practical or concrete manifestations of envy. But more was involved than mere censorship and repression, however effective and complete they were. The ability to transcend envy, and not solely through inner censorship (though this is, of course, included), is part of the moral and psychological drama of Johnson's life.

4

Meanwhile, however confining and depressing the external circumstances, the two years he spent at home after his return from Stourbridge do not seem to have been too unhappy. For the crucial year at Stourbridge, while lifting his horizon, had also provided a momentum of purpose, interest, and confidence that helped to carry the two years that followed, though it might not have been enough to carry a period much longer. The amount of hope present beneath the surface at this time—however generalized rather than specific—can be measured by the contrast to what happened to him psychologically three years later, when he was forced to return penniless from Oxford and all possible doors to the future seemed really closed. Now, however, the year at Stourbridge had reinforced and given sanction to interests that before could seem unrelated, and had shown that there was or could be a vital relation between books and life. In the process it had also started to unify idealisms that had hitherto been random or scattered. Above all, it had given him the concrete experience—and therefore a new confidence—that qualities he himself possessed might have some place in "the living world" and not simply in the schoolroom or on exhibit before Michael's acquaintances.

This appeared especially in the remarkable range of reading he now did, but also in a certain amount of social life that would have been less possible—certainly less fruitful in its effect—without the previous experience at Stourbridge. The effort that went into this reading is partly concealed and partly betrayed by the apparently contradictory ways Johnson later spoke of it. He was tempted, on the one hand, to dismiss it. Even here there were mixed motives. He disliked open boasting; he liked people to believe things came easily to him; and, above all, there was the fact that the hopes of these two years, followed by his year at Oxford, were so appallingly disappointed after the age of twenty—and not for a short while but for another twenty years. The whole effort could, in a way, be considered a failure. It was painful to reflect back on the hopes of these two years, between Stourbridge and Oxford. Boswell—summarizing what Johnson had told him—writes:

> The two years which he spent at home, after his return from Stourbridge, he passed in what he thought idleness, and was scolded by his father for want of application. He had no settled plan, nor looked forward at all, but merely lived from day to day. Yet he read a great deal in a desultory manner, without any scheme of study, as chance threw books in his way, and inclination directed him through them.

As an example of chance combining with inclination, he mentioned having once thought that his brother, Nathaniel, had hidden some apples behind a large folio on an upper shelf of the bookshop. Climbing up in search of them, and not finding them, he found that the large folio "proved to be Petrarch, whom he had seen mentioned, in some preface, as one of the restorers of learning. His curiosity having been thus excited, he sat down with avidity, and read a great part of the book."

But he was expressing only part of his mind when he spoke of this time as being "passed in idleness." However ready he was to condemn himself for indolence and want of "method," he was quite aware that, if there was lack of "settled plan" or "scheme of study," he was—at least at this time—certainly not "idle." In fact, he could be secretly proud of having read as much as he did. As he was to say years later, "All censure of a man's self is oblique praise. It is in order to show how much he can spare." (To which he added oversternly, as he tended to do when he was really reminding himself, "It has all the invidiousness of self-praise, and all the reproach of falsehood.") And even in giving Boswell the account we have just been quoting, he started to add, as qualification, that what he had read was not works of "mere amuse-ment" and then, through this, was led to say even more:

Not voyages and travels, but all literature, Sir, all ancient writers, all manly: though but little Greek, only some of Anacreon and Hesiod; but in this irregular manner (added he) I had looked into a great many books, which were not commonly known at the Universities, where they seldom read any books but what are put into their hands by their tutors.

Uneasy lest he had come too close to boasting—against which, even when he was put on the defensive, he always had a strong inner taboo—he pulled himself back to understatement, and "concluded the account with saying, 'I would not have you think I was doing nothing then.'"

Actually Boswell, with a desire to correct the picture, makes him seem to talk even more strongly in defense of his "desultory" reading than he did on this particular occasion. For, after Johnson's remark that he had "looked into" many books not commonly known by students at the university, he adds to it, without break, a remark Johnson made at another time:

So that when I came to Oxford, Dr. Adams, now master of Pembroke College, told me, I was the best qualified for the University that he had ever known come there.

Johnson's guard was relaxed, when he let this particular remark fall, by their discussion of another compliment Dr. Adams had paid him while speaking to Boswell, and the excuse in mentioning it was partly as another example of Adams's generous attitude toward him.* But he had plainly treasured it for years (by the time he mentioned it, he was sixty-eight), and treasured it because he could feel it had some justice. Aside from these remarks or admissions, there are others that come close to being actual, if oblique, tributes by Johnson to the reading he did at this time, though phrased with a counterbalancing self-depreca-tion about his later life that would make them acceptable to his con-science. For example, he told William Windham (1784) "that he read Latin with as much ease when he went to college as at present," and speaking generally to Boswell about growing older (1763), suddenly added, "In my early years I read very hard. It is a sad reflection, but a true one, that I knew almost as much at eighteen as I do now."[4]

Statements like this betray the degree of hope that he felt at this

---

* See below, pp. 106–7.

time, however adverse the circumstances seemed to be. "Where there is no hope," as he was later to say, "there can be no endeavour."[5] And the hope, in turn, was sustained by the advice and example of Cornelius (the advice would have been of little help without the contagion of living example—or what the young Johnson thought to be "example"): to seek generality, not only in coverage or range but also by trying to penetrate to "leading principles" and "grasping the trunk hard" in order to "shake all the branches" for the fruit of knowledge. It was an advice (and example) that could appeal simultaneously to very different sides of him, whether they were faults or virtues, and justify them—retrieve and rescue them into purpose—by giving them both intellectual and moral direction through a vivid conception of value. It could put to profit and capitalize on his readiness of mind, and his imaginative speed in getting a point, his restless imagination and hunger for novelty, even his impatience and quick capacity for boredom. At the same time it had provided the beginning, at least, of the centrality that his divided nature so craved and valued. But it was a centrality not through mere "system" or "plan," against which his impatient nature was always rebelling anyway, but through *motive*—through moral concern (the question of "how to live," or what can be "put to use") and through eager and direct application to "the living world." Of course, his sense of that centrality was already deepening with a moral sincerity and with a creativity of concern and imaginative strength, if not yet a sophistication, that went far beyond the role model Cornelius had given him. But that is the destiny of role models when they help to awaken hope and purpose in a more capacious nature than themselves.

Accordingly, if he was now acquiring a capital—in the amount of reading he did in these two years—that could conceivably sustain him for the rest of his life, it was not one of sheer "facts" alone. The capital consisted also of habits in the imaginative and intellectual use of reading. It is not the start—that had begun earlier—but the active continuation and development of what Boswell, at the close of the *Life*, tried to describe:

His superiority over other learned men consisted chiefly in what may be called the art of thinking, the art of using his mind; a certain continual power of seizing the useful substance of all that he knew, and exhibiting it in a clear and forcible manner; so that knowledge, which we often see to be no better than lumber in men of dull understanding, was, in him, true, evident, and actual wisdom.[6]

5

Very much a part of the legacy of Cornelius, permanently incorporated in Johnson, was the ideal of active knowledge and experience of "life and manners": the ready and imaginative use of it through conversation; the kind of social life that would permit and encourage it; and the grace and informed nonchalance with which, as John Henley said, Cornelius could put the "quintessence" of things "as smoothly as you rack off a Bottle into a Decanter." The quality of gracefulness eluded Johnson for most of his life, though he never ceased to admire it to a degree that puzzled his friends, who naturally could not help contrasting Johnson's admiration of it with his own awkward and impulsive manner. But getting at the "quintessence" of things— through rather different qualities of mind from those of Cornelius— was already proving to be attainable (as the writing at Stourbridge shows) and was in time to become a distinguishing feature of his thought and expression. In fact, in the combination of exactly this ability with readiness of mind, he was ultimately to prove unequaled, or at least unexcelled, not only in his own century but also in the entire history of verbal intelligence as far as we know it.

More confident than he could ever have been without the year at Stourbridge, and partly because people at Lichfield knew that he had frequented the society he did while he was at Stourbridge, he began to share in the social and intellectual life at Lichfield to a degree that would otherwise have been less possible. Some of the people in whose homes he was welcome included Theophilus Levett, now the Town Clerk, who was a man of some means, and was regarded as having social connections (his godmother had been the Countess of Huntingdon); Stephen Simpson, a lawyer, to whose gifted but later dissipated and unhappy son, Joseph Simpson, Johnson was to remain a loyal and affectionate friend; John Marten, whose house was described as "the *rendezvous* of all the literati of that day or neighbourhood"; and William Butt, the man who had rebuked his children, when Johnson was a student at the grammar school, by saying, "You call him the great boy, but take my word for it, he will one day prove a great man." Perhaps even John Hunter, his old headmaster, began to relent and make peace with his former pupil. For Hunter's grandson, the Reverend Henry White, later claimed—referring to this period generally—that "to the house and table of his intelligent and worthy [former] master, young

Johnson had ever familiar access." In many of the Lichfield families he visited, said Boswell, he "was in the company of ladies." Boswell was naturally eager to learn about Johnson's personal manners at this time, since it was widely assumed that "he was never in good company till late in life": "Some of these ladies have assured me, they recollected him well as a young man, as distinguished for his complaisance."[7] He was also welcome at the home of another family, which was less well off financially but which, because of the social position of army officers at the time, had some standing in the community. This was the family of the delightfully vivacious Captain Peter Garrick. His parents, David and Marie Garric, were French Huguenots who had fled to England from Bordeaux in 1685, after the revocation of the Edict of Nantes. They had bought Peter a commission in the army—Huguenots generally encouraged their sons to enter the British army. His regiment was usually stationed at Lichfield, where he married the smiling and gentle Arabella Clough, the daughter of a vicar choral at the cathedral, and, though living most of the time on half pay, proceeded to father a large family.

The third of Peter's seven children was David Garrick, who was to become one of the greatest names in the history of the theater, and a lifelong friend of Johnson's. At this time David was not quite eleven, seven years younger than Johnson himself, but already brilliantly imitative, clever, and winning in nature. To the end of his life, Johnson—however much he himself might tease Garrick, and speak disparagingly of the dignity of the acting profession—would allow no one else to speak lightly of him. There were reasons for this loyalty. Within a few years, when Johnson's fortunes were at their lowest, at least thus far, Captain Peter Garrick and his son were among the few who showed their confidence in him. The deepest single emotion Johnson was capable of feeling toward others—and he was a strongly emotional man in many ways—was that of gratitude.

6

Most important of all, Johnson was now to find a second role model, helping to reinforce and in important ways qualify the one that Cornelius had given him. This was Gilbert Walmesley, a well-to-do lawyer of forty-seven, whom Anna Seward described as "the most able scholar and finest gentleman in Lichfield or its environs."

Here again, as with Cornelius, the effects were permanent. Even fifty years later Johnson doubted whether a day continued to pass "in which I have not some advantage from his friendship." The mellow and grateful tribute to Walmesley, in which he makes this remark, is often cited as one of the finest examples of Johnson's later prose. It appears in one of the *Lives of the Poets*—the life of the gifted, dissolute Edmund Smith (familiarly called "Rag" Smith, because of his negligent dress), who had died early, back in 1710. Walmesley, who had known Rag Smith, had told the young Johnson much about him. Some of what Walmesley said of Smith may have struck home, and even inspired an element of identification that we sense in this short biography written so long afterward (for example, that Smith "was remarkable for the power of reading with great rapidity, and retaining with great fidelity what he so easily collected"; or that "in his course of reading, it was particular that he had diligently perused, and accurately remembered, the old romances of knight-errantry"). Then, at the close of his account of Smith, Johnson says that he is indebted for much of his information to conversations he had long ago had with Walmesley, and adds:

> Of Gilbert Walmesley, thus presented to my mind, let me indulge myself in the remembrance. I knew him very early; he was one of the first friends that literature procured me, and I hope that at least my gratitude made me worthy of his notice.
>
> He was of an advanced age, and I was only not a boy; yet he never received my notions with contempt. He was a Whig, with all the virulence and malevolence of his party; yet difference of opinion did not keep us apart. I honoured him, and he endured me.
>
> He had mingled with the gay world without exemption from its vices or its follies, but had never neglected the cultivation of his mind; his belief of Revelation was unshaken; his learning preserved his principles; he grew first regular, and then pious.
>
> His studies had been so various that I am not able to name a man of equal knowledge. His acquaintance with books was great; and what he did not immediately know he could at least tell where to find. Such was his amplitude of learning and such his copiousness of communication that it may be doubted whether a day now passes in which I have not some advantage from his friendship.[8]

Walmesley, whose father had been Chancellor of the Diocese and for a short time a member of Parliament for the city, had gone to Trinity College, Oxford, and then prepared for the law at the Inner Temple. Both at Oxford and London, he had a wide acquaintance among men of fashion, some of whom were wits and others merely rakes. After being called to the bar, he was given the attractive and not very onerous position of Registrar of the Ecclesiastical Court at Lichfield, a position he had now held for almost twenty years. It was something of a sinecure—he held some other sinecures as well—and he was able to make extended trips to London in order to see old friends. Often crippled with gout, and forced at times to use crutches, he read widely—works on law, journals of news, both contemporary and earlier literature, and political tracts—and was a valued customer at Michael Johnson's bookshop. He lived in the cathedral close, at the Bishop's palace, which he leased—the Bishop himself living out at Eccleshall Castle.[9]

Walmesley was still a bachelor at forty-seven (in 1736, nine years later, he was to marry Magdalen Aston, whose sister, Mary, Johnson thought "the loveliest creature I ever saw," feeling in her presence what he could only call "rapture").* Walmesley had envied his friend George Duckett for having, as a wife, "such a one as you have, and two or three prating little rogues," whom a father could gradually introduce "to just and noble sentiments." Being lonely as well as generous, he took pleasure in seeking out "rising genius," as Anna Seward said, offering it hospitality at the Bishop's palace, and giving it also "the kind nutriment of attention and praise." He undoubtedly met Johnson at the bookshop, and had also known about him from Peter Garrick, whose ingenious, monkeylike son, with his quick repartees and imitations, had delighted Walmesley and who was already a frequent visitor at the Bishop's palace. Soon, "two or three evenings every week," said Anna Seward, "Mr. Walmesley called the stupendous stripling, and his livelier companion, David Garrick, who was a few years younger, to his plentiful board."[10] Another frequent guest, when the "stupendous stripling" and the vivacious Garrick were there, was Johnson's old schoolmate Robert James, to whose *Medicinal Dictionary* Johnson was later to contribute.†

Something of the freedom and cheerful atmosphere at Walmesley's house is suggested in a story, told by Thomas Davies, of a play put on by David Garrick, when still only eleven, in "a large room," probably the north drawing room at the Bishop's palace. This was in late 1727, shortly after Johnson had become acquainted with Walmesley. Since Davies, in his memoir of Garrick, says that it is to Johnson that "I am

* See below, p. 184.
† See below, p. 219.

indebted for the early part of Mr. Garrick's life," we can assume that the story is really Johnson's. The eleven-year-old Garrick selected Farquhar's *Recruiting Officer*, tried out various "young gentlemen and ladies," distributed the parts (taking himself the role of Sergeant Kite), and put on so fine a performance that the audience at Lichfield remembered it for years afterward. Johnson "was applied to by the little manager for a prologue to be spoken on the occasion." But Johnson, "though willing enough to oblige his young friend," neglected to write one, probably postponing it until it was too late.[11]

7

Without the combined influences of Cornelius Ford and Gilbert Walmesley, it is very doubtful that Johnson would have been at all what he was by the age of nineteen. And without their lasting effect on his tenaciously assimilative nature, it is doubtful that he could have ever survived, in the way he managed to do, the terrible test of the twenty years after he had to leave Oxford at the age of twenty.

In some ways Walmesley and Ford would naturally have appeared similar to a youth of Johnson's own temperament and background. To this extent the ideal now represented by Walmesley could merge with that already incorporated from Ford and strongly affirm it. To begin with, each was a man of the world, with direct knowledge of "life and manners." This included acquaintance, even direct involvement, with what is ordinarily considered a sophisticated portion of the world—both in a social and in a literary or intellectual sense—and with all the imagined pleasures and freedom of movement that a provincial youth, hearing of it from a distance, would attribute to it. That each had a somewhat rakish past—Cornelius especially, and Walmesley more by association with friends like Rag Smith—did not detract from the glamour but added to it. It was safe to admire it, as a part of their varied experience, since it was contained not only by their virtues but also by religious principle (firm in the case of Walmesley, and, though inclined to relaxation in Neely, by no means absent in him). Moreover, both were not only cultivated and widely read but also carried their learning lightly, Cornelius even more than Walmesley, and excelled in the art of conversation. Lastly, both were warm-natured, generous, and free from littleness.

But there were differences, which would have been less significant for Johnson without the parallels. To begin with, Walmesley was inevitably a more authoritarian figure. He was older. Cornelius was only thirty-one when Johnson had met him. Though this could already seem adult and experienced to a youth of sixteen, Walmesley was forty-seven when Johnson met him two years later; and at the age of eighteen, forty-seven can indeed seem—as Johnson himself described Walmesley—"of advanced age." That he was not a relative, like the engaging Neely, could also make him seem less accessible, and his social position—though this was probably less important—was higher. Moreover, he was steadier in character, firmer in aim. The combined effect was of a role model that, once incorporated into conscience and self-expectation, was potentially more rigorous and to that extent more exacting.

More important, by far, were two other differences: Walmesley, unlike Cornelius, was a practical lawyer, skillful in argument and debate; and in addition (for the two do not necessarily go together), he had a warm, even headily partisan, interest in politics. Cornelius disliked argument and dispute, realizing how little they can achieve in all matters human, fluid, speculative, or imaginative—matters that make up the bulk of what interests or engages the passions of mankind, and where interpretation, opinion, early influence, and emotional bias—as contrasted with clearly demonstrable certainty—are inevitably involved. Johnson took this to heart, was to find the truth of it exemplified throughout his life, and, whatever his own practice, was to write about the treacheries and futility of argument with as much insight as any writer on human nature has ever shown. In fact, it was to become a major theme in both his moral and critical writing. He could understand it so well—its "treacheries" as well as its temptations—because another part of him was so actively experienced in doing the exact opposite of what both his conscience and good sense approved: the competitive side of him that now responded eagerly to the example of the admired Walmesley, with his trained lawyer's habits of controversy, forcefulness in dispute, and readiness to take issue and discover flaws in another's argument.

Accordingly, whatever tendency there already was in Johnson toward argument and objection—and Cornelius's gentle advice had implied there was some—it was now drawn out, with permanent effect, through education by "trial at table," and given not only prolonged exercise but direction and even method from a respected example. Perhaps something of mannerism and tone was incorporated as well in this identification. Walmesley, for example, however convivial, could at times be testy, at least partly because of the gout from which he suffered. In fact, Anna Seward said that Johnson himself described Walmesley to her as "a man of strong passions, and, though benevolent in a thousand instances, yet irascible in as many." When she later quoted this back to him, he reaffirmed that though Walmesley "had bright and extensive powers of mind," which had been "cultivated by familiarity with the best authors," it was "no less a fact, that his disposition was irritable and violent." In any case, it was through the challenging pattern of Walmesley that we get the first essential step in the transition from the youth remembered for his "complaisance" (a stronger word at the time than it is now in suggesting courtesy and "eagerness to please or oblige") to that side of Johnson described by Reynolds as "contrary" to all Johnson himself knew of "the folly of this ambition": the Johnson for whom "the most light and airy dispute was . . . a dispute on the arena. He fought on every occasion as if his whole reputation depended upon the victory of the minute, and he fought with all the weapons." And Reynolds added that if he himself were to write a life of Johnson, he would feel it one of his main obligations as a biographer to stress the difference between this aspect of Johnson and the way he really was in "his natural disposition seen in his quiet hours."[12]

8

Two other lifelong influences of Walmesley's should be mentioned. One was a strong ambition to enter the law, just as Walmesley had done. All his life Johnson regretted that he had not been able to do so. As late even as his sixties, long after he had become a famous writer, we see this regret. He and Boswell one day met on the street his old college friend Oliver Edwards. Afterward Boswell repeated a remark "Mr. Edwards had said to me aside, that Dr. Johnson should have been of a profession." Johnson replied that "it *would* have been better that I had been of a profession. I ought to have been a lawyer." And Boswell then adds:

Sir William Scott informs me, that, upon the death of Lord Lichfield [1772] . . . he said to Johnson, "What a pity it is, Sir, that you did not follow the profession of the law. You might have been Lord Chancellor . . . and now that the title of Lichfield, your native city, is extinct, you might have had it." Johnson, upon this, seemed much agitated, and, in an angry tone, exclaimed, "Why will you vex me by suggesting this, when it is too late?"[13]

Finally, more than anyone Johnson had met thus far, and more than anyone he was to know well and respect highly for years to come, Walmesley had a vigorous and sharply informed interest in politics. More than that, he was hotly partisan. Like so many others of both social and intellectual position, he was a Whig, and, as Johnson said, a "violent" one. The Whigs considered themselves the more intellectually respectable party, associated with "enlightened" self-interest, laissez-faire commercial expansion, and the new economic forces generally. To most of them the Tories seemed rural or provincial, romantic and nostalgically backward-looking, unbusinesslike, and bumbling. From the Tory point of view, a thoroughgoing Whig could seem blithely unaware of the need of human nature for institutions that had grown over the years, offering it some measure of protection or shelter; blindly optimistic, and rather inhuman in his schematic and merely theoretical approach; and too concerned with what could most facilitate commercial gain.

Johnson's own political attitudes can be intelligibly discussed only if they are taken up as a unit, in which several factors converge;* and since the greater part of Johnson's life is still before us, this is not yet the place to stop in order to discuss them generally. But a few points can be made at the moment. However attractive and reassuring the new models of Ford and Walmesley (or the combined model of Ford-Walmesley), Johnson's extremely independent nature was bound to reassert itself strongly, and even to revolt, where it could do so with good conscience. Toryism for him was naturally associated with Michael Johnson and people like him, and Whiggism with the more affluent Fords, Crowleys, and now Gilbert Walmesley. However eager he was to share in their world, it was never in him to deny his own origins. He might wish desperately to be a different kind of person from Michael Johnson, psychologically as well as in what he did with his own life. But that did not mean adopting mechanically every attitude associated with the more fashionable world in which the Stourbridge people or Walmesley moved, least of all attitudes that appeared less charitable and less well informed about the humble and unfortunate. He was freer to internalize what was best about them if in at least

* For discussion of the subject, see below, pp. 190–203.

some things—with which they could not possibly be so well acquainted—their attitudes could be detached and kept at arm's length. In particular, that part of him that had earlier incorporated Michael's old-fashioned, quasi-rustic, and High-Church Toryism was now put on the defensive and therefore called into activity, through argument, and made far more assertive than it would otherwise have been. The challenge to react as he did was far greater because of the polemical and argumentative manner of Walmesley himself.

While the youth differentiated himself in political values, he at the same time began to imitate the method of dispute and the sharp tone of this testily partisan man who had stormed out of the city in anger when the Tory Peace of Utrecht was being celebrated in Lichfield (1713). He was, in effect, replying to Walmesley with something of a mirror image, in which the same thing is reflected back in reverse. In Walmesley's letters—and we can assume this was equally if not more so in his conversation—the language with which he speaks of the Tories (*e.g.*, "a pack of abandoned scoundrels") could easily be mistaken for that of the later Johnson, in his headier moments, about the Whigs. Long afterward, when the subject of "difference in political principles" came up during the trip to the Hebrides, Johnson said reflectively, "It is much increased by opposition. There was a violent Whig with whom I used to contend with great eagerness. After his death I felt my Toryism much abated." As Boswell infers, he was doubtless speaking here of Gilbert Walmesley.[14] But it was many years before Walmesley died (1751), and by then the habits of political controversy were thoroughly ingrained.

Chapter 7

Oxford

On October 31, 1728, a few weeks after he became nineteen, Johnson entered Pembroke College, Oxford—the third major event of his life listed in the "Annales" he wrote six years later (*"Novris. 1ᵐᵒ· S. J. Oxonium se contulit"*). He was to remain there for thirteen months. He had neither the money nor probably the wish to leave during vacations in order to return home for a visit.

What suddenly permitted him to go to Oxford was a small legacy that his mother received—enough to pay his expenses for a year—together with the prospect (it proved to be no more) of further help from a former school friend, Andrew Corbet. Sarah Johnson's rich cousin, Mrs. Elizabeth Harriotts, had died in February 1728, in her manor house at Trysull, near Wolverhampton. It was she who had openly showed her disapproval of Michael, on visits to Lichfield, but who had arranged for the well-known oculist Dr. Thomas Attwood, of Worcester, to examine the baby Samuel's eyes. In her will Mrs. Harriotts left Sarah "Fourty pounds for her owne separate use and one pair of my best Flaxen sheets and pillow Coates, A large pewter dish and a dozen of pewter plates." Sarah was not to receive the money until Michael provided his bond not to touch it himself (similar bonds were required of the husbands of Sarah's two sisters, who also received bequests). Whatever his earlier sensitivity to her contempt, and his halfhearted attempts to show his independence, the almost broken Michael, now seventy-two, was eager to oblige. Johnson remembered.

with some poignance, that "mentioning her legacy in the humility of distress, he called her *our good Cousin Harriotts*."[1]

The decision to use the money in order to send their gifted son to Oxford may not have been made at once. The amount was by no means enough to pay all his expenses for much more than a year. Other help would be needed. Fortunately other help was promised. Andrew Corbet, a lad from Shropshire who had been one of Hunter's boarders at the Lichfield Grammar School and a good friend of Johnson's, was now a gentleman commoner at Pembroke College. Corbet's father had been dead for nine years, and his mother—the well-to-do daughter of a Shropshire baronet, Sir Francis Edwardes—died early in 1728, about the time Mrs. Harriotts died. With money of his own suddenly available to do with as he liked, Corbet impulsively offered to pay part of Johnson's expenses at Oxford, said John Taylor, "as his companion in his studies" (or, as Hawkins put it more bluntly, an "assistant in his studies"), and he also offered to let Johnson—at least temporarily—live in his rooms at Pembroke. If there had been any hesitation about using the legacy to send Samuel to Oxford, Corbet's offer resolved the decision. Unfortunately Corbet's new independence also allowed him to be more foot-loose than he had hitherto been. By the time Johnson appeared at Pembroke College, Corbet had suddenly decided to leave. It did not occur to Corbet that he had an obligation to help with Johnson's expenses anyway: he was not providing a scholarship but intending to pay for services as an "assistant" or unofficial tutor in his studies while he was himself at the university. Besides Corbet, there were other inducements to choose Pembroke. Sarah's cousin Henry Jesson had gone there, and so had Dr. Swynfen, Johnson's godfather; and there were still other ties.[2]

Michael, as the only contribution he himself could make, allowed him to choose what books he wished from the bookshop. Johnson selected a surprisingly large number—over a hundred volumes. (A list survives because he left the books at Oxford, and later wrote asking for them to be returned to him.)[3] Since this was well beyond what most students took with them as a library, and could have cleaned out a valuable part of Michael's stock, it was a touching sign of the immense hope invested by the father in this all-important venture. The books and whatever clothes Johnson took were sent by wagon. As Johnson was preparing to leave, Dame Oliver, who had conducted the school for infants he had once attended, came over to say good-bye. She had since opened a small confectionery shop, and now brought him, in the simplicity of her kindness, her famous present of ginger-bread, telling him "he was the best scholar she had ever had"—a compliment he always remembered and "delighted in mentioning." Then, probably on horseback and riding through Birmingham, Stratford, and Chapel House, he and Michael set off for Oxford. The trip was about eighty miles, and they presumably stopped overnight on the way.[4]

2

The day they arrived (October 31), the anxious Michael—eager to have his son start off on what Michael thought was the right foot—arranged to have him that same evening meet his tutor, William Jorden, whom Johnson found gentle if ponderous and later described as "a very worthy but a heavy man." Michael could regard Jorden, who was about forty-three, as an important man whom they should try to impress; for he was also serving as chaplain to the college, and had within the past month become the Vice-Regent of Pembroke. Meanwhile Johnson paid seven pounds as "caution money" to the bursar (customarily paid in order to defray any future unpaid charges) and was allowed to take possession of the same lodgings (according to John Taylor) that Corbet had engaged for them, two flights of stairs above the gateway.[5]

Among the company present that evening at the interview was Jorden's young cousin of twenty-six, William Adams, then a junior Fellow and, much later, Master of Pembroke. It was Adams who long afterward said that he considered Johnson "the best qualified for the University that he had ever known come there." When Adams was in his late seventies, he still remembered that first evening, and told Boswell about it. The son, doubtless already embarrassed by the father's rustic officiousness (or "bustle") in requesting this interview in the first place, obviously became far more so as his old father began to brag about him, affirming to the assembled company that his son was "a good scholar, and a poet, and wrote Latin verses." The son could not now, as he did when he was a child, run off and climb a nearby tree in order to escape being shown off as "the plaything of dotage." Instead he "behaved modestly, and sat silent," which made a good impression on the company, though "his figure and manner appeared strange to them." At one point in the conversation when it seemed apt, he broke his silence and quoted the fifth-century grammarian and philosopher

Macrobius. They were naturally surprised, said Adam, that "a School-boy should know Macrobius."[6]

The following day Johnson attended a lecture on logic given by Jorden, and then neglected to appear during the next four days. He was not aware that attendance was expected, but seems to have assumed that lectures, like books, were to be dipped into and used as one found helpful. On the sixth day he met Jorden, who asked where he had been. Johnson replied that he "had been sliding in Christ-Church meadow." Telling the story to Boswell (1776), he said that he made that remark to Jorden " 'with as much *nonchalance* as I am now talking to you. I had no notion that I was wrong or irreverent to any tutor.' BOSWELL. 'That, Sir, was great fortitude of mind.' JOHNSON, 'No, Sir, stark insensibility.' " After dinner Jorden sent for him. By now Johnson had realized his mistake, and, expecting a sharp rebuke, "went with a beating heart. When we were seated, he told me he had sent for me to drink a glass of wine with him, and to tell me, he was *not* angry with me for missing his lecture. This was, in fact, a most severe reprimand." Immediately afterward Jorden sent for some other students, and they spent a pleasant afternoon. Jorden's kindness was typical, and in time, said Sir John Hawkins, Johnson grew to love Jorden for "the goodness of his nature," though he had little respect for his abilities: "Whenever (said he) a young man becomes Jorden's pupil, he becomes his son."[7]

Meanwhile verses were expected from the students on November 5, the anniversary of the famous Gunpowder Plot to blow up James I and Parliament (1605). On this occasion at Pembroke, there was a special celebration; the Juniors marched "round the fire in the hall"; and the undergraduates handed over their verses. The mention of the requirement could remind us of Johnson's remark in discussing Milton's early writing: "Some of the exercises on Gunpowder Treason might have been spared." Johnson neglected to write the exercise. Since he was always able to compose verse extemporaneously even when he had little or no subject, the explanation is that he probably did not take the request seriously. Instead he submitted some verses with the title *Somnium*, in which he said that the Muse had visited his sleep, "and whispered, that it did not become him to write on such subjects as politics; he should confine himself to humbler themes." About the same time his first declamation in Latin prose was due for his tutor. He neglected to work on it till the morning it was to be submitted. But because this was his first tutorial exercise, and he was a little apprehensive, he went over it twice—which is something he apparently did not bother to do again at Oxford (and rarely thereafter). He had time only to make one finished copy, which he handed over to Jorden as he walked into the hall. Being expected to repeat it orally, he memorized some of it on the way to the hall, said Mrs. Thrale (paraphrasing his own account), but was "obliged to begin by chance and continue on how he could, for he had got but little of it by heart." He was far from displeased that in "trusting to his present powers for immediate supply, he finished by adding astonishment to the applause of all who knew how little was owing to study." To do this certainly involved risk, said someone present who was listening to the account. "Not at all," replied Johnson. "No man I suppose leaps at once into deep water who does not know how to swim."[8]

He was at least half courting that "astonishment" and "applause," as well as the possibility of some approval (if not applause) from himself. He was, in effect, on trial for such time as he might be at Oxford. He was late in coming there. It was only chance that had ever permitted him to be there at all. And he might be early in leaving. Corbet had pulled the rug from under him almost immediately. The money from the small legacy to his mother would not last indefinitely. He could already be thinking of the injunction from St. John 9:4 that was to haunt him most of his life, the first words of which, in Greek, he later had put on the dial of his watch: "That night cometh, when no man can work." He would have to begin working in earnest. It might be some reassurance to know that he could make up, in speed and ready presence of mind, for lack of industry. But any solace this gave was very temporary. Nor did it, even temporarily, go very far except as the applause of others helped to dislodge—or distract him from—the sterner judgment of himself within his own mind.

3

Within a few weeks Jorden, by now quite aware of his pupil's talents, suggested that he translate, as a Christmas exercise, Alexander Pope's poem *Messiah* (1712) into Latin verse. (It was not, as has been sometimes said, a task imposed on him because of idleness, or, as Hawkins claimed, for "absenting himself from early prayers";[9] Johnson himself made this plain.) The premise of Pope's *Messiah* is the medieval belief that Virgil's Fourth Eclogue, which predicts the birth of a child who will bring a golden age, is a prophecy of Christ; and Pope, as he retells the prophecy in Isaiah, deliberately inserts echoes of Virgil. Johnson, writing in Latin, tries to incorporate Virgilian echoes more directly. At the same time he is trying to include every nuance, conceit, or metaphor of Pope himself. The result is verse that is rather crammed, and inevitably not too Virgilian, but is still something of a feat.

He plunged into the translation with remarkable speed. These 119 lines of Latin verse would have been an impressive performance if they had taken him a month or even two. But he wrote half of them in one afternoon, according to Edmund Hector, and finished the poem the following morning. Much of the energy in this burst of effort came from the hope that he might in this way attract enough approval and attention to get some financial help. The success story of Joseph Addison, as a distinguished alumnus of the Lichfield Grammar School, would naturally have been familiar to him—how "the accidental perusal of some Latin verses," as Johnson wrote later in his *Life of Addison*, "gained him the patronage of Dr. Lancaster, afterwards provost of Queen's College; by whose recommendation he was elected into Magdalen College as a Demy," that is, as a "foundation scholar." Three short Latin exercises by Johnson also survive, and he could have written many others. The *Messiah*, however, was a comparatively major effort. But though it brought him "general applause," as Adams said, it brought him nothing more tangible.[10]

He had been also hoping to have the poem presented to Pope himself. Sir John Hawkins said that this was actually done by Charles Arbuthnot, a student at Christ Church and the son of Pope's friend the famous Dr. John Arbuthnot. Pope then praised it by saying that posterity would wonder whether Johnson's Latin version or the English one was "the original." But John Taylor, who really knew Johnson at this time, tells a different story. Johnson must have sent a copy of the poem home, for the delighted Michael had it printed. It did not occur to Michael to ask his son's consent in advance. He would have taken it for granted that Samuel would be pleased, and may have meant it as a pleasant surprise. Just as understandably, the proud father seems to have sent a printed copy to Pope himself. For Johnson "was told that when somebody did shew it to Pope"—probably Charles Arbuthnot—"Pope said it was very finely done, but that he had seen it before, and said nothing more either of it or its Authour." At this the frustrated Johnson became "very angry" at the bumbling if well-meaning interference of his father. Obviously Taylor's account is closer to the facts.

Johnson himself, said Mrs. Thrale, was little inclined to talk about his life at college. But if knowledge of his life at Oxford were wanted, it "lies all between him [Taylor] and Adams," and "he was sure they would always tell the truth."[11]

He was more than angry. In a "violent manner" he told Taylor that "if it had not been his Father [who had done this] he would have cut his throat." The language portrays how much hope he had invested in the poem. By this time some months had passed (for Taylor did not even come to Oxford until March), and it was plain that the Latin version of the *Messiah* was not going to provide any help of a kind that was really needed and was becoming more needed with every month. He could not very well complain about the obtuseness of the authorities at Oxford, and the lack of anyone rushing forward to offer patronage as Dr. Lancaster had done with Addison, and as had happened innumerable times with others besides Addison. He would scorn complaint of this sort. It was his own responsibility. Inevitably the pent-up disappointment turned, for the moment, on poor Michael, of whom nothing was being asked but that he let well enough alone. And Johnson could hardly help exaggerating in his own mind (since there was nothing else to be hoped) the results that might have happened if only a friend had been able "first to introduce it to Pope" in what Johnson considered a proper manner—Pope, whom the brilliant Cornelius had met and who might remember him. But the matter was over.

A year or so after Johnson left Oxford, the work was included in a *Miscellany of Poems* (1731) edited by a young Pembroke tutor, John Husbands, who died a year after the collection appeared. The list of subscribers included almost half of all the members of Pembroke College who were present at the time Johnson was there. But Johnson's own name is not among them, in this book that contains the first surviving publication of any of his works.[12] He may not even have known that the book was appearing. Or, if he did, he could have hardly wished to be reminded—at that time—of the year at Oxford. That year and all it meant, or could mean, was by then hopelessly finished; his ties with it had been cut.

4

Meanwhile the Christmas vacation came and went. He stayed at Oxford throughout the vacation. The expense of the trip home and back was naturally beyond his means. Only three other undergraduates, according to the buttery books, remained in residence at Pembroke during the Christmas vacation. Disliking solitude as he did, he could hardly avoid feeling lonely. It may have been during these weeks that he once thought, "as he was turning the key of his chamber, he heard his mother distinctly call *Sam*."[13] But he probably had no great desire to return anyway. At least he could tell himself this with some truth, and make a virtue of necessity.

Oxford, even if deserted in vacation, was after all the continuation or extension of that magical world to which Cornelius had first introduced him. It was the necessary next step—the third major event in his life: first his birth; then Cornelius; then Oxford. With the momentum of effort and hope he had put into his Latin version of the *Messiah*, he could now turn to that large collection of over a hundred volumes that he had brought with him from Michael's bookshop—the Greek and Latin classics; philosophy and theology; the Renaissance and modern Latin writers, including Sir Thomas More and Erasmus; Vida and the two Scaligers; George Buchanan, William Baxter, and Jean Le Clerc. In addition, about a third of the volumes were books in English literature, particularly poetry from Spenser and Milton down to contemporaries who were favorites of Cornelius's, as well as Gilbert Walmesley's friend Rag Smith. He later said that "what he read *solidly* at Oxford was Greek," and that "the study of which he was most fond was Metaphysics."[14]

In the same burst of ambition and effort, it was probably now—in these solitary weeks—that he drew up an immense plan of study, or "Adversaria," covering all branches of knowledge. It passed after his death into the hands of Sir John Hawkins, who said that "the heads of science, to the extent of six folio volumes, are copiously branched throughout it." Inevitably, considering the magnitude of the task and the time available, the blank pages "far exceed in number the written leaves."[15] This was almost certainly begun before the end of the vacation, or at latest by spring, if only because the cost of the six folio volumes would soon be too high for him.

With his gift for learning to read languages quickly, he at some point—as a by-product of his other efforts—also learned to read French. For while he was at Oxford, he picked up a French translation of Father Jerome Lobo's account of his travels in Abyssinia, which at once caught his imagination. He could have learned French in odd hours while working in his father's bookshop. But the incentive to do so would have been greater at Oxford; and he was more likely to start it now than later, when he was doing assigned work, or talking with others as his acquaintance increased. Another book he is known to have read was one by the painter Jonathan Richardson—probably *An Essay on the Theory of Painting* (1715)—which he told Joshua Reynolds he found by chance on the stairs going up to his room. "I took it up with me to my chamber, and read it through, and truly I did not think it possible to say so much upon the art."[16]

With all this effort it was inevitable that some of the extreme self-expectation and self-demand should spill over or upon his tutor, the kindly, ponderous Jorden, and high-light his inadequacies. True, Johnson in later years would praise Jorden's kindness, and made that remark, "Whenever a young man becomes Jorden's pupil, he becomes his son." And another remark, recorded by Mrs. Thrale, is often quoted, though without attention to the second word: "That creature would (said he) defend his pupils to the last; no young lad under his care should suffer for committing slight improprieties, while he had breath to defend, or power to protect them. If I had had sons to send to college (added he), Jordan should have been their tutor." But these remarks, made so long afterward, could give an exaggerated picture of his reactions at the time. He was later to become far more tolerant of human frailty, and less intellectually arrogant about "standards," than he had been at nineteen. Moreover, Jorden had died (1739) a few years after Johnson was at Oxford, and this, given Johnson's nature, could cause some remorse for having spoken and acted as he sometimes did. Before long he so despised the "meanness" of Jorden's abilities, said Hawkins, that he often preferred to risk paying a small fine rather than to have to attend his lectures, and once told Jorden, when a fine was imposed, "Sir, you have sconced me two-pence for non-attendance at a lecture not worth a penny." There may also have been some disappointment in feeling that Jorden—however much he himself liked the Latin poem—lacked the mental stature, and general standing at Oxford, to do anything for him, or secure the attention of someone who could. In fact, other tutors thought of him as a "pupil-monger," automatically prepared to fight indiscriminately for any of his students, whatever their talents.[17]

Johnson might tell Mrs. Thrale that if he had had sons he would have wanted Jorden to be their tutor, but when he was a student, he had gone out of his way to give opposite advice to his friend John Taylor, and was now half compensating for it in his own thinking about Jorden. For some time he and Taylor, who were writing each other frequently, had been planning to be together at Pembroke. Taylor arrived at Oxford in March, about four and a half months after Johnson had entered, and hurried at once, he said, to his friend's room. But Johnson, rather ostentatiously displaying both his "conscientiousness" and his exacting standards, replied, "I cannot in conscience suffer you to enter here." For Jorden—the tutor to whom Taylor would be assigned—"is such a Blockhead that you will not be five minutes at his lectures till you find out what a fool he is and upbraid me with your looks for recommending you to him." The plans were then changed. Inquiring around, Johnson "from what he collected found that Mr. [Edmund] Bateman of Christ Church was the most celebrated tutor." Taylor therefore entered Christ Church, which was conveniently across the street. The lectures given by Bateman, though he was at this time a man of only twenty-four, did prove excellent (the subjects were classics, logic, ethics, and mathematics), and Johnson began to come over every day to get the substance of the lecture secondhand from Taylor.[18]

5

If at the very start Johnson had seemed indifferent in his work (and that was partly from ignorance of the routine expected, and because he had naturally acquired habits of independent study during the previous two years), he was certainly not so now or into the following summer, after which his hope of staying began to erode. The general impression that he idled away much of his time at Oxford is based largely on a few remarks he himself made. The standard he applied was impossibly high. (He once, when pressed, said he "never knew a man who studied hard. I conclude, indeed, from the effects, that some men have studied hard.") Taking his own remarks literally, one is tempted to notice those of others or incidents that confirm rather than modify them. Hence a composite picture is formed, based on that confused first week (sliding on the ice in Christ Church Meadow—"stark insensibility") and later cutting recitations in order to daydream or pass the day in alehouses, or "vexing the tutors and fellows," as Bishop Percy said:

I have heard from some of his contemporaries that he was generally seen lounging at the College gate, with a circle of young students round him, whom he was entertaining with wit, and keeping from their studies, if not spiriting them up to rebellion against the College discipline, which in his maturer years he so much extolled.

This is the sort of thing, about a man eminent for learning, that could be exaggerated in retrospect ("generally seen lounging . . .") by school or college friends who feel able to give "inside" information that would contradict the stock notions others might have of what he was like as a youth. A kind word from someone he respected could quickly change his attitude for a while. "I have heard him say . . . that the mild but judicious expostulations" of the then young William Adams, "whose virtue awed him, and whose learning he revered, made him really ashamed of himself, 'though I fear (said he) I was too proud to own it.' "[19] In any case, a distinction should be kept in mind between idleness and rebellious attitudes toward regulations. Neither necessarily involves the other. Significantly neither Adams nor Taylor —the two that he said best knew his life at Oxford—stress his idleness.

The spirit of "emulation" was, he thought, one of the best things a university could provide as a means of strengthening or even inciting motivation. This was his thought when forty years later he "expatiated on the advantages of Oxford for learning" because of its "progressive emulation": "The students are anxious to appear well to their tutors; the tutors are anxious to have their pupils appear well in the college; the colleges are anxious to have their students appear well in the University." In his own case emulation was impelled by a hope with something close to desperation. It was only through learning and presence of mind that he could make his way. One of his fellow students struck him as especially able. This was John Meeke, a grandson of John Cooke, who had been Latin secretary to Charles II. The same age as Johnson, he had entered Pembroke two years before, and was to stay on and become a Fellow there for the remainder of his life. So well did he recite that Johnson "could not bear Meeke's superiority, and I tried to sit as far from him as I could, that I might not hear him construe." He confessed this to Thomas Warton, after they called on Meeke at Oxford twenty-five years later. The visit, said Warton, was very "cordial." But Johnson could not refrain from quoting—thinking of Meeke as he was now—"alas! 'Lost in a convent's solitary gloom,' " and adding that at about the same time that the gifted Meeke had graduated and then stayed "to feed on a fellowship," "I went to London to get my living: now, Sir, see the difference of our literary characters!"[20]

Working in his room, Johnson would refuse to reply to the servitor who was sent around at night to check whether the students were present. Knocking on each door, the servitor would ask whether they were there. If there was no answer, he then reported them absent. Johnson, said Hawkins, "could not endure this intrusion, and would frequently be silent, when the utterance of a word would have insured him from censure." Sometimes in exasperation, when he justly considered himself as "profitably employed as perhaps he could be," he would join the others in what was called "hunting the servitor." Seizing pots and candlesticks, and beating them loudly together, they would set off in search of the frightened youth, chanting the lines from the old ballad "Chevy Chase" beginning "To drive the deer with hound and horn."[21]

Naturally, while he was working in his room, his imagination would often leap forward into the future. As he was to say repeatedly—taking it as a fundamental premise of human life—"So few of the hours of life are filled up with objects adequate" to the desires and imagination of human beings that all of us "are forced to have recourse . . . to the past and future for supplemental satisfactions," and in youth, since the past is small in comparison, the imagination especially turns to the future in order to carry us through the present. Moreover, in any kind of continued labor, "he that directs his steps to a certain point, must frequently turn his eyes to that place which he strives to reach; he that undergoes the fatigue of labour, must solace his weariness with the contemplation of its reward." Few enterprises of real labor or risk would ever be undertaken, he goes on, unless we magnified in imagination the rewards. We are all like Don Quixote in this respect. If we are honest, "our hearts inform us he is not more ridiculous than ourselves, except that he *tells* what we have only *thought.*"[22] What he looked forward to was not only the world of the law courts, or of scholarship and literature—the world of Ford and Walmesley—but the chance of travel. The notion that he had little interest in it is one of the strangest of all misconceptions about him.* "He loved indeed the very act of travelling," said Mrs. Thrale, and found it inconceivable that people should complain about the inconveniences of it when the interest and advantages seemed to him so great. According to Adams, Dr. Matthew Panting—the Master of Pembroke, one side of whose house was a few feet across from the windows of Johnson's room—overheard him talking to himself one day "in his strong emphatick voice," saying he had "a mind to see what is done in other places of learning. I'll go to

* See below, pp. 461–62.

France and Italy. I'll go to Padua.—And [instinctively cautioning himself not to be too assertive] I'll mind my business—For an *Athenian* blockhead is the worst of all blockheads."[23]

6

But even at the height of his effort, he was often with friends or acquaintances, especially after John Taylor came in March. Pembroke was then quite small, with not much more than forty men in residence at any one time. Johnson, at least after a few months, may have got to know most of them. On a visit to Oxford late in life (1776), he mentioned two of them as he strolled into the common room at Pembroke with Dr. Adams, then Master, and Boswell. "After a reverie of meditation," he said, "Here I used to play at draughts with Phil Jones and Fludyer. Jones loved beer, and did not get very forward in the church." Jones indeed did not get much "forward": at his death (1764) he was still only a sort of unofficial curate working for another old college friend, Matthew Bloxam, vicar at Overbury, in Worcestershire. In the buttery books at Pembroke—where students would occasionally scribble remarks next to the names—a fair number are allotted Jones ("Ass," "alias Vinegar," "long Gutts"). There are also the start of a doggerel verse ("Philip Jones without any stones") and a picture showing a gaunt young man with unshaven chin. As for John Fludyer (though he seems later to have preferred the name "Fludger"), who was a Low-Church clergyman and a "violent Whig," Johnson said that he "turned out a scoundrel," though "he had been a scoundrel all along, to be sure." Boswell asked whether that meant he had been only a "political scoundrel" or whether it applied in other ways: for example, "Did he cheat at draughts?" Johnson, who apparently did not wish to pursue the subject, simply replied, "We never played for *money*." Quite different from Jones and Fludyer was the kindly William Vyse (1709–70), a gentleman-commoner whose parents were dead and who enters the Johnson story prominently a little later, not long before Johnson left Oxford. He also came from Staffordshire, seems to have had some Lichfield connections, and in time became Treasurer of Lichfield Cathedral and Archdeacon of Shropshire. At Pembroke he grew quite fond of William Jorden, and having a living at his disposal (the rectory of Standon), presented it to Jorden, who, in order to accept it, left Oxford shortly before Johnson himself did.[24]

By far the best remembered of Johnson's fellow students at Pembroke is Oliver Edwards (1711–91) because he reappears almost fifty years later in one of the most delightful scenes in Boswell. It is Edwards who, in the course of the dialogue, makes the famous statement, "You are a philosopher, Dr. Johnson. I have tried too in my time to be a philosopher; but, I don't know how, cheerfulness was always breaking in." After Oxford Edwards practiced for many years as a solicitor in chancery and then retired to a small farm, where he lived an innocent and extremely settled life ("I must have my regular meals, and a glass of good wine. I find I require it"; and a late supper, which "I consider . . . as a turnpike through which one must pass, in order to get to bed"). From one of the things said by Edwards, it is plain that Johnson's dislike of hyperbole ("Don't, Sir, accustom yourself to use big words for little matters") was already apparent at nineteen: "I remember you would not let us say *prodigious* at College. For even then, Sir, (turning to me,) he was delicate in language, and we all feared him"—a remark that led Johnson to say later, "They respected me for my literature; and yet it was not great but by comparison," and then to add, "It is amazing how little literature there is in the world." Though Edwards matriculated in June, he was not in steady residence until the autumn. Because of Johnson's capacity for almost total recall, we have—within this general scene of two elderly men talking—a miniature flashback scene to a moment in those autumn months at Oxford when Johnson and Edwards were sitting in an alehouse. After forty-nine years Johnson had at first not recognized Edwards when he came up to Johnson in the street and introduced himself, nor even recollected the name—they were hardly close acquaintances at Oxford in the short time they were there together. But gradually, as they talked, the memory came back. Then,

Taking himself up all of a sudden, he exclaimed, "O! Mr. Edwards! I'll convince you that I recollect you. Do you remember our drinking together at an alehouse near Pembroke gate. At that time, you told me of the Eton boy, who, when verses on our Saviour's turning water into wine were prescribed as an exercise, brought up a single line, which was highly admired: '*Vidit et erubuit lympha pudica Deum*,' and I told you of another fine line in 'Camden's Remains,' an eulogy upon one of our kings, who was succeeded by his son, a prince of equal merit: '*Mira cano, Sol occubuit, nox nulla secuta est.*' "[25]

He had, of course, been showing off when, at the alehouse, he had capped the line of the Eton boy with another line so completely out of the way. To have remembered both lines after so long a time shows the attention and effort invested even on so slight an occasion. He was by then drawing to the end of his stay at Oxford.

7

Beneath the conviviality and effort, there are darker hints—at least as the year 1729 wore on—that all was not well. His situation was becoming very precarious. By the summer months it was plain that the small legacy his mother had received from Mrs. Harriotts was not going to be supplemented by help from any other source. In fact, even some of that money may have had to be withheld because of needs at home. This is the only way of explaining the extreme poverty in which he found himself that autumn.

Something of his state of mind can be learned by reflecting on the character of two books he was reading—by Bernard Mandeville and William Law—which had an extraordinary impact on him. For these are not books to which we would expect an undergraduate, however gifted, to be drawn. Least of all would one expect an undergraduate to absorb them to such an extent that they would prove permanently influential—the first up to a point, with reservations, and the second in a way nothing less than profound. In a sense, they were diametrical opposites. But they have one thing in common: with complete disdain of easy illusions about human nature, they strip things down to the essential with a directness and satiric realism that struck home to Johnson's own strong essentialism and remained with him.

Mandeville's brilliant *Fable of the Bees,* with the *Enquiry into the Origin of Moral Virtue* appended to it (1714), was widely considered a shocking attack on the growing Romantic idea that man, at bottom, is instinctively good, and will flower into virtue if only the environment is favorable. Mandeville is not content with merely undercutting this notion in favor of the traditional doctrine of "original sin"—that man is naturally corrupt, and that any virtue he is able to acquire comes only through the conquest of reason or religion over the "natural man." He goes further (partly with his tongue in his cheek), and argues that what are called "virtues" are only hypocrisy, that a society in which they predominated would fall into apathy and then paralysis, and that self-love is the sole engine able to keep alive all effort and progress, both economically and intellectually. From this, Mandeville evolves his famous paradox, "Private vices are public benefits."

If Johnson found himself, then and especially later, qualifying

Mandeville, and making distinctions that Mandeville overlooked, at least he found himself now thinking of these matters in a way he would not otherwise have done. As he told Anna Seward, Mandeville "opened my views into real life very much." The sharp satiric reductionism of Mandeville as he cuts through pretenses in his portraits of human character, his ability to reduce things at once to a common denominator that the "cant" of sentimentality and self-deception are always disguising, was to become a permanent part (though only a part) of Johnson's own style, in which compassion and exasperation were so often to wrestle with each other.* Another, more general effect of his reading Mandeville, said Mrs. Thrale, was to increase his own scruples and to make him henceforth "very watchful for the Stains of original Corruption both in himself and others":

> The natural depravity of mankind and remains of original sin were so fixed in Mr. Johnson's opinion, that he was indeed a most acute observer of their effects; and used to say sometimes, half in jest half in earnest, that they were the remains of his old tutor Mandeville's instructions. As a book however, he took care always loudly to condemn the Fable of the Bees, but not without adding, "that it was the work of a *thinking man*."[26]

Far more important than Mandeville as an influence, not only on his thinking, but also even on the form of much of his writing in the years ahead, was the moving devotional work—the finest of its kind written during the century—by William Law, *A Serious Call to a Devout and Holy Life,* which is said to have appeared late in 1728, the year Johnson entered Oxford, but which Johnson almost certainly did not encounter until after the 1729 edition was published. Thus far, as Johnson told Boswell, he had been "a sort of lax *talker* against religion, for I did not much *think* against it." Then, coming across Law's *Serious Call* at Oxford, he began to read it,

> expecting to find it a dull book (as such books generally are), and perhaps to laugh at it. But I found Law quite an overmatch for me; and this was the first occasion of my thinking in earnest of religion, after I became capable of rational inquiry.[27]

Many things about this book, read at this crucial period of his life, remained with him and grew into his habitual feeling in the years ahead.[28] (Nor was it all gain, at least as far as peace of mind was concerned.) For the moment we should notice the most striking thing about the book's influence, at least as far as the form of Johnson's own

---

* See below, pp. 493–96.

writing is concerned. Following the prototype of Ecclesiastes, Law turns on one after another of the desires, ambitions, or possessions at which the human imagination clutches. Time and again Law notes how empty these ultimately prove, how completely they fail to fill the heart, leaving the heart nowhere else to turn for stability and purpose except to religion. With far more psychological clairvoyance than Law, and at the same time with both more charity and humor, this was to become the procedure of Johnson himself in the great decade of moral writing that begins with *The Vanity of Human Wishes* (1748), when he is approaching forty, down through the moral essays, to *Rasselas* (1759). It became, in short, an almost archetypal way of thinking for Johnson himself. Meanwhile it penetrated at once to an imagination already shaken underneath as the disappointment of its own principal hopes began to seem increasingly probable, perhaps inevitable. An example is a strange poem—strange for a youth of his age—called "The Young Author," to which we must turn shortly.

<h1 style="text-align:center">8</h1>

While Johnson was at Pembroke, said Dr. Adams, he "was caressed and loved by all about him and contracted on his part a Love for the College which he retained to the last. This was I am persuaded the happiest part of his Life." Somewhat earlier Adams described him to Boswell as "a gay and frolicksome fellow" when he was first at Oxford. When this was repeated to Johnson, he replied:

> Ah, Sir, I was rude and violent. It was bitterness which they mistook for frolick. I was miserably poor, and I thought to fight my way by my literature and my wit; so I disregarded all power and all authority.[29]

From the beginning he had been haunted by the thought that he was at Oxford only on borrowed time. Now, as his twentieth birthday in September approached, the money from home almost, if not completely, stopped, and throughout the autumn his debts to the college began to increase. What clothes he had brought with him had been wearing out, and he had now, said Hawkins, "scarce any change of raiment," and only one pair of shoes "so old, that his feet were seen through them." Finally "a gentleman of his college," taking pity on him, asked "a servitor one morning to place a new pair at the door of Johnson's chamber, who, seeing them upon his first going out, so far forgot himself and the spirit that must have activated his unknown benefactor, that, with all the indignation of an insulted man, he threw them away." His sense of shame that his need was so obvious was acute. "He could not," said Hawkins, "at this early period of his life, divest himself of an opinion, that poverty was disgraceful," and long afterward—fond as he was of Oxford—spoke severely of the practice there and at Cambridge of using "poor scholars" as servitors or sizars to wait on the rest. "He thought that the scholar's, like the Christian life, levelled all distinctions of rank and worldly pre-eminence."[30]

The story of Johnson and the shoes, told first by Hawkins and then Boswell, passed into legend after Johnson's death, and became one of the most poignant and well-known incidents in literary history. No one after reading or hearing it has ever forgotten it. Boswell, and probably Hawkins, got the story from Johnson's friend John Taylor. Aleyn Reade shrewdly guessed, or rather almost proved, that the unknown "gentleman of his college" was William Vyse, later Treasurer of Lichfield Cathedral and Archdeacon of Shropshire, whom we have already mentioned among Johnson's college friends or acquaintances, and who was also about to become a patron of Johnson's tutor, the gentle and ponderous William Jorden. Now that Marshall Waingrow has made available and brilliantly edited the accounts of so many of Johnson's friends on whom Boswell drew, including Taylor (who confirms Reade's guess about Vyse), we can fill out the picture a little more.

For some months Johnson had been walking over every day to Christ Church in order to see his friend John Taylor, and get from him secondhand the lectures of Taylor's tutor, Edmund Bateman, on classics, philosophy, and mathematics. However, "at last," said Taylor,

> Johnson was so poor that he had not shoes to his feet, but his toes were seen naked. Some of the Christchurchmen smoaked [*i.e.*, ridiculed] this while he stood upon the pavement of Peckwater [Quad] and Johnson saw this. He therefore would never again come to Christ church. His pride or rather dignity of mind was such that it was vain to offer him money and some person (supposed to be [William] Vyse of Lichfield afterwards Canon of that Cathedral . . .) having set a pair of shoes at his door he threw them away with indignation.

This is one of those instances where the embarrassment and diffidence of the giver misfire and produce an opposite effect from what was intended. Not wishing to confront Johnson directly, Vyse—himself only nineteen—could think this a quiet and tactful way of making the present. To Johnson, already shamed by the open ridicule of the students at Christ Church, the anonymous deposit of shoes outside his door could be taken as a crude hint about his appearance or at best as an act of condescension, like a coin tossed to a beggar. Since Johnson would no longer leave Pembroke, and probably kept to his own room as much as possible, Taylor, "without seeming to know his reason for not coming to Christ Church," told Johnson he would "come to him at his own college, and repeat Bateman's lectures," which he continued to do for the rest of the time Johnson stayed at Oxford.[31]

9

Meanwhile, in October, he had decided to keep a sort of diary, or a memorandum of resolutions, written in Latin, which still survives in the Hyde Collection. But he was too halfhearted to make more than three entries during the final two months that remained.

Written as they were with the knowledge that he would soon have to leave—which was something that naturally dominated his thought—we can only think that these jottings, or at least two of them, were made with that in mind. The first (dated simply "October") reads in English, "I bid farewell to sloth, being resolved henceforth not to listen to her syren strains"; and he lists some works on which to start.[32] He is not, as is sometimes thought, merely resolving to snatch the opportunity to finish a few books while he would still be at Oxford. He is understandably beginning to feel something close to despair, and, as he tries to control this—partly by trying to repress his previous hopes—is just as understandably beginning to suffer from the distress of inner protest and self-conflict. One of the things in Law's *Serious Call* to which his strong sense of self-responsibility had immediately responded, and then had incorporated permanently into personal conviction, was Law's emphasis on early rising and on the discipline of industry as a means to "teach you how to exercise power over yourself." As a corollary (for the results were to become very plain in a very few months) he was also beginning to develop his own lifelong conviction—against which another part of him was forever afterward to protest—that indolence is an open invitation to mental distress and even disintegration, and that to pull ourselves together, through the focus of attention and the discipline of work, is within our own power.

Following that first resolution "I bid farewell to sloth" is a second entry, hopelessly mysterious, which reads (in English), "Oct. 22. Remember what I did Sept. 9, 12, 17, 19, 22, 28, and 26." Then, a month later (November 21), a couple of weeks before he left, there is a third entry—a sort of chart (so typical of him, even after he became famous), in which he outlines for himself what reading a certain number of lines per day (10, 30, and so on up to 600) would amount to in a week, then a month, then a year. Since he is about to leave, he can only be thinking of reading that could be done afterward, wherever he would be and whatever else he would be doing. To break it down in this way helped to steady his mind. As Mrs. Thrale said, whenever he felt his imagination "disordered, his constant recurrence was to the study of arithmetic." It was not only the objective exactness of numbers that his turbulent imagination craved as a means of reducing anxiety. It was also the effort to compartmentalize—to break things down into smaller, more manageable units, so that they cease to terrify and overwhelm the human spirit. So in *Rasselas,* when the Prince and his companions despond at the task of piercing their way through the mountains, Imlac tells them that "great works are performed, not by strength, but perseverance." The large palace nearby was raised by one stone laid on another. "He that shall walk with vigour three hours a day will pass in seven years a space equal to the circumference of the globe." Now, in his room at Pembroke, he finds some kind of reassurance—or at least the imaginative suggestion of reassurance to know that a mere 10 lines a day (how little time would be needed) would amount to 60 a week, not counting Sunday, 240 a month, 2,880 a year. A mere 60 lines a day would come to 17,280 a year, and 600 ten times that amount. A little more effort than that, and the classics could be mastered in a few years. There were at least some crumbs of comfort in the thought.

During these last weeks his tutor, William Jorden, left Pembroke in order to become rector of Standon, in Staffordshire (November 14). Jorden had been hoping to secure a living that was open in Wiltshire, and just missed getting it the previous spring. He was naturally disappointed. But William Vyse—the donor of the shoes put outside Johnson's door—had stepped into the breach and secured the living at Standon for Jorden, who was inducted there on December 12.[33]

Johnson was meanwhile transferred to William Adams, whom he so much liked and respected. Referring to that brief time, almost fifty years later (1776), Adams told Boswell, "I was his nominal tutor; but he was above my mark." When Boswell the next year repeated this to Johnson, "his eyes flashed with grateful satisfaction, and he exclaimed, 'That was liberal and noble.' " It was then that he divulged the remark of Adams that he had for so long treasured—that Johnson "was the best Scholar he ever knew come to Oxford."[34]

When he left, some time during the week of December 5 to 12, his fees appear to have been a full quarter in arrears. Then, some time between December 5 and 12 in the list of major events of his life that he wrote at the age of twenty-five (the first three being his birth, his visit to Cornelius, and his entrance at Oxford), the fourth reads starkly: "Decemb. 1729. S. J. returned from Oxford" ("*S.J. Oxonio rediit*").[35]

The inner life that had been going on beneath the surface is openly betrayed in a poem of remarkable psychological interest, called "The Young Author," which also shows how receptive his own condition had made him to his reading of Law's *Serious Call*. It is a sort of miniature version of *The Vanity of Human Wishes*, written twenty years later, and in particular anticipates the magnificent passage on the life of the young scholar that led him, in reading *The Vanity of Human Wishes* aloud to the Thrale family one day, suddenly to "burst into a passion of tears." A note by Edmund Hector says that "The Young Author" was written "in his 20th year,"[36] and the entire tone suggests that it was written near the end of his twentieth year, when the money was running out and he increasingly felt he was skating on thin ice. It is rare to find, in any writer, a short work composed this early in which one of the dominant qualities of his mind and general character throughout his entire life—in this case Johnson's strongly *anticipative* imagination—is so nakedly exposed, with a relatively mature and considered phrasing. At the same time it contains in solution much that Johnson's principal work and thinking—twenty or thirty years later—is both to repeat and, more important, in active inner dialectic, to attempt to correct or counterbalance.

What "The Young Author" shows him doing is to leap ahead in imagination, and to defend himself in advance against the bitterness of broken hope and ambition: to defend himself by turning not against others but against himself, as he instinctively begins to bludgeon his own intense hopes before life itself should leave him broken or stranded. It shows the resolve never again to be fooled, never again to be caught unawares, but to put into practice—to assimilate and domesticate into habitual feeling—the maxim of his "favorite" Horace (the calm and urbane Horace whom he could not imitate with any genuine feeling except in heady extreme): "To be forewarned is to be forearmed" (*"Praemonitum, praemunitum"*). And the only valuable way to be forewarned, and thus forearmed (as contrasted with the chronic "suspiciousness" of petty natures, which he scorned as a way to end up), was to "regulate the imagination by *reality*"—to see things as they are, to widen the context, to overlook nothing, to take it all into account beforehand, from the unconscious or deliberate hostility of others (sheer indifference, self-preoccupation, envy, even treachery), through the general accidents of life that suddenly strike us, such as illness, to the common doom to which death levels us all. This, in effect, is what he is to do twenty years later, on a panoramic scale, in *The Vanity of Human Wishes*. But now, of course, he is very young, and the range of what is covered is relatively small. Even so, the maturity of expression in these firm, clenched couplets in "The Young Author" is striking in the amount of unillusioned experience that they seem to distill. Because so much of the inner self is here involved, not only the general theme itself (the premise, the starting point, the way of proceeding psychologically in this "defense through context"), but also the actual images and even the language seem almost archetypal for him. Every sentence—if not every couplet, with which he tries to stamp in, for himself, this anticipative realization—could be glossed by later ones from *The Vanity of Human Wishes* and the moral essays— the writing that begins to appear once he is finally getting free, at the age of forty, from journalistic hack work, and is able to storm the main gate of human experience.

The poem is essentially one long simile comparing the young rustic, leaving home for the great world, with the young author, fired by idealism and the dream of fame. Just as "helpless man," at the start of *The Vanity of Human Wishes*, is seen as a "traveller"—singing and walking carefree over a heath filled with dangers and snares he does not yet know—the young rustic, long eager to "roam," sets off on what seems to him a "smiling ocean," his hopes high as the boat "dances" on the waves and the "streamers play" in the breeze. But then

> thick clouds invade the skies,
> Loud roars the tempest, high the billows rise,
> *Sick'ning with fear* he longs to view the shore,
> *And vows to trust the faithless deep no more.**

* Italics, in quotations from "The Young Author," here and on next page, are mine.

Johnson is here saying in advance what he is to write in *Rasselas*, thirty years later, where the experienced philosopher Imlac tries to caution the young Prince, Rasselas:

The world, which you figure to yourself smooth and quiet as the lake in the valley, you will find a sea foaming with tempests, and boiling with whirlpools: you will be sometimes overwhelmed by the waves of violence, and sometimes dashed against the rocks of treachery. Amidst wrongs and frauds, competitions and anxieties, you will wish a thousand times for these seats of quiet, and *willingly quit hope to be free from fear.*

Then the poem turns to the young writer. By idealistically placing his happiness in that most intangible of all rewards, "fame"—the futile hope of "filling the minds of others" that we call "fame"—he is far more vulnerable than the rustic who had trusted the sea:

> So the young author panting for a name,
> And fir'd with pleasing hope of endless fame,
> *Intrusts his happiness to human kind,*
> *More false, more cruel than the seas and wind.*

"When once a man has made *celebrity* necessary to his happiness," as Johnson was to write in one of the *Rambler* essays (No. 146), "he has put it in the power of the weakest and most timorous malignity, if not to take away his satisfaction, at least to withhold it." To gloss fully the remaining lines of the poem would involve quoting from one after another of the moral essays that he was to write in his forties. One example would be *Rambler* 2, which speaks of the writer rushing into print, his imagination projecting "forward into future ages" and "the honours to be paid him, when envy is extinct, and faction forgotten," while he forgets that "every catalogue of a library" is "crouded with names of men, who, though now forgotten, were once no less enterprising or confident than himself." Living "only in *idea*," and unaware in his idealism that nothing is more transitory than "fame," even if we think we have attained it—that "the eye which happens to glance upon us is turned in a moment on him that follows us"—the young author is confident that he is moving toward finer and more lasting goals than of those who scramble for riches, material possessions, or social position:

> "Toil on, dull crowd, in extacy," he cries,
> "For wealth or title, perishable prize;
> While I these *transitory* blessings scorn,
> Secure of praise from nations yet unborn."
> This thought once form'd, all counsel comes too late,

He plies the press, and hurries on his fate;
Swiftly he sees the imagin'd laurels spread,
He feels th' unfading wreath surround his head;
Warn'd by another's fate, vain youth, be wise,
These dreams were *Settle's* once and *Ogilby's*.

The names in the cruel final couplet—the forgotten John Ogilby and
poor Elkanah Settle, at one time the official "City Poet" of London,
one of whose functions was to write panegyrics on the Lord Mayor—
betray the fierceness with which this part of Johnson is trying to
undercut his own ambitions. Later, in *The Vanity of Human Wishes*,
there was to be a counterpart to this particular couplet in the warning
to the young scholar: "If dreams yet flatter, once again attend, / Hear
Lydiat's life, and *Galileo's* end." But Galileo and Thomas Lydiat (who
was thrown into prison for debt) were great men. Ogilby and Settle
—the very symbols for Johnson of transitoriness—were to be remembered only because of the contempt with which Pope treated them in
the *Dunciad:* Settle particularly, in a couplet (which Hazlitt thought
so exquisite that it brought tears to his eyes) describing the end of
"Lord Mayor's Day":

Now Night descending, the proud scene was o'er,
But liv'd in Settle's numbers one day more.

But the end that the young author is to face is far worse than
indifference. It is the fearful, perhaps permanent, shock to his idealism
in confronting the frightening omnipresence of envy—the principal
"treachery of the human heart," because the real motives are so easily
disguised, to ourselves if not to others, enabling us in the name of
"criticism" to "gratify our own pride or envy under the appearance of
contending" for standards we are subconsciously eager to find violated.
Implied already is the surprise still persisting twenty years later in the
moral essays that, in a world where we all are facing a common doom,
men should treat each other as they do in such time as they have—that
someone, for example, who "has given no provocation to malice, but
by attempting to excel, finds himself pursued by multitudes whom he
never saw with all the implacability of personal resentment."[37] Almost
immediately the young author is bewildered by attacks:

incessant hisses rise,
To some retreat the baffled writer flies . . .
There begs of heav'n a less distinguish'd lot;
Glad to be hid, and proud to be forgot.

There is not yet the ability to understand this (least of all to modify it with other considerations). For the moment Johnson is simply trying to drive into himself the realization of it as a fact of human existence that must be courageously and honestly faced, and assimilated as a necessary part of living. Naturally, given his desperate situation, he is single-minded in his focus: what he is stamping into his mind is not the truth but one of many truths. Just as naturally, there were several motives just now converging in this single-minded focus. He was preparing himself for the inevitable. In the process he was cleansing his mind of illusion. Yet he was also—as he would be the first to say later—like the fox in the fable dismissing the unattainable grapes as sour. He really cared very deeply. If he somewhat exaggerated the envy of others as a hurdle he had faced and would have had to face even more in the future, he was at least repressing envy in himself. He was not attacking others who were more fortunate. He was accepting full responsibility for "managing himself"—as, in a sense, he had done from the beginning. He did not need others to puncture his illusions about himself. He could do this on his own without help. A part of him could scorn his absurd hopes and pretensions. It was not with the dreams of great scholars or writers who had ended miserably that he is comparing his own, in a self-warning designed to cleanse his mind. It was the dreams of the futile, forgotten Settle and Ogilby. And some pride would be salvaged. He would at least be "managing himself" in not only accepting the inevitable but in courageously arming himself against it in advance. In leaving Oxford, and all that it meant, he could be "proud to be forgot."

Part II

THE
YEARS
OF
TRIAL
AND
OBSCURITY

Chapter 8

Breakdown and Despair;
Psychology of the Young Johnson

When he set out for Lichfield from Oxford in the second week of December, he left "very early in the morning," said John Taylor, "having hid his toes in a pair of large boots." The sturdy, reliable Taylor went with him as far as Banbury.[1] Johnson left behind him, in Taylor's charge, the box of books that he had originally brought with him from Michael's bookshop, after having first made a list of them. There was probably no money at the moment to pay for shipping them home. But there was a deeper reason. To leave them behind could be a gesture—to himself as much as to others—that he hoped to return. It could be no more than a gesture. For his frame of mind within a few weeks was to show him only too aware that a return—if ever—would not be soon. In that case, why not have the books to read in the meantime? Almost certainly he could not bear the finality of bringing them home. That would be a complete admission that everything was finished. Over five years were to pass before he wrote to Oxford to ask for them to be sent to him.

The next two years, to some extent the next five, were perhaps the hardest in the whole course of Johnson's difficult life. He had managed to keep himself afloat during the last few weeks at Oxford. But he now fell into an appalling state of mind, in which feelings of intense anxiety alternated with feelings of utter hopelessness and a lassitude so complete that, as he later confided to his friend Dr. John Paradise, he could stare at the town clock without being able to tell the hour. In desperation he tried to combat his state of mind by rational analysis and by repeated resolves to act, to set himself in motion, but he seemed only to sink further into what he began to fear was insanity. For if he began by blaming himself irrationally for having been forced to leave Oxford, and for having ever allowed himself the hopes that he had in the first place, he was soon blaming himself for the way he met or (from his own point of view) failed to meet the situation in which he now found himself. It was doubtless in despair of his own mind that he may even have come close to suicide. Long afterward John Taylor confided to a friend, Francis Mundy—a county magistrate who lived near Taylor's home at Ashbourne—the secret that Johnson had "at one time strongly entertained thoughts of Suicide."[2] This could possibly have been during the final weeks at Oxford. But much more likely it refers to the period that followed, as his despair of himself continued to deepen, and was something that Johnson confided only later to the stolid Taylor, who, as Johnson told Mrs. Thrale, "is better acquainted with my *heart* than any man or woman now alive." Some thought of the possibility of suicide may lurk behind a cryptic sentence of Edmund Hector's in a letter to Boswell (1785)—a remark Boswell decided not to use—that "when he return'd [to Lichfield from Oxford], I was fearfull that there was something wrong in his constitution, which might impair his Intellects or shorten his Life." And it is possible that this is what Mrs. Thrale is referring to in a mysterious remark that Johnson entrusted to her "a secret far dearer to him than his Life."[3]

In the whirling of the psychological maelstrom in which he now found himself, he learned far more than he had ever suspected, that the mind has "cliffs of fall / Frightful, sheer, no-man-fathomed," as Gerard Manley Hopkins later said out of his own self-experience, and the terror of this realization was afterward always present to Johnson. It may at first seem ironic that Johnson, who was to figure in literary history as its supreme exponent and symbol of practical common sense, of unremitting grip on concrete reality, should have begun his adult life in fear for his sanity. But just this explains the authority of his common sense over other minds and the cleansing power of his utterance. It was no bland virtue, but hard-won, through a fearful and prolonged baptism, and afterward maintained in lifelong struggle with himself. The experience from the age of twenty to twenty-two (and to some extent a few years more) was so terrible that in later years he could hardly be brought to refer to it, except perhaps to old friends on whose discretion he could rely. He would merely say that he "did not then know how to manage it." Only indirectly and by careful inquiry could Boswell—fascinated as he was by this hidden area of Johnson's life—discover some things about this state in which Johnson "felt himself overwhelmed with an horrible melancholia, with perpetual irritation, fretfulness, and impatience; and with a dejection, gloom, and despair, which made existence misery." Yet something that Boswell never wished to dwell upon, as Marshall Waingrow has shown,[4] was Johnson's conviction that there were times in his life when he was close to insanity, and had even passed the line into it. Boswell preferred—as would most others in his own situation—to consider Johnson's fears of insanity as a fanciful delusion resulting from a perfectionistic notion of "sanity" (as they indeed in part were, though we should now be inclined to appreciate the Gordian knot of profound mental distress to which such perfectionistic notions can contribute). To think otherwise of someone who embodied the essence of practical sense and stability of mind was understandably unsettling to Boswell. And of course there were things about Johnson he could never himself have directly seen even when he got to know Johnson over thirty years later. This would include the fearful return in Johnson's fifties of something like his breakdown now. Boswell may have sensed something about his condition at that time, and learned more about it later from others. But he could not have viewed it with the seriousness of the Thrales, when they found Johnson on his knees before a clergyman, Dr. Delap, "beseeching God to continue to him the use of his understanding," and speaking so wildly that Mr. Thrale "involuntarily lifted up one hand to shut his mouth."*

2

Frantically, as he tried to pull himself into self-management—to put at arm's length what was happening to him, and see it for what it was in order to reduce it to size—he at last turned for help to his godfather, Dr. Swynfen, now a physician in Birmingham. Using Latin, which he instinctively tended to fall back on in the hope of getting "distance" and objectivity, as well as privacy, he wrote out for Dr. Swynfen a full statement of his case. Swynfen felt helpless before the account, and his reply (as paraphrased or summarized by Sir John Hawkins, who probably found the letter in Johnson's papers after his death) could only

---

* See below, p. 407.

have increased Johnson's terror. It was that "from the symptoms therein described, he [Swynfen] could think nothing better of his disorder, than that it had a tendency to insanity; and without great care might possibly terminate in the deprivation of his rational faculties." But nothing further seems to have transpired between the two on this matter. For Swynfen, though his motives were of the kindest, was so struck by the brilliance of Johnson's statement, with its desperate effort at control—its "extraordinary acuteness, research, and eloquence"—that he showed it "to several people," possibly with the hope of getting further ideas for help in understanding Johnson's case. Johnson was shocked at this breach of professional confidence, and Swynfen's daughter, Mrs. Desmoulins, whom Johnson in later years helped to support when she became derelict, said that "he was never afterwards fully reconciled" to her father.[5]

At the same time he had also been trying to throw himself into exertions that would pull his mind away from itself into some kind of unified activity. He would force himself to walk to Birmingham and back, a distance of thirty-two miles, in the hope that it could shake him into manageability. "Imagination," as he was later to say, "never takes such firm possession of the mind, as when it is found empty and unoccupied." Any activity—recreation or labor—can be "styled its own reward" if we recognize "how much happiness is gained, and how much misery escaped, by frequent and violent agitation of the body."[6] From this experience began his lifelong conviction that what he had read in William Law at Oxford was not just probably but profoundly true: that effort in daily habits—such as early rising—was necessary to "reclaim imagination" and keep it on an even keel. As he incorporated this conviction more strongly into self-demand, it aroused an even stronger inner protest. And he was never to be free from the struggle, as a glance ahead at entries in the various journals he kept will illustrate. September 7, 1738: "O Lord, enable me . . . in redeeming the time which *I have spent in Sloth.* . . ." January 1, 1753: ". . . To rise early To lose no time." July 13, 1755: "I will once more form *a scheme of life.* . . . (1) To rise early . . ." Easter Eve, 1757: "Almighty God . . . look down with mercy upon me depraved with vain imaginations. . . . *Enable me to shake off Sloth.* . . ." Easter Day, 1759: "Give me thy Grace to break the chain of evil custom. Enable me to shake off idleness and Sloth. . . ." September 18, 1760: "Resolved . . . To reclaim imagination . . . To rise early . . . To oppose laziness . . ." April 21, 1764: "My purpose is from this time (1) To reject or expel sensual images, and idle thoughts. To provide some useful amusement for leisure time. (2) To avoid Idleness. To rise early." Next day (3:00 A.M.): "Deliver me from the distresses of vain terrour . . . Against loose thoughts and idleness."

The following autumn he resolves, on his fifty-fifth birthday (September 18), "to rise early. *Not later than six if I can* . . ."; and, the following Easter (writing at 3:00 A.M.), "*to rise at eight.* . . . I purpose to rise at eight because though I shall not yet rise early it will be much earlier than I now rise, for I often lye till two." Four years later (January 1, 1769, writing after midnight): "I am not yet in a state to form many resolutions; I purpose and hope to *rise* . . . *at eight, and by degrees at six.*" A year and a half later: June 1, 1770: "Every Man naturally persuades himself that he can keep his resolutions, nor is he convinced of his imbecillity but by length of time and frequency of experiment." January 1, 1774 (at 2:00 A.M.): "To rise at *eight* . . . The chief cause of my deficiency has been a life *immethodical and unsettled*, which breaks all purposes . . . and perhaps leaves too much leisure to imagination." Good Friday, 1775 (he is now sixty-six): "When I look back upon resoluti[ons] of improvement and amendments, which have year after year been broken . . . why do I yet try to resolve again? I try because Reformation is necessary and despair is criminal. . . . My purpose is from Easter day to rise early, not later than eight." January 2, 1781 (he is now seventy-one): "*I will not despair.* . . . My hope is (1) To rise at eight, or sooner . . . (5) To avoid idleness."[7]

3

The breakdown at the age of twenty was so crucial an experience in Johnson's life, so important for everything that follows, that it is necessary to see it in as full a perspective as we can.

To begin with, there was its length. In its most extreme form, it lasted about two years, but he was still in a rather shattered condition for at least another three years. Then there was the psychological extent—the number of different aspects of his character that were involved, and the way in which one thing gave rise to another. Before long, everything could seem to be converging on him. The frustration of all his hopes was bad enough, but that was only the beginning. For example, could he not himself be said to have contributed to the whole situation? He had certainly contributed to his present state of mind in ever having allowed himself to have such exorbitant and unrealistic hopes. But he had begun himself to realize this well before he left Oxford, and, as in that poem "The Young Author," had tried to undercut those hopes and stamp into his imagination a more realistic attitude. In doing so, he had paid rent in advance, so to speak. Why had it done him no good? Perhaps that very effort to cut hope back to size had been the wrong attitude, at least if carried too far. Certainly, in later years, he was convinced that the misguided self-protection that leads us to expect the worst can be a fearful misuse of the imagination, creating habits of mind that can have a vicious effect; and he was to write perceptively about it, however much a part of him violated his own precept.

Aside from this, a part of him could seem to have sabotaged the whole effort and betrayed him from the start. True, that magical world Cornelius represented—first as a Cambridge don, so negligent and so brilliant, and then in London, among the authors he had known there—had at first seemed possible to enter. In every way Johnson seemed to have credentials—up to a point; or so at least friends and relatives at Stourbridge had helped him to feel. But inwardly a part of him had, in self-protection, held back. Cumbersome and awkward, half blind and half deaf, he knew he could never be completely of that world. He may not have wanted to be completely of that world—he had found this out as another part of him had begun to assert itself at the table of Gilbert Walmesley. But more than half of him desperately wanted to be of that world, and had felt released by sharing in it and by the thought of all it seemed to represent.

In any case, the alternative was fearful. And the alternative, of course, was the world of Michael Johnson—bumbling, inefficient, perhaps self-destructive, with associations of failure and defeat permeating everything about him. But far more threatening was the incipient "madness" of the old man, who had long since been so incorporated by the young Johnson's assimilative nature, and made so organic a part of him, that he could never disown it, never amputate it. Any scorn or protest against it was henceforth doomed to be self-scorn and self-conflict. He was the opposite of Goethe, who was able frankly and eagerly to shed influences almost as though they were suits of clothes.

And what was Michael doing now? The back of that pathetic "parchment factory" had by now "fallen half down for want of money to repair it." Even so, as Johnson told Mrs. Thrale, Michael would diligently lock the front door every night, though anyone could simply walk into that ramshackle building at the back. "*This* (says his son) was madness, you may see, and would have been discoverable in other instances of the prevalence of imagination, but that poverty prevented it from playing such tricks as riches and leisure encourage." This was the sort of thing, as Johnson saw it, that (with a few gifts added) was probably his own essential self, along with the "vile melancholy" he thought he inherited "from my father, which has made me mad all my life, at least not sober."[8] At least it was his central self now, after he found himself back where he had started and his identification with Cornelius proven to be based on illusion—or perhaps even delusion, self-delusion. And it was a self he felt to be unlovable, just as Michael himself, as far as the son could see, was unlovable.

Not only that. He was also left completely naked and vulnerable to the cruelest of psychological burdens that he was to face throughout life (though it was naturally to prove an indispensable source of his greatness when kept in healthful interplay with other qualities). This was the fierce and exacting sense of self-demand—for which Freud gave the now-common term "superego"—with its remorseless capacity, in some natures, to punish the self through a crippling sense of guilt and through the resulting anxieties, paralysis, and psychosomatic illness that guilt, grown habitual and strongly enough felt, begins to sprout.* "The great business of his life," Johnson told Reynolds, "was to *escape from himself;* this disposition he considered as the *disease* of his mind." The part of himself from which he needed to escape was the remorseless pressure of "superego" demand, of constant self-criticism, and all the unconscious ruses of insistent self-punishment. Arthur Murphy appears to have sensed something of this when he said that there was "danger" for Johnson in indolence; for "his spirits, not employed abroad, turned with inward hostility against himself. His reflections on his own life and conduct were always severe; and, wish-

---

* Freud's term for this strongly internalized self-demand, the "superego" (meaning what is "above or beyond" the ego, hovering over it), was never a happy one. It is especially awkward in English, where "super" also carries the suggestion of the highest excellence (as in "superiority" and "superlative"). But as a shorthand expression for what we are discussing, it is still useful as a supplement to the hopelessly generalized word "conscience." For during the past half century, it has passed into the language and become domesticated not only into general literary usage but also common speech. No possible substitute is remotely so well known. Finally, though the concept itself has begun to seem oversimplified for present-day psychoanalysis, except for unusual individuals, Johnson is pre-eminently one of those individuals.

ing to be immaculate, he destroyed his own peace by unnecessary scruples." And in Johnson's own moral writing, which often anticipates psychoanalysis, he was to show—in a way close to modern psychiatry—how much of the misery of mankind comes from the inability of individuals to think well of themselves, and how much envy and other evils spring from this. One of the aims of biography, he thought, is to inquire into this—to learn how a man "was made happy; not how he lost the favour of his prince, but how he became discontented with himself."[9]

Self-demand to an extreme extent had been the inevitable product, as we noticed, of his first years. It was part and parcel of the more general feeling of complete personal responsibility for "managing" himself: of his proud defiance and disregard of physical limitations; his repression of the experience of early physical ills (the operation on his arm, and the running "issue" kept open till he was six); the beating back of Dame Oliver when she had followed him, in case help was needed, as he nearsightedly tried to crawl across the ditch on the road home. Whatever poor Michael and the nagging Sarah had contributed to the early formation of superego had been quickly subsumed and transcended (though not disowned) by the momentum and habits of independence as these in turn created a far higher level of self-demand and gave it a further reach. At first, when he had gone to the lower grammar school, there had been a sense of release—the cleansing challenge of objective fact, even if it was only Latin grammar, both as a means of getting him out of himself, of lifting his attention, and also as something he could do superlatively (involving the approbation of others than the prejudiced and limited Michael and Sarah), and thus satisfy his own growing and more sophisticated self-demand. But then this challenge, too, was soon met, absorbed, and transcended. A little effort could go a long way simply because others were not too inclined to do the same thing. All the time, of course, there was constant inner protest from another part of him against the pressure of whatever savored of "demand" (which became a pressure, a burden, simply because it could be so quickly transmitted into "self-demand" and therefore both magnified and made more persistent). All his life this inner protest was to be a problem, and the merest hint from others that he should do more than he was doing could bring a strong defensive reaction out of all proportion to their innocent suggestions. So thirty-five years later, not long after Boswell got to know Johnson, Boswell—doubtless thinking it was a compliment—joined Goldsmith in pressing him to get back to writing. When Goldsmith said, "We have a claim upon you," Johnson replied, "I am not obliged to do any more. No man is obliged to do as much as he can do. A man is to have part of his life to himself." Though he is quite justified, he is plainly uneasy in his own conscience as he continues to rationalize; and when Boswell, instead of dropping the matter, says, "I wonder, Sir, you have not more pleasure in writing," there is the testy response: "Sir, you *may* wonder."[10]

4

One of the most valuable things that Cornelius had done for him (Cornelius whom he had now failed) was to help provide for a more integrated identity, in which conflict was less inevitable between unrealistic self-demand, locked into intolerance and rigidity, and mulish inner resistance to it. The superego, however strong, could be made more benign by identification with an admired figure who was so cavalier and free from the exacting pettiness against which, when Johnson met it, he was always to explode in frustrated anger (frustration because of what he felt to be the tyranny of his own exacting "scruples").* That portion of the superego which Freud called the "ego-ideal"—and this is why identification can be so valuable—can serve as a mediator between the harsh exactions of "conscience" and the vulnerable ego, and thus help the self toward unity and confidence. And, in this case, the ego-ideal (at least as the young Johnson envisaged Cornelius, which is the important thing) was in the highest degree salutary, turned as it was with imaginative openness to "the living world." Far from opposing, in the name of "conscience," the "reality principle" so necessary for the healthful survival of the ego, the ideal represented by Cornelius had championed it as the best means of satisfying self-expectation. At the same time it was an ideal that was more than possible. In fact, to attain it involved the liberation, through creative use, of qualities of mind—of readiness, range of interest, and imaginative perception—that he had discovered he might really have.

The shattering of this valuable new sense of identity, held together

---

* On his lifelong struggle against what, in his journals, he calls "scruples" (a shorthand term for obsessive or compulsive acts), see below, pp. 381–83. Cf. a typical remark (Easter 1766): "I prayed in the collect for . . . deliverance from scruples; this deliverance was the chief subject of my prayers. O God hear me. I am now trying to conquer them" (*Diaries*, p. 108).

by living ideal and by hope, was a fearful thing, and even by itself—without further complications—could bring with it, especially to a nature so concerned with self-management, the fear of insanity, of being split apart. And had not that fear been half confirmed by Dr. Swynfen, who had after all known him since birth, and who had also—equally important—known Michael? It was more than half confirmed. Did not Swynfen himself feel helpless before it? But still further complications were inevitable. For with the loss of the ideal of Cornelius as a practicable hope, all the potentiality in Johnson for rigidity and harshness in self-demand, and with it self-scorn, could spring upon him unchecked. He was left to face it alone and without resources. With the situation as it now was, he could feel that all he seemed to have left with which to face it was that now naked, vulnerable part of him permanently identified with Michael ("mad . . . at least not sober") which had been there below the surface all the time, though the protective identification with Cornelius (and with Walmesley superadded to Cornelius) had before allowed him to transcend it and keep it in place. The feeling that this was the essential part of him that was now left could turn into conviction as further complications developed.

For as he desperately tried to pull himself above the surface, the strong aggressive instincts that had been so much a part of him—now defensively aroused to their most extreme degree—inevitably turned on himself. With the iron check that he kept on envy—his scorn of either blaming the system of life or of resenting the good fortune of others—and with his tendency to accept self-responsibility, there was nowhere else for his aggressions to turn except against himself. True, some of his self-detestation spilled over on the family (not only on Michael but somewhat even on Sarah, and certainly on Nathaniel—that unhappy symbol of what Johnson had been trying to get beyond). But that was because they were associated with himself, indeed very much the self to which he had now fallen back. With the aggressive hostility turned against himself, it was perhaps inevitable that he also developed acute psychosomatic ills to such a degree that he was never entirely to overcome them; and there were to be periods in his life when they would return almost as strongly. These essentially dated from about this time ("My health," as he once wrote to Hector—this was when he was seventy-two—"has been from my twentieth year such as has seldom afforded me a single day of ease").[11] A part of him might suspect that this was all in the head—that it was primarily the result of a "disordered imagination." But his efforts to shake himself free of this, as the months continued to pass, seemed as futile as his other efforts.

Another by-product of his attempt to control aggressions by turning them against himself was more conspicuous if less painful. For he now began to develop the embarrassing tics and other compulsive manner-isms that were to haunt him all his life—the sort of thing that led the artist William Hogarth to say that when he first saw Johnson (at the home of Samuel Richardson, standing by a window, "shaking his head and rolling himself about in a strange ridiculous manner"), he con-cluded Johnson "was an ideot, whom his relations had put under the care of Mr. Richardson." Then, to Hogarth's surprise, this figure stalked over to where Richardson and he were sitting, and "all at once took up the argument, and . . . displayed such a power of eloquence, that Hogarth looked at him with astonishment, and actually imagined that this ideot had been at the moment inspired." Johnson was only too aware of the grotesque impression that these compulsive movements and tics made on others, and detested them both for their own sake and as one more example of what could seem to him an appalling inability to control himself. They were also to prove a serious hindrance to employment. Time and again, as we shall notice, he was to confront the sort of reaction implied by a remark of Alexander Pope's, who said he had recommended Johnson as a tutor "but without success"—the explanation being that Johnson had "an Infirmity of the convulsive kind, that attacks him sometimes so as to make him a sad Spectacle."[12]

Discussion of this particular subject should be partly deferred until later, when it became of fascinating interest to some of the people who knew him, and, from what they had to say, passed into the Johnson of legend. But a few points can be summarized at the moment. These tics and convulsive movements—often extreme—were certainly of psycho-neurotic origin and not, as has sometimes been assumed, of organic origin.[13] They almost as certainly date from this period and not at all from early childhood, however "awkward" or "strange" he might sometimes have seemed to others in his earlier years. Otherwise we can be sure they would have been mentioned. Everyone noticed the tics and compulsive mannerisms after they did appear. Had they been pres-ent earlier, they would have especially been noticeable to other chil-dren—who are quick to mark such things—and particularly those who lived to talk about their famous schoolmate at a time when every peculiarity of his had become of wide interest. These obsessional traits took such a variety of forms as to have included almost every major category of tics or compulsive gestures (which itself indicates the massiveness of the trauma he underwent at this time). But they usually tend to have one common denominator: an instinctive effort to control—to control aggressions by turning them in against himself. (As Joshua Reynolds shrewdly said, "Those actions always appeared to me as if they were meant to reprobate some part of his past conduct.") Or they were employed to control anxiety and reduce things to apparent manageability by "compartmentalization," by breaking things down into units through measurement (counting steps, touching posts, and the like), just as he turned to arithmetic, as Mrs. Thrale said, when he felt his mind disordered.

Finally, in the widening complications of guilt that we have noticed, he may for the first time have come seriously to think of himself as both physically and socially incapable of pleasing—in short, of being loved—and to lose the confidence that the period at Stourbridge had given him in this way, too. If there had been doubts before, dating back to childhood—dependent as he was on the often querulous Sarah, difficult to please, or the absent-minded, preoccupied Michael, whose affection appeared most when his son was to be put on exhibit—they were as nothing compared with the feeling he had now. The grotesque gesticulations and compulsive movements, which he abominated and found so difficult to control, intensified this feeling of hopelessness. He once remarked to Henry Thrale that he "never sought to please till past thirty years old, considering the matter as hopeless."[14] But this hardly refers to his first twenty years, in which there were plenty of examples of his own confidence in social groups—especially at Stourbridge—and the quality of "complaisance" that many people were to remember of him in his late teens. The remark refers to his twenties— to the darkening period that begins now, which naturally tended to blot out the memory of earlier hopes and confidence.

The raw material with which he had to work, now and throughout the next twenty years (to some extent throughout the rest of his life), included the effects of this massive breakdown, with its swarm of by-products, psychological and otherwise, and with its long aftermath. To this were added the trials—the challenges as well as the humiliations— imposed on him by the extreme poverty in which he was often to live throughout the following two decades, some of them the product of the five years after he had to leave Oxford. It is an understatement to say that he was never to be the same person he could have been if only he had stayed on at Oxford or, without an interruption of so many years, have been able to reach the sort of life that Cornelius and the year at Stourbridge had led him to idealize. As the years began to pass, the total picture could seem anything but promising. The drama of his life lies in what happens both despite and because of this.

5

If we know very little about the external details of Johnson's life during the first two years after he left Oxford, it is because this time was so traumatic that he naturally had no desire to talk about it in later years but rather to repress it from memory as much as he could.

Obviously he lived off the family, and they were probably not inclined to make an issue of it, despite the extreme need into which they were falling. However much Johnson might have tried to keep it from them, they could sense that there was something seriously wrong. Significantly there seems to have been no pressure on him, during all this time, to get back the large number of books he had taken from the bookshop and had left at Oxford, where they were now lying unused. They had represented a very large investment for Michael, and the expense of shipping them back was nothing in comparison with their value. We can only assume Michael did not dare to bring up the subject to his son, whose state of mind he was afraid to upset any further. That his son did not insist on returning the books, when the family need was so great, indicates how completely he was absorbed or lost in his own psychological struggle.

Certainly Michael, by 1731, was almost a broken man. He continued to retain some standing among his fellow townsmen, as much from their compassion as their respect, and he made a point, the records show, of going to meetings of the Lichfield Corporation. But he was inevitably humiliated in having to accept the grant of ten guineas as "a decayed tradesman" in the late summer of 1731 from the very trust— the Conduit Lands Trust—for which he had earlier been the warden.[15] Meanwhile Johnson had heard that the job as usher was open at the Stourbridge Grammar School. The year at Stourbridge had meant so much to him that to go back again, and touch base, as it were, could be therapeutic. He went to Stourbridge to see what could be done. But aside from any other problem, the mere lack of a degree was a severe handicap, and another man, with a B.A. from Trinity College, Oxford, was chosen (September 6).[16]

At Stourbridge Johnson presumably stayed with Cornelius's half brother, Gregory Hickman. While there he wrote some complimentary verses for Gregory's daughter, Dorothy, a girl of seventeen ("To Miss Hickman Playing on the Spinet"). However distressing his life had been since he left Oxford, he could still occasionally force himself to toss off impromptu verses, and had done so a couple of times earlier that year in order to please others.* Impressed by this, Hickman suggested that Johnson write some verses, presumably satiric, on the situation at the school (Wentworth, the headmaster, the vacant job of usher, the new man chosen because of the degree). The suggestion sounds incredibly stupid and tactless. But Hickman was certainly unaware how shattered Johnson was and had been for over a year and a half, and with how precarious a hold he was keeping himself together during this short visit. Like many people who do not write, he assumed that for people who do, the act of writing is a sort of relief or general panacea. He doubtless regarded this as a very ordinary disappointment, and assumed that Johnson, if he could be brought to treat it lightly by turning it into verse, would feel better.

Johnson did not wish to refuse Hickman at once, but some weeks later wrote asking him to "excuse the composition of the verses you desired"; that "one's own disappointment is no inviting subject," and that, though he had tried to think about it, he could not get started. He had indeed returned with a heavy heart. For while he was still at Stourbridge, or shortly afterward, news came that Cornelius had suddenly died in London (August 22). We can guess at the impact on him of Cornelius's death and the further sense of finality it brought to his earlier life. For in those "Annales" that he wrote down three years later of major events in his life, the fifth entry (after his birth, the visit to Cornelius, his entrance to Oxford, and his departure from it) reads, "In the summer months S.J. lost C.F." ("*Mensibus Aestivis* S. J. C. F. *amisit*").[17]

---

* "Ode on a Lady Leaving Her Place of Abode" and—better known because it was crazily assumed by some to be an actual love poem of his own—a trifle (Johnson himself called it "nonsense") called "On a Lady's Presenting a Sprig of Myrtle to a Gentleman." A friend of Hector's, Morgan Graves, had been given a branch of myrtle by a lady of Birmingham, and wanted to thank her in verse. Graves turned to Hector for help, and Hector to Johnson, who promised to write something and then forgot. When Graves showed up for the lines, Johnson "stepped aside for five minutes, and wrote the nonsense." Hector remembered him as "dictating" the lines. Anna Seward, not knowing the story, inferred—or spread the tale—that they were a love poem from Johnson to Lucy Porter (A, p. 167; W, pp. 439–40, 575–76; L, I, 92–93, n. 2).

During the autumn of 1731, Michael's health began to fail rapidly, and by November he was seriously ill with what Johnson described to Mrs. Thrale as an "inflammatory fever"—possibly pneumonia or some other respiratory infection. He died the first week of December, and is recorded as being buried at St. Michael's Church on December 7. That the arrangements were handled by Catherine Chambers, Sarah's maid, suggests the stunned helplessness and general disarray of the household. Michael left no will. In accordance with the marriage settlement, the house, furniture, and stock went to Sarah for her lifetime. His personal estate came to about £60, of which Johnson the following July received £20.[18]

It was probably during these final months of Michael's life—as James Clifford has persuasively argued—that an incident occurred which Johnson said had "ever since lain heavy on my mind." Fifty years afterward, on a visit to Lichfield, he was to disappear for much of the day. The friends with whom he was staying were reluctant to ask him where he had been, but, after a silence of several minutes, he explained. Michael, who had tried for years to extend his book business to neighboring towns, had a stall at Uttoxeter that he used on market days, traveling there on a horse to manage it. Unable to get out of bed, he asked Samuel to go to Uttoxeter and look after the bookstall for him. (It may tell us something about Johnson's life at Lichfield at this time that the ailing and aging Michael, riding in fatigue and hopelessness from one town to another, should not have felt free to ask his son before to help him in this particular way.) However, "my pride prevented me," said Johnson, and "I gave my father a refusal." Now, on a rainy day exactly fifty years later, he forced himself, in a way that could seem almost like an act of religious penance, to do what he had once denied the helpless Michael. He took

a postchaise to Uttoxeter, and going into the market at the time of high business, uncovered my head, and stood with it bare an hour before the stall which my father had formerly used, exposed to the sneers of the standers-by and the inclemency of the weather.[19]

Chapter 9

Efforts to Begin Again; Birmingham; the First Book

Despite his lack of a degree, he at last got a job the following March as undermaster at the school in Market Bosworth, Leicestershire, a town of about nine hundred inhabitants. The annual salary was £20, and he was to be allowed the free use of a house of his own. He could doubtless have stayed on at Lichfield, working in the bookshop with his mother—whose property it now was—and with Nathaniel, who was now nineteen. But he knew he was not needed. Two were enough to handle the diminished business of the shop. Self-respect demanded that he begin to support himself. Above all, he needed to pull himself out of the combination of morbid lethargy and depressive anxiety that was still continuing after two years. A place with different associations and with set tasks that must not be neglected—as he could neglect things at the bookshop if he wished—could be of help.

Either to save money, or to shake himself into activity in preparation for the new job, or to do both, he set off on foot (March 9) and walked the muddy roads of early spring to Market Bosworth, twenty-five miles away. He at once discovered that the school was not really run by its headmaster, the Reverend John Kilby, a clergyman of sixty-five, who had been there for only a year and a half. It was under the complete control of its chief trustee, Sir Wolstan Dixie, an ill-tempered and coarsely aggressive man of thirty. This had been to Johnson's advantage at first. For Dixie, in appointing him, simply brushed aside the requirement, in the statutes of the school, that the undermaster should have the degree of B.A. In fact, two years before, after the death of the well-known headmaster of the school, Anthony Blackwall, Dixie had boasted at dinner that he could appoint anyone he wanted as headmaster whatever the statutes said. When one of his guests questioned whether he could get away with this, Dixie immediately appointed his butler, a man named Williams, and kept him in the job for a month or so until he finally selected Kilby. With a similar arbitrary spirit, he disregarded the stipulation, when Johnson showed up, that the undermaster should be given a house. Instead he made Johnson live at his own mansion, Bosworth Hall, where "I have been told," said Boswell (paraphrasing what John Taylor told him), Johnson was used

as a kind of domestick chaplain, so far, at least, as to say grace at table, but was treated with what he represented as intolerable harshness; and, after suffering for a few months such complicated misery, he relinquished a situation which all his life afterwards he recollected with the strongest aversion, and even a degree of horrour.[1]

Undoubtedly his own deeply shaken condition of mind had much to do with this sense of horror, which was so acute that many years later he could still tell Taylor that it made him "uneasy" even "to see that side of the town [Ashbourne, where Taylor lived] which leads to Bosworth." For the task of teaching, which used up most of his time, was not intrinsically that unpleasant. Unable to enter into it enough to get out of himself, he naturally found it boring. The words of Martial, he wrote to Edmund Hector (who did not keep the letters but was now trying to recall them), summed up the "dull sameness of his existence": *Vitam continet una dies* ("One day contains the whole of my life"), and, in teaching Latin grammar to the boys, he thought it hard to say who found the difficulty greater, "he to explain Nonsense, or they to understand it." As for Dixie, he was admittedly a trial. A fair amount is now known about him that seems to justify the description of him by John Taylor—who later became acquainted with him— as "an abandoned brutal rascal." One of the stories about him illustrates not only his bullying temper (which led him to become involved in lawsuits and quarrels, which he greatly enjoyed, with neighbors and former servants) but also his ignorance. In the version given by the historian of the school, Mr. Hopewell, Dixie decided to stop further use of what had been a public path through his grounds. A neighboring squire protested this, and fought with Dixie, in which the squire

was battered to insensibility. Years later Dixie was presented to King George II as "Sir Wolstan Dixie of Bosworth Park." "Bosworth—Bosworth:

131

Big battle at Bosworth, wasn't it?" replied the king, referring to the 1485 battle. "Yes, sire. But I thrashed him," replied the baronet.[2]

If stories of this kind indicate how readily Dixie might try to bully or even ridicule him, nothing we know of Johnson suggests that he could not take care of himself when he was attacked by others. On such occasions, his immense capacity for aggression, which he so sternly tried to keep in check, could with conscience be lifted from its usual target, himself. The outburst might not bring complete relief (he could feel keen remorse for it afterward). But Dixie would hardly account for the distress of mind that Taylor described. Nor did Johnson need to crawl for this £20 per year, assuming he was capable of crawling. He had survived before this and would for substantial periods after without £20 per year. Insolence from a bully could not create horror. The real "horror" was within, as it had been for over two years and was to continue even with no Wolstan Dixie hanging over him.

2

In the middle of June, he made a quick journey home, since the personal estate of Michael was now settled. Having received £19 (the amount of the inheritance was £20, but he had been given £1 in advance), he walked back again to Market Bosworth. He was still there on July 17, for he mentions meeting there a friend of whom he had been very fond, John Corbet, the brother of Andrew. Shortly after that, during a quarrel between himself and Dixie, he quit the job at the school (it was like "coming out of prison," he told Taylor), and went back to Lichfield.

What was he to do now? To hang around the bookshop and live off the meager earnings of his mother was anything but attractive to his conscience. Suddenly (July 26) he heard from John Corbet that the usher at the school at Ashbourne had just died, and the next day he wrote to Taylor, Corbet, and the M.P. for Lichfield, George Venables Vernon, to ask their support for the position. For whatever reason, but not because of his lack of a degree (since the man they chose, Thomas Bourne, did not have one), he was passed over not only once but twice; for Bourne almost immediately turned down the position, which then went to a man from Nottingham, Job Sowter.[3] The governors of the school may have heard of Johnson's break with Dixie or have heard rumors of his convulsive gestures. In any case, Taylor and

Corbet, both only twenty, were far too young to have any influence as sponsors.

After this brief flurry of effort, he seems to have sunk back into paralysis and despair, though he may have helped a little at the bookshop, and have continued to see something of Gilbert Walmesley and other friends. In September he became twenty-three, and by December it would be three years since he had left Oxford. But the sense of time passing, always so powerful in his imagination, seemed only to stun rather than arouse him ("Where there is no hope, there can be no endeavour"). For with every month the realization of time passing brought with it, in a vicious circle, still further reason for self-condemnation and the massive self-distrust that had at first so alarmed and now seemed to be paralyzing him. In any case, what was there to do that would use even a fraction of the abilities he had once thought he possessed? He was not only a failure in every hope he had ever had—and, he could feel, a hopelessly grotesque one—but also a failure in the simple matter of self-support, which the bulk of mankind seemed able to face better than he. Of course, the real trouble was in himself, but that was why the matter was hopeless, as Dr. Swynfen had probably realized.

A measure of his paralysis was his continued failure to do anything about the books he had left at Oxford almost three years before. To have them sent back would have made sense. If he could not bear to look into them—associated as they were with all he had lost—they would at least have been a valuable addition to the stock at the bookshop. To contribute them in return for what he had been costing the family all this time would be the least he could do. But he obviously could not bear to bring them back now, three years after, any more than he could during the first year after his return. At first, to leave them at Oxford might have seemed a sort of talisman. But this could hardly be the case any more. It was better to repress the thought of them, as though they had never existed, lest their return upset his effort to strangle and bury forever those exorbitant hopes they had symbolized.

3

During the late autumn Johnson's old school friend Edmund Hector, who had become increasingly worried about him, asked him to come to Birmingham for a visit. Johnson accepted, and stayed on at Birmingham for more than a year. The visit ultimately, though not immediately, was to prove another turning point in his life.

Hector, now a man of twenty-four, had gone to Birmingham the previous year and begun practice as a surgeon. He had an apartment at the home of Thomas Warren, a printer and bookseller, who lived in the High Street across from the Swan Tavern. There was ample room for Johnson if he would come as a guest. They would have their meals with Warren and his family, as Hector was already doing. Whether or not he told Johnson in advance, Hector had in mind a plan for his friend, who seemed to be in as bad shape as when he first came back to Lichfield from Oxford. The important thing was to get Johnson out of himself and engaged in something that would help to occupy his mind. Schoolteaching, for whatever combination of reasons, had failed. But Hector, ever since they were both children, had known and admired Johnson's ability to write rapidly. At such times, even if they were short, Johnson's mind seemed entirely engaged. Moreover, Hector, though far from being a writer himself (even letters were difficult for him to write), could sense that Johnson was secretly proud of that ability, just as he knew that Johnson at this time "had a vanity in concealing that he ever studied. It was all to be from his own mind."[4] And Hector could justly feel that the satisfaction of any sort of pride or self-confidence on Johnson's part was badly needed now.

Thomas Warren, the bookseller at whose house Hector lived, had either just started or was planning to start a small newspaper, the Birmingham *Journal*, to be published each Thursday. The news, aside from local items, would be taken from London newspapers, which was the general practice in the provincial papers. In addition, Warren intended to include an original periodical essay in each number. Hector was obviously hoping that Johnson could contribute to the new paper. When he came—either in October, when the paper was still being planned or in November when it began—Johnson did not know, said Hector, "Whether he might stay a fortnight or a month or what time." But quickly Mr. Warren began to find Johnson—who after all had grown up in a bookshop and had a retentive memory for detail— of "great use" in suggestions and advice, and in return the appreciative Warren was "very civil to him." In fact, the story lingered on among booksellers in Birmingham, during the nineteenth century, that Johnson was for a while an "assistant" to Warren. Moreover, Johnson wrote several essays for the paper. But unfortunately no copy of the paper, during the months Johnson contributed to it, has survived.[5]

4

During the first six months at Birmingham, Hector's hopes began to seem justified. The novelty of contributing to the paper, the change in surroundings and the congenial company, the reassurance to Johnson that he was paying at least part of his expenses all helped to release him from the psychological bind in which he had been. He was also beginning to meet some friends of Hector's and Warren's, including John Taylor (no relation to Johnson's close friend), a young man of twenty-two, who was destined to make a large fortune at Birmingham in the gilding and enameling of metals; and Harry Porter, a mercer or woolen draper of forty-two, whose widow was later to become Johnson's wife.

In later years Benjamin Victor, a theater manager who reveled in anecdote, said that he and Dr. Robert James, Johnson's dissolute school friend, and Johnson himself were all joint lovers of the loose-living wife of the inventor Lewis Paul, of whom we shall hear more later, and that "the Lady told him Johnson was the most seducing man she had ever known." People were always fascinated at the idea of Johnson having any sex life, especially after he became famous as a moralist, simply because of his rigorous self-control in this respect, and anyone who could pretend to give some inside information would at once secure a rapt attention. Unfortunately for the story, Mrs. Paul had died back in September 1729. He may have met her on a visit to Birmingham during the year between Stourbridge and Oxford—for she really was for a while Robert James's mistress, says Hector—and she may indeed have described him to James as "seducing," which then led Victor, hearing it from James, to embellish the story. But the truth is, said Hector, that "Johnson never was given to women" in the sense that the story implies.

Hector, after saying that Johnson "never was given to women," then adds a remark of some interest, to which we must later return: "Yet he then did not appear to have much Religion." In short, it was not religious scruples that inhibited him. On the other hand, in contrast to the rigid abstention from liquor that we associate with him in later life, he at this time often "drank freely, particularly Bishop with a roasted orange in it"—a punch made of port, orange, and sugar. Prizing self-control as he did ("I used to slink home, when I had drunk too much"), he once said that there was no man alive who had seen him drunk. Hector, hearing this, said, "Then he had forgot me," and told of the visit to Birmingham of one of the Ford cousins, possibly an uncle, who invited the two young men to spend the evening with him at the Swan Tavern. Johnson warned Hector that the relative was a heavy drinker, and they would become completely drunk. If they divided the evening—Hector drinking with the cousin first, and then Johnson relieving him—they could get through the night. When Johnson arrived Hector and Ford had gone through three bottles of port, and Hector, unable to get back to his own place, collapsed in a bed at the Swan Tavern. Meanwhile Johnson, "instead of saving himself," had been drinking wine at Mr. Porter's house. As a result, he too ended up drunk in the bed next to Hector.[6]

5

After six months Johnson left Hector's apartment and moved into lodgings at the house of a man named Jarvis (June 1, 1733), in another part of town. There was certainly no quarrel between him and the faithful Hector, who soon moved into a house of his own in which Johnson would have been welcome. Nor could the explanation be that Johnson felt he had abused Hector's hospitality long enough. If he could afford to pay rent to Jarvis, he could certainly have afforded to do so to Hector.

More probably he was beginning to be afraid of himself, and to feel that he was sinking back into the state he was in before he came. If this were so, he would dread inflicting himself on others. He could hardly do without Hector's company and confidence in him. But to be witnessed daily by Hector, possibly for some hours every day, would be inevitable living together in such close quarters, and a cause of distress to both of them. The insomnia that was to afflict him for much of his life, so that he would stay up and read or move about until three or four in the morning rather than lie anxiously in bed, may already have begun. This could become a severe trial to a friend living with him who, as a practicing surgeon, had to abide by settled hours. Finally other people would be dropping by and seeing him far more frequently—Hector's friends, Warren's, even those who were also becoming friends of his own—than if he were off by himself in another part of town, where he would not be on view, with the risk of losing the good opinion of others. Instead he would see them only when he felt he could be at his best.

In any case, after he moved into his lonely room at Jarvis's house, an almost complete relapse occurred. Hector would come to visit him. But he found Johnson in a state of "absence," hardly aware of what was going on, talking to himself, and occasionally turning on his friend with such "abuse" that Hector would leave and "keep aloof" until finally Johnson, said Hector, would come and "coax" him back into their usual friendship. As the months passed Hector really became "afraid of Dr. Johnson's head." He added that "Johnson had been conscious of it all along"—conscious, that is, of Hector's own apprehension—but had been afraid to ask Hector "for fear of an answer in the affirmative." This Hector learned when Johnson made his last visit to Birmingham—November 1784, a month before he died—when he asked Hector if he had at that time, over fifty years before, "observed in him a tendency to be disordered in his mind," and Hector replied that he had. We can only speculate about his means of support during these months from June to the end of the year. He may have continued to do writing for Thomas Warren. (The preface to a volume of sermons by a local clergyman, Edward Broadhurst, published that year by Warren, sounds a little, but not convincingly, like Johnson.) When one of his godfathers, Richard Wakefield, died late in the summer, he left Johnson £5, which at the time could pay the expense of a room for an entire year.[7]

6

Thomas Warren, at the time Johnson came, was also becoming interested in books that he might himself publish. Johnson mentioned a small project that had apparently not yet occurred to any English publisher. Back in the seventeenth century, a Portuguese Jesuit, Father Jerome Lobo, had written an account of his life and travels in Abyssinia. It told about the Jesuit missionary effort there (1625–34), and the customs, religion, and history of the Abyssinians; and there were descriptions of the area—the Nile and its branches, the Red Sea coast— and of the animals and plants. The account seems to have lain unpublished in a Lisbon monastery for years, until a French priest, Abbé Joachim Le Grand, translated it into French and added several "dissertations" on particular topics. The French version had appeared the year Johnson entered Oxford (1728), which is where he had come across it. It was long, and contained a good deal that most readers would find tedious. But a shortened version in English might be "useful and profitable."

Warren at the time may have suggested, without getting much response, that Johnson undertake the project himself. But now, as the months were passing at Jarvis's house, Hector and Warren began to urge him to turn to it, hoping the task would help to pull him out of the despair and dissolving lassitude in which he seemed lost. To get a copy of this little-known book was a problem. But Hector was able at last to get a copy from someone at Pembroke (it was not in the library there). By now it was winter, and Johnson started in, quietly finishing a part of it, which was then taken to Warren's printer. But Johnson again sank into paralyzed indolence. Finally, knowing that Johnson's warm heart would respond to an appeal for charity, if to nothing else, Hector told him that Osborne, the printer, could not get other work till this assignment was finished, and that meanwhile "the poor man and his family were suffering." Though Johnson felt hardly able to move, he tried to arouse himself mentally. Lying in bed, with the large French volume before him, he dictated to Hector, translating and summarizing. Then Hector would make a clean copy, take it to the printer, and correct most of the proof sheets. He finished in January, and was paid £5, which was rather good pay for a month's work (it was a quarter of the annual salary he would have got at the school at Market Bosworth). The book itself was published a year later, at the beginning of 1735.[8]

The work has more interest than the bizarre story of its composition would suggest. It was neglected until recently because it was only an abridged translation, because it was hack work (though hack work from a writer of genius may have points of interest), and because Boswell set a precedent in assuming that the only interest that a translation could have—if you are concerned with the translator—would be style. He found little in the actual translation itself that was typical of Johnson's mature style (though more can be discovered than he thought), but was understandably struck by the style of the Preface, where Johnson is directly expressing his own thoughts. And he prints three paragraphs that do indeed read like a caricature of Johnson's later style, in the use of balance and antithesis, and even in the sentiments (the strong clutch at solid fact and probability in such phrases as "to have copied nature from the life" or "to have consulted his senses, not his imagination"; Johnson's own refusal to equate the "laws of nature" with mere custom; his conviction that human nature is much the same everywhere). For this reason, Edmund Burke, with his almost unrivaled sense of style, was "much delighted," says Boswell, with these paragraphs.* Expecting something similar, the reader who turns from the Preface to the translation itself is naturally disappointed. And, in any case, Johnson's own opinion of the style generally is well known. When Boswell was lent a copy by his friend Sir John Pringle (1776), at a time that the work was almost forgotten, he went to show it to Johnson "as a curiosity":

> He said "Take no notice of it," or "don't talk of it." He seemed to think it beneath him, though done at six-and-twenty. I said to him, "Your style is much improved since you translated this." He answered with a sort of triumphant smile, "Sir, I hope it is."[9]

But there were several reasons why the book caught his attention at Oxford and lingered in his mind. The most general interest is that expressed in the Dedication of the book: "A generous and elevated mind is distinguished by nothing more certainly than an eminent degree of curiosity; nor is that curiosity ever more agreeably or usefully employed, than in examining the laws and customs of foreign nations." In this respect, it typifies, as Donald Greene says, both Johnson's affinity in temperament with those Renaissance Humanists whose subject was mankind in its totality, and the extraordinary range of interests that Johnson's own writing is to begin to show once he finally recovers from this long traumatic period and starts what is in effect a new life. One of the values of range, when used by an active mind, is the help it can give us to "distinguish nature from custom"—to distinguish what

---

* "The Portuguese traveller, contrary to the general vein of his countrymen, has amused his reader with no romantick absurdities, or incredible fictions; whatever he relates, whether true or not, is at least probable. . . .

"He appears, by his modest and unaffected narration, to have described things as he saw them, to have copied nature from the life, and to have consulted his senses, not his imagination. He meets with no basilisks that destroy with their eyes, his crocodiles devour their prey without tears, and his cataracts fall from the Rock without deafening the neighbouring inhabitants.

"The reader will here find no regions cursed with irremediable barrenness, or blessed with spontaneous fecundity; no perpetual gloom, or unceasing sunshine; nor are the nations here described either devoid of all sense of humanity, or consummate in all private and social virtues. Here are no Hottentots without Religion, Polity, or Articulate Language; no Chinese perfectly polite, and completely skilled in all sciences; he will discover, what will always be discovered by a diligent and impartial enquirer, that wherever human nature is to be found, there is a mixture of vice and virtue, a contest of passion and reason. . . ."

is really universal, persisting, or built into man, and what is accidental; and this ability is one of the most striking things about the mature Johnson, especially as a critic of literature. In a sense, he is already beginning to show this interest in the Preface to Lobo's *Voyage.**

7

After finishing the book Johnson went back to Lichfield in the middle of winter (February 1734) with what would appear to be the same hopelessness, the same paralyzing self-detestation and despair, in which so much of the last five years had been wasted. For again the months began to pass with nothing to show for them. It could begin to seem that this radical helplessness would never end, and that nothing could save him. Like everything else since he had left Oxford, the thirteen months or so that he had spent at Birmingham—the same length of time he had been at Oxford—could be regarded as another failure. The last half of it had been almost completely wasted, in his room at Jarvis's, trying to see through what had been threatening him, trying to "manage" his mind.

Increasingly the contrast between what he might have been and what he had become continued to stun rather than arouse him. Finally, during the late spring, in an act of desperation, he resolved on a project that was surprisingly ambitious. The work was something that could occupy even a mature scholar for some years, and it would have been fascinating to see what Johnson—who had spent only a year as an

* Moreover, he is not echoing Lobo's own sentiments (Lobo thinks some of the customs of the natives hopelessly "contrary . . . to the laws of nature"). Instead he is correcting them, but on the basis of Lobo's own facts, stating in effect that if we look at what Lobo actually tells as distinct from what Lobo concludes, we can make generalizations he does not. The same thing applies to another aspect of the book—the extent to which imperialist expansion, which Johnson all his life associated with exploitation, was at least one of the motives, as Donald Greene says, behind the Portuguese missionary attempt: "The ancient Christian state church of Abyssinia was subject to the Coptic Patriarchate of Alexandria, which existed under the protection of the Turkish rulers of Egypt. It was thus greatly to the advantage of the expanding Portuguese empire in the East, whose chief rivals were the Turks, to detach the allegiance of the Abyssinian rulers from the native church and bring them under the control of Rome." Here in Lobo's account the reader could see for himself the way in which political interests could affect religious efforts or hide behind them. Finally, as an abridgment or epitome, the work—considering how quickly it was done—shows a very active intelligence whenever it moves from literal translation to a distilled presentation in a few sentences of a page or so, or is expanded for the sake of clarity.[10]

undergraduate at Oxford—could have done with it, especially considering the short timetable that his impatient nature would have allowed him. The project was to bring out an annotated edition of the
Latin poems of Politian (Angelo Poliziano), the great fifteenth-
century Humanist, scholar, and poet, together with his life, and a
history of Latin poetry from the time of Petrarch, a century before,
down to Politian himself. On June 15 what Hawkins describes as "a
very old and curious edition of the works of Politian" (it was still
among Johnson's own books at his death) was withdrawn from the
library at Pembroke and sent to him. On August 5 printed *Proposals*
were sent out describing the project and soliciting subscriptions, which
were to be sent to "the Editor, or N. Johnson, bookseller, of Lichfield"
(Nathaniel by now seems to have been managing the bookshop). Some
of Johnson's friends responded, but few others did. He was, after all,
completely unknown to the potential market for such a book. Without
the money in advance, the expense of printing could not be met. The
matter had to be dropped.[11]

This project, when we stop to think of it, has at least three points of
interest. It foreshadows again his lifelong fascination with the Renaissance "revival of learning" (of which he later planned to write a
general history)—a fascination that in turn reflects his concern with
whatever can tell us why or how human effort is able to achieve what
it does (or for that matter get anywhere at all). In addition, there was
obviously some identification with Politian himself, who had been a
precocious boy, had grown up in poverty, was physically unattractive
and awkward in form and movement, and who by his thirties became
one of the supreme teachers and scholars of Europe, known for his
range of interests in every field of learning, his astonishing memory,
and the remarkable grace of his Latin style. Finally it was psychologically a good sign. Even if the project came to nothing—through no
fault of his own—merely to go as far as he did, to get the book from
the Pembroke library and write the *Proposals*, showed if not the beginning of a recovery at least the possibility of a beginning. If nothing else
had been gained the previous year, writing the essays for Warren and,
above all, the Lobo book had done something to him. Though far more
time had been wasted than had been used up in writing them, and
though there had been so much inner protest to work against, they had
reopened a part of him that had been locked, and in doing so had
restored some confidence, even if it took some time for the effect to
register in him.

During the autumn (November 10), as if to get his bearings, he started to keep a diary "in a variety of little books," says Hawkins, "folded and stitched together by himself." (Some of these may have been among the many papers Johnson destroyed before his death, or may have been taken by Hawkins himself and then lost when his house burned in February 1785.) It was as a kind of preface to these "Annals," as Johnson named them, that he wrote down that short list—which did survive and which we have been citing—of what he considered the principal events of his life.[12]

In the same spirit of resolve, he also wrote a letter a couple of weeks later (November 25) to Edward Cave, the founder and editor of the new *Gentleman's Magazine*, which within only three years was already becoming famous. In effect, he was offering his services as a contributor. The letter—awkwardly indirect, belligerently and needlessly self-defensive in advance—betrays how uncertain of himself he is. He says, in effect, that the new *Gentleman's Magazine* has considerable room for improvement. Instead of concentrating so much on the "current wit of the month," which could be profitably reduced "to a narrow compass," would not the magazine be interested in original poems, as well as "short literary dissertations in Latin or English, critical remarks on authors ancient or modern, forgotten poems that deserve revival," and similar works? By such means the literary section of the magazine would "be better recommended to the publick than by low jests, aukward buffoonery, or the dull scurrilities of either party." The writer of this letter—which Johnson, probably fearing a rebuff, left unsigned—knows "a person, who will undertake, on reasonable terms, sometimes to fill a column." If Cave is interested, he can write to "S. Smith," in care of the Castle Inn at Birmingham, who will see that it reaches the right person. The letter could have understandably annoyed or been simply disregarded by most publishers. But the calm, sensible Cave was always willing to consider opportunities. According to Hawkins, he sent a favorably reply (December 2) but apparently nothing further developed.[13]

Chapter 10

Johnson's Marriage;
the School at Edial

Meanwhile, in Birmingham, on September 3 (1734), his friend Harry Porter—the mercer and woolen draper to whom Hector had introduced him a year or so before—died at the age of forty-three, leaving a widow two years older than he, Elizabeth Jervis Porter, and three children—a daughter of eighteen, Lucy Porter, and two boys of sixteen and ten, Jervis Henry and Joseph. Mr. Porter, though he had not prospered in business (and in fact lost money) came from an old and fairly well-to-do family. His wife, Elizabeth Jervis, was the daughter of a Warwickshire squire, himself the descendant of a long line of country squires, and she had a rather distinguished ancestry on her mother's side that included members of the royal household. She brought with her what was then a very sizable dowry (at least £600), which, according to the marriage settlement, remained her property in the event of her husband's death before her own.[1]

The Porters had been kind to Johnson and shown him hospitality (it was at their house, for example, that he had been visiting, and drinking wine with Mr. Porter, the night he and Hector were scheduled to provide companionship for the hard-drinking Ford relative at the Swan Tavern). In a way, they could remind him of the people he had known during the year at Stourbridge. And he was grateful for their kindness, and for the respect and confidence in him they showed. They were not put off by his appearance or the convulsive gestures. He could be grateful for this, too; and knowing how he must appear to most women, he could be especially moved by Mrs. Porter's complete disregard of it. Lucy Porter told Boswell that

when he was first introduced to her mother, his appearance was very forbidding: he was then lean and lank, so that his immense structure of bones was hideously striking to the eye, and the scars of the scrophula were deeply visible. He also wore his hair [as distinct from a wig], which was straight and stiff, and separated behind; and he often had, seemingly, convulsive starts and odd gesticulations, which tended to excite at once surprize and ridicule.

But Mrs. Porter was "so much engaged by his conversation that she overlooked all these disadvantages," and told her daughter, "This is the most sensible man that I ever saw in my life."[2]

Johnson, according to Anna Seward, was at Birmingham during Porter's illness, and spent "all his leisure hours at Mr. Porter's, attending his sick-bed." The story is by no means improbable.* Certainly in later life, when so much more is known about him, he proved—as his moral writings have ever since proved—a reassuring friend to those afflicted with fear or sorrow, partly because he himself had undergone so much. At least something of this quality, which is one of the finest things about him, may have already been present at the age of twenty-five—the age he was reaching when Harry Porter died. By this time he had himself endured almost five years of trial and despair.

2

So comforting did the widow find his reassurance, both before and after Mr. Porter's death, that she unquestionably encouraged Johnson in the months of courtship that followed; and Johnson, with his pent-up need for affection and his capacity for gratitude, responded warmly to her own need for help and her confidence in him. The Reverend

* It has been generally discounted because other remarks of hers about Johnson during these years have proved exaggerated or completely fanciful. This was not because of deliberate deceit or delight in creative invention but because she passed on, as assured fact, what was sometimes only speculative gossip on the part of her mother and other older people (she herself was not born until 1742). An example is the story—in which most of the details are known to be wrong—that Johnson had earlier been in love with young Lucy Porter when she had visited Lichfield in Johnson's schooldays (she could not at that time have been more than ten) and tried to overcome her revulsion by writing some verses ("On a Lady Presenting a Sprig of Myrtle"—actually written in 1731 for Morgan Graves, a friend of Hector's, to give a lady friend).[3]

William Shaw said that "the first advances probably proceeded from her, as her attachment to Johnson was in opposition to the advice and desire of all her relations." (Shaw is usually reliable, and his sources were good—in this case probably the daughter of Dr. Swynfen, Elizabeth Desmoulins.)[4]

Johnson would have needed encouragement. To begin with, he was now twenty-five and without the experience of even one moderately successful love affair to give him confidence that any such thing was possible for him. His admiring love for Olivia Lloyd at Stourbridge had naturally been hopeless. It could hardly have been otherwise. But the same thing had apparently been true even of the humbler Ann Hector, Edmund's sister. The years since he had left Oxford, during which it had been a matter of simply staying afloat, had further removed such things from the realm of the possible. In addition, there was the difference in age between Mrs. Porter and himself. Moreover, he was perfectly aware of the way in which it would be regarded by others.

Then there was the disparity in fortune. True, the admired Cornelius had married an older woman from a wealthy family (as had Cornelius's father—it seemed to run in the Ford family); and this could give something of an example, or at least a kind of sanction. If others thought Johnson was marrying her for her money, there was nothing he could do about it (significantly, no one with even the slightest acquaintance with Johnson ever did make or has made the suggestion). Still, he could take it for granted that there would be problems. She would be used to a way of living that he himself, by his own efforts, could not hope to match. There would be a problem in looking after her money, which was something in which he had no experience. Moreover, he was not simply poorer; he was almost penniless. In speaking of Mrs. Porter's money, we should keep in mind what the amount meant at that time—at least £600, probably more. In the early eighteenth century, the purchasing power of a pound (for such things as rents, real estate, or food, though not for clothes or transportation) was worth almost twenty times what it had become even before the inflation that became marked in the 1960's. A clearer way of estimating it is to recall the amount on which a single man or a married couple could live in a modest way: £40 a year would suffice (and one could survive on considerably less). In this case, Mrs. Porter's money was equivalent to at least fifteen times a modest annual income, and the interest alone was almost enough on which to live.

But the principal drawback by far, and one which only warm and continued encouragement on her part could overcome, was the strong opposition of her two sons and of her husband's family. For Johnson was only too aware of what she would be sacrificing, and naturally his pride would also be hurt by their attitude. The older son, Jervis Henry, who had begun training to become a naval officer, was so appalled at his mother's marriage to a grotesque-looking man without any occupation and young enough to be her son that he refused to see his mother again for the rest of her life. We can assume his opposition was made very clear long before the marriage. It was years before the younger son, Joseph—later a prosperous merchant—overcame his "disgust." Lucy, the daughter, combined the sweet nature and impracticality of her father with the firm, warm loyalty of her mother. She quickly accepted the marriage, and before long became a good friend and devoted admirer of Johnson's. Harry Porter, said Anna Seward, had a "rich bachelor brother in London," who left sizable bequests to the three children, especially the older son, but "would never do anything for the worthless widow, who had married 'the literary cub,' as he used to call him." This was Joseph Porter, a London merchant who was indeed rich. According to William Shaw, he "offered to settle a very handsome annuity on her for life, provided she would break her engagement. But nothing would dissuade her."[5]

In comparison, any opposition from Johnson's own family would have been of minor importance if it existed at all. There is sometimes said to have been some, but on the basis of nothing in particular. Anna Seward passed on to Boswell (he did not use it) an amusing account of Johnson's interview with his mother on the matter, in which Sarah refused her "willing consent."* But Miss Seward, though she could speak for the Porter family and was, in fact, connected to them (her

---

* " 'No, Sam, my willing consent you will never have to so preposterous a union. You are not twenty-five, and she is turned fifty. If she had any prudence, this request had never been made to me. . . .'

" 'Mother, I have not deceived Mrs. Porter: I have told her the worst of me; that I am of mean extraction; that I have no money; and that I have had an uncle hanged. She replied, that she valued no one more or less for his descent; that she had no more money than myself; and that, though she had not a relation hanged, she had fifty who deserved hanging.' "

The story need not be an entire invention of Miss Seward's, though the particular woman she remembered as her source denied that she was (the offensive part was the reference to the "uncle hanged," though it is the kind of thing Johnson could easily have said in jest). For the controversy over the story, see W, p. 289, n. 1.

146

grandfather, John Hunter—Johnson's old schoolmaster—had married, after his first wife's death, a sister of Harry Porter's), was hardly in a position to know much about Sarah's sentiments. If Sarah felt that Cornelius had done a good thing in marrying an older woman with money, she may have also thought this marriage satisfactory, at least not impossible, though the wife was older and the fortune smaller. Besides Sarah, there was no one else to oppose the marriage on Johnson's side. Nathaniel's opinion would hardly have been consulted; and the Ford relatives, who had done nothing for Johnson during these years, could claim no proprietary interest in his affairs.

On July 9, 1735, the marriage took place at Derby, in St. Werburgh's Church. Because of the opposition of Mrs. Porter's family and the attitude of her acquaintances at Birmingham, she would naturally not have wished to be married there. Feeling that Johnson's friends might think the marriage strange—she was very self-conscious about her age—she, or possibly both of them, may have also felt that Lichfield was not the place for the wedding. Hence Derby was chosen. In the marriage license the day before the wedding, the bride—forgivably embarrassed at their difference in years, twenty-five and forty-six—gave her age as "forty." A touching indication of her anxiety to be more youthful, married to a man so much younger, was an occasional tendency people later noticed (not entirely in keeping with her character) to play the coquette. She did so now as she and her bridegroom rode horseback to Derby to be married. Johnson told the story both to Boswell and Mrs. Thrale. She had "read the old romances," said Johnson, that inveterate reader of romances himself, and had got it into her head that "a woman of spirit should use her lover like a dog." At first she told the bridegroom he was riding too fast, and she could not keep pace with him. When he slowed up, she would pass him, and then complain that he was lagging behind. Finally Johnson—considering it a matter of principle to remedy this temptation to "caprice"—"pushed on briskly, till I was fairly out of her sight. The road lay between two hedges, so I was sure she could not miss it." Then he stopped, and waited till she came up. "There was a tear or two—pretty dear creature."[6]

Meanwhile, during the preceding months, Johnson's confidence in himself and his general trust in life had at last begun to return, as he was able to turn his mind from self-condemnation and self-distrust to new responsibilities and hopes. With the help of Theophilus Levett, the Lichfield Town Clerk, and a friendly clergyman, John Addenbrooke, he got a job for two months as tutor at the estate of Thomas Whitby (Great Haywood, near Lichfield), preparing Whitby's oldest son for the university. Whitby had wanted his son tutored for six months. Johnson had less than two months free before his marriage. But Addenbrooke assured Whitby that Johnson in that time would be of more help than "a year spent in the usual way at the university." There were four other children in the family, and Johnson taught them as well; and in walking back on Sundays from Colwich Church, which the Whitby family attended, Johnson would surprise them by repeating "the greatest part of the sermon, with criticisms, additions, and improvements."[7]

Most important of all, as a sign that things had made a turn for the better, he wrote to a friend at Oxford (May 18) asking at last for the return of the library of books that he had taken to Oxford and had then left there—almost as if feeling unworthy to reclaim them—for five and a half years.[8]

3

Thirty years later, after Johnson had become famous, people were puzzled about this marriage and have continued to be so ever since. His friends and acquaintances were fascinated at the mere thought of it, and speculated among themselves, partly because of the incongruity resulting from the bits of information they were able to piece together, and partly because of its incongruity with Johnson's own character—as it appeared to them—in his fifties and sixties. If the bride's relatives wondered at the time of the marriage what she saw in him, the situation was now reversed, and has tended to remain so in a way that is cruelly, if unintentionally, unjust to her as well as to Johnson. In effect, she became almost a comic character and the whole situation something of a comic episode, as most things can be if they are viewed with enough detachment. In this case, detachment was not difficult to attain. It was, in fact, inevitable, and ample room was left for the imagination to high-light and enjoy the bizarre.

Since his wife had died in 1752, most of his later friends were, of course, unable to see anything of the marriage at firsthand, least of all as it was at the start. Nor did anyone feel able to ask him directly about details. They knew he had been profoundly shaken by her death. His voice would falter when he spoke of her. Yet it all seemed incredible, judging from the little they knew of it. Marriages in which the wife was so much older were not unheard of. But, rightly or wrongly, the popular mind associated the husband in such cases with an unaggressive type of man—rather mousy, dependent, perhaps slightly infantile. Certainly the idea of such a marriage did not fit one's notion of Johnson, with his huge, unwieldy frame, his immense physical strength, his courage and rhinocerine laughter, his uncanny incisiveness of mind. The sense of incongruity still persists, so that even A. L. Reade—who discovered so much about the background of Elizabeth Porter and her husband—entitled his chapter on the subject "The Amazing Marriage."

In fact, marriage of any kind could seem difficult to associate with Johnson during his last twenty-five years, when he lived, as he said, like an old "straggler," sewed his own buttons, appeared to look after himself in every way, required no more attendance—as Hawkins said—than did Diogenes, and also kept incredible hours. More than that, no moralist had written with shrewder insight about marriage, from which it was inferred that he was not a man to be easily swept off his feet. Moreover, in casual conversation, though he could say persuasively that single life was worse, he would also speak of marriage in a way that could leave a wife a little uneasy if she had been present. When "a gentleman," said Boswell (actually it was Boswell himself), "talked to him of a lady he greatly admired and wished to marry, but was afraid of her superiority of talents," he replied, "You need not be afraid; marry her. Before a year goes about, you'll find that reason much weaker, and that wit not so bright." Of another man's second marriage: it represented "the triumph of hope over experience." The question whether marriage was "natural to man" was discussed at General Paoli's: "It is so far from being natural for a man and woman to live in a state of marriage" that all the motives they have as individuals and all the restraints of society "are hardly sufficient to keep them together." When Boswell asked whether there were "fifty women in the world, with any one of whom a man may be as happy, as with any one woman in particular," Johnson replied, "Fifty thousand": "BOSWELL. 'Then, Sir, you are not of opinion with some who imagine that certain men and certain women are made for each other. . . .' JOHNSON. '. . . marriages would in general be as happy, and often more so, if they were all made by the Lord Chancellor, upon a due consideration of characters and circumstances, without the parties having any choice in the matter.' "[9]

But if there was some difficulty in associating him with marriage generally—living as he did, writing and speaking as he did—it seemed hopeless to reconcile him with what could be learned of the mysterious "Tetty" or "Tetsie" (the nicknames for Elizabeth that he used), so much older than himself and so different from the women in whose company he seemed most to enjoy himself. She was not like Mrs. Thrale—who was small, as Sarah had been, and rather birdlike—nor like the neat and beautiful Quakeress Mrs. Knowles, an Olivia Lloyd grown to maturity, or Molly Aston, whom he thought the "loveliest" woman he had ever known, with her fine, aquiline features: Tetty was large, buxom, highly colored. Yet, as Johnson told his friend Topham Beauclerk, "It was a love marriage upon both sides." (Johnson's honesty was proverbial.) Granted Tetty could have seen something in him, and could have recognized future greatness, what could he have seen in her? It could not have been youthful infatuation of the usual sort. Everything that could be found out about her appearance and manner belied it. Garrick described her to Boswell (and in much the same way to Mrs. Thrale and others) "as very fat, with a bosom of more than ordinary protuberance, with swelled cheeks, of a florid red, produced by thick painting, and increased by the liberal use of cordials; flaring and fantastick in her dress, and affected both in her speech and her general behaviour."[10] True, Garrick exaggerated, as everyone knew. Moreover, he was plainly speaking of her in her later years, as were others like Mr. Levet, who mentioned her drinking, or the people who told Hawkins (Garrick was one) that there was something "crazy" in the way they acted toward each other—"profound respect on his part, and the airs of an antiquated beauty on hers."[11] But even after making allowance for the passage of time, the physical attraction ("Pretty dear creature," he would say, thinking back on her; "pretty charmer") was difficult to conceive. Perhaps (people assumed) the real answer was the one given by Hawkins—that he could not see very well (a remark that is still sometimes made when the marriage is mentioned). Actually, however nearsighted he was, he was extraordinarily noticing, as Mrs. Thrale points out, about every detail of a woman's appearance and dress, and, she adds, extremely critical about those details.

4

The truth is that the years were to be very hard on Tetty. While Johnson went through his thirties, with his fortunes at a low ebb for so long, Tetty, who had given up so much, was passing through her fifties, her sons having rejected her, and her own money largely gone. With so few resources left to give her self-respect, she inevitably changed, and in a way for which no blame can be attached either to her or to Johnson.* In fact, in both of them there is a moving loyalty, a determination to make the best of it, that persists until the end, seventeen years later. Given a few graphic descriptions of her in her last years, it was naturally difficult—even if one tried theoretically to make allowance for the passage of time—to dislodge them without having details of her earlier years that would be equally graphic; and this was impossible if only because the grotesque is by definition more graphic. Mrs. Thrale discounted Garrick, saying, "The picture I found of her at Litchfield was very pretty, and her daughter Mrs. Lucy Porter said it was very like. Mr. Johnson has told me that her hair was eminently beautiful, quite *blonde* like that of a baby." William Shaw, inquiring carefully, said that at the time of the marriage she "was still young and handsome." In fact, she was for a while "so handsome, that his associates in letters and wit [this would have been five or even ten years after the marriage] were often very pleasant with him on the strange disparity" in looks between husband and wife. In addition, she was "so shrewd and cultivated, that in the earlier part of their connection, he was fond of consulting her in all his literary pursuits." She could make a point so well that in some arguments, Johnson told Mrs. Thrale, he would try to get her daughter Lucy on his side in advance. The two of them enjoyed reading plays together. "She read comedy better than any body he ever heard (he said); in tragedy she mouthed too much."[12]

An interesting thing about Johnson that is only superficially difficult to reconcile with his aggressive independence of nature is his enormous capacity for gratitude. It is now becoming more widely recognized, in both human and animal psychology, that loyalty in its more extreme forms (of which gratitude is one) is possible only among the more aggressive species. It is also more prominent among the more aggressive individuals within those species, though an iron ring of taboo, as it were—or, in a more sophisticated being, moral decision—is necessary to turn the strength of emotion back from aggression into the generosity of focused loyalty. If Johnson hated envy, and instinctively created a moral wall of taboo against it, he also detested the smallness of nature in those who cannot feel gratitude. So, in one of the *Rambler*

* See below, pp. 261–64.

essays (No. 4), he was to attack Swift's maxim that men are "grateful in the same degree as they are resentful" ("It is of the utmost importance to mankind, that positions of this tendency should be laid open and confuted"). The freedom to feel gratitude, to express it fully, was itself a sign that one was a "free agent" and, in a fundamental sense, a "moral being."

Certainly gratitude was for Johnson a powerful element in this marriage of seventeen years, which was the first of the three or four things (the next was the new career he was to start in London, largely because of the responsibility he felt for Tetty) that really pulled him out and saved him from the self-destructive state into which he had been sunk for so long. From the start, when she had brushed aside his grotesque mannerisms with that first remark, "This is the most sensible man that I ever saw," and more in the months after Harry Porter's death, Elizabeth Jervis Porter had given him help and confidence. More important, she had given him this confidence when he was nothing, after he had lost five years (and at a crucial time in one's life, from twenty to twenty-five) in a state of what he regarded as near madness. The final confidence was achieved through the marriage itself, when the disadvantages for her were so obvious and the opposition so formidable. Given his immensely assimilative nature, this gratitude became a permanent part of him. As a result, he naturally continued to mourn her loss, long after her death, in a way that would have struck his friends—could they have seen his journals—as even more excessive than they thought. Nothing comparable to what she had done for him was to happen till Mrs. Thrale helped to save him from despair thirty years later.

Of course, there might be other women with whom he would feel he was "in love" (he would never have seen anything wrong in this; what he would have considered wrong would be to start acting in accordance with it as though nothing else mattered). But these attractions were minor in comparison with what Elizabeth Jervis Porter had done for him and had sacrificed for him. Finally, though we should not overstretch the point, her confidence in him had about it something of an aura that could carry him back to that year at Stourbridge—that "second birth" that had been so important as to be almost archetypal for him. The squirearchy from which Elizabeth Jervis had come was not too dissimilar from a world in which Cornelius had moved (not the whole world of Cornelius, of course, but one of them)—the world (naturally idealized) of the people at Stourbridge who had also shown such generous confidence in him. It was almost as though a representative of that world—after he himself could seem to have betrayed it for five years or more—had once again showed confidence in him and had proved that, after all, that world was not completely lost to him.

5

In return, the least he could do would be to proceed without further self-indulgence to do the one thing that he felt was possible for him—becoming a schoolmaster. This meant brushing aside his own personal dislike of the work, which was based on more than one reason. To begin with, as Imlac in *Rasselas* tells the young Pekuah, when she announces her wish to be a student of the astronomer, "Men advanced far in knowledge do not love to repeat the elements of their art." The self-taught in particular (and Johnson was largely self-taught) are rarely the most patient of teachers. The readiness of memory and speed in getting a point that have permitted them to be self-taught are a hindrance to their effectiveness, certainly to their enjoyment, in daily retracing the rudiments of a subject. In addition, he was conscious of the way in which his own tics and convulsive mannerisms would appear to students. His experience at Market Bosworth had been unhappy. Finally his lack of a degree was a barrier, and could subject him to humiliation. Still, there was no alternative.

Moreover, he wanted, if possible, to improve Tetty's small fortune. This led, with the encouragement of Gilbert Walmesley, to the thought of a school of his own. His tutoring in the Whitby family, during May and June before his marriage, could also have suggested that he might succeed at the work if only he were reasonably independent in his teaching. By June plans were developing. For he wrote to a friend, Richard Congreve (June 25), a couple of weeks before his marriage that he was "now going to furnish a house in the country, and keep a private boarding school for young gentlemen"; and since he would like to find out about "the different ways of teaching in use at the most celebrated schools," could Congreve—who had gone as a student from the Lichfield Grammar School to the Charterhouse—tell him "the method of the Charterhouse, and procure me that of Westminster"?[13]

Yet, considering the size of the investment, a school of his own involved genuine risk for his wife's money. And shortly after the marriage, he made one more attempt to get a job that had just opened at another school. This was at Solihull, a village seven miles from Birmingham. The headmaster there, John Crompton—a "morose" man (wrote one of his students, Richard Jago, later a minor poet) who carried "a birchen sceptre, stained with infant gore"—had abruptly left to take on the job of headmaster at Market Bosworth. John Kilby, under whom Johnson had worked at Market Bosworth, was now dead; and Sir Wolstan Dixie, liking what he heard of the birch-wielding Crompton, offered him an unusually large salary (£103 plus house and gardens) to come to Market Bosworth. Gilbert Walmesley wrote to a friend at Solihull supporting Johnson's application to replace Crompton. But the friend, Henry Greswold, wrote back (August 30) that the governors of the school—already irritated by Crompton's manner—were in a cautious mood about a new master, and had wanted to inquire closely into Johnson's character. They had decided not to select him because, though an "excellent Scholar," they had heard he was "a very haughty, ill-natured gent., and that he has such a way of distorting his face (which though he can't help) the gent[s] think it may affect some lads."[14]

This settled the matter, and Johnson and Tetty now went ahead with plans for a school of their own. Even if they had no more than twenty pupils, a sizable building was necessary. At Gilbert Walmesley's suggestion, they rented a large, vacant house—Edial Hall (pronounced "Edjall," and sometimes spelled that way)—in the hamlet of Edial, about two miles west of Lichfield. Despite the size of the house, with its spacious courtyard, the rent was probably not too high because of its unusual shape. It had been built about seventy years before by a prominent citizen of Lichfield named Thomas Hammond, who had rather eccentric architectural tastes. The main part of the house was in the form of a large box with a pyramid-shaped roof. The top of the pyramid was leveled off into a flat square, enclosed by a balustrade, with a tall wooden cupola—apparently a sort of observatory—in the middle. One of the chimneys was shaped like an Egyptian obelisk. (By 1800 it had become a farmhouse, the ornamental parts removed and a large wing torn down. It still survives in its reduced form.)[15]

A large back room was made over into the schoolroom. The loyal Lucy Porter came and lived with them, and there must have been at least a couple of servants, probably more, though the name of only one of them is remembered—Charles Bird, a lad of about sixteen. When he was a very old man, Bird is reported to have been asked whether he remembered those days at Edial Hall, and to have replied only that Johnson "was not much of a scholar to look at" but was remarkably good "in leaping over the styles."[16] It took some time to prepare things, and to furnish the house. Though rents by modern standards were surprisingly low, furniture—in the days before mass production—was comparatively more expensive. Even if the furnishings were modest, their cost could have used up a fair amount of Tetty's money, perhaps £100 or more. Meanwhile they had their own living expenses, and Tetty and Lucy were not used to living in penury. Some of Tetty's capital may also have been drawn on for this. It was during this period of brief affluence—now or early in the next year—that Johnson consented to have a miniature portrait of himself painted to please Tetty (henceforth worn by her in a brooch).[17]

6

Finally, in late autumn (1735), the school was opened. Three pupils showed up—David Garrick, now eighteen; his brother George, who was twelve; and, shortly afterward, Lawrence Offley, a boy of sixteen from a well-known Staffordshire family, who then went to Cambridge the following autumn. Gilbert Walmesley was principally responsible for getting them, though the Garrick family liked and respected Johnson anyway. Offley was the second cousin of Magdalen Aston, the woman that Walmesley—tiring of bachelordom at the age of fifty-six—was about to marry (April 1736).

In rounding up these boys for the school, Walmesley's thought, said Hawkins (who probably heard it from Johnson), was like that of shrewd "country house-wives" who place "one egg in the nest of a hen to induce her to lay more." But the device did not work very well. Johnson had no degree; his convulsive mannerisms were not reassuring to parents; and with the excellent Lichfield Grammar School nearby, Edial Hall naturally seemed to offer very little. Boswell assumed that the two Garrick boys and Lawrence Offley were the only pupils Johnson had. But Hawkins said that a few more appeared, though the total number, at no time, "exceeded eight, and of those not all were boarders." We need not linger on the curriculum. Johnson's summary of it was printed by both Hawkins and Boswell. It was completely conventional, and patterned after that of the Lichfield Grammar School.[18]

Aside from the small number of students, what is principally remembered, when the school is mentioned, is Boswell's remark:

> From Mr. Garrick's account he did not appear to have been profoundly reverenced by his pupils. His oddities of manner, and uncouth gesticulations, could not but be the subject of merriment to them; and, in particular, the young rogues used to listen at the door of his bed-chamber, and peep through the key-hole, that they might turn into ridicule his tumultuous and aukward fondness for Mrs. Johnson, whom he used to name by the familiar appellation of Tetty or Tetsey.[19]

Actually Garrick's imitations of the married pair in their bedroom, with Johnson preoccupied with his tragedy, were among his set parlor pieces. Many of Johnson's friends, including Boswell, saw them. In their more extreme form, they were reserved for men; Mrs. Thrale, for example, says that she never saw them, "though my husband did." However skeptical they might be afterward about the truth of the imitation, they could hardly avoid enjoying such a performance by the greatest actor of his age—a double performance in which Garrick acted the parts of both Johnson and Tetty. Even the noted scholar Edmond Malone had to admit that "Garrick made it entertaining, but doubtless it was all invention." In these skits Johnson would be sitting at a table beside the bed slaving away at *Irene*. Too absorbed to hear Tetty's pleas that he come to bed, he would declaim to her some of the new verses he was writing. At the same time, vaguely aware of the bedclothes dangling next to him and assuming they were his shirttails hanging out, he would be absent-mindedly tucking them into his trousers while Tetty, shivering with cold, would frantically clutch at the departing sheets. Finally, as her situation and her pleas began to get through to him, he would rise and begin running about the room, puffing, blowing, and presumably trailing the bedclothes, as he started to prepare for the night, and crying out, "I'm coming, my Tetsie, I'm coming."[20]

After some months Johnson decided to advertise the school in the *Gentleman's Magazine* (June and July 1736): "At Edial, near Litchfield, in Staffordshire, Young Gentlemen are Boarded, and Taught the Latin and Greek Languages, by Samuel Johnson." But there were still no results. Feeling guilty that—far from improving Tetty's fortune—the school he had started was simply draining it, he turned to the only other alternative, writing: not small pieces, journalistic or in verse, but a full-dress blank-verse tragedy that, if performed, would not only make money but might also make his reputation. The result was his single play—famous at least as a title—called *Irene*.

7

To modern readers—to readers generally during the last two centuries—the mere idea of beginning one's career by trying to write such a play—a quasi-classic tragedy in stiff brocade and with an Oriental or otherwise distant setting—seems strange. But it was for a while, from the 1690's to the 1730's, the normal thing for a really ambitious poet to do. It was a gamble, considering the amount of time and effort you had to invest. But if you succeeded, you were considered to have won your spurs. Johnson remembered the story of the Sultan Mahomet and the Greek Christian slave Irene, which he had read in Richard Knolles's *General History of the Turks* (1603); it had been used as a subject in earlier plays, which he may have read; and, borrowing a copy of Knolles now from Garrick's older brother, Peter, Johnson started in on the play. In Knolles, the beautiful Irene—captured at the fall of Constantinople (1453)—is given to Mahomet as a mistress. He becomes so infatuated that he neglects other matters. His subjects begin to turn against him. In order to prove his firmness as a ruler, he then kills her. In Johnson, Irene is made less passive and the story turned into a moral drama of temptation. Given the choice of renouncing Christianity for Islam in return for safety and power, she wavers, agrees, wavers again, and is finally killed. There is probably no lengthy work (as distinct from mere trifles, or obvious hack work) by any writer of Johnson's standing that has aroused less curiosity, once it is looked into, or provided less enjoyment than *Irene*. If it were not by Johnson, few people, even people with a close interest in literature, would have heard of it during the last two centuries. It would be given a few sentences in the more detailed histories of eighteenth-century drama, along with scores of other plays that the literary historian tries to rescue from oblivion. Yet paradoxically much of the hindrance to the modern reader is the knowledge that Johnson wrote it. If it were picked up at random—particularly after sampling some other tragedies of this type written at that time—it would not seem too bad. But approaching it with the knowledge that it is by one of the masters of English prose style (who also had a powerful command of one kind of poetic style), and that it is also by one of the supreme critics of literature in whatever language, the heart begins after a while to sink except in the most resolute Johnsonian, and sometimes even then.

Several things were working against the play. To begin with, there was the genre itself (as Johnson himself was later to see and to express better than anyone else)—the stiff, stylized kind of tragedy set in a remote place, and remote from common life. Then there was Johnson's own inexperience. This, he understood, was the fashionable thing to do—a way to make money, and secure one's passport into the world of letters; and off in a provincial city, he had started doing what others at least said was the right thing, the way to get a start. But he really knew nothing in a practical way about the theater, and was in no position to do so. Lastly it was against the grain, even this early. He might vary and enrich the nuances, the characters, the moral itself, as three fine discussions of *Irene* have pointed out in differing ways.[21] But it was already, from the start, violating most of the beliefs he was later to develop, and may have already begun developing, about the uses and functions of the drama, or about fiction in general as it could or should present human life. Like Coleridge, another great critic, who was able to learn so much about Shakespeare from his own early attempts (from which he learned, above all, how not to proceed), Johnson was to develop what amounted to nothing less than an obsession against the kind of play that he was writing now and that he continued a year later to try to finish and revise.

The self-consciousness he brought to bear on this play—written as it was for two purposes only, to make some money and to establish his credentials—was enormous. This most rapid of writers, who could later write the equivalent of forty printed pages a day and who could turn out verse impromptu, intimidated himself to a snail's pace. It was indeed in every way against the grain. One sign of this is the versification itself. For there at least Johnson would ordinarily not have had the slightest trouble. But the blank verse reads like heroic couplets from which the rhyme has been removed, and couplets in which the poet has so much anxiety to keep a strict regularity of meter that other considerations—even of style and rhythm alone—become sacrificed. The result is a versification woodenly self-conscious (for a play, especially) in a way Johnson himself in later years would have been the last to tolerate. This is of major psychological interest for us. For Johnson is the first great modern critic to realize what the hurdles of self-consciousness can mean to a writer; and he was here learning it at firsthand.

Naturally, considering the effort he put into it during these months, when he had written about half, he was reluctant to discard it, and with grim resolution took it up again a year later. But he was never on the defensive about it. Asked years later, when it was finally produced, "how he felt upon the ill success of his tragedy, he replied, 'Like the Monument;' meaning that he continued firm and unmoved as that column." When told that a man named Pot considered *Irene* "the finest tragedy of modern times," he replied, "If Pot says so, Pot lies." Yet there is some pathos in the story that when someone was reading it aloud to friends in a country house, Johnson left the room. Asked why, he answered, "I thought it had been better." Meanwhile we should remember the circumstances in which it was begun and half-finished, with the school failing, and with a large part of Tetty's money being drained away. If there is any truth to be wrung from those imitations by Garrick of Johnson in the bedchamber trying to work at *Irene* while Tetty was urging him to come to bed, it is the extent to which Johnson was making an effort to do something that would compensate for what he done to Tetty, and to keep after it, whatever his own internal opposition.

8

As he worked away at *Irene*, he would read parts of it to Gilbert Walmesley, who thought well of it and encouraged him. There is a story that Walmesley told Johnson he was making Irene suffer so much in the first part of the play that there would be nothing left for her to suffer in the latter part. Johnson, in reply (alluding to the delays and abuses of the ecclesiastical court, for which Walmesley was Registrar at Lichfield), said there was "enough in reserve"; for in the final act "I intend to put my heroine into the ecclesiastical court of Lichfield, which will fill up the utmost measure of human calamity."[22]

Aside from his own disadvantages as a playwright, there is the formidable one that he had not even seen many plays (as distinct from reading them), or at least plays well performed. But however anxiously self-conscious he may have been in other ways in writing *Irene*—and the slowness of the work proved that he was—his self-confidence did not seem shaken by any thought that he was ignorant of the practical side of the theater. To judge from later remarks, he probably assumed that this was something of which any intelligent person, using a little imagination, could quickly get the point. And he could feel that he himself had got the point since he had occasionally seen strolling players when they came to Lichfield. In fact, he refers to a performance about this time in a remark to Boswell, when they were in Lichfield in 1776: "Forty years ago," he said, he "was in love with an actress here, Mrs. Emmet, who acted Flora in *Hob in the Well*," a play by Colley Cibber. (Forty years ago, if taken literally, would mean 1736, after he had married Tetty; but he probably meant forty odd, and in any case the remark was made as a sort of jest.) Since no one has yet discovered who Mrs. Emmet was, however carefully stage records have been searched, it suggests a rather humble group of traveling players. Another record of his attending a play at Lichfield is a story Garrick was fond of telling. Johnson, probably because he could not hear well, had a chair on the stage between the side scenes. When he left it briefly for a few minutes, "a Scots officer, who had no goodwill towards him, persuaded an innkeeper of the town to take it." Johnson, on returning, civilly asked the man to let him have his seat. The man refused; argument got nowhere; and finally Johnson picked up the chair, with the man in it, and tossed both chair and man into the pit. Hawkins says he flung them, with "herculean force," entirely across the stage to the opposite side. The Scots officer cried out, "Damn him, he has broke his limbs." But this proved not to be so, and Walmesley interposed to bring quiet. Meanwhile Johnson retrieved the chair, and then "with great composure sat out the play."[23]

9

Meanwhile, to add to the problems of life generally, there was a personal one having to do with Nathaniel about which Johnson, in later life, was to remain completely quiet. We have only two items of evidence to suggest what it was. Earlier in 1736 Nathaniel—by now twenty-three—had opened a small book business in Stourbridge. A short business statement survives that shows this was still going on in June.[24] The second piece of evidence is a letter to his mother, apparently sent from London in late September. From this we can infer that at Stourbridge he got into some sort of trouble (falsifying the accounts, or running up debts and absconding with the money). In this letter to his mother, he says he is forwarding to her the account book for another branch shop, this time at the nearby town of Burton-upon-Trent, which he ran for his mother either before or, less likely, just after he got into trouble at Stourbridge, "and with it all the bills that I can recollect to be due either in Burton side or anywhere else." The crucial part of the letter then follows:

I have neither Money nor Credit to buy one Quire of paper. It is time I did make a Positive Bargain for a Shop at Stourbridge in which I believe I might have lived happily & had I gone when I first desired it none of these Crimes had been committed which have given both you & me so much trouble. I dont know that you ever denied me part of the Working Tools but you never told me you would give or lend them me. As to My Brothers assisting me I had but little Reason to expect it when He would scarce ever use me with common civility & to whose Advice was owing that unwillingness you shewd to my going to Stourbridge. If I should ever be able I would make my Stourbridge friends amends for the trouble and charge I have put them to.[25]

From this we can infer the following. Nathaniel, on a visit to the Ford and Hickman relatives in Stourbridge, got their backing for a branch shop there. Sarah, at her older son's urging, tried to prevent this. Given the way Johnson idealized his own boyhood months at Stourbridge, and the extent to which that time and the people there were built into his own self-expectation and self-demand, he could naturally cringe at the thought of the impression Nathaniel would give if he stayed there. A sensitive man, the twenty-three-year-old Nathaniel covered up his vulnerability with a noisy conviviality, drank freely, and would have no scruples in exploiting the relatives there. Then the worst happened. It is even conceivable (so complete is the silence that hereafter descends about him) that Nathaniel could have slipped into some petty forgery. In that case, there would be an added poignance to Johnson's sympathetic efforts, forty years later, on behalf of William Dodd, when Dodd was sentenced to be executed for forgery. This, rather than mere thievery or falsification of accounts, could explain the despair of Nathaniel, who adds, "I know not nor do I much care in what way of life I shall hereafter live, but this I know that it shall be an honest one." He is thinking, he says, of leaving in two weeks for Georgia—the new colony founded four years before (1732) by General Oglethorpe to help the debt-ridden and the poor.

But Nathaniel did not go to Georgia. He drifted south to Somerset, where no one would know him, and, obviously with some help from his mother, started work as a bookbinder and stationer in the town of Frome. There, a few months later, in early March, he died. Forty-three years afterward, when Johnson was seventy, he wrote to an acquaintance, Mary Prowse, asking whether she could find out anything about him. He does not say the man he is asking about was his brother but simply that "he was my near relation." Aleyn Reade, who discovered the date of Nathaniel's death, suggested the possibility of suicide. There are two arguments against it: Nathaniel was buried in consecrated ground (March 5, 1737); and when Johnson wrote in his old age the epitaphs for his father, mother, and brother, he refers to Nathaniel's "pious death." Neither argument is conclusive. On the other hand, we have Johnson's complete silence about Nathaniel; the unwillingness of others who certainly knew about him to give information in later years; and the fact that Johnson waited so long before he could bring himself to ask about Nathaniel's last months, and, even so, did it only indirectly ("my near relation"). Of course, this could be explained by forgery alone, which was a capital crime. In any case, Johnson was always to feel a strong sense of remorse at whatever he himself had done, or had failed to do, that could have contributed to Nathaniel's unhappiness. In one of his journals, he records a prayer for his mother, who had just died (1759). After this occurs a single sentence—the only reference to Nathaniel in all the surviving journals: "The dream of my Brother I shall always remember."[26]

10

By November (1736), when one of the three original pupils, Lawrence Offley, left to enter Cambridge, no students were left but David and George Garrick and possibly one or two others. Seeing that the end of the school was inevitable, Johnson applied for a job as assistant to William Budworth, the headmaster of the grammar school at Brewood, fifteen miles from Lichfield. Budworth later said he thought highly of Johnson's learning and ability, but felt he had to turn him down because he was afraid that the convulsive motions to which Johnson was subject would "become the object of imitation or of ridicule, among his pupils."[27]

Finally, by the end of January if not before, the school at Edial was closed. Gilbert Walmesley (February 5) wrote to a friend he had known at Oxford—John Colson, now Upper Master of the Free School in Rochester—asking him to take David Garrick as a private student (the school itself was open only to residents), and prepare him to enter the study of the law. Meanwhile the thirteen-year-old George was transferred to the nearby Appleby Grammar School (February 16).[28]

Prodded by the responsibility he felt for Tetty, much of whose money he had lost with his scheme, Johnson resolved to act immediately. A job at another school had proved impossible. *Irene* would take time to finish. If he were actually in London, he might get some work as a writer for journals in a way he could not by mere correspondence. In particular he was thinking of work he could do as a translator.[29] While in London he could finish *Irene* on the side. It would also help to be on the spot when the time came to see whether a theatrical manager would accept it for performance. It would be out of the question for Tetty to go with him at this time. Whatever money she had left was to be used for her own current expenses, not his. Together in London, living in a way she was used to, they would quickly exhaust the money. Alone, he could, if necessary, live from hand to mouth. He would come to get her as soon as he was sure of regular employment.

Since Garrick would be going to Rochester by way of London, Johnson would go along with him. They could give each other company. Courageous as Johnson was, there was naturally some apprehension. The farthest he had ever been from Lichfield was Oxford, and that was eight years ago. Moreover, he was setting off for the unknown world of London in complete ignorance of it, with almost no money (he would use up no more of Tetty's), and with nothing else except the half-finished *Irene*. It would be less lonely to make that long trip toward an uncertain future if a friend were with him at the start.

Chapter 11

The Move to London; First Writings
There; Temporary Separation
from His Wife

When Johnson and Garrick set out for London (March 2, 1737)—a trip of 120 miles—they agreed to travel as economically as possible. Much of the way they "rode and tied," which meant they were able to hire only one horse and would take turns in riding it. One would go ahead on horseback, stop and tie the horse to a tree or post, and then proceed on foot. Meanwhile the other would catch up, untie the horse, and take his own turn in riding. By an unhappy coincidence, as they were soon to learn, not only did Nathaniel Johnson die in Somerset almost on the day they set out, but David's father, Captain Peter Garrick, died suddenly a week later.

When they arrived in London, Johnson had twopence halfpenny in his pocket, and David three halfpence in his.* Actually David had prospects aside from the help Walmesley could give him. An uncle had left him £1,000, which he was to receive in another year when he became twenty-one. But his father, who had just died, was a trustee for this provision of the uncle's will. There was naturally some delay in getting credit, and for a while he stayed in London before going to Rochester to be tutored by the Reverend Mr. Colson. In the meantime

---

* So, at least, Johnson said in later years at a dinner when Garrick was present (L, I, 101, n. 1); and though his intention was to tease Garrick, who did not care to be reminded publicly of such things, we can be confident it was literally true. Yet he could also have carried a letter of credit for a modest amount, however determined he was not to use more of Tetty's money. He could hardly have expected to survive otherwise. But he may have resisted cashing it for a while.

he knew—probably through Walmesley—of a friendly bookseller in the Strand, Thomas Wilcox, and suggested they both apply to him for a loan.

They called on Wilcox, told him of their journey from Lichfield, and their intention to make their way in London. Wilcox was "so moved with their artless tale" that he "advanced them all that their modesty would permit them to ask (five pounds), which was, soon after, punctually repaid." As they left, Wilcox asked Johnson, "How do you mean to earn your livelihood in this town?" "By my literary labours," replied Johnson. Knowing the difficulties, Wilcox shook his head, and, staring at Johnson's powerful frame, said, "Young man, you had better buy a porter's knot"[1]—a pad for carrying burdens on the back with a loop like a horse's collar that came up around the forehead.

2

Meanwhile they had taken a room—though Garrick eventually went on to Rochester—at the house of Richard Norris, a corset- or stay-maker, in Exeter Street, adjoining Catharine Street, in the Strand. They had known of Norris because he was a distant connection, by marriage, of the Garricks. Nothing is known of the household except for a curious memorandum that has survived in which Johnson, a few years later, jotted down for himself memories he was recapturing of the place: "Norris the staymaker—fair Esther [the wife]—w. the cat—children—inspection of the hand—stays returned—lodging—guinea at the stairs—Esther died—ordered to want nothing—house broken up—advertisment—eldest son—quarrel."[2]

Johnson quickly discovered a cheap place to eat—a nearby tavern called The Pine Apple, in New Street, where he dined "very well for eight pence, with very good company." Many of the customers there had traveled, and he enjoyed their talk. "It used to cost the rest a shilling, for they drank wine; but I had a cut of meat for six-pence, and bread for a penny, and gave the waiter a penny; so that I was quite well served, nay, better than the rest, for they gave the waiter nothing." He was trying to put into practice the advice of an Irish painter, Michael Ford, whom he had known in Birmingham and who had lived for several years in London. In later years Johnson, whose own experience left him permanently interested in how little one needed in order to survive, liked to repeat the advice of this man—who had "a great deal of knowledge of the world, fresh from life, not strained through books"—on the way in which one could live on £30 a year "without being contemptible." The largest item was £10 for "clothes and linen." Otherwise,

a man might live in a garret at eighteen-pence a week; few people would inquire where he lodged; and if they did, it was easy to say, "Sir, I am to be found at such a place." By spending three-pence in a coffee-house he might be for some hours every day in very good company; he might dine for six-pence, breakfast on bread and milk for a penny, and do without supper. On *clean-shirt day* he went abroad, and paid visits.[3]

Occasionally he had meals, in radically different company, at the town house of the reckless Henry Hervey, fourth son of the Earl of Bristol. He had met Hervey, through Gilbert Walmesley, back in Lichfield when, as an officer in the Dragoons, Hervey had been quartered there and married an heiress, Catherine Aston, sister of the Magdalen Aston whom Walmesley later married. Hard-drinking, disso-lute, self-indulgent, and described by his father as fit to live nowhere but a jail, Hervey thought Johnson unusual, liked him, and completely disregarded his manners, appearance, and dress. Johnson, for his part, was appreciative, and later helped Hervey with his poems—Hervey fancied himself a poet—and, when he reformed and entered the Church, and was honored by being asked to give a sermon at St. Paul's (1745), wrote the sermon for him. His gratitude to Hervey, like his gratitude generally, was permanent. Speaking of him to Boswell not long before his death, he admitted that Hervey in many ways "was a vicious man"—meaning inclined to "vice" generally rather than cruel—"but very kind to me. If you call a dog Hervey, I shall love him."[4]

3

The misgivings of the kindly bookseller Thomas Wilcox, as he stared at Johnson's huge frame and suggested he work as a porter, were justified. He knew only too well of the hundreds of people who had drifted to London, hoping to make a career of writing, and who were living in unheated garrets on incomes—when they were able to get employment as writers at all—of as little as £5 or £10 a year. At no time in modern history has it been more difficult for an English writer to get started, if he lacked money of his own or influential friends, than during the second quarter of the eighteenth century. He was caught between two worlds. Traditional patronage from individuals or the government, which had supported literature before, was waning rapidly. It had not yet been replaced by the immense expansion of the reading public, throughout the growing middle class, which was to appear in the later 1700's and to transform the entire sociological character of literature in the nineteenth century.

But if there were trials ahead—which Johnson quickly began to sense and, in a few months, understand and take for granted—there were also compensations, at least for him, in the setting: in the variety and concentration of life in London itself, which, whatever the disadvantages, tended now and in the years ahead to help pull him away from self-absorption and self-condemnation. To begin with, there was the sheer size of London. With 650,000 to 700,000 people, it was proportionately far larger at this time than other cities and towns of England, and the contrast this made to a young provincial like Johnson was therefore all the stronger. Birmingham, Manchester, or Sheffield, with 20,000 to at most 30,000 inhabitants, were between a twentieth and a thirtieth of the size. A flourishing town like Lichfield could consider itself a city with a population between 3,000 and 4,000, and even Oxford had only about twice as many inhabitants. For generations the capital had been compared to a head out of all proportion to the size of the body. It was overwhelmingly the center not only of trade and government, but of the arts, the sciences, and fashion. "The happiness of London," said Johnson thirty years later, "is not to be conceived but by those who have been in it. I will venture to say, there is more learning and science within the circumference of ten miles from where we now sit, than in all the rest of the kingdom."

But Johnson could think of London as providing the "full tide of human existence" for another reason as well: the astonishing contrasts of human life that excelled those of any other capital of Europe, and excelled even what London has offered in its long history except during the period from about 1700 to 1830. Before the eighteenth century London was smaller, more manageable, more in tune with the country generally; the slums were less extensive, the Church more active. By the Victorian period the police had become effectively established; the slums, in proportion to the size of the city as a whole, were less extensive and less frightful. Dickens's London is not so much the London of the mid-nineteenth century as that of his boyhood, near the end of the period (1700–1830) we are noting. And even in this period, of 1700 to 1830, the shock effect on London, in its change from the Elizabethan and seventeenth-century city to the far larger modern metropolis, was greatest in the first half of the eighteenth century. In 1783, the year before his death, Johnson talked to Boswell and William Windham "a good deal of the wonderful extent and variety of London," and added that "men of curious inquiry might see in it such modes of life as very few could ever imagine. He in particular recommended to us to *explore Wapping*, which we resolved to do." When they did so a few years later (1792), they were disappointed, probably because of "that uniformity which has in modern times . . . spread through every part of the metropolis." It was at the time Johnson came to London—before the wave of building and improvement in the later 1700's—that we have, in effect, Hogarth's London: the London of unpaved streets, with their mud, garbage, and open sewers; the thousands of thieves, beggars, and prostitutes; the slums with eight or ten people crowded into one unheated, unfurnished room in ramshackle tenements, fighting for crusts or a soupbone; the homeless children sleeping on the ashpits in the hope of keeping warm; the parishes in the East End where infant mortality amounted to 100 per cent; the gin shops, in every fourth dwelling in the slums, with their signs "Drunk for a penny, dead-drunk for twopence"; the violence—especially at night—on the muddy streets, so that few people dared be from home after nightfall (something that never troubled Johnson: his huge frame and the ragged clothes he wore till his fifties were usually enough to give others a second thought about the value of attacking him; and in later years he often carried a club).

But he was not put off by the disadvantages and problems of London. He welcomed the diversity and contrast of this new world, and never stopped doing so. "When a man is tired of London, he is tired of life."

4

He may have done a few pieces of writing for a bookseller during this short period of exploring London and his prospects there.[5] But his first task, he now felt, was to get his unfinished tragedy, *Irene*, out of the way. He could not throw himself into other writing in the way he needed to do if he had *Irene* still hanging over him. And however slowly it came, he naturally did not want to discard it after so much effort had already been invested in it. Moreover, if it could be produced on the stage and did catch on, his prospects for a career in writing would be immensely improved.

Resolved to finish it if possible before going back to Lichfield to fetch Tetty, he tore himself away from the distractions of London and went out to Greenwich, where he got a room in a house next door to the Golden Hart Tavern, in Church Street. There he tried to compose the rest of the play while walking up and down Greenwich Park. But it still came with painful slowness. Finally, in reaction to it all, he suddenly wrote Edward Cave (July 12), the editor of the *Gentleman's Magazine*, proposing a project as radically different from *Irene* as one could imagine—a new English translation of an important work on the Counter Reformation, *The History of the Council of Trent* (1619), by the Venetian priest, scholar, and reformer Paolo Sarpi. It was an imaginative and timely idea.* But Cave apparently took some time to agree to it. For Johnson did not begin on it till the following summer; and, in making the proposal, Johnson's thought may have been less to switch immediately to it from *Irene* than to have an incentive to finish the play more rapidly so that he could turn to something more congenial or at least less obdurate.

In the meantime Johnson doubtless felt that he could finish the play as easily at Lichfield as Greenwich, and certainly at less expense. So he returned home, resolved to complete it before he and Tetty left for London, and hoping it could be done quickly. But it took almost three months. Only one anecdote survives from this period at home when he was absorbed with *Irene*. His mother, when she had been in London, had thought "there were two sets of people"—those who insisted on "taking the wall" (walking next to the wall in order to avoid the slime in the gutters that ran down the middle of the street and also the garbage thrown out from windows above) and those who peaceably surrendered the wall. She "asked me, whether I was one of those who gave the wall, or those who took it. *Now* it is fixed that every man keeps to the right. . . ."[6]

5

In October, with the play finished and after disposing of their effects at Edial Hall, he and Tetty moved to London, took lodgings for a while in Woodstock Street, near Hanover Square, and then moved to 6

* See below, p. 176.

Castle Street, near Cavendish Square. Lucy Porter decided to stay in Lichfield and help the aging and lonely Sarah manage the bookshop. Considering how long and disagreeable the struggle with the play had been, his first interest was naturally to gain what he could from it, and try to get it produced. He found Peter Garrick, who was in London (David had by now gone on to Rochester). They went together to the Fountain Tavern in the Strand to read over the play and discuss it. Johnson did not know at the time that the tavern, though used as a meeting place for writers and lawyers, was also a "notorious bawdy-house."[7] Peter knew Charles Fleetwood, the patentee of the Drury Lane Theatre, and arranged to have it submitted to him. But Fleetwood was not interested in drama of this sort unless it was financially backed by patrons. He did not even trouble to read the manuscript. The play was not produced until several years later (1749), by which time David Garrick was managing Drury Lane. Meanwhile, having opened negotiations with Edward Cave back in July, he began to do writing and other odd jobs during the winter for the *Gentleman's Magazine.*

The *Gentleman's Magazine*, founded six years before (1731), was the first magazine in anything like the modern sense. The magazine—which was to serve as the prototype of all later magazines, and was already being imitated—was the invention of a remarkable man, Edward Cave, who had come from Rugby, where his father was a cobbler. He had shown promise at the grammar school there, but had been forced to leave when the schoolmaster, whose hen roost had been robbed, concluded that the quiet young Cave was the culprit. Working his way up as a printer, a reporter, and an editor, he developed the conception of the magazine, and tried to interest a publisher in it. When no one seemed interested, he started the magazine himself with what little he had been able to save, editing it (under the pseudonym of "Sylvanus Urban") from an office in St. John's Gate, Clerkenwell—an ancient, picturesque building, which had once been the gate of a medieval monastery.

The magazine proved immensely successful. The concept was indeed a brilliant one. (When Johnson first saw St. John's Gate, he said he "beheld it with reverence.") Among the features of the magazine were its reports of debates in the Houses of Parliament—a feature that Johnson was later to handle for Cave. A man of forty-six, the shrewd, thoughtful Cave was deceptively slow and even sluggish in manner. He now rarely left his office. On one of the occasions when he did, we get a picture of Johnson at the time. Offering to introduce him to some of the "luminaries" who wrote for the magazine, Cave took him over to an alehouse near Clerkenwell. Here Johnson, "dressed in a loose horseman's coat" and wearing "a great bushy uncombed wig," was shown a genuine poet, the now forgotten Moses Browne, "sitting at the upper end of a long table, in a cloud of tobacco-smoke." Cave was constantly devising new features or schemes, and, said Johnson, "never looked out of his window, but with a view to the *Gentleman's Magazine*." "Upon the first approach of a stranger," said Hawkins, "his practice was to continue sitting, a posture in which he was ever to be found, and, for a few minutes, to continue silent: if at any time he was inclined to begin the discourse, it was generally by putting a leaf of the Magazine, then in the press, into the hand of his visitor, and asking his opinion of it." Though he appeared to have no interest but the magazine, a similar constancy, though to a lower degree, appeared in his loyalty to people. Johnson was always grateful to Cave, and after his death (1754) wrote a fine biographical sketch of him.[8]

6

While doing small jobs for Cave, Johnson—now that hopes for *Irene* had collapsed—again tried to storm the main gates of literature with a work of his own that would sell. He may have been a little out of date with *Irene*. But he would not be so now. One of the new genres of the previous half century, especially developed by Pope, was the "imitation"—a form that, after two centuries of disuse, has been again revived in our own generation by poets, particularly Robert Lowell. Johnson himself described it, in his *Life of Pope*, as follows:

This mode of imitation, in which the ancients are familiarised by adapting their sentiments to modern topicks, by making Horace say of Shakespeare what he originally said of Ennius . . . is a kind of middle composition between translation and original design, which pleases when the thoughts are unexpectedly applicable and the parallels lucky. It seems to have been Pope's favourite amusement, for he carried it further than any former poet.[9]

At the time Johnson arrived in London, Pope's "imitation" of Horace's satires were being widely read. Aside from Pope's skill as a poet, they had an immediate topical appeal in attacking current social and politi-

171

cal corruptions. Since both the form and the general subject had proved popular, Johnson, who had always liked Juvenal, saw a chance to do for Juvenal what Pope had done for Horace.

The result is Johnson's poem *London*. Taking the Third Satire as a model, he replaces Juvenal's "Spokesman" or persona with a new one ("Thales"), who is appalled by the corruptions and horrors of London and is about to sail off to rural Wales and get away from it all. The significance of the Spokesman's name is often missed because the original of Thales is assumed to be the famous Greek philosopher and geometrician, who is as far from the "injur'd Thales" of the poem as one could imagine. Johnson is plainly referring to the lyric poet Thales (c. 650 B.C.) mentioned in Plutarch's "Life of Lycurgus," whom Lycurgus invited to Sparta to civilize the people and teach them honesty and civic duty. By contrast, this modern Thales ("injur'd Thales")—far from being welcomed by Robert Walpole, and the government—has been treated with a disregard that shows their complete indifference to even the pretense of virtue. (Much of the discussion of the poem has been paralyzed by the question whether or not Johnson is also referring, by "Thales," to his friend Richard Savage.)[10] The bulk of the poem consists of the speech of Thales to a friend as he prepares to enter the boat at Greenwich. In the process of leaving, Thales attacks everything from the prevalence of thieves, arsonists, lawyers, and mimicry of French manners ("Behold the warrior dwindled to a beau") to the stage Licensing Act, "female atheists," and the Committee on Ways and Means ("a cant term in the House of Commons for methods of raising money"). It is all put with a gusto, and at times even a jauntiness, that ill conceal Johnson's own relish of London:

> Here malice, rapine, accident conspire,
> And now a rabble rages, now a fire;
> Their ambush here relentless ruffians lay,
> And here the fell attorney prowls for prey;
> Here falling houses thunder on your head,
> And here a female atheist talks you dead.

The truth is that the poem (in its conception, not its skill of execution) is quite far from all we associate with Johnson, especially in his later years. For example, it is almost pastoral in its appeal to the country as against the city; and no writer has more effectively poured scorn on the whole concept of the "pastoral" than has Johnson. Again, *Lon-*

don is a very conventional poem, indeed deliberately so; and though Johnson, like most truly original people, was not afraid of convention but liked and championed it if it really helped to steady or ease life, he himself was always rising above it (though through and by means of it, as *The Vanity of Human Wishes*, for example, "uses" convention, though in an altogether original way).

Paradoxically the disappointment often expressed about *London* (in the last century and a half, not in his lifetime) comes from people who are fondest of Johnson. Writers as diverse as T. S. Eliot and J. W. Krutch are examples. The reason is that they tend, in imagination, to bracket together *London* and *The Vanity of Human Wishes*, written ten years later. This is understandable. Both poems are "imitations," and not only that, but "imitations" of Juvenal's Satires (the Third and the Tenth). They are the only two long poems aside from *Irene* that Johnson wrote. Inevitably they become seen as "sister" poems, though they really are not. Aware that in the *Vanity* much of Johnson's thought—as well as mastery of poetic expression—is contained in solution, they inevitably feel a disappointment when they turn to *London*. It seems breezy, as if written off the top of the head; it often expresses sentiments that are the reverse of the Johnson we know, especially the later Johnson; and it lacks the sublime moral elevation of the *Vanity*, though there are, of course, exceptions, as in the fine couplets where Johnson prints the last line in capitals:

> Has heaven reserv'd, in pity to the poor,
> No pathless waste, or undiscover'd shore . . .
> This mournful truth is ev'ry where confess'd,
> SLOW RISES WORTH, BY POVERTY DEPRESS'D.

Finally, though there are exceptions, it has little of the unique condensation of phrase of the later poems, or for that matter of the major prose.*

But of course *London* was never really conceived as a "satire"—as a strongly impassioned sense of outrage (or indeed of an impassioned sense of anything else). Instead it was an exercise of talent, understandably designed to make an immediate appeal—to compensate for the failure of *Irene*, and make money for himself and even more for Tetty,

---

* A notable exception is "Slow rises worth, by poverty depress'd," which—though Latin is naturally more concise than English—compressed into six words what Juvenal compressed in nine ("*Haud facile emergunt, quorum virtutibus obstat / Res angusta domi*"). Dryden needed fifteen: "Rarely they rise by Virtue's aid, who lie / Plung'd in the depth of helpless Poverty."

who had placed such trust in him, or at least to get a toe hold on to a shore or bank of reputation. He could (but only if it were done for others, as when he would write prefaces for their works or do other favors) ingratiate himself. And he did so now. He had to make good the loss from the school at Edial Hall, which *Irene* had not helped to recoup. And he succeeded. The poem met with an immediate welcome. It was easy to read. It was packed with appeals to stock responses (the surly but honest English, for example, versus the affected and insincere French). It used common themes, including the desire to get away from the corrupt city to the idyllic country that he so often ridiculed. It was masterly in its versification, and, above all, in its transitions of mood. For Johnson anticipates Goldsmith's *Traveller* and other didactic or quasi-satiric poems in that ability to make transitions which especially inspired admiration in eighteenth-century readers, and which modern poets, especially T. S. Eliot, have singled out for praise. As such, *London* contrasts with *The Vanity of Human Wishes*, in which transition is almost disregarded, and one powerful image or passage is piled on another, with cumulative effect.

It was frankly a bid for success; and, as always when he felt constrained to be insincere, or rather indirect, as a young man (later he found it simpler not to be insincere in most ways except when he was playful), he was awkward in trying to present it to Cave for publication. With needless indirection, he pretended he was submitting it for publication from a friend who was in need, and offered to change anything in it Cave did not like. Soon the mask was dropped. Cave, shrewd and practical, thought the poem would have a better chance if the title page showed the imprint of Robert Dodsley, a publisher widely recognized for his sponsorship of poetry. Dodsley agreed, then decided to assume full responsibility, and paid Johnson ten guineas. Johnson later said he would have accepted less except that Paul Whitehead, a minor poet, recently had been given ten guineas for a poem, "and I would not take less than Paul Whitehead." The poem had luck. It was welcomed as a new political attack on Walpole's administration. Moreover, by coincidence, it was published at the same time Pope brought out his new "imitation" of Horace—the poem *One Thousand Seven Hundred and Thirty Eight* (Boswell says they were published the same day, but actually Pope's satire appeared three days later). This encouraged people to play off the two poems against each other. It gave those who are always jealous of an established reputation a chance to say that a new poet had arisen "greater even than Pope." In any case, *London* could only gain by courting comparison. Pope, to his credit, generously praised the new poem. The writer of it showed such talent he "will soon be déterré." It sold so well that a second edition was called for in a week, a third one later in the year, and a fourth the following year.

7

In April 1738 the House of Commons decided that it was a "breach of privilege" to publish reports of the debates in Parliament. First the *London Magazine* (May)—now a rival publication—and then the *Gentleman's Magazine* (June) adopted the device of pretending their reports were fictitious. The *London Magazine* pretended it was publishing reports of discussions in a political club. The procedure of the *Gentleman's Magazine* was probably suggested by Johnson: to use the first book of *Gulliver's Travels*, the voyage to Lilliput, as a setting. The grandson of Lemuel Gulliver, paying a visit to Lilliput, has found that its government has now been modeled on that of Britain. He has returned with histories, memoirs, and speeches that will illustrate what politics are like now in Lilliput. From these the magazine will start to print reports of "Debates in the Senate of Magna Lilliputia." The speakers' names are easily identifiable ("Walelop" for Walpole, "Ptit" for Pitt, and so on). The reports were written by William Guthrie, a young Scot who worked for Cave. Johnson himself probably wrote the general introduction to these debates, using the opportunity to express his own strong feelings against rampant commercialism and colonial exploitation. In addition, he would revise and edit Guthrie's reports.

By the end of the summer, he was also helping Cave in other ways: judging verses sent in for poetry prizes; helping to select extracts from books for the magazine to reprint; contributing Latin verses to give the magazine a little added tone; doing the preface to the collected volume for 1738; and writing, in four installments (January–April 1739), the life of the famous Dutch physician Herman Boerhaave, who had just died. He also helped in editing and polishing another publishing project of Cave's, a translation from the French, by William Guthrie, of J. B. du Halde's long *Description of China*, a work that had been compiled from accounts by Jesuit missionaries and had been published recently in Paris (1735). More important, Cave had taken him up on

175

that project Johnson had written him about the year before, when he was wrestling with *Irene*—the translation, in two volumes, of Sarpi's *History of the Council of Trent* (1619). Given the religious interests of the public, Cave saw its appeal. For, to begin with, it was a classic, and had been much read throughout the seventeenth century. Because it was written within the fold of the Church, its protests against papal authority and other aspects of the Counter Reformation were still potentially alive for Protestants. Though the book was old, its reputation had revived because of a new French translation (1736), with a new biography of Sarpi and annotation by P. F. le Courayer.

To Johnson, at least, there was a personal interest as well. This is Johnson's fascination—which we have already seen in his project for bringing out the Latin poems of Politian—with the great Renaissance Humanists and scholars who had taken all knowledge for their province. In a way, they were to serve as a lifelong model to him, and he especially identified with them if they had begun life with disadvantages. Sarpi, who had been left an orphan, had become a man genuinely encyclopedic in his interests, versed not only in languages, history, and theology, but the sciences (one of his discoveries was the way in which the iris of the eye contracts and expands).

For some months, off and on, Johnson worked at the translation (August 1738 through the following April) and Cave paid him during that time £49 7s., which was a generous amount. Several thousand "Proposals" were printed for subscribers, and advertisements of the "Proposals" were made in October 1738. Meanwhile, to increase interest, Johnson wrote a short biography of Sarpi for the *Gentleman's Magazine* (November). Ironically another man named Johnson—the Reverend John Johnson, keeper of the library at St. Martin's-in-the-Fields—was at that very time at work on a translation of the same book. Seeing the advertisement, he wrote indignantly to the same newspaper (the *Daily Advertiser*), implying that this was an attempt to capitalize on his forthcoming work, even to the extent of using his own surname to confuse the public. Cave and our Johnson stood firm for a while, while John Johnson became more frantic. But finally they dropped the project (April 1739), and the Reverend Mr. Johnson returned to his slow work, which he still had not finished by the time of his death eight years later.[11]

Another work of translation for Cave was under way in which Johnson became involved. A Swiss professor of philosophy, J. P. de Crousaz, had written two celebrated attacks—an *Examination* and a

Commentary—on the theology (or lack of it) in Pope's now contro-versial *Essay on Man*. Cave rightly thought a translation of these would have a good sale. He asked Johnson to do the *Commentary*, and assigned the *Examination* to that remarkable young woman (she was still only twenty-one) Elizabeth Carter, who was now working for him. The daughter of a widowed clergyman in Kent, she had been educated by her father, and was fluent not only in Latin and Greek (her translation of Epictetus is still standard) but Hebrew and Arabic, as well as several modern languages (French, Italian, German, Spanish, and even Portuguese). Johnson was always to be devoted to her, and enjoyed praising the variety of her accomplishments. (Speaking of another learned lady, many years later, he said, "A man is in general better pleased when he has a good dinner upon his table, than when his wife talks Greek. My old friend, Mrs. Carter, could make a pudding, as well as translate Epictetus.") As she was finishing the *Examination* in November (1738), a rival publisher, Edmund Curll, announced publi-cation of the *Commentary* by a translator of his own, Charles Forman. Johnson thought they might as well give up the *Commentary* them-selves, and push Miss Carter's *Examination*. Cave was unwilling to back down, though Johnson turned to other things, including the Sarpi translation. At length Cave was justified. Curll and his translator got out only the first part of the *Commentary*. Later Johnson turned to it, and, to make up for lost time, wrote with incredible speed, on one day doing forty-eight quarto pages. The notes, which are succinct and penetrating, are valued as Johnson's first writing in literary criticism.[12]

8

During this year and a half of diverse, often desperate hack work (December 1737 to May 1739), something happened between him and Tetty. They had plainly begun to live apart. It had naturally been a shock for her, now in her later forties and with her fortune more than half gone, to leave a place where she had always had some social standing, and to be huddled into more crowded lodgings in this vast London, where no one knew her, and with the husband for whom she had sacrificed so much proving, however gallant his efforts, so little able to advance himself in a way she had earlier taken for granted. Perhaps in these months she had already begun to acquire the habit of solitary drinking that was to remain with her in the years following.

Certainly Johnson felt an acute sense of guilt, and arrangements seem to have been made, before their first year was over, for an informal separation of sorts, as Sir John Hawkins implied. It is ridiculous to think that Johnson, once the novelty of the marriage had passed, was "tired" of Tetty. Their marriage had not been the kind of love match where "novelty" was all-important. For Johnson, it had been based on emotions, especially gratitude, that always tended in him to be permanent. Nor is it likely that Tetty really turned against Johnson in disappointment. Her own affections were more stable. The same firm opinion that she expressed to her daughter when she first knew Johnson ("This is the most sensible man I ever saw") was still unshaken when he began the *Rambler,* twelve years later: "I thought very well of you before," she said, "but I did not imagine you could have written any thing equal to this."

It was doubtless his own sense of guilt, his refusal to live any longer on her money—so much of which he could tell himself he had already lost—that led him to estrange himself, and, with something of self-punishment as well as pride, to live deliberately as a kind of adult waif. The rooms in Castle Street, however confined they might seem to someone from the country, were probably out of the range of Johnson's own limited and unreliable purse; and they may have moved so quickly from Woodstock Street to this much more expensive place, nearer the open fields, because she had been appalled at their first lodgings. Tetty, we know, lived on at 6 Castle Street until January 1740.[13] And everything we can piece together about Johnson's own way of living, at least by the winter of 1738–39, indicates not merely that he was living elsewhere, probably in or near Fleet Street, but also that he sometimes even roamed the streets without settled lodging. Now the fact is that he was earning enough to have a settled lodging, even if he was living apart from Tetty. For example, from August 1738 to the following April, Cave paid him £49 7s. (certainly enough to live on, by Johnson's own calculations) for just the translation of Sarpi's *Council of Trent;*[14] and this was apart from whatever else he earned for work on the magazine itself. We can only infer that he insisted on forwarding to her the bulk of his earnings, pretending that he was getting more from Cave than he actually did, and that he was reserving enough for his own use. That he went to an extreme in reserving so little for himself is suggested by a remark of Richard Cumberland's (though the remark could also have applied to the spring of 1737, when Johnson was alone in London on his first exploratory trip).

Cumberland had heard Johnson "assert (and he never varied from the truth of fact) that he subsisted himself for a considerable space of time upon the scanty pittance of fourpence halfpenny a day."[15]

It was during this time that he became so intimate a friend of Richard Savage's, with whom he would walk the streets all night when neither had enough money even to pay for sitting in a tavern or securing a corner for sleep in one of the crowded "night-cellars." Savage was used to this, living as he did a hand-to-mouth existence, though he would usually end the evening by lying down on the projecting edge of a building in summer or in winter, said Johnson, "with his associates in poverty, among the ashes of a glass-house." Johnson preferred walking. They both enjoyed conversation, and lost no opportunity to vent their outrage at the government. (It is with this background in mind that we should read two outspoken attacks by Johnson on the government in the spring of 1739.)* He told Sir Joshua Reynolds that one night in particular, when they walked around St. James's Square for lack of lodging, "they were not at all depressed by their situation; but in high spirits and brimful of patriotism, traversed the square for several hours, inveighed against the minister, and 'resolved they would *stand by their country.*' "[16]

Richard Savage, at this time a man of forty-two, was one of the more colorful figures of his generation. Back in 1697 the Countess of Macclesfield had an illegitimate son (by Earl Rivers). There had been a sensational trial for divorce because of this, and both she and her husband published accounts of their cases. Savage not only claimed but probably believed himself to be that illegitimate son, and for years had tried unsuccessfully to force the Countess of Macclesfield to acknowledge this and to help him.† He had written both poems and plays, the best known of which was his poem *The Bastard* (1728). Disappointed at not receiving the poet-laureateship, he called himself the "Volunteer Laureate." He had a wide acquaintance, and lived largely by loans, gifts, and getting friends to invite him for meals, repaying them with

* See below, pp. 201-2.
† The general assumption until our own generation was that Savage was a fraud. But after close study of all the evidence, his modern biographer, Clarence Tracy, convincingly argues that "whatever the truth may have been, Savage believed what he said." A probable explanation is that the real illegitimate child (christened "Richard Smith"), who was handed over to a Mrs. Ann Portlock to nurse and bring up, died. Then the nurse substituted a child of her own and brought him up to believe that he was the natural child of Earl Rivers and the Countess of Macclesfield (*The Artificial Bastard* [Toronto, 1953]), especially pp. 11-27).

brilliant talk. He was a chronic spendthrift. Johnson told Adam Smith that at one period when scarlet cloaks with gold lace became fashionable and Savage had just received some money, he met him "with one of these cloaks upon his back, while, at the same time, his naked toes were peeping through his shoes." Gracious, even charming, when his sensitive pride was not aroused, he was also inclined to self-pity and quick to store up grievances; and inevitably he managed to quarrel with all his benefactors. It was "always dangerous to trust him," said Johnson, "because he considered himself as discharged by the first quarrel from all ties of honour or gratitude."[17]

Johnson was fascinated by Savage's knowledge of both low and high life, his anecdotes about writers, and his bizarre history (Johnson completely accepted the story of his birth). Through Savage he came to know even more intimately than before about the London underworld and the large floating body—numbering in the scores of thousands—of the London poor. Much of the atmosphere of this world, and especially of Grub Street and of what we might call the literary underground, is preserved in Johnson's moving *Life of Savage* (1744), which was written after his friend's death and which remains one of the innovative works in the history of biography. Boswell wondered whether, through Savage, Johnson might not have been "led into some indulgencies" (meaning he consorted with prostitutes). This is possible, though unlikely. If Boswell had the slightest evidence—and he was very eager to find out everything he could about Johnson's sexual life—we can be confident it would have been preserved by him, as he did the famous and rather anticlimactic journal entry "Extraordinary Johnsoniana—*Tacenda*."* But his inference is apparently based on four things: (1) That Johnson's "amorous inclinations were uncommonly strong," which, as we have noted, is indeed true. (2) That he "used to take women of the town to taverns and hear them relate their history." He certainly did this, now and in later years, in order to find out more about their lives and to try to encourage them to reform (two of the *Rambler* essays, Nos. 170 and 171, tell the story of such a girl), and was indignant if friends could assume there was any other motive. (3) Boswell was swayed by Hawkins, who said of Johnson, "I have reason to think, that he reflected with as little approbation on the hours he spent with Savage as on any period of his life." Of course, Johnson felt some remorse about this time. With fairly good if confused intentions,

* See below, p. 263.

though also with some pride, he had left Tetty, without yet realizing that she would in a few months be unable to live on the earnings he sent her. (4) Lastly, Boswell, with all his merits, had his own subjective side. He did not understand real poverty, and the extent to which a man like Savage might be more interested in a free meal, free wine, and praise for his abilities than in prostitutes. Hence it was difficult for him—viewing it with the magic of distance—to imagine living this way without snatching the opportunity to do easily what would involve a risk of reputation to someone like Boswell himself.[18]

Finally, to keep Savage free of the debtors' prison, Pope and other friends of Savage's joined to guarantee him an annual pension if he went to Wales. Savage talked enthusiastically of rural delights and the sound of the nightingale. But when he said good-bye to Johnson in July, it was "with tears in his eyes." On his way to Wales, he lingered for quite a while in Bristol, repeating there and later in Wales the same sort of life he had lived in London. Returning at length to Bristol, he died there in a debtors' prison in 1743.

9

Even before Savage left, Johnson was becoming tired and discouraged about his own prospects. He had pushed himself for a year and a half (longer if the struggle with *Irene* is counted), doing everything that he could get assigned to him by Cave as well as some writing on his own. By September he would be thirty—an age by which many writers, whether or not they are yet well known, have written at least some of their principal works—and his own life, given normal expectations, would soon be half over. Yet he was still little more than a waif on the fringes of the literary world, and in Savage's career he could see both a warning and a likely prototype of his own.

Most serious of all was the guilt at what he had done to Tetty, who did not like London and thought the country air necessary for her health. Used as she was to a better style of living than his income from Cave could provide, even if he sent her the whole of it, she had been continuing to draw on what remained of her capital after the failure of the school at Edial. Within a few months she would have nothing left. He could not go back to her now empty-handed. Meanwhile, from May on he seems to have stopped writing for Cave; the proceeds were so small, his personal obligations and his sense of failure so large, that there was little incentive left.*

Suddenly he learned that the headmastership was vacant at Appleby Grammar School, in Leicestershire, a few miles from Lichfield—the school to which George Garrick had gone. This, if he could obtain it, would be an answer to some of the worst problems. The salary was £60 in addition to a residence. Tetty could live more as she was accustomed, and also in the country, as she preferred doing. The favored candidate—Thomas Mould, a man of twenty-five with an M.A. from Oxford—was backed by only five of the thirteen governors of the school. Friends of Johnson's in Staffordshire encouraged Johnson to feel there was a chance, and support was lined up. In some way even Pope—who knew Johnson only through his poem *London*—was induced to write on his behalf to Lord Gower, who, though not himself a governor of the school, was a man of influence in the area. Gower did what he could. Unfortunately the school statutes required the degree of M.A. "A common friend," said Dr. Adams, asked him to find out whether Oxford would grant Johnson an M.A. for this purpose. But the authorities thought this "too much to be asked." Then, though the school's requirement was that the degree be from Oxford or Cambridge, Gower wrote to a friend of Jonathan Swift's in Dublin telling him about Johnson and the job and asking him to "write to Dean Swift, to persuade the University of Dublin to send a diploma to me, constituting this poor man Master of Arts." (The thought was that an M.A. from Dublin would qualify Johnson for one at Oxford—a procedure commonly adopted at the time.) Those who know Johnson, Gower went on,

extol the man's learning and probity. . . . They say he is not afraid of the strictest examination, though he is of so long a journey; and will venture it, if the Dean thinks it necessary; choosing rather to die upon the road, *than to be starved to death in translating for booksellers,* which has been his only subsistence for some time past.

---

*But he did put out some effort for Cave on a matter that showed legal perception for someone without formal training in the law. Cave, in the June number of his magazine, started a series of abridgments from the popular sermons of Joseph Trapp. Threatened with prosecution, he turned to Johnson, who drew up a list of thirty-one "Considerations" for Cave or his lawyer, arguing that abridgment did not violate the rights of the proprietor (this was later upheld in the British courts). See E. L. McAdam, *Dr. Johnson and the English Law* (Syracuse, 1951), pp. 10–14. Cave, however, decided not to continue publishing the abridgments.

Nothing was to develop from Gower's efforts. Swift may never have seen the letter. Though Johnson had no way of knowing it, the odds from the beginning were in favor of Thomas Mould, who, in addition to being an M.A. from Oxford, was "Founder's near kinsman," which gave him precedence; and within a few months, despite the split decision, he was appointed.[19]

Yet so eager was Johnson to get the job, almost entirely for Tetty's sake, that sometime in late July or August, while there still seemed a chance, he responded to the suggestion of friends back home—including one of the school governors, Sir Thomas Gresley, who opposed Mould—to apply in person. We know nothing of the interview. Pope later implied that his convulsive mannerisms, which he had heard made Johnson a "sad spectacle," gave a poor impression. But the lack of a degree was more than enough to prevent him from even being considered. During this time he of course stayed with his mother in Lichfield. Tetty's daughter, Lucy Porter, was now helping Sarah in the bookshop, and out of sheer kindness—for, given her relations through both the Porter and Jervis families, she could move in whatever social circles at Lichfield she wished—considered it no "disgrace," said Miss Seward, "to thank a poor person who purchased from her" something worth only a penny. The bookshop was by now rarely patronized, but Lucy would make no engagement to visit others "on market days lest Granny," as she called Mrs. Johnson, "should catch cold by serving in the shop."[20]

10

While in Lichfield Johnson naturally visited Walmesley and continued to do so as he delayed returning to London. He had no desire to confess his own personal troubles (however frank and direct in all other respects, he was always to be reserved in this one way except to a very few people). Especially entrancing to him was the sister-in-law of the now married Walmesley—Molly Aston, the second of eight daughters of Sir Thomas Aston, one of whom (Magdalen) had married Walmesley, and another (Catherine) Johnson's dissolute friend Harry Hervey, son of the Earl of Bristol. Mary (or "Molly"), who was now thirty-three—Johnson himself was thirty—had fine, aquiline features, and was imaginatively quick, witty, and with rather scholarly interests. Other women sometimes considered her haughty. But she was simply self-confident. She occasionally wrote poems. She was prepared to enter any conversation, whether discussing contemporary literature or a problem in economics. Johnson did not like her less for being (like Walmesley or, for that matter, Olivia Lloyd) not only a Whig but a "Whig intellectual"—he was always attracted to such people, and enjoyed trying to dispel what he thought were their illusions—and he composed a short Latin epigram about her talking of "liberty" while making others captive with her beauty.

There is no doubt that Johnson was in love with her (in the way he had been with Olivia Lloyd at Stourbridge). When Mrs. Thrale once asked him "the happiest period of his past life," he replied it was the year "in which he spent one whole evening" with Molly: "That indeed (said he) was not happiness, it was rapture; but the thoughts of it sweetened the whole year." It was "rapture" partly because of the contrast of Molly—and of the entire way of life that she, like Cornelius, symbolized—to the accumulated indignities and disappointments, the fatigue, disillusions, and self-blame, ever since the school at Edial, three years ago, had begun to fail. Now there was at least temporary release, as he could half identify with men like Walmesley or Hervey, who had been able to marry two of the Aston sisters. But to be "in love" can be and usually is (it certainly was for Johnson) a very different thing from the complex, varying emotions, pulling upon the psyche in every way, that focus into what we subsume in the word "love" when we are using it in any fundamental way. When he spoke as he did to Mrs. Thrale about Molly ("a beauty and a scholar, and a wit and a whig"), adding that "she was the loveliest creature I ever saw," Mrs. Thrale naturally

asked him what his wife thought of this attachment? "She was jealous to be sure (said he), and teized me sometimes when I would let her; and one day, as a fortune-telling gipsey passed us when we were walking out in company with two or three friends in the country, she made the wench look at my hand, but soon repented her curiosity; for (says the gipsey) Your heart is divided, Sir, between a Betty and a Molly: Betty loves you best, but you take most delight in Molly's company: when I turned about to laugh, I saw my wife was crying. Pretty charmer! she had no reason!"[21]

There was also at least one long visit, probably more, to his affluent friend John Taylor at Ashbourne, who was finding the law burdensome and planning to enter the Church. Here even more than in talking at Lichfield with Molly Aston and the Walmesleys (for then he had to return home at night), it was like reliving those first months in Cornelius's house at Stourbridge or visiting in the houses of neighbors like the Hickmans or the Lytteltons at Hagley Park. At Taylor's and at the country houses he would visit with Taylor, everything was at his disposal: good food, pleasant surroundings, servants, leisure, and hours of conversation. And if, in this general spirit of reliving Stour-bridge, there had been a new Olivia Lloyd at Walmesley's in the form of Molly Aston, there was another one here at Ashbourne—Hill Boothby, a year older than Johnson, the niece of Sir William Boothby of nearby Ashbourne Hall. She was, in fact, more similar than Molly to the young Quakeress Olivia Lloyd. She herself inclined toward Meth-odism, and made a point of reading the Bible in Hebrew. (She is the original of "Miss Sainthill" in Richard Graves's novel *The Spiritual Quixote*.)[22] In later years she and Johnson were to correspond regu-larly, and a year after Tetty's death in 1752 he even considered asking her to marry him.*

Other people he now came to know through John Taylor included the rector of nearby Bradley, the learned but eccentric John Kennedy, for whose work, over twenty years later, *A Complete System of Astronomical Chronology* (1762), Johnson was to write the Dedica-tion; the medical family of Chauncey, a daughter of which was to marry Dr. Thomas Lawrence, who was in time to become president of the Royal College of Physicians as well as Johnson's close friend and personal physician; and especially the family, some of whom also ap-pear in *The Spiritual Quixote*, of a rough-tempered squire and sports-man Littleton Poyntz Meynell. The character of "old Meynell" can be quickly suggested by a typical assertion Johnson once quoted from him, "For anything I see, foreigners are fools," and by Johnson's refer-ence to him (which Boswell concealed) when he was denying that another man was really "malignant": "He is mischievous, if you will. He would do no man an essential injury. . . . I, however, once knew an old gentleman [Meynell] who was absolutely malignant. He really wished evil to others, and rejoiced at it." In contrast to "old Meynell" was his virtuous wife, Judith Alleyne, who had been trying to give the children a strict religious upbringing. It produced results. The four-year-old boy, Hugo, inherited one of his father's interests. He became renowned as the greatest fox hunter of his day, and, as the Duke of Beaufort called him, "the real father of the modern English chase." But he was also known for his generosity to the poor. And Johnson

---

* See below, p. 320.

thought highly of Mary, a daughter of seventeen, though he could conceive her virtue as oppressive if one were constantly around her. She married a good-natured but colorless neighbor, William Fitzherbert, whom Johnson liked to cite as an example that "a man will please more upon the whole by negative qualities than positive." He had "no sparkle, no brilliancy," but "I never knew a man who was so generally acceptable. He . . . overpowered nobody by the superiority of his talents, made no man think worse of himself by being his rival, seemed always to listen, did not oblige you to hear much of him, and did not oppose what you said." But even Fitzherbert began to sink before the omnipresent virtue of his wife, standing as she did like "the angel with the flaming sword, to keep the devil at a distance," and, when she died, he "felt at once afflicted and released."[23]

In January (1740) Johnson was back at Lichfield, again visiting Walmesley and seeing Molly Aston. But even if he continued to delay returning to London, something had to be done about money. Lacking any other alternative, he and his mother made arrangements to mortgage the house to their old family friend Theophilus Levett, for £80, from which Johnson was to receive £20 as his share.[24] There is no indication that Sarah herself needed to do this. Living very cheaply, she seemed able to survive on the small income that the bookshop still brought her. The mortgage was certainly made at Johnson's own urging, and his request could hardly increase his self-respect. He was now thirty-one. He had earned nothing for over half a year. Owing to his own indolence, he and—because of him—Sarah were now capitalizing on the sole asset that remained to them.

Chapter 12

Range as a Journalist; Johnson's Politics Generally; *Parliamentary Debates*; Speed in Writing

The euphoria he had been feeling in this very different world with its Cornelius-like associations, and his inability to tear himself away from it, show how much he had been driving himself for two or three years, and how much more discouraged he had been by the results than he admitted to himself or others.

But his feelings of guilt had been accumulating, though on the surface half anesthetized by the relief of these months. Suddenly he heard from Tetty that she had hurt her leg (it was a torn or sprained tendon). January had ushered in one of the coldest winters in British history ("the dreadful winter of Forty"). Each morning, in the London streets, bodies of the homeless poor were found frozen. Doubtless Tetty had fallen on the ice. He wrote to her at once (January 31). Superficially the anxiety he expresses for her health seems out of all proportion to the accident: "After hearing that You are in so much danger, as I apprehend from a hurt on the tendon . . ."; she must have the best surgeons possible, whatever the cost; he cannot "be at rest while I believe my dear Tetty in pain."

Unspoken, but stronger, was his remorse in learning she was in need. In fact, her mention of the injury was doubtless intended (and rightly interpreted by Johnson) as an appeal in more important ways, both financial and emotional. By now she had probably used up her remaining capital, and he could justly consider himself—because of the ill-fated school and his inability to earn more than he had since then—as responsible for her ending in this situation.* He was sending her immediately a guinea to use for the surgeon, and he would forward another £20 in a few days (the money he was receiving as his share after mortgaging the Lichfield house). He goes on: "You have already suffered more than I can bear to reflect upon, and I hope more than either of us shall suffer again. One part at least I have often flatterd myself we shall avoid for the future, our troubles will surely never separate us more." Whether he was trying to allay other apprehensions she had expressed, or was prodded by his conscience, or both, he ends the letter:

> Be assured, my dear Girl, that I have seen nobody in these rambles upon which I have been forced, that has not contributed to confirm my esteem and affection for thee, though that esteem and affection only contributed to increase my unhappiness when I reflected that the most amiable woman in the world was exposed by my means to miseries which I could not relieve. I am My charming Love Yours
>
> Sam: Johnson[1]

Given this letter, and its spirit of new resolve prodded by remorse, he probably returned to London as soon as he could. It is sometimes assumed that he did not return until spring only because there are no certain publications in the *Gentleman's Magazine* till June, when his short "Life of Admiral Blake" appeared. But it takes a little time to get back into harness. Moreover, David Garrick had written him in January that the coyly obstinate Charles Fleetwood, the manager at Drury Lane who had refused even to read *Irene,* was now thawing, and was ready to "give a promise in writing that it shall be the first next season, if it cannot be introduced now." This also would have been an incentive to return, though nothing was actually to come of it.† Ironically,

---

* After her death, referring to the little silver cup his mother had bought him in London when she had taken him there to be touched by the Queen, he said it was "one of the last pieces of plate which dear Tetty sold in our distress" (*Diaries,* pp. 9–10); and this period of their life, if any, he could have regarded as jointly "our distress."

† Johnson himself could have been somewhat to blame. His own growing lack of confidence in the play, and his eagerness to settle for almost anything now, apparently communicated itself to Fleetwood. This is suggested by a letter from Cave to a friend the following year (1741) about Johnson's play: "Both he and I are very unfit to deal with the theatrical persons. Fleetwood was to have acted it last Season, but Johnson's diffidence or [Cave here leaves a blank] prevented it" (L, I, 153). The blank indicates Cave's own puzzlement about what had happened, but the indication is that it had to do with Johnson's own way of handling the affair.

while his own negotiations with Fleetwood were falling apart, he found himself writing a Prologue, as a favor to Garrick, for a work as far from *Irene* as one could imagine: a slight comic skit hastily put together by Garrick called *Lethe: or Aesop in the Shades*, which proved a success when it was produced at Drury Lane on April 15. The irony was by no means lost on him. If the learned professions were completely barred to him because of his lack of a degree, he was beginning to realize that a career as a playwright or poet, without patronage or some other form of support, was equally out of the question, at least for years to come. If he were not responsible for Tetty, he could take his chances. But then—unfortunately for himself—he was responsible for Tetty, and, whatever the temptations to drift in the future, he would never again fail her.

2

As if to make up for lost time, he now at thirty-one turned without further hesitation to the one career possible for him if he was not merely to drift or to take long chances—that of a journalist and a hack writer. For anyone of his ambition and talent, his earlier revulsion after a fair try at journalism was understandable: the hand-to-mouth existence; the lack of choice in what to write; the inevitable scattering of effort; the knowledge that most of what one wrote was by definition ephemeral, and some of it even trivial. Nor, even if one stuck out the course, was there much promise ahead. Journalism, still in its youth, had not acquired the opportunities or prestige it was to develop during the nineteenth and especially the twentieth century. But whatever he was to do in the future would necessarily have to grow from this particular soil. There was no other alternative. Yet as things turned out, the situation by no means proved to be wholly—or even mainly—to his disadvantage. A serious case can be made that it was the second thing to save him from himself after the breakdown of his early twenties—the first being the marriage to Tetty.

The journalistic writings of Johnson during the next fifteen or twenty years, first for Cave and later for other publishers, were "so numerous, so various, and scattered in such a multiplicity of unconnected publications," said Boswell, that it was doubtful whether Johnson himself in later years could make a complete list.* What strikes us most about these publications is the sheer range, however ephemeral, quickly written, or now forgotten some of the pieces. There are short biographies of men noted in medicine, science, literature, naval exploration, and warfare; poems in both Latin and English; monthly articles for the *Gentleman's Magazine*, year after year, on foreign history (that is, political and other current events abroad), and also the section, much of the time, on foreign books. And there are reviews, essays, or other writings that show his knowledge not only of literature, politics, religion and ethics, but also agriculture, trade, and practical business; philology, classical scholarship, aesthetics, and metaphysics; medicine and chemistry; travel, exploration, and even Chinese architecture. Much of it, of course, was hack work, but it was inspired hack work.

Beginning with the 1950's more works have been steadily added to the list of these writings. In the new *Cambridge Bibliography*, without considering further additions that are still being made, there are at least 225 items from 1736 down to 1755, the year in which the *Dictionary* appeared. Some are admittedly quite short but others (leaving aside even the parliamentary debates or the essays for the *Rambler*) are of considerable length. Of these 225 titles down to 1755, well over 30 are concerned primarily with political subjects; over 80 could be bracketed as "literary criticism" and reviews (though often reviews of books of political interest); there are 13 biographies or biographical sketches, and 37 poems; and the rest consist of "Proposals" and other works dealing with history, travel, religion, and other subjects.

This summary does not do justice to the amount of his writing concerned with political and related matters, especially in the years before 1745, during which, in number of titles alone, the writings concerned with political subjects exceed those in any other category. But when we consider the sheer bulk of writing before 1745—the famous "Parliamentary Debates" that he wrote for the *Gentleman's Magazine* from 1741 to early 1744 amount to almost half a million words—the predominance of political interests in his work at this time is even greater.

* It was less a matter of mere indolence than embarrassment, and he did not care to be represented by it. Hence he "declined pointing out any of his earlier performances [in the *Gentleman's Magazine* or elsewhere], when some of his most intimate friends asked it as a favour." To others he acknowledged that "he then wrote many things which merited no distinction from the trash with which they were consigned to oblivion" (Shaw, p. 38).

3

Before turning to the debates and continuing with his other journalistic writing, we should stop to consider briefly the problem of Johnson's politics as a whole. The subject must not only be discussed
generally in any biography of him that is written now, but should
also—ideally speaking—be faced as early as possible in the biography,
even though we must leap ahead chronologically in order to discuss it
as a unit. The reason for confronting the subject both as a unit and also
as early as possible is that the cloud of misconception that surrounded
it for so long still seems to persist to an extraordinary degree. It has
persisted despite the major reconsideration that has taken place in what
we used to call the "Whig interpretation" of British history, and despite two important discussions of Johnson himself in this context—a
seminal essay of Bertrand Bronson's, and a full study of Johnson's
politics by Donald Greene.[2]

The popular misconception of Johnson's "Toryism" is largely the
product of the stock notion of eighteenth-century "Toryism" itself
that developed after the French Revolution, when the general meaning
of the word "Tory" changed, and that then hardened and canonized
during the nineteenth century in the famous "Whig interpretation" of
British history, for which Macaulay was the most eloquent spokesman.
What has kept this stock notion of eighteenth-century Toryism alive,
long after it has been discredited by historians, has been the popular
tendency to use the word loosely as the equivalent of "conservatism,"
even though notions of what is conservative change more radically
than we sometimes choose to remember. In the twentieth century our
tendency to equate "Tory" and "conservative" becomes especially
bizarre if we let ourselves project it back on the eighteenth century,
since much of what has come to be thought of in our own century as
conservative—particularly laissez-faire economics—was the essence of
Whiggism in Johnson's day.[3] Yet such is the control of semantics over
the mind that when words (above all, abstract labels) are learned early
in life, the associations acquired with them at the time seem almost
permanently "imprinted," except for the small number of people who
in each generation try to enlarge or correct them. Hence the mere
mention of "Whig and Tory," when one is speaking of Johnson's
lifetime, still evokes for many of us a conception of two parties with

two distinct philosophies: (1) The Whigs were the "progressive" party. This means they were on the side of reform, advocated a more representative government, and would in general be more "democratic." This usually carries the further notion that they were like modern "liberals." (2) The Tories, by contrast, were opposed to "reform," were nostalgic for the past, were more monarchically minded, and therefore on the side of "privilege" and of what one would think of as the "establishment." Consequently the automatic assumption is that they were "antiliberal." For the American, this conception of Whig and Tory has been reinforced by further associations: the Tories, led by George III and by Lord North (who was in reality a Whig), were the party eager to constrain the colonies, while the Whigs served as advocates of the American interests. Finally, since the Tories are firmly bracketed in the imagination as the party of "privilege," and since "privilege" was obviously rampant throughout the eighteenth century, it is assumed that the Tories were at least as powerful as the Whigs.

Actually the Tories were a minority party in the House of Commons throughout most of Johnson's lifetime. "From 1714 to 1784," as Donald Greene says, "perhaps a fifth of the members of the House of Commons would have so designated themselves."[4] Moreover, it was the Whigs rather than the Tories who represented the interests that the twentieth century has associated with "conservatism." The Whigs were the party of the great landowners and the wealthy merchants, while the Tories were associated more with the small landowners and the country clergy. To Johnson, from his boyhood on, the Tories were the underdogs, unfashionable and considered by others hopelessly outdated; and, if other things did not stand in the way, he was usually tempted to identify with the underdog. After the accession of George III (1760), many of the Tories turned increasingly to the King as a leader in their hope to curb the power of Whig propertied and commercial interests. In doing so they were reviving the old ideal of "King and Commons" versus the nobility. The classic statement of this at the time is by Johnson's friend, the chronically impoverished yet "Tory" Oliver Goldsmith, in the climactic passage of his poem *The Traveller* (1764). There he attacks what he conceives to be rampant Whig commercialism and colonial imperialism (which is what Johnson himself means when he describes Whiggism as a "negation of all Principle"). Two of Johnson's own sentiments, in particular, are echoed here: his lifelong horror of slavery, which he sees as the inevitable extension of the uncontrolled pursuit of wealth; and his detestation of the "cant" whereby those most active in the remorseless "hunt for gain" invoke words like "liberty" and "freedom" simply because they personally resent interference from the Crown. ("How is it," he later asked, "that we hear the loudest yelps for liberty among the drivers of negroes?") The situation, says Goldsmith, is one in which contending Whig leaders

> blockade the throne,
> Contracting regal power to stretch their own.

Accordingly,

> When I behold a factious band agree
> To call it freedom when themselves are free;
> Each wanton judge new penal statutes draw,
> Laws grind the poor, and rich men rule the law;
> The wealth of climes, where savage nations roam,
> Pillag'd from slaves to purchase slaves at home,
> I fly from petty tyrants to the throne.

4

Building upon the popular misconception of what the Tory party was during Johnson's early and middle years, two special factors have further contributed to our stock notion of Johnson's "Toryism" and help to explain the legend's hardy persistence. One of them is quickly stated: the colorful exaggeration of Johnson's "Toryism," for personal reasons, by Boswell, whose *Life of Johnson* has been the natural introduction to Johnson for every reader since the 1790's; and because the impressions of Johnson there are received early, they tend to remain. Moreover, it was from Boswell that the nineteenth-century picture of the "Tory Johnson" was extrapolated, especially by Macaulay, and then incorporated into the textbooks, where it still remains.

To the much younger Boswell, eager to shed some of his Scottish background and to identify romantically with what he conceived to be English "conservatism," Toryism was seen with historical color and the magic of distance. When he discovered that the prevailing intellectual society of London was Whig, it was naturally pleasing to Boswell to feel that he could buttress his own personal sentiments with something that could seem just as "intellectual"—in fact, the authority of a real sage. Starting with his account of Johnson's childhood, where he pictures him as "the infant Hercules of Toryism," Boswell capitalizes on opportunities to cite or interpret remarks by Johnson as both an outlet for expressing and a means of sanctioning his own romantic conservatism. Nor was this done with any intention to mislead. He was happy and reassured to think that he and Johnson shared what he considered a common ground, and was understandably tempted to dwell on it in his own imagination. But the differences, if not always wide, went rather deep. The principal ones are those of individual character and mind. But there is also the important difference of a full generation, during which—especially by the time Boswell's *Life* appeared (1791)—the concept of Toryism was beginning to acquire its nineteenth-century associations. These for Boswell had a snobbish as well as a romantic appeal. As a result, Toryism, as Boswell construed it, provided for himself a socially unimpeachable escape from the rigid Presbyterian Whiggism of his father. There is nothing wrong with the motivation. As Johnson never forgets to remind us, the motivations of all of us are inevitably mixed. But in the case of the emotional Boswell, where this motivation was not too complicated or qualified by other considerations, the effect was to increase both the imaginative appeal and also the simplicity of his own idea of Toryism.

The most dramatic example of their differences is in their attitudes toward slavery. Boswell records Johnson's brilliant defense of the escaped slave who was claiming his liberty in a Scottish court, but prefaces it with condescension:

He had always been very zealous against slavery in every form, in which I with all deference thought that he discovered "a zeal without knowledge." Upon one occasion, when in company with some very grave men at Oxford, his toast was, "Here's to the next insurrection of the negroes in the West Indies."

Boswell, for his part, viewed as "wild and dangerous" the attempt even "to abolish so very important and necessary a branch of commercial interest" as the slave trade. Johnson's own attitude toward it "I will resolutely say . . . was owing to prejudice and imperfect or false information." Boswell himself believed that

To abolish a *status*, which in all ages GOD has sanctioned, and man has continued, would not only be *robbery* to an innumerable class of our fellow-subjects; but it would be extreme cruelty to the African savage, a portion of whom it saves from massacre, or intolerable bondage in their own country, and introduces into a much happier state of life. . . .[5]

5

The second factor is far more complicated: the mixed character of what Johnson himself says, under different circumstances and with very different motives; the interplay of genuine principles with his habitual temptation to take the other side of the argument (most of his friends and acquaintances throughout his life were Whigs); his dislike of the "modish" generally, and of the "cant" that goes along with it; and, deep within one part of his divided nature, a pessimistic feeling—at least a strong temptation to feel—that all forms of government, constructed and managed as they were by fallible man, were equally unfortunate, however necessary.

When we unscramble this, we find one central, indeed profound, principle that persists throughout his life. Though by no means shared by all Tories, it was certainly not "Whig." It is a principle that we can only describe as *protective subordination,* or *subordination for the sake of protection*—protection not only of the society as a whole but also, especially, of the individual. "Subordination" is a favorite word of Johnson's when he is speaking of political matters; and he is using it in its original and literal sense, of a society existing "under" and by means of "order." The attitude is at the opposite pole, for example, from the idea of unbridled laissez-faire economics, which Johnson views as a philosophy of "dog eat dog." To this extent, it has far more in common with some aspects of twentieth-century liberalism, even with socialism, than it has with modern right-wing, capitalistic "conservatism," which—in its claim to "conserve"—looks back for its model to the nineteenth rather than the eighteenth century, and specifically to the heyday of Victorian capitalism. Fitting in with this is the antiimperial, anticolonialist strain that significantly appears in Johnson's first recorded prose (written at the age of sixteen).[6]

This principle of "protective subordination" is sustained by two feelings that pervade all of Johnson's thinking: charity, or compassion; and a dark, unillusioned recognition of the evil—or "original sin"—that is inherent in the nature of man. Leave man alone, he thought, and a "dog eat dog" way of living is sure to take over, as it did in those primitive societies that people were beginning to idealize, he thought, so foolishly. What most struck him about the "Whig" philosophy, in his formative years, was what he considered its smiling acceptance of a potentially savage "state of nature" as the norm for "helpless man." Its response was that of Cain: "Am I my brother's keeper?" And its guilt was the greater because it dishonestly veiled its own selfish opposition to restraint by a curtain of "cant" words like "freedom," which could then be used to entice the bewildered mob into serving as allies. But the poor, with whom Johnson always identified, were in reality the victim. "He loved the poor," as Mrs. Thrale said, "as I never saw anyone else do." This was the Johnson who would flare up, in surprise and horror, when his wealthy acquaintances spoke lightly of the poor, or complained of the inconvenience caused by them. So when Mrs. Thrale spoke sneeringly of the smell of the cheap cookshops, in "Porridge Island" in London, where the poor bought food, he tartly reminded her of the "hundreds of your fellow-creatures" who "turn another way, that they may not be tempted by the luxuries of Porridge Island to wish for gratifications they are not able to attain." Who was to protect these people? Individuals might help a little, as he himself did in a dozen ways, from taking people into his home to slipping pennies into the hands of the beggar boys sleeping on the door steps (in order, he said, that they might at least be able to survive "to beg *on*"). But this was hardly enough. An enlightened society should do something.

The answer, therefore, was not the "negation of all principle" that he saw, or thought he saw, in laissez-faire mercantilism, with its cold and theoretically benevolent confidence in human nature—its confidence that if only the restraints of governmental "order" and regulation ("subordination") were removed, both social and economic blessings would in time follow. He himself expected no such thing. Years later, on the trip to the Hebrides, Lady MacLeod, said Boswell, inquired whether man was not "naturally good." Johnson replied, "No, madam, no more than a wolf." "Lady MacLeod," said Boswell, "started at this, saying, in a low voice, 'This is worse than Swift.'" And Mrs. Chapone, in talking with Johnson, "wondered to hear a man, who by his actions shews so much benevolence, maintain that the human heart is naturally malevolent, and that all the benevolence we see in the few who are good is acquired by reason and religion."[7]

Hence the need of *protective* safeguards for the vulnerable—who comprise the mass of humanity—and the question where the safeguards are to be found. The alternatives were limited. (The voting population, by the middle of the century, was not much more than 200,000.) The principle of "subordination for the sake of protection" could turn only to the Throne as an ally, in the hope once again of alliance of "King and Commons" against powerful special interests ("I fly from petty tyrants to the throne"). As a result, what Johnson means by "order" ("subordination") is inevitably monarchical, and strongly so. Yet even here there are qualifications, and important asides, that would startle an ordinary "monarchist." So, in an argument with Sir Adam Fergusson, he found himself saying, "Why all this childish jealousy of the power of the crown? . . . In no government can power be abused long. Mankind will not bear it. If a sovereign oppresses his people to a great degree, they will rise and cut off his head."[8]

6

The position is neither complicated nor, to say the least, unreasonable. What has complicated and even distorted our *notion* of it in Johnson, aside from misconceptions of what a "Tory" was and aside from Boswell, is the exaggerated tone of which we all think when the subject of Johnson's politics is mentioned—the violence of language, often half feigned ("The first Whig was the devil," "I perceive you are a vile Whig," and the like), most of it, as we have noted, imitated from his second "role model" in his teens, the "violent" Whig, Gilbert Walmesley; the heat, the loud readiness, and the perverse ingenuity with which he would sometimes push a point, as did Walmesley himself; or the absurd pretense at moments that he was a Jacobite.

To discuss this takes us into Johnson's psychology, which, as a subject central to this book as a whole, we have been able to approach only gradually and cumulatively. But a few points should be made briefly in this context. It is important to distinguish them under two headings: (1) psychological factors that intensified his real convictions or feelings on the subject; and (2) those that simply led him, especially in his later years, to embellish his expression of them. The first are immediately relevant. The only reason for even mentioning the latter at this point is to recognize them in advance for what they are, and prevent them from confusing consideration until, in different contexts, they do become relevant—indeed, in their extreme form, psychologically fascinating. Under this latter heading we should include not merely the temptation to contradict, and to argue for the sake of argument (this was, after all, something that could always spring awake in him if he was caught unawares), but something else that was to grow on him: the temptation at times to act a role (which is certainly a large element in the much abused, little-read, and not too typical "political pamphlets" of the early 1770's). This temptation to act a role, and in the process to shock the complacent, is partly the simple willingness of most people to live up to the picture others have of us, provided it does not demand too much effort, and even at times, if our spirits are high, to offer them a self-caricature. But it also involves something else in Johnson, which goes much deeper and which we can only call "self-burlesque": a self-burlesque in which so much of what we find ourselves defending or disputing with such heat is, against the cosmic backdrop, seen as trivial, and as little more than doomed posturings and gestures.* By his middle years, increasing with every decade, we find the conviction growing that he distilled into two of the lines that he wrote for Goldsmith's *Traveller:*

> How small of all that human hearts endure,
> That part which laws or kings can cause or cure.

But this lies ahead. It is the first of the psychological factors mentioned above (those that intensified his real convictions) that are relevant now. These, which are one major theme of Bronson's "Johnson Agonistes," could be subsumed by Bronson's fine remark that "temperamentally" Johnson "is always in revolt." Like his warm, even heady, championship of the poor, or like his emotional identification (or feeling that he should identify) with that part of his family which he exaggeratedly described as "of mean extraction," Johnson's espousal of the "minority," unpopular Tory position was from the beginning one of "revolt." There was, to be sure, what Keats liked to call a "gordian" complication of feelings here. For example, there was a certain pride in the raw, ungainly youth that he was not standing up for obvious self-interest. He may not have been completely conscious of it at the time, when he began standing up to Gilbert Walmesley. But years later he disarmingly admitted that he thought he had "great merit in being zealous for subordination and the honors of birth, for I can hardly tell who was my grandfather," meaning, of course, his paternal grandfather and not "the ancient family of Ford." Moreover, his intellectual conviction of the need for protective order and settlement is constantly being prodded—sometimes given passionate, even explosive, urgency—by his lifelong struggle to control his own rebellious nature, and to pull himself into clarity and balance. (This was something he

---

* See below, pp. 488–89.

had to watch in himself as he grew older—the dangers of too compulsive a finality and certainty, especially in matters that by then seemed far more important than politics.) But the principal psychological factor, by far, was his almost instinctive revolt against the intellectually modish. The aggressive independence with which the half-blind infant had pushed aside Dame Oliver when she had tried to help him was to remain throughout his life as one of the main difficulties in himself that he had to combat. But by adolescence it was also beginning to turn into what was to become, in its more creative aspect, one of his finest qualities, above all as a critic of literature: his refusal to be intimidated by the spurious "authority" of fashion; his scorn of the "cant" of those who are conditioned by attitudes simply because they are current; his tendency to walk immediately up to the tyranny of stock response in the prevailing mode of thinking, and to push directly through it in order to see what is on the other side.

In this, as in other ways, his acquaintance with the "Whig" Gilbert Walmesley, as we have noticed, had been and remained of crucial importance. For Johnson, at eighteen and nineteen, to espouse the position he did provided an honest hold, a purchase for identity, when he was given his second entrance into "polite society"—a society he was grateful to enter—at Walmesley's table in the Bishop's palace. He had already at Stourbridge encountered a polite, even quasi-aristocratic "Whig" society (the Fords and Hickmans, the Crowleys and Olivia Lloyd, not to mention the young George Lyttelton), and, in doing so, retreated a little—so that one part of him could establish a difference, a stance—to the unfashionable "country" Toryism that people like Michael exemplified. But with Walmesley, hotly partisan, delighting in argument and controversy, and made further irascible by gout, Whiggism became a fighting issue. And quickly learning at this formative age to use the same weapons as the admired Walmesley, Johnson fought back across the table—dreaming at the same time of entering the law, as his affluent role model had done, yet keeping, and prepared to defend, his own integrity, his own special insight.

Here was a way in which the young Johnson could, with conscience and personal experience, "correct" Walmesley, "with whom I used to contend with great eagerness." This was to continue throughout his whole life, even though he said that after Walmesley's death (1751), "I felt my Toryism much abated." This is a testimony of how powerfully Walmesley had been incorporated into him as both role model and permanent sparring partner, since he had not seen Walmesley personally for over a decade before this time. It was to continue throughout life, not only because the habit had been ingrained long before the age of forty-two (1751), but also because he was really not just answering Walmesley personally but an entire world of England that he loved and in which one part of him was always living, at times in reality and at other times in imagination. To this extent, he was also answering, or reminding or prodding, a part of himself. Of his closest friends up through his middle years, only his old schoolfellow Edmund Hector and Tetty (both "country" people) were plainly Tory. But starting with the Stourbridge circle—the Hickmans, Fords, Crowleys, and the beautiful Olivia—through Walmesley and Molly Aston, or John Taylor and the wealthy Ashbourne circle and Hill Boothby, whom he may have hoped to marry, the other world in which he moved and to which he was so attracted was "Whig" (intellectual and affluent Whig).

These well-meaning people, of whom he was so fond, had not thought through what they were saying. They had not seen the "real" world, with its cold lack of charity, its depravity, its poverty. He, Johnson, could clear their minds. In a way, it was an act of love. Significantly, when he was to acquire as a friend the greatest Whig statesman of the age, Edmund Burke—whose abilities matched his own, and whose vast knowledge of political detail he could not so easily imagine himself "correcting"—he made a virtue of staying away from politics in talking with him. He could consider this a proof of his own tact.* But it was a tact that included the realization that there was no need to serve as a gadfly—the mere thought was absurd—to such brilliant, warmhearted men as Burke or Charles James Fox, that other great Whig statesman who was a member of The Club and whom Johnson admired. Here things were on a different plane. On essential principles, "a wise Tory and a wise Whig, I believe, will agree."[9]

---

* Thus, talking with Goldsmith (1772) about the question whether "people who disagree in any capital point can live in friendship together," Johnson affirmed they could: "You must shun the subject as to which you disagree. For instance, I can live very well with Burke: I love his knowledge, his genius . . . but I would not talk to him of the Rockingham party." "GOLDSMITH. 'But, Sir, when people live together who have something as to which they disagree, and which they want to shun, they will be in the situation mentioned in the story of Blue-beard: "You may look into all the chambers but one." But we should have the greatest inclination to look into that chamber, to talk of that subject.' JOHNSON. (with a loud voice.) 'Sir, I am not saying that *you* could live in friendship with a man from whom you differ as to some point: I am only saying that *I* could do it' " (L, II, 181).

7

It is with this background in mind that we should turn to the specific political writing of these years, in his early thirties, which is so important not only in bulk and intellectual content but also in the training it gave to his mind.

Outside the mainstream of his political writing are two minor pamphlets (May 1739) that Johnson wrote during the period when he and Richard Savage would walk the streets all night for lack of money to pay for a place to sleep, and would talk for hours about "reforming the world, dethroning princes, establishing new forms of government, and giving laws to the several states of Europe."[10] The inevitable object of their indignation and of their accumulated feelings of injustice was the great Whig, Sir Robert Walpole, certainly one of the most extraordinary Prime Ministers in British history, who had now been managing the affairs of the nation for eighteen years, and whom Johnson later came to admire.

Doubtless encouraged by Savage, and reassured by the success of *London* a year before, Johnson decided to make another attempt at satire, this time in the vein of Swift and directed specifically against Walpole. The result was the ironic pamphlet *Marmor Norfolciense* (May 1739)—the "Norfolk Marble"—in which it is pretended that a large stone had been dug up in Norfolk (Walpole's home county), bearing an old Latin inscription "in monkish rhyme." It is here translated and interpreted for the public by a pedantic scholar who is an admirer of Walpole and is also made purposely stupid. The inscription itself predicts that, when it is discovered, political troubles and abuses will be rampant, and even the King may be deposed. Since it is fairly pointed, it could very well seem inflammatory to the government. But though the implications are obvious to the reader, the pro-Walpole antiquarian finds himself continually puzzled, and proposes that a Society of Commentators be set up to interpret the inscription at an annual cost to the country of only £650,000.

Though we now find the pamphlet tedious—indirect and drawn-out irony was never to be Johnson's forte—it obtained some notice, and there is an unsupported story that a search was made for the unknown author of the pamphlet in order to arrest him, and that Johnson went into hiding for a while. Encouraged by the attention, Johnson quickly followed it with another pamphlet in the vein of Swift (also published in May 1739), which now seems more readable but attracted little notice at the time: *The Compleat Vindication of the Licensers of the Stage*, which is an ironic "defense" of the Stage Licensing Act (1737). In March 1739 the government had prohibited the production of a play (Henry Brooke's *Gustavus Vasa*) that, though the characters were Swedish, was plainly an allegorical attack on both Walpole and George II as anticonstitutional in usurping power, and implying that even a civil war would be justified in order to get rid of them. Though again Johnson's irony is not too successful, the work is a spirited defense of freedom of the press. Hence, whatever its literary value, it has some personal interest, if only because it is so remote from the stock notion of the "Tory Johnson." Its tone, as Greene says, is rather that of "opposition Whig, and 'left-wing' opposition Whig at that."[11]

Of far more importance than these pamphlets, not only politically, but also in what it did for his own intellectual development, was the writing done for the *Gentleman's Magazine*. This consisted particularly of (1) several condensed, factual articles for the section "Foreign History," in other words, "foreign affairs" (at least ten in 1741 and 1742 and a half dozen more during the rest of the decade); and (2), above all, the twenty-seven parliamentary debates, ostensibly consisting of speeches delivered in the two Houses of Parliament from November 25, 1740, to Febraury 25, 1743, and published in fifty-four installments in the *Gentleman's Magazine* from July 1741 to March 1744.

When the House of Commons had forbidden further reporting of speeches (April 1738), the way in which the *Gentleman's Magazine* had circumvented this, as we have already noticed, was by calling its reports "Debates in the Senate of Magna Lilliputia" and using fictitious but easily recognizable names. Naturally this coy device, the charm of which quickly wore off, fooled no one. But the government was not eager to prosecute for fear of ridicule, and care was taken not to publish the speeches during the same session of Parliament when they had been given. Johnson, as we have seen, was involved in the project from the start, and had polished some of the speeches.* Then, when the important debate took place in the House of Lords on the motion to remove Sir Robert Walpole from office, Cave, wanting a more forceful writer, asked Johnson himself to handle it. This Johnson did so effectively that Cave then handed over the whole task to him, and

* See above, p. 175.

the *Magazine* began to prosper as never before, increasing its sale by 50 percent. Cave, naturally delighted, "manifested his good fortune," said Hawkins, "by buying an old coach and a pair of older horses," and, in order to display "to the world the source of his affluence," put on the coach door in place of a coat of arms "a representation of St. John's Gate," where the office of the *Magazine* was housed.[12]

8

The *Parliamentary Debates* remain one of the most remarkable feats in the entire history of journalism. For over two and a half years, Johnson was their sole author, though he himself was never in the gallery of the House of Commons except once. When we consider their total length, their historical importance (the fact that for so long they were considered authentic speeches by some of England's greatest statesmen), the extraordinary resourcefulness and range of argumentative ability they show, his age (thirty-one to thirty-four) and inexperience, the disadvantages under which he worked, and finally the incredible speed with which he wrote them, it is hard to find anything remotely comparable.*

For at least twenty years, the speeches were almost universally regarded as authentic, and for long after that were still assumed to be so. Needless to say, members of Parliament and their close associates knew otherwise. But they had no desire to broadcast their knowledge. They could feel flattered at the command of language they were given; and the speeches were written with surprising impartiality. Johnson's first semipublic admission of what he had done came at a dinner about twenty years later, which Arthur Murphy told about in some detail. An important debate near the end of Walpole's administration (all of this was written by Johnson) was mentioned. Among those present was Philip Francis, who had spent eight years in the study of Demos-

---

* The debates, it should be noted, are not what the word might suggest to us now—the swift give and take of controversy, or of question and answer. Readers are naturally disappointed if they look into them expecting dramatic scenes and dialogue with phrasing adapted to individual characters. (Individuality of character appears in the general attitude of speakers, and in the kind of argument used, as far as could be expected from a writer who had not heard the men himself. But otherwise, like the characters in *Rasselas,* the speakers talk as they would if they had Johnson's style and command of language.) The form, already settled before Johnson took it over, was simply that of "set speeches" focused on an important issue.

thenes, and had just finished translating his orations. Francis said that William Pitt's speech on this occasion "was the best he had ever read," and that even in Demosthenes he "had met with nothing equal" to that speech. At this several members of the company remembered reading the debate, and "some passages were cited, with the approbation and applause of all present. During the ardour of conversation, Johnson remained silent." Finally, after the praise had subsided, he remarked, "That speech I wrote in a garret in Exeter Street." The company was naturally astonished. Then he told them briefly that Cave, who had influence with the doorkeepers, contrived to get himself or his employees admitted. They would then bring back to Johnson "the subject of discussion, the names of the speakers, the side they took and the order in which they rose, together with notes of the arguments advanced in the course of the debate." The implication here is that "notes of the arguments" were generally available to him; and recent research has shown that what Johnson wrote was at times reasonably similar to what was said.[13]

But on many occasions the speeches were spun out of his own head, with no other information given him than the order of speaking and the general point of view taken. Another man might have boasted of this. But Johnson, detesting deceit as he did, became troubled at the way the speeches were increasingly regarded as historical record. He had become uneasy while still writing them, and had at last stopped because he "would not be accessory to the propagation of falsehood." Understandably, when he had started, he could view the matter as innocent. It could be taken for granted that members of Parliament, if they wished, could disown the speeches. He himself was earning a very meager living; he was doing what Cave assigned him; and when materials were not forthcoming, he was still obliged to turn out something. Moreover, the whole thing could be regarded at first as partly a joke. He could justifiably tell John Nichols, six days before his death, that at the time he wrote the speeches, "he did not think he was imposing on the world." But now, as he faced death, he wished to set the record straight, borrowed from Nichols the early volumes of the *Magazine*, and began to turn down the pages at those debates he had written. They were "the only part of his writings which then gave him compunction." For in many cases they had been written "from very slender materials, and often none at all—the mere coinage of his own imagination." Yet few members of Parliament had ever disowned the speeches. Moreover, as time passed, they were incorporated first into quasi-official collections of parliamentary speeches, and later into the

Parliamentary History, of which *Hansard's* was the continuation. From these collections editors would in turn incorporate them into the collected published works of such statesmen as Chesterfield and Pitt—two of them, printed (1777) as examples of "Lord Chesterfield's eloquence," were compared by the admiring editor to the orations of Cicero. Amusingly, some of the speeches—still assumed to be by Pitt, Walpole, or Chesterfield—were to continue to appear over a century after Johnson's death in such collections as *The World's Best Orations* (1899).[14]

Another reason for the wide acceptance of the debates as authentic, or at least a reason why members of Parliament were not eager to disown them, was their impartiality, which contrasted with the strong Opposition bias of the *London Magazine*. At the dinner Arthur Murphy tells about, one of the company rightly brought this up, stating that he had "dealt out reason and eloquence with an equal hand to both parties. 'That is not quite true,' said Johnson; 'I saved appearances tolerably well; but I took particular care that the Whig dogs should not have the best of it.'" But this was a mere jest to cover up his pleasure at the praise. The speeches were made largely by Whigs anyway—Whigs of different kinds. In particular, he presented Robert Walpole favorably, giving him a better speech in his defense than he made in actuality. The more he looked into Walpole, in fact, the better he thought of him, and he ended up, said William Seward, considering him "the best minister this country ever had."[15]

9

The *Parliamentary Debates*, aside from any other interests they might have, were to prove of crucial importance for Johnson's development, both as a writer and as a mind generally. The reason is that, because of the way he himself handled them, they turned into one prolonged gymnastic exercise (approaching half a million words) in readiness of expression, in ingenuity and effective marshaling of argument, and in judicious balance of alternative points of view. If he had these qualities before, he was to have them in far greater degree afterward.

He had always, for example, been able to write rapidly. But now, as John Nichols said, "Three columns of the Magazine, in an hour, was no uncommon effort, which was faster than most persons could have transcribed that quantity." Since a column there contains a little more than six hundred words, this would mean an average rate of at least

eighteen hundred words an hour, or thirty a minute. On one day—
"and that not a long one, beginning perhaps at noon, and ending early
in the evening"—he wrote twenty columns (about twelve thousand
words). On such occasions, said Hawkins,

> his practice was to shut himself up in a room assigned to him at St. John's
> gate, to which he would not suffer anyone to approach, except the com-
> positor or Cave's boy for matter, which, as fast as he composed it, he
> tumbled out at the door.[16]

At least half of all writers, major or minor, have suffered from writing
blocks—from inner resistance to dragging oneself, hour after hour, to
the bar of self-judgment, and forcing oneself, before it, to confront
that most intimidating of objects to any writer: the blank page waiting
to be filled. Johnson especially, whose life was one constant battle with
a demanding superego, had a curiously strong resistance to writing.
But now, prodded by necessity and with some relief from the burden
of self-demand (for the writing was anonymous), he was pushing aside
these inhibitions time and again. Without the assurance through direct
experience that this much writing could be done effectively in the time
it took—that "a man *may* write at any time if he will set himself
doggedly to it"—and without the solace of knowing that it could be
got over quickly, he would certainly have written much less than he
did. Thirty years later, when he and the historian Robert Watson were
talking of "composition," he said he had advised the young Robert
Chambers, who was unable to get started with his lectures on law, and
in fact

> would advise every young man beginning to compose, to do it as fast as he
> can, to get a habit of having his mind to start promptly. It is so much more
> difficult to improve in speed than in accuracy. . . . If a man is accustomed
> to compose slowly and with difficulty upon all occasions, there is danger
> that he may not compose at all, as we do not like to do that which is not
> done easily.*

---

* "BOSWELL. 'We have all observed how one man dresses himself slowly and
another fast.' JOHNSON. 'Yes, sir, it is wonderful how much time some people will
consume in dressing: taking up a thing and looking at it, and laying it down, and
taking it up again. Everyone should get the habit of doing it quickly. I would say
to a young divine, "Here is your text; let me see how soon you can make a
sermon." Then I'd say, "Let me see how much better you can make it." Thus I
should see both his powers and his judgment'" (*Hebrides*, pp. 44–45).

But, of course, it was not speed alone but the penetration and intellectual balance of what was being said so quickly, and the way it was being put, that schooled him as nothing else had yet done for that "promptitude of thought" and resourcefulness of argument in which so few people have excelled him. What Johnson did was to turn the debates into a drama of ideas, and in a way that was to become a prototype for much of his later writing. He quickly found himself using the debates to present particular points of view in counterpoint as they referred to a particular question, whether the Corn Bill, the state of the army and navy, or the motion to remove Sir Robert Walpole. With excited empathy, he began to draw with impartiality on the arguments that occurred to his active imagination, presenting them in the best way he could in the time he had. (The empathy was naturally with ideas and values rather than with individuals that he could know only at second hand.) When he shut himself up in that room at St. John's Gate, and the pages as he wrote "tumbled out at the door" for the copy boy to take to the printer, his imagination, said Hawkins, was raised "to such a pitch of fervour as bordered upon enthusiasm." And because so much of him was caught up in this drama of ideas, the experience proved of permanent value. Almost instinctively, for example, he was here beginning to create the dialectic form of the great moral writing—the essays for the *Rambler*, *Adventurer*, and *Idler*, to some extent *Rasselas*—or even, for that matter, of some of the critical writing, above all the *Preface to Shakespeare:* that is, the powerful back-and-forth movement, where a thing is immediately given its due, stabilized with permanence of phrase, and then qualified with another position given equal justice.

But the principal value of this long gymnastic feat was more general. This came from what it did to develop that astonishing union of ready fertility with judicious balance, that ability to see so many different sides of a thing, which (side by side with his profound honesty to life) is one of the most distinctive qualities of Johnson's mind, and which led Edmund Burke many years later to say that if only Johnson "had come early into parliament, he certainly would have been the greatest speaker that ever was there."[17]

Chapter 13

Lost in Grub Street;
Biography and the World of Books

Meanwhile Johnson's rather waiflike existence in London was continuing. In a sense it was to continue for the rest of his life. For it was not until his fifties—twenty years later—that he was at last free from financial anxiety, and long before then his habits of life had been formed. Now, in his thirties, one of the unforgettable scenes is of Johnson—who had written speeches supposedly by England's foremost statesmen—dining with Edward Cave but, because there was another guest and Johnson was ashamed of his own tattered clothes, eating by himself behind a screen. The guest was Walter Harte, the tutor of Lord Chesterfield's son. During the dinner he praised Johnson's *Life of Savage* (1744), which had just appeared. Meeting Harte later, Cave said, "You made a man very happy t'other day." When Harte asked how that could be since "nobody was there but ourselves," Cave reminded him that "a plate of victuals was sent behind a screen, which was to Johnson, dressed so shabbily, that he did not choose to appear."[1]

He had been deeply contrite when he returned to Tetty, early in 1740, after his long absence from London. But with her own money now gone, it was necessary for both of them, and not merely Johnson himself, to economize. Their lodgings in the fashionable area of Castle Street close to the open fields were out of the question. They moved down to the Strand, and continued to move in and around the crowded area between the Strand and Holborn at least six times during the next six or seven years. Johnson meanwhile fell hopelessly behind on the

mortgage payments for the Lichfield house.² Whatever disappointments Tetty may have felt in this way of life, and the temptation to
feel that she was approaching her middle fifties with little to show for
it, she tried for a while to make the best of the situation. She may not
have thought very highly of Johnson's acquaintances, but she did not
have to see much of them. Given their straitened circumstances and
small lodgings, it was impossible to entertain anyone but an occasional
visitor. Though "both suffered from oddities," said William Shaw,
"which it was impossible to conquer," and though there were naturally
"petty differences, they regarded each other with true cordiality and
affection," and also—especially important to each of them—with "a
steadfast confidence."³

The principal "petty difference" had to do with the efforts of the
still self-respecting Tetty—though she may have felt it a losing battle
—to keep their cheap lodgings clean and orderly, whereas Johnson,
besides becoming more slovenly in dress and eating habits as he ran
about London, left a train of disarray wherever he entered. But argument consisted of little more than hints or mild irony on Tetty's part
and far-from-crushing replies on Johnson's. Being "extremely neat in
her disposition," he told Mrs. Thrale, Tetty was "always fretful that I
made the house so dirty—a clean floor is *so* comfortable she would say
by way of twitting; till at last I told her, I thought we had had talk
enough about the *floor*, we could now have a touch at the *ceiling*."
Asked whether—being so particular about his food—he had "ever
huffed his wife about his dinner," he replied "so often" that at last,
when he was about to say grace one day, she said, "Nay hold, Mr.
Johnson, and do not make a farce of thanking God for a dinner which
in a few minutes you will protest not eatable."⁴

2

One of the things we have seen Johnson acquiring during his first years
in London was an intimate knowledge—matched by very few writers
—of the practical world of books and publishing, of periodicals, reviewing, editing, and printing. But there was also something else in
which no major writer—above all, no major critic of literature—has
equaled him. This was his direct knowledge of what we might call the
underworld of publishing and writing—of the large number of people,
often living in extreme poverty, who did writing and other publishing

work in order simply to stay alive in the most rudimentary way: the world that, in the eighteenth century, was called Grub Street after the street in which some of them lived in unheated garrets. We have already noticed something of this literary underworld as Johnson encountered it in his first two years in London. But when he returned early in 1740, he was really immersed in it, and a few words more about it are relevant. For it remains the primary setting of his life and writing all through his thirties, and is very much in the background of the far greater work of his forties.

A year before Johnson's death, he was talking with John Hoole, who had become well known as a translator of Ariosto. When Hoole said he "had received a part of his early instruction in Grub-street," Johnson congratulated him: "Sir, (said Johnson, smiling), you have been *regularly* educated." Johnson asked who in Grub Street had taught him, and Hoole said it was an uncle, who had been a tailor. Johnson at once remembered him: "We called him the *metaphysical taylor*," and he added that they both had belonged to a little club in the early 1740's that met at an alehouse in Old Street, with "George Psalmanazar, and some others."[5]

Psalmanazar, one of the strangest figures in the publishing underworld at this time, was a man of about sixty (he called himself by this name; his true name was never known), and was a sort of linguistic genius, who had taught himself several languages.[6] He had been born in southern France, and had traveled around Europe as a youth, posing as an Irish pilgrim and begging from priests with whom he would talk in impeccable Latin. He served for a while in a German regiment, and—beginning to delight in changing identities—pretended he was a Japanese. Since no one he encountered had ever seen a Japanese, he got away with it for a while. Then he was baptized in the Church of England, and went to England, where he pretended he was a native of Formosa. There, in a mere two months, he wrote a *History of Formosa* (he was now in his middle twenties), inventing not only descriptions and analyses of the island, but an alphabet and grammar for its "language."

The book sold well, and the Bishop of London arranged for him to go to Christ Church, Oxford, for six months and teach this imaginary language to future missionaries. While there he wrote a study of the coinage of Formosa, and enjoyed himself. After a full day he would keep his candle burning all night as he slept in an armchair by the window, in order to make people think he was constantly working. In time the fraud was revealed. Reading Law's *Serious Call* (1728), he became repentant. Since then he had done hack work for the publishers. He had worked on a *General History of Printing*, begun by and credited to Samuel Palmer, the printer, and was now contributing sections on ancient history for a large publishing project of the time (the *Universal History*). At the time Johnson got to know him, he was about to do the indexes for the huge, seven-volume *Collection of State Papers of John Thurloe*.

Johnson, who was always quick to show compassion for reformed sinners, considered the man to have suffered enough and to have become pious and pure-minded (this was apparently true) as well as genuinely learned. He made a point of seeking him out. In fact, it was usually only with the relatively humble that Johnson, with his temptations toward reverse snobbery, would make such an effort. He was still seeing something of higher social life, and relished the idea of mingling equally with the high and low. But he would not seek it. For example, the Earl of Orrery—a kindly but empty-headed man with literary pretensions—was often a host to Johnson and to others. In later years, when Johnson said "I never sought much after anybody," Boswell asked if Orrery was an exception. "No, Sir, I never went to him," replied Johnson, "but when he sent for me." Boswell then asked about Samuel Richardson, the novelist. "Yes, Sir," said Johnson. "But I sought after George Psalmanazar the most. I used to go and sit with him in an alehouse in the city."[7]

To cite just one other example—this time of the poverty in which writers of Grub Street could live—there was also the colorful poet Samuel Boyse, whom Johnson first got to know around 1740. Boyse, chronically on the verge of starvation, had developed ingenious ruses for raising money to stay alive, one of which was to have his wife report that he was on the point of death and that funds were needed for funeral expenses. If he was working on a book, he would pawn the first few pages, and then retrieve them by pawning the next. At one time (1740) he pawned everything, including his clothes and the sheets on his bed. Naked, and trying to write verses for the magazines—he could turn them out very quickly—he "sat up in bed with the blanket wrapt about him through which he had cut a hole large enough to admit his arm, and placing the paper upon his knee, scribbled in the best manner he could." We are quoting from a short biography (1753) by Robert Shiels, who got much of his information from Johnson. (Shiels was himself a poverty-stricken hack writer, whom Johnson at the time—primarily out of compassion—hired to help him with the *Dictionary*.) Boyse also discovered the use of paper collars and cuffs, which he would wear, even after he had pawned his trousers, with an overcoat hiding his middle section. Once when Boyse "was almost perishing with hunger," said Johnson, some money was given him (probably by Johnson), and he had some roast beef sent up. But he decided he "could not eat it without ketchup," and spent the rest of the money on that, truffles, and mushrooms, which he then ate in bed "for want of clothes, or even a shirt to sit up in."[8]

3

Around the world of Grub Street—mixing freely with it, and with no sense of snobbery about the people actually in it—was another group of people with literary or other intellectual interests. An example would be the young daughter of a Kentish clergyman, Elizabeth Carter, whom we have already met, and who—as Johnson said—could quickly make a pudding in her small lodgings for her Grub Street guests (or for anyone else) with the same unaffected ease with which she could translate Greek or Hebrew. Or another example would be a man he mentioned in later life: "The most literary conversation I ever enjoyed," he said, "was at the table of Jack Ellis, a money-scrivener [a notary who drew up contracts] behind the Royal Exchange, with whom I at one period used to dine generally once a week." Boswell, having heard this, long afterward looked up Jack Ellis and found him, at the age of ninety-three (1790), completely lacking "the discontent and fretfulness which too often molest old age." Ellis, in fact, had written a good deal, including a translation of Ovid's *Epistles*, but from modesty had either not published it or had done so anonymously.

This society, whatever its limitations, was refreshingly free from what Johnson called "cant," professional or social. These people did not receive things at second or third hand, but earned their knowledge through independent experience. What the best of them learned to value, therefore, and what the others at least groped toward, was a healthful essentialism: a scorn of (or more often an oblivion to) those refinements into quibble, or artificial distinctions and complaint (in Johnson's phrase, "imagination operating on luxury"), which are symbolized by the tale of the Princess suffering at the pressure of the pea under the mattress. There appeared to them no reason why the same intelligence that turned upon words, and the hugely varied uses of words that mankind called its "literature," should not also turn to the law, to government, to debates in Parliament, to medicine, or even to mechanics and industry.

For example, one of Johnson's friends at this time was Lewis Paul (the Huguenot inventor he had known in Birmingham before he married Tetty), who, with John Wyatt, had designed a spinning machine that, if it worked, could revolutionize the manufacture of cotton cloth. Johnson was always interested in mechanics to a degree that would now be surprising in a literary man. The appeal of it was as one more example of what human powers could do, and he could quickly grasp the principles of a mechanical work.* Though Johnson himself had no extra money, he had helped in 1740 to line up support for Paul and continued to befriend him. Financial investors in the project included Dr. Robert James and Edward Cave, whose magazine showed his interest in practical science, offering prizes for perpetual-motion machines and giving accounts of Benjamin Franklin's experiments in electricity. The project fell through, at some loss to the investors. But the general principle of the machine was correct, and, when Richard Arkwright later improved on it, he found that Johnson was the only person he knew who immediately, without explanation, got the point of it.[9]

4

One other friend Johnson was acquiring at this time should be mentioned. This was John Hawkins. His interest to us is that he alone—among those who were later to write extensively about Johnson—really knew something of this world in which Johnson was now living, and also knew many of the people involved. A man of strange contrarieties of character, Hawkins was now in his twenties—ten years younger than Johnson—and was preparing to become an attorney.† Though an extremely literal-minded man, Hawkins had an interest in literature and, above all, in music, and occasionally contributed writings—even verses—to the *Gentleman's Magazine*. Over the years,

---

* See below, p. 507.
† Though he began humbly—learning his occupation by being articled as a clerk to an older attorney—he had some success in his business, and in time became Chairman of the Middlesex Justices. It was for this that he was awarded his knighthood (1772).

helped by a wealthy marriage (1753), he acquired a sizable collection of rare pieces of music, and used it to advantage in a history of music (five volumes, 1776), which had the misfortune of being quickly over-shadowed by Charles Burney's classic *History of Music* (four volumes, 1776–89). In a similar way his biography of Johnson (1787), still a valuable source for Johnson's early and middle years, was to be eclipsed by Boswell's *Life*.

Unfortunately, few people—even good-natured ones like Joshua Reynolds and Bishop Percy—ever liked Hawkins. Percy, in fact, considered him "detestable." Though sanctimoniously rigid in his outward religious attitudes, he was contentious, nit-picking, and chronically suspicious. In repressing or hiding from himself his own motives, he projected them on others. So strong was his unconscious desire to foment animosity among others—under the guise of standing up for truth and virtue—that he could even stoop to the use of anonymous letters. At the same time, said Jeremy Bentham, he was "always wondering how there could be so much depravity in human nature." Whatever others thought of Hawkins, Johnson esteemed his religious principles ("Johnson appeared," said Reynolds, "to have little suspicion of hypocrisy in religion"), remained doggedly loyal to him, and appointed him one of the executors of his will. Hawkins used that position to advantage, and quickly got hold of materials that would help him write about Johnson's life. When he attended meetings with the other executors, he would charge the estate for coach hire. His parsimony was a lifelong habit. In the little Ivy Lane Club to which he and Johnson belonged (1749), he would refuse to pay his part of the bill for supper on the ground that he was not in the habit of eating supper anyway. It is this that led Johnson to confess that Hawkins was "a most unclubable man." In fact, despite Johnson's loyalty to him, his defenses of Hawkins could be very halfhearted. Thus, according to Fanny Burney, he found himself saying, "Why really I believe him to be an honest man at the bottom; but to be sure he is penurious, and he is mean, and it must be owned he has a degree of brutality, and a tendency to savageness, that cannot easily be defended."[10]

5

It is rather sad to note that there was some estrangement during these years between Johnson and David Garrick. After Garrick's first appearance in *Richard III* (October 1741), he had risen rapidly. By the following year he was receiving at Drury Lane the highest annual salary (five hundred guineas) that had ever been given an actor, a sum several times as much as his old teacher was able to earn. Disliking envy as he did, Johnson was able throughout most of his life not only to control it but also to plough it under. Yet, in this one case, it could sometimes emerge closer to the surface. They had begun their adventure to London together, with Johnson not only older but intellectually so much more talented. Yet, in a short time, while Johnson was in Grub Street, buffeting with hack work and living with the poor, Garrick was far surpassing him. Inevitably, as Johnson noted the rewards that could be showered on them, he began to think even less of "players" than he had before. If we leap ahead for an example, it is because the example subsumes any number of similar reductive remarks. Boswell puts him somewhat on the defensive by saying, "You are always heretical: you will never allow merit to a player." But what sort of "merit," replies Johnson, is to be allowed a man who simply "claps a hump on his back, and a lump on his leg, and cries '*I am Richard the Third*?'" How is he more deserving than "a rope-dancer, or a ballad singer"? Becoming more heated, he goes on:

"Nay, Sir, a ballad-singer is a higher man, for he does two things; he repeats and he sings: there is both recitation and musick in his performance: the player only recites." BOSWELL. . . . "A great player does what very few are capable to do: his art is a very rare faculty. *Who* can repeat Hamlet's soliloquy, 'To be, or not to be,' as Garrick does it?" JOHNSON. "Any body may. Jemmy, there (a boy about eight years old, who was in the room), will do it as well in a week." BOSWELL. "No, no, Sir: and as a proof of the merit of great acting, and of the value which mankind set upon it, Garrick has got a hundred thousand pounds." JOHNSON. "Is getting a hundred thousand pounds a proof of excellence? That has been done by a scoundrel commissary."[11]

The tension between them was as much Garrick's fault as his own. For Garrick did not at first bear success with negligence and grace. He put on airs. He would speak lightly of well-known figures, while at the same time he was proud of their acquaintance. The habit persisted in later life. One morning, as Boswell informed Johnson,

"when I went to breakfast with Garrick, who was very vain of his intimacy with Lord Camden, he accosted me thus:—'Pray now, did you—did you meet a little lawyer turning the corner, eh?'—'No, Sir, (said I) Pray what do you mean by the question?'—'Why, (replied Garrick, with an affected indifference, yet as if standing on tip-toe,) Lord Camden has this moment left me. We have had a long walk together.'" JOHNSON. "Well, Sir, Garrick talked very properly. Lord Camden *was* a *little lawyer* to be associating so familiarly with a player."

He also had moments of parsimony, despite his income. And when Johnson dropped in for tea, Garrick would scold the actress Peg Woffington for squandering his money by using up too many tea leaves and making the tea too strong. The tea was already "as red as blood." This rather shocked Johnson, a part of whose assimilative nature was forever identified with Garrick, was deeply proud of him, and warmly wished him success. Garrick was as much a part of him now as when, long afterward, Richard Cumberland, the dramatist, saw him standing before Garrick's grave "bathed in tears."[12]

Yet, as Garrick began to command riches, to amass rare editions of Shakespeare, and to act as though he had himself invented Shakespeare, Johnson—with his sense of the undergrowth in literary history, of the thousands of shrubs of effort in every forest needed to produce one or two dominating trees—was naturally tempted to make the remarks he did about "entertainers" who considered themselves (and were considered by the public) as authorities. An almost cruel, if amusing, example is related by Edmond Malone. Garrick, who meant only to express his own sense of the depths of Shakespeare (even though he justly felt he had already increased the public appreciation of Shakespeare), enthusiastically said in company, "Now I have quitted the theatre, I will sit down and read Shakespeare." Before the applause for this tribute (in tribute both to Shakespeare and to his own taste) had time to express itself, it was punctured by Johnson's remark: "Tis time you should, for I much doubt if you ever examined one of his plays from the first scene to the last."[13]

But then, as everyone in later years began to notice—after Johnson himself had become famous, though far from affluent—he would never allow anyone else to abuse Garrick, or to detract from his reputation in any way. He could tell himself (rightly) that he alone had earned the right to criticize Garrick—having started life in London together with him when they were young and poor, and having personally faced for fifteen years or more the contrast between their two lives (a contrast that can become more poignant to the degree that the personal ties are closer). And the minute that others—without a fraction of his own credentials—began to dismiss Garrick, his protective anger was aroused. Even now, in his later thirties, though the difference between their lives was at its most extreme, the unknown hack writer was glad to contribute what he could when his famous young friend—at the age of only thirty—became manager of the Drury Lane Theatre (1747). Garrick wished to celebrate the opening of the theater under the new management. Long ago, when Garrick was only ten or twelve and had put on his first play at Gilbert Walmesley's house, he had asked Johnson to write him a *Prologue*. Johnson, preoccupied with other things, forgot to do it in time. Now he more than made up for it, and wrote the fine *Prologue Spoken at the Opening of the Theatre in Drury-Lane*, for Garrick to recite during the first week of the season (September 15–19).* His own name was not mentioned, and, as far as the public was aware, the author was Garrick himself. Johnson took this for granted. It was done as a personal favor to his friend.

6

It is against this general background—of setting, of friends and acquaintances, of general atmosphere—that Johnson was doing the writing he did in his early and middle thirties: the hack work, so gifted in its way, though now largely forgotten; the writing for the *Gentleman's Magazine*—which he half helped to create in its formative years—and, above all, the *Parliamentary Debates*.

But it was all, as he knew, only too ephemeral. He was now at an age when almost every major writer is at least embarked upon work of the general kind or type that would later establish him if he were not established already. In particular, as he forced himself to turn out the *Parliamentary Debates*, his hunger for essentialism—for the "stability" of concrete experience, the "putting to use" of moral experience, so that we could learn "how to live"—was beginning to assert itself.

In the midst of the political writing and the *Parliamentary Debates*, however brilliantly this was done, another part of him began to register an accumulated fatigue. As he was soon to say, while we discourse

* The sixty-two lines of the poem were "composed before I threw a single couplet on paper . . . I did not afterwards change more than a word in it, and that was done at the remonstrances of Garrick. I did not think his criticism just; but it was necessary he should be satisfied with what he was to utter" ("Anecdotes by George Stevens," *JM*, II, 313–14). On the very first night (September 15), Garrick became ill, and someone else recited the *Prologue* for him. The work was then printed anonymously, together with an *Epilogue*, probably by Garrick, on October 8. The premises and ideas of the *Prologue* are best discussed in the context of Johnson's dramatic criticism generally. See below, pp. 401–6.

so blithely and easily about the "downfall of kingdoms, and revolutions of empire," it is the daily life of individuals that is our real subject if we are seeking to know the "human heart." Very few read about the downfall of kingdoms with excited empathy. In general, the accounts of such things "are read with great tranquillity," without much loss of sleep or with anything approaching the anxiety people would have about getting the next meal if getting the meal were a problem. Whether we are speaking of "the man whose faculties have been engrossed by business, and whose heart never fluttered but at the rise or fall of stocks," or those whose happiness is attached to prestige (which comes from the word meaning "illusion") or to the thought of applause from others, or those who would surrender anything for romantic love, or those whose principal problem is simply to live with themselves, the major concern of the human imagination—the main source of happiness and unhappiness, of hope and fear—is in our personal lives.[14]

It was partly in reaction to the *Parliamentary Debates* and the other journalistic writing he was doing in his early thirties that Johnson discovered (though he was not yet to exploit) another form of writing—biography. That discovery—after it had been sufficiently digested by him—was to have a profound influence on the later development of biography, and to lift it from the humble position it had occupied. One reason is simply that no writer of Johnson's general stature and capacities had ever before turned to this form of writing, and when this much mind is brought to bear on any form—particularly one still relatively undeveloped—the results are naturally creative. Above all, no one had ever turned to biography who had an equally direct knowledge not only of human nature but also of what human (and not merely literary) talent is or can be and of what can permit or encourage its development. A final reason is that no writer has ever approached biography with an interest so strongly personal and so broadly humane, with so searching a concern for the uses of biography "as giving us what comes *near* to ourselves, what we can *turn to use*."[15]

Biography was a "discovery" for Johnson because of the way he started writing the biographical sketches—at first not with deliberate plan or theoretical ideal already in mind, but only as an interesting supplement to the other journalistic writing he was doing. In fact, of the eight short biographies he wrote for the *Gentleman's Magazine* (1738–42), half are little more than translations, with minor changes, of other works: the lives of Father Paolo Sarpi (November 1738), which we have already noticed; the great Dutch physician and scientist Herman Boerhaave (January–April 1739), who had died the year before; the seventeenth-century French physician and botanist Louis Morin (July 1741); and Pieter Burman (April 1742), a famous Dutch scholar who had recently died (1741).* Two others are so heavily indebted to sources as to come close at times to mere paraphrase—the lives of the British Admirals Robert Blake (June 1740) and, with some fine generalizations occasionally added, Sir Francis Drake (August 1740 to January 1741). A seventh biographical sketch (December 1740 and February 1741) is of the precocious young German scholar J. P. Baratier (whose name was Anglicized in Johnson's sketch as "Barretier"). Though he had died at the age of only nineteen, he had already written impressive scholarly studies, and was amassing materials for a large history of the Thirty Years' War. Baratier's father had written a series of letters about the precocious boy; and Johnson draws heavily on these, sweeping them into translation or paraphrase, though often pausing to insert a comment of his own. Somewhat freer in its use of sources is the eighth "life"—that of the seventeenth-century physician John Sydenham, written both for a new edition of Sydenham's works (1742) and for the *Gentleman's Magazine.*

At much the same time he made other minor excursions into biography as a help to his old friend Dr. Robert James, whom we have met before and who spent twenty years, said Johnson, without being sober. This was Dr. James's large *Medicinal Dictionary*, which Johnson helped him to plan. To interest subscribers, Johnson wrote the *Proposals* for this large work, and, in order to launch it—the book appeared in installments, in alphabetical order, starting in February 1742 —contributed at least a dozen short biographies of physicians, mainly at the start (Actuarius, Aegeneta, Archagathus, Aretaeus, and at least eight others).[16] He later said he had learned a fair amount about medicine by helping James, but actually he was a lifelong amateur

---

* "Sarpi" is an abridged translation of Le Courayer's *Vie*, which is in turn translated from the Italian. "Boerhaave" is translated or, in places, heavily paraphrased from the funeral oration (1738) by Boerhaave's friend Albert Schultens; "Morin" is substantially an English version (as it was frankly stated to be when it was published) of the eulogy of Morin by Fontenelle (1724); and "Burman," except for the insertion of occasional comments, is taken directly from the funeral oration (1741) by Herman Oosterdyke Schact (see Bergen Evans, "Dr. Johnson as a Biographer" [Ph.D. diss., Harvard University, 1932], II, 1–23).

student of the subject. These biographical sketches also drew heavily on other sources, from which he translated directly or paraphrased.

To the modern reader, it may come as a jolt to hear that so much in the early "lives" is direct translation or mere paraphrase of other works. Even if we remind ourselves that this was the common journalistic procedure of the time (and that all of these works—like his other writings in these years—were anonymous, and that he himself was far from claiming credit for them), we still feel a disappointment. Knowing of Johnson's later impact on biography, one would naturally have hoped to learn something from these early "lives" about his method or approach. But finding how little in them is original, and dreading lest the passages he singles out for praise or analysis should prove to be by another hand, even the student may be tempted to disregard them. It is true that they can be scrutinized too anxiously; and we ourselves, concerned with so many other aspects of Johnson's life and work, have been citing them for the purpose of notice rather than analysis. Yet at least four points can be made: (1) The interest that led him in the first place—when he was so preoccupied with other matters—to make these voluntary excursions into biography partly as a form of recreation. (2) The subjects he chose (aside from the two British Admirals, doubtless suggested by Cave for patriotic and political purposes): physicians, whom he saw with idealism as "healers" for a humanity condemned to spend far too much of its time in suffering; or scholars and scientists who exemplified what human powers could do—a subject that especially fascinated him. (3) The appeal of most of his subjects, especially Herman Boerhaave, as "role models" of what he himself might have hoped to become. For generations people have pointed out the similarity to Johnson himself in what they regarded as Johnson's portrait of Boerhaave. The fact that the key passages are a translation adds to the interest of the similarity rather than detracts from it. For the portrait could not then be described as a projection onto Boerhaave of qualities in himself. Instead it presented an ideal to which he aspired and which he gradually assimilated. (4) But the primary gain from translating or piecing together these short "lives" was his growing perception of the special ways in which biography—permitting as it does the comparison between life and life, between one person's total experience and our own—can assist us by supporting, encouraging, perhaps clarifying, or at the very least extending, the experience of living.

7

The results were to appear quickly in the *Life of Savage* (1744), which still remains a small masterpiece of biography. Savage had died suddenly in the prison at Bristol (August 1, 1743).* Because of his colorful life, public interest could be easily caught. There was the mystery of his identity—was he or was he not the son of the Countess of Macclesfield?—and with it the famous scandal surrounding his parents or supposed parents. And there were other elements of interest: his trial for murder, the number of prominent people he knew, and his picturesque way of living. Inevitably accounts of his life—eager only to capitalize on the scandalous sides of it—would be rushed into print. "Under the Title of the Life of Savage," as Johnson wrote to Cave, "they will publish only a Novel filled with romantick Adventures, and imaginary Amours."[17] Before this could happen, Johnson wished to present the story and character of his friend in full as far as he could, and also—this was something new in the biography even of authors— to discuss and to do justice to Savage's own writing. Edward Cave, who had known Savage well, was glad to sponsor it, helped Johnson gather materials, and bought from the keeper of the Bristol prison the manuscripts of two plays Savage had left behind when he died. But the autumn of 1743 was a busy time for Johnson. Aside from the *Parliamentary Debates*, he was also at work for Cave on what, in a letter, he refers to as "our Historical Design." Of this (for it was never finished) we know only that Johnson hoped to make it "the most complete account of Parliamentary proceedings that can be contrived," that it was to be a fairly large book, and that it was concentrating especially on the reign of George I.[18] He was also in the midst of other work— the catalogue of the large Harleian Library, discussed below—for another publisher. Moreover, he was not very well, and often lacked money for candles in order to write at night ("The boy," he says in the letter to Cave, mentioned above, "found me writing this almost in the dark, when I could not quite easily read yours").

When he at last set to work on the *Life of Savage* late in the autumn, he wrote very rapidly. On one occasion he wrote "forty-eight of the printed octavo pages," he said later, "at a sitting, but then I sat up all night." This was about a third of the number of pages Johnson wrote

* See above, p. 181.

(of the total of 186 pages in the book, roughly 40 consist of quotations). According to Thomas Tyers, Johnson once said that the amount of time he took for the whole thing ("and valued himself upon it") was thirty-six hours.[19] The work could still be as good as it is, despite the short time he spent on it, because he was writing from a full mind—a direct, personal knowledge of his subject; a sympathetic identification with Savage that stimulated eloquence and gave shape and insightful meaning to his conception of his friend's life; an observant acquaintance with both human nature generally and the literary context in which Savage wrote; and the aroused interest in the uses of biography given him by the exercise of writing or translating the earlier biographical sketches for the *Gentleman's Magazine*. By December 14 he was finished. Cave then paid him fifteen guineas for the copyright, and had the biography published anonymously a couple of months later (February 11, 1744).

Nothing quite like the *Life of Savage* had ever appeared before. As with most forms of writing that prove valuable as well as original, the novelty lay in the unpredictable combination of qualities usually found separately in more specialized and restricted forms: (1) Implied throughout is the high-minded Plutarchian ideal that example is the greatest of teachers (example mainly of what to follow but also of what to beware). In Johnson this becomes transmuted into something more complex: the example of a fellow human being, whose conflicting virtues and weaknesses help to create the web of life in which he is caught. (2) The new realistic fiction, which he prized to the extent that it could "exhibit life in its true state . . . influenced by passions and qualities which are really to be found in conversing with mankind." The only difference is that in biography the people and the incidents must be factually true. But the goal is the same—the presentation of "human life and manners." (3) Because of the character of Savage's own life, some of the details could remind readers of the eighteenth-century genre of "criminal biography" (mystery, a murder trial, the courts, the atmosphere of the slums), except that here they are lifted by the dignity of the context. (4) Still another form coalesced in the *Life of Savage* is the "moral essay" as Johnson was soon to rediscover it (if he was not already rediscovering it now in the process of writing the *Life of Savage*). It is wrapped around, in, and through the narrative; and it appears at its best when Johnson—like the chorus in a Greek drama—stops to comment on human life in a way that anticipates his finest moral essays.* (5) Lastly, by engrafting into

* See below, pp. 494–95.

the story of Savage's life a discussion of his writings—in order both to understand his inner life and to do justice to what was, after all, Savage's principal effort—Johnson invented "critical biography." However strange it may seem theoretically—for what does a writer have primarily to offer except his writings in their totality?—biographical accounts of writers had rarely attempted this. They had tended instead to concentrate on the external details of the writer's life, pausing only to list titles, as they appeared chronologically, with a few sentences of description. Here, in this anonymous, rapidly written *Life*, Johnson created the prototype of his own *Lives of the Poets*, written at the end of his own career, which in turn have served as the prototype of "critical biography."

The novelty of the work was soon felt—and continued to be felt for a generation—by discerning readers. Eight years later (1752), when Joshua Reynolds returned home to Devonshire after studying in Italy, he picked up the book, he said, knowing nothing of its author, and "began to read it while he was standing with his arm leaning against a chimney piece. It seized his attention so strongly, that, not being able to lay down the book till he had finished it, when he attempted to move, he found his arm totally benumbed."[20]

8

In the crowded hack work of Johnson's early and middle thirties, two major interests can be seen emerging that relate directly to the work of his maturity. Together they reflect the twin ideals first represented to him by Cornelius (though transmuted into something rather different by Johnson's moral imagination and his own personal character). One of them is subsumed by his phrase "human life and manners." This appears prominently in the early biographies, especially the *Life of Savage*. After this the line continues through the moral writing of Johnson's forties.

The second interest appears in the application of his omnivorous curiosity and his tenacious memory to the world of books, language, criticism, and scholarship. Here the guiding ideal was Cornelius's advice to seek both "general knowledge" and the "general principles of every science," which over the years had become symbolized for Johnson by the great Renaissance scholars who had taken all knowledge for their province. It is this second interest, reflected also in the numerous articles and reviews, that is to culminate in the *Dictionary*.

Afterward these two ideals—previously distinct yet modifying each other—were to become permanently united.

The most dramatic example of this side of Johnson in his early and middle thirties is a work that is still of some importance to historians. Robert Harley, the Earl of Oxford, who had been Prime Minister under Queen Anne, had assembled a vast library of pamphlets, tracts, rare books, and manuscripts dealing with every aspect of British history in the sixteenth and seventeenth centuries. This had been increased by his son, the second Earl, until the library included about 50,000 books, 350,000 pamphlets, and well over 7,000 volumes of manuscripts. After the second Earl's death, his daughter put up for sale the books and pamphlets.[21] (The manuscripts were bought by Parliament [1753], and placed in the British Museum four years later.) The books and pamphlets were then bought for resale—at what was then an enormous price (£13,000), though this would scarcely have paid for the bindings of the books—by Thomas Osborne, whom Johnson had got to know because he was also the publisher of James's *Medicinal Dictionary*. To dispose profitably of this remarkable library, public interest had to be aroused. This could be done only through a printed catalogue that would do more than simply list titles of books. Yet to provide anything like a real descriptive catalogue of this library could take years. Osborne at present had lined up for work on it only William Oldys, Harley's former secretary. Oldys, a man thirteen years older than Johnson, is now largely forgotten. But he was one of the most gifted antiquarians of the century, and remains one of the pioneers in the scholarship of literary history and biography.[22] Oldys, though industrious and accurate, was not rapid. Osborne had been struck by the speed and grasp of Johnson's mind, and offered to hire him as joint cataloguer. Johnson's imagination was caught by the sheer magnitude of the task. Though he was still writing the *Parliamentary Debates*, this provided a change. He accepted, and, in order to stimulate public interest, immediately wrote a "General Account" of the library (December 1742).

He now "resembled a lion in harness," said Hawkins, as he quickly began work on the catalogue. Within a mere three months (March 1743), the first two volumes of the catalogue were published, covering 15,242 works, digested under particular headings, and occasionally (for the policy of trying to apply this to all the works was soon dropped as impossible) with notes on the author, the edition, and the hands through which the book had passed. Within another year (January

1744), the next two volumes were ready, covering 20,724 more titles. After that their work on the catalogue stopped.* Meanwhile, as these two volumes were going to press, Johnson and Oldys began (December 1743) to select and prepare for publication the collection of pamphlets, in eight volumes, known as the *Harleian Miscellany* (published in installments, 1744–46), which is still a standard reference work and for which, as a Preface, he wrote the penetrating manifesto on the study and uses of documents later known as his "Essay on the Origin and Importance of Small Tracts and Fugitive Pieces."[23]

The famous occasion when Johnson knocked Osborne down with a folio, and put his foot on Osborne's neck, happened while Johnson was working on the *Miscellany*. Osborne was a bull-like, thickset man, with a loud voice and a domineering manner. Many stories were also told of his ignorance. (One of them, hard to believe, is that he was unaware Milton's *Paradise Lost* was an English poem, and coming across a French translation of it, he hired one of his "garreteers"—hack writers living in garrets—to translate it into English prose.)[24] Naturally, in his work for the *Miscellany*, Johnson had to look through the pamphlets in order to judge their value. While doing so, he would sometimes read quickly on out of curiosity. Given the speed with which Johnson was doing the work, Osborne was getting a tremendous bargain for the small pay provided, and Johnson knew it. Yet Osborne, said Hawkins, at once upbraided him "with inattention and delay, in such coarse language as few men would use." When Johnson replied that the delay was necessary, Osborne told him he lied. At this, Johnson picked up a huge sixteenth-century Greek Bible, felled Osborne to the floor, placed his foot on him, and told him not to be in a hurry to rise lest he next be kicked down the stairs. The story

---

* A final volume was published by Osborne in 1746. But it was simply a list (15,284 titles) of his unsold stock. Estimates of the comparative work of Johnson and Oldys on the first four volumes vary widely. They are all based on hearsay or speculation. Boswell's sole remark is in his very incomplete list of Johnson's works. Referring to the catalogue, he adds the words (I, 17) "in which the Latin Accounts of the Books were written by him." This has been interpreted overhastily to mean that the English commentary was done only by Oldys. Two other extremes are represented by Yeowell, in his memoir of Oldys (n. 23, above), who conjectured that Johnson was responsible for the bibliographical and biographical remarks in Vols. I and II, and Oldys for those in Vols. III and IV; and Hawkins (p. 133), who said that Oldys stopped after Vol. II, possibly from a falling out with Osborne, and that Johnson went on alone for the next two volumes. Hawkins tends to be reliable in his facts for this period of Johnson's life. On the other hand, if Oldys quarreled with Osborne, he was back at work for him by December 1743.

became widely known only because Osborne himself was foolish enough to broadcast it with loud complaint.[25]

9

His work on the *Harleian Miscellany* could have carried him well into 1745, providing a supplement to the salary he was receiving for helping Cave to edit the *Gentleman's Magazine*—a job that also continued into this year, but apparently not longer. In this latter capacity, which naturally took him often to Cave's office at St. John's Gate, one little scene from his closing months with the *Magazine* survives (January 1745). They were putting together the February number, and Cave, as guests for dinner, had Johnson and Stephen Barrett, a young curate who had been recently at Oxford, and who later told the story. After the cloth was removed, Cave, going through the items to be assembled for the next issue, picked up a Latin translation of a poem by the now-forgotten John Byrom. It was the right length, but an "indifferent performance." Could either of his two guests "brush it up"? Johnson said, "Give it to Mr. Barrett"—Barrett had distinguished himself at Oxford in writing Latin verse—"he'll correct it for you, in a minute." Barrett was diffident, and said that if Johnson would alternate with him—each doing a couplet—he would do what he could. "Very well," said Johnson, "do you begin." Barrett pleaded that elders came first, and tossed the paper to Johnson across the table. "He return'd it, in a moment; and so it passed from the one to the other, like a shuttlecock; Cave chuckling all the while to see it pass and repass, so rapidly."[26]

Two other small items may be mentioned. His old friend Harry Hervey, who had been such a notorious rake that his family had wished to disown him ("He was a vicious man, but very kind to me. If you call a dog Hervey, I shall love him"), had suddenly changed his life, and entered the Church as a clergyman. His wife, Catherine Aston (sister of both Molly Aston, whom Johnson had found so entrancing, and Magdalen, Walmesley's wife), had brought him a large fortune. Out of gratitude toward her family, Hervey had taken the name "Aston" and had become rector of Shotley, in Suffolk. To Hervey's distress, he was suddenly asked to preach the annual "Festival Sermon" for the "Sons of the Clergy" at St. Paul's Cathedral (May 2). It was always a splendid occasion. The Archbishop of Canterbury and other dignitaries of the Church would attend. So would the Lord Chief

Justice. After this, there was a feast. The sermon, of which the subject was usually "charity," was then published. In panic, Hervey turned to Johnson, who quickly wrote the sermon for him, which the reformed Hervey, in full regalia, then delivered at St. Paul's to an appreciative audience.[27] Another bit of ghost-writing was done for an Irish clergyman, Samuel Madden, who had written a long poem, called *Boulter's Monument*, in praise of the former Primate of Ireland, Hugh Boulter. Johnson cut it down by some hundreds of lines, and tried to make it less bad. Madden, he said later, "was very thankful, and very generous, for he gave me ten guineas, which was to me at that time a great sum."[28]

10

But his real effort, which began in the winter of 1744–45, was very much in the wake of his work on the Harleian Library. Looking as he had (however quickly) through thousands of books and pamphlets from the sixteenth and seventeenth centuries, his imagination had been caught by the possibility of editing the works of the greatest English poet. The men who had been editing Shakespeare, he could see, were far from acquainted with the full context of his age. They were often working in a vacuum. A new edition, in which he would follow up the kind of thing he had learned in helping with the *Harleian Catalogue* and the eight-volume *Miscellany*, and combine it with his own literary knowledge of sources, poetics, and language, would not only establish his reputation but would be profitable to Cave or any other publisher who would sponsor it.

During the winter of 1744–45, he began to work on it, taking some scenes from *Macbeth* to provide a specimen of what could be done. From this he put together a short work with the modest title *Miscellaneous Observations on the Tragedy of Macbeth*. He also added some remarks on a new sumptuous edition of Shakespeare (by Sir Thomas Hanmer), which had recently appeared. (If we do not discuss the *Observations* in more detail at the moment, it is because the premises and values are subsumed in Johnson's edition of Shakespeare twenty years later.)* At the end of this specimen there was an announcement of a new edition of Shakespeare (in ten small volumes, at a low price, for which subscriptions could now be taken). The *Observations*, to-

* See below, pp. 398–406.

gether with the announcement, was published on April 6. But the announcement of another new edition of Shakespeare alarmed the publisher, Jacob Tonson, who quickly wrote to Cave (April 11) that the copyright of Shakespeare was controlled by himself and his associates, and that they were ready to begin suit. Cave at once backed down. Any thought of going further with Shakespeare was put aside. The reason for Tonson's alarm, and why he took a stand so quickly, is that he and his associates were themselves planning a new edition. It was being edited for them by the formidable scholar and theologian William Warburton, now in his late forties. When that edition appeared (1747), the cantankerous Warburton dismissed as beneath serious notice "all those things which have been published under the title of Essays, Remarks, Observations, &c on Shakespeare," with one exception. That exception was an anonymous pamphlet of "some critical notes on *Macbeth*, given as a specimen of a projected edition, and written, as appears, by a man of parts and genius." Though Warburton did not mention him by name (the work was published anonymously), Johnson was always grateful for the remark: "He praised me at a time when praise was of value to me."[29]

Part III

IN
THE
MIDDLE
OF
THE WAY:
THE
MORAL
PILGRIMAGE

Chapter 14

Entrance into Middle Age;
Uncertainties;
Problems in the Marriage

Suddenly, as he approached thirty-six (September 1745) the astonishing flurry of activity, which he had sustained for so long, began to subside, and within another year Gilbert Walmesley was writing to Garrick, now a celebrity, asking him to tell Johnson, "I esteem him as a great genius—quite lost both to himself and the world."[1]

Most of the past eight years (and he had made a late start) had been spent in the midst of Grub Street, which he was to define in the *Dictionary* as a place "much inhabited by writers of small histories, dictionaries, and temporary poems, whence any *mean production* is called Grub-street." The psychological gain, as he was later to realize, had been enormous. After the long breakdown, from twenty to almost twenty-five, followed by the failure of the school at Edial, another life had become engrafted on the first. Through it, and his responsibilities to Tetty, he had been able for years to fight off—and perhaps conquer for good—that fearful combination of anxiety, self-punishment, and helpless apathy that excessive self-demand could create within his divided nature, and which had so darkened his twenties that he had almost despaired of his sanity. Grub Street had its lacks, but he owed it a great deal.

Yet by now this second life could understandably begin to seem a dead end. The work of these years—as we ourselves look back on it now, knowing what it included—was remarkable not only in bulk and range but also in unpredictable talent. Yet one thing about it is often forgotten. None of these writings had carried his name, not even the more personal ones like the poem *London* or the *Life of Savage*. This was partly his own decision, at least for some of them. It was as though he were refusing to make any claim, and denying that all this was a serious bid, a serious effort. (Significantly the first work to carry his name was to bear the title *The Vanity of Human Wishes*.) As a result, he was still unknown to the general public. He took this for granted. More important: he had done nothing that he himself felt had used his talents (throughout his life he was always thinking of the parable of the talents in the Bible)—nothing to which he even wished to affix his name. Yet he was now about to enter middle age.

During all these years—in fact, ever since he had known Gilbert Walmesley—law had seemed to him the ideal profession for someone of his own interests and talents. More than ever, the thought of the law was now returning to haunt him as the missed ideal, "the road not taken." His life, given even optimistic expectations, was at least half over. If there was to be a new start, it could not be further delayed. True, he lacked the necessary entrance ticket into the profession, a degree in law (or, for that matter, a degree of any kind). But much of his work had shown his ability to handle the subjects dealt with in law. How many lawyers could have written the *Parliamentary Debates* in the time he did?

Late in 1745, or early the next year, he made a final effort, and wrote to his old friend Dr. Adams. Johnson knew, if only slightly, young Richard Smallbrooke, son of the Bishop of Lichfield. Smallbrooke had just taken the degree of D.C.L. (Doctor of Civil Law), and was now practicing as an advocate in "Doctors' Commons." This court, which was concerned with canon and civil law, was self-governing, and might be willing to make exceptions to the requirement of a degree. Johnson himself would be embarrassed to approach Smallbrooke directly, and especially to speak of his own qualifications, whereas Adams could do so with some authority. Could Adams sound out Smallbrooke and discover "whether a Person might be admitted to practise as an Advocate there" without the degree of D.C.L.? Adams quotes him as saying that though he was admittedly a stranger to the formal study of the subject, yet "whatever is a Profession and maintains numbers must be within the reach of common Abilities and some degree of Industry." Adams thought the idea excellent, and did what he could. But "the Degree was an insurmountable Bar," and though Johnson was not a complainer, Adams could tell that he felt this "as a great disappoint-ment."[2]

2

Wondering what he did at this time (from the autumn of 1745 to the spring of 1746), people have for generations speculated about causes. Did he quarrel with Cave, and is that why no more writings appeared every month in the *Magazine?* Or had he perhaps—the thought, though insane, persists—joined the Jacobite rebellion of 1745 and hur-ried north to support the Stuart cause, or, staying in London, served as a sort of underground agent?* There is a tendency in human nature, whenever we are considering the lives of others, to expect them to proceed at a far brisker pace than we ourselves do, not because we are uncharitable but because our vicarious interest is better able to notice results than to share the actual process and daily crawl of other people's experience. In viewing others, however well-intentioned our empathy, our imaginations are naturally less fatigued and clogged with the distractions, uncertainties, and inner resistances that make up so much of daily life. Hence even the sympathetic biographer or critic, who may take ten years for a book, can become puzzled or suspicious if his subject seems to tarry for ten months between writings, and is ready to assume that only something very specific or concrete could have intervened. Especially if his subject had written rapidly before, it does not now seem "in character"—it is not at all like him—to stop suddenly in this way. What could have happened? Or perhaps he did not really stop. Perhaps there were works hidden away that can yet be discovered?

Above all, when we come to the onset of middle age, a curtain descends on any consideration of the obvious. It is a commonplace of psychology that few people care to dwell consciously on the problems of middle age. To those in their twenties and early thirties, the prob-lems are not yet real. Those already entered on middle age would

---

* On April 16, when the climactic Battle of Culloden occurred ("I have heard him declare," said Boswell, "that if holding up his right hand would have secured victory at Culloden to Prince Charles's army, he was not sure he would have held it up"), he was hard at work on his "Short Scheme for compiling a new Dictionary," which he was preparing to submit to the publishers at the end of the month. For a charming fictional account of Johnson supporting the Jacobite rebellion, see John Buchan's *Midwinter.*

prefer not to have their attention riveted to it directly lest, like the head of Medusa, it rob them of their stamina and leave them paralyzed. Their first concern is to keep their own balance on what has begun to seem a sort of tightrope, and not look down but rather across—to an end, aim, or purpose. Nor, afterward, is there much interest in dwelling on the traumas of middle age, for the simple reason that few people are confident they are safely past them. Too often the fifties—to some extent the sixties—seem only an extension of the "dark middle years," with the further disadvantage that the half-consoling word "middle" has now ceased to apply. So in the fine passage on middle age in T. S. Eliot's *East Coker*, where, echoing Dante, he begins:

> In the middle, *not only in the middle of the way*
> *But all the way*, in a dark wood, in a bramble,
> On the edge of a grimpen, where is no secure foothold . . .
> . . . They all go into the dark . . .

What has happened to us is not only the first massive shake to human identity since adolescence, but probably the strongest we receive after becoming adults—aside from individual calamities—until we suddenly find ourselves in old age. True, it can be deferred, if not avoided, provided we are able to distract ourselves and keep busy enough in our late thirties and throughout our forties, as Johnson himself managed to do. But even if we push it aside through the artifices of what he liked to call "bustle" ("getting on horseback in a ship"), we begin to feel more acutely that time is passing; and this is to become a perennial theme of the *Diaries* that soon begin.

3

If we are laboring the obvious, it is because the obvious is often forgotten. As Johnson was soon to say, people in general "more frequently require to be reminded than informed."[3] More than that of most human beings, his life from thirty-six into his early fifties—and most of what he wrote—must be seen in the light of all that we know of what it means to enter and pass through middle age. The great writing on human nature and destiny—from the age of thirty-nine to fifty—is in large part a comment on this experience.

What he shares with us all is the feeling he had of being at sea as he entered the later thirties; the sense of time passing, of the melting away of alternative choices, of the lessening of chances to make a fundamentally new start. Yet he was always to deny fiercely—as if in an effort to drive the thought into himself—that a new start was impossible in anything, provided one really cared. What he shares with many of us, if not all, is the desperate energy with which he was soon to plunge into fourteen years of astonishing effort, thus forestalling the more personal results of the inevitable "middle-age reconsideration" until, in his fifties, the pressures toward it became very strong. And the way in which he was like at least some of us was in the fearful experience of his fifties, when, after keeping things at bay by the achievement of his forties, life caught up with him, and—with the revenge of what has accumulated through postponement—exacted a fearful psychological toll.

But Johnson was almost unique in combining an external preoccupation with a work of the most demanding sort, the famous *Dictionary*, with an internal awareness of all that could be suggested by the phrase "middle-age reconsideration" (while at the same time having the ability to see this almost retrospectively). At least he is almost unique in having expressed his sensibilities so powerfully in the decade of moral writing that begins with *The Vanity of Human Wishes*, written at thirty-nine, and continuing down to *Rasselas*, when he was approaching fifty. What is especially involved in the inner life, and expressed profoundly in the writing, is the recognition that begins to deepen in middle age that our "choices" in life, in careers, in marriage, in everything else, are now—with our lives at least half over—bringing completely unexpected and unwelcome chickens home to roost. Or, to change the metaphor, because we selected one fork in the road rather than another—and did we really "choose" it?—we have not merely forfeited the chance of taking that other fork (though we might like to think we could still do it, yet, as Robert Frost said, "knowing how way leads on to way," we really doubt that we can "ever come back"). But, more distressingly, we find that our "choice" of each fork of the road has brought with it so much that we had never bargained for—so much that we never wished for, or even dreamed of as an inevitable by-product, in that original idealism or hope that had inspired or hovered about the choices we had made. We must defer discussion of this until we turn to the actual writing that moves in, through, and refreshingly beyond all we have been saying. But the point, at the moment, could be put in a single line from *The Vanity of Human Wishes*, which condenses so much of this inner experience: "*Fate wings with ev'ry wish the afflictive dart.*"

4

In Johnson's personal situation, as he entered his later thirties, there was a special complication—and a daily rebuke to his conscience—in the disintegration beginning to take place in Tetty. She was increasingly turning to drink, hypochondria, and occasionally opium (we should remember how freely opium was taken then for illness of any sort, usually in the liquid form of laudanum, in which it is mixed with alcohol). Like nothing else, the daily sight of this impressed upon him his failure to live up to what had been expected, the ironic unpredictability of life generally, and the remorseless speed with which time was moving through their lives.

What Tetty was essentially doing now was to retreat from life. She had at first been able to defy her family as she did—when she had married Johnson back in her mid-forties—because of the confidence of her romantic nature that she was acquiring a new lease on existence, a second chance. In return, she had surrendered family, friends, her small fortune, and the comfort of familiar surroundings. Wrenched into the strange world of London at the age of forty-nine (1737), with no friends of her own and with her remaining money rapidly melting away, she had still tried to retain her self-respect, as we have noticed, and had kept her good humor and managed to repress her disappointment. But she stayed indoors, within their crowded lodgings, and—at once rustically proud and timid—remained aloof from what she doubtless considered the motley crowd of Grub Street figures with whom her husband worked. She tried to present him with a pleasant home when he returned ("A clean floor is *so* comfortable," she would say).

But now, in her middle fifties, the disappointments were catching up. Soon after she had come to London she may have started to drink a little during the day in order to soften the sense of loss about her old life and the disappointment in what had followed. About this time Johnson abruptly stopped drinking. Doubtless he was trying to set an example. But the habit for Tetty had by now begun to deepen. Always uneasy about the difference in their ages, she became more so now, and pathetically began to use rouge and make-up. It is from this period (in the late 1740's) that the descriptions of her—always quoted—date:

Garrick's cruel gibe about her as "a little painted Poppet; full of Affectation and rural Airs of Elegance," with "swelled cheeks of a florid red, produced by thick painting, and increased by liberal use of cordials; flaring and fantastic in her dress"; or, still later, the remark of Robert Levet's, when he was pumped by Mrs. Thrale (Levet, a reliable witness, was under no temptation to exaggerate), that "She was always drunk & reading Romances in her Bed, where She killed herself by taking Opium."[4]

But the defeated Tetty was putting on the make-up and the "flaring and fantastic" clothes as much for Johnson as from fright and ebbing self-respect. Johnson, of course, knew this, just as he knew why she drank. And his sudden anger at the airy blitheness with which, much later, Anna Williams could dismiss the temptation to drink (however firmly he himself abstained from it) was because he thought that, as a friend of his wife's, she should have known better: "I wonder, Madam, that *you have not penetration to see the inducement . . .*" When he returned at the end of the day—if he was not out dining with Cave at St. John's Gate, or snatching a meal at a tavern with his writing friends —she knew he would be spreading papers around, as the night wore on, half-talking to himself as he dashed down writing in order to meet a deadline, and not coming to bed until 3:00 A.M. or later. Still, when he came home, there was a considered courtesy—stylized, but with mutual understanding and a sense of helplessness—as they met each other, each trying to lift from the other any burden, however light, of self-blame: "profound respect on his part," said Hawkins (repeating what other friends told him, since he himself never saw her), "and the airs of an antiquated beauty on hers." The impression was of something almost "learned by rote."[5]

Johnson funneled all the money he was able to get into the support of Tetty in the hope of approximating, as far as he could, what she had been used to having before he had married her. For example, she always had a maid, perhaps even in their worst poverty (1739–41), and certainly afterward. Out of an income of about £100 or £125 a year, in the middle 1740's, he may very well have devoted two-thirds of it to Tetty while keeping his own personal expenses to a minimum.* Yet

---

* Some notes left by his friend Richard Farmer, later Master of Emmanuel College, Cambridge, stated that Cave paid him an annual salary of £100 for serving as unofficial "editor" of the *Gentleman's Magazine* during at least the latter half of the period 1738–45. (See the reference to Farmer's notes on Alexander Chalmers, *General Biographical Dictionary* [London, 1812–17], xix, 53.) In addition, there

Tetty had never learned to live economically. If rent or food were proportionally much cheaper in the eighteenth century than now, dress was far more expensive. With just a little indulgence or even relaxation there, one's annual expenses—if one's income were in the £100-a-year range—could leap 50 percent. To this should be added the growing expenses for laudanum and, in particular, for doctors' bills. For, repressing her disappointments as she did, Tetty was sinking more deeply into hypochondria and psychosomatic illness. The usual physician's fee at the time—incredible as it may seem—was a guinea per visit.[6] If you were an invalid, or considered yourself so, a visit every two weeks is quite imaginable. This, at over £27 a year, could itself almost equal the entire yearly income of the ordinary hack writer. Moreover, Tetty increasingly stayed in bed. This, of course, meant many things for Johnson himself: it deepened his sense of guilt; he was the more eager to provide what he could to ease her; and it also meant the virtual end of sexual relations between the two, despite a touching persistence on Johnson's part.*

5

True, he had seen enough of the world thus far—and, more importantly, had thought about it—to take for granted much, if not all, that was happening now in the marriage (for which no one was to blame): or, for that matter, to take for granted what was happening to *him*, to his own way of thinking and feeling, and all that it meant to be entering one's middle years, above all in the situation in which he himself now was. One of the distinctive peculiarities of Johnson's, of which we have been able to say very little after the long breakdown that followed Oxford, is the immense inner life—the strong imaginative digestion and assimilation of experience into thoughtful centrality. That is because, starting with the school at Edial and continuing through the years thus far in London (except for that short truancy to the country in late 1739), he was, in effect, constantly running. The hack work he was turning out, on so many different subjects, was done largely to

was whatever Osborne paid him for the *Harleian Catalogue* and *Miscellany*, in the early 1740's, together with odd sums for other writing. That he fell behind on the mortgage for the Lichfield house, despite his frugality in his own personal expenses, suggests that everything was going to Tetty, directly or indirectly.
* See below, p. 263.

order. Except for moments, we rarely have had, during his thirties, a glimpse into his inner life. The extent to which the inner life was there—surveying and digesting so much, taking for granted and antici- pating still more—was soon to be shown in one of the two forms of writing in which he is at his greatest: the decade of moral writing that is to begin in three years with *The Vanity of Human Wishes,* which already—though it was written at thirty-nine—seems to distill a life- time of experience. But meanwhile he was facing the specific, practical problem of what to do in his own life.

Chapter 15

Storming the Main Gate: the *Dictionary*

Early in 1746, five or six months after his thirty-sixth birthday and with the possibility of entering the law permanently closed, Johnson pushed aside his hesitations and started on his monumental *Dictionary of the English Language.* The finished work, nine years later, easily ranks as one of the greatest single achievements of scholarship, and probably the greatest ever performed by one individual who labored under anything like the disadvantages in a comparable length of time.

A constant rebuke to national pride for over half a century—and a growing embarrassment to the English intellectual world in particular—was the lack of a major English dictionary. There was nothing even remotely to compare with the great national dictionaries of France and Italy, both of them the product of learned academies with many members. The standard had been set by the Italian dictionary (six volumes, 1612), which had taken the Accademia della Crusca twenty years to prepare. With this standard in mind, the French Academy—established primarily to "purify" and bring order to the French language—spent four years deliberating how to proceed with a dictionary that could match or excel the Italian. Then, in 1639, with its original eight members expanded to forty, it began the actual work and finished it fifty-five years later (1694). The revision, begun soon afterward, took another eighteen years (1700–1718).

The thought of creating an English dictionary that could stand in comparison with these works had long depressed the spirits of any individual qualified even to begin on such a project. For of course it would have to be an individual. There was not only no academy in Great Britain similar to the French Academy but also, given the pride in British individualism, not much prospect of one. If scholars with any real sense of what was involved were intimidated by the magnitude of the task, writers who were less scholarly were willing to play with the idea until they began to think about it closely: Pope; Addison, who was said to have been offered £3,000 for the job; and Ambrose Philips, who brought out "Proposals for Printing an English Dictionary," and then dropped the project. Moving into the vacuum over the years had been approximations to a dictionary by men who felt they had little to lose. Usually these were little more than lists of "hard words." A commendable exception was the dictionary (1721) by a Stepney schoolmaster, Nathan Bailey, which had been revised (1736) to include around sixty thousand words. But it was concerned primarily with the origins of words. Since etymology was still in its infancy and often simply wrong, this limited the value of the book. Moreover, the definitions were often casual (*e.g.,* "horse"—"a beast well known" and "dog"—"a quadruped well known").

2

The London publishers were quite aware of the need. In fact, Robert Dodsley, according to his brother James, had earlier suggested the project to Johnson when he was sitting one day in Dodsley's shop. Johnson "seemed at first to catch at the proposition, but, after a pause, said, in his abrupt decisive manner, 'I believe I shall not undertake it.' " Yet actually, said Johnson, before Dodsley had ever mentioned the matter to him, "I had long thought of it."[1]

Of course, he would have thought of it. Here, as much as in any other project (at least as he envisaged it, with scores of thousands of quotations drawn from every branch of learning to illustrate different shades of meaning), he would be fulfilling the Renaissance ideal of the polymath that had haunted him ever since the year at Stourbridge and the year at Oxford. As the late Renaissance was creating and beginning to pass into the "Enlightenment," the Academies themselves were a product of that ideal. Yet they also marked the dilution of that ideal through the assumption that it was less possible to the individual than to group enterprise. To try to do for England, as an individual and in a fraction of the time, what the Academies had done for Italy, France, and, most recently, Spain was a tempting challenge to Johnson, who for fifteen years had found one door after another barred to him for lack of a degree. If he succeeded, it would permanently establish his reputation and change the whole course of his life. Still, only a fool could deny the immense disadvantages under which he would be working, particularly the absence of libraries. Most important of all, the kind of work involved and the length of the project were at complete odds with his nature and habits. At every step of the way he would be fighting an enemy—his own impatient temperament, his rebellious fits of indolence, the overwhelming desire he felt whenever he began any kind of work to get it over with as soon as possible.

It is a measure of his inner desperation at the sense of time passing that the balance of indecision (and the occurrence was one of the most important events of his life) suddenly tipped in the winter of 1745–46. If he was condemned to hack work in Grub Street, he might as well face up to what a part of him could regard as the supreme job of hack work, and the very essence of Grub Street (the residence and workplace of "makers of small dictionaries") carried to its highest degree. And there was some grim satisfaction to his humor as well as to his pride to know that it was in this least likely of settings (or what those in the comfort of "academic bowers" might regard as the least likely of settings) that he as one individual would be "rivaling the Academies" if only he could keep himself at the job. Nor was he underestimating the difficulties. Boswell, forty years later, suggested he might have: "You did not know what you were undertaking." Johnson justly answered: "I knew very well what I was undertaking, and very well how to do it, and have done it very well."[2]

After reaching a tentative agreement with Robert Dodsley early in 1746, he prepared "A Short Scheme for compiling a new Dictionary of the English Language" to submit to a group of publishers (April 30, 1746).[3] Because of the size of the undertaking, no one publisher wanted to take complete responsibility for the work. The group that combined to sponsor the new dictionary consisted of Dodsley, Charles Hitch, Andrew Millar—whom Johnson praised for his generosity to writers and for having "raised the price of literature"—and the firms of Messrs. Longman (Thomas Longman and his nephew) and of the brothers John and Paul Knapton.

Then, on June 18, the contract was signed at a breakfast held at the Golden Anchor near Holborn Bar. Johnson was to be paid £1,575 in installments, out of which he was himself to defray expenses and the cost of any help he received.

3

With some of the money he rented the house (17 Gough Square) that still stands and is visited by thousands of tourists every year. Any money spent on furniture other than that which came with the house was devoted to the rooms Tetty would be using. The garret was meanwhile considered the "dictionary work-shop." There were small tables and chairs for the amanuenses who were copying out quotations he had marked. The place looked like a small, crowded countinghouse. Books were strewn all over the floor. He himself probably used the same chair and table he was using later, when Joshua Reynolds brought the French sculptor Louis Roubiliac to meet him: an "old crazy deal table" and an elbowchair with only three legs. The chair, as he sat in it, was next to the wall, which "served to support it on that side on which the leg was deficient." Reynolds's sister, Frances, added that Johnson was still using the chair when he was writing the *Idler* (1758–60). On rising from it, he "never forgot its defect, but would either hold it in his hand, or place it with great composure against some support, taking no notice of its imperfection to his visitor."[4]

The six humble assistants (five Scots and an Englishman) were almost derelict when he hired them. He seems to have chosen them as much out of compassion as for any other reason. Perhaps no more than three or four were working with him at any one time, and, given the size of the house, it would have been like him to have supplemented their pay—about twelve shillings a week—by lodging and boarding some of them.* The Englishman was V. J. Peyton, who tried to keep alive by teaching French. After the *Dictionary* was finished, Peyton wrote a few works on language, and Johnson himself was occasionally able to hire him when he made revisions in the *Dictionary*. But after Peyton's wife had a stroke, he was reduced to complete penury,

* Fairly good pay for this kind of work at the time would be seven or eight shillings a week. But there is a receipt in the Hyde Collection, signed by Francis Stewart, one of the assistants, that reads, "June 18th [1746] I received by way of advance three pounds three shillings a week for which I contract to assist in compiling the Work [the *Dictionary*], and which is to begin to be paid from Midsummer next." On the probability of Johnson's lodging and boarding the assistants, see R. W. Chapman's note in *Letters*, No. 38.

said Johnson, and "sat starving by the bed of a Wife not only useless, but almost motionless, condemned by poverty to personal attendance. . . ." Johnson's rough friend Giuseppe Baretti described Peyton as "a fool and a drunkard." But Johnson thought Peyton's life as moving as those of others that "fill histories and tragedies" only because they are better known. When Peyton's wife at last died (1776), he was immediately "seized by a fever" and died himself, and Johnson paid the burial expenses of both.[5]

The five Scots included Alexander Macbean and his brother William, an obscure "Mr. Maitland," and two who died while the *Dictionary* was still under way—Robert Shiels and Francis Stewart, the latter of whom helped with "low cant phrases" and words having to do with gambling and card-playing. The unworldly Alexander Macbean, said Johnson, knew "several languages" but "nothing of life." He is remembered because of Johnson's remark, after encouraging him to write the *Dictionary of Ancient Geography:* "I have lost all hope of his doing anything properly, since I found he gave as much labour to Capua as to Rome." Nevertheless, when the work came out (1773), Johnson wrote one of his splendid Prefaces for it. And when Macbean soon afterward was starving, Johnson raised money to support him and also got him admitted to the Charterhouse as a "poor brother." Robert Shiels, about whom more is known, was an unsuccessful poet (he wrote two hopeless poems, "Marriage" and "The Power of Beauty"). Johnson felt "much tenderness" for him. A little scene, while they were working together on the *Dictionary*, survives in a moment of reminiscence by Johnson years later (1776). Shiels was a great admirer of the blank verse in James Thomson's *Seasons,* whereas Johnson felt Thomson had

such a cloud of words, that the sense can hardly peep through. . . . I took down Thomson, and read aloud a large portion of him, and then asked,—Is not this fine? Shiels having expressed the highest admiration, Well, Sir, (said I,) I have omitted every other line.[6]

It was Shiels who, with Johnson's aid, wrote the life of the colorful and impoverished poet Samuel Boyse, whom we described earlier. This was a small part of a larger project for which Johnson took off time to help him during poor Shiels's final year or two, while he was ill of consumption (and Johnson may even have suggested the project at the start, with assurances of help, as a means for Shiels to raise both money and his own self-respect): a collection significantly called *Lives of the*

Poets (five volumes, 1753), published shortly before Shiels died in the bleak tenement known as May's Buildings (December 27, 1753).*

4

The following March (1747) the publishers announced the preparation of the *Dictionary* in advertisements. They did this not because the work itself would appear soon but because they assumed Johnson was finishing for publication the *Plan of a Dictionary of the English Language,* which was necessary to stake out the territory. Actually Johnson, though he had begun work on the *Dictionary* itself, had deferred getting around to the *Plan.* But he now turned to it, and it was published in early August, with a dedication to the Earl of Chesterfield, and the background was thus laid for Johnson's famous letter eight years later (1755), which, reprinted thousands of times since then, remains as one of the most celebrated letters in the English language. The result is that Chesterfield, ever since, has been popularly and unjustly considered a sort of villain in the Johnson story.

Chesterfield, at the time he entered the story of the *Dictionary* (1746), was approaching fifty-four, and had already had a distinguished career as a statesman—as a member of the House of Lords, as Ambassador to The Hague, and, most recently, as Lord Lieutenant of Ireland. In this last and very difficult position, he served with such rare ability, as well as integrity of character, that the Irish people were for a generation or more to look back on his brief administration with admiration and nostalgia. Because of Chesterfield's prominent position, his union of good sense with tact and elegance, and his knowledge of both ancient and modern languages, he was widely respected in England as something of an arbiter of taste. Robert Dodsley, who was on friendly terms with him, thought that the *Dictionary* would receive an immense boost with the public if a man with Chesterfield's prestige could publicly serve as its sponsor or patron. Chesterfield was ill for

* Shiels got up the materials (many provided by Johnson, who could also have dictated some of the passages) and wrote almost the entire work. Since Shiels was unknown, the booksellers arranged a clever ruse. They paid Theophilus Cibber (currently in prison for debt) ten guineas, said Johnson, for agreeing to "revise, correct, and improve" the work, and then printed as the author on the title page "Mr. Cibber," hoping the public would assume it was by his better-known father, Colley Cibber. (Johnson's story is confirmed by the publisher's agreement, which is now in the Hyde Collection; the sum, however, was £21.)[7] On Shiels's life of Boyse, see above, p. 211.

some months after he returned from Ireland (April 1746). But after he came to London in the autumn to take on a new job (as one of the principal Secretaries of State), Dodsley sounded him out, found him receptive, and carried the news to Johnson, who was hard at work on the *Dictionary* but had neglected to start on the *Plan*, which the booksellers wanted to publish soon. When Dodsley proposed that the *Plan* be publicly addressed to Chesterfield, Johnson said, "I laid hold of this as a pretext for delay, that it might be better done"; and he told Richard Bathurst, "Now if any good comes of my addressing to Lord Chesterfield, it will be ascribed to deep policy, when, in fact, it was only an excuse for laziness."[8]

The idea could well have attracted him. Aside from the practical advantages, there was the fact—symbolically important—that Chesterfield had been not only the friend but also the patron of Cornelius, whose example (at least as the adolescent Johnson had seen him) had been so firmly absorbed as to remain a permanent part of him. True, Johnson would never himself have taken the initiative, and presented himself before Chesterfield as an impoverished cousin of Cornelius's seeking Chesterfield's help. But then it was Dodsley who had taken the first step, and without prompting from Johnson. Hence he could afford to warm a little to the symbolic significance. For he could feel that he was at last—in this large, perhaps unrivaled work—fulfilling the dream, forever associated with Cornelius, of moving through every field of learning. In a way, the wheel had come full circle. It is because of these feelings that he was to prove far more sensitive to bruising, real or imaginary, than he would otherwise have been. Revising the "scheme" to the formal *Plan*, he sent it to his friend John Taylor, who was about to come to London anyway for the season. Unfortunately, shortly after Taylor arrived, he left the copy on a table at his house. The poet William Whitehead (later poet laureate) saw it when he dropped by for a call on Taylor, admired it, and took it away with him. He passed it on to another friend, who in turn showed it to Chesterfield. This naturally annoyed Johnson, who was planning to have it presented to Chesterfield with what he thought would be appropriate ceremony. It was like the time that old Michael had sent to Pope a copy of Johnson's translation of Pope's *Messiah*, which led Johnson to say that if it had not been his father who had done this, he "would have cut his throat." But Johnson now, not wishing to rebuke his old friend Taylor for his carelessness, said only that the *Plan* would "have come out with more bloom if it had not been seen before by anybody."[9]

The busy Chesterfield expressed his interest, made a few minor suggestions, and sent a gift of £10. After the *Plan* was published (August
1747), Johnson paid a courtesy visit to Chesterfield, discovering that
he was not only "exquisitely elegant" but had "more knowledge than I
expected." One or two other visits then followed during which, as he
was to say in the celebrated letter, "I waited in your outward rooms or
was repulsed from your door." A famous historical painting—still used
to advertise dictionaries—shows Johnson sitting in gloomy irritation
outside Chesterfield's office. Part of the folklore of the incident is the
story that on the final day, when he waited in the outward rooms, he
was told that Chesterfield was engaged. After an hour's waiting out
came poor Colley Cibber, the poet who had been the hero of Pope's
Dunciad. At this, Johnson left for good. Boswell asked him whether
this story was true. Johnson, always scrupulous about fact, denied it.
He said that the real cause was Chesterfield's "continued neglect,"
though—given Johnson's pride—his threshold for what he might call
"continued neglect" could have been low. At this point Chesterfield
passes out of the story until a few years later, when the *Dictionary* was
about to be published.[10]

5

In order to conceive the *Dictionary* for what it was, we should keep in
mind what is involved when even a middling dictionary is prepared
now, though there are dozens of previous works to build on, incorporate, or often merely manicure while quibbling with minor details.
Grants are secured from foundations; scholars are lined up by the
score; other help is abundant, and mechanized filing systems are available.

All this contrasts dramatically with that upper room in Gough
Square, where, with no real library at hand, Johnson wrote the definitions of over 40,000 words (not only of them, but of different shades
of meaning), illustrating the diverse senses in which these words could
be used by including about 114,000 quotations drawn from English
writing in every field of learning during the two centuries from the
middle of the Elizabethan period down to his own time. (Actually he
may have gathered over twice this number, but was forced to drop
somewhat more than half of them lest "the bulk of my volumes would
fright away the student.") In doing this he was following the example
of the Italian dictionary prepared by the Accademia della Crusca, ex-

247

cept that the variety of writing that he covered was greater (it was less exclusively "literary" and included more examples from philosophical, scientific, and technical works). This practice had been rejected by the French Academy with the excuse that membership in the Academy automatically indicated that one was already an "authority," and that other authorities did not need to be cited. Long afterward (1778), Voltaire, just before his death, was to urge the Academy to revise its procedure and follow Johnson's example.[11]

From the conception of the *Dictionary* until its conclusion, his concern was not with "originality" but with doing the work as well as possible within the time he was giving it, drawing on all of the best ideas and aspects of earlier major dictionaries, including the lexicons of Greek and Latin. James Sledd and Gwin Kolb rightly stress the mistake of looking primarily for what is innovative, original, or different about the *Dictionary*.. The achievement is in "the continuity of the development" from previous dictionaries, "especially those of the academies." The aim was to select and then include the best that tradition could offer. And his remark to Dr. Adams was not wholly whimsical when Adams called on him soon after the *Dictionary* was started, and wondered that Johnson could think so great a work possible in only three years, since "the French Academy, which consists of forty members, took forty years to compile their Dictionary." This for Adams, or for anyone else at the time, above all for Johnson, was the real context—the magnificent dictionaries of the Academies. Not stopping to remind Adams that the French Academy took fifty-five years, Johnson replied, "Let me see; forty times forty is sixteen hundred. As three to sixteen hundred, so is the proportion of an Englishman to a Frenchman."[12]

6

The method of carrying out a work of this size is naturally of interest. He used about eighty large notebooks. From what he had learned of Johnson's procedure, Boswell inferred that he first got up a master list of words with the help of other dictionaries, wrote the words down alphabetically throughout the notebooks, and then afterward—having left ample space—prepared the illustrative quotations and inserted them and the definitions. But to have started with a master list, as Bishop Percy said, and then for each word to "hunt through the whole compass of English literature for all their significations, would have taken the whole life of any individual."* Actually his procedure, "as he himself described" it to Percy, was very different:

He began his task by devoting his first care to a diligent perusal of all such English writers as were most correct in their language, and under every sentence which he meant to quote, he drew a line, and noted in the margin the first letter of the word under which it was to occur. He then delivered these books to his clerks, who transcribed each sentence on a separate slip of paper, and arranged the same under the word referred to. By these means he collected the several words and their different significations; and when the whole arrangement was alphabetically formed, he gave the definitions of their meanings, and collected their etymologies. . . .

Only after this was done, and the material arranged alphabetically, did he look at other dictionaries "to see if any words had escaped him."[13]

In short, as W. K. Wimsatt says, what he did first was to embark "on a huge program of reading English poetry, drama, prose essays, history, biography, science and arts" (among other things, the *Dictionary* is a veritable "magazine of contemporary science"). The books he used, said Hawkins, were "what he had in his own collection, a copious but a miserably ragged one," together with whatever he could borrow from friends. To judge from those that survive, he did not underline the whole passage to be quoted in the way Percy says. Instead he usually drew vertical lines to mark the beginning and the end of the passage for the clerks to copy, and then underlined the key word. Though he used a black lead pencil with the thought that the marks could be easily erased, the books often came back to their owners "so defaced as to be scarce worth owning, and yet, some of his friends were glad to receive and entertain them as curiosities."[14] In many cases, when the works of a poet were not readily available, he quoted from memory. He had two criteria in mind in selecting the quotations. The primary one, of course, was to illustrate the meaning (or meanings) of the word. But where possible he also hoped to give quotations of some interest in themselves either in quality of language or in content of thought. ("I therefore," as he said in the Preface,

* The same objection applies to Hawkins's remark (p. 175) that Johnson used "an interleaved copy of Bailey's dictionary" as both a starting point and as "the repository" of the information and quotations that he gathered. Moreover, though he may have used an interleaved copy of Bailey at some point, it could hardly have served as a file for more than the minutest fraction of the material for which eighty large notebooks were needed.

"extracted from philosophers principles of science; from historians remarkable facts; from chymists complete processes; from divines striking exhortations; and from poets beautiful description.") Since the number of quotations actually used is about 114,000, and since he cut them by more than half, the total number assembled could well have amounted to 240,000. Then the slips of paper on which the amanuenses had copied out the passages were pasted in the eighty large notebooks under the key word. Here a final feature was added. In order to indicate something of the history of the word, Johnson arranged the passages according to the time they were written.

Before pasting the slips in the notebooks, Johnson wrote down first—or perhaps occasionally inserted afterward—the etymologies (inevitably the least valuable part of the work in any dictionary before the development of historical linguistics)* and the superb definitions. No qualified student of the subject in our century, now that no lexicographer needs to feel in competition with Johnson, has failed to agree with H. B. Wheatley that the definitions are "above all praise" and "can never be superseded." In one major dictionary after another since Johnson's, they have served as a model.[16]

It is through the definitions and the happy selection of authorities that the *Dictionary* achieved its aim—to provide a pragmatic standard for correctness and propriety. It is a popular legend that the *Dictionary* abounds with quaint definitions. Examples frequently cited (often only a part of the definition) are: *oats*—"A grain, which in England is generally given to horses, but in Scotland supports the people"; *pension*—"An allowance made to anyone without an equivalent. In England it is generally understood to mean pay given to a state hireling for treason to his country"; *patron*—"One who countenances, supports, or protects. Commonly a wretch who supports with insolence, and is paid with flattery"; *lexicographer*—"A writer of dictionaries, a harmless drudge. . . ." And there is the famous polysyllabic definition of *network* (probably in reaction to Bailey's definition of *net*—he did

---

* In the following century it became fashionable to echo Macaulay's remark that "Johnson was a wretched etymologist" without stopping to ask who at the time could have been superior. As is often the case with such complaints, the charge came not from the major figures who were creating the new field of historical linguistics and were in a position to appreciate what Johnson did, but from those who knew only that the study of linguistics was progressing and wished to show that they were not unaware of it. Even with the limitations he faced, Johnson managed, as Sledd and Kolb have shown, to gather "the best available resources and made better use of them than many alleged professionals."[15]

not attempt *network*—as "a device for catching fish, birds, etc."): "Anything reticulated or decussated at equal distances with interstices between the intersections." There is also the famous slip in which *pastern* is defined as the "knee" of a horse rather than the part of the foot between the fetlock and hoof—famous because of his answer to a lady at Plymouth who asked him why he so defined it, and expected a learned explanation. His reply was simply, "Ignorance, Madam, pure ignorance." But if all such definitions are put together—the very few slips, and the larger number that are somewhat puckish—they amount to about fifteen out of a total of forty thousand, and the reader who is looking for them finds that he is going through scores of pages before encountering one.[17]

So well did he succeed that, for over a century, the work was without a serious rival. Other dictionaries were little more than a modification or partial development of Johnson's. The various editions of Noah Webster's *Dictionary* are typical.[18] He devoted his life to little else. Moreover, he had Johnson to build on, which was a considerable help, and, though he was always jealously protesting his originality and looking for excuses to snap at Johnson, he took over thousands of the definitions, with minor changes, as well as an immense number of the quotations.

Significantly, the *Dictionary* that was finally to replace Johnson's, and that now serves as the basis of all other dictionaries in English, was again the product—like those of the Academies—of many individuals working over a long period of time, except that now the time was even longer and the number of people involved was far larger. This is the great *New English Dictionary*, in ten volumes (1888–1928), which has since served as the basis of all dictionaries in English. As originally planned by the Philological Society, it was conceived as a supplement to Johnson and the other dictionaries that followed him. When the plan was enlarged, and it was decided to provide a distilled history of every word known to have been used in the language since the middle of the eleventh century, the word *New* was used in the title because it was the only really "new" dictionary since Johnson's (in the second edition of thirteen volumes, it was retitled the *Oxford English Dictionary*). This *New* dictionary, for which work was begun in 1858, was by the 1880's drawing on the help of thirteen hundred scholars (it was to draw on at least another thousand before it was finished), and was to take seventy years to complete. Johnson, working in a cluttered room with the most meager help and with few resources, finished his two monumental volumes in nine years. These volumes were not only the creation of one man, but of one man who had not been a professional lexicographer, who was emotionally impatient and turbulent in imagination, who was distracted by psychological and other problems, and who—well before the work was half done—was also writing some of the profoundest reflections on life and human experience that exist in any language. In some ways, the task could seem to demand no "higher quality than that of bearing burdens with dull patience, and beating the track of the alphabet with sluggish resolution." But considering the comparatively short time in which the *Dictionary* was done, and the range of talents needed, this remarkable work is essentially a by-product of what Johnson himself defined as "true Genius"—"a mind of large general powers, accidentally determined to some particular direction."[19]

7

By October 20, 1750, the first 120 sheets (containing the first three letters of the alphabet) were printed. Actually Johnson was further along than this might at first suggest. For the authorities were all collected, and the work now consisted largely of writing the definitions. Repeatedly Johnson clung to the conviction (it is also one of the themes of his moral writing) that employment and activity beget activity; that the momentum of effort, if once under way in any direction, is more easily transferred than summoned out of nothing. Certainly this was true of his own experience. The work on the *Dictionary*, far from inhibiting effort in other ways, proved a spur to his imagination by keeping his mind, as he said, "on the stretch."[20]

Because the moral writing, beginning with *The Vanity of Human Wishes* (1749), is of major importance, it is discussed separately. But a few words should be said about the other writing, aside from that mentioned elsewhere (*e.g.*, the Drury Lane *Prologue*, 1747). For example, he did two pieces as a favor to Robert Dodsley. He might balk at the mere idea of a "patron" in any serious way, but with someone like the kindhearted Dodsley it was different. As he once said in another context, "Doddy, you know, is my patron, and I would not desert him."[21] On this occasion "Doddy" wanted to capitalize on a growing public interest in "home" or self-education with a work, part textbook and part anthology, to be called *The Preceptor* (1748), with sections on literature, elocution, mathematics, ethics, and so on. For this book, Johnson stayed up one night to write a general Preface. On another night, returning after an evening out, he dashed down a short allegory, "The Vision of Theodore, the Hermit of Teneriffe," to swell out one of the sections. The main moral is the insidious power of habits, pictured as pigmies that smooth one's path up the "mountain of existence," valuable and docile when in the service of Reason and Religion, treacherous when allied with Passion and Appetite, and capable of swelling to gigantic size as one fights against them. (It is amusing to see him, even at this busy time, as apprehensive as ever at the capacity of Indolence to hand one over to Melancholy and Despair.) Except for those resolved to find transcendent merit in everything Johnson ever wrote, the "Vision of Theodore" is usually read with disappointment because of the remark (which Boswell paraphrased from Bishop Percy) that Johnson once said "he thought this was the best thing he ever wrote."*

Of minor importance (except for the attention given it later by others trying to embarrass him) was his brief involvement in the so-called "Lauder controversy." William Lauder, a Scottish Latin scholar with a curiously twisted nature, was eager to convince the public that *Paradise Lost* had been plagiarized by Milton from a group of modern Latin poems. Actually, what he did was select lines from a little-known Latin translation of the poem by a man named William Hogg, and then pretended they were passages from the earlier works from which Milton supposedly took them. Lauder got hold of Cave to see whether the *Gentleman's Magazine* would publish his results. Cave turned him over to Johnson, who, though busy and preoccupied, was always interested in seeing the background of any great work, and did not suspect deceit but considered Lauder "too frantic to be fraudulent." He wrote a short essay to accompany Lauder's *Proposals* (1747), which Lauder then used as a Preface to his full book on the subject (1750). The fraud was soon exposed and Johnson dictated and forced Lauder to sign a retraction, and himself published an apology. In later years, when he became famous as a critic, people would cite Johnson's Pref-

* The statement is so absurd that we can forgivably assume one of two things. On some occasion when Percy was praising Johnson's allegories, which he genuinely admired, Johnson could have pulled his leg by making a remark of this sort. Or Johnson may have been referring only to Oriental tales and allegories, and stating that he thought this the best of the lot (the remark was made before he wrote *Rasselas*).[22]

ace as an example of his readiness to believe the worst of Milton. This was far from the case. He was admittedly careless, but his interest, as far as it went, was in whatever could show "the progress of his mighty genius in the construction of his work"—to note "whence the scheme was taken, how it was improved, by what assistance it was executed." In fact, during the very month Lauder's book was published, Johnson was persuading Garrick to put on a benefit performance of *Comus* for Milton's impoverished granddaughter, and wrote a Postscript to Lauder's book asking for funds for relief, stating, "It is yet in the power of a great people to reward the poet whose name they boast . . . whose works may possibly be read when every other monument of British greatness shall be obliterated."[23]

Such writings took little time. Of more importance is that in 1747, according to John Nichols, he resumed editorial work for the *Gentleman's Magazine* and, busy though he was with the *Dictionary*, "was frequently, if not constantly, employed to superintend the materials."[24] Moreover, he again started to contribute pieces himself to the magazine down through 1754. The number of these contributions, as we have recently discovered, is impressive (at least eighty, though most of them are quite short).*

8

By 1751 work on the *Dictionary* had begun to slow up to a point that disturbed the publishers. It was a rather distressing time for Johnson, as we shall see when we turn to his personal life. Tetty had become gravely ill; her expenses the previous four years had been higher than he could originally have expected; he had by now used up most, if not all, the money due him for the *Dictionary;* and after Tetty's death (March 28, 1752), it took him a few months to pull himself together.

---

* They include, among other works, at least a half-dozen poems, one or two of which may have been school exercises or written back in his early twenties (*Poems*, pp. 80–87, 367–71); the section on foreign history for November 1747, for February 1749, and for December 1750; Johnson's short *Life of the Earl of Roscommon* (May 1748); his Prologue (April 1750) for the benefit performance of Milton's *Comus;* an editorial note on the controversy over "Milton's imitation of the Moderns" (December 1750); "Proposals" for printing the works of Anna Williams (September 1740); at least fifty reviews or short notices down through 1755 (in particular of Edward Moore's *Gil Blas*, William Mason's *Elfrida*, Charlotte Lennox's *The Female Quixote*, and Hogarth's *Analysis of Beauty*); the Preface to the general Index to the first twenty volumes of the *Magazine* (1754); and, immediately after the death of his old employer, Edward Cave, a fine short life of him (February 1754).[25]

Finally, in a burst of energy, he completed the first volume (April 1753). Meanwhile, prodded by what amounted on Johnson's part to a threat to strike, the publishers had arranged to pay him additional money, but this time by the piece—a guinea per sheet of copy. For a while he was supplying copy faster than the printers could set it up. Within another fourteen months (July 1754), he had finished the second volume. It was now a little more than eight years since the contract had been signed. When the last sheet was rushed to Andrew Millar, who was handling things for the publishers as a group, Johnson was curious to know what he said: "Sir," answered the messenger, "he said, thank GOD I have done with him." "I am glad," replied Johnson with a smile, "that he thanks GOD for any thing."[26]

He had been planning to go to Oxford and use the libraries there while preparing the "front matter"—the history and the grammar of the language. Dr. Adams had not been in residence at Oxford for some years. But the young Thomas Warton, who was just beginning his long and famous career as a Fellow at Trinity, was eager to smooth the way for Johnson, and arranged to have him put up at Kettel Hall, then a sort of annex to Trinity. Though he stayed for five weeks, he never —said Warton, who saw him daily—collected materials at the library. After his marathonlike race of the last two years, there had been a sense of finality in dispatching that last sheet to Andrew Millar. (He apparently deferred writing the history and grammar till he returned to London, and then wrote them quickly, forgivably rationalizing that they were not the essential thing.) Moreover, he had not been at Oxford for almost twenty-five years, and was naturally eager to revisit places he had remembered and to see people he had known. Those anxious final months as a student, culminating in that early morning when he had left quietly, having first, as Taylor said, "hid his toes in a pair of large boots," had left him with no feeling of bitterness toward Oxford. Like his inability for years to have the books he left there sent back to him, this had been a tribute to how much he cared—and was permanently to care—for the place. He called on the present Master of Pembroke, John Ratcliff, who had been bursar when Johnson was a student, and who "received him very coldly," said Warton. But Johnson was pleased that the old college servants still remembered him. He had a "most cordial" meeting with John Meeke, whose "superiority" had seemed almost overwhelming to him when they had been students, and who had been a Fellow of Pembroke ever since 1731.* Forgivably he felt that, though he had not been able to stay on "to feed on a

* See above, p. 97.

Fellowship," but had lived such a radically different life, he had not done badly in comparison. He took long walks with Warton in and around Oxford, during which he reminisced about his year there. A new friend to whom Warton introduced him was Francis Wise, the Radcliffe librarian. It was through the help of Wise and Warton that within a few more months—because of the forthcoming *Dictionary*— he was awarded a degree (Master of Arts, conferred February 20, 1755). For years, time and again, the lack of a degree had proved painfully important. Now at last it had come, and it arrived in time for him to have it put on the title page of the *Dictionary*. As Wise told Warton, the compliment was a mutual one. "It is in truth doing ourselves more honour than him, to have such a work done by an Oxford hand."[27]

9

In the autumn Lord Chesterfield, after seven years, re-entered the picture. Caught up in his work as Secretary of State, and with other worries, not to mention the number of people seeking his patronage, Chesterfield had naturally forgotten about the *Dictionary*. Nothing more would have happened had not the ever-hopeful Dodsley got hold of him, informing him that the great work was about to appear. The *Plan*, after all, had been addressed to him. Now that the *Dictionary* itself was finished, would not some puff or recommendation from him still be possible?

Chesterfield had been ill most of the past year. Not only was he almost crippled by arthritis, but he was also afflicted with a growing deafness that involved something like Ménière's disease, or a disturbance of the semicircular canals. "It seems," he wrote in a letter around this time, "as if all the complaints, that ever attacked heads, had joined to overpower mine. Continual noises, headache, giddiness, and impenetrable deafness . . ."[28] More from courtesy and a belated stirring of conscience than any thought of the honor of being associated with the work, the aging and weary Chesterfield tried to oblige Dodsley. He had been for some time writing occasional essays for a weekly paper called the *World*, and he now sent off two letters to the *World* (November 28 and December 5) praising the forthcoming *Dictionary*, and Dodsley happily carried the news to Johnson of Chesterfield's endorsement.

The result was Johnson's memorable reply, from which, however familiar, at least a few sentences must be quoted:

Seven years, my Lord, have now past since I waited in your outward rooms, or was repulsed from your door; during which time I have been pushing on my work through difficulties, of which it is useless to complain, and have brought it, at last, to the verge of publication, without one act of assistance, one word of encouragement, or one smile of favour. Such treatment I did not expect, for I never had a Patron before. . . .

Is not a Patron, my Lord, one who looks with unconcern on a man struggling for life in the water, and, when he has reached ground, encumbers him with help? The notice which you have been pleased to take of my labours, had it been early, had been kind; but it has been delayed till I am indifferent, and cannot enjoy it; till I am solitary, and cannot impart it; till I am known, and do not want it. I hope it is no very cynical asperity not to confess obligations where no benefit has been received, or to be unwilling that the Publick should consider me as owing that to a Patron, which Providence has enabled me to do for myself.

Chesterfield accepted the rebuke with good nature, and was also quite impressed by the letter. It lay on his table where any visitor could see it, and, reading it aloud to Dodsley, he said, "This man has great powers," and "pointed out the severest passages, and observed how well they were expressed." Nor is there any reason to doubt the sincerity of his remark to Dodsley that he "would have turned off the best servant he ever had, if he had known that he denied him to a man who would have always been more than welcome." And when Dr. Adams quoted that to him, Johnson had no better answer than to assert, "That is not Lord Chesterfield; he is the proudest man this day existing." "No," said Adams, "there is one person at least as proud; I think, by your own account, you are the prouder man of the two." "But mine," replied Johnson, "was *defensive* pride."[29]

The letter is misconstrued if it is thought of as anger because of neglect or, least of all, complaint about it. He was used to neglect. There would have been no letter had not Chesterfield belatedly written the two pieces he did. The real explanation of the letter, as Sledd and Kolb point out, is that Chesterfield's tardy endorsement was placing Johnson in the false position "of a man who was soon to declare, in a Preface perhaps already written, that his great work had been written, without the 'patronage of the great.' " The public inference would be that since Chesterfield had been addressed in the original *Plan* (1747) and was now recommending the work (1754), he had been patronizing it all along (and exactly this inference was made, despite Johnson's letter, with one review actually charging that he wrote a new Preface instead of reprinting the *Plan*—which could have served as a Preface—merely in order to conceal his debt to Chesterfield).[30] Before long Johnson's attitude toward Chesterfield began to soften. Boswell tried for years to extract from him a copy of the letter. But Johnson continued to put him off. Finally (1781) he gave up and dictated it to him (for of course he knew it by heart). But this was a rare occasion. A year before Johnson died, his friend John Douglas, the Bishop of Salisbury, also tried to get a copy, pointing out to him "the Expectation of the Public to have that masterly Composition, preserved." Johnson said he did not have a copy (he did not say he could dictate it), and Douglas later learned that a message sent by Chesterfield before his death had "melted the Heart of the Writer of that epistolary Philippic."[31]

10

The *Dictionary* was published April 15, 1755, in the middle of his forty-sixth year. Naturally there were people eager to express reservations or disapproval, and to disguise envy—not only to themselves but, as they thought, a listening world—by showing that their standards were too high to allow them to be easily impressed. Nothing is more common, as Johnson once said, than the belief that we are displaying judgment or taste by "unwillingness to be pleased," and—given man's chronic uneasiness about himself and with so much of life generally—it is always "much easier to find reasons for rejecting than embracing."[32] But of course the achievement was undeniable, if only because this was a work in which national pride could be, if not flattered, at least relieved and reassured. Though he still had to struggle for a livelihood (and this is important to remember for the next seven years, for a time was to come when he was about to be arrested for debt), his reputation was now established. Before long the consensus among the informed (and within another decade far more widely) was close to the tribute paid almost immediately by the Marquis Nicolini, the President of the Accademia della Crusca, which more than a century before had fathered the first great dictionary of Europe. This "very noble Work," he said, will be "a perpetual Monument of Fame to the Author, an Honour to his own Country in particular, and a general Benefit to the Republic of Letters throughout all Europe."[33]

As for Johnson himself, these final months were pervaded with the sense of contrast, in all that he himself was feeling, with the hope in which he had started, and, above all, with the death of Tetty three years before (1752). In the near-empty house in Gough Square, with Tetty dead, with the amanuenses gone from the garret workshop, the triumph of this long wrestle with an achievement that would match the "academies" could seem very barren. The Preface he now wrote remains one of the monuments of English prose. After surveying the whole enterprise, he turns briefly—and for almost the only time in all his formal writing—to his own personal situation. Even the most envious of his attackers—the now-forgotten philologist Horne Tooke—confessed that the conclusion brought tears to his eyes:

In this work, when it shall be found that much is omitted, let it not be forgotten that much likewise is performed; and though no book was ever spared out of tenderness to the author, and the world is little solicitous to know whence proceeded the faults of that which it condemns; yet it may gratify curiosity to inform it, that the English Dictionary was written with little assistance of the learned, and without any patronage of the great; not in the soft obscurities of retirement, or under the shelter of academick bowers, but amidst inconvenience and distraction, in sickness and in sorrow.

If the lexicons of ancient Greek and Latin—though the languages are now dead and therefore fixed—are still, after centuries of work, in the process of being corrected; if the co-operative effort of the Italian academicians for twenty years could not be secure from attack on details; and if the embodied French Academy, after fifty years of combined labor, were at last compelled to start a revision,

I may surely be contented without the praise of perfection, which, if I could obtain, in this gloom of solitude, what would it avail me? I have protracted my work till most of those, whom I wished to please, have sunk into the grave, and success and miscarriage are empty sounds: I, therefore, dismiss it with frigid tranquility, having little to fear or hope from censure or from praise.

Nothing so high-lights this moment in Johnson's own life as the parallels one could draw between the end of the Preface and the writers who have since been haunted by it. The best example is the "Advertisement" by Noah Webster, seventy-three years later, of his own dictionary. For here Webster is speaking of a life that has "insensibly" passed away in the pursuit of a great work of scholarship. Yet, for Johnson, the far larger and more creative work was done in a fraction of that time, during years that were painful beyond anything in Webster's experience or imagination. But so hypnotic was Johnson's example that Webster (however much he fought or quibbled with the example of Johnson) could not help echoing the conclusion to the great Preface: "In my endeavors," said Webster,

a long life has passed insensibly away; and, in now submitting it to the scrutiny of the world, I am feelingly reminded how near these labors have brought me to that period, when I shall be beyond the range of censure or applause.

Chapter 16

Personal Life; Tetty's Illness and Death; a Straggler

Among Johnson's incentives to undertake the *Dictionary* was an immediate and personal one. With the income, he could at last offer Tetty something she had always had before he lost so much of her money in the school at Edial—a house of her own, and perhaps a way of living comparable to that she had given up because of him.

He had been aware from the start of what it meant to this daughter of a Warwickshire squire, who had shown such faith in him, to find herself in cramped city lodgings at the age of forty-nine, when it is not easy to readjust. Yet, however chagrined and guilty he felt about it, there had been no alternative. He could only devote every shilling he could to her comfort and spend as little as possible on himself, wearing clothes, almost as if in self-imposed penance, that struck his friends as little better than those of a beggar. But now the situation was becoming urgent. Tetty's deterioration the last few years tore at his conscience. She was almost sixty, and time was running out. Besides retreating to bed and turning for solace to laudanum, gin, and books of romances, she had begun to use ill health as an excuse to go out for days at a time to Hampstead, which was becoming something of a resort—a place where members of the upper middle class who could not afford a country house could get away from the smoke and noise of the city. Considering that he himself regarded country life as comparatively dull (and was soon—partly in reaction to Tetty—to write satiric sketches of people flying to the country for relief and finding it dull), he could not believe that it was the country per se—or even "country air"—that was the attraction. It was the lack of space and of a house in which she could live with some dignity. Now at last, when she was almost sixty, he could provide her with this.

The house at 17 Gough Square, which he would never have considered taking for himself alone with twice the income he received from the *Dictionary*, was at least as large and handsome as that of a moderately prosperous tradesman. When he arranged to rent it, he doubtless thought back to Harry Porter's house in Birmingham. In the basement was the kitchen, with two small adjoining cellars or store-rooms. On the ground floor were the dining room and a sitting room, which, with folding doors, could be made into a large room for entertaining. Above it were a bedroom and another sitting room, which Tetty could use for herself, and, on the third floor, two other bedrooms. Then, at the top, there was the large garret that could be used as the study and general workshop, conveniently remote from the living quarters on the first two floors that he hoped Tetty would enjoy. A house of this sort would cost at the time about £700, and would rent for about £50 a year.[1]

<h2 style="text-align:center">2</h2>

It did not seem to occur to him, at least for a while, that Tetty had another motive for going to Hampstead under the shelter of illness. That was to make herself less available to her still gratefully devoted younger husband. It allowed her to avoid more easily, without repeated excuses, what had become a trial, given not only her age but her obsession with it: her erosion of self-confidence, and her growing desire to hide from the world, wrapped in a cocoon of inviolability. Moreover, the impoverished amanuenses trooping up and down the stairs to the garret could have struck her—if she still retained her old interest in comedy—as rather like the squad of ragamuffins and waifs (Mouldy, Shadow, and the rest) that Falstaff recruited for battle, and the whole idea of the "workshop" as a bit like what she may have heard of Michael's "parchment factory."

Continuing to use illness as an excuse, she seems to have spent little time at Gough Square, at least until the last year or so of her life (1751–52). Instead a small house was rented for her in Hampstead, behind the church. (It was still standing in the 1890's; and at that time it was called—and may have been called in Johnson's time—Priory Lodge.) In effect, Johnson was supporting two households. Since there was now more money, Tetty soon had living with her, besides her Scottish maid, a companion and general nurse. This was Elizabeth Swynfen, the daughter of Johnson's godfather Dr. Swynfen, for whom he had written the Latin statement of his case after his breakdown. She had known Tetty in Birmingham, was now in her early thirties, and is generally referred to as Mrs. Desmoulins (apparently pronounced "De Mullin" or "De Mullins") because she later married a Huguenot writing teacher of that name.

Long afterward (1783), a year or so before Johnson's death, Boswell and another friend, Mauritius Lowe, snatched the opportunity to interview her about Johnson's relations with Tetty. Considering the frank details, Boswell decided not to use the interview, which is still unpublished, but labeled it as something "to be kept silent" ("Extraordinary Johnsoniana—*Tacenda*"). In the *Life* he merely said that, according to Mrs. Desmoulins, Tetty "indulged herself in country air and nice living, at an unsuitable expence, while her husband was drudging in the smoke of London."[2] Actually she stated that Tetty was by now drinking heavily and, using the excuse that she was not well, had refused for years to have sexual relations with Johnson. What is also plain from the interview is that, while the fatigued and unhappy Tetty wished to be left alone, Johnson, who felt no diminution in his own fondness, was starved for affection.*

Often, during the week, he would come out to Hampstead for two or three days. (It was there, one morning late in 1748, that he wrote the first seventy lines of *The Vanity of Human Wishes*.) Being lonely, since Tetty would have been in bed most of the day and have gone to sleep early, he would spend the evening talking with his friend Richard Bathurst, who for a while lived nearby, until two or three in the morning. Because the maid would have gone to bed long before he returned, Mrs. Desmoulins would sit up to warm his bed with a pan of coals and let him in the house. As he was preparing to retire, Johnson would often ask her to come to his room, after he had got into bed, and sit and talk with him till he was ready to sleep. Sitting on his bedside, she would occasionally rest her head on his pillow. This at

---

* Permission to paraphrase and quote from the *Tacenda* has been granted by Yale University and the McGraw-Hill Book Company. The *Tacenda* will be printed in full in the forthcoming eleventh volume of the reading edition of Boswell's journal, Yale Editions of the Private Papers of James Boswell.

once led Boswell to ask whether Johnson had ever expressed himself in an amorous way. She replied that he had, immediately adding that, for her part, she "always respected him as a Father" (she was, in fact, only seven years younger). Boswell and Lowe tried to find out whether Johnson made any direct sexual advances. At this, Mrs. Desmoulins protested that "he never did anything that was beyond the limits of decency." As they continued to question the now elderly Mrs. Desmoulins, she confessed she herself might have gone further had Johnson urged her strongly enough. But, struggling with himself, he would push her away and ask her to leave.

Naturally, after a while, the situation began to wear on Johnson. But except for Mrs. Desmoulins, and perhaps his new friend Richard Bathurst, probably no one else but John Taylor knew what a trial it was for him. Long afterward Taylor told some friends that Tetty "was the plague of Johnson's life, was abominably drunken and despicable. . . . Johnson had frequently complain'd to him of the wretchedness of his situation with such a wife."[3] Taylor was naturally partisan about his friend, whom he considered as foolishly submitting to unnecessary indignity. In addition, he was blunt and uninterested in psychological subtlety or excuse. But that he was not exaggerating for effect (he was not much inclined to do that anyway), but expressing his own conviction, is shown by his obstinate refusal to preach the funeral sermon for Tetty—he considered it too hyperbolic in its praise—that Johnson wrote with the hope that Taylor would deliver it.*

It also tells us something about Tetty's condition—real or imaginary—and about her growing timidity before the world that she was not even present at the opening night of *Irene* (February 6, 1749).[5] For this would naturally have been an occasion in the Johnson household. Moreover the play, as she knew very well, had been written almost entirely for her sake. She had seen it grow from nothing; they had read it aloud as it was written; it was closely associated with their first years together; she had shared his disappointment when no theater would accept the play.

---

* See below, p. 273. It should be added that Taylor, at the time Tetty died, was extremely annoyed by an unpleasant marriage of his own. Amusingly, when Taylor's wife left him (1763) and he was preparing on principle to be generous about money, Johnson in turn began to lecture him not only about bearing the troubles of marriage generally (*e.g.*, "To have an unsuitable or unhappy marriage happens every day to multitudes, and you must endeavour to bear it like your fellow sufferers . . ."), but also against a financial settlement that would be "paying [her] for her disobedience."[4]

Now at last the play was being rescued from oblivion by David Garrick, who was using his new position as manager of Drury Lane to help his old schoolmaster in this way. Written back at Lichfield when Johnson was twenty-eight and knew little of the theater, it could by now, when Johnson was almost forty, seem even more old-fashioned to a London audience. For this and other reasons, Garrick wished to make some changes. It was also to have a new title, *Mahomet and Irene*. There were some heated arguments, Johnson, for example, complaining that Garrick "wants me to make Mahomet run mad, that he may have an opportunity of tossing his hands and kicking his heels" (actually Garrick took another part). But Garrick got John Taylor to mediate, and Johnson finally agreed to some of the changes, one of which proved mildly unfortunate (Garrick thought to enliven the play by having Irene strangled before the audience instead of off stage).[6]

Johnson himself thought the first night such an occasion that, believing his character as the author required some "distinction of dress," he appeared in a scarlet waistcoat with gold lace and a gold-laced hat. Dr Adams, who was present, said there were catcalls and whistling before the curtain rose. Johnson's Prologue "soothed the audience, and the play went off tolerably, till it came to the conclusion," when Hannah Pritchard, as Irene, appeared with a bowstring round her neck, ready to be strangled. At this there was such an uproar, with cries of "Murder!," that she finally had to leave and be killed off stage, and later performances were changed accordingly.[7] Garrick kept the play going for nine nights. Asked later, said Boswell, "how he felt upon the ill success of his tragedy, he replied, 'Like the Monument;' meaning that he continued firm and unmoved as that column." But nine nights made a respectable run for a new play. He made a total of almost £300: £195 from the production, while Robert Dodsley, who published it (February 16), gave him another £100. Except for the *Dictionary*, this was considerably more than anything he had yet received for his writing. Moreover, it was by itself almost half the sum Tetty had brought with her when she had married him. It is conceivable that he devoted the entire amount to her.

3

With Tetty out at Hampstead most of the time, the house was naturally lonely at night. By the autumn of 1748, the men helping with the

Dictionary were said by a friend to have almost finished transcribing the authorities to be quoted.[8] The information is not conclusive. When one is collecting over 200,000 citations and continuing to read, one has second thoughts. Moreover, there was other work for at least some of them to do; and for this, as well as reasons of charity, Johnson may have been reluctant to discharge them. But unless one or two were being lodged and boarded there, the place was empty at night. In any case, the house was associated not merely with work but with an extremely demanding work, done under pressure and against the strong inner opposition that a part of him always felt before persistent self-demand.

To ease the loneliness and give himself some change from the atmosphere of the *Dictionary*, he founded a small club in the winter of 1749. It met once a week, on Tuesday evenings, at the King's Head (sometimes called Horseman's, after the landlord), a tavern and beefsteak house in Ivy Lane, near St. Paul's. Here, said Hawkins, "he constantly resorted, and, with a disposition to please and be pleased, would pass these hours in a free and unrestrained interchange of opinions, which otherwise had been spent at home in painful reflection." Here, to an extent he had never been able to do before, he found the means—if only once a week—of approaching the ideal of conversation he had caught from Cornelius. For it was a talented, diverse group, and the conversation ranged over every subject. Johnson, responding to the challenge, "made it a rule to talk his best," said Hawkins, though he would often change the side on which he argued from one week to another. Above all, in his pleasure at their meetings, "he was a great contributor to the *mirth* of conversation," and did so with a "talent of humour" that proved infectious to the others.[9]

In contrast to the famous club (The Club) of Johnson's later years, the atmosphere of the Ivy Lane Club was quite youthful. The majority of the ten members consisted of men with professional or intellectual interests who were still in their twenties or early thirties. There were three physicians: a young Scottish doctor, William McGhie, whom Johnson, said Hawkins, "may almost be said to have loved," and who, "failing in his hope of getting forward in his profession, died of a broken heart, and was buried by a contribution of his friends"; Edmond Barker, aged twenty-eight, who professed himself a Unitarian, was widely read in literature, was deliberately slovenly in dress, and later drifted away; and Richard Bathurst, already a close friend of Johnson's. Then there was a clergyman, Samuel Salter, considerably older than the others. One of the problems for the younger members, said Hawkins, was "to keep alive in Johnson's mind a sense of the decorum due to the age, character, and profession of Dr. Salter, whom he took a delight in contradicting, and bringing his learning, his judgment, and sometimes his veracity to the test."[10]

Several of the members were to remain lifelong friends of Johnson's. One in particular was the endearing and talented young publisher John Payne. It was he who was to publish the series of Johnson's essays during the next decade that comprise the core of his moral writing (the *Rambler*, the *Adventurer*, the *Idler*). Payne also worked for the Bank of England, and in time became Chief Accountant there. The two men, who were physically such a contrast (Payne was "very diminutive"), always delighted in each other's company, and with a cordiality that could seem to others almost playful. Other permanent friends included John Hawkins, whom we discussed earlier in some detail; a young West Indian merchant, John Ryland; and Samuel Dyer, who came from a wealthy Dissenting family (his father was a well-known jeweler) and, though only twenty-four, already combined such learning with a modest and gentle character that Johnson, said Hawkins, "might almost be said to have looked up to him." Later, as a member of *The* Club, he was described by Burke as "a man of profound and general erudition; and his sagacity and judgment were fully equal to his learning." Somewhat less attractive was John Hawkesworth, a miscellaneous writer who worked for the *Gentleman's Magazine*. He attached himself to Johnson as a man on the way up, and became quite good at imitating Johnson's style. He continued the *Parliamentary Debates* after Johnson stopped composing them, and eventually made a good deal of money as a writer. Reynolds thought him "an affected insincere man," rather empty, and something of a "coxcomb," and even Johnson—stubbornly loyal though he was to old friends—had to admit he was among those "whom success in the world had spoiled."[11]

4

Richard Bathurst, who died young (1762), has a special place in any mention of Johnson's friends. If little is known of their relationship, it is because Johnson—who "hardly ever spoke of Bathurst," said Arthur Murphy, "without tears in his eyes"—could rarely bring himself to do more than mention him. But there is a revealing remark to Mrs. Thrale. Speaking of his childhood attempt to search "for evidences of the truth of revelation" (see above, p. 42), he added that he had never told the story to anyone else "except Dr. Taylor, not even to my *dear dear* Bathurst, whom I loved better than ever I loved any human creature; but poor Bathurst is dead!!!" "Here," she said, "a long pause and a few tears ensued," after which she tried to cheer him up by going back to the original story and treating it lightly. This is all she says in her published *Anecdotes*. But in her original notes from which she extracted this, she added something else that indicates how strongly he had felt and still continued to feel about Bathurst:

Speaking once of His friendly Affection for me, he said kindly, I do certainly love you better than any human being I ever saw—better I think than even poor dear Bathurst, and esteem you more, though that would be unjust too, for I have never seen You in distress, & till I have I cannot rank you with a Man who acted in such trying circumstances with such Uniformity of Virtue.—You would (added he) have lov'd Bathurst as well as I did, if I would have suffer'd you ever to see him, but that I would never have done, I should have lost somewhat of each of you.[12]

Given such affectionate language, which is almost without parallel in Johnson, one is naturally eager to find out what one can about Bathurst. His family had settled as planters in Jamaica back in the 1660's or 1670's, but his father, Colonel Richard Bathurst, the proprietor of the Orange River Estate, was not a good businessman. In particular he disliked slavery. Near the end of his life, he returned to England and settled in Lincolnshire (1750). Meanwhile his son Richard had gone to Peterhouse, Cambridge (1738–45), where he took the degree of Bachelor of Medicine, and was now in London hoping to qualify for practice. Peterhouse was the college where Cornelius had been a Fellow, and for this and other reasons Johnson, who was struck by "his endowments and engaging manners," was prepared to associate Bathurst with Cornelius. Despite his father's financial problems, Bathurst's family were landed gentry; he "dressed well," said Hawkins (which Johnson, however careless about his own clothes, liked in others); he was well read in both literature and the sciences; and he scorned "cant" and thought for himself. Above all, like Cornelius, but fortunately without being addicted to drink or gambling, he combined four qualities: a refreshing and unillusioned toughness about human nature (*e.g.*, a remark Johnson once quoted from him: "how seldom, on occasion of coming into the company of any new person, one felt any wish or inclination to see him again"); a fundamentally warm and convivial nature; and, in particular (what Hawkins said made him especially "beloved" by Johnson), the union of "pregnancy" or fertility of imagination with "elegance" of manner.[13]

From here on, as his acquaintanceship begins to extend beyond Grub Street, we note Johnson's fondness for men who could remind him of Cornelius (or rather Cornelius as Johnson at fifteen had idealistically viewed him). He was surprisingly tolerant if their frailties were similar to those of Cornelius's. Bathurst, who had few frailties to forgive, was the first and by far the most affectionately regarded of them. Moreover, he was stepping into Johnson's life when the onset of middle age was leading Johnson not only to question all that he had done but to question life generally in a more serious way than he had ever done before. And, in a way, Bathurst was filling the vacuum created by the change in Tetty. This close relationship continued through Johnson's forties—a period of immense trials. The extent to which he was shaken by Bathurst's death (1762)* is shown not only by the passages cited from Mrs. Thrale, but also in what survives of the diaries and journals, where, in mentioning special prayers at church, he cites Bathurst along with his immediate family: "I recommended Tetty in a prayer by herself, and my Father, Mother, and Bathurst in another."[14]

5

Other friends he was acquiring—typical in their diversity—included a former actress of about thirty, Charlotte Lennox, who was hoping to become a writer; and two of the interesting waifs who were later to become members of his personal household, Robert Levet and the blind Anna Williams.

Mrs. Lennox had a colorful background.[15] She had begun life in the frontier post of Albany, New York, where her father, James Ramsay, was an army officer (in later life she pretended he was Governor or—her story varied—Lieutenant Governor). Sent to England at fifteen to complete her education, she found that the aunt who was to look after her had become incurably insane. Meanwhile her father

---

* Discouraged at his unsuccessful practice in London, Bathurst went back to the West Indies (December 1756), became a physician in the navy, and died of fever, like hundreds of others, in the expedition against Havana, in Cuba (October 1762).

died, and she was left to fend for herself. Failing as an actress, she had recently married a man who worked for William Strahan, the printer for Johnson's *Dictionary*, and had a small book of poems to her credit. She was now finishing her first novel, *Harriet Stuart*, which was being published by John Payne (December 1750). Johnson proposed that the club celebrate the birth of her "literary child" by "a whole night spent in festivity." The story is told with some gusto by Hawkins, who thought the occasion something of a "debauch." They all met at the Devil Tavern around eight in the evening—the club, Charlotte and her husband, and a few others:

Our supper was elegant, and Johnson had directed that a magnificent hot apple-pye should make a part of it, and this he would have stuck with bay-leaves, because, forsooth, Mrs. Lennox was an authoress, and had written verses; and further, he had prepared for her a crown of laurel. . . . About five Johnson's face shone with meridian splendour, though his drink had been only lemonade; but the far greater part of us had deserted the colours of Bacchus, and were with difficulty rallied to partake of a second refreshment of coffee, which was scarcely ended when the day began to dawn.[16]

Johnson, who liked her courage and admired her uphill struggle to establish herself, remained permanently fond of her and continued to help her, writing six dedications for her to use in later publications.* This was to become an increasing practice on his part—writing fifty-odd dedications and prefaces as a favor for other writers, not to mention other contributions to their works. The psychological interest resides in the obvious vicarious pleasure he took in this, while at the same time—using a very different standard—he absolutely refused to write dedications for any of his own works (with the notable exception of the *Plan for the Dictionary* addressed to Chesterfield).

Robert Levet, whom Boswell describes as "an obscure practiser in physick amongst the lower people," was a ruggedly honest and silent man, whom Johnson first got to know in 1746. Like Anna Williams, he was later to prove—and would remain for the rest of his life—a comfort and reassurance to Johnson in what would have otherwise been a painfully lonely life at home. Born in Yorkshire of poor parents, he

---

* He wrote the Dedication and contributed one chapter (Bk. 1, Chap. 11) for her best novel, *The Female Quixote* (1752), which is about a young girl who became crazed by reading romances; the Dedications to her book on Shakespeare's sources, *Shakespeare Illustrated* (1753), her closet drama *Philander* (1757), the second edition of her *Henrietta* (1761), and her translations of Sully's *Memoirs* (1755) and Pierre Brumoy's *Greek Theatre* (1760), to the latter of which he also contributed two sections.

worked in London, probably as a servant, and then in Paris, where, as a waiter in a coffeehouse, he caught the interest of some French surgeons who patronized the place, and through them was allowed to attend lectures on pharmacy and anatomy. Since his return, he had developed a wide practice among the London poor, walking long distances every day, from Houndsditch, near one end of the city, to Marylebone, at the other, ministering to them for a small fee, or, if they could not afford that, for anything they felt they could give him. Often this was no more than a drink of gin or brandy. Rather than go away unrewarded—though he never demanded payment—Levet would quietly swallow the drink, though he really did not want it; and he would occasionally end up drunk ("Perhaps the only man," said Johnson, "who ever became intoxicated through motives of prudence"). An account of him in the *Gentleman's Magazine* (1785), after his death, describes him as a thin, middle-sized man, with a swarthy and "corrugated" face. "When in deshabille, he might have been taken for an alchemist, whose complexion had been hurt by the fumes of the crucible, and whose clothes had suffered from the sparks of the furnace."[17]

After Johnson became famous, most of the people getting to know him—particularly if they were affluent and of some social position—were fascinated by the inmates and pensioners of his household, and would try to get Johnson to tell about them. They were particularly curious about Levet, who, with his stiff silence and "uncouth" manner, seemed the opposite of all that Johnson enjoyed in company. Whoever called on Johnson around midday, said Hawkins, "found him and Levett at breakfast, Johnson in dishabille, as just risen from bed, and Levett filling out tea for himself and his patron alternately, no conversation passing between them." Johnson's new friends were aware of the principal explanation for the presence of Levet, as well as the others—Johnson's charity toward the unfortunate. As Goldsmith said, when Boswell (1763) was questioning him about Levet, "He is poor and honest, which is recommendation enough to Johnson."[18] In addition, a few were aware what it meant to Johnson not to go back to a empty house. But Johnson also found Levet a stabilizing influence. Here was a man who, despite serious disadvantages, performed a useful and charitable function not impulsively or occasionally but with unwavering constancy. It was an example to frail human nature of what could be done. Always haunted by the parable of the talents, he applies it in the finest of his short poems, the lines "On the Death of Dr.

Robert Levet": "Obscurely wise, and coarsely kind . . . The single talent well employ'd."

Anna Williams, who was later to serve as a sort of hostess for Johnson, was the daughter of an elderly Welsh physician, Zachariah Williams, who had come to London hoping to compete for a prize offered by Parliament for a better method of determining longitude at sea.* As the years passed he became completely impoverished. Meanwhile his daughter, who wrote poems and knew French and Italian, developed cataracts. Tetty, who knew about her from Lucy Porter, befriended her. When Tetty died, she committed Miss Williams to Johnson's special care. He accepted the charge seriously, took her into the house at Gough Square, arranged for an operation (it proved of no help), and assisted her in revising her poems and getting them published.[19]

6

Around 1751, Tetty became more seriously ill, and she moved to Gough Square. A touching story of this period was told by Miss Williams, who was visiting Tetty at the time. During all these years Tetty's son, Jervis Henry, a captain in the navy, had abided by his threat never to see his mother again if she married Johnson. He was now a rich man, having inherited the fortune of his uncle, Joseph Porter. One day he knocked at the door and asked the maid if her mistress was at home. The maid replied:

"Yes, Sir, but she is sick in bed." "O!" says he, "if it is so, tell her that her son Jervis called to know how she did;" and was going away. The maid begged she might run up to tell her mistress, and without attending his answer, left him. Mrs. Johnson, enraptured to hear her son was below, desired the maid to tell him she longed to embrace him. When the maid descended, the gentleman was gone and poor Mrs. Johnson was much agitated by the adventure: it was the only time he ever made an effort to see her.[20]

Near the very end, Tetty again went back to the country. We know about this from a remark Johnson made to Fanny Burney three weeks before he himself died. From this, we can infer that the house at Hampstead had been given up and that it was a different place to which she was now taken. "He told me," said Fanny, that

* See below, p. 318.

he was going to try what sleeping out of town might do for him. "I remember," said he, "that my wife, when she was near her end, poor woman, was also advised to sleep out of town; and when she was carried to the lodgings that had been prepared for her, she complained that the staircase was in very bad condition, for the plaster was beaten off the walls in many places. 'Oh,' said the man of the house, 'that's nothing but by the knocks against it of the coffins of the poor souls that have died in the lodgings!' He laughed, though not without apparent secret anguish, in telling me this."[21]

7

When she died (March 17, O.S., 1752), he was distracted. In one of the prayers he wrote after her death, he mentions the resolves he made to her as she was dying (promises of "reformation" in regularity of life and in religious devotion), and which he repeated "when she lay dead before me." Then, though it was at night, he sent in desperation for his old friend John Taylor, who was currently living in Westminster. The letter, said Taylor, which was carried to him immediately, "expressed grief in the strongest manner he had ever read." Dressing himself at once (it was now about 3:00 A.M.), Taylor hurried to Johnson, whom he found "in tears and in extreme agitation." They prayed together. The next day he again wrote Taylor briefly: "Let me have your company and instruction. Do not live away from me. My distress is great."[22]

Pulling himself together, he wrote a sermon that he hoped Taylor would preach at the funeral. But Taylor, as we noted before, refused, finding the sermon's praise of Tetty's virtues too excessive for him to stomach. Johnson was in no condition to argue. The sermon was not delivered. John Hawkesworth then took charge of things for Johnson, and Tetty was buried at Hawkesworth's parish church in Bromley, Kent, where Hawkesworth had recently buried his own wife, a friend of Tetty's. The melancholy that now seized Johnson, said Hawkins, "was of the blackest and deepest kind," and at times seemed "hardly supportable." Only "company and conversation" gave him some relief. Lacking these, "he was miserable." When the Ivy Lane Club broke up at eleven, the usual hour for departure, he would wander the streets. For some time, said William Shaw, he seemed "almost insensible to the common concerns of life."[23]

Henceforth, for years to come, the diaries record his grief for

Tetty, and his prayers for her (especially on each anniversary of her death, and on Good Friday and Easter). April 25, 1752: "Enable me to begin and perfect that reformation which I promised her." March 28, 1753: "I kept this day as the anniversary of my Tetty's death with prayer & tears. . . ." March 28, 1756: "I beseech thee, that the remembrance of my Wife, whom thou hast taken from me, may not load my soul with unprofitable sorrow. . . ." September 18, 1760: "Resolved . . . To consult the resolves on Tetty's coffin . . ." Easter, 1764: "Thought on Tetty, dear poor Tetty, with my eyes full." March 28, 1770: "When I recollect the time in which we lived together, my grief for her departure is not abated, and I have less pleasure in any good that befals me, because she does not partake it. When I saw the sea at Brighthelmston I wished for her to have seen it with me." March 28, 1782: "Perhaps Tetty knows that I prayed for her. . . . We were married almost seventeen years, and have now been parted thirty."[24]

Naturally, in a grief so strong—above all, this continued—several elements converged to reinforce it. Certainly there were guilt and remorse—remorse that she had lost so much at the start because of him (though he had more than paid it back); remorse far more that, because of him, she had been forced to live for seventeen years—and her final seventeen years—in a way radically different from all that she had expected (and this he could never redress); and also some guilt that he had himself at times resented—when another part of him could consider it so understandable—the way she had withdrawn from him, as she had for so many years. Then there is the extent to which, in later years, the grief is self-imposed, significantly on particular occasions like the anniversary of her death. Here the feeling is the familiar one—when the direct responsibility for another person has been a large part of our own lives—that it would be nothing less than treachery not to retain a full sense of what that loss involved. He would blame himself bitterly if he felt his grief growing cool. It would be as though he personally were allowing her to die again.

But the central factor is that he was now—for the first time since he was twenty-six—without the sense of purpose that being needed by another person can give us. Who else had really needed him before Tetty entered his life, and who else needed him now? Something irreplaceable had gone out of his life. For seventeen years she had been the principal responsibility for his effort—at once the motive and, equally important, the excuse for doing what he had done. Given his almost impossible standards for himself, would he—without her as an object of responsibility—have written all those things to which he did not wish to append his name? Certainly it was for her that he had dressed like a beggar all these years, and had so denied himself that he had become radically (and as it proved permanently) incapable of spending anything on himself beyond the barest necessities. In the future he would be unable even to retain a house unless it was filled with the needy. Moreover, that responsibility for her had moved into a fearful vacuum in his life when, for those five years after Oxford, he had been the victim of paralyzing self-despair. Now he was almost back where he had been before he married her. At least he could understandably feel as though he were. Inevitably, his grief, as the profoundest grief always is, was partly for himself. But of course his inner moral censor could not permit him to think of it this way, at least for a while. So little inclined to project unhappy emotions rather than to face and assimilate them directly, in this one case he did, though only enough to help soften the change that had happened to him. Here was another motive for the stated remembrances, the focusing of thoughts back to Tetty.

8

Meanwhile his entire image of himself changed in the next year or two. Henceforth he began to think of himself as a "straggler"—to use his own term about himself much later, when he told old Mr. Edwards, "I am a straggler. I may leave this town and go to Grand Cairo without being missed here or observed there." As Mary Hyde says, he seemed the "young Johnson" until Tetty died, and then suddenly, within a short time, he was much older and much more like the Johnson familiar to us in the memoirs and accounts of his later years.[25] In a way, he was to remain young until the end (this is part of the fascination of his later years), just as he had often seemed older than his years in his twenties and thirties because of the extent to which he had assimilated experience. But this rather sudden change does take place in our image of him, partly because of the change in his image of himself. Needless to say, it could not have taken place so suddenly had it not already been there in solution or *in potentia*, accumulating with his way of life ever since he had come to London—for that matter, ever since he had left Oxford. But responsibility for Tetty had kept the balance from tipping too far. Now the balance tipped permanently.

The three books of which he never tired, said Mrs. Thrale, were *Robinson Crusoe, Pilgrim's Progress,* and *Don Quixote.* "Alas," he would say, "how few books there are of which one can ever possibly arrive at the *last* page"; and "Was there ever yet any thing written by mere man" that one could wish longer than these three books?[26] He would have gone on reading them, he would never exhaust them, because here—as in no other works—his identification was almost complete. These three wanderers—one a castaway, one a pilgrim, and one on an impossible quest—were prototypes of what he felt to be his own life.

Chapter 17

The Moral Landscape: *The Vanity of Human Wishes* and the *Rambler*

While he was in the midst of the *Dictionary*, still another career for Johnson had begun. It was not deliberately selected. He was simply turning now, more directly than ever before, to the human condition and the central problems of living. From this writing, which continues for twelve years (1748–60), Johnson was ultimately to emerge as one of the supreme moralists of modern times—as one of the handful of writers who, in what they have to say of human life and destiny, have become a part of the conscience of mankind. Of such central importance is this writing that we have deferred discussing it until, with the larger part of it under way, it could be considered as a unit.

It begins with that strangely powerful poem *The Vanity of Human Wishes*, an imitation of the Tenth Satire of Juvenal, which he wrote in the autumn of 1748, two and a half years after he had started on the *Dictionary*. He was then thirty-nine, and was on one of those hopeless visits to Tetty at Hampstead that were constantly driving into him how different life becomes from all one would have expected. There, as he told George Steevens, he wrote the first seventy lines "in the course of one morning, in that small house behind the church."[1] Walking up and down, he composed the whole section in his mind before putting it down on paper, which was his general practice in composing verse.* He continued to write it rapidly, and on November 25 sold the copyright to Robert Dodsley for fifteen guineas.

* In writing verses, he told Boswell, "I have generally had them in my mind, perhaps fifty at a time, walking up and down in my room; and then I have written

That so concentrated a poem could be written with such speed indicates how much a part of the inner life it expresses. To begin with, he had for years had all of Juvenal's satires "in his head."[2] As with anything completely assimilated, experience had accrued about these poems and had meshed with them and enriched them. The Tenth Satire in particular had coalesced with a way of thinking that went back to the year at Oxford—to his formative reading of Law's *Serious Call* and the lines he wrote, "The Young Author," which already anticipate the vein of *The Vanity of Human Wishes*.*

The result is a poem that (as was once said of Burke) dazzles the strong and educated intellect far more than the feeble, and sways intelligent and cultivated readers as a demagogue would a mob. Even in the Romantic period, when the condensed intellectual poetry it typifies was not in favor, Sir Walter Scott could praise the imaginative and moral depth of this poem, which "has often extracted tears from those whose eyes wander dry over pages profoundly sentimental."[3] As the twentieth-century reconsideration of poetry began to mature and seek a new relation to the past, T. S. Eliot, on the basis largely of *The Vanity of Human Wishes*, eloquently argued Johnson's claim as a major, in some ways unique, poet. Within our own generation the poem has justly come to be regarded as a landmark. There is indeed nothing else like it in the English language, or indeed any other language. Johnson's own opinion of it could be expressed by the fact that when it was published (January 9, 1749), it was the first work in which he put his name on the title page.

2

The Vanity of Human Wishes discloses the inner landscape of his mind—that is, it reveals the image of reality that was fixed in him, and to which his experience naturally assimilated itself—more completely than any other single work. It is the somber vision of things from which he was often deliberately distracting himself when he talked or

---

them down, and often, from laziness, have written only half lines. I remember I wrote a hundred lines of *The Vanity of Human Wishes* in a day (L, II, 15). The manuscript of the poem (now in the Hyde Collection) confirms the remark about writing "half lines." The first part of many lines is in a different ink from the latter part.
* See above, pp. 107-11.

wrote on more particular topics, though, at the same time, it partially determined what he would say on these subjects. The same vision, diffused through all his other writings, expressed itself in a total way in one other work, *Rasselas*, which he wrote ten years later. If the longer prose fiction could include more characters and pass more topics in review, *The Vanity of Human Wishes* may have fetched Johnson forth more complexly and from deeper down for the simple reason that it was poetry. In fact, *The Vanity of Human Wishes* has a denser, more active texture than would be tolerable in essayistic writing. There is more activity within phrases, and there are more interwoven strands of connection between phrases. All that is going on helps form and refine our sense of Johnson's imagination, its habitual processes and vision.

Though *The Vanity of Human Wishes* is a deeply personal utterance, it also embraces tradition and convention, so much so that it might at first seem almost anonymous to readers habituated to Romantic and post-Romantic modes. Loosely based on a satire of Juvenal's, it adopts the closed heroic couplet of Dryden and Pope. The argument itself is a traditional one in religious apologetics, put unforgettably in the Biblical book of Ecclesiastes, and in such works, among others, as Augustine's *Confessions*, Jeremy Taylor's *Holy Living* and *Holy Dying,* and William Law's *Serious Call:* the complete inability of the world and of worldly life to offer genuine or permanent satisfaction, and our need to turn from this world in order to seek safety and joy in religious faith and in another world. That *The Vanity of Human Wishes* forms itself out of tradition and convention does not make it any the less Johnson's. For, in the first place, the personal re-experiencing of the known and familiar is itself characteristic of Johnson, and is an essential part of his greatness. He authenticates the traditional and conventional by keeping in mind their grounds in practical human needs. Quite apart from this, moreover, tradition and convention do not necessarily make poetry impersonal. They may release quite as much as they guide a poet's own insight and emotion. And, of course, a poet also shows himself in the way he modifies the structures he receives. Johnson omits, for example, Juvenal's coarseness of imagery, and he voices less anger and contempt. He has less playfulness and wit than Dryden and Pope, but far more meditative weight and power of direct emotion. His poem is formally a satire, but his irony differs essentially from that in most classical or Augustan satiric writing, for it articulates a vision more essentially tragic than comic. In most satire, that is, the irony is in the author, who thus stands above his subject. Frequently in the poem Johnson also adopts this stance. But pervasively through *The Vanity of Human Wishes,* the irony is in the world, in the way of things, and the author is as helpless before it as the persons he writes about. In this respect Johnson is closer to Hardy than to Pope.

The perspectives overlap. Because it is following Juvenal's Tenth Satire, it has strong affinities with Roman Stoicism as it relentlessly exposes the slipperiness or emptiness of all the supposed goods through which men and women strive to win happiness. And, at the same time, it exemplifies, as we noted, a traditional mode of religious discourse that seeks to detach the heart and hopes of man from this world by showing that the world offers nothing that can long or deeply satisfy. With these two perspectives, the latter of which begins to subsume the first, passages of generalization alternate with concrete examples, some of which, like the summary narratives of the careers of Wolsey and Charles XII of Sweden, are extended set pieces. Gradually the poem works its way through a wide catalogue of possible human lives in which "schemes of happiness" shipwreck—the wealthy man, the statesman, the soldier, the scholar, the beauty, the man whose wish for "length of days" is granted, even the person of wholly virtuous and benevolent life. The poem awakens an increasingly more powerful response as the examples remorselessly accumulate, but the structure is open-ended, and the examples could theoretically be continued indefinitely. Suddenly, thirty-five lines before the end, the question that had been implicit throughout is allowed to emerge explicitly:

> Where then shall Hope and Fear their objects find?

And the meaning of the question, all that is at stake in it, is driven home by a series of further questions that reveal what must be the situation of man if hope and fear can find no real and valid object:

> Must dull Suspence corrupt the stagnant mind?
> Must helpless man, in ignorance sedate,
> Roll darkling down the torrent of his fate?

The passage defines, as it goes on, a state of stoic or even nihilistic apathy, a lack of engagement in life, which would prevail, in Johnson's opinion, in the absence of religious faith. Then Johnson, who had himself been the questioner, suddenly puts the questioner at a distance by addressing him as though he were another person ("Enquirer, cease, petitions yet remain"), and steps forward himself to remind the almost despairing "Enquirer" that religious love and faith have not been proved vain, but, on the contrary, offer the only solid ground of hope:

> With these celestial wisdom calms the mind,
> And makes the happiness she does not find.

3

As the poem traces the condition of man, two themes strike us as particularly characteristic of Johnson. In the first place, he dwells on the helpless vulnerability of the individual before the social context, the tangled, teeming jungle of plots, follies, vanities, and egoistic passions in which anyone—the innocent and the virtuous no less than the vicious—is likely to be ambushed. The sense of this was already present in the satire of Juvenal's he was imitating. Yet we also recognize a side of Johnson's own temperament in this scene of headlong competition. His characters are "athirst for wealth" and "burning to be great." Even the scholar is motivated by "the fever of renown" that "burns" through "all his veins." As they rise, they jostle others aside, and if they attain the wealth, power, or fame for which they pant, they are at once dogged by the envy and hate of rivals, who soon bring them down.

In the second place, far more than any earlier writer in this tradition, Johnson traces the inevitable "doom of man" to inward and psychological causes. He emphasizes, as was common all the way back to the author of Ecclesiastes, man's incapacity to be filled, to be long satisfied with anything. But he goes further, and the confused jostle he depicts in the outer world finds an analogy in the nature of man himself—in the medley processes of "hope and fear, desire and hate" intercepting each other and making it impossible for the heart to be satisfied if only because its own basic impulses are in conflict. More than this, Johnson makes clear the inevitable self-deception by which human beings are led astray. We see objects through the fog of our own passions, and chase or fly distorted images that lack reality—"fancied ills" or "airy good." We substitute a hot pursuit of fame or wealth as unconscious proxies for what, without knowing it, we really seek. Even in religious devotion the heart may be incorrigibly and perilously self-deceiving, at once creating, and at the same time falling into, the "secret ambush" of its own "specious prayer." What is most immediately striking, as Johnson reveals the principal source of man's misery to be in his own inward nature, is the sheer multiplicity of psychological responses by which he says human hopes are ambushed. Yet the power and panoramic sweep come not from the mere amassing of detail (the poem has only 368 lines) but rather from the extent to which the psychologizing of the theme is organically built into the approach:

> Then say how hope and fear, desire and hate,
> O'erspread with snares the clouded maze of fate,
> Where wav'ring man, betray'd by vent'rous pride . . .

In these tremendous lines from the opening of the poem, it is not sickness, crime, or war—though these figure prominently elsewhere in the poem—that spread the snares, but the natural passions of man; and the arrangement of them in antithesis enforces the recognition that all passions—the positive and innocent, such as hope, as much as the destructive or reprehensible, such as fear and hate—are equally fatal. In the alchemy of man's nature as it interacts with his world, each wish, Johnson goes on, and each "gift of nature" and "grace of art" become sources of disaster. Because the betrayal is from within, the human being seems peculiarly defenseless before it. Johnson would never, of course, have admitted that the mind cannot be "managed," at least to some degree. But because he intuited and emphasized the built-in fatalities of human psychology, he anticipates the pessimistic sense of inevitable self-betrayal that was later to be powerfully expressed in the writings of Schopenhauer and Freud.

When at the end of the poem Johnson turns to religion as the only true and lasting source of hope, the turn of feeling and argument is expected, magnificently handled, and yet also raises central problems of interpretation. Ultimately they are problems in interpreting the character of Johnson's religion, and naturally cannot be explored in the context of this poem only. For if in this poem Johnson had focused, for example, on the figure of Christ, or had centered attention on heaven or eternity as opposed to this world, he would have violated his prototype in Roman satire. The question, however, is the extent to which that prototype imposed a genuine limitation, or, alternatively, allowed him to express, perhaps unconsciously, some of the more essential dynamics of his faith.

Without seeking to answer the question at this point, we can observe that, in the poem itself, the approach to religion is essentially by a negative path. The poem says nothing, in other words, about positive motives to faith, such as the love of Christ, but dwells rather on the incapacity of anything except religion to rescue man from his helpless and doomed condition. As an approach to religion, it is empirical and analytic, and assumes that when one has cast off all illusions, what one has left is the truth. Since it seeks to achieve trust through a basic attitude of mistrust, it clearly entails psychological costs, however strong the intellectual justification may be. Moreover, though it is a religious argument, its focus, as Johnson handles it, is on the problem of happiness in this world. True, the answer is religious resignation to the will of God, trust, patience, obedient passions, a will resigned, love, and faith. The weight of emphasis is on the need to abandon hope and fear, to resign ourselves to God's will; but the point is that what can be gained through heaven's help is happiness on this earth. It is still that to which the imagination is fixed. (Moreover, "happiness," we should note, is Johnson's own word. Juvenal, in fact, says simply that we should leave things in the hands of the gods, who, "in place of what is pleasing, will give us what is best.") Johnson's characters are miserable because they cannot achieve what they strive for, or long keep it when they have it, or long relish it if they keep it. But if we could imagine Cardinal Wolsey continuing through his whole life at the height of his power, and continuing also to be pleased with his power as much as ever—though both conditions are impossible—he would not be, as far as anything in the poem itself would indicate, an example of the vanity of human wishes.

We can illustrate the point quickly if we turn to another poem of religion for comparison, T. S. Eliot's *Four Quartets*. There we find a similarly "negative" mode of argument developed along with other, quite different ones. But the central anxiety of the *Four Quartets*— what is most deeply hungered for and not to be found outside religion—is not so much happiness as such, but rather meaning; that is, a total structure of belief that will integrate unhappiness with the rest of life and give it a positive content or purpose. To the extent that Johnson himself is here taking the problem of happiness as fundamental (and is not entirely forced to do so by the character of the poem), he is, of course, very much a man of his age, speaking directly to one of its central preoccupations.

4

In all his writing Johnson tended to concentrate his vision of things into weighted generalization. His poetry, moreover, is usually rhetorical and declamatory, and it gives a sturdy welcome to known and familiar associations. But this could be said of many neoclassic poets; and what particularly characterizes Johnson's style is the combination of weighted and generalizing declamation with a texture that is remarkably active, varying, and unpredictable, and one that compels close attention and constant minute adjustments of feeling. A miniature example is the well-known couplet he revised (1755) after his experience with Chesterfield (he had originally written, "Toil, envy, want, the garret, and the jail"):

> There mark what ills the scholar's life assail,
> Toil, envy, want, the *patron*, and the jail.

Amid the procession of abstract nouns the new word "patron" bristles unexpectedly with satiric attack.

The combination of diverse energies that makes the texture of his poetry can be shown most easily in the adjectives and verbs that accompany and particularize his general nouns. On the one hand, stock epithets abound, expressing Johnson's confidence in the cumulative wisdom of inherited culture. They organize human experience into its typical and recurrent elements—the "rival kings," the "insidious rival," "restless wishes," "the young enthusiast," the "virtuous friend," and so forth. But, on the other hand, he is just as likely to provide an epithet that arrests attention, energizing, deepening, or sharply individualizing the typical situation. Thus, for example, he speaks of the toiling statesman's "*gaping* heir." The theme is familiar in satiric writing, but the particular epithet "gaping" spreads lurid implications: at the most literal level, the heir might almost be a driveling idiot; at the outer reach of suggestion, there is a half-activated image of the grave, gaping hungrily to swallow the father.

The verbs that go with these nouns commonly lend them a concrete force. We may call this personification, but to think of it as a figure of speech is inadequate. When Johnson writes "nations sink," "envy seizes," "fears invade," "fate wings," "hate dogs," "insult mocks," and the like, he embodies the depth of his response to these abstractions. In other words, both the typically Johnsonian element and the powerful effectiveness of such phrases lie in the extent to which Johnson absorbed these abstractions as concrete realities or presences. To put it still another way, he transformed what in other writers would ordinarily remain abstract into something concretely pictured and felt. Hence also his continual use of allegorical metaphor and illustrative imagery:

> Love ends with hope, the sinking statesman's door
> Pours in the morning worshiper no more.

The lines are typical of Johnson because they give the abstract generalization and also pin it at once to concrete human behavior. Although such imagery could be called "illustration," we should not conceive it as derived and subordinate to the abstract statement. The dynamics of Johnson's style certainly involved the transmuting of the abstract into the concrete, but this does not imply that the craving for concrete purchase and impression was less strong than the need and instinctive clutch for the stability of generalization. In fact, the two tendencies were equally powerful, and were locked in productive conflict.

Johnson's ordinary speech teemed with images, apt, pithy, and surprising. In his critical writings he repeatedly regrets the relative lack of original and forceful imagery in the poetry of his own time, and he uses the term "image" more frequently and favorably than any other critic before the twentieth century. The imagery of *The Vanity of Human Wishes* is constant, condensed, concretely pictorial, and expressed with gusto. There is, for one example, the haunting image we have already quoted from the concluding lines of the poem:

> Must helpless man, in ignorance sedate,
> Roll darkling down the torrent of his fate?

What is typical of Johnson is that his imagination follows up and completes the rather conventional metaphor (torrent of fate) so that now man is pictured as actually rolling down it. "Darkling" (in the dark) adds a further element to the scene, and is at the same time one of Johnson's typical doublings, since it translates into concrete terms a meaning already given in "ignorance." Meanwhile a crosscurrent of feeling comes to the fore in the word "sedate." For man to be ignorantly sedate in a situation so lamentable is ridiculous in the extreme. And, of course, "sedate" also keeps here its root Latin sense of "sitting," so that ignorance becomes the boat, as it were, in which man is both swept along and (though only temporarily) protected. The concreteness of this imagery, the complex interactivity of it, the bold heaping up, and the multiple meanings and feelings evoked are all characteristic.

Throughout the poem there are recurrent images of cloudiness and darkness that conceal lurking danger. At the start of the poem, man is seen treading a "clouded maze," on "dreary paths without a guide," and deluded by "treach'rous phantoms in the mist." As the images accumulate, they suggest a visionary and perilous landscape. Later in the poem Wolsey, for example, builds near the "steeps of fate," and falls into the "gulphs below." The other landscape that the imagery suggests throughout the poem is essentially an urban one. There are repeated suggestions of thronging jostle. Rivals and competitors start up on all sides. The poem sees men and women in mobs of "suppliants," vulnerable and dependent like the "clients" of the ancient patricians in Rome. "Unnumber'd suppliants crowd Preferment's gate"; after Wolsey's fall "his suppliants scorn him." And the theme of man as suppliant returns movingly in the religious content at the end of the poem in the context of religious need: "Still raise for good the supplicating voice."

Another theme of the imagery throughout the poem is the constant rising and sinking in both the inner and outer lives of human beings. There is the slippery scramble of men and women for wealth, reputation, or preferment, in which "They mount, they shine, evaporate, and fall." But there is, to repeat, the even more ominous psychological instability and insatiability rooted in human nature. We see the voter primed with election ale, briefly feeling himself important, "full." And at the other extreme of the social scale Wolsey appears in "full-blown dignity," so "great" that "his nod" alone turns "the stream of honour. . . . His smile alone security bestows." But his wishes are still "restless," he aspires to "new heights" of power. The theme is not just of rising and sinking, but, more generally, of unresting inner and outer transition, inevitably frustrating the clutch of human beings for permanence and security.

5

Johnson had to a pre-eminent degree the quality that Hazlitt called "gusto," that is, an imaginative grasp and response so strong that it is not expressed in a single epithet, but, instead, while coming to focus in an epithet or image, also spreads itself through the adjacent context. Speaking of the "gusto" in Milton's diction, Hazlitt notices that he "repeats his blow twice; grapples with and exhausts his subject," and he quotes for illustration:

> Or where Chineses drive
> With sails and wind their *cany* waggons *light;*

and, as another example:

> Wild above rule or art, *enormous* bliss.[4]

No passage in *The Vanity of Human Wishes* is more characteristic in this respect than that on the "sinking statesman." The opening couplet has already been cited:

> Love ends with hope, the sinking statesman's door
> Pours in the morning worshiper no more.

The powerful verb envisions worshipers in streaming spate; the bold exaggeration in "worshiper" drives in how excessive and wrongly directed the hopes of these "suppliants" are—

> For *growing* names the weekly scribbler *lies*,
> To *growing* wealth the dedicator *flies*—

for it is ironically assumed that the scribbler will naturally lie, the dedicator will naturally flatter, and also, as the passage goes on, that the statesman's followers will of course, when his day and influence have passed, take down his portrait from their walls:

> From every room descends the painted face,
> That hung the bright Palladium of the place,
> And smoak'd in kitchens, or in auctions sold,
> To better features yields the frame of gold.

The demotion of the portrait makes the satiric point; the scenes of its afterfate in kitchens and auctions are an imaginative supplement put with bitter and comic vigor. And then comes the ironic justification:

> The form distorted justifies the fall,
> And detestation rids th' indignant wall.

The four-syllable "detestation" adequately conveys the feeling, but Johnson throws himself into it with such energy that it is further attributed by transference to the wall, as though the wall were bristling with indignation to repel the picture. Again, in the couplet on the way in which human emotions constantly "O'erspread with snares the clouded maze of fate" that man is condemned to walk, we must think of *fate* not only as a *maze* but as a *clouded* maze, and, furthermore, a clouded maze that contains *snares* and is, in fact, *overspread* with snares.

If any passage in the poem is closely analyzed, it will be found that the couplets are composed of two integral units, the individual lines, while the lines themselves are normally divided into two half lines by a caesura. Moreover, the units formed by the versification normally co-incide with the units of syntax, and the integrity of these units is further assured by alliteration and assonance, and by figures of syntax.

> Fate wings with ev'ry wish th' afflictive dart,
> Each gift of nature, and each grace of art.

This firm and shapely modeling should be kept in mind when we read Johnson's critical strictures on the art of eighteenth-century poetry, for example, his doubtful attitude toward blank verse as a vehicle for poetry, and his feeling that Pope, though far from being the greatest of English poets, might well represent an ultimate refinement of versification.

Finally, in Johnson's great generalizing passages, the nouns and adjectives tend often to convey a tone and feeling even if they are lifted from their context. We may take for example the magnificent passage with which *The Vanity of Human Wishes* first announces its theme:

> Remark each anxious toil, each eager strife,
> And watch the busy scenes of crouded life;
> Then say how hope and fear, desire and hate,
> O'erspread with snares the clouded maze of fate,
> Where wav'ring man, betray'd by vent'rous pride,
> To tread the dreary paths without a guide,
> As treach'rous phantoms in the mist delude,
> Shuns fancied ills, or chases airy good.

The abstract nouns are toil, strife, life, hope, fear, desire, hate, fate, man, pride, ills, good. In comparison with other poets, they are unusually many, and in their aggregate weight they create an impression of solemn concern for the ultimate, general character of man's existence. The shading of these nouns is pessimistic, for the notes of "hope" and "good" are outnumbered by "toil," "strife," "fear," "hate," "ills." The adjectives suggest emotional restlessness: anxious, eager, busy, crowded, clouded, wavering, venturous, dreary, treacherous, fancied, airy. Moreover, the adjectives are often interchangeable. Johnson could have written, "Remark each *eager* toil, each *anxious* strife," or, "*dreary* toil" and "*treach'rous* strife," and so forth, although there would always be some loss of tension or propriety from the interchange. That they can be repositioned in this way does not, of course, indicate loose writing, but rather the extent to which a dominant, general feeling governs the whole passage. Finally, the adjectives express Johnson's attitude to his subjects as much as they characterize the subjects themselves. To concentrate on each adjective would be tedious, but if the passage is examined from this point of view, one finds that the adjectives convey alternatively (or in some cases combine) Johnson's sympathy and participation, on the one hand, and, on the other hand, his judgment and warning. In the first case, we have adjectives that express what the person caught up in the toil or strife feels—anxious, eager, dreary, and the like. In the second case, we have terms such as treacherous, fancied, airy, which pronounce the judgment of an onlooker, who sees not just the eager, toiling individual, but also the whole context in which he strives, and utters accordingly his somber but firmly held truth. It is exactly this combination, when both tendencies are present in an extreme degree and—in Coleridge's phrase—locked in a "war-embrace," that is an essential part of Johnson's greatness as a moralist.

6

The moral writing of the following decade, which continues throughout Johnson's forties, could be described as an extended prose application of *The Vanity of Human Wishes*. This is especially true of a large proportion—almost half—of the more than two hundred periodical essays that he now began to write (1750) twice a week for the series he called the *Rambler*.[5] They were published every Tuesday and Saturday for two years, whether he was well or ill, busy or doing nothing, from March 20, 1750, to March 14, 1752. The booksellers who combined to sponsor it were his old friend Cave, his new friend John Payne, from the Ivy Lane Club, and Payne's partner, Joseph Bouquet.

The *Rambler* essays were written, he said, partly as a "relief" from his work on the *Dictionary* and partly because he needed the money. But he also intended the work as a serious moral effort. The name *Rambler* has always seemed a little strange for a work of this character. But titles that would disarm readers had been a convention for periodical essays since the *Tatler* (1709-11) and the *Spectator* (1711-12). However serious Johnson's other intentions, he wanted the work to sell, and a title that would openly proclaim it at the start as a series of moral discourses would have at once cut it off from the popular journalistic prototype on which he hoped to capitalize. Moreover, Arthur

Murphy had a point when he suggested that Johnson was thinking of Savage's poem *The Wanderer*. For years a part of himself had identified with those, like Savage, who lived on the fringes of society, just as another part of him identified with the wanderers in those three books of which he never tired—*Pilgrim's Progress, Don Quixote,* and *Robinson Crusoe*. Between a pilgrim, who travels with "settled direction" or aim, and the "straggler" he at bottom felt himself to be ("one who *rambles without* any settled direction")—the definitions are from the *Dictionary*—there was a middle position, a "rambler," which would not be claiming too much but which would also not preclude moving at times into purpose and direction. From Johnson himself, the only account of the title is a remark to Reynolds—that he "was at a loss how to name it," and, sitting at the edge of his bed one night, resolved that he "would not go to sleep till I had fixed its title. The Rambler seemed the best that occurred, and I took it."[6]

Though the essays did not sell much at the start, and Johnson for a while considered writing them only until he had finished a complete year, they were soon being widely read because other periodicals began to take them over (without pay).* Within another fifteen years they had become something of a classic. From here on Johnson is often referred to as "the author of the *Rambler*." He himself is quoted by Samuel Rogers as once saying, "My other works are wine and water; but my *Rambler* is pure wine." But he was really thinking of the best of them (though there are many good ones), for the series is naturally uneven. As he said in the final essay, the periodical writer who condemns himself twice a week to "compose on a stated day, will often bring to his task an attention dissipated, a memory embarrassed . . . a mind distracted with anxieties, a body languishing with disease." It is not always easy to find a subject quickly twice a week, to change it in time if the topic proves barren, or to correct and revise the essay before the deadline. Moreover, he felt some attempt should be made at variety, and that he should occasionally provide a lighter touch. (In this he is generally less successful.)

Certainly the *Rambler* essays were written more rapidly and with less leisure to outline, consider, or improve them than the works of any other major moralist. Many were written without even being read over

---

* The sale rarely exceeded five hundred per number at twopence a copy. But it was a common practice for periodicals of the time to draw on each other without payment, and many magazines and newspapers soon began to reprint sections or whole numbers as they appeared, with some being published as far away as Boston and Nova Scotia. Afterward the *Rambler* was to go through ten numbered reprintings in Johnson's lifetime (Y, III, xxii).

once by him before they were printed. It is typical that one of the finest discussions in English of idleness and procrastination (No. 134) was "hastily composed," said Mrs. Thrale, "in Sir Joshua Reynolds' parlour, while the boy waited to carry it to the press." But, as in *The Vanity of Human Wishes*, he was drawing upon a large internal fund of assimilated experience and reflection. The best of them—in fact, substantial parts of the majority of them—are saturated with thought to a degree unexceeded by any writer of English prose since Francis Bacon. Boswell was not expressing merely his own opinion when he said that "in no writings whatever can be found more bark and steel [quinine and iron] for the mind."[7]

The distinctive combination is one of psychological shrewdness and somber elevation, of humor and weight of experience, of irony and compassion. Hence the ring of authority even in single sentences that read like proverbs and are quoted time and again:

We are more pained by ignorance than delighted by instruction. . . . The natural flights of the human mind are not from pleasure to pleasure, but from hope to hope. . . . Men more frequently require to be reminded than informed. . . . The safe and general antidote against sorrow is employment. . . . Merit rather enforces respect than attracts fondness. . . . Many need no other provocation to enmity than that they find themselves excelled. . . . The vanity of being known to be trusted with a secret is generally one of the chief motives to disclose it. . . . Among other pleasing errors of young minds is the opinion of their own importance. He that has not yet remarked, how little attention his contemporaries can spare from themselves, conceives all eyes turned upon himself, and imagines everyone that approaches him to be an enemy or a follower, an admirer or a spy. . . . The cure for the greatest part of human miseries is not radical, but palliative. . . . Whatever is proposed, it is much easier to find reasons for rejecting than embracing. . . . Almost every man has some real or imaginary connection with a celebrated character. . . . Discord generally operates in little things; it is inflamed . . . by contrariety of taste oftener than principles. . . . So willing is every man to flatter himself, that the difference between approving laws, and obeying them, is frequently forgotten; he that acknowledges the obligations of morality and pleases his vanity with enforcing them to others, concludes himself zealous in the cause of virtue.

This aphoristic power, which makes him so quotable, was henceforth to be a distinguishing feature of his prose style, both written and spoken. The desire to "manage" experience by compressing it into condensed generality is something we have been noting in him since the verse exercises he wrote as a boy in Stourbridge. But until the

Rambler, we find it mainly in the poetry. By contrast (though only by contrast), the earlier prose, despite exceptional passages, seems almost diluted.

Longinus speaks of the influence of great models in enabling us to become our best selves. The formative influence here was the greatest master of compression in English style, Francis Bacon, whose works Johnson had been reading for the first time while gathering quotations for the *Dictionary,* and "from whose writings alone," he said, "a Dictionary of the English Language might be compiled." In fact, he at one time planned an edition of Bacon's works together with "the Life of that great man." The extent to which he assimilated Bacon has not been recognized. Yet one of his primary themes, from *The Vanity* of *Human Wishes* (1748) to *Rasselas* (1759), is a development of Bacon's treatment of the whole psychology of wishing and of hope, and in particular of boredom and satiety.* But, above all, Bacon gave him an ideal of style involving a union of compression and metaphor, of practical wisdom and imagination. And the tribute he pays to Bacon's *Essays* is one that eminently applies to the *Rambler* and all of his own greater writing henceforth: "Their excellence and value," Reynolds quotes him as saying, "consisted in being the observations of *a strong mind operating upon life.*"[8]

A year after he finished the *Rambler,* Johnson began to contribute essays (roughly every two weeks, from March 3, 1753, to March 2, 1754) to the *Adventurer.* This was a periodical started in imitation of the *Rambler* by John Hawkesworth, of the Ivy Lane Club. Among other contributors was Johnson's friend Richard Bathurst. So close are these twenty-nine essays to the style and theme of at least some of the *Rambler* that, though Johnson may have ghost-written them (or some of them) for Bathurst, we may for our own purposes regard them as in effect a continuation.†

---

* For example, the famous passage in *Rasselas* on the motives behind the building of the Great Pyramid (see below, p. 299), and the "insufficiency of human enjoyments" to the "hunger" of the human imagination is an *exemplum* of the opening section on kings in Bacon's essay "Of Empire."

† Anna Williams told Boswell these papers were really done for Bathurst, who was hard pressed for money, and that "as he had *given* those essays to Dr. Bathurst, who sold them at two guineas each, he never would own them; nay, he used to say he did not write them: but the fact was, that he dictated them, while Bathurst wrote." When Boswell repeated this to Johnson, "he smiled, and said nothing" (L, I, 254). To me, this has the ring of truth and could be accepted as fact (Mrs. Thrale also confirms it). But the distinguished editor of the *Adventurer,* L. F. Powell, has argued against taking it too literally.[9]

7

Though we discuss the moral writing generally in the chapter following this, a few words more should be added about the *Rambler* in particular. It is, after all, the first and largest of the moral writings that follow in the comet's tail of *The Vanity of Human Wishes*. And there was a special sense of dedication about it. He even wrote a prayer on beginning the work:

Almighty God . . . without whose grace all wisdom is folly, grant, I beseech Thee, that in this my undertaking thy Holy Spirit may not be witheld from me, but that I may promote thy glory, and the Salvation both of myself and others.

The sense of the *Rambler* as something special is also shown in his decision at the start (though within a few weeks the effort proved futile) to keep the authorship secret. He was aware that his own appearance and way of life could seem to others grotesquely incongruous with what he would be saying. He wished the purity of the work to be accepted objectively, without the personal comparison people are naturally eager to make between the writings of a moralist and his own life. Less than six years before, when Cave invited him to dinner to meet a man who admired the *Life of Savage*, he had eaten behind a screen because his clothes were so shabby. Now, after the first few *Ramblers*, a gentleman wrote a letter, said Cave, "directed *to the Rambler*, inviting him to his house . . . to enlarge his acquaintance." Johnson was embarrassed, avoided the meeting, and then, uneasy at what he had done, wrote one of his best essays (No. 14) on the inevitable differences between a writer's life and work if the writer conscientiously puts the best of himself into the work.[10]

He was taking no more than a mild gamble in adopting the "external" form he did—the eighteenth-century periodical essay. This was not only an extremely popular form (well over three hundred different periodical series were published during the century) but was also already a fairly flexible one, in which it was quite possible to be serious, though no one had been as persistently serious as Johnson intended to be. Moreover, if it sold even modestly, it would bring in one year more of an income than a book alone would ordinarily bring (Johnson received four guineas a week); and, if it caught on, an audience was meanwhile being created to buy it later in book form. On the other hand, after years of "topical" journalism, his hunger for essential-ism and disdain for "the local and temporary" had deepened. This work was to be different. On the whole, he made few concessions to the "lighter" type of periodical essays,* and was able to say, with some bravado in the last paper, that he had "never complied with temporary curiosity" or tried to exploit "the topic of the day." That he got away with it is a tribute to the flexibility of the periodical essay and also to its audience. But we must also recognize what literary historians forget when they start to bracket works by "genre": that our conception of the *Rambler* is trivialized if, in thinking of its literary ancestry and type, we concentrate merely on the periodical essay. This is what most of the Victorians did. They had a stock notion of what the periodical essay should be, which they based on Addison's *Spectator* and its many imitations. Then, finding the *Rambler* radically different in tone, and so much weightier in thought, they assumed Johnson had "failed," meaning that he must have tried to be like Addison and his imitators, and that he did not "succeed." That assumption is still found in school or college textbooks, and is repeated even by admirers of Johnson who tend to think of him as a sort of Dickensian character in the pages of Boswell.

The truth is that he was doing something quite novel in the periodi-cal essay, with a result that lifts the form into permanent universality. He was combining several things. One is the tradition of "wisdom literature" from the Greek aphorists and the book of Ecclesiastes, through the Renaissance Humanists, down into the seventeenth cen-tury. We have been noting, since he reached the age of twenty and planned to edit Politian, his strong affinity with the Renaissance Hu-manists. He was steeped in their writing. Of the hundreds of literary allusions and quotations that stud the *Rambler*, it is extraordinary how much of the references are to the Humanists (for example, Erasmus, Fabricius, Lipsius, Pontanus, the Scaligers, and Thuanus) and to writers generally from the start of the Renaissance to the end of the

---

* Almost half of the *Ramblers* (ninety-two) consist of direct moral essays. Of the remainder, a large proportion consist of short narrative sketches or "portraits," allegories, and "Eastern tales." But most of these are not just indirectly but frankly didactic, and several are included only as parts or *exempla* within a general frame of discussion. About a seventh (thirty-one) of the essays are concerned with literary criticism. But they tend to be specifically technical and analytic (*e.g.*, on Milton's versification), or else moral in the broadest sense (*e.g.*, concerned with the problems and frustrations of the literary and learned world).

seventeenth century.[11] Because of the speed with which he wrote, these citations were by no means got up for the occasion, but (usually quoted from memory) reflect what came readiest to mind. The tradition of "wisdom literature" and the eighteenth-century periodical essay comprise the warp and woof of the *Rambler*. Further interwoven are elements of the sermon, particularly of the century before (Johnson, as A. N. Whitehead said a generation ago, "is still of the essence of the seventeenth century"). In the rich medley that makes up the style, we look back not only to Bacon, but also to the period of Bacon generally (as Sir John Hawkins said we should if we wanted to know how Johnson's style was formed). At the same time, as Wimsatt has shown, he was incorporating—from his reading for the *Dictionary*—technical and scientific words that he applied metaphorically to psychological and philosophical concepts. Used in this way, they have become part of our modern vocabulary.[12]

Finally, the "portraits" have something timeless about them that transcends the external form of the eighteenth-century periodical essay. In general conception they go back through the "Theophrastan character" of the seventeenth century to the classical writers of *exempla*. But they have been sharpened by the combined influence of the "portraits" in those two writers—radically unlike each other in aim—who had so impressed him when he first read them at Oxford twenty years before: William Law, in the *Serious Call;* and Bernard Mandeville ("his old tutor," as Mrs. Thrale called him), whose satiric reductionism—assimilated long ago by Johnson—remains constantly stirring within him as one element in the habit and dynamics of his expression. The result is something unpredictably and uniquely his own, which cannot be discussed apart from his genius in general and of his humor in particular. In effect, he was developing further a new form of writing, already begun in the *Vanity*, which we could describe as "satire *manqué*"—a form in which protest and satire, ridicule and even anger, are essential ingredients at the start but then, caught up in a larger context of charity, begin to turn into something else.*

* See below, pp. 494–96.

Chapter 18

The Condition of Man: Johnson
as a Moralist

It is as a moralist, in the broad sense of the word, that Johnson regarded himself. In the moral writings as a whole during this period of
his life—from the age of thirty-nine (1748) when he wrote *The Vanity of Human Wishes,* to the age of fifty-one (1760)—we have the
essence of Johnson. It is appropriate to discuss these writings as a unit.
What is most important in any one of them cannot be isolated. As soon
as we more than glance at a central idea in the *Rambler,* for example,
we are led at once to the other moral writings. If we artificially compartmentalize each work, our alternatives are either to avoid the major
ideas generally, and, as we come to each work, concentrate largely on
dates and other external details, or else to fall into repetition of these
ideas when we come to his later periodical series, the *Idler* (1785–60),
and, above all, to *Rasselas* (1759), which, as a kind of prose poem,
serves as a distilled Epilogue to this writing, just as *The Vanity of
Human Wishes* serves as its Prologue. Moreover, it is appropriate not
to wait until these twelve years of moral writing are over and then
look back on it retrospectively, but to turn to this subject now, which
so closely reflects his inner life in his forties, and discuss it at a point
when the larger portion of it has just been completed.

2

What is almost unique about Johnson's writing on human life and
experience is the immense reassurance and trust it inspires. Hence, for

generations, people reading him have found themselves not merely cleansed and steadied in the head, and at times deeply moved, but often smiling or even laughing with what can only be called a sense of "relief." This is especially the secret of the appeal that Johnson's moral writing has begun to make to our own troubled generation, so suspicious of abstractions and slogans, of systems and mere theory, and so quick to distrust and mock whatever has not been personally tested.

In this ability to arouse—and sustain—an immediate and permanent trust, no other moralist in history excels or even begins to rival him. To begin with, few moralists have lived as he did—so close to the edge of human experience in so many different ways. We are speaking of "experience" in the vivid Latin sense as something genuinely won the hard way—*ex periculo*, "from danger" or "from peril." (From the Greek *peràn*, to "pass through," and *peira*, "trial" or "risk"; cognates range from "fare," in the sense of making a journey, to "pirate" and "pilgrim.") Hence the ring of authority in so much that he says. We know that he has gone through it himself at genuine risk or peril, and that his assimilative nature—most aroused when turned to the personal problem of "how to live"—has digested it. This is one reason why, next to Shakespeare, he is by far the most quoted writer in the English-speaking world. But there is another reason. For what distinguishes him still further among moralists (and it is significant that here again one must leave professional moralists and turn to Shakespeare for comparison) is the incredible range—from the hopes and fears of the inner life to the most practical concerns of worldly existence, from anxieties shared by everyone to the more specialized ideals and generosities, stratagems and envies, of the learned, professional, and political milieus. Nothing is left untouched. And yet, when he is through, we find ourselves discovering—what we had never realized before to the same degree—how much of a piece humanity is, and how common the lot we all share in such short time as we have.

Finally, in the assimilative strength of Johnson as what Sir Walter Raleigh called an "experiencing nature," we have distilled the union of four qualities of character constantly operating upon experience—his massive honesty, his unrivaled if often desperate courage, his compassion, and his refreshing humor. Since the result is greater than the mere sum of the parts, any attempt to condense the moral writing (as also the critical writing) into system or formulas always becomes frustrated. As we anatomize, abstract, categorize, and label (with the best of intentions), we inevitably lose what is essential: the active interplay of qualities—of compassion and anger, of humor and moral profundity, of range of knowledge and specialized focus, of massive moral honesty and specific technical or psychological acumen—that come together so refreshingly and reassuringly in Johnson's conversation and moral writing.

For example, we could extract from Johnson's essays as pessimistic a view of the human condition as anyone has ever presented. Viewed in isolation, this would naturally leave us puzzled at the extraordinarily *tonic* effect Johnson always produces. But when we accept it as part of the general *Gestalt* or human totality of Johnson as a moral searcher or pilgrim through the wilderness of life, we realize that an indispensable basis for the trust and reassurance he inspires is precisely this awareness of evil knit up in the very nature of the human situation, of the frightening omnipresence of egotism, greed, and envy; and, above all, of what he called the "treachery of the human heart" in our almost infinite capacity to delude ourselves (while imagining we are deluding others) about our own motives. If we start with the Greek Cynics and go through the long line of writers who have focused most sharply on the radical self-centeredness of human nature, it is hard to find anyone who excels him even in this one respect. The well-known, unilluded moralists who flourished during the sophisticated century just before he wrote—men like Thomas Hobbes, La Rochefoucauld, Swift, or Bernard Mandeville—are more "pessimistic" than Johnson only in the sense that they are more one-sided. In general, Johnson takes what they say for granted, includes and subsumes it. In two ways he goes even further. His suspicion of human motives and his knowledge of the unconscious is even more psychologically informed (in some ways, as we shall notice, it is close to twentieth-century psychoanalysis). Secondly, the sense of evil extends further beyond human nature itself into a more comprehensive attitude toward life and the universe generally. Hence our confidence, which never wavers after we have begun to read him, that he—least of all writers—is not overlooking, disregarding, or falsifying anything at all. He has returned to us with credentials apparent on every page.

3

In *Rasselas*, the Prince and his little group, traveling in search of a fuller understanding of human nature and the world, visit the Great Pyramid in Egypt. As they rest before returning, the philosopher

Imlac speculates why the huge monument was ever built. If the motive were secrecy for the tomb or treasure, this could easily have been secured by less costly and more effective means. What, then, compelled a Pharaoh "whose treasures surmounted all real and imaginary wants" to "amuse the tediousness of declining life, by seeing thousands labouring without end"? The answer is typically Johnsonian: the Pyramid

seems to have been erected only in compliance with *that hunger of imagination which preys incessantly upon life.* . . . Those who have already all that they can enjoy, must enlarge their desires. He that has built for use, till use is supplied, must begin to build for vanity. . . . *I consider this mighty structure as a monument to the insufficiency of human enjoyments.*

The "hunger of imagination" puts in a strong metaphor a perception that pervades Johnson's moral writing: that "so few of the hours of life are filled up with objects adequate to the mind of man"—which can conceive and therefore want so much more than any moment of the present can ever supply—"that we are forced to have recourse every moment to the past and future for supplemental satisfactions." Scarcely an hour passes that we are not looking ahead to the next hour, the next day, the next week, or looking back in the same way. "No mind is much employed upon the present: recollection and anticipation fill up almost all our moments." Time and again, in making excuses for human nature, he would recur to this observation, as Mrs. Thrale noticed. The phrases appear on every page: we are forced to "relieve the vacuities of our being by recollection . . . or anticipation of events to come"; riches fail to "fill up the vacuities of life"; the attempts of visitors at summer resorts to "rid themselves of the day"; literary quarreling for many people "relieves the vacancies of life":

The *vacuity* of Life [said Mrs. Thrale] had at some early period of his life struck so forcibly on the Mind of Mr. Johnson, that it became by repeated impressions his favourite hypothesis. . . . One Man for example was profligate, followed the Girls or the Gaming Table,—why Life must be filled up Madam, & the man was capable of nothing less Sensual. Another was active in the management of his Estate & delighted in domestic Economy: Why a Man *must do* something, & what so easy to a narrow Mind as hoarding halfpence till they turn into Silver?[1]

This is the starting point of Johnson's psychological approach to what it means to be a human being—the nature of the human imagination, the capacity of which is so much larger than any possible enjoyment. It is essentially the theme of the opening chapter of Ecclesiastes: "The eye is not satisfied with seeing, nor the ear filled with hearing." Whatever we have, we are always able to imagine more (or something different); and to imagine more is very soon to want more, or, if despair or fatigue prevent our desires coming again into focus, at least to lose pleasure in what we have. This inexhaustible capacity of the imagination (and, through it, of wishing) is the source of practically all human desires, barring a few biological ones. If it is an indispensable ingredient for human happiness, when it is sufficiently kept open and "regulated by reality," it is also the source of most of human misery— aside from obvious calamities and genuine privation or loss—and of that state into which man can so easily fall, where "many of his faculties can serve only for his torment," as well as the torment of others. The universal scramble for wealth or possessions, for position, reputation, or fame; and—most serious of all—the complex of emotions, like "envy" or the desire "to pull others down," that grows out of the tendency of the imagination to leap over to another person, and then to start comparing what we imagine his situation to be with what we more directly and comprehensively feel to be our own. The whole procedure is thought of by Johnson in dynamic terms, in which, as he says (*Rambler* 2), "The natural flights of the human mind are not from pleasure to pleasure, but from hope to hope."

As in no other classical moralist, we have a profound anticipation of what was to be the wide-scale nineteenth- and twentieth-century discovery about the mind that went on from the major Romantics down through the clinical exploration of the unconscious that follows Freud. That is, the discovery that the mind—far from being either a serene, objective, rational instrument, or, as the radical materialist thought, a sort of recording machine that works in mechanically happy union with whatever outside experiences press the button—is something unpredictably alive in its own right. And when something outside stimulates or pokes it into activity, it can start moving in any number of unforeseen ways that are by no means in harmony with things outside it.

4

The large, tragic knowledge of this is always present in Johnson. It is one of the things that keep him from quick answers about human nature. Those only, said Coleridge, "can acquire the *philosophic imagination* . . . who within themselves can interpret and understand the symbol, that the wings of the air-sylph are forming within the skin of the caterpillar. . . . They know and feel that the potential works *in* them, even as the actual works *on* them."[2] By reaching down to the active process of desiring itself, Johnson attains a deeper level of generality, brushing aside the labels and static concepts of those more conventional moralists and more primitive psychologists who confuse the process of emotion with the particular objects on which desire or obsession happens to fix. Having seized upon the essential, the problem always confronting him is how to use this hungry, preying capacity—the human imagination—in such a way as to get the most happiness or the least misery.

It is in this light that he is constantly looking at the things for which human beings, in their brief lives, compete, grow ill and pine, or fall into envy and hate; and he does so with a shared sense that not only prevents him from cynicism, in any strict sense of the word, but also spreads an arch of charity over his thinking. So in the essays that deal with the desire and struggle for riches, we have something different from the usual answers about the emptiness of wealth. As he once said, "When I was running about this town a very poor fellow, I was a great arguer for the advantages of poverty; but I was, at the same time, very sorry to be poor." Nor could he stand the usual comfortable talk about poverty that comes from people who no longer have to worry about it, nor the nostalgic feeling that the life of the poor has enviable compensations; it was like Marie Antoinette playing the shepherdess. When the wealthy Mrs. Thrale "dwelt with peculiar pleasure" on a line by Garrick, "I'd smile with the simple and feed with the poor," Johnson could not help interrupting: "Poor David! Smile with the simple! What folly is that! And who would feed with the poor that can help it? No, no; let me smile with the wise, and feed with the rich." So with easy talk about poverty from philosophers, especially if they are supported by endowments in colleges and churches that save them from that destitution which is a real "impediment to virtue" because it does not allow "the mind to admit any other care." Nor should we forget that many who pride themselves that they are above the pursuit of wealth neglect it not because "they value riches less, but they dread labour or danger more." Few of them, as he says, would deliberately *refuse* to be rich if to be rich were suddenly in their power.[3]

5

Hence our confidence as he probes, in the moral writings, the "fallacies of imagination" that latch themselves to the images of possessions or wealth. Here, as in other ways, he persuades because nothing that can hypnotize the imagination or distort judgment is merely dismissed. The recurring debate on marriage versus single life is another example, from common and daily experience, of the way in which the imagination is constantly defeating or souring happiness for many people because of its tendency to project an oversimplified image (whether of marriage or of single life) and then to become disappointed. The married who look back nostalgically on their single years, and "blame the rashness of their own choice," are not keeping in mind that the days they wish to call back "are the days not only of celibacy but of youth, the days of novelty and . . . of hope." The truth is that "marriage has many pains, but celibacy has few pleasures"; that "every animal revenges his pains upon those who happen to be near"; and that "we see the same discontent at every other part of life which we cannot change":

Every man recounts the inconveniences of his own station, and thinks those of any other less, because he has not felt them. Thus the married praise the ease and freedom of a single state, and the single fly to marriage from the weariness of solitude. . . . Whoever feels great pain, naturally hopes for ease from change of posture. . . .[4]

In a lighter vein, another subject that fascinates him as an example of the working of the imagination could be expressed in his remark: "The general remedy of those, who are uneasy without knowing the cause, is change of place." In the essays we are always coming across people who fly off for privacy, get bored, feel sudden release when they meet people they knew back home, complain of the discomforts of the journey and the service at inns, and then promptly do the same thing again the next year. All this is put with such comic insight that Macaulay, in his famous essay on Johnson, said that he dismissed travel "with the fierce and boisterous contempt of ignorance." Macaulay's essay—reprinted in scores of schoolbooks and anthologies—popularized the notion of Johnson, which is still common, as a confirmed Londoner who could not be budged from Fleet Street. Actually, as

Mrs. Thrale said, "he loved indeed the very act of travelling," and was "an admirable companion on the road, as he piqued himself upon feeling no inconvenience, and on despising no accommodations."*

What he is doing here, as he illustrates again the working of the imagination, is to select an example so nearly universal that almost anyone can recognize it, and so innocent that people are not afraid to admit it. The point is put best in *Rambler* 6, where he discusses the announcement of the now almost forgotten poet Abraham Cowley that since fame was bringing him no rest, he intended to sail to a plantation in the West Indies, and "foresake this world forever, with all the vanities and vexations of it, and to bury myself there in some obscure retreat." Actually, as Johnson says, he could have buried himself in his own country. There is enough pride in the human heart to prevent our seeking the acquaintance of those by whom we are certain to be neglected. But Cowley, when interrupted and fatigued by attention or social life, began to feel it impossible to be far enough away from what he thought "the cause of his uneasiness," and letting his imagination fly by contrast to an image of leisure and retreat, forgot

that solitude and quiet owe their pleasures to those miseries, which he was so studious to obviate . . . that day and night, labour and rest, hurry and retirement, endear each other . . . we desire, we pursue, we obtain, we are satiated; we desire something else, and begin a new pursuit.

If he had proceeded in his project . . . it may be doubted, whether his distance from the vanities of life, would have enabled him to keep away the vexations. It is common for a man, who feels pain, to fancy that he could bear it better in any other part. Cowley, having known the troubles and perplexities of a particular condition, readily persuaded himself that nothing worse was to be found, and that every alteration would bring some improvement; he never suspected that the cause of his unhappiness was within. . . .[5]

6

As with these simple things common in most people's experience, so with careers, professional ambition, the hunger for power or for "reputation," and the pathetic hope that we are "filling the minds of others" with a sense of our own "importance." The theme again is the

* For Johnson's attitude toward travel generally, see below, pp. 461–62.

way in which the imagination extrapolates from the chaotic welter of possibility a specific aim that it thinks will answer the heart's desire. Hope, and with it fear, begins to narrow obsessively.

Inevitably, since he is partly reminding himself, he enjoys focusing on the writer or scholar, who likes to think his motives are purer but secretly "places happiness in the frequent repetition of his name." It is this more than anything that underlies what Johnson (and few writers have more earned the right to the phrase) delightfully calls "the epidemical conspiracy for the destruction of paper" that is constantly going on in thousands of rooms at any one moment. But once a man has made "celebrity necessary to his happiness, he has put it in the power of the weakest and most timorous malignity, if not to take away his satisfaction, at least to withhold it." We find it difficult to remember how little "renown" is possible anyway, with people universally preoccupied with their own hopes and fears, "engaged in contriving some refuge from calamity, or in shortening the way to some new possession." If the writer stopped to reflect a moment on it, he would remember that "every catalogue of a library" is crowded with "names of men, who, though now forgotten, were once no less enterprising and confident than himself"; that names which "hoped to range over kingdoms . . . shrink at last into cloisters or colleges." And even in these "last retreats of fame," the attention of the "few solitary students" that may read or copy down a name is very casual, except for those authors "whom the present mode of study happens to force upon their notice."[6]

In one of the finest essays (*Rambler* 2), he mentions how much like Don Quixote we all are, dreaming of projects, exaggerating the rewards, and living "in idea." "Our hearts inform us that he is not more ridiculous than ourselves, except that he *tells* what we have only *thought*." Yet at the same time he points out that few efforts of labor or risk would ever be undertaken "if we had not the power of magnifying the advantages" in the way Don Quixote himself did. It is not a matter of suppressing or bludgeoning imaginative wish. In the first place that is not possible. The stoic belief that this can and should be done is itself an example of the "fallacies of imagination." We cannot so completely fly in the face of our own nature. In the second place, as moral beings we are effectively motivated through the imagination, that is, through the concrete envisioning that activates emotion. "Without hope there can be no endeavour"; and "it is necessary to hope, though hope should always be deluded; for hope itself is happiness, and its frustrations, however frequent, are less dreadful than its extinction."[7] The problem remains: what are we to do after accepting what we are? "Where, then, shall hope and fear their objects find?"

7

In most of what we have touched on, there is usually—up to a point—a genuine, if precarious, innocence. No one else need be hurt, nor do we ourselves need to be mortally wounded, by the incorrigible habit of the imagination in clutching at images of wealth and security, of "change of place," or of "filling the minds of others" (whether in romantic love or in the thought of audiences "panting with expectation"). And frequently it is treated with a light touch, as in Cowley's dream of an island retreat; or the idea of the moralist "swelling with the applause which he has gained by proving that applause is of no value" (in contrast to Johnson's own honest admission that "the applause of a single human being is of great consequence"); or in the picture of the lecturer who torments himself as he imagines an audience filled with admiring expectation, hushed with attention. Terrified with "the dread of disappointing them," he strains his imagination to prove that

his reputation was not gained by chance. He considers that what he shall say or do will never be forgotten; that renown or infamy is suspended on every syllable; and that nothing ought to fall from him which will not bear the test of time. Under such solicitude, who can wonder that the mind is overwhelmed . . .? Those who are oppressed by their own reputation, will, perhaps, not be comforted by hearing that their cares are unnecessary. . . . While we see multitudes passing before us . . . we should remember, that we are likewise lost in the same throng; that the eye which happens to glance on us is turned in a moment on him that follows. . . .

So in the hilarious sketch of the young author (*Rambler* 146) who, with beating heart on the day of publication, walks out "like a monarch in disguise" to the coffeehouse, prepared to overhear comments on his new book with thoughtful attention and receptive good nature, and then finds that no one is even aware of the book but talking of other matters. True, the process by which the imagination—reacting from the comparative emptiness of the present—oversimplifies an aim, leads us to work or ingratiate our way to it, and then finds it is not the answer to happiness, is one that can prove, in really serious matters, tragic. Yet (up to a point) the troubles and disappointments remain our own, and need not complicate or distress the lives of others.[8]

But discontent and frustration, in the human heart, rarely remain either simple or final. Unless they are being purified by moral or religious principle (though, as the line in *The Vanity of Human Wishes* says, one of the sad lessons of experience is "How rarely reason guides the stubborn choice"), or unless they are being supplemented with other considerations that bring us closer to the larger context of reality, they retreat into the self and begin to fester. Johnson had "studied medicine diligently in all its branches," said Mrs. Thrale, "but had given particular attention to the *diseases of the imagination*."[9] The moral writings become more penetrating as Johnson also turns on the way in which the human imagination and human desires, when blocked or repressed, begin to grow claws and start to tunnel their way out into the various forms of envy and hostility, while at the same time deluding us into thinking we are standing up for virtues or standards (in moral conduct, in art, in intellectual works, or anything else).

His clairvoyant sense of the complex "treachery of the human heart," and its capacity to destroy both its own peace and its own perception of reality, provides an anticipation of Freud that we are only beginning to recognize.[10] Psychiatrists for years have been fond of quoting him: "Children are always cruel. . . . Pity is acquired and improved by the cultivation of reason"; "Abundant charity is an atonement of imaginary sins"; "We do not so often endeavour or wish to impose on others as on ourselves"; "There is a kind of anxious cleanliness . . . characteristic of a slattern; it is the superfluous scrupulosity of guilt, dreading discovery, and shunning suspicion." But the part of Johnson that really anticipates psychoanalysis is not to be found in simple thrusts that cut through a complacent sentimentalism about human nature. It is to be found in Johnson's studied and sympathetic sense of both inner "resistance" and what in psychoanalysis are called "defense mechanisms," or, in Johnson's phrase, "the stratagems of self-defence." In particular, he anticipates the concept of "repression" as he turns on the way in which the human imagination, when it is frustrated in its search for satisfaction, doubles back into repression, creating a "secret discontent," or begins to move ominously into various forms of imaginative projection. The result, of course, is not a series of formal analyses. The moral writings consist of reflections on a wide variety of topics. The insights they contain are to be interpreted by the frequency of themes and the pattern into which they fall as Johnson touches on problems only superficially different.

We may start by noticing the extent to which Johnson dwells on the multiform rivalries and secret resentments that divide human beings not only from each other, but also from what they really want. Grudge and malice are surveyed in every context, from the ingrown rancor of rural and village life to the "stratagems of well-bred malignity" in fashionable society, from the mutual animosity of different callings—such as the "malignity of soldiers and sailors against each other"—to the far more alert and individual jealousies of writers, scholars, and critics, which naturally fascinate him and evoke some of his sharpest satiric phrasing. We see this in the ease with which gossip (though begun with other motives—we can think of nothing else to say, we wish to avoid topics that might kindle argument, we need to fill "the vacuities of life") can slip into disparagement or censure of others. A few moments of praise and admiration of someone not present often prove as much as a company can endure. Censure is more "willingly indulged because it always implies some superiority," both in our ability to discern faults and in the supposedly high standards that we can parade to ourselves and others as being violated. Of special interest is Johnson's perception that the restless need of the human psyche to censure, as it becomes more pronounced or focused, is really "the symptom of some deeper malady within ourselves"—a warding off and projection away from ourselves of our own "secret discontent." For example, a sense of our own fearful and anxious nature, vigorously repressed, easily projects itself into a constant and uneasy suspicion of others, a suspicion in which—unless we have been extraordinarily victimized in the past—we really betray our own inclinations. Or there is the projection by which a man, consciously or not, tries to inflict "on others" what he "formerly endured himself," as if to dispel, Johnson remarked, his own misgiving that his sufferings were wasted. Or there are those who seek to enforce on other people moral or legal obligations that they themselves have broken or secretly resent having to follow. They begin to "extenuate their own guilt" or resentment by making "vague and general charges upon others," or by circulating more particular suspicions in the hope that attention—including their own—will "be employed on any rather than themselves." But the imagination can take still more "artful subterfuges." An individual can ease his guilt by magnifying or dwelling on faults or habits that seem different from his own: "He then triumphs in his comparative purity, and sets himself at ease." Even here Johnson notes how commonly the quality we censure in another is the counterpart to an "opposite fault" in ourselves, as if we hoped to transform our own lack into a virtue.[11]

8

In all this a fundamental motive is the desire to relieve our sense of any unfavorable disparity between ourselves and others. Instead of "lowering others," we could, of course, try to raise ourselves, or we could at least try to measure more objectively the supposed disparity to see whether it actually exists, and to discover—if it does—how seriously we are being harmed. But to lessen others is far easier, particularly since we have an almost unlimited capacity to delude ourselves about our motives in doing so.

Johnson points out that all other vices, except indolence, at least require special opportunities. But it is the advantage of envy that it can operate "at all times, and in every place." Even in the Happy Valley, where all desires are satisfied, Rasselas finds himself envying the animals if only because, unlike them, he has nothing "to desire." A further temptation to envy is that it can usually act "without expense or danger. To spread suspicion . . . to propagate scandal, requires neither labour nor courage." Only when a man has "given no provocation to malice, but by attempting to excel," and nevertheless finds himself pursued "with all the implacability of personal resentment," does he learn to "abhor those artifices at which he only laughed before" and discovers "how much the happiness of life would be advanced by the eradication of envy from the human heart."[12]

In professional as well as social life Johnson notes how envy contributes to the cult of mediocrity, smoothing the path for those who make us better "pleased with ourselves." The acrimony of literary critics is often excited merely by "hearing applauses which another enjoys"; the palm of popularity in drawing rooms goes to persons whose conversation is "unenvied insipidity." Envy is naturally all the greater in professions where performance cannot be objectively measured, and where the main external reward is (or is thought to be) that most elusive of things, "reputation." Merchants can judge themselves by their income, physicians by their cures, but writers and scholars—except for the really generous of heart—too often allow themselves to fall into the same psychological situation as that of celebrated "beauties," where, "as both depend for happiness on the regard of others, on that of which the value arises merely from comparison, they are . . . both incessantly employed in schemes to intercept the praises of each other." And because of the perennial debatability of all things that cannot be strictly or numerically measured, the door is more widely open to the temptation to delude ourselves about our own motives and to release our aggressions in what we quickly convince ourselves is a righteous cause. But "he that knows the treachery of the human heart" is also aware "how often we gratify our own pride or envy under the appearance of contending" for standards of excellence.[13]

Envy is of all vices closest to "pure and unmixed evil" because its object is "lessening others, though we gain nothing to ourselves." To this extent, it violates "the great law of human benevolence" more than "self-interest" does. We may rationalize and say there is some profit from envy (profit to the individual morally in being "pulled down" or deservedly chastised, or, if we are insane enough, profit to ourselves, in the thought that the attention we are trying to prevent being given to another will be freer to turn with admiration and delight to ourselves). But the real motivation in "the cold malignity of envy" is "not so much its own happiness as another's misery." As Johnson recurs to this, we sense an incredulity that people can treat each other thus in "a world bursting with sin and sorrow," where all face the same doom. That incredulity is reflected in an episode in *Rasselas*, where Imlac tells the Prince of his early life. When he first joined a caravan as a merchant, he found that his fellow merchants deliberately exposed him to frauds, or led him into situations where he would face difficulties with officials. In doing so, there was no "advantage to themselves, but that of rejoicing in the superiority of their own knowledge." The young Rasselas cannot believe that a man would wish to "injure another without benefit to himself." Also, though men are certainly pleased by feeling superior, yet Imlac's ignorance and naïveté were "merely accidental," and could afford his fellow merchants "no reason to applaud themselves": "the knowledge which they had, and which you wanted, they might as effectually have shown by warning, as betraying you." But Imlac can give no answer except to say, "Pride is seldom delicate, it will please itself with very mean advantages; and envy feels not its own happiness, but when it may be compared with the misery of others."[14]

9

There is a special psychological interest for us in the way Johnson approaches envy. One of the fascinating things about him, as we noted earlier, is his almost complete freedom from it. Yet the temptations to envy, as we also noted, had been unusually strong—especially in so aggressive and competitive a nature—as he saw, in his later teens, one schoolfellow after another, with a fraction of his talent, go on to a university while he had to stay in Michael's bookshop. If the temptations were strong in his teens, they became little short of massive when he left Oxford with such a feeling of humiliation. Yet what we find during the five years following this is the opposite of envy in any ordinary sense of the word: a desperate effort to turn his aggressions against himself rather than against others, and to assimilate and digest the "disease of comparing oneself to others," rather than to project it into jealousy and antagonism toward the more fortunate or toward the social system generally. So also through his thirties, except for the rather innocent resentment of the young Garricks' meteoric rise to wealth and fame through the arts of "mimicry" and "gesticulation."

We are naturally curious how he did it, and how this taboo against envy succeeded to such a degree that it remains as one of the permanently refreshing and admirable things about him. The answer is that he did it through a combination of two things: pride and charity. "Reformation," as he says, is rarely achieved through only one means. There are occasions when the only way to drive out a "passion" is by another passion. Pride can be a fearful thing. But it is possible for pride (as distinct from "envy") to rise in quality and aim to a point where it can disdain and free itself from the degrading "malignity of envy." He is speaking from the experience of at least twenty years when he says that philosophy has proved helpless to pull out this "stubborn weed of the mind." Hence any means is justified that can help us, if not to eradicate it, at least to "overpower and repress it":

I have hitherto avoided that dangerous and empirical morality, which cures one vice by means of another. But envy is so base . . . that the predominance of almost any other quality is to be preferred. . . . Let it, therefore, be constantly remembered, that whoever envies another, confesses his superiority, and let those be reformed by their pride who have lost their virtue.[15]

This is one way, and it is not to be disdained. But what makes him uneasy now—what made him uneasy for years—is that this is essentially the "high classical" and "pagan" appeal to a nobler pride. The true Christian will achieve freedom from envy through the humility exemplified in the life of Christ. In the dialectic of Johnson's own nature, the more creative and therapeutic uses of pride are constantly wrestling with the Christian preaching of humility and charity before the fact that all mankind, in this world "bursting with sin and sorrow," is facing the common "doom of man." Accordingly, Johnson's moral writing, starting with *The Vanity of Human Wishes* and continuing down through *Rasselas*, is in one of its most important aspects an eloquent reminder—to himself as well as others—that "there are none to be envied." If we can see envy for what it is, it and the huge "bustle" of activities into which it seduces us are at best another of man's doomed "stratagems of self-defense"—a self-made prison, or web, built largely by projections, fears, and wants, in which the desire is not so much "to impose on others as on ourselves," and in which, as "helpless man" becomes enmeshed in it, his faculties begin to "serve only for his torment."

By his forties, the panoramic sweep with which he looks at the condition of man is so thoroughly ingrained as to become habitual and to appear at every occasion, giving depth and resonance. To give just one example, he begins what seems to be a light essay on sleep (*Idler* 32). As he mentions the need of human beings for oblivion at least once a day, he remembers the remark of Alexander the Great that he knew himself to be a man rather than a god by his need for sleep. Johnson wonders whether anything could help more to cleanse the mind and "repress all the passions that disturb the peace of the world" than for all of us to keep in mind how all—the high and the low, the favored and the destitute—unite in their need to sink for a time "into insensibility," and not merely through sleep alone. Even Alexander, in order to endure "the sovereignty of the world," had to add drink to the amount of daily "stupefaction" afforded by sleep:

All envy would be extinguished if it were universally known that there are none to be envied, and surely none can be much envied who are not pleased with themselves. . . . Such is our desire of abstraction from ourselves, that very few are satisfied with the quantity of stupefaction which the needs of the body force upon the mind. Alexander himself added intemperance to sleep, and solaced with the fumes of wine the sovereignty of the world. And almost every man has some art, by which he steals his thoughts away from his present state.[16]

10

When we consider all that religion meant to Johnson, the relative absence of explicit discussion of it in the moral essays indicates, for one thing, that though the moral essays put us into intimate contact with Johnson's mind, they do not contain his whole mind. We should note something else. As far as *specific* discussion is concerned (in contrast to general injunctions), the moral writings are far more concerned with what to beware of and avoid than what to do positively. In all serious moral writing, of course, from the Ten Commandments down, the values are quickly stated and implied. The problem is how to avoid slipping from them, and the procedure is therefore admonitory. Even so, the difficulties of living tend, as Johnson treats them, to pile up to so formidable a degree that the general picture is indeed one in which "human life is everywhere a state in which much is to be endured, and little to be enjoyed."[17]

It is therefore the more striking that the total effect of the moral writings, despite their searching awareness of all that cumbers and darkens the heart and life of man, is to create hope as well as the trust we mentioned at the start. The hope is what we ourselves catch from Johnson's own resolute belief that the tangled mess of human nature is not beyond help. Men and women can become wiser and more aware: moreover, what they understand as intellectual beings can make a difference in the dynamics of emotion and instinct, clarifying and guiding them to some degree. But it is not only or even primarily through arguments in favor of hope that one effectively gives hope to others. What matters more is his whole style as a person.

So with Johnson. He energizes hope not only by what he thinks, but also by the way he goes about thinking it, and the hope his example activates is a hope for human nature, for ourselves. Merely to list the topics of the essays that deal with human weaknesses, temptations, and trials is to list what he spent a lifetime in battling in himself. Since he had a capacious and varied nature, the list is long, ranging from the hunger for fame or praise—"reputation" or "importance"—to the reading of escapist romances (in which he could lose himself for hours); from the self-defeating folly of anger, when his own heady temper was one of his principal enemies, to the inability of the imagination to remain content with the present moment, but to leap ahead, if not in hope, at least (as he was constantly doing) in order to anticipate imagined future calamities and steel oneself against them. He could write as well as he did about grief or despair, about remorse and guilt, about boredom, satiety, and the hunger for novelty, about pride, aggressive competition, and the habit of arguing "for victory," because he himself was so susceptible to all of them and yet was constantly putting them at arm's length in order to see them for what they were. The insights into the psychology of indolence come from a man who could write the *Dictionary* singlehanded, but who also knew what it was to fall into a state of blank apathy for weeks at a time (or, in his twenties, for months at a time) and who could honestly say that he had not just occasionally but "*always* felt an inclination to do nothing." The religious James Beattie once confessed to him that he was "at times troubled with shocking impious thoughts." If he was startled by Johnson's reply, he could also have been reassured: "If I was to divide my life into three parts, two of them have been filled with such thoughts." So in every aspect of life: when he is discussing the need and ways of bringing thoughts "under regulation," he is speaking with the direct knowledge of what it means not only to wrestle with inner resistance and a turbulent imagination but also to have feared at times for the preservation of his own sanity.

Yet he is never defeated. He emerges on the other side of a question, peers around it, and then goes beyond it to more fundamental problems, confronted with equal courage, including even the question:

whether to see life as it is, will give us much consolation, I know not; but the consolation which is drawn from truth, if any there be, is solid and durable; that which may be derived from error, must be, like its original, fallacious and fugitive.[18]

There is a refreshing dauntlessness in the way he cuts through to the essentials of human psychology and need, and while keeping all of them steadily in mind, pushes aside (with cleansing and unforgettable comment on them as well) the incessant quarreling over superficial points and labels that always goes on in the intellectual world. Even the testiness and comic impatience of phrase are therapeutic for us. We begin to feel as though a mine sweeper were moving in front of us, clearing the path of so much that we had darkly feared. Or, if dangers remain, they now seem more reduced to size, because of that marvelous union of two forms of perspective that Johnson combines—the union of comic reduction (which would never succeed for us unless we were also aware that he was overlooking and dismissing nothing) and of sympathetic understanding and compassion (which again would never convince, and never prove contagious, unless we knew it had been hard-earned). Finally there is the example of what we can only call the *purity* of his thinking. Though what he writes is pervaded with his own experience and emotion, he is constantly able to keep them from imposing subjective distortions.

11

Hence in the moral writings—as in all of his greater writing or as in the parable of his life generally—we always sense two fundamental values, not because they are preached but because they are coming to us with the force of example. One is the potential freedom of man: the conviction that man is to a large extent—or at least can be to a greater degree than he realizes—a "free agent," even though everything seems to combine against it, including the traps human nature is forever making for itself.

Before he is through, we ourselves begin to share his antagonism to any form of the belief, such as that popularized by Hobbes a century before, that human motives are determined by a mechanical, inner calculus of pleasure that ministers to our own egos. In one of the first issues of the *Rambler* (No. 4), he turns at once upon Swift's statement that men are "grateful to the degree that they are resentful":

> This principle, with others of the same kind, supposes man to act solely from a brute impulse . . . without any choice of the object. . . . It is of the utmost importance to mankind, that positions of this tendency should be laid open and confuted.

The "laying open" and "confuting" of all determinism, of all thinking that seals over man's hope for freedom of choice, is carried through every aspect of Johnson's writing on human life.

The second value, sustaining and rendering practical the first, is expressed in the simplest and finest of his maxims: "The first step in greatness is to be honest." He had written this back in that early "Life of Sir Francis Drake" (1740), soon after he had come to London and begun the long period of struggle there. More than anything else, his own courage to move toward and into honesty is what had at least partly freed him from the prison house of a crippling self-involvement—from the paralysis that an overwhelming superego or self-demand had pummeled him into during the terrible years of his early and middle twenties. Though it is as easy to trivialize the ideal of honesty as of anything else, the truth is that many qualities are necessary for genuine honesty, and that is why it is so difficult in the sense

Johnson means ("the first step in *greatness*"). It is impossible without a perspective (and, more than a perspective, an active imaginative and emotional response to value) that can take us beyond ourselves. It may be possible without humor, though without humor it can quickly hit a ceiling where our potentiality for sincerity is unable to go beyond mere earnestness, with the myopia that mere earnestness, naked or alone, inevitably creates. But honesty is certainly not possible without courage. For "unless a man has that virtue," as Johnson says, "he has no security for preserving any other." Above all, it is impossible without charity and compassion. It is necessary, in English, to use both words, though they overlap. For the ideal of *caritas*—of caring and feeling responsibility—is traditionally (and was for Johnson) a religious and moral principle. While including "compassion," it involves more, and, because of that more, provides direction and value. On the other hand, "compassion" (or "with-feeling") is a psychological act, involving sympathy or empathy—the ability to get out of ourselves and into and with others—but is still incomplete except as it moves into actual caring and responsibility. "All joy or sorrow for the happiness or calamities of others," he said, "is produced by an act of imagination . . . placing us, for a time, in the condition of him we contemplate."[19] The *projective* capacity of the imagination is a major theme in Johnson, as we have been noting in detail. We are all, as he shows time and again, living vicariously "in idea" anyway—hoping to astonish or impress others (and, through them, ourselves). In one of the satiric sketches (*Adventurer* 84), six travelers enter a coach with "supercilious civility" and, "collecting importance" into their faces, try to impress their companions. By degrees they begin to assume certain roles—a butler talks about his titled friends, a stockbroker's clerk begins to talk about his investments as he scans the newspaper, a woman who runs a small eating place begins to complain of inferior service at the inns in comparison with what she is used to having. The point is that, since they will never see each other again, they have nothing to gain in the way they impose on each other except their own momentary satisfaction, through a kind of play-acting, of living vicariously in a more vivid semblance of what they wish. In other words, we are dealing with something so ingrained in human nature that it is going to find an outlet no matter what the circumstance. But the same outward leap of imagination that leads the people in the coach to do this, or that leads us to look ahead to the next hour, the next month, to our future condition and interest (or that leads us back, with nostalgia, to the past), is also capable of sympathetic identification with others, with moral values, or with anything else that can release man from the subjective prison of self. The problem is to use this yearning, this capacity to leap forward—or in any other direction—in a moral way: to "regulate" it with "reality."

12

Over a century before Freud, the plea is for the release and freedom of the psyche through what Freud, himself deeply classical, called the "reality principle," and Johnson, in the *Preface to Shakespeare*, called "the stability of truth." True, it is taken for granted that the frail human ego can only too readily, if unconsciously, fight against the admission of truth, and is astonishingly resourceful in the devious ways it can discover for doing so. Still, in the broadest sense, the "heart naturally loves truth." At least it naturally wants the security, the reassurance and anchorage to fact, that only reality can give. Of course, we can quibble about "reality" forever while the world passes by. Hence Johnson, though he delighted especially in "metaphysical reasoning," finally kicked the stone in answer to Berkeley's idealistic argument against the existence of matter, saying "I refute it *thus*." Here he was like the philosopher Hazlitt mentions who, weary of the arguments about the impossibility of motion based on "Zeno's paradox," finally got up and walked across the room. As we read through Johnson, we begin to share his conviction that "truth such as is necessary to the regulation of life, is always to be found where it is honestly sought."[20] The essential phrase is "*honestly* sought." And, of course, it is a process, and, in our pursuit of it, we find ourselves only pilgrims and searchers. But as Whitehead said, in his great manifesto for modern science and philosophy, "The process *is* the reality." Every new experience we face will be in some ways different.

In Johnson's moral writing we are dealing with a drama in which different parts of him are in dialogue with other parts. The drama is an honest commentary on the drama of life itself, in which doubts, perplexities, repressions, pride, and charity all are a part of the medley of what "helpless man" confronts in his own pilgrimage, whether he considers himself a "Rambler," an "Adventurer," or even—as Johnson called his last series—an "Idler." "For us," as T. S. Eliot said in *East*

Coker, "there is only the trying." But when conviction finally emerges (if only for a part of what we conceive or hope to attain), the honesty that results is such that our own experience begins to thaw from defensive numbness into co-operative confidence, and moves closer to the only freedom possible to us—the freedom that comes through the harmony of the inner life with truth.

Chapter 19

Later Forties: Growing Difficulties; the Start on Shakespeare; *Rasselas*

In September of 1755, the year the *Dictionary* was published, Johnson became forty-six. The money paid him in installments (£1,575) had been used up as it came in, and so had the smaller amount that he got from the *Rambler* (1750–52). Much of the other writing had been done as a help to others. One such work, written as the *Dictionary* was appearing, is so typical in both its compassion and unexpected talent that it deserves a kind of immortality. It was done for an aged Welsh physician, Zachariah Williams, the father of the blind Anna Williams, whom Johnson, at Tetty's request, had taken into his household in 1752. For years—since 1714—Parliament had offered a large prize for a more accurate way of determining longitude at sea. Williams, who had studied navigation in his free hours, had worked out a method based on variations of the magnetic needle of the compass in different parts of the world. He came to London and submitted his plan. It received no attention and he was soon helplessly adrift in the city, though for a while he had been allowed to live in the Charterhouse as a "poor brother pensioner." He had been bedridden since 1746, and now, at eighty-two, was fatally ill.

Johnson had already ghost-written several letters and petitions from Williams to the Admiralty, but with no success. Now, in order to give the dying Williams some feeling of self-respect, Johnson quickly studied the subject of navigation in more detail, and wrote up Williams's ideas in a little book, *An Account of an Attempt to Ascertain the Longitude at Sea* (1755), with Williams on the title page as author. He then got Giuseppe Baretti to make an Italian translation to be printed with it (the thought was that this would give the booklet a quasi-international status). Meanwhile he arranged for his friend "Doddy" to publish it, almost certainly paying the expense himself, though he had hardly any income now except what he was paid for making an abridgment of the *Dictionary*. In June, just before Williams died (July 12), he made a quick trip to Oxford, deposited a copy in the Bodleian Library, and, said Thomas Warton, who was with him, "for fear of any omission or mistake, he entered in the great Catalogue, the title-page of it with his own hand."[1]

By the end of 1755 Johnson was finding it difficult to meet his bills. It was doubtless foolish to cling to the large house in Gough Square, which he had rented at the beginning only to please Tetty. But it was associated with so much of the past eight years—with the hopes of establishing for Tetty a new "respectability," with the *Dictionary* and the amanuenses working with him on the top floor, and with the *Rambler*. Meanwhile, during the lonely Christmas season, he became ill with a severe case of bronchitis, possibly even pneumonia, with "a cough so violent," as he told a friend (December 29), that in his weakened condition he "once fainted under its convulsions." To add to his troubles, his single good eye became inflamed with an acute conjunctivitis that went on for weeks, making it difficult to read or write. This continued throughout much of February.

2

Just as he was becoming ill in late December, he received news that shook him—of the serious, perhaps fatal, illness of a woman he had hoped, almost three years before, to ask to marry him; the religious and high-minded Hill Boothby, that "second Olivia Lloyd" whom he had met in 1739 when he stayed with John Taylor at Ashbourne. That was when, after his first year in London, he had returned to Lichfield to apply for a schoolmaster's job, and had lingered in the area for so long, unwilling to return to London.*

We have only recently learned that, back in 1753, a year after Tetty died, he had seriously considered marrying again. We know this now from two short entries in a diary he kept for this crucial period of his

---

* See above, pp. 182–86.

life (1753–65), probably the most extensive diary he ever kept. This is one of the journals he burned before his death. But one day at Johnson's house (May 5, 1776), Boswell secretly copied several entries, which still survive in Boswell's handwriting. He decided not to mention these two, perhaps out of delicacy and with the thought that they might reflect on the picture he felt he should give of Johnson's first marriage. The first entry is on Easter (April 22, 1753):

> As I purpose to try on Monday to seek a new wife without any derogation from dear Tetty's memory I purpose at sacrament in the morning to take my leave of Tetty in a solemn commendation of her soul to God.

Then, the next day (April 23), he states that he went down to Bromley, where Tetty was buried, and, "during the sermon which I could not perfectly hear," made a prayer for her and another prayer "against unchastity, idleness, & neglect of publick worship." He adds that "during the whole service I was never once distracted by any thoughts of any other woman or with my design of a new wife." Plainly he was eager to convince himself that his intention was in no way disloyal to Tetty's memory, though another part of him—aroused by guilt and protective loyalty—now began to dwell on her memory to such an extent that he writes a few days later (April 29): "I know not whether I do not too much indulge the vain longings of affection."[2]

Almost certainly the wife he had in mind was Hill Boothby.[3] But any thought of marriage was quickly dropped. Miss Boothby's close friend Mary Meynell, who was married to William Fitzherbert, had died in March (1753). Miss Boothby, her executor, had long promised to take over the management of the Fitzherbert household and the six Fitzherbert children. Meanwhile she and Johnson corresponded. In fact, he once told John Taylor (1756), while apologizing for being a poor correspondent (for he never enjoyed writing letters), that "I never did exchange letters regularly but with dear Miss Boothby." Most of these private letters have not survived. Johnson had ample opportunity in later years to get them returned from the Fitzherberts and then to destroy them. More likely, Miss Boothby herself may have destroyed them, considering them private. But a few do survive from the weeks of her final illness, when she had no opportunity to put them away. They express the deepest tenderness in language rarely found elsewhere in his letters ("My Sweet Angel," "Dearest Dear," "none but you on whom my heart reposes"). Though he was himself ill, he wrote her almost daily during these weeks. In his last letter (as always when emotion becomes so overpowering that he instinctively strives to control it through formality), he stops addressing her as "My Sweet Angel" or "Dearest Dear," and begins "Honoured Madam—I beg of you to endeavour to live . . . if you can write three words to me, be pleased to do it." But then he ends: "I am afraid to say much, and cannot say nothing when my dearest is in danger."[4]

When she died (January 16), said Giuseppe Baretti, who saw him frequently at this time, Johnson "was almost distracted with his grief," and his friends "had much ado to calm the violence of his emotion."[5]

3

Then, in the middle of March, he was suddenly put under arrest for debt (£5 18s.). The prospect of the debtors' prison in the eighteenth century—so difficult for us to imagine now—was a fearful one, especially in the winter, when scores of debtors would be thrown together in the Marshalsea Prison with only scraps to eat, a thin blanket to cover them as they lay on the floor, and of course with no heat. The arrest completely surprised Johnson, sunk in loneliness and grief and still not well. Immediately he tried to reach his friend William Strahan, who had been the printer for the *Dictionary*. Not finding him, and perhaps unwilling from embarrassment to approach the other booksellers connected with the *Dictionary*, he wrote to Samuel Richardson, whose novels had been a success, and who had loaned him money in the past and had offered to do so again whenever Johnson needed. Richardson at once sent six guineas—in other words, eight shillings more than the sum for which Johnson was being arrested. That tiny extra touch of generosity—a round sum slightly above the amount of the debt—naturally tells us something about Richardson, who, as distinct from his own fictional heroes, was being very close, and yet doubtless felt he was showing he did not count pennies too exactly. But it could also explain why Johnson, who understood him very well, applied to Richardson rather than someone else. Johnson was never to forget the favor, and, though at bottom he always regarded Richardson as something of a prig, he had an additional incentive in standing up for him against rival novelists.

Obviously something had to be done, and not only because he needed money. He also needed a project to help him get out of himself. Hill Boothby's death drove in the sense of loneliness that had been deepening since Tetty's death. The loneliness had been modified by the sense of purpose in his work at the *Dictionary*, and palliated by the Ivy Lane Club, but the *Dictionary* was now finished and the members of the club had begun to disperse.[6] He had, of course, been acquiring new friends. Three of special importance should be mentioned: Arthur Murphy, Bennet Langton, and Joshua Reynolds. They were quite unlike each other. The enterprising young Murphy, the son of a Dublin merchant, was a talented actor who was later to become a well-known dramatist. Indirectly he was to have an enormous influence on Johnson's life and happiness, for it is he who later introduced Johnson to Henry Thrale and his wife. Murphy was twenty-seven when he had first met Johnson in the summer of 1754. At this time he was single-handedly writing a periodical patterned after the *Spectator* called *The Gray's-Inn Journal*, though he was also entranced by the stage (the following autumn he acted Othello at Covent Garden). On a visit to the country early in June 1754, he told his friends he had to hurry back to town to prepare a new number of his *Journal*. One of the company—Samuel Foote, the actor—said there was no need, and pointed to a French magazine that contained "a very pretty Oriental tale" that Murphy could simply translate and send to the printer. Murphy followed the suggestion, but on returning to town discovered that the tale in the French magazine was itself a translation from one of the *Ramblers* (No. 190). He felt he should call on Johnson and explain what happened. He was fond of telling the story in later years, and once did so in Johnson's presence. Happening to arrive when Johnson was at work on one of his chemical experiments, he

> found our friend all covered with soot like a chimney sweeper, in a little room, with an intolerable heat and strange smell, as if he had been acting Lungs in [Ben Jonson's play] the Alchymist, making *aether*. "Come, come (says Dr. Johnson), dear Mur, the story is black enough now; and it was a very happy day that brought you first to my house, and a very happy mistake about the *Ramblers*."[7]

Another lifelong friend, though Johnson could hardly have guessed it at the time, was young Bennet Langton—a conscientious, earnest, somewhat prim youth with scholarly interests, from a wealthy and established family in Lincolnshire. In later life "Lanky," as Johnson called him, reminds one of those people from old New England families about whom George Santayana writes in *The Last Puritan*. He even looked like them—tall, thin, long-faced, "much resembling," said an acquaintance, "a stork standing on one leg, near the shore, in Raphael's cartoon of the miraculous draught of fishes. His manners were in the highest degree polished; his conversation mild, equable, and always pleasing." When still only fourteen or fifteen, he had read and admired the *Rambler* essays, which were beginning to circulate in bound volumes, and a year or so later (1754 or early 1755), while studying to enter Oxford, he visited London mainly with the hope of being introduced to the author. Mentioning this hope to the landlady of the house where he took lodgings, he learned that by good luck Mr. Levet often visited the house. The landlady introduced him to Levet, who in turn took him to see Johnson. No one had told him of Johnson's appearance, and it would hardly have occurred to the silent Levet to enlighten him as they walked to Gough Square. From reading the *Rambler*, Langton had fancied to himself

a decent, well-drest, in short, a remarkably decorous philosopher. Instead of which, down from his bed-chamber, about noon, came, as newly risen, a huge uncouth figure, with a little dark wig which scarcely covered his head, and his clothes hanging loose about him. But his conversation was so rich, so animated, and so forcible, and his religious and political notions so congenial . . . that he conceived for him that veneration and attachment which he ever preserved.

At some time during the year 1756, Langton persuaded his father, who controlled a rectory of some value in Lincolnshire, to offer it to Johnson if he wished to take orders in the clergy. Johnson, despite his need, turned it down, and not merely because of his attachment to London. He knew how incongruous he and his whole way of life would seem to his parishioners. Moreover, if his scruples and distrust of his own imagination inhibited him from discussing religion in his moral writing (discussing it in any really specific way), they certainly prevented him from considering himself qualified to be a clergyman.[8]

A third new friend was the still relatively young Joshua Reynolds, now in his early thirties, who within the next ten years was to become the principal portrait painter in England.[9] Reynolds, whose family lived in Devonshire, had spent two and a half years in Italy (a severe cold caught while painting in the Vatican brought on the partial deafness—hereditary in the family—from which he suffered the rest of his life). He settled in London early in 1753, first in St. Martin's Lane and then later in the year at a house in Great Newport Street. With him was his young sister Frances, then in her mid-twenties, who was to keep house for her bachelor brother for many years. In time, because she was disappointed in love, Frances proved a trial to her brother and moved to separate lodgings. But Johnson always remained devoted to his "dear Renny," as he called her, and her "Recollections" of Johnson, which she was too timid to publish, are probably the most delightful, certainly the most amusing, of the short memoirs of him.

Johnson and Reynolds first met at the home of the two daughters of Admiral Charles Cotterell, Frances and Charlotte, whom Johnson had known for years and who kept a kind of salon. On this occasion the Miss Cotterells were lamenting the death of a friend to whom they had been deeply obligated. Reynolds remarked, "You have, however, the comfort of being relieved from a burthen of gratitude." The Miss Cotterells were shocked. But Johnson, whose readiness to attack the cant of affected or exaggerated grief was one of the instinctive defenses by which he tried to control his own feelings, was pleased with "the *mind*" the remark "exhibited." It showed that Reynolds "had the habit of thinking for himself." Reynolds, for his part, had admired the *Life of Savage*, which he had recently read, and found that Johnson more than fulfilled his expectations. That same evening Johnson went home and had supper with Reynolds, and their friendship quickly grew. An incident occurred shortly afterward—again at the Miss Cotterells'—which both Reynolds and his sister thought amusingly characteristic. While Johnson was following some ladies upstairs on this visit, the housemaid, noticing his shabby dress, seized him by the shoulder and tried to pull him back, exclaiming, "Where are *you* going?" Startled into shame and anger, Johnson roared out like a bull, "What have I done?" Meanwhile a gentleman behind him quieted the maid, and Johnson "growled all the way up stairs, as well he might." Already chagrined, he became more offended when two ladies of rank suddenly arrived (the Duchess of Argyle and Lady Fitzroy), and the Miss Cotterells, engrossed in their titled visitors, neglected to introduce him or Reynolds. Inferring that this was because they were ashamed of him and Reynolds as "low company," he sat for a while in silent meditation and then, "resolving to shock their supposed pride," called out to Reynolds in a loud voice, "I wonder which of us two could get most money by his trade in one week, were we to work hard at it from morning to night." "This incident," said Frances Reynolds, "Dr. Johnson used to mention with great glee—how he had *downed* Miss C., though at the same time he professed a great friendship and esteem for that lady."[10]

Becoming acquainted with Johnson at this crucial period (later in the year he was to paint the first of his portraits of Johnson), Reynolds got to know him in a way that few others among Johnson's later and famous friends could possibly know him, and during one of the darkest periods of Johnson's life—in 1764, before he knew the Thrales—he could think of Reynolds as "almost the only man whom I call a friend." Everything Reynolds later wrote of Johnson is the result of direct knowledge considered over a period of thirty years. Significantly, when Boswell published his great *Life of Johnson*, he dedicated it to him.

4

Of course, the time he spent with such friends was limited (Langton, in fact, went back to Lincolnshire, and then in 1757 went to Oxford as a student). The time he spent with all his friends put together was limited, though the number, as we have noted, was large and included people of every sort. It was not the same thing as having a family to which one could turn at any time, and it was in this way that Johnson was especially lonely. Even his makeshift family at home was at this time smaller than we later think of it as being. Besides Miss Williams and the Scottish "maid" she inherited from Tetty—one imagines someone like the "orfling" in the Micawber household—there was apparently a cook. Possibly the roughly silent apothecary Mr. Levet, carrying on his practice in the poor areas of the city, had already joined the company, though he may simply have been a daily visitor, joining Johnson for breakfast around noon each day. Finally there was Francis Barber, a black youth of twelve or thirteen, who as a child had been brought to England from Jamaica (1750) by Colonel Bathurst, the father of Johnson's close friend Richard Bathurst. Colonel Bathurst, who hated slavery, had in effect given Frank Barber his freedom when they left Jamaica (he had obviously brought the child to England only because he was an orphan), and in his will (1756) reasserted this lest Barber have trouble in the future. After sending him to a school, which Frank disliked, Colonel Bathurst asked his son Richard to take over responsibility. But Richard's attempt to start a medical practice in London was proving hopeless. He was living a hand-to-mouth existence, and in desperation decided to join the navy as a physician. After Tetty's death, knowing how lonely Johnson would be in the big house at Gough Square, Richard in turn transferred Frank (now about ten) to Johnson, who, if he could not afford to send him to school, could at least give him employment as a kind of valet.

The mere idea of a personal servant for Johnson was laughable, not only now but in later years. As Sir John Hawkins said, "Diogenes himself never wanted a servant less than he seemed to do." But Johnson was not thinking of a servant when he accepted responsibilty for Frank. The youth was simply being added to the family of the compassionate and lonely Johnson, and increasingly he was valued both for his own sake and, above all, because he was associated with the beloved Bathurst. Very quickly Johnson felt he should arrange for Frank to attend a new and friendly school—one conducted by Mr. Desmoulins, the Huguenot writing master who had recently married Elizabeth Swynfen, the daughter of Johnson's godfather Dr. Swynfen. This, Johnson could feel, was a help not only to Frank but also to the struggling Desmoulins. But Frank was getting restive and wanted to become an apprentice to an apothecary, a Mr. Farren, who had a shop in Cheapside. This was the situation at the point where we are now (1756).

Since Frank was later to be a permanent member of the household, we should add a few words more about the intervening years. Money was needed to article Frank as an apprentice. Later in 1756 Johnson arranged this. But Frank found shopwork dull, resented the way apprentices were treated, and ran off to sea (July 1758) as a sailor in the navy, where he stayed two years. Life as a sailor at this time, when a third of a ship's company could perish on a long voyage, could well prove a shock to the gentle Frank, accustomed all his life to kind treatment and more recently to the Bohemian permissiveness and disarray of Gough Square. As Johnson later put it: "No man will be a sailor who has contrivance enough to get himself into a jail; for being in a ship is being in a jail, with the chance of being drowned. . . . A man in a jail has more room, better food, and commonly better company." This was not wholly a joke. In 1759 the worried Johnson, at the cost of some embarrassment, tried to get Frank released from the navy (it involved getting the notorious John Wilkes to use his influence at the Admiralty). After Frank was released (August 1760), he was to remain permanently with Johnson, except for a five-year period of schooling (1767–72) which, complained Miss Williams, cost Johnson £300. He later married an English girl (1776), and Johnson in his will made him his principal beneficiary.*

5

His small household, aside from whatever other comfort it gave him, had the further value of providing him with obligations. Sunk in despair during January and February, he occasionally tried to pull himself into shape. In a prayer after Hill Boothby's death (January 16, 1756), he asked for help to "apply myself earnestly to the duties which thou hast set before me." When the inflammation of his eye seemed over (February 15)—actually the respite lasted only four days—he made another prayer: "Almighty God, who hast restored light to my eye . . . teach me, by the diminution of my sight, that whatever I possess is thy gift," and to use the gifts granted him. His arrest for debt (March 16) finally jolted him into firmer resolution.

He determined to embark without further delay on two projects. The more immediate one, chosen with the idea of earning money as soon as possible and enabling him to get his bearings for a different and larger project (an edition of Shakespeare), was a new magazine. The previous year he had toyed with the thought of something already well developed in France: a *Bibliothèque,* or general digest and review of works, particularly foreign, appearing in all learned fields. Dr. Adams said he was quite serious about it. Johnson's experience with the huge *Harleian Catalogue* had proved that something of this kind was not only well within his powers but could be handled without usurping too much time. But of course he would need financial backing, and no publisher at the moment was much interested.

A compromise of sorts seemed possible when two or three publishers approached him to supervise and help with a journal to be called *The Literary Magazine, or Universal Review.* Business details would be handled by William Faden, who had been the printer of the *Rambler.* Moreover, since Johnson—who had never liked to appear to the public

---

* Johnson asked Tobias Smollett, the novelist, who knew navy procedures, for help, and Smollett then got Wilkes to intercede. The school to which Johnson later sent Frank was the excellent grammar school of Bishop's Stortford, Hertfordshire (a school later attended by Cecil Rhodes).[11]

as a "mere journalist"—had developed almost an obsession about anonymity in work of this sort, Faden could also serve as nominal editor. The first number came out on May 19, 1756. Within a few months there were political disagreements between Johnson and the owners. The Seven Years' War had begun. In political articles, he strongly attacked the policy of imperial and commercial expansion. The quarrel of the British and the French in America, as he viewed it, was the quarrel of "two robbers" for the land stolen from the Indians. Of the two, the French had at least the credit of treating the victim—the natives—with more consideration. He also swung against public clamor and the press generally in his spirited defense, for two numbers, of Admiral John Byng, who had failed to lift the French siege of Minorca, and was then hounded by the press, accused and condemned for "cowardice," and finally executed (March 1757). Johnson rightly pointed out that Byng was being made a scapegoat for the Admiralty's incompetence and that neither the press nor the court was giving him a fair hearing. Johnson's political position soon proved embarrassing to the owners of the magazine (there was also apparently some change in ownership), and he began to lose interest, though he continued to write some reviews. The magazine was not very successful anyway, and lasted only another year and a half (till July 1758).[12]

Considering the time he was willing or able to give it, the work he did for the *Literary Magazine* is something of a tour de force in range and variety. Like Bottom, he was willing at first to play all the roles—as editor and as contributor on every subject, including a biography of Frederick the Great. A special feature of the magazine, salvaged from his plan for a *Bibliothèque*, was to be its reviews. During the first year, especially the first six months, he wrote at least thirty-four reviews of works ranging from Sir Isaac Newton's proofs of God to Francis Home's *Experiments on Bleaching*, and from Jonas Hanway's attack on the consumption of tea (with which Johnson, already an inveterate tea drinker, naturally took issue) to Hoadley's and Wilson's *Observations on a Series of Electrical Experiments*. There were reviews of works on beekeeping, the use of ventilators in ships, and distilling sea water; on Ben Jonson, the court of the Emperor Augustus, dealings with the Mohawk Indians, Polybius, and the national debt. Two major reviews are among the better-known short essays of Johnson: the review of Joseph Warton's essay *The Writings and Genius of Pope* and, above all, of Soame Jenyns's *Free Inquiry into the Nature and Origin* *of Evil.* We must come back to this last essay when we turn to the subject of Johnson's religious attitudes.*

Apart from the *Literary Magazine*, he was doing other miscellaneous writing. Shortly after he had finished the *Dictionary*, he had mentioned, as a project to some publishers, a special dictionary dealing with trade and business, and may have made a start on it. But it turned out that one was already being completed—Richard Rolt's *New Dictionary of Trade and Commerce* (1756). The publishers got Johnson to write a Preface for it. Later questioned about it, he said that he "never saw the man and never read the book. The booksellers wanted a Preface . . . I knew very well what such a Dictionary should be, and I wrote a Preface accordingly." Aside from this and the little book on Longitude for Zachariah Williams, mentioned at the start of this chapter, he also wrote Dedications for his friend Giuseppe Baretti's *Introduction to the Italian Language* (1755), for William Payne's *Introduction to the Game of Draughts* (1756), and for Charlotte Lennox's translation of the memoirs of the Duke of Sully (1756). He revised an older edition of Sir Thomas Browne's *Christian Morals* and prefixed to it a "Life" of Browne, which tends to be rather testy and is remembered now largely for its perceptive remarks on Browne's style. Partly for the money, but even more to help his unfortunate friend Christopher Smart, who started up a new magazine that lasted only for the year 1756—the *Universal Visiter*—he wrote three pieces, characteristic in their diversity: "Further Thoughts on Agriculture"—so called because it continued from another writer's article in a previous number; "Dissertation on the Epitaphs Written by Pope"; and a penetrating essay, to which we shall return later, "Reflections on the Present State of Literature."[13]

6

But writing of this sort was not what he expected of himself, however resistant part of him might be to his own self-expectation. Nor would it be what others expected. (As he wrote a friend at Oxford, he was willing to send him copies of the *Literary Magazine*, "But you must not tell that I have anything in it.") What was really needed, as he realized even while he was agreeing to take over the *Literary Maga-*

* See below, pp. 375–76.

zine, was another large work—something that, in its way, would be comparable to the *Dictionary*.

On June 2, 1756, after the first number of the *Literary Magazine*, he had signed a contract to prepare an eight-volume edition of Shakespeare within eighteen months—a volume every two months, with a mere two months at the end to wrap up the edition, insert any further notes that seemed needed, and add a Preface. In preparation he published (June 8) his *Proposals for an Edition of Shakespeare*. It had been ten years since he had first thought of doing this. The plan had been dropped because the publishers of William Warburton's projected edition of Sharkespeare had threatened to sue Johnson's own publisher, Edward Cave. But now things were different. Because of the *Dictionary*, Johnson's position as an authority on the language excelled that of anyone in England, and it was Warburton's publishers themselves who now turned to Johnson. His own thought was that he could draw rapidly on what he had learned of the language and writing of Shakespeare's time, while working on the *Harleian Catalogue* and, above all, the *Dictionary* itself. In fact, he could tell himself that he had already done a fair amount of the work.*

Even so, the target date of eighteen months was so absurdly short as to suggest that he was deliberately imposing it on himself with less concern for the demands of the project itself than for fighting what he knew to be an enemy—his own inner opposition to exacting self-demand. How often he had learned that he could write most fluently when he could do it vicariously—when he was writing prefaces, dedications, sermons, or anything else for another person, or doing it anonymously as "assigned" hack work for Edward Cave or another publisher. Then any possible "blame" could be deflected. By this is meant "self-blame," for of course, as he said (as no one has ever said better), the rest of the world is not much preoccupied with the slips, mistakes, or inadequacies of an author.

He would now learn from his own experience. The time he had spent on *Irene*, self-consciously working over each line—grotesquely out of all proportion to its value—was only one graphic example from his own experience, contrasting wildly with a work like the *Parliamentary Debates*, written as fast as the human hand could write them,

* Among the index slips of passages for the *Dictionary*, only half of which had been used, were some thousands from Shakespeare alone illustrating his use of words, and comprising, as Bertrand Bronson says, a "relatively complete Shakespeare Glossary." Moreover, there are indications that when he planned that earlier edition years before—the one blocked by Warburton's—he had already done some work on it.[14]

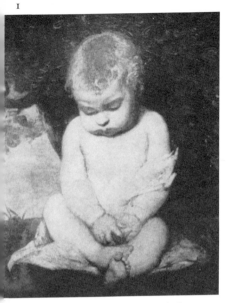

Imaginary portrait of the infant
Johnson by Sir Joshua Reynolds

Michael Johnson

The Lichfield Grammar School

Midnight Modern Conversation by Hogarth. The man third from the right is thought to represent Cornelius Ford in his middle thirties.

The school
at Stourbridge

Gilbert Walmesley

The Bishop's Palace, Lichfield, where Walmesley lived

The school at Market Bosworth

Elizabeth Jervis Porter
a few years before
marrying Johnson

Edial Hall

St. John's Gate,
containing the office of the *Gentleman's Magazine*

Temple Bar

Priory Lodge, where Tetty lived in Hampstead

Gough Square
in the Victorian period

Stairway to the garret in Gough Square

Imagined scene of Johnson waiting to see Lord Chesterfield.
(Here and below Johnson is portrayed more as he might have looked
twenty years later.)

Imagined scene of Johnson reading the manuscript of *The Vicar of
Wakefield* when Goldsmith was about to be arrested for debt

Anna Williams

Johnson in his late thirties

Frank Barber

20

Inner Temple Lane, where Johnson lived in his early fifties

Boswell at twenty-five

Imagined scene of some members of The Club at Reynolds's house.
From left to right: Boswell, Johnson, Reynolds, Garrick, Burke, Paoli,
Burney, Warton, Goldsmith

Johnson's Court, where Johnson lived from 1765 to 1776

Hester Thrale
as she looked in the years
Johnson first knew her

Henry Thrale at forty-five

The Thrale Brewery, Southwark. Part of the "Round Tower," containing Johnson's room, is shown on the right behind the lamp.

Mrs. Thrale and Queeney

Streatham Park

Bolt Court, No. 8, Johnson's
residence from 1776 to his death

John Taylor

32

Johnson
in his seventies
by John Opie

Ashbourne Hall now

33

Reynolds's last portrait of Johnson (1782–84)

Death mask of Johnson

though in as just and balanced a way as some of his *Ramblers*, which were also written—as if half by calculation and self-daring—with the printer's boy at the door. Not till *The Vanity of Human Wishes*, as we have seen, was there a work to which he would openly put his own name. The poem was perhaps overly concentrated, almost self-defensively too clenched. How clearly he saw through this shadow-battle with oneself, and how acidly he could write—in his struggle for perspective—of this overconcern for "reputation"! And, of course, in this internalized ideal of expectation, it was not really what "others" thought. It was himself. True, no one knew better how "rarely reason guides the stubborn choice"—how rarely even the most honest introspection can alter the long habits (however blindly and stupidly defensive) of the "stubborn" self. As he once said about "plans" of resolve or reformation, "Every man naturally persuades himself that he can keep his resolutions, nor is he convinced of his inbecillity but by length of time, and frequency of experiment."[15]

But now it would be different. There would be no excuse. In the huge file of words prepared for the *Dictionary*, he already had much of what he would need. Time and again, he had seen—and written on effectively—the needless ways by which authors and scholars intimidate themselves. He would at last practice what he preached. The deadline of eighteen months would insure it. In contrast to those "oppressed by their own reputation," he would cut the thing down to size. There would be no nonsense, from himself or others, about pretending the work was other than a routine chore and thus allowing it to appeal too much to the conscience. When John Hawkins "congratulated him on his being now engaged in a work that suited his genius" and assumed that this work at least would be "executed *con amore*," Johnson startled him by saying, "I look upon this as I did upon the Dictionary: it is all work, and my inducement to it is not love or desire of fame, but the want of money, which is the only motive to writing that I know of."[16]

In a burst of effort, he began to send material to the printer for one play after another, and several were set up in type. Meanwhile he wrote the short pieces we have mentioned, including the extraordinary array of reviews for the *Literary Magazine*. Even so, his writing during this year, said Arthur Murphy,

engrossed but little of Johnson's time. He resigned himself to indolence, took no exercise, rose about two, and then received the visits of his friends. Authors, long since forgotten, waited on him as their oracle, and he gave responses in the chair of criticism. He listened to the complaints, the schemes, and the hopes and fears of a crowd of inferior writers, "who," he said, in the words of Roger Ascham, "lived, men knew not how, and died obscure, men marked not when." He believed, that he could give a better history of Grub-street than any man living. His house was filled with a succession of visitors till four or five in the evening. During the whole time he presided at his tea-table.

Then, as 1757 continued to pass, his speed in working on the Shakespeare began to slacken. By December, the date when it was due to be completed, he told his new friend Charles Burney that he would have the edition ready by the following March. He had a special reason now for getting back to the edition. In February 1758 he was again about to be arrested for debt—for what he described to the publisher of the edition, Jacob Tonson, as "about forty pounds." Tonson, the preceding year (June 8), had loaned him £100 to pay off the mortgage of the Lichfield house, perhaps writing it off as an advance for the Shakespeare edition, and then had given him another £26 5s. in September. Now, in February, to forestall Johnson's arrest, Tonson at once advanced the £40 necessary. Resolving to get to work, Johnson wrote Burney that the Shakespeare edition would definitely be published "before summer," and, when Burney made a trip to London soon afterward, showed him "some volumes of his Shakespeare already printed, to prove that he was in earnest." After this he seems to have stopped telling others when the edition would appear.[17]

7

So things were to continue for another five years, by which time he was approaching a serious psychological crisis. In a way utterly unlike him, when he had to do with any mere literary work (but in a way similar to his resolutions for "moral" reform), he continued—however silent he was about it to others—to defer it, to set new target dates, and then to defer again.

Plainly, within the theater of his own imagination, the edition of Shakespeare was in a deep, essential way a form of "moral" resolve in which the self-demand was so great that the inner resistance began to mount almost in proportion to it. Of course, other things complicated the picture. However effectively he could ridicule those who felt "oppressed by their own reputation," that was the way he felt now. He would have to live up to the *Dictionary*. But with the *Dictionary*, things had been so different. He was only at the onset of middle age when he began it. Now he was ten years older, and the problems of middle age had accumulated. Then he had a personal incentive—to support Tetty—that helped to anesthetize or push aside perfectionistic hesitations. Now it was very different.

But if he began to slow to a halt with the Shakespeare, a rush of energy, as if in compensation, shows itself in other writing during the next five years (1757–62)—writing in which "self-commitment" is not involved, but rather something that could be done, as it were, on the side. Some of it brought money that was badly needed, but often it was done for purposes of charity or friendship. Very few people, at any time in his life, appealed in vain to him for help. And, like the hack work of his thirties, or the writing done for others in his early and middle forties, this miscellaneous writing shows the same variety of talent.

For example, he helped the young William Chambers—later one of England's foremost architects—with a Preface for his *Designs of Chinese Buildings, Furniture, Dresses, etc.* (1757). Another piece of writing shows an unexpected knowledge of the problem of stresses in engineering, though he could not have devoted more than a short time to studying it for the occasion. This is found in three letters written in support of another architect, his friend John Gwynn, "On the plans for Black-Friars Bridge" (in the *Daily Gazeteer*, 1759). Gwynn, who was to become a great bridge builder, planned to construct this bridge with circular arches, while his rival architect, Robert Mylne, advocated elliptical arches (Mylne's design was the one chosen). In addition, for his friend John Payne, who was at the Bank of England, Johnson contributed a Preface to Payne's *New Tables of Interest* (1758); for Charlotte Lennox he provided Dedications for her translation of Brumoy's *Greek Theatre* (1760) and her novel *Henrietta* (1761); and for the publisher John Newbery—in this case he at least was paid something—an Introduction to a collection of voyages and travels called *The World Displayed* (1759). One of his more recent friends was Giuseppe Baretti, the son of an architect in Turin. He had come to England in 1751, when he was thirty-two, and opened a small school where he taught Italian. Charlotte Lennox was one of his pupils, and through her he met Johnson (1753). Though Baretti did not seem likable to many people—he was at once timid, heady, and liable to violent prejudices—Johnson felt protective toward him, and before long his protective feelings ripened into friendship. Besides his Preface for Baretti's *Introduction to the Italian Language* (1755), mentioned earlier, he gave him some help with his *Italian Library* (1757), an account of the lives and works of Italian authors; wrote "Proposals" (1758) for a contemplated volume of Baretti's poems (the volume was apparently not published); and provided a Dedication for his *Dictionary of the English and Italian Languages* (1760).

8

But the major writing of this period of his life after the *Dictionary*— though he would not have considered it at any time as "major," and certainly not when he wrote it—consisted of another group of periodical essays, the *Idler*, a sort of briefer and less serious *Rambler*, and the remarkable philosophical tale *Rasselas* (1759).

In beginning the *Idler*, as Sir John Hawkins shrewdly guessed, his principal motive "was aversion to a labour he had undertaken"—the edition of Shakespeare, the *Proposals* for which had been issued two years before. But Johnson could also justly say that he needed the money. ("No one but a blockhead ever wrote, except for money.") Unlike the *Rambler*, these essays were to have a light touch and to be rather short. There was nothing like the sense of commitment he had felt with the *Rambler*. There was no "prayer" on beginning this series, and—another difference—he was glad to have others contribute (twelve—that is, one of eight—are by other people).[18] Nor, in contrast to the *Rambler*, did he want to think of these essays as an important effort that would appear alone and naked. Hence some publisher friends (probably they took the initiative in making the original proposal to Johnson to write the essays, and then tailored the paper to fit his modest ideas of what he was willing to do) created a new weekly newspaper, *The Universal Chronicle:* his old friend of the Ivy Lane Club John Payne, working at the Bank of England but still retaining his interest in publishing, was one; another was the warmhearted John Newbery, whom Goldsmith portrays in *The Vicar of Wakefield* ("a red-faced, good-natured man, always in a hurry"); and in time others joined in or took over—Robert Stevens, and then William Faden, who had printed the *Rambler* and helped supervise the *Literary Magazine*. The paper was published every Saturday from April 15,

1758, to April 5, 1760. News of the week and stock reports were tacked on after the leading essay. These embellishments proved of little or no interest to the public—there were already too many better newspapers. But the *Idler* essays themselves did prove of interest—so much so that very quickly they were seized on as they appeared and reprinted, without pay, by numerous newspapers and magazines not only in London but also throughout Britain and Ireland. In a gently ironic tone, Johnson inserted an "advertisment" several months after the *Idler* started, suggesting that if this continued, the *Universal Chronicle* would respond in kind, and pirate articles from the offending journals. But he was not greatly displeased.

The choice of title illustrates his decision to view these essays in a casual spirit. If a "rambler," compared with a "pilgrim," travels without "settled direction," an "idler" makes no claim, either to himself or others, of traveling or doing anything at all. In keeping with this decision, he made a deliberate attempt to depart from the *Rambler* in both subject and style. The *Rambler* had frankly disdained the "local and temporary" and sought a high level of universality. The *Idler*, at the start, talks about events of the day and writes on casual subjects with attempted whimsey (*e.g.*, No. 6, about a lady who won a bet by riding one thousand miles in one thousand hours). This is kept up for about thirty issues, though there are half a dozen exceptions. As a result, the confirmed Johnsonian finds them thin. But then, from habit and perhaps with some feeling of relief, the familiar Johnson begins to return, and not only to return but to stay for the rest of the course as well. Even so, there are differences when compared with the *Rambler*. For example, few of the character "portraits" in the *Rambler* could be called favorable. Beneath many of them is an exasperation that comes very close to anger, though the anger becomes blunted by charity. But in the *Idler* they are frequently favorable (and often based on real people), and if there is satire, it tends to be gentle and even sweet-tempered.

At the very start of the *Idler*, Johnson tried in style to catch the easy, conversational tone of Addison and Steele. In contrast to the *Rambler*, the diction is simple and the sentences are short. Even if the subject matter begins to deepen in seriousness after the first thirty numbers, this new style remains. Like the *Rambler* and *Adventurer*, the *Idler* is a repository of some of the finest proverbial wisdom in the language. But now the phrasing is simpler, less probing and less metaphorical:

He that never labours may know the pains of idleness, but not the pleasure. . . . The great differences that disturb the peace of mankind are not about ends, but means. . . . Pain is less subject than pleasure to caprices of expression. . . . Man has from nature a mode of utterance peculiar to pain, but he has none peculiar to pleasure, because he never has pleasure but in such degrees as the ordinary use of language may equal or surpass. . . . Nothing is more hopeless than a scheme of merriment.

. . . Reformation is seldom the work of pure virtue or unassisted reason. . . . Much of the pain and pleasure of mankind arises from the conjectures which everyone makes of the thoughts of others. . . . There are few things not purely evil, of which we can say, without some emotion of uneasiness, this is the last.

9

On Saturday, January 13, 1759, Johnson suddenly received word from Lucy Porter that his aged mother (now eighty-nine) was seriously ill. He was so completely without money that he was at last planning to give up the house in Gough Square. He had already let the cook go, and, when Bennet Langton sent him a present of some game, he had given it away to friends since "I have left off housekeeping" (January 9). His first thought, on hearing of his mother's illness, was to raise money to pay for the trip to Lichfield to see her and meet the expenses of her illness. He was able to get together only twelve guineas, which he immediately sent her.

Meanwhile he arranged with the publisher William Strahan, by now an old friend, to send to him in a week or two a philosophical story in the popular form of the "Eastern tale." Readers had liked the "Eastern tales" in the *Rambler*, particularly that of Seged, lord of Ethiopia (Nos. 204 and 205). The new tale would be called (he had not yet decided on a name for his main character) "The Choice of Life, or the History of —— Prince of Abissinia." He knew he could write it quickly. If the ideas he had in mind had been long considered, the setting was also familiar. Ever since he translated Father Lobo's *Voyage to Abyssinia*, he had continued to read works about the country and had in mind details—historical as well as geographical—that now helped provide concrete body to the story. In fact, even the name he selected, "Rasselas," was the name of an actual Prince of Abyssinia, though Johnson doubtless chose it because of its generality (*Ras* is the root word for "chief" in Hebrew, Arabic, and Semitic languages generally). There was a short negotiation about price. The sum finally agreed on was £100, though he afterward received another £25 when the second edition appeared. Just as he finished, or shortly earlier, he learned, on January 23, that his mother had died a couple of days before, and had been buried almost immediately. There was now no point in making the trip to Lichfield. Hence William Strahan's remark to Boswell, which applies only to the result and not the intention, that Johnson wrote the book to "defray the expense of his mother's funeral, and pay some little debts she had left." There was now no hurry. But Johnson had no incentive to expand the tale, though he had probably ended it more abruptly than he intended when he began it.[19]

In effect, then, as he later told Sir Joshua Reynolds, he "composed it in the evenings of one week, sent it to the press in portions as it was written, and had never since read it over" until, in 1781 (twenty-two years after the book appeared), he found it accidentally in a post chaise with Boswell, and then read it with close attention.[20]

10

Despite the circumstances and speed in writing, the result is one of the short classics of world literature, *The History of Rasselas, Prince of Abyssinia* (published on April 19 or 20, 1759). Its appeal was almost immediate. Within the next generation the book was being read—and has continued to be read—in every part of the English-speaking world. It has been estimated that an English or American edition has appeared almost every year since it was first published. Meanwhile it was translated almost at once into French (1760), Dutch (1760), German (1762), and then Russian (1764) and Italian (1764). In time it was to be translated into other languages, including Spanish, Hungarian, Polish, Greek, Danish, Armenian, Bengali, Japanese, and Arabic.

This "little story book"—as Johnson described it to Lucy Porter frankly and without false modesty—begins like a fairy tale from folklore, though it also has some historical background.[21] It is the story of the Prince Rasselas, who, with his sister Nekayah and other companions, lives in a sort of protective prison, the Happy Valley, where he is to stay until he is called to take over his ancestral duties (he is the fourth son of the Emperor). Here in the Happy Valley every pleasure is anticipated and satisfied and every external cause of anxiety or grief is removed. In this ultrapermissive world, Rasselas and his companions have long since become listless and bored and want to escape from it. With the help of the philosopher Imlac, a widely traveled man who has found his way there, they manage to get out of the Happy Valley and then eagerly explore the world in search of what will bring happiness. They inquire into every condition of life. They find the rich suffering from anxieties or boredom, restlessly seeking new interests in order to make life more attractive, while at the same time they are subject to the envy of others. Political power, which had seemed to the young travelers to provide the ideal means of doing good, proves not only precarious but far more impotent to change the condition of man than they had ever imagined. The world of learning, at first so promising to idealistic youth, is found to be torn by petty rivalries and vested interests. While the social world of idle pleasure proves empty and ridiculous, the hermit who has tried to get away from it is found to be just as dissatisfied as those caught up in the chase of social pleasures. The philosopher who discourses bravely about the way to confront death and calamity proves as vulnerable as anyone else. At the end the little party decides to return to Abyssinia (though not to the Happy Valley), hoping to confront the duties of life with more understanding.

In short, *Rasselas* is a story of a "pilgrimage"—of the questing intellect and restless heart of man for something that will give "purpose" or "meaning" to life. But implied throughout the story—only implied, never stated—is the radical mistake we make when we self-centeredly equate "happiness" with any particular object or condition. For "happiness" cannot be obtained if we search for it. It proves a mirage as we move toward it. In moments when we awake to a feeling of happiness, we find it has come only as a by-product, only when we are in the active process of lifting our focus of interest to something beyond our own condition and losing ourselves in something else. If this is implied rather than stated, it is partly because the story (forgivably under the circumstances) ends abruptly, though at the same time it is able to make a virtue of remaining "open" at the end. (The last chapter is called "The Conclusion, in which Nothing is Concluded." There is some evidence that he considered writing a continuation of the tale.) Another reason the moral is only implied is Johnson's own inner taboo —which we have noticed already in *The Vanity of Human Wishes* and the *Rambler*—against specific religious discussion on his own part in his writing: a deep sense that he himself is not qualified to speak of it too explicitly, at least in his own person (as distinct, for example, from ghost-writing sermons for others). That taboo is stronger now, as he is approaching fifty, and as he is also approaching what was to prove psychologically the most difficult time of his life except for the long breakdown after he left Oxford.

Part of the secret of the book's appeal lies in the variety of archetypal forms that it combines. Each by itself, if used by an intellect that has strongly assimilated experience, could have a potentially strong interest to the human psyche. But as they are here coalesced, they reinforce each other into a still denser unit of appeal: (1) The traditional fairy story. (2) Its sophisticated cousin, the "Eastern tale," with its frankly moral aim, which had now been familiar for half a century. This gave "distance," through its remote setting. More than that, it predisposed the mind to seriousness through a quasi-Biblical setting. The English, as one French writer after another remarked, were a nation of Bible readers (as the Anglicized German Handel quickly discovered when he found that oratorios, based on the Bible, appealed to an English audience as no opera possibly could). Yet this quasi-Biblical setting need not commit one to specific religious discussion. It was enough to invoke it. (3) The idea of "pilgrimage," so ingrained in Johnson's own deepest responses to literature (*e.g.*, those three "favorite" works, *Don Quixote*, *Pilgrim's Progress*, and *Robinson Crusoe*). (4) Another "form," itself a mixed one, is that of "satire *manqué*"—of satire blunted by compassion and then turned into something else. This is so distinctive a feature of Johnson's moral writing and also of his humor generally that it is discussed as a separate subject. (It also accounts for the principal differences between *Rasselas* and Voltaire's famous *Candide*, which appeared at almost the same time, and with which it has often been compared. Significantly Voltaire, in his praise of *Rasselas*, regarded its "philosophy" as warm and lovable—"*aimable*"—rather than satiric.)* (5) In addition, we have in miniature the concept of the *Bildungsroman*, which was soon to capture the imagination of the greatest novelists of the nineteenth century. Those who are to be educated (Rasselas and his sister) have a teacher, the philosopher

* On "satire *manqué*," see below, pp. 494-96. *Candide* (published at Geneva in January) was not issued in England until May. The books are similar enough in general plan so that Johnson himself said that, if more time had elapsed between them, "it would have been vain to deny that the scheme of that which came latest was taken from the other" (L, I, 342). But the differences are more interesting than the somewhat accidental similarities (*e.g.*, the rapid movement of *Candide*, its brilliantly mocking tone, and the fact that the philosopher Pangloss—in contrast to Imlac—is a subject of ridicule). For Voltaire's remark (1760) on *Rasselas*, see *Oeuvres Complètes* (1880), XL, 390.

Imlac, who has already seen the world. Naturally he is something of a spokesman for Johnson himself. The story of his life, which he tells Rasselas near the start, is a kind of prologue to what they will learn. But, of course, one cannot pass on to others the fruit of one's experience. One can at most provide a suggestion of what they might look for and of a way they might think. Otherwise, they must learn by themselves. And this is what Rasselas and his sister do (though with Imlac often entering, like the chorus in a Greek drama, to comment on what is happening). For, by the later part of the story, they themselves have progressed to the point at which they think and talk about experience in the way that Imlac would. Finally, in the structure of this deceptively simple tale, there is far more "art" than used to be thought, even by its warmest admirers.[22]

But the main reason *Rasselas* quickly became—and remains—the classic it is, though the time he devoted to it was so short (less than the time devoted to any other classic in the history of literature, for which we know the actual timetable, except the "great odes" of Keats), is that here we have distilled, in this brief, richly brooding story, so much of the total character of mind—the power of subsuming, the sweep and readiness of intellect, the appealing humanity, the general style and tone—of one of the most refreshingly practical of reflective natures ever to write about human experience. On almost every page we have what Johnson praised in Francis Bacon—"the observations of a strong mind operating on life." Haste in writing was often an advantage for Johnson, enabling him to brush aside hesitations or doubts and to tap at once his internal fund of both accumulated experience and richness of expression. It also acted as a challenge. But the value of haste was always greater when the subject was such that he was encouraged to storm the main gate of human experience without stopping to approach it (in Bacon's phrase) by a "winding stair." To discuss *Rasselas* with the concentrated attention it deserves would be to repeat our discussion of his moral thought as a whole. For *Rasselas*, in its union of archetypal forms, subsumes Johnson's moral thought generally. If *The Vanity of Human Wishes* serves as the Prologue to the great decade of moral writing, *Rasselas* serves as its Epilogue.

Chapter 20

Into His Fifties; the Pension;
Boswell; The Club

Johnson's decision to give up the house in Gough Square, after all its associations of the past twelve years, shows how badly off he was now. Though his original hope in renting it had been to reconcile Tetty to living in London, he had clung to the place another seven years after she died. It provided a sense of anchorage and stability after the years of drifting from one cheap lodging to another. It was associated with the *Dictionary* and the moral writings—with what, in fact, was the most productive period of his life generally—and it had seen him pass from lower to upper middle age. To surrender the place and return to lodgings inevitably represented a defeat. It was almost as though he were back where he had started, except that there is less hope at fifty than at thirty-seven.

But there was no alternative. He arranged for rooms at Staple Inn, the old half-timbered Inn of Chancery now used as an appendage by Gray's Inn. Miss Williams was put into lodgings nearby where he could visit her every day. On March 23 he wrote Lucy Porter, "I have this day moved my things." (Since the quarters into which he was moving were small, we can infer that most of the furnishings in Gough Square had either belonged to the owner of the house or else, more probably, were sold by Johnson when he left.) Later the same year (1759) he moved to Gray's Inn. Within still another six months, he moved to slightly larger lodgings on the first floor of 1, Inner Temple Lane. Here he was to stay for the next five years (August 1760 to July

1765)—the larger part of the crucial time of his life to which we should now turn.[1]

The move to Staple Inn marked the end of a period of his life with more symbolic poignance than he could afford to admit. "There are few things not purely evil"—as he was to write a year later, in the last issue of the *Idler*—"of which we can say, without some emotion of uneasiness, *this is the last*. . . . The secret horror of the last is inseparable from a thinking being." Always susceptible to the emotional appeal of symbols, his immediate defense was to deny them in order to prevent them from pressing too tyrannically on his feelings. Above all, he was always quick to scorn the idea of being affected by "change of place." It was like resigning oneself to the influence of the weather ("imagination operating on luxury"). To admit the influence, on either one's work or happiness, of "change of place"—unless real "destitution," real poverty and privation resulted—meant giving up the belief that one is a "free agent." "Do not," he once told Boswell, "accustom yourself to trust to *impressions*. . . . A man may gradually come to yield to them, and at length be subject to them, so as not to be a free agent, or what is the same thing in effect, to *suppose* that he is not a free agent." He could feel this kind of surrender particularly absurd in his own case. For had he not always been a "straggler"? Could he not take in his stride this "change of place" as he had so many other changes in the past? Yet, with all these defenses against "impressions," we sense his anxiety in a prayer he wrote late at night just after he moved from Gough Square to Staple Inn, where he twice refers—as he tries to control his feelings—to this "change which I am now making in *outward* things." His hope in this prayer is that the change now forced on him might be joined by an inner change, by a genuine "reformation."[2]

The truth is that something very serious was beginning to happen to him, and he was quite aware of it. The general reconsideration of life so common in middle age and the problems inevitable to it were something he had foreseen long before this. He had taken them into account and half assimilated them in advance, in protective preparation, in *The Vanity of Human Wishes* and in the *Rambler*, while managing to postpone some of their worst effects when he plunged into work on the *Dictionary*. But now, as he was entering his fifties, he was more vulnerable. The larger part of middle age could seem already behind him; and instead of his life being half over, as it was when he began the *Dictionary* and rented the house in Gough Square, it could now, by any optimistic calculation, appear two-thirds over, and most of it could seem a waste—a history of disappointments, frustrations, regrets, and mistaken choices, none of it to be blamed on the world but only on himself.

Worst of all was the growing sense of paralysis since the *Dictionary* was finished. True, this had been punctuated by bursts of activity, which could be excused as a means of meeting expenses or of helping others. But the fact remained that these had not consumed much time. In any case, they had been growing less frequent, and now he was not even meeting expenses, as his need to surrender the house amply showed. The one serious project he had set for himself, the edition of Shakespeare—and he had been telling himself that was a small project compared with the *Dictionary,* in a sense no more than a kind of appendix to it—was to have been finished over a year ago. He had known long in advance that his only enemy was himself, and had taken precautions to see what that meant and had taken steps to guard against himself. But the result, as he failed to make headway, was only more self-condemnation; and to condemn one's own self-condemnation was only another form of self-conflict and hence of self-preoccupation. On his last birthday, after squandering, he felt, "another year of proba- tion," he had prayed for help "to improve the time that is yet before me. . . . This year I hope to learn diligence." Now, with this change in "outward things," no further hesitation could be allowed: "Give me thy Grace [April 15] to break the chain of evil custom. Enable me to shake off idleness and sloth . . . that I may support myself and relieve others."[3]

Because he was still writing the *Idler*—though the series could hardly go on forever—he should have been able to meet the more modest expenses he had now. (The rent at Staple Inn was at most a third of the rent for the Gough Square house,[4] and Miss Williams had enough, from her own small income, to pay for her simple lodgings.) Yet on May 19 he was forced to borrow £42 19s. 10d. from John Newbery. The amount, instead of being a round sum, is so strangely precise that it was obviously for a specific debt. Since it is close to what we know to be the approximate rent of the Gough Square house, one is tempted to infer that payments for the rent had accumulated for about a year, possibly with interest, and that this was the reason for the loan. (We are reminded that the previous year he was arrested for a similar sum he describes as "about forty pounds" and had to be extri- cated by his publisher, Jacob Tonson.) Certainly he had been living beyond his means for some time, largely because of his generosity. Though he was a good arithmetician, and able to give sound financial advice to others, there was a side of him that felt a proud disdain about being too mindful of his own expenses. He preferred instead, and found it more compatible with his pride, to go without things and live as simply as he could. The sole personal extravagance had been the house, retained because of sentimental and symbolic reasons. But this particular form of economy—merely to shut off expenses—was not something he could apply to others who were in need.

In an effort to divert the melancholy he felt at this move to Staple Inn, he left in June for a visit to Oxford, where he stayed several weeks. This was not the expense it might seem. He had what amounted to a standing invitation from his old friend Thomas Warton, now professor of poetry, who could put him up at Kettel Hall. Part of the time he spent with a new friend, Robert Vansittart, a young legal scholar from a noted family, who was a Fellow of All Souls and was to become in a few years Regius Professor of Civil Law at Oxford (1767). Vansittart was almost exactly the same age (approaching thirty-one) that Cornelius had been when he had arrived at Lichfield and taken the fifteen-year-old Johnson back with him to Stourbridge. Like Cornelius, Vansittart was also renowned as a rake, and was, in fact, a member of the famous Hell-Fire Club. Johnson delighted in his company, and at the end of one convivial evening challenged him to climb over the wall with him at All Souls. Though nineteen years younger (Johnson within two months would be fifty), Vansittart declined the challenge.[5]

Besides the Cornelius-like qualities of Vansittart, there was another attraction—his similarity to that second model of the young Johnson, Gilbert Walmesley (though only in field, not temperament). The year before, Vansittart had taken the degree—Doctor of Civil Law—that Johnson had hoped he might himself get in order to practice in "Doctors' Commons," the lack of which finally led him to turn to the *Dictionary*. Far from being envious of younger men who achieved what he had been frustrated in doing himself, his generous nature took a vicarious pleasure in them and in their opportunities. So with a still younger legal scholar, Robert Chambers, to whom Francis Wise—who had helped Johnson get his M.A. from Oxford—had introduced him on an earlier visit. Johnson had enjoyed talking law with this industrious undergraduate, who was quite different from Vansittart. The year before his present visit, he had written letters of recommendation in support of Chambers when he was chosen Vinerian Scholar (1758). Chambers was to enter the Johnson story more prominently when he was appointed Blackstone's successor as Vinerian Professor of Law (1766), and Johnson helped the frightened Chambers prepare his lectures.* Chambers was now at University College, and it was probably at his place that Johnson, usually so abstemious, performed a feat for which Cornelius had been famous—drinking three bottles of port without showing any effect. Vicariously living the life of both a student and a don, as he had imagined it as a youth at Stourbridge, he might suggest climbing the wall at All Souls, but at the same time—as at last an M.A.—he enjoyed wearing his new academic gown. William Scott later said that when Johnson visited Oxford he prided himself on being very "academic in all points; and he wore his gown almost *ostentatiously*"; and, when the new Chancellor of the university was installed, took part in the grand procession of the Masters and "clapped his hands till they were sore" at William King's speech at the end of the ceremony.[6]

2

During these exuberant weeks he also went swimming for the first time in many years. Bennet Langton, now a student at Trinity College, swam with him, and warned him "against a pool which was reckoned particularly dangerous; upon which Johnson directly swam into it." Once a week Johnson would stop to write an essay for the *Idler*, which he would then send to the printer in London. One evening, said Langton, he learned that the last post would leave in half an hour. "Then we shall do very well," said Johnson:

> He upon this instantly sat down and finished an Idler, which it was necessary should be in London the next day. Mr. Langton having signified a wish to read it, "Sir, (said he) you shall not do more than I have done myself." He then folded it up, and sent it off.[7]

Through Langton he acquired another lifelong friend, Topham Beauclerk, whose grandfather was the Duke of St. Albans—the son of Charles II and Nell Gwynne. In some ways Beauclerk looked like Charles II, and though already a libertine (he was now only nineteen), he had "so ardent a love of literature, so acute an understanding, such

* See below, pp. 418–20.

elegance of manner," that not only the serious Langton but Johnson himself soon forgave him. "Thy body," he said once, "is all vice and thy mind all virtue." Though capable of acid sarcasm, Beauclerk was a man of open and generous nature, his conversation was easy as well as brilliant, and to Johnson he could seem almost a caricature of Cornelius. "What a coalition," said Garrick when he heard of this new friendship. "I shall have my old friend to bail out of the Round-house." A year or so later, when Langton and Beauclerk were in London, the two young men sat drinking in a tavern until 3:00 A.M., and then decided to rouse up Johnson to join them in a "ramble." They pounded on his door, and he appeared in his nightshirt with a poker in his hand, as if he assumed some ruffians were trying to break in the door. When he saw who they were, he smiled and said, "What, is it you, you dogs! I'll have a frisk with you!" As soon as he dressed, they went to Covent Garden "where the green-grocers and fruiterers were beginning to arrange their hampers, just come in from the country. Johnson made some attempts to help them." But the grocers, surprised by his figure and manner, stared at him, and he gave up. They went to a tavern and drank the punch called Bishop that Johnson so liked—wine, oranges, and sugar—and then went down to the Thames, got a boat, and rowed to Billingsgate. Johnson and Beauclerk wanted to continue throughout the day, but Langton was engaged for breakfast with some ladies—"a set of wretched *un-idea'd* girls," said Johnson.[8]

3

Returned to London and the bleak lodgings in Staple Inn, he confessed in a letter to Lucy Porter that, however well treated he had been at Oxford, "I have no great pleasure in any place." He had to face the fact that, through this visit of seven weeks, which he had extended as much as he decently could, he had still further postponed that immediate "reformation" that was to take advantage of and redeem his change in "outward things." Within a month he would be fifty. His birthday was always a time for considered stocktaking. It would be especially so now, as he passed the half-century mark. But any reflections he wrote then or for the next year generally were among the journals he burned before his death.

For the first time since he had come to London twenty-three years before, he virtually stopped writing after he finished the last *Idler*

(April 5, 1760), though in March he was again forced to borrow from John Newbery (£30). A move to different surroundings—to rooms in Gray's Inn, in November 1759, did not help to jolt him into activity, nor another move a half year later to Inner Temple Lane. During the next three years, what little work he did was mainly of a charitable nature, or consisted of a few prefaces and dedications written for friends.* Special mention should be made of two of these works. One was a short Introduction to the *Proceedings of the Committee to Manage the Contributions . . . for Cloathing French Prisoners of War* (1760). Struck by its combination of good sense and charity, the International Red Cross, learning of it in the period after World War II, had it translated into French and published in its *Revue Internationale* (Geneva 1951) as a notable anticipation of the principles on which the Red Cross was founded.[10] Soon afterward, the kindly Thomas Davies —the man who later introduced Boswell to him—aroused Johnson's interest in the plight of James Bennet, an impoverished schoolmaster in Hertfordshire. Bennet had been struggling with an edition of the *English Works of Roger Ascham*, the noted Elizabethan writer on education. Bennet was slow, lacking in confidence, and his large family was in need. Johnson added some succinct notes and also wrote a brief, perceptive *Life of Ascham* to be prefixed to the edition. Any profits from the work went largely, perhaps entirely, to Bennet.[11]

4

In September 1760, on his fifty-first birthday, he made a new list of injunctions to himself: "Resolved . . . To apply to Study. To reclaim imagination . . . To study Religion. To go to Church . . . To op-

* For Charlotte Lennox, who was ill and trying to complete a translation of Brumoy's *Greek Theatre*, he translated two of the dissertations and wrote a Dedication (1760). Aside from the Preface for Baretti's *Dictionary of the English and Italian Languages* (1760), he wrote Dedications for Charlotte Lennox's *Henrietta* (1761), John Hoole's translation of Tasso's *Jersualem Delivered* (1763), and a book by the eccentric John Kennedy—whom he had met years ago (1739-40) on his visit to John Taylor—*A Complete System of Astronomical Chronology, Unfolding the Scriptures* (dated 1762 but published 1763). Two short pieces for which he was probably paid include an *Address of the Painters, Sculptors, and Architects to George III on his Succession to the Throne* (1761), the opening paragraphs of John Gwynn's *Thoughts on the Coronation* (1761), and a Preface for John Newbery to Lenglet du Fresnoy's *Chronological Tables of Universal History* (1762).[9] For the brief piece on "The Imposture in Cock-Lane" and the discussion of William Collins, see below, pp. 353, 383.

pose laziness, *by doing what is to be done*," and—suggesting there had been a recent lapse after in general abstaining from wine for so long—to "drink less strong liquors." He ends with four specific resolves to begin at once:

> To morrow
>> Rise as early as I can.
>> Send for books for Hist. of war.
>> Put books in order.
>> *Scheme life.*

The "Hist. of war"—possibly of the Seven Years' War, now going on—suggests a new project (it remained merely that). The resolve to "put books in order" was a beginning step to counteract the messy way of life that, when depressed, he so disliked as a projection of his disorderly self. Such small things, he increasingly reminds himself, are not to be disregarded (*e.g.*, after a solemn prayer on Good Friday some years later, he writes, as an immediate practical step to take, "I hope, To put my rooms in order," and then, going back to the remark, adds as a sort of note, "Disorder I have found one great cause of Idleness").[12]

His friends were naturally puzzled by the lassitude into which he was falling. A few sensed that something more serious lay beneath it. To a very few—Reynolds and his sister, for example—he confessed, said Miss Reynolds, that he had "inherited from his Father a morbid disposition both of Body and Mind": a "terrifying melancholy," she added, "which he was sometimes apprehensive bordered on insanity."[13] But so firmly did he hold himself in control when he talked, and so convivial could he be in company, that such confessions—kept as they were on a very general plane—were of course discounted. The assumption was only that he was liable to severe but still manageable lapses into depression when he was alone, and that this was a lifelong trouble he had always had to face, no more acute now than before. Certainly company, as far as they could judge, gave him effective relief, at least for the time being, and they tried to provide it for him.

One such friend was John Douglas, later Bishop of Salisbury, who "endeavored, by constant attention," said Murphy, "to soothe the cares of a mind which he knew to be afflicted with gloomy apprehensions," and made a point of asking Johnson to parties at his house where he could meet people Douglas hoped would interest him. At one of these parties, Douglas invited him to meet the celebrated Jesuit Father Roger Boscavich, who had recently introduced the study of Sir Isaac Newton's mathematics at Rome, and was now visiting England, where he had just been made a Fellow of the Royal Society. Boscavich could not speak English, and so the conversation at first was in French. However fluently Johnson could read or even write French, his knowledge of it—since he was self-taught—was naturally visual rather than aural. He found it difficult to follow the pronunciation and did not feel he could "speak it himself with propriety." Hence the conversation continued in Latin, which, after a short delay, he was speaking "with as much facility as if it was his native tongue." With "a dignity and eloquence that surprized that learned foreigner," Johnson discussed Newton's accomplishments in detail, maintaining his superiority over other scientists and mathematicians. Boscavich was himself an accomplished Latinist—he had in fact written a fine Latin poem on the Newtonian philosophy—but the experience of this conversation, as well as their second meeting in Reynolds's home, when they again conversed in Latin, left him with a feeling of "astonishment."[14]

5

Meanwhile, at Inner Temple Lane, he lived in what Arthur Murphy, who saw much of him, called the "poverty, total idleness, and the pride of literature." Typical of all three qualities, he thought, was the story of William Fitzherbert's, who stopped by to pay "a morning visit to Johnson, intending from his chambers to send a letter into the city; but, to his great surprize, he found an author by profession without pen, ink, or paper." Of course, it was partly "pride"—a combination of inner rebellion at writing further, of inability to overcome it, of not wishing to be reminded of his resolutions to return to work, masking themselves with—or seeking support from—a proud and affected indifference to the arts and "bustle" used in "the destruction of paper." A day rarely passed that he did not give beggars on the street more than the equivalent of what he would need for writing materials. He could afford to go to the theater, and in fact was doing so, as he told Baretti, "more than in former seasons," though "I have gone thither only to escape from myself." And during the winter of 1761–62, he paid a five-day visit to Lichfield, where he "found the streets much narrower and shorter than I thought I had left them, inhabited by a new race of people, to whom I was very little known. My play-fellows were grown old, and forced me to suspect that I was no longer young."[15]

For that matter, he could at least once during these years afford—according to Bishop Percy—a new suit of clothes, though more probably it was a suit bought long before and kept in reserve that simply struck Percy as "new" because of the contrast (for before his pension, as Miss Reynolds said, "he literally drest like a Beggar"). This was on May 31, 1761, when the struggling young writer Oliver Goldsmith invited friends for a supper at his lodgings in Wine Office Court, Fleet Street. After his wanderings on the Continent, Goldsmith had come to London and tried to make a living from his writing. He lived in complete poverty. Percy, in 1759 (the year in which Johnson had also got to know Goldsmith), found him writing his *Enquiry into the Present State of Polite Learning* "in a wretched dirty room, in which there was but one chair, and when he, from civility, offered it to his visitant, himself was obliged to sit in the window." Now, when he was about thirty, he was becoming a little more affluent. Hence the supper on May 31—the first occasion when he felt able to invite friends. Percy, stopping at Inner Temple Lane to pick up Johnson, was struck with the "studied" neatness of Johnson's dress—"a new suit of clothes, a new wig nicely powdered"—and asked the reason. Johnson replied that he had heard that "Goldsmith, who is a very great sloven, justifies his disregard . . . by quoting my practice, and I am desirous this night to show him a better example."[16] It was the year following this that one of the famous incidents in English literary history took place (1762). Johnson received word from "Goldy"—as he was soon to call him—that "he was in great distress," and begging that "I would come to him as soon as possible." This was in the morning, and Johnson was not yet up. He at once sent a guinea, then dressed himself, and hurried to Goldsmith's rooms. Goldsmith's landlady had had him arrested for his failure to pay rent:

I perceived that he had already changed my guinea, and had got a bottle of Madeira and a glass before him. I put the cork into the bottle, desired he would be calm, and began to talk to him of the means by which he might be extricated. He then told me that he had a novel ready for the press, which he produced to me. I looked into it, and saw its merit; told the landlady I should soon return, and having gone to a bookseller, sold it for sixty pounds.[17]

The novel was *The Vicar of Wakefield*. One of the famous historical paintings still reproduced in histories and anthologies of English
literature shows Johnson nearsightedly reading the pages of this work,
which was to become so famous, while Goldsmith, hovering over the
corked bottle of Madeira, stares at him, and while the frowning landlady also stares from the doorway. The publisher took the work because of Johnson's testimony, though with "faint hopes of profit by his
bargain," said Johnson. Goldsmith was not yet well known; the book
was unusual. Only after Goldsmith's poem *The Traveller* (1764) sold
well—a poem Johnson helped him with, and for which he wrote several lines at the end—did the publisher feel confident in producing *The
Vicar of Wakefield* (1766).

6

People of every sort began dropping by Johnson's rooms in Inner
Temple Lane about noon, when he rose, and often before then, while
he was still in bed. "I have been told by his neighbors at the corner,"
said Hawkins, "that at the time he dwelt there, more enquiries were
made at his shop for Mr. Johnson, than for all the inhabitants put
together of both the Inner and Middle Temple." William Maxwell, a
clergyman attached to the Temple, said:

He generally had a levee of morning visitors, chiefly men of letters;
Hawkesworth, Goldsmith, Murphy, Langton, Steevens, Beauclerk, &c. &c.
and sometimes learned ladies, particularly I remember a French lady of wit
and fashion [Mme. de Boufflers] doing him the honour of a visit. He seemed
to me to be considered as a kind of publick oracle, whom everybody
thought they had a right to visit and consult. . . . I never could discover
how he found time for his compositions.

Around four in the afternoon he would go out and, if he was not
paying visits, have dinner in a tavern with any company that would
join him. A favorite place was the Mitre Tavern in Fleet Street. "He
frequently," said Maxwell, "gave all the silver in his pocket to the
poor, who watched him, between his house and the tavern where he
dined." Within an hour after eating, said Reynolds, he would begin
drinking tea, continuing until after midnight. Then, before returning
home at two in the morning or even later, he would drop by to drink
tea with Miss Williams, who "always sat up for him." He did this as

much from his unwillingness to return to the solitude of his lodgings as from regard for her. Occasionally a companion who had been with him at the tavern would be invited to join him in paying this late call. Boswell, soon after meeting Johnson, envied Goldsmith for having this privilege, when, after an evening together, Goldy went off with Johnson, "strutting away, and calling to me with an air of superiority . . . 'I go to Miss Williams.' . . . But it was not long before I obtained the same mark of distinction."[18]

Some indication of what the rooms in Inner Temple Lane were like is given in a letter from the artist Ozias Humphry to his brother describing his first visit to Johnson: "We passed through three very dirty rooms to a little one that looked like an old counting-house." (The top floor at Gough Square, where he had written the *Dictionary*, had been described as like a "counting-house," and Johnson may have fitted up this room to remind him of it.) The furniture, said Humphry, consisted of "a very large deal writing-desk, an old walnut-tree table, and five ragged chairs of four different sets." Johnson, who was sitting there "waving over his breakfast" (it was one in the afternoon), was dressed in a dirty brown coat and breeches that were also brown, though Humphry could tell that they had once been crimson. His collar and sleeves were unbuttoned, and "his stockings were down about his feet, which had on them, by way of slippers, an old pair of shoes." As he continued waving over his breakfast in silence, Humphry "could hardly help thinking him a madman" till he suddenly began to talk with wonderful precision—"everything he says is as *correct* as a *second edition*." The books he had collected over the years were too numerous for the small apartment. They were kept in two garrets, up four flights of stairs, which Henry Lintot, a bookseller, had once used as a storehouse. It had a view of St. Paul's over the rooftops. The books—when Mr. Levet showed the place to Boswell (July 19, 1763)—were lying about in confusion and dust; the floor was strewn with "manuscript leaves, in Johnson's own handwriting," and "I observed an apparatus for chymical experiments, of which Johnson was all his life very fond."[19]

7

Early in 1762 there occurred a small incident—the affair of the "Cock-Lane Ghost"—often given an importance out of all proportion to what it deserves. The explanation for the attention given it is that it was distorted by a popular satirist, Charles Churchill, to indicate a superstitious streak in Johnson. It then got incorporated into the popular legend of Johnson, and accounts of him ever since have either mentioned it in the same spirit or, when more informed, felt obliged to clear up the misunderstanding.

At the house of a man named William Parsons, in Cock Lane in Smithfield, mysterious knockings and scratchings had been heard for some time, supposedly made by the ghost of a woman, Fanny Lynes, who had died a couple of years before and was now trying to tell the world she had been poisoned by her brother-in-law, William Kent, against whom Parsons had a grudge. Parsons had an eleven-year-old daughter who pretended she was a medium. Lying in bed in a trance, she would ask questions and get answers (one knock meant yes and two no). The story became widespread and crowds of people began to show up at the house. Then Stephen Aldrich, the rector of St. John's, Clerkenwell, invited a group of men—including Johnson, Sir John Fielding, and John Douglas, "a great detector of impostures"—to investigate the matter with him. They concluded rightly that the noises were made by Parsons's daughter. For the group investigating the matter, Johnson then wrote up a brief "Account of the Detection of the Imposture in Cock-Lane," which was then published in the *Gentleman's Magazine* (February 1762). Meanwhile Charles Churchill, resenting Johnson's lack of enthusiasm for his verse, snatched the occasion to portray him—under the name of "Pomposo"—as one of the credulous people taking the matter seriously. Johnson, of course, paid no attention to this. But what certainly did sting him was the caricature provided of him in another part of *The Ghost*, published later in the year, where Churchill—while portraying him as a hideous, unwieldy creature ("Not quite a Beast, nor quite a Man")—mentions the long-delayed edition of Shakespeare, for which so many of Johnson's friends had subscribed:

> He for *subscribers* baits his hook
> And takes their cash—but where's the Book?
> No matter where—*Wise* fear, we know,
> Forbids the robbing of a Foe,
> But what, to serve our private ends,
> Forbids the cheating of our Friends?[20]

Suddenly, in July, Arthur Murphy stopped by at Inner Temple Lane with news that took Johnson some time to digest. On behalf of the Crown, the Earl of Bute, then Prime Minister, wished to present him with an annual pension of £300. The man directly responsible for getting Bute to award the pension was Bute's intimate friend Alexander Wedderburn, the noted lawyer, later Solicitor-General and, as Lord Loughborough, Chief Justice of the Common Pleas and eventually Lord Chancellor. The honor of being the first to urge Wedderburn to make the award was claimed both by Murphy and by Thomas Sheridan, an Irish actor and theatrical manager with scholarly interests, whose son, Richard Brinsley Sheridan, became the famous orator and dramatist. Thomas Sheridan (called "Sherry" to Johnson, a nickname later improved to "Sherry-derry") had already become an authority on pronunciation and elocution. His writings during the next two years (1762–63) and his later dictionary of pronunciation (1780) remain our richest single source of information on these subjects during this period. Sherry was in a particularly good situation to interest Wedderburn in the pension. He saw him frequently. Wedderburn, shy about his Scottish accent, had put himself in Sheridan's hands some time before. Boswell in later years tried to get Wedderburn to say who was "the prime mover in the business." Wedderburn replied simply that "all his friends assisted," though when Boswell mentioned Sheridan's claim, Wedderburn granted that "he rang the bell."

After Bute agreed to the pension, Wedderburn asked Murphy to sound out Johnson. The definition of "pension" in the *Dictionary* was widely known and quoted ("An allowance made to anyone without an equivalent. In England it is generally understood to mean pay given to a state hireling for treason to his country"). Wedderburn added, half in jest, that "having heard much of his independent spirit, and of the downfall of Osborne the bookseller, he did not know but his benevolence might be rewarded with a folio on his head." Actually the more Wedderburn thought about the pension, the better it seemed as an idea, and he did not want Johnson, in a moment of heady independence, to brush it aside. Bute's pensions, especially those given to Scottish friends and dependents, were being criticized as both self-serving and undeserved. Now, at small cost, the government could begin to improve its image and appear as more of a disinterested patron of literature and the arts. The *Dictionary* had become a source of national pride. Yet Johnson's need was not only acute but well known to people of importance in London. Above all, for a man of indisputable integrity to accept a pension from this particular government, when his own insulting definition of "pension" had become a byword, would be the surest sign of the purity of the government's motives and its freedom from prejudice. Finally, political considerations, though they may not have entered prominently, at least presented no obstacle.*

Murphy was as worried as Wedderburn about Johnson's reaction, though for another reason. The rooms at Temple Lane were beginning to strike him as the veritable "abode of wretchedness." Quite understandably, he assumed that much of Johnson's "melancholy" was associated with poverty and the loss of his house; that, in any case, he deserved a pension as no one else in England did, and that it would mark a turning point in Johnson's life (as indeed it proved to do). He therefore disclosed the news with what he considered "slow and studied approaches." After a long pause, Johnson asked first "if it was seriously intended," and then "fell into a profound meditation." After a while he mentioned his own definition of a "pensioner," to which Murphy replied that "he, at least, did not come within the definition." Johnson arranged to meet Murphy the following afternoon at the Mitre, when he would give an answer. Meanwhile he went over to Joshua Reynolds's house in Leicester Square. Reynolds, within the last few years, had become very successful. His income was now £6,000 a year—an astonishing sum, especially for a painter, when we recall the cost of living at the time. He was by now completely at home in the sophisticated world of London. Johnson told him of the offer, which could seem rather small to Reynolds, and said he wanted to "consult his friends as to the propriety of accepting this mark of the royal favour, after the definitions which he had given in his Dictionary of *pension* and *pensioner*." He knew he would be attacked for hypocrisy in accepting a pension—as indeed he was (*e.g.*, Churchill's "He damns the pension *which* he takes"). But this did not bother him. What worried him was whether there would be a grain of truth in the charge. He would give Reynolds time to think it over, and would return the next day for his opinion. Reynolds said he did not need time, and that the matter was clear to him: the reward was for "literary merit," and the definition (which Johnson was to leave unchanged in future editions of the *Dictionary*) was simply "not applicable to him."

When Johnson saw Murphy that afternoon, he "gave up all his

* Sentiments Johnson had expressed in the past—particularly his opposition to the Seven Years' War, which Bute was now trying to end—were not uncongenial to the government; and to the older, independent Tories, who were not embracing the government with the warmth originally hoped for, the pension could appear as a gesture of good will (Greene, pp. 189-90).

scruples." The next day Murphy arrived a little after nine, "got Johnson up and dressed in due time," and took him to Wedderburn, who then conducted him to Bute. Johnson, in expressing his appreciation, said he considered himself "the more highly honoured, as the favour was not bestowed on him for having dipped his pen in faction." Bute replied that this was indeed so: "It is not offered to you for having dipped your pen in faction, nor with a design that you ever should." In a more general way, he twice repeated, so that there could be no misunderstanding, "It is not given you for any thing you are to do, but for what you have done."[21]

8

Small as £300 might seem to friends like Reynolds or Garrick, for Johnson it represented affluence. He had for so long been accustomed to living simply that he was never to spend more than a fraction of the pension on himself. It was to be three years before he even left the rooms at Inner Temple Lane and once again rented a house.

He did, however, agree to a suggestion of Reynolds's, made almost immediately after the pension was awarded, that they take a trip of six weeks to Devonshire, Reynolds's home county. Johnson had always wanted to travel. Now at last he could do so, and this was a part of England he had never seen. True, he might need prodding, since he had been accustomed for so long to depriving himself of any pleasure that cost money. Moreover, for some time he had plainly been far from happy. Reynolds, in fact, was becoming seriously worried about his state of mind, of which the continued delay of the Shakespeare edition was only a symptom. He may have hoped that this trip would drive into Johnson the reality of the pension, give him some experience of the potentialities of a new *modus vivendi,* and help jolt or entice him out of himself and into a more hopeful state of mind. Moreover, he could put it to him that Johnson would be doing him a favor; that he wanted to make this visit anyway to his home county, and would welcome his companionship.

Johnson mentioned the forthcoming trip with some self-defensive dubieties in a letter to Baretti (July 20), now in Milan. After referring to the gloomy five-day trip to Lichfield the previous winter, he added, "I think in a few weeks to try another excursion; though to what end?" Yet he went. The trip did indeed help him get out of himself. It also gave him, in the dark four years ahead, a pleasant experience to look back on—for, like every other experience, it was firmly remembered and incorporated—and, because it meant so much, it provided him, as he said, with "a great accession of new ideas."

They set off together on August 16, stopping that night and the next day at Winchester, where Johnson certainly must have visited his friend Joseph Warton, then undermaster of Winchester School. They then went on to Salisbury (August 18), where they visited Wilton, the country seat of Lord Pembroke, whose portrait Reynolds had painted, in order to see its collection of paintings, and spent the night at Longford Castle, the seat of Lord Folkstone, who also had an impressive collection of paintings. Later, at Kingston Lacy, they visited the home of John Bankes, in order to see the portraits collected by his family. Johnson startled Bankes, soon after they entered, by the strange convulsive movements to which he was suddenly liable.

As Bankes conducted them into the first apartment, said Frances Reynolds, who got the story from her brother, Johnson began

stretching out his legs alternately as far as he could possibly stretch; at the same time pressing his foot on the floor as heavily as he could possibly press, as if endeavouring to smooth the carpet, or rather perhaps to rumple it, and every now and then collecting all his force, apparently to effect a concussion of the floor.

Bankes stared at him with silent astonishment, and then said, as if to assure him, that "though it was not a new house, the flooring was perfectly safe." Johnson pulled himself together, and made no reply. As they entered another apartment, Bankes called special attention to the fine shading of a picture. The nearsighted Johnson, probably still a little embarrassed, is said to have replied, "It is all one to me, light or dark." From here they went to Dorchester, then Bridport and Exeter. We need not trace the entire itinerary in detail; this has been carefully done by James Clifford, using Reynolds's own record as a basis.[22] But mention should be made of a three-day visit in Torrington with Reynolds's two married sisters—Mary (Mrs. John Palmer) and Elizabeth (Mrs. William Johnson). The Palmers' fine Palladian house is still standing. It was now fairly crowded, for there were five children, and Frances Reynolds had also arrived for a visit. The children remembered their mother asking Johnson whether he would like pancakes for dinner. When he replied, "Yes, Madam, but I never get enough of them," she made an especially large number and he ate thirteen of them. A very different scene was remembered by Frances Reynolds. As they were driving in a carriage past the village churchyard of Wear, outside Torrington, she mentioned a striking monument raised there by a widowed mother over the grave of her only child. As she was telling the story behind the monument, she suddenly heard Johnson sobbing, and, turning to him, saw his face bathed in tears.

When they reached Plymouth they stayed for three weeks at the home of Reynolds's former schoolmate Dr. John Mudge, a cheerful, talkative physician with wide interests and a house full of small children. His father, Zachariah Mudge, the vicar of St. Andrews, was one of the most celebrated preachers in the west of England, and gave a special sermon so that Johnson might hear it. Zachariah—learned, high-minded, charitable and unaffected—came close to Johnson's ideal of what a clergyman should be, and, when he died a few years later (1769), Johnson wrote a tribute to him for the London *Chronicle*.[23] Perhaps in an effort to compensate for the unworldly Zachariah, his wife was not only practical, but, according to her son, overthrifty. She was disturbed at the amount of tea Johnson would drink when he visited them. But to please her son and husband, she would pour it out for him, though, once, after he had finished seventeen cups and again presented his cup, she could not refrain from saying, "What! another, Dr. Johnson?"—to which he is said to have replied, "Madam, you are rude."[24] But he was also drinking more than tea, at least on one occasion. One night after supper, said Reynolds, Johnson drank three bottles of wine and then found "he was unable to articulate a hard word which occurred in the course of his conversation." He tried it three times and failed. Then he finally succeeded, stood up, and said it was obviously "time to go to bed." It was the only occasion, said Reynolds, that he ever saw Johnson affected by drink.

Meanwhile the maritime life of Plymouth—"the magnificence of the navy, the ship-building and all its circumstances," the busy mercantile activity—gave him an experience of human nature and manners in a new and different setting. The Commissioner of the Dockyard, Sir Frederick Rogers, took him out in a special yacht through the harbor and past the fleet. He enjoyed talking with one of the senior magistrates of Plymouth, Henry Tolcher ("full of life, full of talk, and full of enterprise. To see brisk young fellows of seventy-four is very pleasing to those who begin to suspect themselves of growing old"). Because of the growing dockyard, a rival town had arisen two miles away that excited the jealousy of the old one. Partly to humor Mr.

Tolcher, Johnson set himself "resolutely on the side of the old town, the *established* town . . . considering it as a kind of duty to *stand by* it" and oppose the "dockers" as "upstarts." For example the "Dock, or New-town," was trying to get Plymouth to direct to it some of the Plymouth water supply, and Tolcher was one of those who had reservations about allowing them the water. In the spirit of burlesque that would often surprise his friends, Johnson, "affecting to entertain the passions of the place, was violent in opposition; and half-laughing at himself for his pretended zeal, where he had no concern, exclaimed, 'No, no! I am against the *dockers;* I am a Plymouth-man. Rogues! Let them die of thirst. They shall not have a drop!' "[25]

The height of his holiday mood is shown in a charming story told by Miss Reynolds, when he was being entertained at a country house with a large company (the same place where the hostess at dinner asked him why he had defined *pastern* as the "knee of a horse," and he replied, "Ignorance, Madam, pure ignorance"). Before the house was a spacious lawn. When someone remarked that the lawn was ideal for racing, a young lady who was present boasted that she could outrun anyone there. At this, Johnson rose and said, "Madam, you cannot outrun me":

> The lady at first had the advantage; but Dr. Johnson happening to have slippers on much too small for his feet, kick'd them off up into the air, and ran . . . leaving the lady far behind him, and . . . returned, leading her by the hand, with looks of high exultation and delight.[26]

9

On Wednesday, September 22, they left for London, stopping for the day to see Plympton, where Reynolds had been born and gone to school. While they were at the school, Reynolds left him for a while to pick up an apple in the orchard next to it where he had often as a boy stolen in to get apples. Then, by rapid coach, they reached London on September 26.

Back once more at Inner Temple Lane, he again sank into uneasy lethargy, and as winter approached the chronic bronchitis from which he increasingly suffered became acute, with a cough "sometimes very violent." December brought news of the death from fever of the beloved Richard Bathurst in the siege of Havana.* Hoping for a lift in

* See above, pp. 267–69.

spirits and health, he left for a visit to Oxford. In the gray months through which he was living, his unwillingness to change his residence—now that he could afford it—is curious and could be interpreted as a form of self-punishment. He could certainly have used larger quarters. Frank Barber was now back with him; Miss Williams was available as a permanent inmate; and Mr. Levet, after a disastrous short marriage to a streetwalker and pickpocket (she thought he was a prosperous physician and in turn convinced him that she was likely to inherit money), was soon adrift and needed the consolation of a home.

On Monday, May 16, when he dropped into the small bookshop kept by his friend Tom Davies, there occurred one of the famous meetings in literary history, which began an acquaintance that was ultimately to result in one of the masterpieces of world literature—James Boswell's *Life of Johnson* (1791). The admiring young Scot was the son of Alexander Boswell, Laird of Auchinleck, a man about Johnson's age, who had studied law at Leyden and was now a judge on the Scottish bench. Though Boswell's name, because of his great work, was to become a household word not long after his death, he himself was drastically underrated until our own generation. He has proved, at the very least, to be a far more complicated person than was ever imagined. The most celebrated literary discovery of this century was the vast journal—or series of journals—he kept through most of his life, chronicling with complete frankness his own personal experiences and, more important, recording conversations and interviews with noted people he met. When published, the writings—*The Private Papers of James Boswell from Malahide Castle* (1928–34)—filled eighteen volumes, and they were later to be supplemented by other material.[27] The conversations in the *Life of Johnson*, together with those in Boswell's earlier *Journal of a Tour to the Hebrides with Samuel Johnson* (1785), are carved from this enormous collection of diaries.

We should remind ourselves (it is often forgotten) how extremely young Boswell was when he met Johnson—he was only twenty-two; Johnson was fifty-three—just as we should remind ourselves that he had many interests, and spent most of his adult life as an able and busy lawyer in Edinburgh, visiting London only on vacations. In some ways, he was even younger than twenty-two at this time, and was generally to remain younger than his years. The identity for which the young Boswell was searching—and continued to search—was one that could define itself against the example of his father, Lord Auchinleck, who was firm and moralistic, a Whig and a Presbyterian, and who proudly spoke broad Scots. In reaction, the son was all the father was

not: romantically imaginative, sexually promiscuous, impulsively idealistic and open-natured, pliable, and with an impressionable genius for
mimicry.

In his search for identity, a shadow in the background was always
there to make him uneasy if he allowed himself to think of it. There
was a strain of mental instability in his family; and Boswell's own
younger brother John, after the age of nineteen, was to suffer from
marked insanity for most of his remaining life. The stability for which
Boswell was always to crave was something that his gregarious nature
could acquire only through others. And his profoundest enjoyment, if
not at the start, certainly as the years passed, was the company, example, and if possible the approval, of older men whom he admired—
men of acknowledged standing who were also interesting in themselves, knew the world, and, like Johnson, symbolized the moral rectitude he wanted desperately to impose on his own wayward nature.

Hence his injunctions to himself in his journal to identify with
admired models, and acquire a stronger mind and character (*"be* Johnson"). At first the ideals suggest conventional notions of sophistication
and elegance. After arriving in London, for example, he writes, "I felt
strong dispositions to *be a Mr. Addison.*" Months later—he has by now
met and talked a good deal with Johnson—the rather frightened youth
is to set off for Harwich to get the boat to Holland, where he is to
study law. And the models now, basically so different from each other
(the father from whom he is in part fleeing, Lord Chesterfield, and
Johnson), show what he really wants most to acquire—inner strength,
reserve, calmness, and courage: "[Be] like Father, grave . . . composed. . . . Go abroad with a manly resolution. . . . Never despair.
. . . Study [to be] like Lord Chesterfield, *manly. . . . Resemble
Johnson . . . your mind will strengthen*" (August 1763); or, later in
the year, "*Be* like the Duke of Sully." As he approaches and enters
his thirties, there are moments of satisfaction (when he says "you," he
is addressing himself—a common practice in his diaries, and typical of
his attempt at detachment):

> "You felt yourself . . . *like a Johnson* in comparison of former days"
> (1766). "Was *powerful* like Johnson, and very much satisfied with myself"
> (1767). "I was in such a frame as to *think myself an Edmund Burke*" (1774).
> "Fancied myself like Burke, and drank moderately . . ." (1775).

One of the touching entries is near the end, toward the close of his life.
Much of his despair—he is now fifty—is that he felt he had no more
inner strength to meet difficulties now, when he needed it badly, than

he had as a youth—that he seemed to have gone through life "without any addition to my character from my having had the friendship of Dr. Johnson and many eminent men."[28]

10

This was Boswell's second visit to London. Two years before this, he had become a Catholic, which meant at the time that he would be legally prevented from the occupations he might otherwise enter—a public career in the law, standing for Parliament, or getting a commission in the army. When his father sternly summoned him, he ran off to London, and thought of going to France and becoming a monk or a priest. A family friend in London, Lord Eglinton, talked him out of the idea and got him interested in becoming an officer in the Guards. His Catholicism lasted only a month, and his ideal of an ascetic life disappeared when he threw himself into the pleasures of the town and caught gonorrhea. By now his father decided it was time to go to London personally and bring him back. Boswell went back unwillingly to the study of law, got a serving girl pregnant, and, with other young Scots eager to shed their accents, took lessons in speech from Thomas Sheridan, who was lecturing in Edinburgh at the time. After passing his examination in civil law (July 1762), he got his father's reluctant assent to what was presumably to be a more serious visit to London. With an allowance of £200 a year, he had arrived in November, half hoping he might become a writer before having to yield to family pressure to go on with law. One of the people he was most eager to meet was Johnson.

From reading Johnson, a special image of him had grown up in the young Boswell's mind. With "a kind of mysterious veneration," he had pictured to himself "a state of solemn elevated abstraction, in which I supposed him to live in the immense metropolis of London." Thomas Sheridan, while improving Boswell's accent in Edinburgh, had mentioned how he and other friends would talk with Johnson until two or three in the morning, and had told Boswell he would have ample chance to do the same thing when he came to London. But now Sheridan was not speaking to Johnson. Sheridan himself had been given a pension (£200) in recognition of his plan for a *Pronouncing Dictionary*, and Johnson, always ready to take a dig at the "performing" arts of acting and elocution, had let himself remark, though largely in jest,

"What! have they given *him* a pension? Then it is time for me to give up mine." James Macpherson, the author of the "Ossian" poems, had repeated this to Sheridan without telling him that Johnson added, "However, I am glad that Mr. Sheridan has a pension, for he is a very good man." "Sherry," who had helped Johnson get his own pension, was naturally hurt. He had an unforgiving nature anyway (for years he refused to speak to his famous son after an argument over the son's marriage). He now refused to meet Johnson again.

But Tom Davies, the actor, came to Boswell's rescue. Davies, as a sideline, kept a bookshop (8 Russell Street, Covent Garden) that Johnson occasionally visited. More than once he invited Johnson especially to meet Boswell. But Johnson's unhappiness with his own state of mind was deepening, and the months passed without his accepting Davies' invitation. Then, on May 16, by sheer chance, he stopped at the bookshop when Boswell was drinking tea with Davies in the back parlor. Seeing Johnson through the glass door between the back parlor and the shop, Davies announced his approach "in the manner of an actor in the part of Horatio, when he addresses Hamlet on the appearance of his father's ghost, 'Look, my Lord, it comes.'" Boswell, much agitated as he was introduced, remembered hearing of Johnson's "prejudice" against the Scots, and said to Davies, "Don't tell him where I come from." "From Scotland," cried out Davies. "Mr. Johnson," Boswell hurried to say, "I do indeed come from Scotland, but I cannot help it." The famous reply—"That, Sir, I find, is what a very great many of your countrymen cannot help"—left him stunned for a moment and apprehensive about what would be said next. The conversation, however, moved ahead rapidly; the vigor of Johnson's talk was all that he had imagined. When Boswell left, Davies followed him to the door and reassured him, "Don't be uneasy. I can see he likes you very well." Eight days later (May 24) he "boldly repaired" to Johnson's rooms and paid his first call.

Boswell had only about two months left in London. He was to leave in August for Holland, where he would study law at the University of Utrecht (a common procedure for young Scots, since the Dutch universities were noted centers for the study of Roman law, with which Scottish law had close connections). But busy as he was with other engagements and with what he now called disapprovingly his "promiscuous concubinage," he managed to see Johnson several times and talked with him at length, often sitting up all night to record everything that was said. He told him about his own life—his sins, follies, and resolutions. (One entry, June 18, reads, "At one call Johnson. Be fine and appoint him to sup with you next week. Think of telling him your imbecility, your disposition to ridicule, and take his advice.") Johnson, though feeling sorry for what he felt was a confused and lonely youth, preferred speaking in generalities. He knew how little people profited from good advice. He finally suggested a day's excursion to Greenwich, during which he promised to talk with Boswell about his future. The record of the talk that day does not provide much "advice." To give him further moral support, Johnson also went with him to Harwich (August 5–6), from which Boswell was to take the packetboat to Holland.[29]

11

Two and a half years were to pass before Boswell returned. After his course of study at Utrecht, he traveled throughout the Continent. Memorable sections of his journal record his interviews with Rousseau, Voltaire, and other celebrities; and he spent six weeks in Corsica, to which he went in order to interview the famous Pasquale Paoli, who was leading the fight for Corsican independence. Soon after his return, in February 1766, he went back to Edinburgh to practice law, though he was to make frequent trips to London. Many readers assume that he was constantly in Johnson's presence. But during the twenty-one years he knew Johnson, the total number of days he spent in Johnson's company amount to 325, plus another 101 during their trip to Scotland and the Hebrides in 1773.[30]

Even so, by 1772—ten years after he met Johnson—he had accumulated what he justly called "a vast treasure of his conversation at different times," and decided that he would someday try to write a life of Johnson using these materials. It was to be a new kind of biography—a "life in Scenes," as though it were a kind of drama. And when the "life in Scenes" did appear, nothing comparable to it had existed. Nor has anything comparable been written since, because that special union of talents, opportunities, and subject matter has never been duplicated. If there were writers who had Boswell's opportunities of knowing their subject as well, they have not had his unusual combination of talents. If they had his talents, they have lacked his opportunities. The talents include his gift for empathy and dramatic imitation, his ability to draw people out and get them to talk freely, his astonishing memory for

364

conversations, his zest and gusto, his generous capacity for admiration, and his sheer industry as a reporter—qualities that are by no means often found together. Bringing these qualities into focus and sustaining his industry was his prevailing sense of what he called "the *waste* of good if it be not preserved," of the rapid erosion and loss of human experience through life's enemy, time, and the need to rescue it as far as possible through the recorded word. But the final indispensable element in Boswell's great work is Johnson himself. Fascinating as they are, the interviews with others—David Hume, Voltaire, Rousseau, the elder Pitt—rarely approach in range of topics and personal interest any section of equal length dealing with Johnson.

The picture of Johnson, which for better or worse remains permanently imprinted because of this classic work, is inevitably, given the circumstances, somewhat specialized. Most important, it is a picture of Johnson in his later years. The first half of Johnson's life occupies little more than a tenth of the work. Less than a quarter takes him up to fifty-three, when his life was more than two-thirds over; and a full half of the book is devoted to Johnson's last eight years, from sixty-seven to seventy-five. There are also personal sides of Johnson even after fifty-three of which Boswell could never know, but of which others—above all, Mrs. Thrale—knew or suspected a great deal, though they did not always care to proclaim their knowledge. Moreover, it is a very masculine world in which Boswell presents him—the world of The Club and the taverns. In addition, he saw Johnson through the spectacles of his own romantic Toryism, with the result that Johnson has been—and perhaps will unfortunately always be—viewed as an "arch-conservative." Even his minor dramatic touches have proved permanent: for example, his exaggerated insertion of "Sir" before so many of Johnson's remarks, as if to give them a kind of thunderous and formal authority; or his decision to change his references to him from "Mr. Johnson" to "Dr. Johnson," with the result that Johnson alone, of all great writers who have ever received a doctor's degree, is forever known to most people as "Dr. Johnson." (Ironically Johnson himself—according to Hawkins—rather disliked being called Dr. Johnson. At least, as even Boswell once admitted, he hardly ever assumed it in formal notes or on cards—"but called himself *Mr.* Johnson"; and when Boswell once noticed a letter addressed to him with the title "Esquire," and said he thought it a title inferior to "Doctor," Johnson "checked me, and seemed pleased with it.")[31] Yet whatever its limitations, large or small, the work remains unique among all writings by one human being about another—unique in the way Boswell himself foresaw when he decided as a mature man to undertake it: that is, in the drama, fidelity, and range of interests in the conversation of one of the most fascinating individuals in history.

12

Before turning to the later Johnson, one other incident should be mentioned, from the year that Boswell met him, which also helped to create the picture of him that literally millions of people, from the 1790's to the present, have had. This was the founding of The Club, the prototype of all dining and conversational clubs.

Joshua Reynolds first proposed it to Johnson in the winter of 1763–64, when they were sitting at Johnson's fireside. He was certainly thinking of Johnson's own frame of mind and of the psychological help to him of a regular meeting with challenging company. The original group was small, and rather different in character from the large, distinguished group it soon became. The first members, aside from Johnson and Reynolds, included Goldsmith, the still relatively young Edmund Burke, who was not yet the famous figure he was to become; Topham Beauclerk and Bennet Langton; the physician Dr. Christopher Nugent, Burke's father-in-law; the "unclubable" John Hawkins, from the old Ivy Lane Club, brought in by Johnson at the start because of his loyalty to old friends (Hawkins later withdrew); and Anthony Chamier, a stockbroker of Huguenot descent with literary interests. The plan was to meet every Monday night at seven, at the Turk's Head in Gerrard Street, Soho. Within a few years, The Club was to become the most sought-after and prized informal society in England. And within a few more years, it was to include the most remarkable assemblage of diverse talents that has ever met so frequently for the sole purpose of conversation.*

Meanwhile, in January (1764), before the new club began meeting in February, Johnson finally accepted the invitation of young Bennet Langton to visit the family seat in Lincolnshire. He was in need of a vacation. He was, in fact, rapidly entering a psychological crisis in which all that he had most dreaded in his past seemed at last to be catching up with him. But no one would have guessed it. He was watching himself very carefully. He charmed Langton's parents, and

* See below, pp. 504-5.

he talked very well to everyone. Of course, he had immense resources to help him to remain open to what Freud called "the reality principle": above all, courage, freedom from self-pity, generosity of spirit, and humor. Time and again, when he was with others, he could climb out of the prison house of self that he so loathed, and emerged with an exuberance and a childlike love of fun for which, said Mrs. Thrale, she never saw an equal. One little episode during this visit was typical. For whatever reason, Langton never told it to Boswell, though he passed on so much other information to him. Perhaps he simply thought Boswell would not have understood it. But he always remembered it, and as an elderly man told the story to a friend of his son when they were out walking and came to the top of a very steep hill. Back in 1764 Johnson and the Langtons had also walked to the top of this hill, and Johnson, delighted by its steepness, said he wanted to "take a roll down." They tried to stop him. But he said he "had not had a roll for a long time," and taking out of his pockets his keys, a pencil, a purse, and other objects, lay down parallel at the edge of the hill, and rolled down its full length, "turning himself over and over till he came to the bottom."[32]

Part IV

THE
JOHNSON
OF
LEGEND

Chapter 21

Approaching Breakdown; Religious Struggles; Fear of Insanity

We are at last approaching the Johnson—from the age of fifty-five, in 1764, to his death twenty years later—who was to become the subject of the largest and most fascinating group of memoirs ever devoted to a writer, and of whom Boswell could justifiably say that his "character . . . nay his figure and manner, are, I believe, more generally known than those of almost any man." But the transition to the Johnson we see, and hear quoted, in the memoirs—and it was never a complete transition anyway—was far from apparent to most of those who were to write about him.

In particular, he kept to himself the distressing state of mind into which he had been gradually sinking since his fifty-first year (1760), when he virtually stopped writing. Entries in his journal betray a growing helplessness at his inability to attain "superiority over my habits"; and by 1761 the sense of paralysis into which he felt himself falling becomes crossed with an anxiety and despair that begin to remind us of the breakdown thirty years before:

Easter Eve, 1761. "Since the communion of last Easter I have led a life so dissipated and useless, *and my terrours and perplexities have so much increased*, that I am under great depression. . . . 'Come unto me all ye that travail.' *I have resolved . . . till I am afraid to resolve again.* . . . Almighty and merciful Father look down upon my misery with pity. . . ."

Nothing else from the next three years remains of the journal he was keeping except an entry for the following spring (March 28, 1762), on the anniversary of Tetty's death. When he burned so many of his papers and journals before he died, it was these especially, having to do with the crucial years 1762 to 1768, that he wanted to destroy, including those two quarto volumes at the loss of which he said he would have "gone mad." Beginning with the spring of 1764, a few more entries survive (by now The Club was founded and he was attending its weekly meetings). April 21, 1764. 3:00 A.M.: *"A kind of strange oblivion has overspread me, so that I know not what has become of the last year,* and perceive that incidents and intelligence pass over me without leaving any impression. . . . *Yet I will not despair."* Easter Day, 1764, 3:00 A.M.: "Almighty and most merciful Father . . . Let me not be created to misery. . . . Deliver me from the distresses of vain terrour. . . ." September 18, 1764: "I have done nothing; the need of doing therefore is pressing, since the time of doing is short." Easter Day, 1765 ("about three in the morning"): "Since the last Easter . . . my time . . . seems as a dream that has left nothing behind. *My memory grows confused, and I know not how the days pass over me."* March 28, 1766: "I was twice at church, and went through the prayers without perturbation." March 29, 1766: "O God! . . . Grant that I may be no longer disturbed with doubts and harrassed with vain terrours."[1]

2

By 1764 and for at least another three years, he was constantly on the verge of a breakdown, and only by the most heroic effort, exerted day after day, could he pull himself together. Any suspicion or anxiety on the part of his friends was dispelled as soon as he began to talk. They then felt the same relief that the young artist Ozias Humphry felt on first meeting Johnson in his rooms at Inner Temple Lane (September 1764) when, during the long silence at the start, he thought himself in the presence of a "madman" until at last Johnson began to talk, and "faith . . . everything he says is as *correct* as a *second edition."**

But there were occasions—and not just at night, when he was alone, but for days at a time—when he was afraid to see anyone whom he did not trust completely. One such occasion was described by Dr. Adams, after Johnson's death, to Boswell, who rather softened the account in

* See above, p. 352.

his own paraphrase of the story. Adams, who had not seen him for some time, was now in London and dropped by his lodgings. Miss Williams answered the door. She said "nobody had been admitted to him for some days now but Mr. Langton. But he would see Dr. Adams." When Adams went in, he found Langton sitting silently with him. Johnson "looked miserable; his lips moved, tho he was not speaking; he could not sit long at a time . . . walked up and down the room, sometimes into the next room, and returned immediately." Finally he turned to Dr. Adams, saying only "I would suffer a limb to be amputated to recover my spirits." The whole situation, said Adams, was "dreadful to see."[2]

3

As in the breakdown in his twenties, what was making the situation so serious for him now was not any one thing—the more shattering experiences of life are rarely so simple for anyone—but the convergence of several, all of them reinforcing each other.

To begin with, he was reaping the harvest—always known by him to be accumulating, but deferred throughout the busy years of early middle age—of his most deeply ingrained habit of self-defense (however treacherous and self-destructive he knew it to be): the habit of leaping ahead in imagination into the future and forestalling disappointment and hurt by anticipating, taking for granted beforehand, and assimilating all that could produce them. Beneath this was that resolution never again to be fooled, never again to be caught off guard, which we saw put so firmly at only twenty in those lines in "The Young Author," written when he knew he had to leave Oxford and go back to Lichfield to a life of what seemed total defeat; that early *Vanity of Human Wishes* in which, with distilled bitterness, he turned on himself by trying to club his own ambitions and hopes. There we were already confronting a form of self-defense that was threatening to become not only internalized but also dangerously agile and resourceful; and the long breakdown that followed was a result, involving inevitable self-division and a savage turning of aggression against himself. We have been noticing the deepening of this whole habit of mind—however many other things in Johnson warred against it—until it becomes one major element in the dialectic of *The Vanity of Human Wishes* and the moral writings generally. True, it is the *dialectic*

373

that is important when we come to evaluate the moral writings themselves. Time and again he turns on the treachery of the human temptation—common to us all and especially chronic in himself—to overprepare ourselves for future disasters by refusing to surrender to the present lest we lose stamina and be taken unawares. No one knew better, and he had found it out the hard way, that—beyond a certain point—the result is the erosion rather than the increase of stamina; that to have learned to live well today is to be better able to live well tomorrow; and that the "frustrations" of hope, "however frequent, are less dreadful than its extinction." But the answers in the moral writing are as convincing and resonant as they are precisely because what they have to answer is so powerfully present in him at all times—his own lifelong compulsion to get all possible evils anticipated in advance, shrewdly, realistically, and digested into habitual response in order not to lose his ability as a "free agent" and become the helpless victim of chance, caprice, or malignity. Not that the result had been any of the usual by-products of this form of defense common in more timid, less generous natures (paranoid suspicion, envy, and the like, all involving projections on other individuals, who, Johnson never forgets, are all in the same boat with himself). The attitude—and with it the anger and sense of protest—was one that skipped over rather than focused on his fellow participants in life, and was something that extended instead to the universe at large.

This massive attitude of distrust toward life generally and of inner protest against the way it went (in short, the whole problem of evil) was to create his greatest single difficulty by far in his religious struggles, preventing that "resignation" and "reposal of myself upon GOD" that he feared himself unable to give. We should recognize the psychological complications of something rarely even mentioned when the subject of Johnson's religious attitudes is discussed. This is the surprising *anger* (no milder word will do) that he can suddenly show to anyone who denies—or may not even fully admit—the radical unhappiness of human life. It can be almost brutal in its heady suddenness, though in later years he learned to ease it for himself and others by humor or wit. When anger flares up so easily at a subject—and it could be evoked, as Mrs. Thrale said, by an innocent remark of "a friend whom he loved exceedingly"*—it expresses a deep and abiding frustration.

What is being frustrated is the ability to discharge in effective pro-

* See below, p. 490.

test (rather than try to absorb and internalize) what we can only call a massive resentment at the fact that "the only thinking being of this globe is doomed to think merely to be wretched, and to pass his time from youth to age in fearing or suffering calamities." It was a resentment that another part of him feared in himself, which is why he so recoiled from what he thought was the example of Jonathan Swift ("He was not a man to be either loved or envied. He seems to have wasted life in discontent . . .") Because of his taboo against bringing it as a charge to the door of orthodox, revealed religion, it usually appears as an eloquent inner protest pressing upward against the surface, yet still firmly contained, as in *The Vanity of Human Wishes*. But if it can be expressed in what he considers a good cause, the bitterness becomes frank and open. We see this in his famous review (1757), one of his finest short pieces, of Soame Jenyns's *Free Inquiry into the Nature and Origin of Evil*. Jenyns's was admittedly a foolish book and foolish in many ways. But it is hard to believe Johnson would have bothered to focus on it such an array of artillery had not its glib optimism—the old argument that evil is an inevitable part of the picture, that it helps good to shine out by contrast, that the suffering of the individual helps out the larger good—been expressed within the frame of deistic or "natural" religion rather than of Hebrew-Christian teaching. Hence, in facing this particular attempt to excuse or reconcile the evils of life within a larger picture, all the taboos for Johnson are immediately dropped. The luckless Jenyns, hoping for philosophic "detachment," imagines "superior beings" who could regard us—and our struggles with each other and the conditions of life generally—as we do the lower animals. Johnson, as he works into his analogy, begins to push the argument into the open. Jenyns might have carried the argument further:

He might have shewn that these hunters whose game is man have many sports analogous to our own. As we drown whelps and kittens, they amuse themselves now and then with sinking a ship, and stand around the fields of Blenheim or the walls of Prague, as we encircle a cock-pit. As we shoot a bird flying, they take a man in the midst of his business or pleasure, and knock him down with an apoplexy. Some of them, perhaps, are virtuosi, and delight in the operations of an asthma, as a human philosopher in the effects of the air pump. To swell a man with a tympany is as good sport as to blow a frog. Many a merry bout have these frolic beings at the vicissitudes of an ague, and good sport it is to see a man tumble with an epilepsy, and revive and tumble again, and all this he knows not why. As they are wiser and more powerful than we, they have more exquisite diversions, for we have no way of procuring any sport so brisk and so lasting as the paroxysms of the gout and stone which undoubtedly must make high mirth, especially if the play be a little diversified with the blunders and puzzles of the blind and deaf.[3]

Unquestionably a major element in the crisis he was now entering was the intense self-conflict involved in his religious struggles, though in the interests of space we defer discussion of his religious attitudes until we can consider this subject in a more general way.* The conflict was essentially one between the Christian ideals of self-surrender, resignation, and "reposal upon God," and the powerful unconscious need—with which he had lived for so long—to take whatever steps he himself could take independently not to be caught off guard. And if the philosophical range and horizon of this ingrained habit of mind had widened by his middle years, and with it the compassionate sense of the shared "doom of man" that we all face, this hardly made the accumulated psychological legacy—itself so firmly internalized as to be a part of him—any easier to carry in a world where "without hope there can be no endeavour," and where "hope is itself a species of happiness, and perhaps the chief happiness which this world affords." Of course, this can be said to be the inevitable price paid by those in the spearhead of human consciousness—by those who, without complete religious confidence, follow Socrates' injunction about the "examined life" and examine it closely, honestly, without illusion but still with values, and, in the words from *King Lear*, "see it feelingly."

4

But the special burden for Johnson was his refusal to slough off responsibility for his own frame of mind. "Reasonable with regard to others," said Mrs. Thrale, "he had formed vain hopes of performing impossibilities himself." However strong the suppressed anger against life being what it is—"a state in which much is to be endured, and little to be enjoyed"—he would not "whine." Nor would he blame or project on others, or on society, or even, beyond a point, on the universe generally lest it become a charge against God Himself.

It was up to him personally to digest these feelings and force them into moral and mental perspective—just as it had been up to him to

* See below, pp. 449-60.

bludgeon envy or to throttle his strong aggressive instincts, and just as it was up to him now to digest any psychological conflicts, or by-products of them, that might be afflicting him. Long ago, in his attempt at "self-management," he had written that Latin statement of his case to show Dr. Swynfen. So now and for years he had himself been studying "medicine diligently in all its branches," as Mrs. Thrale said, "but had given particular attention to the diseases of the imagination, which he watched in himself with a solicitude destructive to his own peace, and intolerable to those he trusted." "Will anybody's mind," she once asked in desperation, "bear this eternal microscope that you place upon your own so?"[4] And the more closely he probed into his own state of mind, the more hopeless the gulf between what he found there and what he demanded from himself. Only company could relieve him. As soon as he was alone and unoccupied, as he was so often now at night, "his spirits," said Murphy, "not employed abroad, turned with *inward hostility* against himself." In one of the *Idler* essays (No. 31), he had written a little sketch of "Sober"—largely a self-portrait—whose "chief pleasure is conversation," which frees him "for the time from his own reproaches":

But there is one time at night when he must go home, that his friends may sleep. These are the moments of which poor Sober trembles at the thought. But the misery of these tiresome intervals he has many means of alleviating. He has persuaded himself, that the manual arts are undeservedly overlooked . . . and supplied himself with the tools of a carpenter, with which he mended his coal-box very successfully. . . .

He has attempted at other times the crafts of the shoemaker, tinman, plumber, and potter; in all these arts he has failed. But his daily amusement is chemistry. He has a small furnace . . . draws oils and waters . . . which he knows to be of no use; sits and counts the drops as they come from his retort, and forgets that, whilst a drop is falling, a moment flies away.

That was six years ago, in 1758, when he was only a few months behind the deadline he had given himself for the Shakespeare edition. But now the nights were becoming more fearful as a part of him battled to stay awake—unable to let go his clutch at objective reality as the sole means of steadying his mind, unable not to keep all guards posted and retain "self-management" rather than to relapse into the unconsciousness that another part of him (a part he feared) deeply craved.

Now, as in his twenties, when he had to leave Oxford, what was happening to him was that the full force of his powerfully aggressive nature—blunted by compassion and philosophy from turning on others —was directed toward himself. Murphy shrewdly sensed this when he spoke of the "inward hostility" Johnson suffered when alone. The only thing that could beat him to his knees and bludgeon him without opposition for months at a time was himself. Fear, in the usual sense of the word, was something to which Johnson—as those who knew him repeatedly testified—seemed impervious. With most things that cause fear to human nature, his automatic tendency was to face them at once. But these "fears" now were self-created and self-inflicted. They had all the strength of his own character behind them. What was left to oppose them, within his divided nature, was afraid to resist lest what it resisted and fought back against was "conscience" itself. And the result of such a radical split in the psyche is inevitably one of horror, which in turn has to be fought, but with the further fear that the horror is justified.

5

True, *work*—as he had been the first to say—can make a great difference; work that he could himself consider of real value (though, as another part of him never forgot, so little that one did seemed to make much difference to the world). "Work and love," said Freud near the end of his own life, in *Civilization and Its Discontents*, are the only ways in which human nature can come closest to happiness or at least avoid misery.[5] Freud adds, of course, that far fewer people really "love" than think they do. But still more neglected—and something that will "raise more difficult social problems" if a world of leisure lies ahead—is the "human aversion" to that other necessary form of therapy, "work." Johnson did indeed love—very much throughout his life. True, from the experience of *mutual* erotic love—of "romantic love," as he defensively called it—his appearance and entire history from the age of twenty on had shut him off, except for the very unusual relationship he had with Tetty. Any isolated episodes, such as those pathetic demonstrations of affection to Mrs. Desmoulins, were brief and infrequent. Even if they had not been, they would hardly have been a substitute for the experience of mutual erotic or "romantic" love; and by his fifties, the long suppression and frustration of this whole aspect of human life, joined with the long conviction that he was essentially "unlovable" in this way, had naturally taken its psychological toll. Still, he was able to distinguish between "loving" and "being loved" and to value the first without demanding equal payment through the latter. Above all, his conception of love was by no means narrow. Even so, in these years he was very lonely. (To whom, among all his close friends, could he really talk frankly and openly now, except—a little—to Reynolds, whose situation was so different, who was now earning £6,000 a year and moving in a different world? The immense rush of affection and confidence when the Thrales took in Johnson shows how much had been dammed up inside him.)

But, if he could love, constructive release or health through "work" was denied him. The profession he had always most wanted to enter—the law—had been closed to him. By the bitterest irony, the form of "work" to which he had been forced to turn—the sole form of "work" he could do now in his mid-fifties—was writing. That we ourselves know he could do it supremely well is aside from the point. The fact remains that it is one of those very few forms of work that—if one has exacting enough standards sharpened by an unsleeping remorselessness of self-demand—is constantly splitting the self and pitting the parts of it against each other. With every sentence one writes, one part of the divided self is dragging another to the bar of self-judgment. True, Johnson could smash through the inhibitions. We have been repeatedly noticing the speed with which he would do so, in exasperated impatience, and his innocent pride—especially in his earlier years—that he could do this. It could be done easily if one did not care too much, or when (as was the case with much of his writing) it was done anonymously as a favor for others. But the truth is that a part of him did care—if he was really going to be forced to turn out a major work under his own name. Then the inner resistance was massive—especially after the accumulated fatigue from having fought that inner resistance for so long. He might say, and mean it, that "a man might write at any time if he will set himself *doggedly* to it." But as with Coleridge—so different from him in other ways, and different too in the way he faced this problem—the crushing burden of self-demand could make almost any other activity pleasant by contrast. Again as with Coleridge, talking was infinitely preferable. For there one's powers of expression could be exercised in the highest degree, and yet the result was constantly flying away instead of remaining there on paper to rebuke him. Hence his dislike of revision, and his eagerness (concealed under a certain bravado) to dispatch a work to the press without rereading it, or his reluctance to reread it later (a notable exception was the cherished *Rambler*, conceived in a spirit of dedication and prayer, which he did agree to revise).

No, he was already facing the bar of self-judgment quite enough as soon as he was alone. There was no need to court it further. Even when he wrote *The Vanity of Human Wishes*—the first work to which he had been willing to put his name—he had stopped to count how many lines were finished and how many still had to be done. And that was fifteen years ago. "I wonder," said Boswell, who lacked that inner censor, "you have not more pleasure in writing." Johnson: "Sir, you *may* wonder."

6

It was no consolation—quite the reverse—that he had known about all this beforehand, and written about it so well.

The time-honored injunction *"Physician, heal thyself!"* was perhaps the most bitter of all things that he had to digest now, and was one of the distinctions between his present state and the breakdown in his twenties. There was not a single thing now afflicting him of which he had not already written with honesty, psychological insight, and balanced judgment. Take only one instance of the most elementary sort. The commonest of commonplaces is that "happiness" can never be found if consciously and deliberately looked for (and weighed in the balance against the expectant imagination), but occurs only as a by-product when we lose ourselves in something else. Yet, after all he had written, and though he had rediscovered the truth of this time and again, he was himself repeatedly using "happiness" as a yardstick with which to measure and evaluate life. That he should be so passionate in maintaining the futility of "happiness" as a goal or end in itself showed only how persistent an obsession it was. And was he following any of the ways he had known—and so often said—could get one started on a better path? Above all, and at the very least, "employment" or work of any sort? "Nature abhors a vacuum"; "imagination never takes such firm possession of the mind, as when it is . . . unoccupied"; labor itself "may be styled its own reward."

Yet now—as Hawkins said, referring to the edition of Shakespeare—"such a torpor had seized his faculties, as not all the remonstrances of his friends were able to cure: applied to some minds, they would have burned like caustics, but Johnson felt them not."[6] To say that there were other forms of work he would have preferred was no excuse to his own conscience. Most of mankind could say the same thing. The fact remained that the work was not too onerous, and that a man *can* write "at any time if he will set himself doggedly to it." To say that he especially, beyond most people, was afflicted with an overwhelming resistance to this work (or to his own self-demand about it) was again no excuse, but rather another sign of the hopeless mental state in which he was now. So with his hypochondria: his physical illnesses, even if not caused by psychological factors, were certainly intensified by them. But this itself was an indictment of his state of mind and of his inability to do anything to cleanse it.

What he had ended in becoming, especially in these hours alone at night, was not a defeat for what he had *said* in the moral writings (which could now seem to have been written long ago). Instead it was an indictment of himself and what he had done about it. And as he struggled alone against the self-conflicts, the paralysis, the inner resistance, he once again—as in his twenties—found himself also having to battle with the swarm of psychological by-products that rose up from them, especially from his suspicious, watchful efforts at "control" and "self-management." They could become so compulsive and yet be so trivial that he could feel that their tyranny over him was itself a form of "madness." Much of this is suggested by the word "scruples" (from the Latin *scrupulus*, meaning "a small sharp pebble") that becomes so important in the *Diaries*, indicating hesitations and doubts focusing obsessively on minute matters in what he could feel a disease of conscience and self-demand. In effect they involved a morbid growth in the impulse to *correct* oneself, and to keep on "correcting" till the act of correction becomes an end in itself, and nothing can exist that the now overburdened psyche does not feel *has* to be corrected: 1759 (undated): "Enable me to *break the chain of my sins* . . . and to overcome and suppress vain scruples." September 18, 1764: "I resolve . . . *To drive out vain scruples*. . . . God help me . . . to combat scruples." Good Friday, 1766: "Scruples distract me, but at church I had hopes to conquer them." March 29, 1766: "Scruples still distress me. My resolution, with the blessing of God, is to contend with them. . . ." Easter Day, 1766: "I prayed in the collect for . . . deliverance from scruples; this deliverance was the chief subject of my prayers. O God hear me. I am now trying to conquer them."[7]

What his more rational self thought of these "vain scruples" against which he was battling is shown in a story he later told Mrs. Thrale of a half-mad clerk who haunted his lodgings for five weeks. It turned out that the clerk was in the habit of occasionally stealing paper and pack-thread from his employer rather than buying any for his own use. Johnson told him to tell his employer, who would doubtless regard the matter as trivial. The clerk said he had told his employer, who bade him help himself. Yet the clerk was still bothered by what he had been doing. Finally, discovering the man left work at 7:00 P.M. and retired at midnight, Johnson burst out:

I have at least learned this much . . . that five hours of the four-and-twenty unemployed are enough for a man to go mad in; so I would advise you, Sir, to study algebra . . . your head would get less *muddy,* and you will leave off tormenting your neighbours about paper and packthread, while we all live in a world that is bursting with sin and sorrow.

More to remind himself than for any other reason, he "quoted this scrupulous person with his packthread very often," said Mrs. Thrale, and once applied it to a friend who saw some birdcatchers on Streatham Common on Sunday morning and lamented the "wickedness of the times":

While half the Christian world is permitted to dance and sing, and celebrate Sunday as a day of festivity, how comes your puritanical spirit so offended with frivolous and empty deviations from exactness? Whoever loads life with unnecessary scruples . . . incurs the censure of singularity without reaping the reward of superior virtue.[8]

Meanwhile the tics and other compulsive habits had increased. As we noted when they first began to afflict him to a marked extent, during the breakdown of his twenties, the compulsion neurosis behind them showed a powerful unconscious need to release nervous tension through order, pattern, or rhythm and keep it from overwhelming the psyche—a need to "divide up" the welter of subjective feeling and reduce to manageable units, which we also see in his constant resort to arithmetic and counting.* Examples would be his touching the posts as he passed, and going back if he missed one; adjusting his steps so that his foot would touch a threshold at a particular moment; blowing out his breath loudly like a whale when he finished a lengthy remark or a dispute, as if to punctuate it and give it finality; treading the floor as if measuring it and also testing its firmness or stability; or making patterns with his heels and toes, as Miss Reynolds said, "as if endeavouring to form a triangle or some geometrical figure."[9]

* See below, p. 415.

Naturally this subconscious compulsion to "order" subjective experience—to divide it up, round it off, or give it "manageable" pattern—could seem to him ridiculous, and as "mad" as old Michael Johnson's habit of scrupulously and compulsively locking the door of the parchment factory even though the back part of the place had fallen in and was open to anyone who wanted to enter. Hence his resolutions in the journals "to avoid all singularity" and an "aversion" to "gesticulation in company" so strong that he once seized the arms of a man, who was gesticulating as he spoke, and held them down.[10]

7

As he reached his middle fifties, the wild disparity between his own life, as he saw it, and all that he demanded of himself had increased to such a point, and had created such a further swarm of psychological by-products, that he could feel that the "madness" he had inherited from old Michael—the potentiality for "the heaviest of human afflictions"—was at last beginning to catch up with him.

What was emerging, in short, was the "negative identity" he had loathed and feared from the start and had suppressed for so long throughout his thirties and forties: the sum total of everything he wanted, at all costs, *not* to be. The proof that it was winning out—that it may have been destined to be the winner all along—was his complete paralysis before it; and by now an enormous fatigue at the constant self-struggle was beginning to add a further reason for fearing his own state of mind. In 1763 he had written—very much from the heart—a short "character" of the poet William Collins, who suffered mental collapse and died fairly young. There he mentioned "that depression of mind which enchains the faculties without destroying them, and leaves reason the knowledge of right without the power of pursuing it."[11] He was speaking partly for himself. That compulsion, for example, to "manage experience" in his own mind—to stay in the driver's seat and leave nothing to chance: had he not always known what the morbid excesses of this could mean, and half burlesqued himself when he wrote of the mad astronomer, in *Rasselas*, who at last ended up convinced that he was personally responsible for directing the weather for the world and dared not leave his post lest chaos result? True, unlike the mad astronomer, he could still see what was "right," even though he seemed as powerless now as Collins to "pursue" what he knew was right. But who knew how much longer this could continue before that part of him that could still see the "right" simply let go, in overwhelming fatigue, and let the whole "negative" self well up and permanently engulf him?

He even found himself clutching at the sense of guilt itself in order to pull himself back to the surface. Admittedly this could be treacherous. "No disease of the imagination," he had said in *Rasselas*, "is so difficult of cure, as that which is complicated with the dread of guilt; fancy and conscience then act interchangeably upon us, and so often shift their places, that the illusions of one are not distinguished from the dictates of the other." When the imagination lures us to things immoral or irreligious, we can at least try to drive these thoughts away. But when they "take the form of *duty*," they lay hold of the mind without opposition because we are then "afraid to exclude or banish them." And now, almost five years after *Rasselas*, because of the growing fatigue of watching and punishing himself, he began to feel guilt at not feeling guilty enough: "I perceive [April 21, 1764] an insensibility and heaviness upon me. I am less than commonly oppressed with the sense of sin and less affected with the shame of Idleness. Yet I will not despair." And again next year he tries in a prayer to enforce the feeling of guilt more sharply, lest he relapse from effort (April 7, 1765): "*Fill me with such sorrow for the time mispent*, that I may amend my life."[12]

He had, he felt, learned nothing, old as he now was—learned nothing in any way that really counted, in his ability to incorporate and apply it to his own life. And the reason was the raw material he himself had brought to the "positive identity" he had tried so hard to become after the terrible time of self-punishment and despair in Birmingham thirty years before: the characteristics he had inherited from Michael and the querulous Sarah. Time and again, with fierce satiric reductionism, he would suddenly surprise others by dismissing all ills, other than "*real* privation," as only "in the head." That was the problem he himself now faced. His ills were really "in the head," and in a way that deeply frightened him. "Of the uncertainties of our present state, the most dreadful and alarming is the uncertain continuance of reason."

8

At the sale in 1823 of Mrs. Thrale's library and other belongings after her death, an item listed in the catalogue was a padlock, with a note attached in her handwriting: *"Johnson's padlock, committed to my care in the year 1768."* If we are trying to understand Johnson's situation in these years (1764–67), we must face the implications of this item surrendered to Mrs. Thrale in 1768, and also of a cryptic footnote in her journal for 1779: "the Fetters & Padlocks will tell Posterity the Truth."*

The insane, in this period, were still frequently kept in chains. Plainly the fear of insanity, hypnotically working on his imagination, had mounted to such a degree that he finally, in exhausted despair, bought the fetters and padlocks lest the enemy that seemed to be winning against him pass beyond control. It was a sign not only of shattered self-confidence but of a fearful self-condemnation. Only after he came to trust Mrs. Thrale as he had no one else since Richard Bathurst did he confide in her what had happened to him and surrender these items to her (1768) with the request that they be kept in case they were needed again. In a passage she did not print but which has been known for some time, she wrote (1779) that

Johnson trusted me about the Years 1767 or 1768–I know not which just now–with a Secret far dearer to him than his Life: such however is his nobleness, & such his partiality, that I sincerely believe he has never since that Day regretted his Confidence. . . . Well does he contradict the Maxim of Rochefoucault, that no Man is a Hero to his Valet de Chambre. – Johnson is more a Hero to me than any one–& I have been more to him for Intimacy, than ever was any Man's Valet de Chambre.[13]

With touching historical naïveté, our minds leap to sex–in biographies if not in sober histories–at the mere mention of anything connected with either "secrecy" or "guilt" in any human being from the ancient Greeks to the end of the eighteenth century. The way in which this passage from Mrs. Thrale's journal has been misinterpreted is typical. About what else, we ask, could anyone be deeply secretive or ashamed (unless about some serious crime like murder)? Were not our parents and grandparents that way, and do they not represent "the past"? This inference is strengthened by the thought of the biographer that he is bringing "modern" psychoanalytic understanding to his sub-

* Knowledge of the padlock and of relevant passages in the diary was first made available by Katharine Balderston in her important edition of *Thraliana* (1942), especially I, 384–85, 386, n. 2, 415, n. 4; II, 625. But it was disregarded until Miss Balderston's famous article, "Johnson's Vile Melancholy," in *The Age of Johnson*, F. W. Hilles and W. S. Lewis, eds. (New Haven, 1949), pp. 3–14. Since then it has been mentioned without acknowledgment to Miss Balderston or much reflection on the general context.

ject. Unfortunately that hope is based on a very naïve idea of psychoanalysis. In fact, it flies in the face of one of the central insights of psychoanalysis, and one that especially applies to the entire psychological history of Johnson: that a pervasive, incorrigible sense of "guilt"—as distinct from specific "remorse"—is the inevitable result of the structural character of the human psyche, in which aggressiveness is taken over by a portion of the ego, and then internalized and directed back against the rest of the ego by a "superego"; and the punishment of the vulnerable ego from this rigid internalization of oppression into self-demand is essentially through a chronic sense of "guilt." The more highly developed the "superego," the more severely exacting and the more sleepless the punishment of the ego through irrational and chronic "guilt" (unless, of course, it is projected on others, which Johnson was in general incapable of doing). Hence, as Freud emphasized, those who have carried "virtue" farthest, to the point even of saintliness (*Heiligkeit*), will inevitably—not because of what they have done (for the ego can never win in such a struggle) but because of the structure of their character—feel chronic guilt the most strongly. In fact, as Freud mused near the end of his life, they serve as a kind of spearhead illustrating that "the price we pay for our advance in civilization is a loss of happiness through the heightening sense of guilt."[14]

In the case of Johnson, a new legend of sorts has grown up in our own generation, based on tentative suggestions originally made by Katharine Balderston but now hardened into an assumption without looking specifically again at the actual evidence. The assumption is that Johnson had a deeply masochistic nature, which was seeking erotic expression, and that he developed an arrangement with Mrs. Thrale whereby she would chain and perhaps flog him, or else he was trying—at least unconsciously—to maneuver her into a situation where this could happen. The evidence from which this has been drawn consists of: (1) The passages quoted above from Mrs. Thrale and the existence of the padlock. (2) A short note in the *Diaries* (1771) saying merely "De pedicis et manicis insana cogitatio" ("Insane thought about foot-fetters and manacles"). Now, the imagery of being dragged down and shackled or chained is a recurring figurative expression of dread on Johnson's part when he is speaking of what he *fears*: for example, depression ("that depression of mind that *enchains* the faculties without destroying them") or the power of habits against which one must struggle to become free (*e.g.*, the nephew in *Rambler* 135, waiting for his wealthy aunt to die, "drags the *shackles* of expectation"; in sorrow "the faculties are *chained* to a single object"; "the shackles of habitual vice"; or Johnson's prayer, echoing the Book of Common Prayer, to be "loosed from the *chain* of my sins"). Similarly the note about "foot-fetters and manacles" suggests dread of mental paralysis and loss of liberty rather than erotic craving or desire—the loss of what he valued above all else for himself, the ability to be "a free agent." (3) A letter in French to Mrs. Thrale, obviously more often referred to than read, which he wrote some years later (1773), by which time he was approaching sixty-four.

We should defer a more detailed discussion of the letter till the appropriate time.* For it can be understood only in the special context in which it was written—the fatal illness of Mrs. Thrale's mother, with whom Johnson felt a strong rivalry, and a childlike sulkiness and feeling of hurt that Mrs. Thrale is neglecting him when he himself is ill and lonely. Isolated from its background, the letter has been wildly misinterpreted not only as an appeal to be kept locked up in his room but—because of a remark Mrs. Thrale makes in her reply—as a plea for physical punishment. It would doubtless add zest to a biography of Johnson if we could honestly regard the letter in this way, and the present biographer would by no means be unwilling to pursue the subject if the facts justified it. The less picturesque—though psychologically more interesting—truth about the letter is the strong element of infantilism, always potentially present in individuals subject to constant "superego" demand, which has been repressed for so many years and is at last, in Johnson's sixties, given a chance to express itself. Mrs. Thrale, who has by now understood this in him, writes a reply as though she were a governess or stepmother addressing a child. In the process she adds an innocent, figurative remark: "Farewell *and be*

---

* See below, p. 440. For the sake of completeness, we should mention one final item cited in support of the argument, though apparently for what it contributes in general flavor, since it can hardly qualify as "evidence." In *Thraliana*, which we should remember was available to the family for reading, Mrs. Thrale mentions the infatuation of a man, James Hackman, for a woman he killed when she refused to marry him. The woman (a cast-off mistress of Lord Sandwich, by whom she had nine children) was extremely unattractive, adds Mrs. Thrale: "And yet says Johnson a Woman has *such* power between the Ages of twenty five and forty five, that She might Tye a Man to a post and whip him if she will. This he knew of himself was literally and strictly true I am sure." "This he knew of himself" means, in idiomatic English, "This he himself knew" rather than "knew about himself." Moreover, he is saying only that a woman (at least with a man like Hackman) has such power that she could get away with doing *even* this to a man, against his will, not that he would crave it as a favor or a pleasure (T, I, 386).

good; and do not quarrel with your Governness for not using the Rod enough"—meaning for not having taken a firm enough stand with him as he wandered about the house distracting her when she was trying to nurse her dying mother. Plucked out of context, that half-playful, semimaternal remark—"for not using the Rod enough"—has been forced, naked and alone, to bear as evidence the full weight of the argument, since the French letter itself has a very different implication.

Not only is the "evidence" so slender and disconnected as to come close to nonexistence, but it flies in the face—if we feel urged to consider it *erotically*—of both psychological probability and practical good sense. His demonstrations of erotic affection tend to be closer to what Anna Seward, speaking of his fondness for Mrs. Thrale, cruelly called "cupboard love" (desire to be fed and looked after). Finally, if we are thinking of anything even remotely overt, we should remember the immense respect and affection that the grateful Johnson felt toward Henry Thrale as well as his wife. Hester Thrale may not have exaggerated when she said years later that Johnson had really "loved" her husband more than he had her. To this we should add Johnson's fondness for their children, his delight in their family life, and the virtual impossibility of anything illicit, especially of anything so bizarre, in a home full of servants as well as children. True, Johnson himself was capable of immense self-flagellation, if we wish to use the term figuratively. But this was part of the burden of being a divided soul, in which one portion of him punished another with such astounding success that it needed no co-operating flagellation from others. What he needed from others—in companionship, respect, or affection—was something that would help to get him out of himself, and free him from the immense capacity for self-punishment that could so exhaust him.

9

But whatever supplementary inferences we wish to make, it is clear that "*the* secret" he confided to Mrs. Thrale (the secret that left Johnson "more a Hero to me than any one" and that she was confident he had "never since that Day regretted" telling her) was his belief that he had been, from his own point of view, actually insane for a while. Hence her apprehension when she read a remark by Thomas Tyers in the account he wrote for the *Gentleman's Magazine* just after Johnson's death: "He was afraid of his disorders seizing his head, and took all possible care that his understanding should not be deranged. . . . His imagination often appeared to be too mighty for the control of his reason." In her diary she wrote:

> I see they will leave *nothing untold* that I laboured so long to keep secret; & I was so very delicate in trying to conceal his fancied Insanity, that I retained no Proofs of it—or hardly any [meaning that she has by now, in 1785, kept only one single padlock]—nor ever mentioned it in these Books, lest by dying first they might be printed and *the Secret* (for such I thought it) discovered.[15]

Of course, he kept up a magnificent front. The letters he wrote at this time and his conversations continued for most people to be, in Ozias Humphry's words, "as *correct* as a *second edition.*" Only those who themselves have come close to mental breakdown—and not merely for a short while but for a period of some years—know how easy it is to disguise their situation from others unless living with them constantly (and even then it can be concealed to a surprising extent). Few people otherwise ever believe this is possible. It is too far from their own experience. But the truth is that most people, as Johnson often said, are far too preoccupied with their own problems, whether large or small, to pay close attention to those of others unless they are almost thrust into their faces. With Johnson in particular a curtain was dropped before others—especially before anyone he could not trust completely, and there were very few of them. Dr. Adams, finding him in that state of collapse so "dreadful to see," was an exception. What Mr. Levet and the blind Miss Williams knew, they carried to their graves: they owed far too much to this man whom the world admired to talk loosely to the people who were eager in later years to learn everything about him. But to at least one other friend—the physician Dr. Thomas Laurence, a high-minded and sweet-natured man—he did speak frequently and perhaps openly, though we know only of Laurence's despairing remark that if Johnson "would come and beat him once a week he would bear it; but to hear his complaints was more than man could support."[16]

Chapter 22

Shakespeare

It was in the midst of this crisis (1764–67) that Johnson, with heroic effort, finally finished the Shakespeare edition and wrote the noble *Preface* (1765) that serves as one of the landmarks in the history of literary criticism. It was done through what Boswell called a "Caesarian operation," though he was far from aware of Johnson's condition at the time and was mistaken in thinking that the surgical "knife" was the satiric attack by Charles Churchill. To the extent that there was a "Caesarian," Johnson performed the operation himself.

Despite the mere eighteen months he had given himself· for the Shakespeare edition back in 1756, and despite all the other writing he was doing, especially for the *Literary Magazine*, he had at first made rapid progress. By April 1758 he was probably at least two-thirds finished—if one did not apply too high a standard. But one of the difficulties he faced, aside from the growing general psychological distress we have been tracing, was that he was himself beginning to apply a higher standard than he had been using—not in explanatory annotation, where he was superb and could draw immediately on the capital of his knowledge of words, but in establishing a sound *text*. In his *Proposals* (1756) he had perceptively outlined the only ways in which a sound text could be obtained. But this involved securing early copies of the plays and collating them carefully. In short, it involved time and patience—necessities for which no amount of brilliance could serve as a substitute. Inevitably his conscience began to rebuke him; and as he rebelled inwardly against this further self-demand, his progress ground to a halt, and he started to write the *Idler* essays, half mocking himself in the title. Soon the texts and notes printed up by William Strahan, the printer, began to lie around in his rooms without much being done either to alter or to add to them. Yet occasionally they were at least being corrected. And by the end of 1761—it was now four years after the original deadline—the printer's ledgers show that the publishers had paid him for the corrected sheets of six of the eight volumes that were to make up the edition (a total by this time of about £270).[1] Probably most of the work that had gone into these first six volumes was what Johnson had done so rapidly during the first year or so (June 1756 to December 1757).

By 1762 Charles Churchill had written his famous gibe: "He for subscribers baits his hook, And takes their cash—but where's the Book?" But it was not Churchill who aroused in him a brief effort to get started again. It was the receipt of the pension that seems to have shamed him temporarily into trying to justify it. The day after he received the first payment, he wrote to thank the Earl of Bute (July 20, 1762), saying he now hoped to provide "the only recompense" he could—"the gratification of finding that your benefits are not improperly bestowed." That same day he also wrote to Giuseppe Baretti in Milan, and, in his first reference for some time to the edition, says, "I intend that you shall soon receive Shakespeare."[2]

But the thought of the pension could cut both ways. If it was an incentive, it was also a further burden to self-expectation. For if and when the Shakespeare was finished—and he still might live another twenty years—what other real project was left ahead? How could he hope to begin on another project of comparable magnitude, starting from the ground up, when his state of mind was such that he could hardly continue with what was already at least half done? It was better to try to do well what was already in hand, and to get himself into a frame of mind where he could start doing that. Once again the months began to pass.

It was a year later (1763) that a young bookseller, after bringing Johnson a new subscription for the edition, wondered that he did not write down the man's name and address for his "printed list of subscribers." Johnson, with "great abruptness," said, "I shall print no List of Subscribers." Then, noting the youth's dismay, he said that he had two reasons for not doing so: "one, that I have lost all the names, the other that I have spent all the money."[3] This is very unlike Johnson, usually so punctilious in his integrity about financial and business matters. It betrays, of course, his strong unconscious desire to forget, and even half sabotage, the whole thing. Inevitably his self-defeating loss of the list of subscribers—when ordinarily he would have passed on the names to the publishers for safekeeping—disturbed him in a way completely at odds with this defensively cavalier remark.

2

Hawkins might comment on the "torpor" that had "seized his faculties" and the anxiety of his friends that he finish the work. But their anxiety was as nothing compared with his own. They were worried merely about his reputation. He was beginning to worry about his sanity. In November 1763 Reynolds got him to spend a few weeks—perhaps three or four—at a house Reynolds had in Twickenham in order to "finish" the work; and he went there, said Bishop Percy, "resolved not to return to London" until he was finished. He made some headway, but contrived to get back to London by early December. Then came the founding of The Club—Reynolds's other hope to help him psychologically—and the trip to Bennet Langton's place in Lincolnshire, where he rolled down the hill in that memorable scene.

Then, in June 1764, he accepted Percy's invitation to visit him for several weeks up in Northamptonshire, at Easton Maudit (June 25 to August 18). The original thought had been to do some work on Shakespeare and perhaps catch some contagion of diligence from Percy, who was himself hard at work editing; and while there he did correct the sheets for *Othello*. Yet as if to guard himself against pressure, and to make it more of a social occasion, he brought Miss Williams with him for the first six weeks of the visit. They took several drives around the countryside, all of which are recorded by Percy. There is a touch of comedy in the thought of these drives—with Johnson half blind and Miss Williams completely so. Of special interest is the way in which he would snatch at Percy's large collection of old romances and ballads and retire with them for a part of every day (choosing for "his regular reading" the old Spanish romance of *Felixmarte*). The romances were all that Shakespeare—as Johnson viewed him—was not, or rather had transcended: Shakespeare, who gave a true "map of life," showing "manners and life" in their "real" state. This was probably when he confessed to Percy his lifelong habit of reading "these extravagant fictions" and his belief that they had contributed to his "unsettled turn of mind."

Meanwhile Percy had looked forward to the visit for another reason besides social pleasure. He was now finishing his famous *Reliques of Ancient English Poetry* (1765)—the principal source for generations to come of early English and Scottish ballads. He wanted concrete help as well as moral support from Johnson, who had encouraged him to publish the work in the first place and who now aided him with a Glossary and wrote the Dedication for the *Reliques*. We should remember this when we come across all those references, in scores of books, to Johnson's "prejudiced ignorance" of ballads, his "scorn" of the ballad revival of the time, and the little spontaneous parody of ballads—quoted *ad nauseam*—

> I put my hat upon my head,
>   And walk'd into the Strand,
> And there I met another man
>   With his hat in his hand.

He was, of course, only teasing Percy and other antiquarians, as when he also—at a tea with Percy at Miss Reynolds's—said that to compose ballads was as easy as mere talking and began to address her ("Renny dear") in ballad stanzas until Percy begged him to stop.[4]

3

Early in 1765 (January 9), he met the Thrales; and the day after this meeting—which was to prove so important for his life and happiness generally—we have the first reference in the *Diaries* to the Shakespeare edition during all these years: the simple statement, "Corrected a sheet." In February he made a weekend visit to Cambridge to get some help from his friend at Emmanuel College, Richard Farmer, who was preparing an *Essay on the Learning of Shakespeare*. Since Farmer was busy with official duties, he could only promise to help later in the year. Throughout all this time Johnson was not simply doing the last two volumes of the plays. He was also trying, as far as possible, to improve what he had already done. A total of over 550 additional notes were inserted after the eight volumes were supposedly done. By spring it was too late to insert more without reprinting the pages; so any further notes (about 220) were packed into an Appendix. Meanwhile, in July, he received the degree of LL.D. from Trinity College, Dublin. He had published an advertisement in June that the edition would appear on August 1. But he did not get around to the *Preface* until August. This was finished by early September, and printed up by September 29.

During these final months he had the voluntary help of an aggressive and personally unattractive young scholar named George Steevens, who was quick to see what Johnson's situation was and, as 1765 went on, began to make himself useful. Steevens was not working for money. (He received a comfortable income from his father, a director in the East India Company, and in another two years was to become his heir.) But neither was his help pure altruism. He was eager to rise in literary circles; Johnson was by now a famous man, and Steevens knew an opportunity when he saw it. He had been acquiring a good antiquarian library at his home in Hampstead Heath, where a cousin, Mary Collinson, and her daughter kept house for him. Though only twenty-eight, he was already quite methodical in his habits. He would rise early every morning and walk to London, arriving by seven at Staple Inn, where the scholar Isaac Reed kept a room for him. After a morning conference with Reed and then another scholar, John Nichols, he would stop at the celebrated watchmakers Mudge and Dutton to have them check and regulate his watch. Other calls followed, including one on Johnson, who would be getting up around noon. Then he would walk back to Hampstead and work in his library.

Few people seem to have liked Steevens. He had a jealous and acrimonious nature, was quick to quarrel, and by his forties was capable of real malice. But he could keep a rein on this side of himself if he had a purpose. Moreover, he genuinely admired Johnson, whom he thought of as an "old lion." Meanwhile he set to work. Nor, to his credit, did he boast of it. In his published account (1785) he kept himself anonymous when he said (referring to the story that Johnson usually wrote at night) that most of the *Preface to Shakespeare* was "composed by daylight, and in a room where a friend was employed by him in other investigations." The "friend" was, of course, Steevens, working on the Appendix. Whatever others thought of Steevens, Johnson stood up for him just as he always stood up for Hawkins. He considered Steevens to have proved himself a friend. He was grateful for his help in this trying period and for even more help later;* and in 1774 he even got Steevens elected to The Club.[5]

Finally, on October 10, the edition was published: *The Plays of William Shakespeare, in Eight Volumes . . . To which are added Notes by Sam. Johnson.* A thousand copies were printed, and sold so quickly (there had been almost that many subscribers, who now showed up with receipts) that a second edition was published almost immediately.

4

Even if we knew nothing of the state of mind he was forced to battle during this psychological crisis, the edition of Shakespeare—viewed with historical understanding of what it involved in 1765—could seem a remarkable feat; and we are not speaking of just the great *Preface.* To see it in perspective, we have only to remind ourselves what Johnson brought to it—an assemblage of almost every qualification we should ideally like to have brought to this kind of work with the single exception of patience; and at least some control of his impatience, if not the quality of patience itself, might have been possible if this period of his life had not been so distressing.

To begin with, there was his knowledge of books in every field of learning from the Renaissance to his own day—the kind of knowledge we first noticed in detail when he helped pull together the *Harleian Catalogue* back in his early thirties. More specifically there was the reading (and close, if rapid, perception of shades of meaning) that had gone into those 240,000 quotations for the *Dictionary*, less than half of which had been used. To this we should add his extraordinary sense of *Gestalt* and syntax in a language so that he could quickly penetrate to

---

* The greatly improved edition "by Samuel Johnson and George Steevens" in ten volumes (1773; revised, 1778), which gave Johnson's earlier work a new lease on life while at the same time it established Steevens's reputation. For this joint effort Steevens had carefully prepared. In 1766, a year after Johnson's edition, Steevens brought out his own edition of twenty of Shakespeare's plays collated from the quartos. It was designed not to compete with Johnson's (*e.g.*, it was without critical annotation). But it was also designed to transcend Johnson's in proceeding further toward a sound text. This having been done, an open coalition between the two editors was arranged, as Steevens had hoped for all along. Johnson, regarding his own work on Shakespeare as past history, was glad to let Steevens perfect the edition as he would, though he himself changed some notes and added about eighty new ones.

the heart of what a writer was saying and catch the drift of its implications, however incomplete or garbled the version. Operating in and through these qualities was his own extensive knowledge of human nature and life. No Shakespearean critic or editor has ever approached him in this respect. It is apparent not only in his more general criticism but also in his notes, and includes, one should add, a perceptive insight into the psychology of editors themselves, enabling him time and again to avoid the pitfalls that editors can dig for themselves as well as each other.

The total result—as Edmond Malone, the patron saint of all modern literary scholars, was to say twenty-five years later—is that Johnson's "vigorous and comprehensive understanding threw more light on his authour than all his predecessors had done." There was only one fault, or rather lack, compared not with his predecessors but with the ideal he had announced at the start (1756) and with what later editions were to do. None of his plays had been presented under Shakespeare's own supervision. The versions we have are inevitably secondhand at best, and often more remote than that. His works, as Johnson said,

> were transcribed for the players by those who may be supposed to have seldom understood them; they were transmitted by copiers equally unskillful, who still multiplied errors; they were perhaps sometimes mutilated by the actors, for the sake of shortening the speeches; and were at last printed without correction of the press.

For no classic in the entire history of modern literature were the texts more inadequate and corrupt. Johnson, aware of all the reasons why this was so, had said in his *Proposals* that "the corruptions of the text will be corrected by a careful collation of the oldest copies." Moreover, as we noted before, his technical perception of the ways to proceed—since supported by modern bibliographical study—kept sharpening and clarifying itself as he went on from play to play.[6] Despite his psychological situation acting on his impatient temperament generally, he might have made more progress than he did with the thorny problems of the text if people who possessed early copies had been more willing to let him take them back to Inner Temple Lane. But they were by no means eager to let him do this, having heard how he had treated books loaned him for the *Dictionary*.

From Garrick's valuable collection alone, he could have acquired a good deal of help if he had been willing to stomach his pride. Garrick assured him he was welcome to use the collection at any time. He left the key to it with a servant, "with orders to have a fire and every convenience for him." Johnson disregarded the offer, considering it affected and presumptuous on the part of a player to be so possessive about Shakespeare. Garrick, by seeking to make him come there to work, was expecting Johnson to "court" him. This Johnson would not do. If Garrick had really wanted to help, he would have bundled up and sent him "the plays of his own accord." Johnson was to remain troubled in conscience about this neglect, even though, in a way quite at odds with his original *Proposals*, he could slip into a defensive dismissal of its importance. When Edward Capell's edition appeared—which was superior to his own in this one respect—Johnson was asked, said George Steevens, what he thought of Capell's abilities. "Just sufficient," replied Johnson, "to enable him to select the black hairs from the white ones, for the use of the periwig-makers. Were he and I to count the grains in a bushel of wheat for a wager, he would certainly prove the winner."[7]

Where his annotation especially excelled was in his ability to penetrate at once to the sense of a difficult or mangled passage. Even when the transcribers of the early copies had not lost or distorted Shakespeare's phrasing, other factors combined to create the obscurity the modern reader often finds in him—particularly Shakespeare's use of common colloquial speech, which admitted allusions and elliptical or proverbial expressions now unfamiliar; "to which might be added that fulness of idea, which might sometimes load his words with more sentiment than they could conveniently convey, and that rapidity of imagination which might hurry him to a second thought before he had fully explained the first." Lacking all the equipment of the modern Elizabethan specialist, Johnson—as Walter Raleigh said two generations ago (1908)—is able in one passage after another to "go straight to Shakespeare's meaning, while the philological and antiquarian commentators kill one another in the dark." Inevitably the results of this kind of annotation have long since been taken over and subsumed in the notes available to the general reader in any good edition of Shakespeare. But what Raleigh goes on to add still remains true of all major Shakespearean scholars and editors in our time: in using the variorum editions, the practiced scholar "soon falls into the habit, when he meets with an obscure passage, of consulting Johnson's note before the others."[8]

Occasionally Johnson simply let himself pause and comment generally on a passage or on a change of action in the play. Two notes of this sort are typical in different ways. In *All's Well That Ends Well* (V, iii, 21), everything speeds up and much ingenuity could be devoted to excusing or explaining this. But Johnson writes with common sense, "Shakespeare is now hastening to the end of the play, finds his matter sufficient to fill up his remaining scenes, and . . . contracts his dialogue and precipitates his action." Johnson mentions the threads still hanging loose, and adds, "Of all this Shakespeare could not be ignorant, but Shakespeare wanted to conclude his play." Utterly different is the distilled or miniature *Rambler* on some lines from the speech of the Duke in *Measure for Measure* (III, i):

> *Thou hast nor youth, nor age;*
> *But as it were an after-dinner's sleep,*
> *Dreaming on both*

This is exquisitely imagined. When we are young we busy ourselves in forming schemes for succeeding time, and miss the gratifications that are before us; when we are old we amuse the languour of age with the recollection of youthful pleasures or performances; so that our life, of which no part is filled with the business of the present time, resembles our dreams after dinner, when the events of the morning are mingled with the designs of the evening.

5

But it is, of course, the *Preface* of which we all think when the edition of Shakespeare is mentioned. It falls roughly into four sections: (1) The greatness of Shakespeare, who by now may be considered a classic comparable to any poet in history. The primary stress is on Shakespeare's portrayal of human nature in all its ramifications. His characters are "the genuine progeny of common humanity, such as the world will always supply," and "act and speak by the influence of those general passions and principles by which all minds are agitated." (2) He then turns to the faults or weaknesses (Shakespeare "sacrifices virtue to convenience," and neglects moral purpose; the plots are often loosely and rapidly constructed, and the language sometimes unwieldy). This section bothered the Romantics and their Victorian followers, who felt anything less than the highest eulogy inappropriate for Shakespeare and resented even the suggestion that Shakespeare might have faults or shortcomings. The special interest of this section to us now is the part in which Johnson denies as a "fault" Shakespeare's neglect of the neoclassic "unities of time and place." (3) He then considers Shakespeare in relation to the poetry and drama of his age. (4) Finally he surveys the history of Shakespearean criticism and editing down to the mid-1700's and describes his own way of proceeding.

One can sense what the *Preface* meant to his own century by citing the remarks of two very different people. Adam Smith, even though he did not much like Johnson, described the *Preface* as "the most *manly* piece of criticism that was ever published in any country." And Edmond Malone thought the *Preface*—both in the wealth of what it said and the power of style with which it was put—"the finest composition in our language," meaning the finest piece of prose writing of any sort.[9] This is going rather far. But it is true that Johnson is one of the supreme masters of English prose, and the *Preface*, simply as prose, is unexcelled by anything else Johnson wrote except for parts of the *Lives of the Poets*. Here we have continuing for pages what before we found more often in particular sentences or paragraphs: a grasping, against strong internal pressures, for certitude, control, balance, and order. We sense the whole body being involved, as though he were trying to pull himself above the surface. Hence the tamped-down finality as he phrases convictions based on a lifetime of experience. But then, with equal justice, he moves over to other considerations, for contrast or supplement. This underlies one of the distinctive qualities of his mature style—its active balance. It moves back and forth dialectically, using every form of balance and antithesis, stabilizing one step before moving to the next one. An interesting by-product is a form of sentence that is now beginning to be more common with him and that becomes more so in the later writing.* In it we see the centrifugal reaching out for further explanation or nuance gradually expanding within the body of the sentence itself, and then, at each step within the sentence, pulled back and incorporated before still further qualification is begun. The procedure, in short, is one of progressive assimilation—of expansion, return, further expansion, and return. An example would be:

This therefore is the praise of Shakespeare,
  that his drama is the mirrour of life;
  that he who has mazed his imagination . . . may here be cured . . .
    by reading human sentiments in human language,
    by scenes from which
      a hermit may estimate the transactions of the world,
      and a confessor predict the progress of the passions.

* See below, pp. 542–44.

But the same procedure can carry over into an expanding series of balancing phrases:

> The great contention of criticism is to find
> > the faults of the moderns,
> > and
> > the beauties of the ancients. . . .
> To works, however, of which the excellence is not
> > absolute and definite,
> > but
> > gradual and comparative;
>
> to works not raised upon principles demonstrative and scientifick
> > but
> > appealing wholly to observation and experience,
>
> no other test can be applied than
> > > length of duration
> > > and
> > > continuance of esteem.

Or, to cite part of another, more extended example:

> The work of a correct and regular writer is a garden
> > accurately formed
> > and
> > diligently planted,
>
> > varied with shades
> > and
> > scented with flowers;
>
> the composition of Shakespeare is a forest, in which
>
> > oaks extend their branches,
> > and
> > pines tower in the air,
>
> > interspersed sometimes with
> > > weeds and brambles,
> > and sometimes giving shelter to
> > > myrtles and to roses;
>
> > filling the eye with awful pomp,
> > and gratifying the mind with endless diversity.

It is partly because the *Preface* is one of the monuments of English prose that people who try in our own generation to discuss it briefly feel so frustrated. They are still smarting from the tendency in the nineteenth century (which Johnson would have understood and taken for granted) to focus, with hypnotic astonishment, on his short discussion of Shakespeare's weaknesses. But how does one begin to suggest the abundance present in the *Preface to Shakespeare*? It is impossible to put in briefer language what Johnson already distills so superbly. The natural desire is to quote, and to let it as much as possible speak for itself. Yet the thought of excerpting a few sentences (for one cannot quote the entire work) reminds one of Johnson's own remark—that anyone who tries to illustrate Shakespeare with selected quotations "will succeed like the pedant in *Hierocles*, who, when he offered his house to sale, carried a brick in his pocket as a specimen."

6

T. S. Eliot once said of the *Preface to Shakespeare* that "no poet can ask more of posterity than to be greatly honoured by the great; and Johnson's words about Shakespeare are great honour." In fact, any poet "would willingly resign the honour of an Abbey burial for the greater honour of words like the following, from a man of the greatness of their author." And he goes on to quote, from the opening part of the *Preface:*

The poet, of whose works I have undertaken the revision, may now begin to assume the dignity of an ancient, and claim the privilege of established fame and prescriptive veneration. He has long outlived his century, the term commonly fixed as the test of literary merit. Whatever advantages he might once derive from personal allusions, local customs, or temporary opinions, have for many years been lost; and every topick of merriment or motive of sorrow, which the modes of artificial life afforded him, now only obscure the scenes which they once illuminated. The effects of favour and competition are at an end; the tradition of his friendships and his enmities has perished; his works support no opinion with arguments, nor supply any faction with invectives; they can neither indulge vanity nor gratify malignity, but are read without any other reason than the desire of pleasure, and are therefore praised only as pleasure is obtained; yet, thus unassisted by interest or passion, they have past through variations of taste and changes of manners, and, as they devolved from one generation to another, have received new honours at every transmission.[10]

What Eliot is saying—that in the *Preface* we have the encounter of one great experiencing nature with another—is perhaps the only way to approach the *Preface* unless we forget that we are in the midst of a biography, shift our context, and, as the writer of this book has done more than once before, concentrate on those issues technically most relevant to that more specialized context. Yet, as Thomas Tyers wrote after Johnson's death, he belonged not to criticism or even to the world of learning, superb as he was in these ways, but "belonged to the world at large."[11]

For of course Johnson is bringing his entire self to bear on this subject, as he does in no other work except the moral writings as a whole and, much later, the *Lives of the Poets*. Here, in solution, is all that his idealism as a boy had associated with the world of Cornelius, when he had praised "his acquaintance with *life and manners*": "Shakespeare is above all writers . . . the poet that holds up to his readers a faithful mirrour of *manners and of life*." This was an ideal that had stayed with him all through the breakdown after Oxford, the Grub Street years, the moral writings, the near breakdown now in the 1760's. So with that phrase "living world," which he also associated with Cornelius, and which—used time and again before—is once more brought to bear, charged with a lifetime of meaning, as he approaches this poet who "caught his ideas from *the living world*."

And always this *essentialism*—for no other word will do—has been completely earned, not just in one but a variety of ways. So, in that astonishing paragraph where he suddenly lays down the premise from which he is going to proceed, we have distilled the years of reading— with exuberant release—in the hundreds of romances and "extravagant fictions" that he told Bishop Percy had given him for life an "unsettled turn of mind":

> The irregular combinations of fanciful invention may delight a-while, by that novelty of which the common satiety of life sends us all in quest; but the pleasures of sudden wonder are soon exhausted, and the mind can only repose on the stability of truth.

7

The *Preface* is drenched and permeated—creatively, magnificently— by this one supreme value, "the stability of truth."* As he confronts

---

* To such an extent that writers on the history of criticism have sometimes leapt to the conclusion that Johnson was generally uninterested in the "formal" as formal hesitations and misgivings still being expressed about these remarkable dramas, he pulls from under them the static premises on which they were built and substitutes one more functional and dynamic. The essential function of poetry—taking precedence over everything else—is to "instruct by pleasing": that is, to heighten awareness and deepen or extend the experience of life, through the magical power of language at its greatest. In the process we see the "classical tradition" of criticism, which extends from Aristotle to the later eighteenth century, and which Johnson inherits, becoming more alive and self-corrective. Typically, as he rescues and revitalizes classical values (the uses of art for knowledge—that is, for the deepening of experience), he sweeps aside three major regulations of "neoclassic" theory—the so-called rules of decorum—that had acquired a stranglehold on the theory of the drama for 150 years. They had been among the many by-products of the effort of literary criticism in the late Renaissance—haunted by its dream of classical antiquity—to rival that dream and create and systematize a "new classicism." As so often happens, the systematization had replaced the imaginative conception of the general aim; and though there were protests and arguments against it, the strangle hold remained in theory if not in practice.

One of the "rules of decorum," the "decorum of type," had to do with the portrayal of character. In a drama you should try to emphasize the general "type" of person—to give it "universality"—and cling to that, disregarding personal idiosyncrasies. This, theoretically, was a good idea: behind it were the three values of "economy," "general meaning," and "form," all coalescing in a persuasive way. But like every other general idea, it was capable of being interpreted with routine simple-mindedness. Hence critics and writers by the score assumed that if you were portraying a Roman, you should concentrate most heavily on what was "Roman"; or, if a miser, his miserliness; or, if a king, what was appropriate to him *as* a king:

---

against the "representational" values of literature. But we should keep in mind two considerations: (1) The *Preface*, profound as it is, is only one of his many critical writings; and it was written under very special circumstances, when Johnson's clutch at what Freud calls "the reality principle" is especially strong. (2) Johnson was born at the height (and is writing near the close) of the longest and most intensive period of literary formalism in English literary history—the "high neoclassic mode" from the 1660's to the 1750's. As a result, he is taking for granted formal and stylistic values (see below, pp. 534-42) with the single exception of conventions having to do with stage performance and the practical theater.

His adherence to general nature has exposed him to the censure of criticks, who form their judgments upon narrower principles. Dennis and Rhymer think his Romans not sufficiently Roman; and Voltaire censures his kings as not completely royal. Dennis is offended, that Menenius, a senator of Rome, should play the buffoon; and Voltaire perhaps thinks decency violated when the Danish usurper [in *Hamlet*] is represented as a drunkard. But Shakespeare always makes nature predominate over accident; and if he preserves the essential character, is not very careful of distinctions superinduced and adventitious. . . . He knew that Rome, like every other city, had men of all dispositions; and wanting a buffoon, he went into the senate-house for that which the senate-house would certainly have afforded him. He was inclined to shew an usurper and a murderer not only odious but despicable; he therefore added drunkenness to his other qualities, knowing that kings love wine like other men, and that wine exerts its natural power upon kings. These are the petty cavils of petty minds; a poet overlooks the casual distinction of country and condition, as a painter, satisfied with the figure, neglects the drapery.[12]

So with the "neoclassic" rule against mingling tragic and comic elements in the same play. It was based originally on two arguments, both of which sound good until one really examines them: (1) intellectual cleanliness of *form* and *genre;* and (2) imaginative and emotional unity of impact. Tragedy is obviously different from comedy. Hence, if you are portraying a tragic character or tragic event and then suddenly move over into comedy, will this not destroy the unity of impact and cancel the effects of both the "tragic" and the "comic"? The compartmentalized formalism of this way of thinking, says Johnson, has proved to be so seductive that it still continues to be repeated by critics who in their own "daily experience" (if they would only consult it) know it to be "false." The tragic and comic in our reactions to every aspect of life are constantly intermeshing. If we agree that the aim of the drama is to "instruct by pleasing," the "mingled drama" of Shakespeare "instructs" more by showing life as it really is—a life in which "the reveller is hasting to his wine, and the mourner burying his friend"; and, at the same time, it also "pleases" more because of that closer approximation to our daily experience and because "all pleasure consists in variety."

So, finally, with the "unities of time and place" that had dominated the critical imagination for over a century and a half. According to the "unity of *time*," what is being shown in a drama should itself ideally take place only in such time—say, three hours—as we ourselves spend in looking at the play; or at most it should not last more than a day. Here the aim again was cleanliness and unity of impact, but with the further argument of *credibility* added. We know that during these three hours, a total of five years have not passed. The "unity of *place*" had a similar argument. If you start a play at Alexandria, and then shift to Rome, this especially strains human credibility. We know, sitting in our seats at the theater, that we have not suddenly left Alexandria for Rome. It sounds incredible to us now that this sort of reasoning should have hypnotized critical thinking as much and for as long as it did. But—like so many other criteria in art—it got mixed up with the notion of "form" and hence became sacrosanct. To attack "form" in art (or what a large number of people equate with "form") is like attacking "virtue." Through a quick, common-sense analysis of "poetic illusion," Johnson brushes aside the criteria brought to bear, pointing out that, if we are able, while sitting in a seat at Drury Lane, to imagine ourselves at Alexandria, the imaginative feat of transferring ourselves to Rome is minor. Occasionally others with smaller voice had said similar things. But no one was paying much attention to them. What Johnson did was something that, as T. S. Eliot said, "only Johnson could do." And he did it so effectively that sixty years later Stendhal, in his *Racine et Shakespeare* (1822), took over and incorporated what Johnson wrote into what Stendhal considered a "romantic manifesto."

8

The perennial value of Johnson's example is that the *real* issues are still not dead. For the real issues are not these particular formalistic ones, so effectively plowed under by Johnson, but the ways in which the "hunger of the imagination" generally—in criticism, as in everything else—is always extrapolating particular qualities in the name of a larger end, and in the process complicating as well as impoverishing the broader uses of literature.

As in his moral writing, the drama of his literary criticism lies in the power with which he moves at once to that rarest of all things for frightened and confused human nature—the obvious. The catharsis, or relief, as in all good drama, lies in the fact that nothing is being disregarded as he walks toward the forgotten obvious. While he matches any other critic in technical expertise and strength of close analysis, he is unequaled in his grasp of the psychological temptations of criticism—through dispute and the desire to take issue—to concentrate on a part rather than the whole or in any other way to erect barricades between mankind and the large written record of experience we call "literature." The *Preface* is one of the great classical affirmations of the highest uses of literature. But the affirmation is genuine because we also have distilled the shared sense of all the other uses—trivial or important, malignant or generous—to which literature can and daily is being put. Back in his "Reflections on the Present State of Literature"—written when he had begun the Shakespeare edition (1756)—he had said that "whatever may be the cause of happiness, may be likewise made the cause of misery," and that "there is no gift of nature, or effect of art, however beneficial to mankind," that cannot be perverted into results that are trivial, burdensome, or mischievous. If humane letters were considered "only as a means of pleasure, it might well be doubted, in what degree of estimation they should be held; but when they are referred to *necessity* the controversy is at an end; it soon appears that though they may sometimes incommode us, yet human life could scarcely rise, without them, above the common existence of animal life." For every civilization, there was a time before it existed; and it would not have developed without the "intellectual light" that literature—taken as a whole—was able to provide. That "intellectual light" may certainly "enable us to see what we do not like; but who would wish to escape by condemning himself to perpetual darkness?"[13]

Chapter 23

Toward Recovery: the Thrales;
Law Lectures

Through the next few months, the despair in which so much of Johnson's inner life was now being spent continued to increase until the following June (1766), when a distressing scene occurred. His new friends, Henry and Hester Thrale, unexpectedly dropped by to see him one morning. For over a year they had known and entertained him frequently—Arthur Murphy had introduced him to them—and they had delighted in his company.

To their horror, the Thrales now found him on his knees before a clergyman, Dr. John Delap, "beseeching God to continue to him the use of his understanding." Delap, seeing the new visitors, hurried to excuse himself, while Johnson called after him to beg his prayers, and then, turning to the Thrales, spoke so "wildly" in self-condemnation that Mr. Thrale "involuntarily lifted up one hand to shut his mouth." Shortly after this they took him out to their country place in Streatham for three months and there tried to nurse him gradually back to health.[1]

2

Throughout the previous year he had tried as never before to pull himself together. He had not even waited until the Shakespeare was finished before planning the next stage of his effort to remake what was left of his life. While he was still writing the *Preface*, he had at last taken the step—in August or early September—he had been deferring for so long. He had moved back into a house, for the first time in six years (7 Johnson's Court, Fleet Street—the name of the court is pure coincidence), taking with him Frank Barber, Miss Williams, who was given an apartment on the ground floor, and Mr. Levet, who had a room on the top floor. Moving back to a house was to be a symbol of the fresh start he was now to make at fifty-six. A large upper room—perhaps to remind him of that upper room at Gough Square where he had written so much—was fixed up as Johnson's study.

Meanwhile he was resolved not only to capitalize at once on the momentum of work but also to turn to a new form of it that would really "steady" his mind and give him a sense of purpose. What this new form of work would be is shown by a prayer he composed on September 26, while the *Preface to Shakespeare* was being printed—a prayer he entitled "Before [Beginning] the Study of Law"—and by another some weeks later with the title "Engaging in Politicks with H------n."

This new work on which he started was, in effect, to serve as unofficial adviser to William Gerard Hamilton, who was known at the time —and is still remembered in British history—as "Single-Speech" Hamilton. He was called Single-Speech because, in the golden age of British oratory, he had begun his career in Parliament back in 1755 with a three-hour speech widely admired (even Horace Walpole, never eager to praise, thought it "perfection" in style and argument); and after that one great speech, intimidated by the burden of having to live up to its reputation, Hamilton rarely—and then only briefly— spoke again. Thomas Birch, who had good sources of information, said this remarkable speech had been written for Hamilton by Johnson.[2] In any case, Hamilton had an eye for talent. For some years now he had been employing Edmund Burke as a private secretary. But Burke, who resented having his brains picked constantly by Hamilton and who was hoping to enter Parliament himself, had quit the job, and Hamilton wanted someone else who at the very least, according to Malone, would "furnish him with sentiments on the great political topics that should be considered in Parliament." This could have amounted to a good deal of help from September 1765 to the following April. One of Burke's complaints about Hamilton was his knack for squeezing one like a sponge. Nothing still survives in written form of what Johnson did for Hamilton except some pages of notes called "Considerations on

Corn" (that is, the Corn Laws) that Malone found when he went through Hamilton's papers half a century later. But there was no reason for Hamilton to keep all of Johnson's notes until the end of his own life; and much of Johnson's help was probably given in conversation. The urgency with which Johnson started on this work is shown by the two prayers mentioned above, which also reflect a touching idealism about this renewed "study of law": "Qualify me to direct the doubtful, and instruct the ignorant, to prevent wrongs . . . to do good, and to hinder evil."[3]

3

At the same time that he began this "study of law," his divided self hoped to overcome his aggressive obsession for "self-management" in one way at least: "To consider the act of prayer as a *reposal of myself upon God* and a resignation of all into his holy hand."

After years of resolving to rise early and never succeeding except for a few days at a time, he now began to rise at eight, however late he went to bed. This was to be a symbol and test of his ability to avoid total disintegration; for if he could not succeed in this one small thing, he was really hopeless. By March 29 he felt he could draw some comfort from the fact that for three months "I have risen every morning at eight; at least, not after nine. Which is more superiority over my habits than I have ever been able to attain." He had also stopped drinking wine. For years he had abstained from it almost entirely, finding abstinence from drink far easier than moderation. Then he had started drinking more often as he approached and passed the age of fifty. He would drink a full bottle of port, for example, when talking with Boswell back in 1763, while at the same time speaking of the treacheries of drink for anyone disposed to "melancholy." Boswell, returning from his long stay abroad and stopping briefly in London on his way back to Edinburgh (February 1766), learned from Johnson—for he gave him no further details—that "there was now a considerable difference in his way of living. Having had an illness, in which he was advised to leave off wine, he had, from that period, continued to abstain from it, and drank only water or lemonade."[4]

He was also keeping his resolution to "read the Bible through in some language this year," devoting part of each Sunday to it. On the other hand, by the second Sunday his impatient nature was already finding this a task rather than an interest or consolation. For, in order to steel his resolution, he began to fall back into his old habit of breaking up "work" into small units that would seem more "manageable." A mere twenty-one pages each Sunday, he found, would get him through the Bible in a year. For the time he was allotting himself for this, he figured that the speed needed to be only "6 verses a minute," which would allow plenty of time for meditation. As a part of his effort "to live methodically," his study upstairs was refurnished in February; and that this was to be another symbol of a fresh start is shown by a special prayer on hoping to take advantage of these "new conveniencies for study" (March 7).[5]

4

Aside from his work for Single-Speech Hamilton, he was even doing a little writing, though only as a favor for others—a preface, a couple of sermons, short dedications, and, more important, some ghost-writing for Miss Williams.

Back when he first knew Miss Williams, he had, in a charitable moment, written proposals (1750) for a book of poems she was writing. She naturally regarded this as an authoritative stamp of approval, and assumed that her all-powerful protector would also arrange for them to be published as soon as she herself felt the poems were ready. To her annoyance the years had passed without his doing so. Instead, whenever she brought up the subject, Johnson (as she complained to Lady Knight) "always puts me off with *Well, we'll think about it;* and Goldsmith says, *Leave it to me.*" Johnson lacked the heart to tell her that her collection of verses was far too slight, in both size and quality, to interest any publisher. Finally, early in 1766, he gave in to her urgings. He revised her poems, added some verses of his own that could appear to be by her, and also secured contributions (naturally anonymous) from a few friends—Mrs. Thrale, Frances Reynolds, and John Hoole, as well as a stray sonnet from Bishop Percy. He then arranged for the kind Tom Davies to publish it (April 1) as *Miscellanies in Prose and Verse* "by Anna Williams."[6]

But before it went to press, he felt the volume was still too slight, and "for the purpose of filling up" the book, said Mrs. Thrale, he added "The Fountains"—a strange, bittersweet fairy tale, rarely if ever noticed now, which becomes rather ominous at the end. It is worth attention if only as an indication of Johnson's state of mind at this

410

time. Though written in a deceptively gentle and disarming style, the story expresses a profound hopelessness about human life, for which the only relief is death.* It could be described as a child's version of *The Vanity of Human Wishes,* but without even the suggestion (though it could perhaps be said that this is taken for granted) of religious consolation. The story, innocent as it is on the surface, illustrates Mrs. Thrale's remark that, when she first knew Johnson, he seemed like one who had "looked on life till he was weary" and had seen through it to such a point as to become "sincerely sick" at any further perusal. Certainly, to anyone who assumed this story was by Miss Williams, it could come as a surprise, even something of a shock. This was true of Elizabeth Carter, who found the "conclusion so unsatisfactory and melancholy, that it left only a gloomy impression on my mind."[7]

5

By April—certainly by early May—his condition, said Mrs. Thrale, had grown "so exceedingly bad, that he could not stir out of his room in the court he inhabited for many *weeks* together, I think months." She was in a position to know. For over a year he had been dining with them about once a week when they were in town, and sometimes more frequently in the winter of 1765–66. Then his visits stopped.

The Thrales, naturally concerned at this sudden change in someone usually so fond of company, began to call on him at his house. He now began to confide to them "the horrible condition of his mind, which he said was nearly distracted," while at the same time charging them "to make him odd solemn promises of secrecy" about what he was telling them.[8] The state she is describing, which is similar to that described by Dr. Adams, is by no means disproved by the fact that he was able to

---

* A girl, Floretta, rescues a little bird (in reality a fairy). In return, she is shown two fountains, one of "joy" and a bitter one of "sorrow." To drink from the first will grant wishes (some, not all), while to drink from the second will remove, if painfully, the unforeseen evil effects of those first wishes. Floretta wishes in turn for beauty (which brings her the envy and hostility of other women); riches (which pall, while leading to fawning insincerity from others); intelligence (which makes others uneasy and tend to shun her, while at the same time it makes her more sharply aware of the hypocrisies of life and the emptiness of ambition). She in turn renounces each wish except intelligence, which she cannot bring herself to give up, however painful. A wish for long life brings decay, loss of novelty, the death of friends. Finally she renounces this too in order to accept the ordinary "course of nature" (death).

attend The Club a few times, to write an occasional letter that makes no mention of his condition, or to write three short pieces for others—the Preface to James Fordyce's *Sermons to Young Women* (1766) and a couple of Dedications.* We can only remind ourselves again of what seems incredible to most people who lead normal lives but is a commonplace to those who have gone through long periods of despair or depression—that it is possible even for those who lack Johnson's courage to steel themselves to get through particular tasks until they are at the very edge of collapse.

The Thrales for their part found "the horrible condition of his mind" incredible until the day in June when they found him on his knees before Dr. Delap "beseeching God to continue to him the use of his understanding." The breakdown in control was the more ominous since Delap was not someone to whom Johnson would ordinarily turn in such a condition. Though Delap was a clergyman, he was a rather superficial person who was principally interested in advancing in the literary world and fancied himself a poet and dramatist (in later years his tragedy *The Captives*, said John Philip Kemble, was performed "amidst roars of laughter").

The Thrales decided that something had to be done at once. The obvious answer was to take him out to their country house at Streatham. The helpless and broken Johnson seems to have offered no objection. He did go to Streatham and stayed there for more than three months (from late June to October 1), after which he became virtually a member of their family. Mrs. Thrale did not exaggerate when she said that in undertaking "the care of his health"—and it was a long and gradual process—she "had the honour and happiness of contributing to its restoration." The Thrales did more than "contribute" to the restoration of his "health." They made it possible.

6

Mrs. Thrale, whose maiden name was Hester Maria Salusbury, was at this time only twenty-five. We need to remind ourselves—it is often forgotten—how young the Thrales were in comparison with Johnson

---

* Fordyce, a Presbyterian clergyman, had earlier shown these sermons to Johnson, who advised him to publish them and suggested the title (the book sold widely throughout the eighteenth century). Doubtless, when Fordyce now came to him for a Preface, he felt he could not refuse. The Dedications were for a work by his old friend the architect John Gwynn, *London and Westminster Improved* (1766), and George Adams's *Treatise on the Globes* (1766).

(now approaching fifty-seven) if we are to get a true picture of his relations with them in the years ahead. Hester came from a Welsh family that was proud of its lineage (it traced descent from Henry Tudor) but had gradually lost its money. An only child, she had been something of a prodigy. She read French fluently at seven, and soon afterward learned Latin, Greek, Italian, and Spanish. She also wrote poetry, and at sixteen translated some Spanish works, including part of *Don Quixote*. She was very short and birdlike, with a sharp nose, a wide mouth, and large hands (her "Salusbury fists," as she called them). But, if not a beauty, she was vivacious, charming, and warm-hearted.

While her hot-tempered, unbusinesslike father drifted toward financial collapse, her mother and uncle began planning a wealthy marriage for her and found a candidate in Henry Thrale, twelve years older than Hester. Henry's father, a self-made man, had inherited a flourishing business as a brewer, developed it further, and became a member of Parliament. Determined to raise his son as a gentleman, he sent him first to Oxford, where he was encouraged to associate with the nobility, and then on the Grand Tour, ostentatiously paying the expenses not only of his son but his son's companion, William Henry Lyttelton, the future Lord Westcote. After his return Henry lived the life of a rake and a man about town until his father died (1758), leaving him his fortune and his brewery, which was in Southwark on the site of the old Globe Theatre. Henry changed his way of living, plunged into the business, looked about for a wife, and, with Mrs. Salusbury's encouragement, decided on Hester. The marriage, in short, was not a love match; nor, like so many other eighteenth-century marriages, was it expected to be. Moreover, Thrale was already attached to Polly Hart, the daughter of a dancing master, and he was to continue to have attachments to other women. Mrs. Thrale, like other wives of the time, accepted this, and, at least externally, did not seem too hurt.

Hester's father opposed the marriage, considering Thrale unworthy of his daughter. But Salusbury died suddenly, and the marriage took place in October 1763. The following September the first of their children was born. This was Hester Maria, whom Johnson called "Queeney" after Queen Esther; and henceforth the family always referred to her as "Queeney." For years her mother's life was to consist of a dreary round of pregnancies. Mrs. Thrale, in fact, was to bear her husband twelve children, eight of whom died in infancy or childhood, including the boy (Henry) whom Thrale had hoped would be his heir to the brewery.

The Thrales had been married a little more than a year when they first met Johnson. As a girl, Hester had often heard of Johnson from her father's friend William Hogarth, who would praise the *Rambler* and describe Johnson's conversation in comparison with that of others as being "like Titian's painting compared to Hudson's"—Thomas Hudson, a middling painter but with some reputation in his time. Now Arthur Murphy—one of Thrale's close friends from his bachelor days—offered to introduce him to them, warning them "not to be surprised at his figure, dress, or behaviour." Hester was especially eager to meet Johnson. The tall, stately Thrale was himself far from being a good conversationalist, though he had the merit of keeping quiet when he had nothing to say. Johnson, out of friendship, somewhat exaggerated when he later stood up for him to another friend who asked about Thrale's silence: "His conversation does not show the minute hand; but he strikes the hour very correctly." But the self-contained Thrale genuinely enjoyed listening to others who could talk well, and in time—through contact with Johnson and people he came to know through Johnson—he became addicted to it.[9]

The Thrales looked for a pretense to invite Johnson, and decided to ask at the same time James Woodhouse, the "Poetical Shoemaker," who had been taken up by fashionable people. They thought Johnson would be curious to meet him. The dinner went off well, and soon Johnson was being invited regularly every Thursday when they were at their town house, which was in Southwark, next to the brewery. For a while he and Mrs. Thrale carried on a small literary project—a translation into English verse of the *Metres* of Boethius. She would prepare one for him before he came to dinner on Thursday, and sometimes they would collaborate, with each doing alternate parts. The thought was to publish them. But then Johnson found out that a poor author was engaged on this work, and "fear'd our Publication would be his Hindrance"; so the matter was dropped. Meanwhile Thrale decided to run for Parliament and was elected in December 1765 (Johnson wrote some of his election addresses, which were published in the *Public Advertiser*).[10]

7

It was to their country house—Streatham Park (or Streatham Place), six miles from the city—that the Thrales took Johnson when they found him in such distress the following June. For a while he tended to confine himself to his room, trying to pull his mind into focus. It was probably on one of these occasions that Mrs. Thrale discovered his tendency, when he felt his imagination "disordered," to turn to mathematics, especially arithmetic. Going to his room to see what he was doing, she found him in the midst of an elaborate series of calculations. He was taking the national debt, computing it at 180 millions sterling, and then calculating whether it "would, if converted into silver, serve to make a meridian of that metal, I forget how broad, for the globe of the whole earth."[11] But soon, with Mrs. Thrale's gentle encouragement, he began to leave his room and become familiar with the house and grounds.

Streatham Place was a large three-story brick house, surrounded by a hundred acres of land. Behind the house were greenhouses, stables, and other farm buildings, as well as frames for growing melons, peaches, and other fresh fruit. (Johnson was to become very fond of the peaches, and would eat several before breakfast and again after dinner.) Within the next few years, as Thrale's income increased, he turned the place into a showpiece. The rooms, including Johnson's, were remodeled; a large library wing was built; and on the grounds a lake with a small island in the center was added.

For the first time in his life, Johnson was surrounded not for a few days but for months with every convenience and attention. It was like the boyhood visit to Stourbridge, which had been permanently imprinted in Johnson's mind as an archetypal experience, except that even Cornelius did not live in this way. True, Johnson was now forty years older, with very little of the hope he had then. Even so, the situation could seem almost ideal. He was given the best of food. His hours were his own if he wanted them to be. There were servants available to attend to every want (though he was careful never to abuse this). A coach was at his service whenever he wished.

More important was the attention given him by Mrs. Thrale, who in size and general appearance was not unlike his mother, Sarah Johnson. Mrs. Thrale tried to be ready for conversation at any time, even if it meant sitting up until 3:00 or 4:00 A.M. pouring tea for him. It was not easy for her. Johnson's eyes "of a light blue Colour were so wild and at Times so fierce; that Fear I believe was the first Emotion in the hearts of all his beholders." But she also felt complimented in having, in her household, a genuine lion. The rewards made the effort worthwhile. Moreover, he was plainly so helpless that, besides the respect she gave him, she also began to baby him, though he was thirty-one years older than she. Johnson, ordinarily so fiercely scrupulous and self-examining, in turn began to accept this without quite knowing he was doing so. One of the first results was the almost childlike competition he fell into for her attention—a competition not with her daughter or future children, for whom he was to feel a strong parental or grandfatherly affection, but with a woman closer to his own age, Mrs. Salusbury, Hester Thrale's mother. They quickly began to view each other with annoyance and to complain of each other to Mrs. Thrale. Nor was the situation helped when he took advantage of Mrs. Salusbury's intense interest in foreign politics by fabricating details of battles between Russia and Turkey, then at war, or would "feed her," as Mrs. Thrale said, "with new accounts of the division of Poland." Later, Mrs. Salusbury's severe illness was to move his compassion and they became firm friends.[12]

A radical change took place in Johnson's life as a result of this summer at Streatham. However well known he had become, he had still been living the life of a waif during his forties and fifties. It is not too much to say that the Thrales adopted him, and within a year he was to think of their town and country houses—the italics are his own—as "my *home.*" There was something almost filial in the grateful devotion he showed to Henry Thrale, whom he often called, till the end of Thrale's life, "my Master," while Mrs. Thrale was "my Mistress." When any worry bothered Thrale, Johnson hung around him, "left him scarce a moment, and tried every artifice to amuse as well as every argument to console him." He would accept any correction of his manners from Thrale as he would from no other person. If he became dogmatic at the table, Thrale could stop him at once with a firm remark: "There, there, we have now had enough for one lecture, Dr. Johnson; we will not be upon education any more till after dinner, if you please." Thrale even got him to improve his appearance, persuaded him to change his shirt more frequently, arranged to have his clothes kept clean, and had silver buckles put on his shoes. He also got him a special wig to wear at dinner. Johnson always read in bed at night. Because of his poor eyesight, he would lean his head so near the candle that his wig—which he often forgot to take off—was singed. The same thing would happen to new wigs. Finally Thrale had his personal valet stand outside the dining room with Johnson's "company" wig, which was presented to him before he entered and taken away from him afterward.[13]

At the end of the summer, when he went back to London, it was arranged that he henceforth would spend at least half of his time, often more, with the Thrales when either he or they were not away on trips. In general he stayed with them throughout the middle of the week. As time went on, he often spent as much as five days a week with them, coming on Monday night after The Club and remaining till Saturday, when he would return to his own house and look after his charges there, who were to become increasingly quarrelsome as they got older and more numerous. Since the Thrales were at their Southwark house at least as often as at Streatham, a new apartment for Johnson was fitted up there, over the counting house, and called the Round Tower.[14]

In short, the Thrales saw far more of Johnson in his later years and knew him better than anyone else did. We fail to remember this because the picture of Johnson engraved on our minds tends to be that of Boswell or of writers like Macaulay who extrapolate from him. Though Boswell gradually learned about Johnson's life with the Thrales, he saw little of it at first hand; and later on, his sense of rivalry—as Mary Hyde shows in her book *The Impossible Friendship* (1972)—led him to minimize Johnson's life with the Thrales as much as he felt he could.

8

The healing process begun at Streatham was a gradual one, and it was the result of no one thing. It was a combination of several things, all of which could be implied by saying that for the first time since boyhood he had a real family—one that could at last help fill his heart and help get him out of himself, especially in the years ahead, as the children kept arriving and he was drawn more closely into a feeling of responsibility and concern for the happiness and well-being of the family. Moreover, this was something that came to him very late. He was approaching sixty. Time was necessary for him to assimilate it in opposition to a lifetime of experience that had been so different. But though the healthful effect was gradual, he had already taken a large step forward when he returned to his own house on October 1. And, of course, he was not really "returning" except for a part of each week.

In another way—less essential but still important—his recovery was to be furthered by an intellectual interest that touched his oldest ambition, the study of law, in a way that his work for Single-Speech Hamilton did not (for he had resumed helping Hamilton). He had idealized that work in thinking it might have to do with "the law." It had merely involved being a general consultant on anything that interested Hamilton politically. But now (though he did not at first realize what it would lead to) something far more directly concerned with the law presented itself. And in a way no other work would have done, it was to help him get his thoughts off himself onto a challenging subject, and also give him confidence that he still—however shattering the last few years—retained his mental faculties.

In effect, he was about to help prepare a three-year series of lectures (and personally dictate large sections) given by the new Vinerian Professor of Law at Oxford, Robert Chambers, who had just succeeded the celebrated William Blackstone. At Johnson's request (and needless to say at the frantic desire of Chambers) his help was kept secret. Boswell never learned about it. Only Mrs. Thrale (and doubtless her husband) learned of it, and even they were probably unaware of the scale of Johnson's help. It is only in our own generation that E. L. McAdam, following clues in Mrs. Thrale's diary, unraveled the secret.[15] Even then the facts did not become widely known, and the authoritative history of the Vinerian professorship (1958), in its account of Chambers, makes no mention of what Johnson did.

The background is briefly as follows. When the professorship of law had been founded by the bequest of Charles Viner, the first appointment (1758) had been William Blackstone. The first volume of Blackstone's great *Commentaries on the Laws of England* (1765) was expanded from his Vinerian lectures—an example that could easily overwhelm the heart of anyone who immediately followed him in the chair. When Blackstone resigned the professorship in order to return to the practice of law, the next choice was Robert Chambers, who was only twenty-eight but had been Blackstone's understudy and was expected to have a brilliant career before him.

Johnson had first met the young Chambers back in 1754 when visiting Oxford while he finished the *Dictionary*. As so often when he met young men entering the law—such as Robert Vansittart, who also reminded him of Cornelius—his own frustrations at not entering the law led him to identify himself with them, and to take a generous, vicarious pleasure in their careers. Since then he had seen Chambers on other visits to Oxford. They had corresponded a little, and he had written letters of recommendation for him.

9

Chambers was appointed Vinerian Professor in May 1766—the month when Johnson's breakdown was at its worst—and was also made Principal of the New Inn Hall (later merged with Balliol). He tried to start at once on the lectures due the following year. There was an added embarrassment. The Vinerian Professor was required to lecture. If he failed to do so, he was fined for each lecture missed, and to such an extent that if he missed all of them, the fines amounted to almost the full salary.

Over the summer Chambers began to panic. Try as he would, he could not get started. He was a timid man anyway, and inclined to self-distrust.* He was paralyzed at the thought of the comparison people would make between his lectures and those of Blackstone. Moreover, since Blackstone had already covered the whole field so authoritatively, how could he avoid simply repeating Blackstone unless he fell back on one of the two alternatives, neither of them commendable, to which human nature resorts under such circumstances? That is, to give up comprehensiveness, and retreat to a specialized corner and develop that; or else to try to turn some of Blackstone upside down for the sake of novelty and carry on a running quibble with him. It was the age-old problem Johnson himself had raised fifteen years before (*Rambler* 86) when he quoted Pliny, "The burthen of government is increased upon princes by the virtues of their immediate predecessors," and then pointed out that the same thing is true in the intellectual and literary world.

In early autumn, with the term about to begin, the desperate Chambers turned for help to Johnson, who had just returned to his house from Streatham (October 1). Johnson then took the coach to Oxford, and stayed for a month with Chambers at New Inn Hall, looking through Chambers's source books, and helping him outline four introductory lectures (on the law generally, the rise of feudal government, feudal law, and the "general division of the laws of England"). Then,

* So timid that, over thirty years later (1798), in his presidential address to the Asiatic Society of Bengal, he had to resurrect and reuse the opening paragraphs Johnson had written for his inaugural lecture as Vinerian Professor (S. Krishnamurti, *Modern Language Review*, XLIV [1949], 236–38).

in order to prime the pump, he dictated about two-fifths of the first lecture. At the same time he could hardly help reflecting on the low opinion he generally had of lectures as a form of education. As he had said not long before, he doubted that lectures did as much good as "reading the books from which the lectures are taken." Of course, not everyone who sat at a lecture would bother to read the books. Even so, he thought nothing could be best taught by lectures "except where experiments are to be shewn. You may teach chymistry by lectures.— You might teach *making of shoes* by lectures!"[16]

After Johnson left (November 8), Chambers again became terrified. He felt he needed still more help. At the same time he was haunted with a new fear—the profound humiliation if it were known that the Vinerian Professor at Oxford, the successor of Blackstone, had been forced to rely on a man who was not only without legal training but also one who had attended college for scarcely more than a year. Johnson, completely understanding the situation, gently wrote to Chambers (December 11) to bring him his notes and law books. They would work together, and "I doubt not but Lectures will be produced. You must not miss another term."[17] (Though Johnson conscientiously destroyed Chambers's letters to him, the uneasy Chambers, for whatever reason, never destroyed Johnson's.) A fresh start was made, and Chambers returned to Oxford hoping to continue the momentum.

But Chambers soon reached another snag and sent another appeal. Johnson now realized he would simply have to do more of it himself or Chambers would never be able to face the next term. Hence, this time (January 22, 1767), "I shall expect abundance of materials. . . . There will be no danger, and needs to be no fear." Together they now prepared the lectures for the coming term, and they were publicly announced to begin on March 17. The unexpected talent Johnson showed in whipping the materials into shape is little short of amazing. Moreover, for this and the next two series, he dictated the sections already mentioned in order to pull the lectures into generality and to make crucial transitions. (In logical cleanliness and forcefulness of phrase, the passages contrast sharply with Chambers's own rambling, diffuse style.)[18] For this first series (spring 1767) there are the four introductory lectures already mentioned, and then sixteen on the "Public Law," that is constitutional law, of which four concentrate on Parliament, three on the monarchy, and the rest on the judiciary, the civil divisions of England, and constitutional issues concerned with the union with Scotland and the government of Ireland and the American colonies.

10

We should interrupt the story—which extends for another two years —to notice that Johnson's health, which had taken a dramatic turn for the better during the months at Streatham, continued to improve. Even the insomnia that had bothered him for years was disappearing, and he was beginning to wonder whether the unaccustomed sleep he was now getting was a form of self-indulgence. A prayer at the start of the New Year (1767), which significantly lacks all his usual self-prodding resolves, now asks to be preserved "from unseasonable and immoderate sleep" (with the result that he managed to get "little rest" the next night). This is put in the context of hoping generally "to use all enjoyments with moderation."[19] And the fact that there are now "enjoyments" to moderate, though only sleep is specifically mentioned, indicates a radical change in outlook.

He was also going out frequently, and would walk over to Buckingham House to use the splendid library there, probably in order to consult books on law. The young librarian, Frederick Barnard, who did everything he could to contribute to Johnson's ease and convenience there, told the King of these visits. The King wanted to meet Johnson. On Johnson's next visit, in February, Barnard stole around to the King's apartment and told him Johnson was now reading in the library by the fire. Barnard then picked up a candle, led the King through some rooms and a private door into the library, and presented Johnson to him. Throughout the interview, Johnson stood with dignity and talked in a courteous but firm and sonorous voice rather than in the subdued, deferential tone customary among those presented to the sovereign. The King asked him about the libraries at Oxford and Cambridge, about various scholars, and about a strange but ingenious quack doctor, John Hill, who had attained some notoriety. Johnson started to describe the sort of thing Hill did, but suddenly considered he would be "depreciating this man in the estimation of his Sovereign, and thought it was time for me to say something more favorable." The conversation then turned to the comparative merit of literary journals.

The King at one point asked him if he was now writing anything. Johnson replied that he "had pretty well told the world what he knew," and that he "thought he had already done his part as a writer." "I should have thought so too," said the King, "if you had not written so well." Asked by a friend later whether he had replied to that compliment, Johnson answered he had not: "It was not for me to bandy civilities with my Sovereign." Near the end of the interview, the King "expressed a desire to have the literary biography of this country ably executed, and proposed to Dr. Johnson to undertake it." Johnson indicated his willingness to comply with this, and in the *Lives of the Poets* was to come closer than anyone else to doing so.[20]

11

Throughout the spring he made two more short visits to Oxford (in late March and in early May) to help Chambers, who was now giving the Vinerian lectures at a rapid rate, and on the side wrote a couple of Dedications for friends—one for William Payne's *Geometry* (1767) and one for John Hoole's translation of the *Works of Metastasio* (1767). In between these visits he received news of the serious illness, almost certainly terminal, of the old family servant of the Johnsons at Lichfield, ironically named Catherine (or "Kitty") Chambers, who was asking for him. He hurried to Lichfield in May to do what he could for her, stopping at Oxford for a few days to give some last-minute help to Robert Chambers on his final lectures that term.

When he arrived at Lichfield, he found Kitty almost completely helpless. The weeks passed, while Johnson remained with her at the new house of his stepdaughter, Lucy Porter. For years Lucy had lived with old Mrs. Johnson helping to look after the bookshop. Then her brother Captain Jervis Porter—the one who had vowed never to see his mother after she married Johnson—died (1763); and the fortune he had inherited from his rich uncle, Joseph Porter, passed to Lucy. She had built an attractive new house and recently moved there (1766) taking Kitty with her. Though Lucy as always was pleasant to Johnson, she had become somewhat prissy; and feeling his own age, he thought her—though he was six years older—already "a little discoloured by hoary virginity."

To kill time, he started to reread Homer, but it did not really occupy his mind. Having so little to do, his immense capacity for self-dissatisfaction began to prey on him. As the summer wore on, he became desperate to return from this "exile." "My old melancholy has laid hold upon me to a degree sometimes not easily supportable." Yet his tender heart would not allow him to leave Kitty. In August she seemed to be dying. Johnson, so fond of asserting in self-protection that grief is a "species of idleness," was greatly shaken. He took Communion with her. "I was for some time distracted but at last more composed." Then she seemed to recover (she was not to die until November 3).[21]

Finally, on October 17, when he had been at Lichfield for five months, he felt he really must leave, and wrote in his journal:

I desired all to withdraw, then told her that we were to part for ever, that as Christians we should part with prayer, and that I would, if she was willing, say a short prayer beside her. She expressed great desire to hear me, and held up her poor hands, as she lay in bed, with great fervour, while I prayed, kneeling by her, nearly in the following words. . . .

I then kissed her. She told me that to part was the greatest pain that she had ever felt, and that she hoped we should meet again in a better place. I expressed with swelled eyes and great emotion of tenderness the same hopes. We kissed and parted, I humbly hope, to meet again, and to part no more.

Reading this account fifty years later (1816), Mrs. Thrale, then an old woman, wrote in the margin:

Johnson told me this tender Story with many tears; & cried *Poor Kitty! Poor dear Kitty!* so often in the Course of the Evene—I rejoyced to see new Faces come in, & turn the Course of his Ideas.[22]

12

Meanwhile, with Robert Chambers, the pattern was repeating itself. He seems to have made little headway over the summer with his second series (this time on the subject of criminal law). Johnson stopped at Oxford on the way back from Lichfield, and they started to work. There were probably other visits of Johnson to Oxford or of Chambers to London, and the lectures were scheduled to begin on February 20. Around the close of the year, he also wrote a short Prologue—a rather gloomy one—for Goldsmith's new comedy, *The Good-Natured Man* (performed January 20, 1768).

Though he was not well, he dutifully went to Oxford in February to help see Chambers through the new series of lectures, and while there wrote an election address for Henry Thrale. He became quite ill during this long visit of more than two months, and as a result the series on "Criminal Law" was shorter than it was expected to be. Even so, he and Chambers managed to put together fourteen lectures, which begin with the concept and history of punishment, and move rapidly through the entire range of English criminal law with some detail but especially with philosophical perspective. The first series had been rather similar in structure and theme to Blackstone. But this one shows a growing independence and develops ideas more freely.

While he was at Oxford, Boswell arrived in London (March 22) after an absence of two years, partly to take a cure for gonorrhea and partly to enjoy what he hoped was his new fame as an author. His *Account of Corsica* had just been published and been well received (he was hoping to be popularly known as "Corsica Boswell"). He expected Johnson to congratulate him, unaware that Johnson—who had not answered his letters for a long time and assumed he was in Scotland— was at last about to write him a short letter saying, "I wish you would empty your head of Corsica, which I think has filled it rather too long." He dropped around to Johnson's house, and was surprised to learn he was staying with Chambers at Oxford. He had a fixed notion of Johnson's life based on his two previous visits to London, and as- sumed he was forever either at home or at a tavern talking with friends. He went to Oxford (March 26) for a few days. Johnson, touched that Boswell made this special trip to see him, talked readily, and Boswell recorded the conversations. Now, or soon after he re- turned to London for the "cure," Boswell for the first time learned about the Thrales and became very curious. In early June, shortly before he left for Scotland, he again stopped by at Johnson's house, and found him waiting outside for Mrs. Thrale, who was to pick him up in her coach to take him to Streatham. When the coach arrived and Johnson entered it, Boswell also leapt into the coach (explaining to Mrs. Thrale later that he did so by "that agreeable kind of attraction which makes one forget ceremony"). Johnson then introduced him to her, and Boswell made a point of talking in such a way as "to shew her that I was as Johnsonian as herself."[23]

13

The long visit to Lichfield the year before, in order to be with the dying Kitty, had seriously upset Johnson's new way of life, and his illness throughout the spring of 1768 was partly psychosomatic. He was far better than he had been in 1766. But after the radical improvement that had taken place, a slip backward naturally frightened him.

Hoping that it would do him some good, the Thrales, in September, took him on a tour through Kent. The night of his birthday (September 18), which they spent at Townmalling in Kent, he wrote in his journal:

I have now begun the sixtieth year of my life. How the last year has past I am unwilling to terrify myself with thinking. This day has been past in great perturbation. I was distracted at Church in an uncommon degree, and my distress has had very little intermission.

Soon after their return, Mrs. Thrale, while checking to see that his room was all right, started to close an open drawer when she saw in it his journal and read these lines. It is possible that he hoped she would discover it. In any case, now and during the weeks that followed, she talked with him about his state of mind, and he confessed to her more frankly than ever before the fear of insanity with which he had been wrestling—that "Secret far dearer to him than his life." At her request he surrendered to her the fetters and padlocks that he had kept at home.[24]

The following year was spent—as he was to write on his next birthday—"in a slow progress of recovery." Meanwhile, in December, he again went to Oxford to start on the third and last series of the law lectures—this one, "On Private [*i.e.*, civil] Law"; and he made another trip in February when the lectures were under way. For this final series, which consists of twenty-two lectures, Chambers was at last becoming more self-confident, and Johnson's help was less necessary until they came to the concluding lectures (late May and June). Then Johnson again went to Oxford and sequestered himself with Chambers, though, in a celebrative mood, he also brought with him Miss Williams. Boswell, when he tried later to find out the reason for this mysterious trip, learned from her only that "he seldom or never dined out. He appeared to be deeply engaged in some literary work."[25] Meanwhile he was given an honorary position at the newly founded Royal Academy of Arts. Reynolds, its president, had suggested that honorary professorships be established there, and Johnson was made "Professor in Ancient Literature." It carried no duties as well as no salary. In later years, when he was again to become lonelier, he would attend some of its exhibitions and annual dinners. Goldsmith was also given an honorary professorship and said that, for someone in his position, it was like presenting "ruffles to a man that wants a shirt."

14

A word should be added about the later history of the lectures. Chambers continued to deliver them six more times, and was soon regarded as one of the most eminent lawyers in the kingdom (he was knighted in 1777). When he was appointed to the Supreme Court of Bengal (1774), the King's Librarian, Mr. Barnard, asked him before he left to present a copy of his Vinerian lectures to the Royal Library (now in the British Museum). There the copy still remains, a manuscript of about sixteen hundred pages.

Naturally Chambers had no desire to publish the lectures. When Mrs. Thrale's *Anecdotes* appeared (1786), she mentioned how liberal Johnson was "in granting literary assistance to others," and added, "Innumerable are the prefaces, sermons, lectures, and dedications which he used to make for people who begged of him." Since Chambers could have known of no other lectures in which Johnson gave help, he could well have been startled when he read this and have wondered what rumors were current. But out of respect for Johnson's wishes rather than Chambers's feelings, she said nothing more. The secret remained a secret, except (and then only possibly) in Chambers's family. For a short selection of twelve lectures was made and published twenty-one years after Chambers's death by his nephew, Sir Charles Chambers, also a lawyer, and given the title *A Treatise on Estates and Tenures* (1824); and the lectures selected were ones in which Johnson had little or no hand, at least in any obvious way. Then Chambers's personal copy, from which the selection had been made, was apparently destroyed.

Chapter 24

Early Sixties

Henry Thrale, whose father left him a house at Brighton, had been going there for vacations since he was a boy. He had recently bought a larger house with the thought that he and the whole family would spend the last part of the summer there each year. He enjoyed hunting on the Downs, and Hester was fond of sea bathing. This summer (1769) the Thrales naturally asked Johnson to come with them. He would have far preferred it if they had stayed at Streatham. But, dreading loneliness, he hastened to accept, and, after a short visit to Lichfield and to his old friend John Taylor at Ashbourne, joined the Thrales for their last six weeks at Brighton (August 21 to the end of September). Though the weather was warm, the chronic bronchitis from which he suffered, together with emphysema, was growing worse. Consequently, "my lungs seem encumbered, and my breath fails me, if my strength is in any unusual degree exerted."

Even so, he went swimming. He would also join Thrale at hunting and ride fifty miles or more without admitting he was tired, while deploring "that the paucity of human pleasures should persuade us ever to call hunting one of them" (he later concluded that it was "because man feels his own vacuity less in action than when at rest"). He was greatly pleased when William Gerard Hamilton called out one day on the Brighton Downs, "Why Johnson rides as well, for aught I see, as the most illiterate fellow in England." And once, when Thrale leapt over a stool to show he was not tired after a chase of fifty miles,

Johnson immediately jumped over it to show he too was not tired "but in a way so strange and so unwieldy, that our terror lest he should break his bones, took from us even the power of laughing."[1]

Meanwhile David Garrick had been busily preparing his "Shakespeare Jubilee" at Stratford (September 6–8), designed to call attention to Shakespeare as a national hero. There were to be feasts, a pageant, music, a horse race for a "Jubilee Cup," and a masquerade. A large rotunda was built next to the Avon. Garrick had hoped Johnson would write an ode to be delivered on the occasion. But Johnson was uninterested, and Garrick had to write the ode himself. He also designed special "Shakespeare ribbands" for the visitors, with rainbow colors and the line about Shakespeare from the *Prologue* Johnson had written for Garrick years before (1747), "Each change of *many-colour'd* life he drew."

Boswell arrived in London shortly before the Stratford Jubilee. He needed to renew the treatment for venereal infection he had undergone a year and three months before. Moreover, he was planning to get married and wanted to hear Johnson—to "hear the Oracle," as he wrote—discuss marriage generally. To his surprise he learned from Miss Williams that Johnson was at Brighton, without the slightest thought of going to the Jubilee. This seemed perverse. Boswell thought his "connection both with Shakespeare and Garrick founded a double claim to his presence. . . . The absence of Johnson could not but be wondered at." Caught up with the idea of the masquerade, Boswell deferred his medical treatment for a few days and decided to go himself, celebrating his book on Corsica of the previous year by appearing in the costume of a Corsican war chief with a headband in gold letters reading *Viva la Libertà*.[2]

It was not merely proud disregard of the Jubilee that kept Johnson at Brighton. In the "slow progress of recovery" he was at last experiencing (September 18), his sense of "home" with the Thrales was proving all-important. True, he took for granted that the Jubilee would be a trivial, probably an absurd, affair. Events more than confirmed him. To begin with, though the magistrates at Stratford hoped to make something of the occasion, the townspeople were suspicious and antagonistic. The carpenters sent from London by Garrick to make the rotunda lacked materials, and local carpenters, regarding stage machinery as the contrivance of the devil, refused to lend their tools. The Drury Lane lamps Garrick dispatched to Stratford arrived broken to pieces by the rough journey. Adequate lodging was lacking for the crowds, and they were forced to pay an exorbitant price merely to sleep on a blanket on the floors of sheds or stables. Worst of all, the weather was becoming very uncertain, and rains in the area were causing the Avon to rise almost to the level of the open plain where the rotunda had been built.

The cloudy first day dawned with the boom of cannon and the appearance of Drury Lane actors in costume walking the streets strumming guitars and singing ballads in honor of Shakespeare ("Let beauty with the sun arise, / To Shakespeare tribute pay . . ."). A festive breakfast followed, where Garrick was awarded a medallion—previously paid for by himself—carved from the inexhaustible "mulberry tree" Shakespeare was said to have planted. Next came a performance of Thomas Arne's oratorio, *Judith,* to an audience that naturally failed to see the connection with Shakespeare, and after this there was a ball. On the second day, for which the pageant had been planned, the rain began streaming down, much to the delight of townspeople who regarded it as a righteous judgment. The pageant had to be canceled, and the crowd hastened to the rotunda where Garrick delivered his *Ode to Shakespeare.* Pressed to comment later on Garrick's ode, Johnson would only say that it *"defied* criticism." Unfortunately the barber who had shaved Garrick that morning had been badly drunk at the ball the night before, and cut a large gash in Garrick's face, which continued to bleed profusely; and throughout the day Mrs. Garrick and ladies from the theater tried vainly to staunch the blood with styptics. This was followed by a dinner at which a huge turtle, weighing 327 pounds, was eaten.

By now the Avon had overflowed, and the horses had to wade knee-deep to get to the rotunda. Fortunately the rotunda itself was not flooded, and it was possible to go ahead with the masquerade (11:00 P.M. to 4:00 A.M.). The visitors had looked forward to this as their principal chance to participate creatively, and many had designed costumes for themselves as Shakespearean characters, including Lady Pembroke and two friends, who appeared as the three witches in *Macbeth.* Boswell waited till midnight to make a dramatic appearance as "Corsica Boswell," and noted in his journal that "my Corsican dress attracted everybody." On the third and last day, the rain stopped. The horse race for the Jubilee Cup, followed by damp fireworks, went ahead as scheduled, though the racecourse was a foot deep in water.[8]

2

When Johnson returned to London at the end of September, Boswell, who had to return to Scotland in a month, made special efforts to see him. They had a reunion at the Mitre Tavern. Partly because he half believed it and partly to see what Johnson would say, Boswell fell into the cant of the day about the "superior happiness of savage life" and argued for it. Johnson ridiculed the notion. Savages "have not better health; and as to care or mental uneasiness, they are not above it, but below it, like bears." Boswell persisted: "Sometimes I have been in the humour of wishing to retire to a desart." Johnson: "Sir, you have desart enough in Scotland."

Boswell was also seeing as much as he could of the famous Corsican leader General Pasquale Paoli, who had now arrived in England as an exile after the French conquest of Corsica. He arranged for Johnson to meet Paoli (October 10). The two men, who were later to become good friends, were impressed with each other. (Johnson afterward said Paoli had "the loftiest port of any man he had ever seen.") But at this first meeting they found communication difficult. Paoli spoke in Italian, which Johnson could understand but not speak, while Johnson spoke English, which Paoli could only partly follow. Johnson then tried French. But his pronunciation of it was never good, and he was forced to write out some of his remarks. A few days later (October 16) Boswell held a dinner at his lodgings in Old Bond Street, to which he invited Johnson, Reynolds, Garrick, Goldsmith, and a few others. Garrick, bearing Johnson no grudge for his absence from the Jubilee, "played round him with a fond vivacity, taking hold of the breasts of his coat, and, looking up in his face with a lively archness, complimented him on the good health which he seemed then to enjoy," while Johnson, "shaking his head, beheld him with a gentle complacency."[4]

Meanwhile a friend of some of those present—the headstrong, near-sighted Giuseppe Baretti—had been charged with murder (October 6). The short trial two weeks later is still remembered because of the array of eminent men who showed up to testify on behalf of the poor Italian teacher. This "constellation of genius" included Johnson, Burke, Reynolds, Beauclerk, Goldsmith, and Garrick. It was through Johnson that the others had come to know Baretti. What happened is that Baretti, on his way back to Soho, was accosted by a woman of the town, and, as he moved away, she put her hand to his breeches and grasped him painfully by the genitals. Startled, he struck her. There-upon three bullies, rallying to the woman's scream, started to descend on him. As Baretti tried to run from them, he drew from his pocket a little fruit knife of a kind habitually carried in Italy because—as Garrick was to explain to the jury—only forks were provided for dinner at inns. When the men reached him, he stabbed at them, and one died from the wound. He was put in Newgate Prison, where a rival Italian teacher soon called on him, saying he wanted to take over Baretti's pupils after his execution and asking Baretti to write him a letter of recommendation. Johnson and Burke also visited him there. Taking the hands of each, he asked, "What can *he* fear that holds two such hands as I do." At the trial (October 20), Johnson described Baretti succinctly as a man who "gets his living by study. . . . A man that I never knew to be otherwise than peaceable, and a man that I take to be rather timo-rous." "How is he as to his eye-sight?" "He does not see me now, nor I . . . see him." Baretti would have been incapable "of assaulting any-body in the street without provocation." The evidence was over-whelmingly in Baretti's favor, and he was discharged.[5]

During the month Boswell also had a chance to see Streatham. The Thrales, at Johnson's suggestion, invited him for dinner (October 6). It is the first scene of Johnson's life there as recorded by an outsider. Boswell thought Streatham an "elegant villa," with "every circum-stance that can make society pleasing." He was struck by the affection of the Thrales for Johnson. "I rejoiced at seeing him so happy." The conversation ranged from Scottish gardeners to Whitefield's preach-ing, and from history to light verse. Sitting there in that "elegant villa" after a lifetime of experience so different, Johnson could not refrain from teasing his wealthy hostess when she praised the light poetry of Garrick and dwelt with "peculiar pleasure" on a line from one of Garrick's songs, "I'd smile with the simple, and feed with the poor." That is when Johnson made the reply we quoted earlier, in another context: "Nay, my dear Lady, this will never do. Poor David! *Smile with the simple!* What folly is that! And who would *feed with the poor* that can help it? No, no; let me smile with the wise, and feed with the rich."[6]

3

The social life of the Thrales, much to their delight, was becoming transformed because of Johnson. When they had taken him into the family, his situation was so desperate that their thought had not gone much beyond that. They were far from consciously aware that he could—though only, of course, if they themselves wished it—turn their home into something of an intellectual center. Despite their wealth, their place in Southwark next to the brewery was hardly in a fashionable location. In general, the guests of the young couple had been limited to Thrale's bachelor friends, acquired in his twenties, when he fancied himself a rake. But now (1769–72) they found themselves beginning to entertain some of the most gifted men in the London world of literature and the arts—the foremost painter and the foremost actor, Sir Joshua Reynolds and David Garrick; the talented Oliver Goldsmith; and the finest political mind of the generation, Edmund Burke. When Thrale, for his new library wing at Streatham, commissioned Reynolds to paint portraits of his new friends, he was doing something that no other man in England of his age and situation could do. He and his wife were by now quite aware of this, and realized that it could never have been done without Johnson.

Nor did it bother Mrs. Thrale that the company tended at the start to be almost wholly masculine. The Victorian obsession with "pairing off" men and women and anxiously trying to make the number of them match, as if to maintain a formal "truce" between the sexes, was still in the future. A single man or a group of two or three thought nothing of dining, taking tea, or even breakfasting (as Johnson often did) with a group of several women; and vice versa. And, in any case, with such distinguished members of The Club as frequent guests, the attractions of Streatham as a place to visit became overwhelming, and women of intellectual interests soon became eager for invitations.

But we get a distorted picture of Johnson's life in the two Thrale homes—Streatham and the house in Southwark—if we think of him as living there in a perpetual salon. There was also an active family life going on all this time. During a period of nine years, Mrs. Thrale was bearing a child almost every year. By the autumn of 1769, there were already five, one of whom had died soon after birth. Of the four remaining children, Hester ("Queeney") was now five, Henry two and a half, Anna Maria one and a half, and Lucy Elizabeth four months (the "Elizabeth" was to please Johnson, who wanted one of the girls to be named after Tetty). Other children continued to appear once a year: Susanna (May 1770), Sophia (July 1771), Penelope (September 1772), and Ralph (November 1773). Much of their distracted mother's time had to be spent in the nursery; and very soon she was to be closely involved with their education. Moreover, with so many children, sickness was a perpetual problem, and in March 1770 little Anna Maria died after a long illness.

All this was very much a part of Johnson's life, and represents a side of him that we rarely see in Boswell or in most of the other accounts, which naturally tend to concentrate on Johnson's conversation. In fact, one of the famous comic scenes in Boswell gives exactly the opposite impression. Putting Johnson to the question ("I know not how so whimsical a thought came into my mind"), he asks:

"If, Sir, you were shut up in a castle, and a newborn child with you, what would you do?" JOHNSON. "Why, Sir, I should not much like my company." BOSWELL. "But would you take the trouble of rearing it?" He seemed, as may well be supposed, unwilling to pursue the subject: but upon my persevering in my question, replied "Why yes, Sir, I would; but I must have all conveniences."

And so it continues, ending:

BOSWELL. "Would you teach this child that I have furnished you with, any thing?" JOHNSON. "No, I should not be apt to teach it." BOSWELL. "Would not you have a pleasure in teaching it?" JOHNSON. "No, Sir, I should not have a pleasure in teaching it." BOSWELL. "Have you not a pleasure in teaching men?—There I have you. You have the same pleasure in teaching men, that I should have in teaching children." JOHNSON. "Why, something about that."[7]

But behind this is Boswell's attempt to find out what is drawing Johnson to the Thrales (this is a couple of weeks after Boswell's first visit to them). Daily life in this family does not match his impressions of Johnson as a sage discoursing on life at the Mitre Tavern. He knows the Thrale children are very young. That "castle" could refer to Johnson's new apartment (called the Round Tower) in the Southwark house of the Thrales; and Johnson, quite aware of Boswell's interest, is putting him off ("You pursue me," he said, "with question after question very idly, without seeming to care about the matter"). Later, Boswell was to notice and mention his "love for little children." But it was not something that lent itself to quotable remarks or picturesque scenes, though he does provide one charming incident, in the *Tour of the Hebrides*, where Johnson delights a little girl, Stuart Dallas, by pretending he is a giant, and, talking in a "hollow voice," tells her he will take her with him to the cave where he lives, and where he has "a bed in the rock, and she should have a *little* bed cut opposite to it."

The Thrale children were devoted to him, and viewed him as a combination of friend and a sort of toy elephant. Every year Queeney's birthday (September 17) and his (September 18) were celebrated together in one big party. Then, as at other times, he was the first to "join in childish amusements, and hated to be left out of any innocent merriment that was going forward."[8]

4

Though he still had immense human resources despite his age—resources in humor, compassion, and imaginative understanding generally—there was also some conscious effort on his part. For he was now sixty. Even if we leave aside the accumulated pile of psychological distress from which he hoped he was at last emerging, he was often physically far from well (a painful combination of three illnesses the following spring—lumbago, muscular inflammation around the loins and belly, and a bronchial inflammation that spread to the trachea—led him to seek relief in opium, which he took in the form of laudanum). He was only too aware that he was entering the final period of his life, during which problems of health alone—not to mention problems of every other sort—were bound to multiply.

The thought haunting him now was that expressed in a line of Robert Frost's, "what to make of a diminished thing." This, as he had realized long ago, was the central problem of aging. It is already a problem in middle age, when we must begin to come to terms, as Johnson says, with what it means to be a "finite being," whose life is at least half over. But it becomes more acute as we pass from upper middle age into our sixties. Back when Boswell had first met him and tried to get him to talk about "managing" the mind, he had said "It is by studying *little things* that we attain the great art of having as little misery, and as much happiness as possible." He was repeating with more feeling what he had said some years before in the *Rambler* (No. 68), that the "main of life" is "composed of *small* incidents, and petty occurrences." So much of our bitterness about life comes from impossible expectations and demands. The "refusal to be pleased"—because of soured expectation, or because of our projections on others of the self-demands we have created for ourselves—became almost an obsession of his as something to avoid and fight against, however obdurate his own impatience and quickness to irritability or despair. *"Delicacy,"*

Mrs. Thrale quotes him as fond of saying, "does not surely consist in impossibility to be pleased." And before long, even "cards, dress, and dancing," she says, "found their advocate in Dr. Johnson"—at least theoretically, since in his own practice he remained as grotesquely remote from them as ever. In his hope to make "readiness to be pleased" more of an active principle of life, circumstances were at last helping him. The Thrale family was not a completely happy one, of course. But it was now, in a way, *his* family. For the first time since the death of Tetty, when he was entering "young" middle age almost twenty years before, he at last had responsibilities that helped to get him out of the prison of self-exaction and self-condemnation—responsibilities aside from the unfortunates he had taken into his home, like Levet and Anna Williams. And in this new family, a growing knot of mutual trust was binding them together.

Yet, as was fitting in someone his age in the home of people so much younger, he on the whole trod softly, at least for him. He never completely forgot that he was their guest. Above all, a complete curtain descended before any criticism or adverse reaction about Henry Thrale, or the way in which Thrale managed the house or his own personal affairs.

5

With the Thrales' home as a base, he now began to take some trips with less inner demand and hence less readiness for disappointment than he had done before, visiting Lucy Porter at Lichfield and John Taylor at Ashbourne without the old feeling that he was forever adrift; and during the coming three years, each trip was a little longer (July 1770; June 20–August 5, 1771; October 15–December 17, 1772). He knew he would be coming back—though he knew also that he was entering his sixties. And he felt free to write, on one of these trips, asking for Mr. Thrale to have the builders who were remodeling the house set aside a hundred loose bricks so that he could construct a special oven in the kitchen garden for his chemical experiments. The children and servants would flock around him as he performed these experiments. The flames of the oven could become quite fierce. And with the delighted Johnson, absorbed in the work and not seeing very well, there was constant danger of explosions. Finally Mr. Thrale, after returning home unexpectedly and seeing a particularly dangerous experiment that made him fear for Johnson's life, decided to put a stop to any more experiments.[9]

Meanwhile there were personal sides to Johnson's life at Streatham that no one else saw to the same degree as the Thrales. There was the time that the family asked him to read the passage about the life of the scholar, in *The Vanity of Human Wishes*, and he "burst into a passion of tears" as he tried to do so. No one beside the family was present except George Scott—a large, heavy man, similar in build to Johnson—who suddenly clapped Johnson on the back, saying, "What's all this, my dear Sir? Why, you and I, and Hercules, you know, were all troubled with *melancholy*." Johnson, brushing away his tears in delight at this "odd sally," leapt up and embraced Scott. Or there was the time that Johnson (1771) went with Mrs. Thrale to an oratorio at Covent Garden, because he dreaded being alone. Though he usually talked during performances, his impatient mind being always restive at them, he was now—to please her—"surprisingly quiet." She thought he was really listening. But when they got home, he repeated to her a poem of sixteen lines in Latin verse ("*In theatro*") he had composed there on the inadequacy of theatrical exhibits to "fill" the mind and heart. And though all his friends knew of his demonstrative nature—and though this was something far more common in his time even than in our own, despite our pretenses of being free from nineteenth-century inhibitions—he could be especially open in his affection for Mrs. Thrale as well as the children. "How many Times has this great, this formidable Doctor Johnson kissed my hand, ay & my foot too upon his knees." Though she suspects it is largely "interest"—the nursing and other things she has done for him—and adds, with more pique than conviction, "he loves Miss Reynolds better."[10]

Of course he was "in love" with Mrs. Thrale. His openness of temperament was such that he could always quickly—however old he was, however suffocating the accumulated experience and disillusion—fall "in love." And of course a strong element in this, as we noted before, was what Anna Seward, using an old proverbial phrase, called "cupboard love" (*i.e.*, love in return for provisions from the "cupboard"), though Miss Seward also felt that an idealistically "Platonic" streak, as well as his response to her flattering attention and concern, entered into it. But it was also "cupboard love" in the sense of home, which Johnson, throughout most of his life, lacked and hungered for; and uniting with it—as there had been with Tetty—was the gratitude that, as we have seen, was so strong an element in his desperate and profoundly assimilative nature.

6

In June the Thrales received a shock. They suddenly found themselves confronted with the prospect of complete financial ruin.

An old friend of Thrale's—a chemist named Humphrey Jackson—thought he had discovered a new way of brewing that made it unnecessary to use malt and hops. Thrale had trusted Jackson implicitly for years. Moreover, despite his apparently lethargic temperament, he was capable of making quick decisions. Without confiding in his family—for it was his practice until now to keep his business affairs to himself—Thrale snatched at this chance to outdo his competitors, borrowed heavily, bought land in East Smithfield, and built thirty enormous copper vats, at great expense, each holding one thousand barrels. Through this scheme, he lost his entire year's output as well as the capital spent on equipment. Unless he found credit to begin brewing again and to sustain him for some months, he was bankrupt. But, suddenly, in June 1772, just as he was beginning to realize his situation, the great London banking house of Neal, Fordyce, and Company failed, which created financial panic in the city and led to the rapid collapse of one business after another. Credit on the scale that Thrale needed was almost impossible to attain.

Thrale—without beer, without customers, without credit—seemed completely stunned. Then his clerical force—despite the efforts of his head clerk, John Perkins—became rebellious and decided to desert the firm, and Thrale sank into torpid apathy and began to think of suicide. Though Mrs. Thrale was six months pregnant (a child was born in September and died a few hours later), she threw herself, with Johnson's help, into the task of saving the brewery. While her mother offered her entire life savings (£3,000), an act that deeply touched Johnson, Mrs. Thrale addressed the mutinous clerks, and hurried to Brighton to borrow £6,000 from a friend. Soon another £11,000 was raised. This kept the brewery going; and though there was still an enormous debt (£130,000), it was paid off in a few years. From here on, Thrale was never the same man he had been. His self-confidence was badly drained. John Perkins, with Mrs. Thrale's backing, became virtual manager of the brewery, and she and Johnson continued to take an active role in supervising Perkins's management.

To add to their trials, the Thrales also suddenly found themselves (from March to June 1773) the object of a newspaper scandal. Henry Thrale, ever since his Oxford days, had fancied himself a member of the fashionable world and, as we noticed, occasionally kept mistresses. The *Westminster Magazine* dug up details of his early amours and embellished them in such a way as to make him look ridiculous. Thrale at this sank further into morose silence, while his wife, already worn by their financial problems, was badly shaken. Having discovered that Thrale's amours provided a fertile field of interest, another newspaper decided to see what it could do with his home life, and in early April published a short account of "an eminent Brewer" who was "very jealous of a certain Authour in Folio [i.e., the *Dictionary*], and perceived a strong resemblance to him in his eldest son."[11]

7

Meanwhile Mrs. Thrale's mother, Mrs. Salusbury, who had been suffering from cancer of the breast for some time, had become seriously ill. The cancer was plainly entering a terminal stage, and she was in continual pain.

Naturally Mrs. Thrale, when she was not having to attend to the children or trying to raise money to save the brewery, wanted to devote her time to nursing her mother. Under the circumstances, Johnson would be in the way at Streatham, and the most helpful thing he could do would be to stay at his own house. He himself recognized this, and he could hardly resent the attention Mrs. Thrale now needed to give her mother. In fact, he himself had become very compassionate in his feelings about Mrs. Salusbury. But a part of him—the half-child part that from the beginning had been in competition with this woman of his own age for the attention of the daughter—began to develop symptoms that might deserve a comparable sympathy and concern from Mrs. Thrale. The early months of the year had not been easy for him physically. A bad cold he had caught before Christmas, which he disregarded at first, hung on for over two months. His chronic bronchitis, in short, became acute, and he was coughing constantly. In April and May he tried to "learn the Low Dutch language," but then his one good eye became badly inflamed from the strain of reading small print.

Unable to read because of the eye inflammation, he began to complain to Mrs. Thrale. Because of his eye (May 29) he had been unable to read the note she had just sent; "I wish you would fetch me. . . . I long to be in my own room"; he assures her he will "not add much to your trouble. . . . I long to be under your care."[12] Though she was almost distracted with worry, she took pity on him and sent the coach to bring him to Streatham (Henry Thrale during this period had sequestered himself in the house at Southwark).

8

As soon as he got to Streatham, he of course found it a very different place. There was no one to talk with him. No company was being invited. Mrs. Thrale could hardly sit and pour tea for him. Inevitably he felt like an intruder, and his conscience told him he really was an intruder. With a defensiveness not far from sulking, he ostentatiously retreated to his room, and then found that his self-conscious retreat was hardly noticed. His feelings were hurt. At the same time, sitting alone in his room with his inflamed eye (which, however, was improving), his capacity for self-condemnation was completely unleashed. He felt guilty in imposing on her at such a time, and needed reassurance that he was not doing so. In fact, with his imaginative ability to make connections, he could very well feel guilty in having imposed on her all along—as he knew he had done—and thus stood doubly in need of reassurance. Finally he sent her a letter, which he wrote in French, partly to prevent the servants from reading it but partly—for what he had to say was embarrassing—to give himself "distance."

We should linger on the letter because it (and one sentence of Mrs. Thrale's reply) comprise the principal exhibit in the speculation that his relationship with Mrs. Thrale had erotically masochistic overtones.* It is an extraordinary document—self-defensive, ironic, coy,

---

* See above, pp. 386-91. The French text is as follows: "Madame trés honorée/ Puisque, pendant que je me trouve chez vous, il faut passer, tous les jours, plusieures heures dans une solitude profonde, dites moi, Si vous voulez que je vogue a plein abandon, ou que je me contienne dans des bornes prescrites. S'il vous plaît, ma tres chere maîtresse, que je sois lassè a hazard. La chose est faite. Vous vous souvenez de la sagesse de nôtre ami, *Si je ferai & c.* Mais, si ce n'est trop d'esperer que je puisse être digne, comme auparavant, des soins et de la protection d'une ame si aimable par sa douceur, et si venerable par son elevation, accordez moi, par un petit ecrit, la connoissance de ce que m'est interdit. Et s'il vous semble mieux que je demeure dans un certain lieu, je vous supplie de m'epargner la necessitè de me

disguising complaint under the appearance of excessive courtesy and self-abasement, and filled with signals asking for reassurance that he was not in the way but rather a cherished member of the family. He begins with hurt implications of her recent neglect of him, and ironically asks whether—since it is now "necessary to spend several hours in a profound solitude"—he is permitted to "wander *a plein abandon*" (by which he could have meant wander "abandoned, or neglected," or "freely, without care"); or should he confine himself to "prescribed limits" in the house (as he was now doing) so he will not be interrupting her other duties and interests? If she wishes, she can simply leave him to whatever happens to come (*a hazard*), which is what she has been doing thus far. But if she still thinks him "worthy, as formerly, of the cares and protection of a soul so amiable in its sweetness," he would like her to send him a note telling him "what is permitted me and what is forbidden." And if she decides he has to keep out of her way and stay in his room, where he will not be a nuisance to her, he would prefer that she take the initiative and "spare me the necessity of constraining myself." This would cost her "only the trouble of turning the key in the door twice a day." He is sure she can invent a routine for him that will not, as he adds with hurt irony, cause "peril" to the harmony of the household. He then puts her on the defensive in order to relieve his own sense of guilt in having blundered in upon her at this dreadful time. If she is going to be the "mistress" of this household, she could profitably make an effort to be "mistress over *herself*" and try to rein in that "inconstancy" of nature that leads her to neglect all her previous policies in running the household, forget her promises of help, and—worst of all—force him to the indignity of having to make "so

---

contraindre, en m'ôtant le pouvoir de sortir d'ou vou voulez que je sois. Ce que vous ne coûtera que la peine de tourner le clef dans la porte, deux fois par jour. Il faut agir tout a fait en Maîtresse, afin que vôtre jugement et vôtre vigilance viennent a secours de ma faibless. / Pour ce que regarde la table, j'espere tout de vôtre sagesse et je crains tout de vôtre douceur. Tournez, Madame tres honorèe, vos pensèes de ce côte la. Il n'y a pour vous rien de difficile; vous pourrez inventer une regime pratiquable sans bruit, et efficace sans peril. / Est ce trop de demander d'une ame telle qu'est la vôtre, que, maitresse des autres, elle devienne maitresse de soymême, et qu'elle triomphe de cette inconstance, qui a fait si souvent, qu'elle a negligèe l'execution de ses propres loix, qu'elle a oublièe tant de promesses, et qu'elle m'a condamnè a tant de solicitations reiterèes que la resouvenance me fait horreur. Il faut ou accorder, ou refuser; il faut se souvenir de ce qu'on accorde. Je souhaite, ma patronne, que vôtre autoritè me soit toûjours sensible, et que vous me tiennez dans l'esclavage que vou scavez si bien rendre heureuse. / Permettez moi l'honeur d'être Madame Vôtre très obeissant serviteur."[13]

many repeated solicitations for her attention" that the memory of them, excruciating for his pride, horrifies him. With the opportunity that the use of French gives him, he ends with one of those awkward gestures of gallantry that Miss Reynolds, fond as she was of him, thought hilarious, though it is also a little tinged with hurt sarcasm: he regards Mrs. Thrale as his "patronness" and hopes she will continue to keep him in that "slavery you know so well how to make happy."

It is, of course, the sort of letter that a highly gifted child, suffering guilt or remorse, might write, if he had the resources and vocabulary, in order to get a reply—any reply that would give him the confidence and reassurance that he was needed and that he was not a mere encumbrance. The quickness with which he recovered, and within a short time went off to the Hebrides, shows how far from desperate his situation really was. Mrs. Thrale, however distracted with other anxieties, shows herself completely aware, in her reply, of what he is really craving ("care," "tenderness," "attention"): "What Care can I promise my dear Mr. Johnson that I have not already taken? What Tenderness that he has not already experienced?" On the other hand, the "generous Confidence which prompts you to repose all Care on me . . . tempts you to neglect yourself." For she justifiably feels he is indulging himself, and is tactfully turning on him the remark he had made to her about being "mistress of herself." If he wishes it (she hastily so interprets what he says, or deliberately pretends to do so, for he has clearly stated that he does not wish to stay in his room, as he is now doing), he can remain confined there. Yet this is not at all the best thing for him. Diversion is the medicine he most needs, "and I believe Mr. Boswell will be at last your best Physician," meaning the trip he and Boswell would soon be taking to Scotland and the Hebrides. She ends as though she were addressing a child: "Farewell and be good; and do not quarrel with your Governness for not using the Rod enough."[14]

9

The difficulty was quickly resolved. He had received the needed reassurance. Soon afterward, on Friday, June 18, Mrs. Salusbury died, and Johnson was in her room, noting (as he wrote the night she died) that "she had for some days lost the power of speaking":

Yesterday as I touched her hand and kissed it, she pressed my hand between her two hands, which she probably intended as the parting caress. At night her speech returned a little. . . . This morning being called about nine to feel her pulse I said at parting God bless you, for Jesus Christs sake. She smiled, as pleased. She had her senses perhaps to the dying moment.[15]

Meanwhile Boswell's arrangements for the tour they were to take through part of Scotland to the Hebrides had gone forward. He had been giving a great deal of thought to this trip, and was worried lest Johnson pull out of it at the last minute. He was worried about Johnson's eye inflammation; and, in any case a trip of this sort was a major effort for a man approaching sixty-four. But Johnson decided to go ahead with it, and it was soon settled that he would meet Boswell in Edinburgh in early August.

Chapter 25

Writings; Continuing Religious Struggles

It was largely as a by-product of his life with the Thrales at this time and his friendly empathy with Henry Thrale as an active member of Parliament that Johnson wrote his four famous "political pamphlets"— *The False Alarm* (1770), *Thoughts Concerning the Late Transactions Respecting Falkland's Islands* (1771), *The Patriot* (1774), and *Taxation No Tyranny* (1775).

The pamphlets have for generations been singled out for special and usually unfavorable attention. There seem to be three reasons for this: (1) Until recently the overwhelming bulk of Johnson's political writing, which he did much earlier, was known, if at all, only superficially. (2) In contrast to such works as the *Parliamentary Debates* or the Vinerian lectures, these short polemical pamphlets, if one did not look too closely, might seem to fit in with the stock nineteenth-century picture, extrapolated from Boswell, of the "Tory" Johnson supporting "Tory" government (though, as a matter of fact, the pamphlets were really written in defense of policies of a Whig administration). (3) Because they appeared to spring out in a way so unmotivated, people were tempted to assume he was at last "earning his pension." In the days before speculation about a writer's sex life gave one an opportunity to appear to "have his number," this thought—though no one could demonstrate it—was so alluring that, repeated often enough, it entered into the pipeline of Johnson legend.

Actually he would never even have begun these pamphlets had it not been for the urging of the Thrales, who were constantly involved in the issues that engaged a conservative member of Parliament from the turbulent borough of Southwark. Even then Johnson needed prodding, as Baretti told Thomas Campbell (Baretti became Queeney's Italian teacher in 1773, and now lived out at Streatham); nor would Johnson, he said, have written the last two at all—*The Patriot* (1774) and *Taxation No Tyranny* (1775)—"had it not been for Mrs. Thrale & Baretti who stirred him up by laying wagers."[1] Even if we disregarded the background and decided to concentrate on the pamphlets for their political substance, they "tell little about his basic political attitudes," says Mr. Greene, "not expressed more thoughtfully elsewhere."[2] It is the earlier writing, supplemented by the Vinerian lectures, that provides the proper context for discussing Johnson's political views, and the broader implications of the thinking or general spirit behind these pamphlets is therefore subsumed by our earlier discussion.*

The first pamphlet, *The False Alarm* (1770), was written, said Mrs. Thrale, "at our house between eight o'clock Wednesday night and twelve o'clock on Thursday night; we read it to Mr. Thrale when he came very late home from the House of Commons."[3] This pamphlet, even more than the others, is distinguished by its vigor and sharp-pointed invective. That he thought it the best of the lot may tell us something of the spirit in which they were conceived—as frankly polemical pieces, that is, rather than as considered political discussion. *The False Alarm* is a defense of the decision of the House of Commons to reject the election of John Wilkes by the Middlesex voters. The engaging Wilkes had been prosecuted for libel and obscenity (the obscenity charge was for publishing at his private press an "indecent parody" of Pope's *Essay on Man* called *Essay on Woman*, with learned notes supposedly by Bishop Warburton). Abroad at the time, visiting his daughter in Paris, he did not return to receive sentence. He was consequently expelled from the House. Though he repeatedly got himself re-elected by the Middlesex voters, who cheered him on as a challenger to the Establishment, the House stood its ground.

The False Alarm, written in a knockabout style more popular in Johnson's younger days than it was now, cites precedents for the power of the House to pass on its own membership, and pokes fun at mob rule and populism generally. A remark on petitions is typical. As they are circulated from town to town, the inhabitants flock to stare at

---

* See above, pp. 191–200.

what they have heard will be "sent to the king." Signatures are easily collected:

One man signs because he hates the papists; another because he has vowed destruction to the turnpikes; one because it will vex the parson; another because he owes his landlord nothing; one because he is rich; another because he is poor; one to shew that he is not afraid, and another to shew that he can write.[4]

The remarks on riots and mobs are particularly amusing when we find that a few years later—by then he was sixty-five (1774)—Johnson himself, said George Steevens, served as the "ringleader" of a small riot. He and Steevens went to a performance of fireworks at Marylebone Gardens. Because of the wet weather, the crowd was small. The performance was canceled because the fireworks were said to be damp. "This is a mere excuse," cried Johnson, "to save their crackers for a more profitable company. Let us but hold up our sticks, and threaten to break those coloured lamps that surround the Orchestra, and we shall soon have our wishes gratified." And immediately a group of young men, hearing what he said, began to riot, though it turned out that the fireworks really were damp.[5]

Of more intellectual interest is the second pamphlet, dealing with the quarrel with Spain over the remote Falkland Islands, off the southern coast of South America. The administration had finally arrived at a peaceful agreement with Spain, in which the islands were to be regarded as Spanish yet administered by the British. But some of the opposition was clamoring for war. It is against this unthinking clamor that Johnson turns the best of the polemical passages in these pamphlets. In his *Thoughts on the Late Transactions Respecting Falkland's Islands* (1771), he speaks of the shocking unawareness with which most of humankind will see a war started. The drab horror and suffering of war is completely beyond their experience. What little they know of it has been picked up from colorful accounts of battles in "heroic fiction":

Of the thousands and ten thousands that perished in our late contests with France and Spain, a very small part ever felt the stroke of an enemy; the rest languished in tents and ships, amidst damps and putrefaction; pale, torpid, spiritless and helpless; gasping and groaning, unpitied among men made obdurate by long continuance of hopeless misery; and were at last whelmed in pits, or heaved into the ocean, without notice and without remembrance.[6]

2

Of the two remaining pamphlets, *The Patriot* (1774) is essentially a short election pamphlet written during a single day for Henry Thrale. It is worth notice because of its plea for religious toleration in defending the Quebec Act (1774), which, against the opposition of many of the American colonists, had tried to protect the religious and other rights of the French people in Canada.

Then came the fourth and last pamphlet, *Taxation No Tyranny* (March 8, 1775), in which, with a combination of heady impatience and legalistic ingenuity, he tried to answer the arguments of the American Congress. This final pamphlet is famous because of the historical importance of the issue—the first great threat of internal quarrel within the British Empire through the deepening division between the mother country and the American colonies. For two centuries both British and American readers, and curiously British more than American, have felt their reactions to Johnson caught on a minor snag when they come to this short pamphlet. It could seem so completely against history—not only history as it was to develop later, but as it was already in the process of being seen by so many people in England.

Two or three considerations should be kept in mind. One is Johnson's lifelong detestation of colonial and imperial expansion, and his conviction—which we have already been noticing—that the conquest of America was a gigantic form of European exploitation and robbery of the natives. To this was added his hatred of slavery, typified by that famous toast with which he suddenly startled a group of "very grave men at Oxford": "Here's to the next insurrection of the negroes in the West Indies!" No one of his time more consistently opposed slavery, and he viewed the procedure of the American Congress in appealing to abstract human rights as a form of profound hypocrisy ("How is it that we hear the loudest *yelps* for liberty among the drivers of Negroes"?). Moreover, he felt it only just for the colonists to help pay for their own defense against rival colonial powers. They had, he thought, been well treated compared with most of those who had stayed at home. They were no more deprived of "representation" than the majority of Englishmen at the time; and it was the taxation of these "unrepresented" Britons that was helping to pay for the colonists' security while they were gathering the advantages of a land peopled only by helpless natives. Finally the pamphlet could be considered partly as an attempt to score a debating point with a man he admired intellectually more than any other he knew—Edmund Burke ("the first man everywhere"; "a great man by nature"; "his stream of mind is perpetual"). The year before had seen Burke's memorable *Speech on American Taxation* (1774), and Johnson's pamphlet is in part trying to answer that speech, though he naturally avoids mentioning Burke by name. Nor did Burke, who equally admired Johnson, name him personally in the great speech *On Conciliation with the Colonies* (March 22, 1775), delivered shortly after *Taxation No Tyranny* appeared, though it systematically answers almost every point Johnson makes.

3

But the principal work of this period of recovery and comparative relaxation was very different from the pamphlets. This was a revision of the *Dictionary* for a new edition, at which he worked, off and on, from the summer of 1771 to October 1772.* In concluding this revision—for there was very little likelihood he would ever make another—he was giving a final farewell to the only thing he had done, as he himself viewed his life, that no one else in the English language had done: the one work in which he had approached his old ideal of the Renaissance scholar-Humanist, which went back to Cornelius and the two years he spent in Michael's bookshop, after the visit to Cornelius.

The thought of what lay ahead for him now, at sixty-three, haunted his mind as he took off a few weeks, after finishing the work, to make a visit to Lichfield and to John Taylor at Ashbourne. Returning to London on the coach in early December, he composed a poignant Latin poem that he wrote down (December 12) the day after he arrived home—a very private poem, for which he instinctively fell back on Latin to give himself formal distance: "Γνωθι σεαυτον (*Post Lexicon Anglicanum Auctem et Emendatum*)"—"*Know Thyself* (After the Revision and Correction of the English Dictionary"). It falls into two halves, the first of which turns to one of his Renaissance models, the

* The fourth edition, published in March 1773. He also wrote a Dedication for William Payne's *Elements of Trigonometry* (1772), a Preface for Alexander Macbean's *Dictionary of Ancient Geography* (1773), and helped John Hoole with the Preface to his *Present State of the East India Company's Affairs* (1772). For the revision of the Shakespeare (1773), left largely to Steevens, see above, p. 394.

great scholar Joseph Scaliger (1540–1609), who among many other works compiled an Arabic dictionary. "Bored with the slender achievement" of this kind of work, Scaliger (writes Johnson in this poem) prescribed the writing of dictionaries as a task "for condemned criminals." He was right. Scaliger was "fit for greater works"; and, when he was finished, a new and larger life indeed opened up for him. In comparison with that model, Johnson then weighs himself. Naturally the model is idealized largely in order to rebuke himself (and the Arabic lexicon was a minor work in comparison with Johnson's *Dictionary*).

By contrast with Scaliger, as Johnson now finds himself freed from his own task, "the harsh lot of slothful idleness awaits me, and black and gloomy leisure, more burdensome than any labour . . . and the bad dreams of an empty mind." He is now "forced to know myself better," with deeper honesty than before—to come back in his old age, as Yeats was later to say of himself, to the "foul rag-and-bone shop of the heart." And what does the heart tell him? "The Heart, now reviewing its gains, does not see the wealth of Intellect accumulated"— that is, wisdom genuinely assimilated and put to active use. Nor, serving as "its judge," does it—or can it—"accept" the honors offered by others. Instead (and the imagery, so often starkly existential in his major poetry, becomes more so now) the "Heart," surveying its own very personal kingdom, the self, "shudders at the wide regions silent in the night, where empty appearance and fleeting shadows . . . flit through the void." In what time remains to him,

What shall I do? Is it left to me to condemn my sluggish old age to darkness? Or should I gird myself boldly for weightier studies? Or, if this is too much, should I at last ask for—new dictionaries?[7]

4

When he had turned sixty-two, the year before he finished this revision, he was at last beginning to feel that the healing effect, in this new life with the Thrales, was proving more than temporary. And on the night of his birthday (September 18, 1771), he had written, "I am now come to my sixty-third year. For the last year I have been slowly recovering from the violence of my last illness"—the long breakdown of hope and finally of will that had reached its lowest point in his later fifties—"and, I think, from the general disease of my life." That hope was to continue throughout the year that followed, in which he finished revising the *Dictionary*.

But though the traumatic period of his fifties could now seem behind him (and perhaps even the "general disease" of his life, of which his mental distress at that time was an extreme manifestation), the fact remained that the years were beginning to close in on him. Long ago he had remarked, partly to warn himself, on the way in which hope is increasingly replaced by memory as we move into upper middle age and beyond, if only because the years that might provide hope begin rapidly to shorten. So with him now during the coming months. Though it could seem to him particularly absurd in his own case, since so little of his past life was a joy to recall, his mind was turning too often "with a very *useless* earnestness upon past incidents. I have yet got no command over my thoughts."[8]

Now more than ever it seemed to him necessary, in such time as remained, "to confirm myself in the conviction of the truths of Religion." Significantly this comes at the start of a list of the usual "resolutions" ("To rise by eight, or earlier"; "To form a plan for the *regulation* of my daily life"). That it should take the form of a "resolution" is one of a hundred reminders of how grotesquely far from the truth is the stock notion of Johnson as a conventional Church of England man who differed from others only in the superior firmness of his beliefs and his militant sectarianism (actually he thought that "all Christians, whether Papists or Protestants, agree in their essential articles, and that their differences were trivial, and rather political than religious," and he could remind Mrs. Mary Knowles, "Have we heard all that a disciple of Confucius, all that a Mahometan, can say for himself?").[9] In one way only does the stock picture of Johnson's religious life have much truth: that is, in the *importance* of religion for him. But religion for Johnson, at least in its deeper implications, involved far more of inner struggle (as well as being a far more private concern) than the conventional picture of him could even begin to suggest. Significantly this deeply religious man never felt qualified to write directly or at any length about religion itself, at least under his own name. Here more than with any other subject, the inner censorship imposed by his conscience was almost complete. Hence the only writing specifically concerned with religion—as distinct from what he states briefly or indirectly in his other writing—is confined to the "Prayers and Meditations" that survive from his private journals or the sermons he ghost-wrote for others. Of these sermons (he said that he wrote at least forty), the greater number consist of those written for his friend John Taylor, which were published after Taylor's death.[10]

5

At the center of his religious struggle were two things in particular, both of which we have been noticing in other contexts as well. Neither of them proved a determining obstacle, but, acting in combination, they greatly complicated his hope for religious understanding and acceptance, and turned it into more of an effort (with the further psychological complications that "effort" involves) than it would otherwise have been. One was the problem of evil, which, as he tried to digest or assimilate it and to turn his aggressive protests inward rather than outward, had been a strong element in the long period of psychological distress during his fifties. More than most people, he found it difficult to accept calmly Elihu's answer to Job's protest—that the wisdom and justice of God are unsearchable to the human mind; that we must accept the fact of evil as a "mystery." Not that Johnson did not try ("Enquirer, cease"—as he wrote at the end of *The Vanity of Human Wishes*—"petitions *yet* remain, / Which heav'n *may* hear . . ."). But the language is always restive and seethes with inner protest. Moreover, any attempt to accept "mystery" ran counter to a quality that years of having to fight his own way had built into him. Mrs. Thrale remarked on Johnson's "fixed incredulity of everything he heard," and said that it "amounted almost to disease." Naturally he drew a line when he came to revealed religion. But it was not easy to suppress completely a habit so thoroughly ingrained, and on one occasion, as Boswell noted, he came "near Hume's argument against miracles." In any case, it was a line he himself drew consciously and with some effort, and to which he could come very close. When Lord Lyttelton's prediction of the time of his own death was mentioned, Johnson said, "I am so glad to have every evidence of the spiritual world, that I am willing to believe it." Dr. Adams: "You have evidence enough; good evidence, which needs not such support." Johnson: "I like to have more."[11]

Since his nature was such that he could never remain content with "mystery," his tendency for years—and increasingly now in his sixties —was to grasp at the idea of an afterlife as the principal, almost the sole possible, means of justifying the fact that "the only thinking being of this globe is doomed to think merely to be wretched, and to pass his time from youth to age in fearing or suffering calamities":

It is scarcely to be imagined, that Infinite Benevolence would create a being capable of enjoying so much more than is here to be enjoyed, and qualified by nature to prolong pain by remembrance and anticipate it by terror, if he was not designed for something nobler and better than a state, in which many of his faculties can serve only for his torment. . . .

"Fear," said Mrs. Thrale, "was indeed a sensation to which Mr. Johnson was an utter stranger, except when some sudden apprehension seized him that he was going to die." But it was a fear, as his friends noticed, that started up at the *idea* of death; for at the same time he could show an imperturbable courage in the face of dangers (if he feared death, said Boswell, "he feared nothing else, not even what might occasion death").[12] In short, it was strongest when he was considering it theoretically or *in abstracto,* and doubt had a sudden chance to express itself about what death could prove or disprove. As a boy (as he told Mrs. Thrale in his story about reading Grotius's *De Veritate Religionis*), he had first begun "to deduce the soul's immortality" from "the pain which guilt had given him" after neglecting to try to find out more about religion.* The conception of "immortality"—"the point that belief first *stopped* at" for him—made him suddenly more open to the truth of religion. Since then the years had confirmed in him a habit of mind in which he unconsciously, and sometimes more than unconsciously, came close to demanding proof of immortality as a proof of religious truth.

The deepening anxiety about death in his later years is greatly over-simplified, therefore, when we attribute it merely to a literal belief in damnation (prompted by guilt for secret and colorful sins), and become too literal ourselves in interpreting passages like the following:

JOHNSON. ". . . As I cannot be *sure* that I have fulfilled the conditions on which salvation is granted, I am afraid I may be one of those who shall be damned." (looking dismally). DR. ADAMS. "What do you mean by damned?" JOHNSON. (*passionately and loudly*) "Sent to Hell, Sir, and punished ever-lastingly." DR. ADAMS. "I don't believe that doctrine." . . . [Johnson] was in gloomy agitation, and said, "I'll have no more on't."

But the truth is that for Johnson there was a far worse alternative to damnation. It could be expressed by a remark John Wesley once made in a letter to his brother Charles (1766): "If I have any fear, it is not

* See above, p. 41.

of falling into hell, but of falling into nothing." For years, said Arthur Murphy, one could sometimes hear Johnson muttering to himself the lines from *Paradise Lost*,

> for who would lose,
> Though full of pain, this intellectual being . . .

and the passage from *Measure for Measure* beginning,

> Ay, but to die and go we know not where;
> To lie in cold obstruction and to rot. . . .

And when Anna Seward said that at least one fear of death was groundless, "the dread of annihilation, which is only a pleasing dream," he replied, "It is neither pleasing, nor sleep; it is nothing. Now mere existence is so much better than nothing, that one would rather exist even in pain. . . ."[13] And beneath those uneasy outbursts, in which he is trying to convince himself rather than someone else ("passionately and loudly"), is a far deeper anxiety: a need, through conviction of a future after death (at whatever risk), to find an explicit purpose or meaning for human suffering in this world; a strongly suspicious and starkly existential dread, which he needed constantly to repress, that this purpose might not be found; and a "displacement" of that larger anxiety by a more simplified, partly self-imposed dread in which, though he himself might be weighed in the balance and found wanting, the universe would at least make sense.

Given his nature, and his lifelong habit of expecting the worst (however much he condemned the habit), he could hardly impose on his skeptical and turbulent nature a concept of afterlife in which he had only to contemplate, with smug self-satisfaction or thoughtless abandon, a state of eternal bliss as a reward for this strange purgatorial tramp he had made through life. Everything in his experience had taught him to resist any thought that happiness was just around the corner. A future life could be driven into him and felt as *real* only if there were also something to dread. Hence the startling remark he jotted down in one of the journals (1777), where it appears without any context: "Faith in some proportion to Fear."[14]

6

The second continuing hurdle for him personally—though it would have presented fewer problems to a less turbulent and rebellious nature

—was his constant temptation to become impatient at "publick worship" and to rely on private devotion, particularly prayer. This naturally meant that the task of controlling and focusing thoughts became far more a matter of self-responsibility than it would otherwise have been, and that opportunities for self-examination and self-blame, in the very act of religious devotion, were immensely increased. To say such a thing flies in the face of the cherished stereotype of Johnson standing up for ritual (as close to half of him could sincerely do, and much more than half could do theoretically, with only too close a personal knowledge of what he thought the "dangers" of "private worship"); or of Johnson declaiming against the Dissenters, particularly the Quakers or some of the Methodists, with their belief in the "Inner Light" ("a principle utterly incompatible with social or civil security"; for "If a man pretends to a principle of action of which I know nothing, nay, not so much as that he *has* it . . . how can I tell what that person may be prompted to do?"); or of Johnson reproving those, like Milton, who rely too much on private devotion, and stressing the importance of organized and communal worship: "To be of no church is dangerous. Religion, of which the rewards are distant and which is animated only by Faith and Hope, will glide by degrees out of the mind unless it be invigorated and reimpressed by external ordinances, by stated calls to worship, and the salutary influence of example."[15] Other remarks could easily be quoted that appear to justify the stereotype. In his religious life Johnson's battle to resist the temptations of excessive self-reliance—one of his most deeply implanted characteristics—was unceasing.

But the struggle was hardly one he cared to reveal publicly, and what others saw were the victories, real or apparent, or the ideal to which he clung rather than what he was trying to oppose in himself. By 1773, for example, he had taken a seat at St. Clement Danes, in the balcony over the pulpit. Boswell, on a spring visit to London, attended two services with him there on Good Friday, noting that "his behaviour was, as I had imaged to myself, solemnly devout." Johnson's own remark in his journal for that day (April 9) gives a different impression. He had been very irregular, he says, in attending church that winter, but "did not wholly omit it." Today "I found the service not burthensome nor tedious, though I could not hear the lessons. I hope in time to take pleasure in publick Worship." Similarly, he was fond of maintaining, said Miss Reynolds, that "Man's chief merit consists in resisting the impulses of his nature." He accordingly attacked Lord Kames for arguing that "virtue is natural to man, and that if we would but consult our own hearts we should be virtuous. Now after consulting our own hearts . . . we find how few of us are virtuous." Yet despite his resolutions to resist "impulse" and attend church regularly, another part of him felt he should go only if properly receptive and, said Hawkins, "from an opinion peculiar to himself, seemed to wait for some secret impulse as a motive to it."[16]

The hope to "take pleasure in publick Worship" (sometimes better described as a "resolve") persists all through the journals. But it is a hope that runs counter to his lifelong habit of trying to "manage" his own mind. He once admitted to Boswell that he "went more frequently to church when there were prayers only than when there was also a sermon." The reason for this, he added, was that people generally "required more an example" when there were only prayers, "it being much easier for them to hear a sermon, than to fix their minds on prayer." In giving this as his reason, he apparently neglected to see the implication of what he was saying—that his primary motive for attendance was to serve as an "example" for others. But it was largely a rationalization. The truth is that, to someone who had thought as much about religion and human life as he had, most sermons at church could be regarded as an affront to the intellect, distracting him from his habitual efforts to answer his own inner objections and settle his mind. At the least it could create a feeling of extreme impatience. In a disarming moment he confessed as much to George Steevens:

> I am convinced I ought to be present at divine service more frequently than I am; but the *provocations* given by ignorant and affected preachers too often disturb the mental calm which otherwise would succeed to prayer. I am apt to whisper to myself on such occasions—How can this illiterate fellow dream of fixing attention, after we have been listening to the sublimest truths, conveyed in the most chaste and exalted language.

But he at once added:

> *Take notice, however*—though I make this confession respecting *myself*, I do not mean to *recommend the fastidiousness* that led me to exchange congregational for solitary worship.[17]

The word "fastidiousness" is typical. For of course he is trying to remind himself—as a part of him never ceases to do in other contexts— of the futility of the attenuated tastes and of gestures of disdain ("elegance refined into impatience") of intellectuals who forget, for the moment, how completely and helplessly they share the collective "doom of man" ("Nor think the doom of man reversed for thee," as he tells the young scholar in *The Vanity of Human Wishes*).

7

Johnson is probably the most extraordinary example in modern times of a man who in his own character concretely and dramatically exemplifies the Augustinian tradition of individualism and "interiority"—that "it is within the soul itself that man must search for truth and certitude" (*in interiore homine habitat veritas*)—and yet, far from welcoming it or turning to it with conscious choice, distrusted and in many ways tried to resist it. In this respect, he is of enormous interest in illustrating the transition to the modern inwardness of the religious life and the problems of elusiveness and self-doubt that attended it. His instinctive sympathies were with those forms of Protestantism that had found Augustine the most congenial of the early Church writers precisely because of Augustine's stress on the irreplaceable subjectivity of the religious experience and a theology of grace conceived in terms of the *personal* conversion to God of the reflectively conscious individual.[18] But if the Augustinian emphasis on personal responsibility is carried far enough, public worship (as Johnson knew or rather feared from his own experience) can begin to seem a distraction or at least a dilution. The burden is rather on individual prayer, as it was very much for Johnson.

Yet "prayer," of all forms of devotion, was by definition the most vulnerable to "the treachery of the human heart," as he had long ago said in that ominous line in *The Vanity of Human Wishes*—"The secret ambush of a specious pray'r." Coming from the subjective self, it could only too easily carry with it the contaminations, the stains or sediment of the irrational—the greed, the self-destructive impulses, the conflicting and shortsighted obsessions and fears. We noticed before that remark he made, with transparent candor, when James Beattie confessed he was "at times troubled with shocking, impious thoughts": "If I was to divide my life into three parts," said Johnson, "two of them would have been filled with such thoughts." In "solitary worship," unless one was genuinely sharing in God's grace, one could end by trying to fight the subjective with the subjective.

Moreover, in his own case, too exclusive a reliance on "solitary worship" could also mean a constant wrestle with what Lucy Porter thought his most characteristic quality—with his almost habitual tendency to disagree and, if not to resist or contradict, at least to start to qualify; with his profound distrust of the fearful unpredictabilities of life; and with his habitual feeling of self-responsibility for preliminary scanning and having all his guards posted in preparation for the next catastrophe. Here especially he was in danger, as he knew, of falling into a psychological bind: of assuming an almost personal responsibility for learning not to be too responsible but for learning instead (what he had listed as a "resolution" in 1765) "to consider the act of prayer as a reposal of myself upon God, and a resignation of all into his holy hand."

Of course, one solution—and it was a solution to which he was always turning in practice, since he was incapable of surrendering "private" meditation and prayer as the principal means of controlling his thoughts—was to reconsider the proper function of "prayer": to limit and focus it in such a way as to exclude from it the abuse of prayer for what is really nothing more than another expression of the universal "disease of wishing." If prayer is no more than the impulsive projection of the impurities of personal wish, it can hardly deserve the "reversal" of the universal process. Moreover, if prayer is only a stylized expression of wish, who, if he really probed his heart, could be confident of the complete sincerity of his prayer—confident that he was really praying with a whole rather than a divided mind that would not quickly be wanting to supplement, qualify, or correct that original wish, like the girl in his little allegory, "The Fountains"? Had not all of his moral writing turned, time and again, on all that was implied in the title of *The Vanity of Human Wishes* ("Fate wings with every wish th' afflictive dart")? Hence, developing a conception of prayer from a man he greatly admired, Robert South (prayer should be "an *act of dependence* upon God"), he himself stresses that the principal use of prayer is "to preserve in the mind" a "constant dependence on God." The quote is from one of the sermons he wrote for John Taylor. Personal "wish," in short, is to be excluded. If this could lead to a very austere ideal of prayer, it at least avoided (or could help one to avoid) "the secret ambush of a specious pray'r." Moreover, his own prayers—as distinct from the personal "resolutions" often printed with them—are in keeping with this conception, which is why they have often struck readers as rather stark. Specific wishes, on the whole, are scrupulously kept out of them lest they sully the purity of prayer (even when he is most ill, he tends to be reluctant to let prayer turn into a request for recovery, though he afterward gives thanks when recovery comes). Almost invariably the prayers for help (as distinct from purely formal prayers or prayers of thanks) have one central theme—his search for help in learning to "live more in accordance with God's law" and thus for becoming in actual practice more "dependent upon God." Even here care is taken not to trivialize them by focusing on specific acts of moral reform (which are presumably his own personal responsibility) but to keep such prayers on a general plane: to learn repentance, to learn hope and not to despair, to learn not to waste his "remaining days" but to "use thy gifts to thy glory," and to acquire a deeper sense of God's "mercy and forbearance."

Beneath this firmly confined conception of prayer was also the hope that it could itself, if one strictly adhered to it, *create* the "trust in God" that he wanted so deeply to find. Of the sermons he wrote for John Taylor—the nearest thing we have to a considered statement of his religious convictions—only one is devoted to trust in God (No. 14), a subject on which he did not feel he could speak with authority; and significantly, even in this sermon, the bulk of it is devoted—as in *The Vanity of Human Wishes* and in so much of his writing generally—to saying, in effect, that no other trust is possible. We have nowhere else to turn. But in one place in this sermon he does try to state, as much to himself as to anyone else, *how* this "trust" can be achieved. It can come to us only in the hardest way: "He that hopes to find peace by trusting God, must *obey* him."

In other words, we must not demand "trust" in advance as a reason or incentive to obey religious dictates. We begin by obeying, by *acting* in conscience, with the result that the trust then follows, creatively earned and acquired by ourselves. The thought is somewhat like the famous "James-Lange theory of emotion," where feeling need not proceed but can follow and be itself created by *act* (*e.g.*, to act with courage begins to give us courage, or to act lovingly begins to give us the feeling of love). "This constant and devout *practice*," said Johnson, "is both the effect, and cause, of *confidence* in God"—the assumption being that the growing "confidence" in ourselves, as we obey the dictates of conscience, allows us to be more "confident" in God Himself. In this important sermon, we find in solution all of Johnson's own struggles for "trust in God"—his eagerness to find "grace," and yet his immediate wariness lest the subjective self be deluded; his clutch at anxiety about damnation and the future life as a means of offering *testimonials* to the sincerity of his belief (as though agonizing enough about it—like clubbing his pride and standing in the rain at Uttexeter market, "exposed to the sneers of the standers-by"—would prove that he was not "wishing" but rather genuinely "fearing"):

Trust in God . . . is to be obtained only by repentance, obedience, and supplication, not by nourishing in our hearts a confused idea of the goodness of God, or a firm persuasion that we are in a state of grace; by which some have been deceived. . . . We are not to imagine ourselves safe, only because we are not harassed with those anxieties about our future state with which others are tormented, but which . . . so far from being proofs of reprobation . . . are more frequently evidences of piety, and a sincere and fervent desire of pleasing God.[19]

8

Yet this, as he knew, was only a partial answer. However strictly hedged the conception of prayer, he was still placing, in practice if not theory, the overwhelming weight of religious obligation upon "private" devotion.

He could feel caught in a dilemma. For his basic approach to religion was so profoundly moral—and moral in a way that could not be amputated from self-responsibility—that it was inevitably private between himself and God. In this respect, a large part of him felt that he no more needed to be prodded or "encumbered with help" from other people or even from "congregational worship" than he had needed Dame Oliver to help him as an infant over the muddy road home from his school. Yet no one knew better the liabilities of "solitary worship." In fact, the "solitary mortal," as he once said impulsively to Mrs. Thrale, is "probably superstitious, and possibly mad."[20]

There were still further complications for a nature trying by itself to digest and turn inward a massive protest against the suffering of human life. Up to a point this was desirable in a being that has free will and can be truly "moral" only if it is willing to accept responsibility. But beyond that point it was a form of "pride," and ultimately even a form of madness, as he had shown in the astronomer in *Rasselas* who ended up feeling responsible for controlling the weather of the whole world. In this reliance on reaching God in and through moral conscience (*in interiore homine habitat veritas*, as Augustine said), there is inevitably some projection in which "fancy and conscience . . . so often shift their places that the illusions of one are not distinguished from the dictates of the other." Certainly in his own case he was in constant danger of projecting upon God not "a confused idea of the goodness of God," based on unthinking self-satisfaction, but a harshness created by his own fierce self-demand. Hence the "scruples" of conscience constantly stealing over him that he had to battle in himself. He could only pray for help in learning to *accept* the fact of "God's mercy and forbearance," and to use his good sense in trying to remember what he had Imlac tell the astronomer: "Keep this thought always prevalent, that you are only one atom of the mass of humanity, and have neither such virtue nor vice as that you should be singled out for supernatural favors or afflictions."

9

He had no choice but to continue to wrestle with the situation—a struggle, year after year, that was nothing less than heroic, especially since he was bringing to it qualifications that, from his own point of view, were far from ideal.

If he was on a quest or a journey, he could at no point feel that he had arrived. Least of all was he qualified to teach others on this all-important subject of religion, though people were already beginning to look on him as a father figure who could and should do so. Twenty years before, when he began the *Rambler*, he had thought to keep his authorship secret lest he bring disgrace on what he wrote (No. 14). But then he was writing only of moral concerns. That same reticence was immeasurably deepened when he came to the subject of religion. He could write directly about it only when he could speak vicariously with a different voice, and his capacity for self-blame and for noting anything in himself that savored of hypocrisy or self-delusion could be deflected. It was particularly easy to write sermons when the persona was gratifyingly different from his own character—as when he wrote one for the carefree Henry Hervey or the whole group of sermons for the worldly John Taylor, who had always brushed aside Johnson's mental problems and who seemed refreshingly free from the burdens of excessive conscience.

In his own life—as he was soon to tell Mr. Edwards, whom he had known a half century before at Pembroke College—he was an old "straggler." But however reductively he described himself—a "Rambler," then an "Idler," and finally a "straggler"—his life for years had really been that of a "pilgrim," which is why he so deeply identified, as we saw, with *Pilgrim's Progress*. A "pilgrim," he had said in the *Dictionary*, is "a wanderer, particularly one who travels on a religious account." He was to remain, by his own definition, a "pilgrim" until the end.

Chapter 26

Travel: the Hebrides;
Wales

The idea of travel had haunted Johnson's imagination since he was a boy, when his father had put in his hands a copy of Martin's *Description of the Western Islands of Scotland*. It was about travel that the Master of Pembroke College heard him musing aloud to himself one day ("I'll go to the universities abroad. I'll go to France and Italy. I'll go to Padua . . ."), and it tells us something that Johnson's first book was a translation of a *Voyage to Abyssinia*.

But until his fifties, when he received the pension, travel—which cost relatively much more in the eighteenth century than now—was completely out of the question. Inevitably he would at times become self-defensive about his lot. He would praise the variety of London life, and would make remarks about the futility of travel as it was pursued by most people (he was usually referring to those who flocked like sheep to fashionable resort areas). Because of this, the Victorians extrapolated a sort of caricature of him, which is still a part of popular Johnson legendry, as a "confirmed Londoner" who dismissed travel, as Macaulay said, "with the fierce and boisterous contempt of ignorance." A more truthful picture is found in the little sketch Johnson wrote of "Omar, the son of Hussan" (*Idler* 101), which is partly a self-portrait. Omar all his life had "wished to see distant countries," and was now entering old age having "always resided in the same city."

When the pension was finally awarded him, Johnson said, "Had this happened twenty years ago, I should have gone to Constantinople to learn Arabick." By now he had become constitutionally incapable of spending money on himself. Moreover, during his middle and late fifties, he was in such psychological distress that he was reluctant to be away from the Thrales. But there were, of course, short trips. "He loved indeed the very act of travelling," said Mrs. Thrale, and was "an admirable companion on the road, as he piqued himself upon feeling no inconvenience, and on despising no accommodations." Any discomforts seemed so minor in comparison with the advantages of travel that he would dismiss complaints from others about "the rain, the sun, or the dust," or about inns or long confinement in a coach, as "proofs of an empty head, and a tongue desirous to talk without materials of conversation. A mill that goes without grist (said he) is as good a companion as such creatures." He was surprised that a visitor at the Thrales' who had been in Bohemia seemed unwilling to talk about anything. "Surely," he said later, "the man who has seen Prague might tell us something new and something strange, and not sit silent for want of matter to put his lips in motion." If he had enough money, he told Mrs. Thrale, the first use to which he would put it, old as he was, would be to go to Cairo, and then sail down the Red Sea to Bengal and journey through India. A recurring daydream was to visit someday the Great Wall of China, and one of his cherished possessions was a stone from the Wall.[1]

2

On Boswell's first trip to London, Johnson told him (July 1763) he would like to visit the Hebrides, mentioned how he had read Martin's book about them when he was a boy, and suggested that they take a trip there together when Boswell returned from the Continent. Boswell thought this a "very romantick fancy." Even to most Scotsmen, the islands, as Johnson said, seemed as remote as "Borneo or Sumatra."[2] Inevitably, given the pressures and problems both were facing in their own lives, the matter was postponed.

But in a few years Boswell realized not only that Johnson was in earnest but also that the trip would provide a valuable opportunity for himself. He was by now planning a biography of Johnson that would consist as far as possible of Johnson's actual talk. Yet compared with other people, especially the Thrales, he was not seeing much of Johnson. If they did make this trip to the Hebrides, he would have at least three months in Johnson's company, and in picturesque situations where he could record conversations in a way no one else would ever be in a position to do. There was an added attraction to Boswell's poetic imagination and also to his vanity. A trip of this kind could seem almost a re-enactment of Johnson's own *Rasselas*—journeying to strange lands in the company of a sage. The difference would be that in the story it was the sage Imlac who conducted the tour, whereas now it would be as though the young Rasselas were serving as guide and escort to Imlac—in fact, the "original" Imlac—while inducing him as they went along to comment on "men and manners."

In the spring of 1773, almost ten years after Johnson first mentioned to him this "very romantick fancy," Boswell was in London for several weeks (April 2 to May 10). By now he was thirty-two, and Johnson was sixty-three. If only because of Johnson's age, the trip should not be postponed much longer. Boswell could see that he was often far from well this spring. Moreover, the journey would be arduous once they got into the Highlands. Much of the time they would be traveling on horseback over wild and mountainous country. The weather could be stormy when they reached the Hebrides, and they would often be in places where there would be no inns. Boswell urged that they start on the trip in August this year (he himself, as a lawyer, was not free until the Court of Session rose on August 12). Johnson agreed. This visit to London was a happy one for Boswell. To his delight, he was made a member of The Club (April 30). Though Burke and a few others doubted whether he had the mental qualifications, everyone valued his good nature.

As soon as he returned to Scotland, Boswell began to make arrangements for the trip and to line up people for Johnson to meet. He was worried about the serious inflammation in Johnson's good eye. But Johnson, partly at Mrs. Thrale's urging, did not back down. He wrote that he would leave on Friday, August 6. He traveled as far as Newcastle with Robert Chambers, who had been appointed a judge of the Supreme Court of Bengal and who wanted to visit his family in Newcastle before leaving for India. Then, with another friend, the lawyer William Scott, he went on to Edinburgh.

3

He arrived in Edinburgh at Boyd's Inn Saturday evening, August 14, and sent a note to Boswell, who immediately came to fetch him. William Scott told Boswell that, while they were waiting for him, Johnson had just experienced a bad introduction to "Scottish cleanliness." He had ordered lemonade, and then asked for more sugar for it. The waiter, whose fingers were greasy, lifted up a lump and dropped it in the glass. At this, Johnson indignantly tossed the lemonade out of the window and Scott was afraid he was about to knock the waiter down.

As they walked to Boswell's house, where Johnson was to lodge, the "evening effluvia of Edinburgh," said Boswell, was very strong. There were no covered sewers at that time. As they walked, Johnson said in his ear, "I *smell you* in the dark." When they arrived, Mrs. Boswell had tea ready for him. He was pleased at this attention, and touched that she insisted on giving up her own bedroom for him. But she soon became annoyed at his irregular hours and such habits as turning the candles upside down so that they would burn more brightly when he read. She did not approve of the trip they were making, and said a little heatedly to her husband, "I have seen many a bear led by a man; but I never before saw a man led by a bear." During the next three days, they made a tour of the city, and Johnson met and talked with several people, including the eminent historian William Robertson, the pioneer sociologist Adam Ferguson, and the blind poet Thomas Blacklock.[3]

On Wednesday, August 18, they set off, taking with them Boswell's servant, Joseph Ritter, a tall Bohemian who could speak several languages. Johnson wore boots and a wide brown greatcoat with enormous pockets in which he could carry miscellaneous items. He also had a large oak stick that he had fixed up to do double duty as a measuring stick (a nail was driven in it at the length of a foot and another at a yard). Partly as a guide and partly for sentimental reasons, he brought along Martin's *Description of the Western Islands* (1703). The Highlands were no longer the violent place they had been in Martin's time. Of course, Johnson had read later books, especially Thomas Pennant's *A Tour in Scotland* (1772). Even so, from a mistaken notion that they might be meeting robbers, Johnson had brought with him a pair of pistols and a supply of gunpowder and bullets. Boswell persuaded him to leave these in a drawer at his home, where Johnson also deposited a "full and curious Diary" that he later destroyed (Boswell wished his wife's curiosity "had been strong enough to have it all transcribed . . . the theft, being *pro bono publico*, might have been forgiven," but she did not bother to look at it).[4]

The plan of the trip, which was to take about twelve weeks, was to go straight north through Aberdeen along the eastern coast of Scotland

and then turn west and follow the northern coast to Inverness. After this they would have to give up the carriage and change to horseback, dip south along Loch Ness, and at Fort Augustus turn and go directly to the west coast. From there they would cross over to Skye and the Hebrides, and then return to Edinburgh through the Lowlands, stopping briefly at Auchinleck, the house of Boswell's father.

Their first stop (August 18–19) was at St. Andrews, which Johnson had longed to see as the seat of the oldest university in Scotland and the place where George Buchanan taught—the Renaissance Humanist whom Johnson thought the greatest Latin scholar Britain had yet produced. The professors at the university were very cordial. But St. Andrews had lost its former splendor; the university had shrunk; the cathedral, since the change of religion in Scotland, had gone to ruin and been dismantled; the town itself had lost population. The appearance of decay and depopulation, at this first place where they stopped, made a vivid impression that was to continue to haunt him throughout the trip so that, when he finally wrote about his journey, the depopulation of the Highlands becomes one of his prevailing themes.

From St. Andrews they went north to Aberdeen, stopping for part of a day (August 21) to visit Lord Monboddo (James Burnett) at his estate. Monboddo, a Scottish judge who was also a pioneer anthropologist, had just brought out the first volume of his celebrated work *Of the Origin and Progress of Language* (1773–92), which maintained that man and the higher apes belonged to the same species. He was also an ardent "primitivist," who extolled the superior health and virtue of primitive life and believed that the human race, cut off from "natural" life, was in a state of decline. In the country he enjoyed the opportunity to live simply as "Farmer Burnett," and he was wearing a rustic suit and "a little round hat." Johnson always instinctively resisted any notion of "decline" as a reflection on man's freedom of will, and they had a short but friendly dispute whether a savage or a London shopkeeper had the better existence—Monboddo taking the side of the savage and Johnson the shopkeeper, though, as he said later, he would probably have argued for the savage "had anybody else taken the side of the shopkeeper." They also talked of Homer, of the value of the "history of manners" and of biography. Within a few weeks Johnson was to begin to refer affectionately to Monboddo as "Mony."[5]

From Aberdeen (August 22–23), where Johnson talked with professors at the university and was given the freedom of the city, they went along the northern coast through Elgin and Fort George to Inverness (August 28–29), where they made a tour of the city. One of the most delightful moments in the tour—at least to read about—took place at this time. For whatever reason, Boswell did not record it. Perhaps he was not present at this particular moment, or he may not have wished to record it. At the inn where they were staying, some people came in to visit Johnson on the evening of a solemn Scottish Sunday, including the Reverend Alexander Grant. During the conversation, said Grant, Johnson was in "high spriits," and mentioned that Joseph Banks (afterward Sir Joseph) had discovered in Australia an "extraordinary animal called the *kangaroo*." In order to render his description more vivid, Johnson rose from his chair and

volunteered an imitation of the animal. The company stared . . . nothing could be more ludicrous than the appearance of a tall, heavy, grave-looking man, like Dr. Johnson, standing up to mimic the shape and motions of a kangaroo. He stood erect, put out his hands like feelers, and, gathering up the tails of his huge brown coat so as to resemble the pouch of the animal, made two or three vigorous bounds across the room![6]

4

Leaving Inverness on horseback, they rode south along Loch Ness, and at one place saw an old woman at the door of a hut. Johnson wanted to see the inside of the hut, which was very primitive—a fire of peat, with smoke going out of a hole in the roof. They had brought with them two Highlanders, on leaving Inverness, who could help guide them and also speak Erse—the only language many of the people here knew. Johnson, looking about the hut, asked where the old woman slept. When the guide translated this into Erse, she became very indignant. She thought this meant Johnson wanted to go to bed with her. So ludicrous a notion amused Johnson greatly. But he would not "hurt her delicacy" by inquiring further. However, Boswell—his own curiosity now aroused—lit a piece of paper and poked his head into the place, behind a wicker partition, where she slept.

By September 1 they reached Glenelg on the west coast, from which they were to cross over to Skye. It had been an exhausting day. They had to get over a very steep mountain, Mam Rattachan, and for the first time Johnson—in his effort to suppress thoughts of growing age and decrepitude—began to fall into ill humor. As he grumbled to himself, one of the guides made an effort to cheer him, and, as though Johnson were a sulky child, called out "See such pretty goats!" and then whistled to make the goats jump. Johnson retreated into silence. When they descended from the mountain it was dusk, and because there were several miles still to go, Boswell—without thinking to mention his reason—started to ride rapidly ahead to Glenelg to make sure there would be accommodations for them. Johnson "called me back with a tremendous shout, and was really in a passion with me for leaving him." Boswell tried to explain, but Johnson brushed it aside, saying, "I should as soon think of picking a pocket" as doing what Boswell had done, adding that "such a thing made one lose confidence in him who did it, as one could not tell what he would do next."[7]

The next day they sailed over to the Isle of Skye, by far the largest of the Inner Hebrides, where they were to spend the next month, except for a short visit to the adjoining island of Raasay (September 8–12). Their hosts at Armadale, where they landed, were the miserly Sir Alexander Macdonald and his strange wife, Elizabeth. Lady Macdonald fascinated Johnson, and she kept recurring to his mind throughout the rest of the trip. Though she occasionally "made a kind of jumping," as if to express joy, she in general seemed half dead, or like someone "cut out of a cabbage." "The difference between that woman when alive," said Johnson, "and when she shall be dead, is only this. When alive she calls for beer. When dead she'll call for beer no longer." In fact, she so intrigued Johnson that he added her to his repertoire of imitations, "leaning forward with a hand on each cheek and her mouth open."* She tended to talk at the table with her mouth crammed with food, and Johnson later created another imitation of her addressing the butler ("Thomson, some wine and water!") while her mouth was still full.[8]

Throughout September, as they traveled about Skye, the weather was often stormy, and they began to realize that they had made the trip a month or six weeks too late. September, as Johnson said, marks "the beginning of the Highland winter"—consisting largely of rain and wind—and by October, when they were planning to see some of the smaller islands, the seas could become very rough.

5

The trip—despite the change in the weather, which Johnson viewed with proud disregard—was proving an immense success. At times he was not well, though he kept this to himself. When physical effort was

* For an account of it, see below, p. 487.

needed, his rheumatism and bronchitis could remind him that he was no longer young. He was not pleased when Boswell, "with some of his troublesome kindness," informed the McLeod family that September 18 was his birthday, the mention of which (he is writing to Mrs. Thrale) "fills me with thoughts which it seems to be the general care of humanity to escape"; and as they passed "mountains which I should once have climbed . . . I am now content with knowing that by a scrambling up a rock, I shall only see other rocks. . . ."[9] But he was plunging into things with a gusto almost incredible in a man of his age.

As a result, the conversations were going as merrily as Boswell could ever have wished. The detailed journal he was keeping proved so rich a record of Johnson's talk that he sensibly decided, after Johnson's death, to publish it (or a revised version of it) in advance—*The Journal of a Tour to the Hebrides with Samuel Johnson, L.L.D.* (1786)—as a sort of trial balloon before going ahead with his *Life of Johnson.* Because of the exuberance Johnson felt, and the stimulus of new surroundings and new people, he could be led, as never before, to speak about anything, sometimes with Boswell alone but far more often with the Scots, High and Low, whom he was meeting. He would talk about law and jurisprudence, the nature of genius, and the problem of evil; laziness, food and cooking, education, and the psychology of gratitude; the genuineness (which Johnson had long doubted) of James Macpherson's supposed translations of early Gaelic poetry;* "primitivism" and the effect of "luxury"; stage-acting, threshing grain and thatching roofs, economics, the Trinity, and the uses of biography. The most casual thing could be lit up as he spoke. As an admiring physician on the island of Mull said—Dr. Alexander Maclean—"This man is just a *hogshead of sense!*" The subject of smoking, for example, would come up. Though he himself did not smoke, he had a "high opinion" of it as one more means of composing the mind. It had recently taken a sudden decline as a habit. Johnson could not believe this disappearance of smoking could possibly last ("I cannot account why a thing which requires so little exertion and yet preserves the mind from total vacuity should have gone out. Every man has something by which he *calms* himself: beating with his feet or so").

They talked of the act of writing—of the hesitations and burdens of self-expectation and perfectionism that inhibit writers—and the advantages to an author to have his book attacked as well as praised since

* See below, pp. 519–22.

"Fame is a shuttlecock. If it be struck only at one end of the room, it will soon fall to the ground. To keep it up, it must be struck at both ends." At one moment he might speak of the motives people have, aside from hunger, for elaborating dinner as a major event of the day ("vacuity of mind"), or the amount of time people can consume in dressing themselves, "taking up a thing and looking at it, and laying it down, and taking it up again. Everyone should get the habit of doing it quickly." Just as easily he could switch to more serious talk of empirical versus a priori reasoning, or maintain that good humor, or good nature, can be acquired by people as they grow older. "It is *music* to hear this man speak," said Alexander MacLeod of Ullinish. As never before Boswell began to look on Johnson as being "like a great mill, into which a subject is to be thrown to be ground." And at least once (September 7) he confessed he did not exert himself "to get Mr. Johnson to talk, that I might not have the labour of writing down his conversation."[10]

Aside from the conversations, there are the engaging personal details—Johnson, in a gloomy place, trying to frighten Boswell; strutting about the room with a broadsword and a Scottish war bonnet; the colored handkerchief he wore around his head instead of a nightcap; his fondness, so unusual at the time, for fresh air ("He sets open a window in the coldest day or night, and stands before it"); refusing to be treated like an old man, so that when they were landing at Iona and Boswell and Allan Maclean allowed themselves to be carried by the men from the boat to the shore, the far older Johnson "sprang into the sea and waded vigorously out"; or trying to prove, half in fun, that he had good eyesight (when Boswell, for example, spoke of a mountain as shaped like a "cone"—no, said Johnson, "it is indeed pointed at the top. But one side of it is much longer than the other"; or, of a mountain Boswell called "immense," "No, but 'tis a considerable *protuberance*"). And there are the scenes of Johnson, at a Highland dance, smiling, talking, and at moments glancing through Hooke's *Roman History*, or, when Dr. Mac Leod at Raasay tried to show them some early bones of an "uncommon size," Johnson refusing to look at them and starting back from them "with a striking appearance of horror." And there is the transparent moment when Johnson begins to talk in detail about the capacity to hold dirt in cloth made from animal fiber, such as wool, as compared with vegetable fiber, such as linen, and then said meditatively, "I have often thought that if I kept a seraglio, the ladies should all wear linen gowns, or cotton; I mean stuffs made of vegetable substance. I would have no silk; you cannot tell when it is clean. It will be very nasty before it is perceived to be so. Linen detects its own dirtiness." The company was naturally struck by that phrase "I have often thought," and Mr. Macqueen, picking it up, asked if Johnson would admit Boswell into the seraglio. Startled back to reality, Johnson unkindly said (annoyed that Boswell had told everyone his birthday was approaching), "Yes, if he were properly prepared; and he'd make a very good eunuch."[11]

6

Just before they had arrived at the west coast of Scotland and crossed to Skye, Johnson himself had decided to write a short book about the journey. He was not to get around to doing so until he had been home for several months, and it was not published until January 1775. But its principal interest is now, while he is making the trip, rather than later, when he wrote the book in about three weeks, using the letters he had written to Mrs. Thrale as a means of refreshing his memory.

Naturally his *Journey to the Western Islands of Scotland* is in a radically different genre from Boswell's *Tour to the Hebrides*. Boswell's book is a brilliant cross between three literary forms—an actual "journal," a biographical memoir of Johnson, and, above all, a record of conversation. Johnson's *Journey* is a straightforward travel account, focusing on places that would be of interest to other travelers and inquiring into general social conditions. Like everything written by a great man, it has already a built-in interest, and there are also, as Robert Orme said to Boswell, thoughts in this book that "had been rolled and rolled in Johnson's mind, as in the sea."[12]

Several themes coalesce. A major one, inevitable to anyone as concerned as Johnson with what we now call sociology, was the destitution and general atmosphere of decline in the Highlands as compared with the vigorous social health of the Lowlands. The heavy emigration of the Scots from the Highlands, which had begun thirty years before Johnson and continued for a generation afterward, was itself a haunting lesson to a moralist of the Enlightenment aware of the effect of economics on society. There was the added interest to the social historian that in the Highlands and the Hebrides one saw, as nowhere else in the British Isles, a dying feudalism at wrestle with the new mercantilism, and, inevitably, so drastic a social transition had left serious scars.

It was Johnson's special concern with these problems and also with local customs and manners that, for readers of the time, distinguished his book from other travel accounts. But this also made the book more controversial than if it had dwelt only on the picturesque. For a foreigner to discuss social conditions among a people always runs the risk of offending unless the discussion is interwoven with praise, and Johnson's picture, though generalized, was straightforward. But it is a tribute to the intelligence of his Scottish readers that most of them thought well of the book. The number of those annoyed by one detail or another has been greatly exaggerated. In general, the Scottish public realized that his attention to social problems was a far profounder act of sympathy than that shown by a traveler concerned only with antiquities or a view. Symbolic of the whole tone is the moving final page of the book, where, after his return to Edinburgh, he is speaking of something "which no other city has to shew"—Thomas Braidwood's school for the deaf and dumb. It is as though the thought of all the disadvantages under which the inhabitants of the Hebrides had been suffering were typified by an even worse fate, but one about which something could and was being done. He mentions the smiling faces and sparkling eyes with which the pupils were waiting for their teacher, and the eagerness with which a girl, with quivering fingers, worked out on her slate a sum Johnson asked her to do:

It was pleasing to see one of the most desperate of human calamities capable of so much help: whatever enlarges hope, will exalt courage; after having seen the deaf taught arithmetick, who would be afraid to cultivate the Hebrides?[13]

7

Late in September the young Laird of the Isle of Coll, Donald Maclean (who was to drown during a storm the following year), joined them and offered to conduct them to the smaller islands. But for a few days the weather was so bad that no boat would leave the harbor. Finally they set off for Coll (October 3), though the waves were still high. Johnson became seasick, and Boswell, delighting to find himself "a stout seaman, while Mr. Johnson was in a state of annihilation," devoured boiled mutton and salt herring, washed down by beer and punch. He then became seasick himself and, as a violent storm arose, recalled all he had heard of the proverbial dangers of sailing at this time of year among what Milton called "the stormy Hebrides." Boswell prayed and vowed reform if he lived. Meanwhile, despite the tempest, Johnson had recovered and lay in his bunk, unconcerned and tranquil, with one of Maclean's greyhounds at his back to keep him warm.

In Coll (October 3–14) the stormy weather continued. Johnson had never "heard the wind so loud in any other place." But they made occasional excursions from Maclean's house, saw the castle, and then sailed over to Mull, which struck them as really desolate. While they were crossing Mull on horseback, their baggageman, who was riding behind them, lost (or sequestered) Johnson's large oaken stick, which he was carrying with the other luggage. Since there were hardly any trees in Mull, Johnson suspected the stick was stolen: "It is not to be expected that any man in Mull who has got it will part with it. Consider, sir, the value of such a *piece of timber* here." From Mull, after a brief stop at Ulva, they went on to the little island of Inch Kenneth— "inch" being the Gaelic word for island—where they were cheered by "the sight of a road worked with cart-wheels, as on the mainland; a thing we had not seen for a long time."[14]

Here, at the home of Sir Allan Maclean, the chief of his clan, Johnson "showed so much of the spirit of a Highlander that he won Sir Allan's heart." He was by no means eager to leave. But Boswell, who had to be back for the Court of Session by November 12, was worried lest they get detained in the Hebrides by the weather. He had even been thinking of giving up one of the spots he had himself most wanted to see—the nearby island of Iona (or Icolmkill), where St. Columba in 563 had founded the famous monastery from which missionaries later went out to convert Scotland and northern England. Johnson felt he should leave the decision to Boswell, who decided to go on to Iona and was glad they did. They arrived at night (October 19), slept in a barn with their clothes on, and the next morning went to see the ruins. While Johnson was studying them, Boswell went by himself to the cathedral, of which a portion of the walls and the tower was still standing. There, as he wrote in his journal (though omitting it from his published account), he offered a prayer to St. Columba, hoping that "ever after having been in this holy place, I should maintain an exemplary conduct," and then "read with an audible voice the fifth chapter of St. James, and Dr. Ogden's tenth sermon." (He had brought along with him, on the trip, Samuel Ogden's *Sermons on Prayer*, which he greatly admired.) "I had a serious joy in hearing my voice, while it was filled with Ogden's admirable eloquence, resounding in the ancient cathedral of Icolmkill." Johnson, for his part, was usually tempted to resist the influence of places, with a feeling that to surrender to "impressions" was to surrender one's ability as a "free agent," able to pursue what is right at any time or place. In his own famous remark in Iona, he is answering himself:

To abstract the mind from all local emotion would be impossible, if it were endeavoured, and would be foolish, if it were possible. Whatever withdraws us from the power of our senses; whatever makes the past, the distant, or the future predominate over the present, advances us in the dignity of thinking beings. Far from me and from my friends, be such frigid philosophy as may conduct us indifferent and unmoved over any ground which has been dignified by wisdom, bravery, or virtue. That man is little to be envied, whose patriotism would not gain force upon the plain of Marathon, or whose piety would not grow warmer among the ruins of Iona![15]

8

Returning again through Mull, they crossed to Oban on the mainland (October 22), and then, going rapidly, passed through Inveraray, Cameron, Dumbarton, and Glasgow, on the way to Auchinleck in Ayrshire.

They were now in a different world. At Inveraray they were entertained by the Duke and Duchess of Argyll, the Duchess making it plain that it was Johnson in whom she was interested and not Boswell. In Glasgow some of the professors at the university called on Johnson at his inn and breakfasted and dined with him. He was particularly pleased at a visit Boswell induced him to make three days later to the Dowager Countess of Eglinton, who had been celebrated as a beauty, a wit, and a patroness of poets, and was now eighty-four. She had lost her son, the Earl Alexander, four years before and said that since she had married before Johnson was born, "she might have been his mother, and that she now adopted him," and, as he left, she embraced him, saying, "My dear son, farewell." Later, at Sir Alexander Dick's in Edinburgh, Boswell mentioned this to the company but, by a slip, said that the Countess had been married "after" rather than before Johnson was born. Johnson corrected him, saying that he was "defaming" the Countess. "For, supposing me to be her son, and she was not married till a year after my birth, I must have been her *natural* son." At this "a young lady of quality"–Lady Anne Lindsay, according to Malone–

said, "Might not the son have justified the fault?" Johnson was so delighted by the compliment that, in a way unlike him, he would resort to a ruse to hear it again (and thus be reminded of what pleased him still more—that Lady Eglinton had "adopted" him). For sometimes, when they would be speaking of the trip to Scotland, he would ask Boswell, "What was it that the young lady of quality said to me at Sir Alexander Dick's?"[16]

Having hurried during the past week, they were able, as Boswell had hoped, to spend almost a week at Auchinleck (November 2–8), where his autocratic and testy father was waiting for them with no expectation of pleasure at meeting Johnson. "His age, his office, and his character had long given him an acknowledged claim to great attention, in whatever company he was; and he could ill brook any diminution of it. He was as sanguine a Whig and Presbyterian as Dr. Johnson was a Tory and Church of England man." Boswell urged Johnson to stay off topics that might inflame his father, and Johnson replied that he would "certainly not talk on subjects which I am told are disagreeable to a gentleman under whose roof I am." But on the fourth or fifth day they came into collision, during which "Whiggism and Presbyterianism, Toryism and Episcopacy, were terribly buffeted." Boswell understandably did not go into details, saying he disliked the idea of exhibiting his father and Johnson as "intellectual gladiators, for the entertainment of the public." Peace was re-established, and the two men parted with courtesy. But the elder Boswell's reaction to Johnson was typified by the name he soon gave him—"the great bear," or Ursa Major. And according to Sir Walter Scott, he told a friend, "There's nae hope for Jamie, mon. Jamie is gone clean gyte [crazy]. What do you think, mon? He's done wi' Paoli . . . and whose tail do you think he has pinned himself to now, mon?" Here he sneered with sovereign contempt: "A *dominie*, mon"—that is, a schoolmaster—"an auld dominie: he keeped a schule, and cau'd it an acaadamy."[17]

9

After several crowded days in Edinburgh, during which they were "harassed by invitations" ("But how much worse would it have been," as Johnson said, "if we had been neglected"), he took the coach for London (November 22) and arrived home four days later. He was to remember these three months as one of the most pleasant episodes in his life. True, in his annual stocktaking on New Year's Day ("near 2 in the morning"), he said—in mentioning the trip—"my mind was not free from perturbation." But his remark is unusually mild—"the chief cause of my deficiency has been a life immethodical, and unsettled . . . and perhaps leaves too much leisure to the imagination."[18]

On his return he found that his old friend Tom Davies, the book-seller—now in straitened circumstances—had taken a liberty that would have infuriated most writers. Davies had published a two-volume anonymous work, called *Miscellaneous and Fugitive Pieces,* and advertised it in the newspapers as "by the Authour of the Rambler." It consisted partly of pieces known to be by Johnson, partly of short works he had written for others, and—most annoying of all, since readers would infer they were by Johnson—some writings by other people to fill out the second volume. Learning of this at Streatham, he decided he should be really angry and left for London, said Mrs. Thrale, "in all the wrath he could muster up," resolved to have the matter out with Davies. But his heart melted as soon as he discovered how badly off Davies was, and he returned to Streatham trying to think up other ways to help Davies, one of which was to offer him some more pieces, free of charge, for a third volume. Such is the history—unplanned, a little grotesque, and altogether typical in its charity—of what is, in effect, the "first collected edition" of Johnson's works.[19]

Meanwhile he caught a bad cold, which aroused the bronchitis that was always ready to flare up and which kept him coughing for several weeks in January and February. This caused him to defer work on his book about the trip to the Hebrides. Much of the time he spent at Streatham trying to get in shape.

The Thrales, since the brewery was again becoming prosperous, began to talk of taking a long trip. At first they thought of the continent, since both Johnson and Mrs. Thrale were especially eager to see Italy. But Thrale finally decided they should defer this larger trip and go instead to Wales. His wife, at the death of her uncle, had inherited the old Salusbury property of Bach-y-Graig, and Thrale wanted to take possession of the place and make sure everything was in order. They could leave in early July and need not be back till the end of September, and they could do a good deal of sight-seeing. With them would go Johnson and their oldest child, Queeney, now almost ten. The other children would be left in the charge of Giuseppe Baretti and their nurse.

In June—with the trip almost ready to begin—Johnson decided that if he was ever going to write his *Journey to the Western Islands of Scotland*, it would have to be now. If he delayed until after this next trip, it might have grown stale as a subject, or he might have other projects to occupy him. Plunging into the book, he wrote it in twenty days, according to Thomas Campbell, sending it in batches to the printer as he wrote it, which meant that he had no chance to make detailed revisions.[20] (Because he had not quite finished before they left, the printing of the book slowed up while he was gone, and it was not published till the following January.)

10

We need not trace the trip in detail. It has little of the interest of the journey to Scotland and the Hebrides. For those who wish to follow it, there are two detailed accounts. One, quite readable, is a journal kept by Mrs. Thrale, though it does not tell us anything very significant about Johnson. Secondly, Johnson himself jotted down notes, in diary form, of places they saw.[21]

Leaving Streatham on July 5, with Johnson reading Cicero's *Letters* some of the time in the coach, they reached Lichfield at midnight of the following day, and put up at the Swan. Johnson was eager to show his native city to the Thrales. He also wanted Mrs. Thrale to appear at her best, and when she came down in casual dress the next morning, he urged her to go back and "change my apparel for one more gay and splendid." They saw Lucy Porter, Molly Ashton, David Garrick's brother Peter, saw the famous museum collected by Richard Green, and had breakfast with Erasmus Darwin, the grandfather of Charles Darwin. After this they paid a long visit to Ashbourne (July 9–20), where John Taylor entertained them liberally at his handsome estate, and then, proceeding west toward Wales, they stopped for a few days at Combermere Hall to see Mrs. Thrale's uncle, Sir Lynch Salusbury Cotton.

At Chester (July 27), where they stopped before entering Wales, Mrs. Thrale was getting tired of sight-seeing, and Johnson annoyed her by keeping Queeney up after her bedtime and taking her for a walk along the wall, "where, from the want of light, I apprehended some accident to her—perhaps to him." Entering north Wales, they went to Bach-y-Graig, the house Mrs. Thrale had inherited, and found it in a rather dilapidated condition. They stayed in the area for almost three weeks, and visited Denbigh Castle and Ruthlan Castle. Then they continued west to Carnarvon, stopping to see Beaumaris Castle, which Johnson found fascinating, and visiting Bodville, where Mrs. Thrale was born. There were times when Johnson was not well and became grumpy. Nor were Mr. Thrale and Queeney ideal traveling companions at all times. On one occasion Johnson startled Mrs. Thrale by saying, "Why is it, that whatever you see, and whoever you see, you are to be so indiscriminately lavish of praise?" "Why, I'll tell you, sir," she replied. "When I am with you, and Mr. Thrale, and Queeney, I am obliged to be civil for four!"[22]

They returned to England, going by way of Shrewsbury, Worcester, and Birmingham, and stopped to see Burke in his country home at Beaconsfield. During the next day Burke had to leave with Lord Verney to attend to some election matters. Burke and Verney came back that night, said Mrs. Thrale, "much flustered with liquor." The visit with Burke, to which Johnson and Thrale had been looking forward, was cut to two days. This was because Parliament suddenly dissolved, and a new election had to be held. Thrale decided to go at once to the Southwark house and campaign. The trip was over. Returning to Southwark, Johnson quickly wrote an election address for Thrale, and also dashed down for him the pamphlet called *The Patriot*, while correcting the last proofs of the *Journey to the Western Islands*.

11

Of as much personal interest to us as anything else that occurred on this trip is a remark Mrs. Thrale made in her journal when she learned at Burke's house in Beaconsfield that they had to hurry back to Southwark: "I thought to have lived at Streatham . . . and here I must be shut up in that odious dungeon, where nobody will come near me, the children are to be sick for want of air, *and I am never to see a face but Mr. Johnson's.* Oh, what a life that is! And how truly I abhor it!"[23]

It was no more than the trace of a cloud on the horizon. Yet, considering what the next few years were to bring, the remark could seem ominous. We should not read too much into it. This had been a fatiguing trip for her; they had all been penned up together closely where the irritations or boredom of any one of them quickly spread to the others; she had been worried about the children left at home; she was once again pregnant; and she had come to detest the Southwark house, with its associations of noise, trade, problems, and nearby slums. Still, the phrase starts out from what she is writing here—"and I am never to see a face but Mr. Johnson's."

The truth is that Johnson was gradually being caught up in a situation that, with all his insight into human nature, he may not have understood simply because his surrender to the Thrale family had been so complete that his internal guard, when he was with them, had long since disappeared. Or, even if he had sensed it, he was helpless to do anything about it. It had been ten years since the Thrales had taken him into the family. Except for being much happier, his essential character had not changed, as was natural between the ages of fifty-five and sixty-five. But the Thrales, much younger, had both become somewhat different people. Henry Thrale had entered middle age, and Hester, after having borne nine children, was approaching it. She could begin to feel that life as she had once hoped it would be was passing her by. She had tried valiantly—and was to continue trying—to make the best of a marriage with a man she did not really love and who, she thought, took her for granted. But the strains were accumulating. With Johnson so often present, some of her dissatisfactions with Thrale and her life generally were naturally projected on him or at least associated with him.

Meanwhile Johnson secretly regarded the trip as an anticlimax after the journey to the Hebrides. This was partly because Wales did not seem very different from England. But it was also because there was no Boswell to smooth the way, searching out interesting people to meet him, and providing a constant lubricant of ebullient good nature. Instead Johnson was with a family unused to extended travel, worried about accommodations, carrying with them a good deal of luggage, with Mrs. Thrale anxious about the children at home and with Thrale and Queeney often stiff, self-defensive, and easily bored. Of course, Johnson could not let himself think in this way about "his" family. He preferred to explain it to himself as he did in a letter to John Taylor— that Wales had "nothing that can much excite or gratify curiosity. The mode of life is entirely English."[24]

But he had really made an effort to enjoy the trip, and if only his companions had been happier, he would have succeeded. Even so, he was often able to infect them with his own enthusiasm. It was on this trip especially that Mrs. Thrale learned what "an admirable companion on the road" he could be however "cruelly tired" she herself had become during the last month. Time and again the oldest of the group of travelers could prove the most lighthearted. One little episode, too charming to be omitted, should be mentioned, especially since Mrs. Thrale did not record it or was not present at the moment. At Gwaynynog, they were visiting Colonel John Myddelton, whom Johnson liked ("the only man who in Wales has talked to me of literature"). While he and Johnson were talking, said Myddelton, the gardener caught a hare among the potato plants and brought it to Myddelton, who ordered it to be taken to the cook and prepared for dinner. As soon as he heard this, Johnson begged to hold the frightened hare in his arms for a moment, "which was no sooner done, than approaching the window then half open, he restored the hare to her liberty, shouting after her to accelerate her speed."[25]

Chapter 27

Humor and Wit

Johnson's humor is so important to our understanding of him that we need to pause and look at its implications as a whole rather than merely allowing them to be inferred in a scattered way. The best place for doing this in a biography of him is during the account of his later years. This is partly because the information available becomes so plentiful for his later years that we could by no means neglect it; and, if we took up the subject earlier in any detail, we should be constantly having to leap ahead in order to get it into perspective. There is another reason for deferring our discussion until this point. For most readers during the last century and a half, his humor (together with his common sense, to which it is related) has been at the heart of the fascinated attraction they have felt for the Johnson they have known best—the familiar Johnson of his sixties. The biographer has an obligation to try to explain a quality with so strong and persisting an appeal and to discover, if possible, its relation to the larger context of Johnson's mind and character.

The importance of the subject has at least three aspects. To begin with, there is the sheer range and variety of his humor—from the playful to the aggressive, from the naïve to the intellectually complicated, and from his unexpected talent for buffoonery and mimicry to almost every kind of wit. In other words, it is not a special or minor aspect of his personality but something interwoven with it at almost every point. A second interest is the connection of his humor with some of his most serious psychological problems—his attempts to gain "distance," to curb or "displace" aggression, and with his lifelong struggle for mental health and his ability, under the most trying circumstances, to retain his hold on reality. Humor, as Freud said, is by far "the highest of the defensive processes" against the psychological trials and anxieties of living, and, in its genuine state, the most healthful. For in contrast to the common "neurotic" forms of defense that cripple the psyche, humor does not rigidly repress and deny—thus "quitting," said Freud, "the ground of mental sanity"—but openly acknowledges threats and anxieties, and allows them to propel themselves by their momentum, while creatively steering and "displacing" them into a new context.[1]

Finally Johnson's humor is intimately related with the secret of his genius generally and with what is, of course, a part of his genius, his style and powers of expression, especially in the conversations of his later years. In fact, he could serve as a paradigm for one of the most fascinating subjects that psychology is only now beginning to explore—the close connection between humor and creative genius as a whole. This connection is essentially the theme of Arthur Koestler's valuable work *The Act of Creation:* that all creative activities of mind (scientific discovery, originality in the arts, or comic inspiration) have in common a basic psychological pattern for which humor serves as a prototype—a creative, "bisociative" leap between two or more frames of reference, or matrices of experience, previously unconnected and even regarded as incompatible. Comedy occurs in the sudden collision of frames of experience or reference ordinarily assumed to be separate. In scientific or philosophical discovery, this same collision and element of surprise are followed by a new fusion, creating the possibility of a new matrix. In art the principle is the same, though here the leeway is greater. For, depending on taste, the originality we prize in art may involve—as in humor—the collision of different matrices (in motif and medium), or a more solemn and purely aesthetic "confrontation," or—as in classical art—a fusion (*i.e.,* Aristotle's principle of *harmonia*) after the confrontation or collision. But in every case—humor, science, art—we find ourselves experiencing reality on more than one plane. The creative act is thus "an act of liberation—the defeat of habit by originality."[2]

2

Johnson would often say, according to Mrs. Thrale, that "the size of a man's understanding might always be justly measured by his mirth."

As for Johnson himself, "No man," she said, "loved laughing any better, and his vein of humour was rich and apparently inexhaustible." Most of his friends agreed with her.

Arthur Murphy, for example, in trying to sum up Johnson's genius after a close friendship of thirty years, decided that, joined "with great powers of mind, wit and humour were his shining talents." As a comic playwright and actor, Murphy was a good judge, and he added that Johnson—quite unexpectedly to those who did not know him—was "incomparable at buffoonery." Even the dour Sir John Hawkins thought that "in the talent of humour there hardly ever was his equal, except perhaps among the old comedians." Boswell is an interesting exception. He was very much aware of Johnson's humor. But he was often frankly puzzled by it, and, though the conversations he records provide a delightful compendium of it, he does not linger on the subject. It did not quite fit the father image he had of "the authour of the *Rambler*," and, when he drew on his journal for his published account of his first meeting with Johnson, he decided to omit a sentence he had originally written: "He has great humour." Moreover, despite his own merry and uninhibited nature, humor was not Boswell's strongest point. Mrs. Thrale, grading thirty-eight men on different qualities, and using 20 as a perfect score, gave Boswell 19 for "good humour," that is "good nature," but decided she could give him only 3 for humor itself.*

When Johnson's own friends spoke of his gift for humor, they were thinking of a combination of four things. First and mainly they were referring to his ready and fertile wit. He said even "the most common things," wrote Thomas Tyers, "in the *newest* manner." As another friend remarked to Hawkins, "In general you may tell what the man to whom you are speaking will say next: this you can never do with Johnson."[4] It is his wit of which posterity also immediately thinks at the mention of Johnson's humor—almost exclusively, since, without his physical presence, what we ourselves are left to encounter directly are only his actual words; and for almost two centuries, in any company, a remark beginning "As Johnson says . . ." usually brings a smile even before the quotation gets under way: learning in Scotland "is like bread in a besieged town: every man gets a little, but no man

---

* She gave Johnson 16 for "humour," giving only Garrick a higher grade (19), not because he "loved laughing any better" but because of his histrionic gifts. Murphy came third (15). She was using a strict standard. For example, Reynolds, Burke, and her husband all got 0, though she gave 10 to Reynolds for "good humour."[3]

gets a full meal." "A woman's preaching is like a dog's walking on its hinder legs. It is not done well; but you are surprized to find it done at all." When some Methodists were expelled from Oxford, Boswell said he was told they were "good beings." "A cow," said Johnson, "is a very good animal in the field; but we turn her out of the garden." Pressed to say whether Derrick or Smart was the better poet, he replied, "There is no settling the point of precedency between a louse and a flea." Of a woman who continued to sit next to him "desperately silent": she "takes away the confidence one should have in her chair if she were once out of it." Or to cite an example Boswell decided not to publish: in the tower of an old castle in the Hebrides, he discovered a "necessary" room, where a long shaft carried the refuse to "the outside of the rock at the bottom." Pleased at this early example of sanitation in Scotland, he pointed it out to Johnson, who laughed heartily and said, "You take very good care of one end of a man, but not of the other." We could quickly fill an entire chapter with remarks of this sort, most of them so familiar that they have passed into the language. It is enough, as a reminder, to add a few more in a note.*

What we see in these remarks is a simple example of the "bisociation" described by Johnson in one of his own definitions of wit: "the *unexpected* copulation of ideas, the discovery of some occult relation in images in appearance remote from each other" (learning, where there are few books, and bread in a besieged town; a woman's preaching and a dog walking on its hind legs; a pallid personality and an empty chair). The same general principle applies to what would at first seem to be a different form of wit—the sharp but effortless distinctions he is always making, however small the matter. Here the disparate elements are not brought together from a distance, so to speak, but instead are suddenly discovered to be already there and are being

---

* A young man was lamenting one day that "he had lost all his Greek." "I believe it happened at the same time, Sir," said Johnson, "that I lost all my large estate in Yorkshire." Mrs. Thrale mentioned an acquaintance who had been expecting a large estate and was now disappointed, and then spoke sympathetically of still another woman who, when she heard the news, would grieve deeply "at her friend's disappointment." "She will suffer as much perhaps (said he) as your horse did when your cow miscarried." At a party, said Miss Reynolds, a lady was asked to propose a toast to the ugliest man she knew, and at once named Oliver Goldsmith. Just afterward a second lady rose on the other side of the table and reached across to shake hands with her, "expressing some desire of being better acquainted with her, it being the first time they met." Observing this, Johnson remarked, "Thus the Ancients, on the commencement of their Friendships, used to sacrifice a Beast betwixt them."⁵

plucked apart and seen in opposition. Boswell asks whether Bishop Burnet, remembered for his long death scene of the Earl of Rochester, had not written "a good Life of Rochester." Johnson: "We have a good *Death:* there is not much *Life.*" Boswell inquires, "Is not the Giant's Causeway worth seeing?" Johnson: "Worth seeing, yes; but not worth *going* to see." Thomas Newton's *Dissertations on the Prophecies,* said Dr. Adams, "is his great work." Johnson: "Why, Sir, it is *Tom's* great work; but how far it is *great,* or how much of it is *Tom's* are other questions." Reynolds says of Elizabeth Montagu's *Essay on Shakespeare,* "I think that essay does her honour." Johnson: "Yes, Sir, it does her honour, but it would do nobody else honour. I have, indeed, not read it all. But when I take up the end of a web, and find it packthread, I do not expect, by looking further, to find it embroidery." Or, later on: "Mrs. Montagu has dropt me. Now, Sir, there are people whom one should very well like to *drop,* but not wish to be *dropped by.*"[6]

3

There was another aspect of his humor that never ceased to surprise and divert his friends. With "a form less inflexible," said Mrs. Thrale, "he would have made an admirable mimic." Actually the bisociative surprise and appeal of mimicry is heightened to the extent that there is a radical difference beforehand, as Coleridge said, between the raw material used in the imitation and what is being imitated. Johnson's face, said William Cooke (known as "Conversation" Cooke from his poem *On Conversation*), was "composed of large coarse features, which, from a studious turn, looked sluggish, yet awful and contemplative." But it was also a face "capable of great expression," and the sudden contrast of his features with the play of expression that took place over them made his imitations all the more amusing, as he himself was certainly aware. This contrast was what so struck the company at Inverness when Johnson gave his imitation of the newly discovered kangaroo.* So with another incident on the trip to the Hebrides. One morning, after meditating a new imitation, Johnson called Boswell to his bedside,

and to my astonishment he took off Lady Macdonald leaning forward with a hand on each cheek and her mouth open—quite *insipidity on a monument*

* See above, p. 466.

grinning at sense and spirit. To see a beauty represented by Mr. Johnson was excessively high. I told him it was a masterpiece and that he must have studied it much. "Ay," said he.

When Hawkins said that "in the talent of humour" Johnson never had an equal except "among the old Comedians," this was what he was mainly thinking about—Johnson's ready empathy in seizing on peculiarities of character and then (despite or because of his own distinctive features) imitating them with the "nicest exactness"; and he goes on to mention how much this gift of Johnson's could disconcert the grave and pompous William Warburton, especially in company where Warburton was hoping himself to be regarded as "a man of pleasantry."[7]

A third element—and here he was extremely unusual for a man of his intellectual stature—was the refreshing and contagious gusto with which he could throw himself into things, even in his old age, and the willingness to share, to participate, which we see in a scene that took place one morning, on the trip to the Hebrides, when he hears that James Beattie has received a pension. Sitting upright in bed, with a knotted handkerchief on his head as though it were a crown, and half burlesquing himself as though this were a royal levee, he clapped his hands with joy, and cried out "*O brave we!*"—"a peculiar exclamation of his," said Boswell, "when he rejoices." This is what so captivated Fanny Burney, who thought Johnson (1779) had "more fun . . . and love of nonsense about him than almost anybody I ever saw." As with his mimicry, part of the appeal was the contrast with what one would have expected. A magazine account after his death, in trying to show the public a side of him familiar only to those intimate with him, spoke of his sudden transitions "from the contemplation of subjects the most profound to the most childish playfulness." It mentioned his love of racing, climbing, and jumping, and is the source of a charming story of a race he once proposed in the country with his friend, the tiny John Payne, who had published Johnson's moral essays and who later became chief accountant at the Bank of England. Before they had gone half the way, Johnson caught up the diminutive Payne in his arms and placed him on the branch of a tree they were passing. He then "continued running as if he had met with a hard match," releasing Payne from the tree "with much exaltation" on his way back.[8]

Particularly fascinating were moments when two or more forms of humor would suddenly coalesce, as they did one afternoon in the

Hebrides. Some young women had been discussing among themselves how ugly Johnson was, and one of them took a bet to go over and sit on his knee and kiss him. The company stared, wondering what would happen. No one could have predicted what he would say, and yet—carrying with it his unsleeping sense of the transitoriness of all things—it could have been said only by him: "Do it again," he said, "and let us see who will tire first."[9]

4

Finally there was his own gift for laughter, which often—though not always—proved so "irresistible," said Mrs. Thrale, that others would catch it by contagion, even if they did not see the point, and would start to laugh "purely out of power to forbear it." "Rabelais and all other wits are nothing compared to him," said Garrick. "You may be diverted by them; but Johnson gives you a forcible hug, and *shakes* laughter out of you whether you will or no."[10]

But there were times when no one followed him at all, even Garrick—moments when the charity and excuses he is always finding for human nature get suspended, and he suddenly seems to be looking at the whole scene with the detachment and mockery we find in a great satirist like Swift. An example is the incident of "Langton's will," back in 1773 (May 10), told by Boswell, who thought it a strange contrast to what one would expect from the "melancholy and venerable Johnson." Johnson had been ill for some weeks. Forcing himself out into company, he went with Boswell to call on Robert Chambers, by then a prominent lawyer because of the Vinerian lectures Johnson had helped him write, and with a London apartment at the Temple.

That very day Chambers had made a will for Johnson's friend, Bennet Langton, in which "Lanky" left his estate to his three sisters ("three dowdies," said Johnson) rather than the nearest male relative. Half laughing at himself for his "feudal" zeal, Johnson—trying to forget his illness—began to talk enthusiastically about the need to keep up male succession in noble families, though "for an estate newly acquired by trade, you may give it, if you will, to the dog *Towser,* and let him keep his *own* name." Then the crucial passage follows:

> I have known him at times exceedingly diverted at what seemed to others a very small sport. He now laughed immoderately, without any reason that we could perceive, at our friend's making his will; called him the *testator,*

and added, "I daresay, he thinks he has done a mighty thing. He won't stay till he gets home to his seat in the country . . . he'll call up the landlord of the first inn on the road; and, after a suitable preface upon mortality and the uncertainty of life, will tell him that *he* should not delay making his will; and here, Sir, will he say, is my will, which I have just made, with the assistance of one of the ablest lawyers in the kingdom . . . (*laughing all the time*). He believes he has made this will; but he did not make it: you, Chambers, made it for him. I trust you had more conscience than to make him say, 'being of sound understanding;' ha, ha, ha! . . . I'd have his will turned into verse, like a ballad."

In this playful manner did he run on. . . . Mr. Chambers . . . seemed impatient till he got rid of us. Johnson could not stop his merriment, but continued it all the way till we got without the Temple-gate. He then burst into such a fit of laughter, that he appeared to be almost in a convulsion; and, in order to support himself, laid hold of one of the posts . . . and sent forth peals so loud, that in the silence of the night his voice seemed to resound from Temple-bar to Fleet-ditch.[11]

Boswell was just as puzzled as the prim Chambers, and says that he mentions this incident only so that his readers "may be acquainted even with the slightest occasional characteristics of so eminent a man." But in the context of Johnson's whole life we see what is breaking through, in a moment when he has so much else on his mind. Behind it is the accumulated sense, put so powerfully in *The Vanity of Human Wishes* and the moral essays, of the triviality of all our posturings and stratagems for "importance" against the large backdrop of the general "doom of man." For a moment, through Johnson's eyes, we see the still young Langton, swelling in his new importance as "the *testator*," and, sobered by the responsibilities of this new role, eager to inform others —as the author of *The Vanity of Human Wishes* was himself always doing—about "mortality and the uncertainty of life," but with the illusion that, through a will, he was in some way "controlling" events, and to that extent surviving his own death. At the same time ("everyone has a real or imaginary connection with a celebrated character") we have Langton contriving to mention, to the awed innkeeper, that his own will has just been made up "with the *assistance* of one of the ablest lawyers in the kingdom," though actually it was not he who made it—"*you*, Chambers, made it *for* him" (as the celebrated Chambers had his Vinerian lectures largely made "for him"). And when Johnson adds, "I'd have his will turned into *verse*, like a ballad," the spirit is the same as when he made up a ballad stanza on the spur of the moment, and cried it out to young Queeney Thrale as she was talking with great seriousness to a friend about the gown and hat she would wear to an assembly:

> Wear the gown, and wear the hat,
> Snatch thy pleasures while they last;
> Hadst thou nine lives like a cat,
> Soon those nine lives would be past.[12]

But it was especially himself at whom he was laughing—sitting there ill, fighting away thoughts of death, and talking with enthusiasm about male succession and the need of keeping up noble families, as if, under the aspect of eternity, it mattered at all, and, least of all, should matter to himself. However solidly based his conservatism, there could also, as he knew, be something ludicrous in an old and ailing man, whose life had been a continual struggle, becoming so "zealous for subordination and the honours of birth," when he could "hardly tell"—or rather liked to pretend he could hardly tell—"who was my grandfather." As he plunges now into this role, we see something of the self-burlesque with which, during the trip to the Hebrides, he clapped a Scottish war bonnet on his head, or the outburst of merriment—just as puzzling to the company—when MacLeod of Skye offered to give Johnson the tiny island of Isay provided Johnson would go and live there for a month each year: "I have seen him please himself with little things, even with mere ideas. . . . He talked a great deal of this island—how he would build a house, how he would *fortify* it." And, imagining himself with the noble title, "Island Isay," began telling

how he would have cannon . . . how he would sally out and *take* the Isle of Muck; and *then he laughed with a glee* that was astonishing, and could hardly leave off. I have seen him do so at a small matter that struck him, and was a sport to no one else. Langton told me that one night at the Club he did so while the company were all grave around him; only Garrick in his smart manner addressed him, "Mighty pleasant, sir; mighty pleasant, sir."[13]

So with a scene at Streatham one day, which the young Fanny Burney recorded in her diary. She was flattered at the friendly praise given her novel *Evelina* by so many people who in reality viewed her mainly as a sort of pet. The praise, all of it recorded in her diary, continued for weeks, and Mrs. Thrale and Johnson joined in it (though when John Opie was painting his portrait and asked whether Johnson really considered *Evelina* as good as he had been reported to think it and had really sat up all night to finish it, he replied, "I never read it through at all, though I don't wish this to be known"). Then, one morning after breakfast, Mrs. Thrale again started to flatter Fanny, telling her she should now turn her satiric talents to a *dramatic* "comedy." Suddenly the two women noticed that Johnson,

> see-sawing in his chair, began laughing to himself so heartily as to almost shake his seat as well as his sides. We stopped . . . hoping he would reveal the subject of his mirth; but he enjoyed it inwardly, without heeding our curiosity,—till at last he said he had been struck with a notion that "Miss Burney would begin her dramatic career by writing a piece called *Streatham.*"
>
> He paused, and laughed yet more cordially, and then suddenly commanded a pomposity to his countenance and his voice, and added, "Yes! *Streatham—a Farce!*"[14]

Fanny, familiar as she was with Johnson's humor, did not see the point, though she naturally suspected he was laughing at her. But it is the whole scene at which he was laughing, and above all himself as a character in a comedy—joining in the flattery, when he could hardly get through the book, grotesque and ailing, dreading loneliness, annoyed and fretful if the ladies went to a ball without him, and inventing ruses to keep their company.

5

One of the surprising things about Johnson is that, with his immense powers for ridicule, he had never turned more than he did to satire, but, on the contrary, as Mrs. Thrale said, had "an aversion to general satire." Certainly the general atmosphere was favorable. Satire was easily the most brilliant mode of writing from the 1660's to the 1740's, and to a writer who grew up in the latter part of that period and who possessed even a fraction of the endowment of Swift or Pope, the attractions of satire were almost irresistible.

It is hard to think of a single qualification for satire that Johnson did not possess. His uncanny ability to sense incongruity and pretense in every aspect of life exceeds Pope's and equals that of Swift. Add to this the pent-up aggression that could leap out with astonishing readiness, though he was now trying so hard to contain it. Richard Cumberland ("Cumby") compared him to a savage who "never came into suspicious company without his spear in his hand and his bow and quiver at his back." Or, as Mrs. Thrale put it, "Promptitude of thought, indeed, and quickness of expression, were among the peculiar felicities of Johnson: his notions rose up like the dragon's teeth sowed by Cadmus already clothed, and in bright armour too, fit for immediate battle." The readiness and aggressive strength at least match, and possibly exceed, what we find in any satirist of whose life we know anything at all. The same may be said of Johnson's personal temptations to make full expressive use of them—the irritabilities and impatience of temperament, the eagerness to confute, the large floating dissatisfactions, the physical suffering; all of which he strove so hard to control, though the struggle to do so naturally produced its own further tensions. Significantly this immediate ability to draw on every weapon was an instinctive response rather than a considered one (the effect of consideration being to blunt or muffle it with other reflections); and it leapt into action not when he had time to prepare himself but when he did not, and when he was suddenly taken off guard, especially on small matters. For example, disliking idle talk about the ease of being happy in "a world bursting with sin and sorrow," he became heated when a friend, said Mrs. Thrale, continued to push the argument. As if to clinch the matter, the friend pointed to his wife's sister, who was present, and said she "was *really* happy, and called upon the lady to confirm his assertion." When she did so with a smug and pert superiority, Johnson burst out:

"If your sister-in-law is really the contented being she professes herself . . . her life gives the lie to every research of humanity; for she is happy without health, without beauty, without money, and without understanding." [When Mrs. Thrale later] expressed something of the horrour I felt, "The same stupidity (said he) which prompted her to extol a felicity she never felt, hindered her from feeling what shocks you on repetition. I tell you, the woman is ugly, and sickly, and foolish, and poor; and would it not make a man hang himself to hear such a creature say, it was happy."[15]

Then there is the power of *reductionism*—of quickly, through an exasperated brush of the fingers, sifting a thing down to the lowest common denominator. Reductionism is the essence of satire, and it is as habitual in Johnson as it is in the greatest of satirists, Jonathan Swift. If we go through the records of the conversations, at least a quarter of the memorable remarks—the replies or observations that have passed into legend—are severely, even drastically, reductive. Take one of a score that would occur at once to a Johnsonian, and selected precisely because it is unfair both to the subject and to Johnson. For the point is the way in which this habit of expression is so ready that it can arise immediately, as a stock response, before he has even had a chance to consider a matter. Goldsmith, back in 1766, teased him for going so little to the theater any more. (Johnson, who had loved the theater when he was younger, was now neither hearing nor seeing very well.) The reply is: "Why Sir, our tastes greatly alter. The lad does not care for the child's rattle, and the old man does not care for the young man's whore." In this quick, impatient jostle, not just one thing is being reduced but the whole lot. The lad with his whore and the child with his rattle are not much luckier than the playgoer. This sort of thing happens time and again through the recorded conversations, though frequently supplemented (as is the case with the remark quoted above) with second thoughts.

We have already seen the same temptation to reductionism constantly stirring throughout the moral essays. Thus, in speaking of the specialization and isolation of scholars and scientists: "He who is growing great and happy by electrifying a bottle, wonders how the world can be engaged by trifling prattle about war and peace." Here we have the satirical habit. Or the whole frantic zeal and scramble of writing, scholarship, criticism, and reviewing is suddenly brought to heel in that magnificent phrase "the epidemical conspiracy for the destruction of paper." The reduction is often to the physical, and to the physical of the most elementary sort—even to mere space to be filled. Open the essays at random: Fame, the "desire of *filling* the minds of others"; "*filling* the vacuities of his mind with the news of the day"; or Zephyretta, who, after marriage, had "in four and twenty hours spent her stock of repartee." Or there is the quasi-mechanical, as in the account of poor Tim Ranger (*Idler* 64), who, after learning that laughter is necessary for success in society, struggled hard to acquire the art, suffering often from bad timing or deficiency in loudness and length, until "I attained at last such flexibility of muscles, that I was always a welcome auditor."

Then there are the almost brutally concrete verbs. Speaking of the effect of custom and familiarity on feeling, and the tendency of men to grow less tender with age because of this (*Rambler* 78): he who when young melted at the loss of every friend begins, in age, to look with less concern "upon the grave into which his last friend was thrown, and into which himself is ready to fall. . . ." But more often (as in his style generally) we have the immediate clutch into condensed abstractions, but invigorated and jostled into a new combination through an unexpected verb, as in "elegance *refined into* impatience," or in the phrase with which he dismisses the notion that one can write better at one season of the year than another—"imagination *operating upon* luxury." (The formula could prove contagious to his friends: *e.g.,* Mrs. Thrale's own remark on another occasion, "arrogance acting upon stupidity.") Often the effect is close to a slap: the fortune hunter's opportunity to "walk the Exchange with a face of importance"; "a frown of importance"; the travelers in *Adventurer* 84, thrown together in the stagecoach, whose first effort, in order to inspire each other with the proper veneration, is "employed in *collecting importance* into our faces"; or Lady Bustle, "who has no crime but luxury, nor any virtue but chastity." Or think of that "unwillingness to be pleased" which always so infuriated him with its stock assumption that superiority is more effectively demonstrated by disapproval than by praise: the "cultivation of the powers of dislike"; "the stare of petulant incredulity"; "the stratagems of well-bred malignity."

These fidgety, tart phrases that bristle through the moral essays and the conversations are often joined by something darker that shows Johnson's kinship with Hobbes, Swift, and Mandeville: a deeply pessimistic conviction of the frightening and unsleeping strength of human egotism and vanity. Sometimes it is fairly innocent. There is that blustery group in the *Rambler* rushing out to the countryside, with the rest of the fashionable world, who, in missing the coach, lose the pleasure of "alarming villages with the tumult of our passage, and disguising our insignificancy with the dignity of hurry." There is the moral philosopher discoursing to his audience, and "swelling with the applause which he has gained by proving that applause is no value." But this sense of the power of egotism can lead to sharper attacks. One of many is *Rambler* 188, where the modest, good-natured man is pictured as loved only because he cannot be envied: "His only power of giving pleasure is not to interrupt it," and by keeping quiet and concealing his imbecility leads his companions to think that his silence comes "not from inability to speak but from eagerness to hear"—to hear *them*. (Here we recall Johnson's own struggle to attain "good humour," and how he despondently admitted to Henry Thrale that he had never even "sought to please till past thirty years old, considering the matter as hopeless.") But again what we are mentioning is found mainly in phrases or individual sentences: critics, whose "acrimony is excited merely by the pain of seeing others pleased, and of hearing applauses which another enjoys"; "the treachery of the human heart" that can lead the critic to gratify his "own pride or malignity *under the appearance* of contending for elegance or propriety"; "Many need no other provocation to enmity than that they find themselves excelled"; "We are inclined to believe those we do not know, because they have never deceived us"; or most of *Rambler* 183 on envy. Mrs. Chapone, after talking with Johnson, "wondered to hear a man, who by his actions shows so much benevolence, maintain that the human heart is naturally malevolent, and that all the benevolence we see in the few who *are* good is acquired by reason and religion"; and when Johnson, in the *Tour to the Hebrides*, denied that human feelings were any more automatically or "instinctively" directed to the good than those of a "wolf," Lady MacLeod, said Boswell, muttered, in a "low voice," "This is worse than Swift."[16] Lastly there are the prolonged outbursts of laughter (as in the incident of Langton's will) where Johnson's intellect is piercing through the pretensions and self-delusions that make up so much of life and placing them against a background that almost nihilistically shrinks them into triviality.

6

Yet Johnson was not and could not be a satirist. He had not only the "aversion" to it mentioned by Mrs. Thrale, but also a hatred and fear of it, which is what led him to be so antagonistic and unfair to Swift. Against this background, Johnson's lifelong struggle for good humor (a "willingness to be pleased") and his efforts to check or suppress anger suddenly light up. They show that he did not dare to release the satiric impulse partly because it was so strong. But something else is involved—the charity and justice he is always bringing to "helpless man." He could not simply watch. He had to participate; and his own willing participation sets a bar to satire.

What happens, therefore, is that ridicule, anger, satiric protest, are always in the process of turning into something else. It is this process that is important. We have here what amounts to another genre or form of writing, the essence of which is not satire at all but which begins with satiric elements and an extremely alert satiric intelligence (indeed, an imagination that often seems most fertile and concrete when stung by exasperation). But then the writer—still fully aware of the satiric potentialities, still taking them all into account—suddenly starts to walk backward and then move toward something else. Much of Johnson's greater writing on human nature and human life falls into a distinctive literary type, eminently characteristic of him, that we might call "satire *manqué*" or "satire foiled." It involves a kind of double action in which a strong satiric blow is about to strike home unerringly when another arm at once reaches out and deflects or rather lifts it.[17] So deeply ingrained is this as a habit of thought that we see it throughout the whole course of his adult life. Something very close to it was already in solution even in the earliest poems, where a restive satire wrestles with both sympathy and philosophical "distance," especially in "The Young Author," written when he knew he had to give up Oxford; and in a relatively gentle form, we find it constantly stirring throughout the most personal work of his thirties, the *Life of Savage* (1744).

A condensed example, itself almost a miniature *Rambler* essay, occurs during one of those moments in the *Life of Savage*, where Johnson begins to generalize about human nature and destiny, in a sort of dialogue between two sides of himself. He is speaking here of the only work of Savage that could boast of a wide reception (his poem *The Bastard*), the sale of which was therefore "always mentioned by Savage as an incontestable proof of a general acknowledgement of his abilities":

> But though he did not lose the opportunity which success gave him, of setting a high rate on his abilities, but paid due deference to the suffrages of mankind when they were given in his favour, he did not suffer his esteem of himself to depend upon others, nor found any thing sacred in the voice of the people when they were inclined to censure him; he then readily showed the folly of expecting that the public should judge right, observed how slowly poetical merit had often forced its way into the world; he contented himself with the applause of men of judgment, and was somewhat disposed to exclude all those from the character of men of judgment who did not applaud him.
>
> But he was at other times more favourable to mankind than to think them blind to the beauties of his works, and imputed the slowness of their sale to other causes; either they were published at a time when the town was empty, or when the attention of the public was engrossed by some struggle in the Parliament, or some other object of general concern; or they were by the neglect of the publisher not diligently dispersed, or by his avarice not advertised with sufficient frequency. Address, or industry, or liberality, was always wanting; and the blame was laid rather on any person than the author.

But then the whole tone changes as the growing satiric exposure is swept up and put within another frame in the sentences that begin:

By arts like these, arts which every man practices in some degree, and to which too much of the little tranquility of life is to be ascribed, Savage was always able to live at peace with himself. Had he indeed only made use of these expedients to alleviate the loss or want of fortune or reputation, or any other advantages which it is not in man's power to bestow upon himself, they might have been justly mentioned as instances of a philosophical mind, and very properly proposed to the imitation of multitudes, who, for want of diverting their imaginations with the same dexterity, languish under afflictions which might be easily removed. . . .[18]

In its most concentrated form, the form or process of "satire *manqué*" pervades the brilliant decade of moral writing from *The Vanity of Human Wishes* (1748) to *Rasselas* (1759). In this as in other ways, *The Vanity of Human Wishes* serves as the prototype. Nowhere in literature is there a more panoramic view, condensed in a work so short, of the competition for riches and power, for fame and reputation, and the busy efforts of short-lived man to undercut others. And yet, as this huge, greedy struggle goes on, something begins to happen to all these people. They start to stumble and weaken; disease, the envy of others, and old age club or push them into weariness, despair, and finally death. (One thinks of the remark Johnson was sometimes heard to mutter to himself: "And then he died, poor man.") And this strange "satire," which—as Sir Walter Scott said, has drawn tears from people who would scorn sentimental poetry—softens its mockery by dissolving it within a profound compassion and a wider understanding. This is equally true of the prose writings of Johnson's forties, beginning with the *Rambler*. We see it most obviously in the "satiric portraits" that so often and with compassion or excuse (for example, the aging legacy hunter, in *Rambler* 73, who finally receives the money only after long habit has permanently corrupted him "with an inveterate disease of wishing" and therefore made him unable to live happily in the present).

But in the straightforward expository esssys as well there is a drama of thought and expression always moving from the reductive to explanation and finally to something close to apology. For almost every impatiently reductive phrase we cited earlier there is more than supplement. That remark "He who is growing great and happy by electrifying a bottle" comes from a man whose interest in science is equaled by few humanists of the past three centuries. The hunger and scramble for "reputation"—socially, intellectually, or in any other way—are repeatedly burlesqued, sometimes in the concrete example of a portrait but more often in a few sentences: the young who think that everyone who approaches them must be either an "admirer or a spy," when the cruel truth is that no one is even thinking of them; the lecturer who agonizes with the fear that renown or infamy is suspended on every syllable when, as a matter of fact, whatever he says will be only too quickly forgotten; the author in *Rambler* 146 who on the day of publication, with beating heart, walks out to the coffeehouses, like a monarch in disguise, expecting to overhear remarks about his book, prepared to bear with stoicism or good humor any censure, and he then finds that no one is even aware of the book. And yet the excuse, or at least explanation, is quickly at hand: the need of everyone to conceal his own unimportance from himself, and the doomed struggle of that need with the brute fact that the bulk of mankind—occupied, as Johnson reminds us, in shortening their way to some new possession or trying to ward off some expected calamity—have very little time to spare for the "reputation" of others, past or present. So even with the evils that sprout from envy and the readiness of the human animal to try to pull others down, most strident in its *Schadenfreude* (and therefore most evil) when it can release itself through the guise of maintaining virtue or "standards." In minds not constantly "corrected," by reason or religious belief, or preferably by both, this becomes the source of most of the daily anxiety and misery of human life. And yet (as Johnson concludes *Rambler* 76): "It is generally not so much the desire of men sunk into depravity to deceive the world as themselves. . . ."

Johnson's later work, from the *Preface to Shakespeare* to the *Lives of the Poets*, is as great as it is partly because it is the product of a mind—the product of a *life*—that has for years been subsuming some of the strongest temptations to satire of any major intelligence in history, while at the same time moving beyond them. This also explains much of the dramatic appeal of the conversations—the constant interplay between impatience, reductionism, turning a thing upside down and shaking the nonsense out of it, and, on the other hand, openness of empathy, participation, excuse and charity for others, relish, and eagerness in learning "to be pleased."

What we have been noticing is interesting not only in its own right but also as the most graphic example of something we find in Johnson's thinking generally: a habit of mind that, for shorthand purposes, we might call "trisociative." There is the original act of "bisociation," leaping across or bringing together two different frames of experience. Apart even from the psychological pressures that can carry him further into open ridicule, this "bisociative" jostling of the familiar into the new, simply because of its unpredictability, already involves or moves toward some form of humor or wit. It is partly this to which Thomas Tyers referred when he remarked that Johnson "said the most common things in the *newest* manner." But he was also referring to something else: a still further process of mind in which the original shuffling of perspectives, already surprising us with elements we had overlooked or forgotten, is joined by considerations drawn from other matrices of experience that can only be described as "moral," that is, having to do with the condition of man—with human hopes and fears; with value, purpose or aim; with the shared sense, never forgotten, of the "doom of man"; and with an unsleeping practical urgency in considering concretely what to do and how to live.

It is through this completing process that Johnson's refreshing *essentialism*, which is the secret of his "common-sense," is always emerging—refreshing because it is always coming to us through the vestibule of a new context. While it cleanses the mind, as Reynolds said, "of a great deal of rubbish," it also leads us back again to the fundamental, and in such a way as to release the human spirit rather than restrict it.

7

One by-product, in his own personal life, of what we have been discussing is Johnson's touching and unending struggle—especially beginning with his early sixties—to acquire something quite different from humor and often at odds with it. This is the combination of qualities suggested by the phrase "good humor," meaning "good nature," which in the *Rambler*, twenty-five years before, he had defined as "a *habit of being pleased;* a constant and perennial *softness* of manner, *easiness* of approach, and suavity of disposition." Without it, "learning and bravery can only confer that superiority which swells the heart of the lion in the desert, where he roars without reply, and ravages without resistance."[19]

For most of us, what is ordinarily meant by "good humor" or "good nature" embraces qualities that can, of course, include "humor" itself, and is often far better for it if it does; and it can also (though it need not) include compassion or something approaching it. But beyond a certain point, both "humor" and "compassion" could theoretically begin to violate or work against "good nature," especially as Johnson saw it. For both "humor" and "compassion" are by definition protests, in different ways, against the *status quo* and a refusal to accept what is happening with placid approval or sunny indifference. That form of smiling acceptance, without at least inner protest, was one of the things he naturally found hardest to acquire—harder even than learning to "surrender" himself to God's will and learning to find "repose" in that "surrender." And at times, when he had referred to it in the past, there could be real bitterness, as when he says with impatience that "good humor" is essentially a negative thing that involves neither intelligence nor virtue but, by its lack of both, puts envy to sleep and "pleases principally by not offending." But there was despair as well, as in his touching admission to Henry Thrale that he had never even "sought to please till past thirty years old, considering the matter as hopeless."[20]

The truth is that he had never lost his wistful admiration of the smiling good temper of his boyhood model, Cornelius Ford, however terrible the first five years after Johnson had to leave Oxford, when life seemed a constant battle for sanity, and however grim the long struggles in Grub Street that followed those years. In his late fifties, after recovering from the second breakdown that had darkened his life for at least two or three years, he had again tried more deliberately to acquire "good humor"—that elusive quality for which Mrs. Thrale, in her list of grades for her friends, gave him "O," however high the grade she gave him for "humor" itself. On the other hand, even with the help given him by his new life with the Thrales, he could feel that most of the habits he had acquired by middle age were hopelessly in conflict with this ideal: the aggressiveness he could often control only by turning it against himself; the habit of "talking for victory"; his instinctive tendency to face the miseries of life directly, emphasize them to their fullest extent and retain them in mind with the defensive feeling that "to be forewarned is to be forearmed." Yet this was not the way—as another part of himself kept maintaining—to go through life. Increasingly after his middle years we find him turning against these habits of mind with the desperation that breaks out when, in the *Lives of the Poets*, he speaks of Swift—always a frightening example for Johnson of what not to be: "He was not a man to be either loved or envied. He seems to have wasted life in discontent, by the rage of neglected pride and the languishment of unsatisfied desire."[21]

The most treacherous to his own happiness of all the habits of mind mentioned above was the one that he knew underlay and largely sustained the others—the firmly ingrained habit for over forty years of dwelling in his own imagination on the universal unhappiness of human life, partly in order to blunt or repress any temptation to envy others, partly in order to curb aggression against them and to realize they were equally vulnerable, but, above all, in order never again to be fooled and caught off guard and to be forced to endure again the horror he had lived through in his early twenties. Over and over in the moral essays he had tried to control this habit of "anticipating evils," to realize its insidious effect when it was carried too far, and to replace it with the "*habit* of being pleased." But this habit had long since become too closely interwoven with his own sense of identity and self-preservation. Now in his later years he could still burst out angrily, as we have noticed, if people talked lightly of the evils of life. Yet on one occasion he was checked if not checkmated. One day, said Miss Reynolds, he was again asserting that "the pain and miseries of human life far outweighed its happiness and good." At this particular moment he was sitting comfortably in a chair, and the company was friendly and pleasant. Doubtless thinking of this, a lady who was present gently asked him "whether he would not permit *common ease* to be put into the scale of happiness and good." At this, Johnson "seem'd *embarrassed* (very unusual with him), and answering in the affirmative, instantly rose from his seat to avoid the inference."[22]

Partly because of Johnson's open capacity for gusto and humor, but partly also because of his courage and intellectual honesty, he was able to prevent himself from being self-defensively sealed off from a quality he felt he almost completely lacked—that "readiness to be pleased" that he thought the essence of good nature. He hoped not only to understand it but also to keep it before him—however obdurate his own temperament—as a formative ideal about which he continued to think carefully, angrily, eagerly, and with something closer to love than he felt for almost any other human quality.

Chapter 28

Indian Summer

Johnson in his early sixties had entered a sort of Indian summer, and was now at sixty-five (1774) in the midst of it. If "summer's lease," as Shakespeare said, "hath all too short a date," that of Indian summer is far shorter, and its brevity for Johnson was all the more poignant since he had never had, in personal happiness at least, much of a summer.

Yet however brief it was, there has always been a timeless quality about this period of his life. If it is Johnson from his middle fifties till his death who is the "Johnson of legend," it is Johnson in his middle and late sixties who is the quintessence of it. Forever, by millions of people, he will be imagined as talking on any and every subject at taverns or at the Thrales'. What he said will be quoted time and again, from the richest collection of conversation in history; and books every year will be written, retelling the story of this period of his life.

2

"He loved the poor," said Mrs. Thrale,

as I never yet saw any one else do, with an earnest desire to make them happy.—What signifies, says some one, giving halfpence to common beggars? they only lay it out in gin or tobacco. "And why should they be denied such sweeteners of their existence (says Johnson)? it is surely very savage to refuse them every possible avenue to pleasure, reckoned too coarse for our own acceptance. *Life is a pill which none of us can bear to swallow without gilding. . . .*"

As a result, she goes on, he for years "nursed whole nests of people in his house, where the lame, the blind, the sick, and the sorrowful found a sure retreat from all the evils whence his little income could secure them." Asked once by a lady why he so constantly gave money to beggars, he replied with great feeling, "Madam, to enable them to beg *on*." Nor could he refrain from rebuking Mrs. Thrale when she once spoke in ridicule of the unpleasant odors of "Porridge Island" (a street filled with cheap "cook-shops" used by the poor): "Hundreds of your fellow-creatures, dear Lady, turn another way, that they may not be tempted by the luxuries of Porridge-Island to wish for gratifications they are not able to obtain." And just as he would give all the silver in his pocket to the poor who watched him as he left the house, so, on returning late at night, he for years had been putting pennies into the hands of children lying asleep on thresholds so that they could buy breakfast in the morning.[1]

Johnson's house had more than ever taken on the appearance of an informal home for the destitute and infirm. The inmates during these years, apart from others who came and went, consisted of a steady corps of six to eight people, including two elderly servants whose duties were light and who could themselves be viewed as pensioners. At the top in seniority and prestige—both were a few years older even than Johnson—were the blind Anna Williams, general hostess and pre-sider, and Mr. Levet, the "obscure practiser in physick amongst the lower people," still at seventy walking miles every day to look after the London poor and, while at home, serving as doctor-in-residence, said Mrs. Thrale, to "the whole Ship's Company."[2] As in the old days, the stiff and silent Levet continued to return to the house for a while, just before noon, in order to join Johnson for breakfast. There they would sit quietly, saying little or nothing, while Levet poured out tea alternately for himself and his patron and while Johnson, in disha-bille, would be preparing to meet the day. In the afternoon and again at night before going to bed, Johnson would punctiliously continue to have tea with Miss Williams, who would wait up for him however late the hour. With Levet and Miss Williams especially, after more than twenty years, he felt at home, and their ancient rivalry, though in-grained, had become externally subdued and redirected toward more recent inmates. Meanwhile (March 1776) Johnson moved to his final house—8, Bolt Court, just off Fleet Street—where there was a little garden behind, which he enjoyed watering. Miss Williams had her lodging on the ground floor, with Mr. Levet on the top floor.

Next in order of dignity, after Miss Williams and Levet, was the widowed Mrs. Desmoulins, who long before, as Elizabeth Swynfen, had served as a companion to Johnson's wife, and to whom Johnson had occasionally made fumbling advances, back in his late thirties, when his wife refused to let him sleep with her. Mrs. Desmoulins, who was now entering her sixties, had only recently entered the fold. She was given charge of the kitchen, to the disgust of Mr. Levet, who would periodically inform Johnson that the kitchen "is not now what it used to be." Besides her room and board, Johnson paid her what was then a high allowance—a half guinea a week. She also persuaded Johnson to take in her daughter, a woman about thirty, and at a particularly crowded time, to judge from a remark of Boswell, who, on arriving in London, "was informed that the room formerly allotted to me was now appropriated to a charitable purpose; Mrs. Desmoulins, and I think her daughter, and a Miss Carmichael, being all lodged in it!"[3]

The mysterious Poll Carmichael was almost certainly the prostitute Johnson late one night found lying sick and exhausted in the street. Of this prostitute we know only what Mrs. Desmoulins, without naming her, told Boswell after Johnson's death—that Johnson, taking pity on her, picked her up, carried her home on his back, had her nursed back to health, took care of her "for a long time, at considerable expense," and tried to "put her into a virtuous way of living." If Poll was the prostitute, it would explain why Johnson, whenever Mrs. Thrale tried to find out about Poll's origin, would evade answering lest she be prejudiced against her (even so, Mrs. Thrale may have learned the story, since in her unpublished journal she refers to her as "a Thing that he called Poll"). From some letters of Johnson's, we learn that Poll had been deprived of a little legacy she had hoped to get from her father, and that he got the eminent Chambers and later Arthur Murphy (who had by now entered the law) to take her case. But nothing came of it, and she remained as one of his pensioners, with her own pocket money as well as room and board.[4]

Especially after the advent of Mrs. Desmoulins and Poll, the quarreling became constant. ("Williams," as Johnson wrote to Mrs. Thrale, "hates everybody. Levet hates Desmoulins and does not love Williams. Poll loves none of them.") Often he was afraid of going home, said Mrs. Thrale, "because he was so sure to be met at the door with numberless complaints . . . every favour he bestowed on one was wormwood to the rest." But if she spoke of their ingratitude, he at once began to excuse them and to say, "I knew not how to make allowances for situations I never experienced." When pressed to explain why he went on helping them, said Hawkins, his answer was "If I did not assist them, no one else would, and they would be lost in want." Sometimes, when the rancor became most bitter, his only relief was to plunge into the fray and try to push it into comedy. Fanny Burney's diary records a discussion one day at Streatham (September 1778) when Mrs. Thrale tries to get him to talk about what Macaulay called his "menagerie," which he does with dramatic gusto—describing their feuds, and the general anarchy of the kitchen under Mrs. Desmoulins's charge. Mrs. Thrale then unsuccessfully tries to get him to tell them how Poll came into the family:

Mrs. T.—But pray, sir, who is the Poll you talk of? She that you used to abet in her quarrels with Mrs. Williams, and call out, *At her again, Poll! Never flinch, Poll?*

Dr. J.—Why, I took to Poll very well at first, but she won't do upon a nearer examination.

Mrs. T.—How came she among you, sir?

Dr. J.—Why, I don't rightly remember, but we could spare her very well from us. Poll is a stupid slut; I had some hopes of her at first; but, when I talked to her tightly and closely, I could make nothing of her; she was wiggle-waggle, and I could never persuade her to be categorical. I wish Miss Burney would come among us; if she would only give us a week, we should furnish her with ample materials for a new scene in her next work [a comedy called *The Witlings*].[5]

Frank Barber, the black youth Johnson had taken over from his friend Richard Bathurst back in 1752, had a special position. Now about thirty, he was only theoretically a servant—he was a sort of personal valet to Johnson (which occupied very little time), answered the door, waited on table on the few occasions when Johnson gave formal dinnners, and was in charge of ordering provisions for the house. Since Johnson regarded him almost as though he were a son, the others treated him with respect, except for Miss Williams. She had resented the £300 Johnson spent on his schooling, and now complained constantly of "Frank's neglect of his duty," while he in turn would complain to Johnson of "the authority she assumed over him, and exercised with an unwarrantable severity." In 1776 he married an English girl named Betsey, and for a while they lived outside in a nearby house in order to minimize friction with Miss Williams. Later, after Miss Williams's death, they moved in, with their two infant daughters. A third child, Samuel, was born after Johnson's death and became a well-known Methodist preacher in Staffordshire.[6]

Finally there were at least two real servants. Miss Williams had a maid—probably the Scottish maid she had inherited from Johnson's wife twenty-five years before—and there was also "a wretched Mrs. White" (as Mrs. Thrale cruelly called her in her journal), an elderly woman who served as general housekeeper. Johnson was always thoughtful about the feelings of anyone who worked for him. For example, when his cat, Hodge, got old and sick and could eat nothing but oysters, he always went out to buy them himself in order that Frank's "delicacy might not be hurt at seeing himself employed for the convenience of a quadruped."[7]

3

Counterpointing with this aspect of his life were the other worlds in which he lived: the half or more of every week that he spent with his "other family," the Thrales, from Monday night or Tuesday morning to Friday; the conversations with friends at taverns and at dinner parties.

The Club, originally consisting of nine members (1764), was now much larger. In the 1760's Bishop Percy, Robert Chambers, and the dramatist George Colman had been added. In the 1770's new members included David Garrick and the greatest linguist at this time in the whole of Europe, Sir William Jones; Adam Smith, Edward Gibbon (previously blackballed), and the dramatist Richard Brinsley Sheridan; two of the most notable statesmen in England, Charles James Fox and William Windham; and the famous naturalist Sir Joseph Banks. (There was also one serious loss—Goldsmith died in April 1774.) In 1773 the membership had been enlarged to twenty. In 1777 it was increased to twenty-six, in 1778 to thirty, and in 1780 to thirty-five.* In 1772 the

* A complete list of new members after the original nine and down to Johnson's death may be convenient, with dates of election: Samuel Dyer (1764), Bishop Percy and Robert Chambers (1765), George Colman (1768); in 1773 Garrick, Sir William Jones, Boswell, the Earl of Charlemont, and Agmondesham Vesey; in 1774 C. J. Fox, Gibbon, Sir Charles Bunbury, George Fordyce, and George Steevens; in 1775 Adam Smith and Thomas Barnard, later Bishop of Limerick; in 1777 Joseph Warton, R. B. Sheridan, Lord Ashburton, the Earl of Upper Ossory, and Richard Marley; in 1778 Joseph Banks, William Windham, Sir William Scott,

meetings were changed from Monday to Friday and were held fort-nightly instead of once a week. The chair was taken in rotation by each member in alphabetical order. Johnson had always felt that nine was as large as any group should be if general discussion was to be maintained. Otherwise conversation inevitably became split up among separate groups, as in any large dinner party. As The Club enlarged, Johnson, whose deafness was increasing, began to attend it less often.

Even so, Johnson saw his friends at The Club in other ways, at their homes or those of mutual friends, or at his own place in Bolt Court, or at the Thrales'. Some of the scenes in Boswell most often reprinted in anthologies are of social occasions spent in this way, though this is partly because he may have felt more restrained in reproducing con-versations at The Club itself. The discussion could at times become explosive. Typical would be the dinner at General Paoli's where they argued about the advantages of drinking wine, and Johnson—who, from abstaining from it so long, assumed everyone who drank wine was intoxicated—finally shouted to Reynolds, "I won't argue any more with you, Sir. You are too far gone" (at which Reynolds actually made Johnson blush by saying, "I should have thought so indeed, Sir, had I made such a speech as you have now done").[9]

An excerpt from at least one of these scenes may be pardoned, despite its length, to illustrate the dramatic ebb and flow that an argu-ment could take. At a dinner at Bishop Percy's, Johnson praised Thomas Pennant's *Tour in Scotland*. Percy, who liked to fancy him-self related to the noble Percys of Northumberland and was attached to them for personal favors, resented the disrespect with which Pen-nant had spoken of Alnwick Castle and the Duke's pleasure grounds, and "therefore opposed Johnson eagerly":

JOHNSON. "Pennant in what he said of Alnwick, has done what he in-tended; he has made you very angry." PERCY. "He has said the garden is trim, which is representing it like a citizen's parterre, when the truth is, there is a very large extent of fine turf and gravel walks." JOHNSON. "Ac-cording to your own account, Sir, Pennant is right. It is trim. Here is grass cut close, and gravel rolled smooth. Is not that trim? The extent is nothing against that; a mile may be as trim as a square yard. Your extent puts me in mind of the citizen's enlarged dinner, two pieces of roast-beef, and two puddings. There is no variety, no mind exerted in laying out the ground,

and Earl Spencer; in 1780 Jonathan Shipley, Bishop of St. Asaph; in 1782, Edmond Malone, Thomas Warton, Lord Eliot, Richard Burke, and the Earl of Lucan; in 1784 Sir William Hamilton, Viscount Palmerston, and Charles Burney.[8]

no trees." PERCY. "He pretends to give the natural history of Northumberland, and yet takes no notice of the immense number of trees planted there of late." JOHNSON. "That, Sir, has nothing to do with the natural history; that is civil history. A man who gives the natural history of the oak, is not to tell how many oaks have been planted in this place or that. A man who gives the natural history of the cow, is not to tell how many cows are milked at Islington. The animal is the same, whether milked in the Park or at Islington." PERCY. "Pennant does not describe well; a carrier who goes along the side of Lochlomond would describe it better." JOHNSON. "I think he describes very well." PERCY. "I travelled after him." JOHNSON. "And I travelled after him." PERCY. "But, my good friend, you are short-sighted, and do not see so well as I do." I wondered at Dr. Percy's venturing thus. Dr. Johnson said nothing at the time; but inflammable particles were collecting for a cloud to burst. In a little while Dr. Percy said something more in disparagement of Pennant. JOHNSON. (pointedly) "This is the resentment of a narrow mind, because he did not find every thing in Northumberland." PERCY. (feeling the stroke) "Sir, you may be as rude as you please." JOHNSON. "Hold, Sir! Don't talk of rudeness; remember, Sir, you told me (puffing hard with passion struggling for a vent) I was short-sighted. We have done with civility. We are to be as rude as we please." PERCY. "Upon my honour, Sir, I did not mean to be uncivil." JOHNSON. "I cannot say so, Sir; for I did mean to be uncivil, thinking you had been uncivil." Dr. Percy rose, ran up to him, and taking him by the hand, assured him affectionately that his meaning had been misunderstood; upon which a reconciliation instantly took place. JOHNSON. "My dear Sir, I am willing you shall hang Pennant."[10]

4

Now more than ever before—though perhaps it is because he had become so famous that there were more people eager to record it—Johnson was living up to the ideal given him as a boy of fifteen by his admired cousin Cornelius Ford—to possess "the general principles of every science," to "grasp the Trunk" of knowledge and "shake all the Branches," and then, in speaking, to be like Cornelius himself, who could pour out the distilled quintessence of the fruit "as smoothly as you rack off a Bottle into a Decanter." If the example of Cornelius's easy good nature still eluded him, Johnson far excelled his model in wit and humor; and the range of what he could discuss exceeded anything that Cornelius, as he spoke to the boy, had ever had in mind. Meanwhile Johnson received his second doctor's degree (March 1775), this time the degree of Doctor of Civil Law from Oxford—the very degree he had so badly wanted thirty years before so that he could fulfill his long dream of practicing civil law in the "Doctors' Commons." But he still continued to call himself "Mr." Johnson, nor was he eager to show his friends the diploma, which he thought effusive, though it obviously pleased him.[11]

Boswell, before they had taken their trip to the Hebrides, had already seen that there was no aspect of literature and language, of philosophy, theology, psychology, medicine, or history, that Johnson could not immediately illuminate (Johnson's supposed antipathy to "history" was only a pose—partly an attempt to remind himself and others that we are "free agents" and not the passive products of history, and partly a rebuke to historical pedants); and as for law, Johnson had already dictated to him the first of what were to be many legal briefs for cases Boswell was to argue in court. But only when Boswell was seeing Johnson day after day, on the trip through the Highlands and the Hebrides, did he fully realize what other friends of Johnson knew—the extent of Johnson's knowledge of science, the "useful arts," and practical trades. We noticed examples earlier, and may add a few more: "He this morning gave us all the operation of coining, and at night he gave us all the operation of brewing spirits," and so clearly that Mr. McQueen said that when he heard the first, he thought Johnson had been brought up in the Mint, and when he heard the second, that Johnson had been "bred as brewer." At Fort George he talked with the officers in such detail about the process of making gunpowder that he afterward, with a pang of conscience, felt he had spoken too "ostentatiously." Or again: "Last night Mr. Johnson gave us an account of the whole process of tanning, and of the nature of milk and the various operations upon it, as making whey, etc. . . ." Boswell at this point tried—as an experiment—to draw out Johnson on a subject that he thought furthest possible from a poet or philosopher—"the trade of a butcher"—and found that, despite Johnson's "horror of butchering," he could explain it in detail.[12]

It is perhaps less surprising that one of the three or four greatest critics in the history of literature should write lectures on law for William Blackstone's successor at Oxford, or dictate legal arguments to be presented at the House of Lords and the Court of Session, than that he should also arouse admiration by his discussion of mechanics before the Society of Arts and Manufacturers, the principal group in England concerned with the practical application of science. But earlier, in fact, he had been a member of at least five committees in that society. A fellow member of one committee was Benjamin Franklin (1761), whose electrical experiments Johnson had closely followed and whom he had first met in 1760 in a charitable organization to which they both belonged. The inventor Sir Richard Arkwright said that Johnson was "the only person who, on a first view, understood both the principle and powers of his most complicated piece of machinery" —his famous spinning machine (long before, as we noticed, he had been a sponsor of Arkwright's predecessor, Lewis Paul). As he grew older, he made a more conscious effort to avoid "stagnation" through "new images" and "new topics." He was rarely inclined to speak favorably of any quality in himself, but on one of the few occasions he did, he let himself admit:

"I value myself upon this, that there is nothing of the old man in my conversation. I am now sixty-eight, and I have no more of it than at twenty-eight. . . . Mrs. Thrale's mother said of me what flattered me much. A clergyman was complaining of want of society in the country . . . and said, 'They talk of runts;' (that is, young cows). 'Sir, (said Mrs. Salusbury) Mr. Johnson would learn to talk of runts.'" . . . He added, "I think myself a very polite man."[13]

It was not so much the detailed knowledge that mattered—though this showed his credentials—but the ability to make connections, to see the human experience as a whole, to revert to central premises and values, while using the detail as a means of illuminating the general thought, that made everyone who heard him acknowledge him the most gifted talker of his time. Burke, for example, was perhaps the greatest speaker—in richness of language and thought if not in elocution—in the history of Parliament, and he was no less able in ordinary conversation. But everyone knows his remark to Bennet Langton after an evening when topics on which Burke himself could speak with unrivaled knowledge were repeatedly taken up by Johnson "in a most masterly manner." Johnson, said Burke on the way home, had been "very great." Langton agreed, but added he would have liked to "hear more from another person," meaning Burke. "O, no," said Burke, "it is enough for me to have rung the bell to him."[14]

5

On the other hand, the greatest single disservice to Johnson as a *mind* —as a guide to the human spirit to whom posterity could turn for courage and wisdom—was his own fame, after his death, as a talker. For it was the dramatic picture of Johnson as a supreme conversationalist that, more than anything else, swept attention away from his works to this one aspect of his life. The result, however engaging and picturesque, was to impoverish immensely his meaning and value as a fellow participator in human experience; and it is only within our own generation that we have at last begun to rediscover his real greatness.

What the nineteenth century substituted in place of Johnson's own writings—a conception of Johnson as talker, with quotations drawn largely from Boswell and, to some extent, Mrs. Thrale—was inevitably more limited in intellectual content than what he himself wrote. Even if everything he had said had been transcribed, this would still be so. As he himself was always saying, the best part of any author is naturally to be found in his works, or he would not be an author worth reading. But this is especially the case when those who tried to report what he said wrote it down only afterward and thus were forced to rely on memory. Inevitably what they tended to recall were short and crisp remarks, usually phrased with some wit. Otherwise, however brilliantly he may have talked, we know of it partly from general testimony rather than from direct quotation ("He this morning gave us all the operation of coining, and at night he gave us all the operation of brewing spirits," etc.). Often the testimony is from the most impressive sources—from Burke, for example. Yet we have only to glance at the reviews he wrote for the *Literary Magazine* on every subject, over twenty years before, to get a far more direct insight into his range of knowledge, or to glance at a dozen essays for the *Rambler* to find him speaking about human experience generally and with a massive relevance to every aspect of our lives that the recorded conversations could never equal.

This is why any collection or anthology of "Johnsoniana" that tries to represent the "mind of Johnson" becomes very thin if it remains only with the spoken remarks, and is more than a mere curiosity only if it also turns—however superficially—to the writings. The point is not to derogate the recorded conversations. Far from it. But their intellectual and moral value is as a supplement to what he wrote. Viewed in this light, they can often be seen to distill thoughts or feelings put more richly and strongly in his writings; and they have the further interest to us of doing so after a period of his life (the breakdown in his fifties) when all that he had written had already—in the severest and most literal way—been tested in the fire, and was now, ten or twelve years later, being further tested at a time when he knew that his life (as he never ceased to remind himself) was inevitably drawing to an end. "When I survey my past life," as he wrote (March 30, 1777) in his journal, "I discover nothing but a barren waste of time with some disorders of the body, and disturbances of mind very near to madness." But he will not despair ("despair is criminal"), and the resolutions continue. April 20, 1778: "In reviewing my time from Easter—77, I find a very melancholy and shameful blank. . . . My health has indeed been very much interrupted. My nights have been commonly not only restless but painful and fatiguing. . . . *I am now with the help of God to begin a new life.*" April 13, 1779 (11:00 P.M.): "Of resolutions I have made so many with so little effect, that I am almost weary, but, by the Help of God, am not yet hopeless. Good resolutions must be made and kept. I am almost seventy years old, and have no time to lose."[15]

6

With accumulating infirmities constantly reminding him that time was evaporating, he made even stronger efforts to acquire that mysterious combination of qualities that he considered to make up "good humor" —"readiness to be pleased," "easiness of approach," and "softness of manner." He tried harder to resist the temptation to "talk for victory," though time and again he would relapse into doing so. "That is the happiest conversation," he would say, "where there is no competition, no vanity, but a calm quiet interchange of sentiments." A remark he had made in the Hebrides expresses a sort of credo of which he kept reminding himself: "A man grows better-humoured as he grows older, by experience. He learns to think himself of no consequence and little things of little importance; and so he becomes more patient, and better pleased. All good-humour and complaisance is acquired." And five years later (1778) he was putting it even more strongly: "A man's being in good or bad humour depends on his will."[16]

"It is by *studying little things*," he had told Boswell soon after he met him, "that we attain the great art of having as little misery, and as much happiness as possible." Now, thirteen years later (1776), when Boswell tried to get him to talk again about the "management of the mind," he came back to this. We must "*divert* distressing thoughts, and not *combat* with them." Could you not "think them down?" asks

Boswell. "To attempt to *think them down*," said Johnson, "is madness." The only effective procedure is to deflect or displace them. Boswell, knowing of Johnson's experiments in chemistry at late hours of the night when he could not sleep, artfully asks: would it not be a good idea for a man so afflicted to "take a course of chymistry?" "Let him take a course of chymistry, or a course of *rope-dancing*"—anything that will get the mind off itself. It is the focusing of the mind on specific interests—the ability, in short, to live in the moment—that prevents it from preying on itself, which it will otherwise surely do.[17]

Repeatedly he would continue to tell himself that the "main of life" consists of "little things"; that happiness or misery is to be found in the accumulation of "petty" and "domestic" details, not in "large" ambitions, which are inevitably self-defeating and turn to ashes in the mouth. "Sands make the mountain," he would quote from Edward Young. In past years he would speak with irritation of anyone who could "shuffle cards and rattle dice from noon to midnight without tracing any new idea in his mind." But now he said (whether or not he wholly meant it) that he was "sorry I have not learnt to play at cards." Simply by being a communal activity, it has a social function that, in its way, "generates kindness and consolidates society"—consolidates in the sense of bringing people together as a unit—whereas "intellectual" conversation leads to debates, heated talk, and disagreement followed by heady dislike. When Boswell complained that at an elaborate dinner there had not been "one sentence of conversation worthy of being remembered," and added "Why then meet at table?," Johnson replied, "Why to eat and drink together, and to promote kindness; and, Sir, this is better done when there is no solid conversation; for when there is, people differ in opinion, and get into bad humour, or some of the company who are not capable of such conversation are left out, and feel themselves uneasy." He would say that women were lucky because the "general consent of the world" would allow them to do "little things, like knitting or knotting, without disgracing themselves"—occupations, as he told Mrs. Thrale, that contributed to "lengthening their lives, and preserving their minds in a state of sanity." He himself privately "tried knotting. Dempster's sister undertook to teach me; but I could not learn it." He even bought a small flute in order to learn to play it, though he finally gave up because "I never made out a tune." But after he moved to Bolt Court, he had more success with a little garden, which, says Hawkins, "he took delight in watering," and he then began to prune the vines and look after them with new interest. On only one thing did he inevitably face complete defeat—the ability, in conversation, to talk mildly and at length about trifles without pushing them into comedy and burlesquing them. Talk of the weather especially annoyed him. When anyone spoke of it, said Charles Burney, he would burst out, "You are telling us that of which none but men in a mine or a dungeon can be ignorant."[18]

What especially complicated his efforts to acquire "good nature"— the healing "balm" of human existence—is that he rightly saw it as a twofold thing. There was the subjective element of his own state of mind—of learning to "be pleased"—which was already struggle enough. But "good nature" was also, and above all, a *social* quality (perhaps, he at times suspected, the supreme social quality). As such, it had long since become further intermingled with exacting notions of "good manners," "good breeding," and "politeness" that, as he viewed them, could be especially demanding for someone who had lived as he had. With his wide and sympathetic knowledge "of what we call low or coarse life," said Mrs. Thrale, he would resent it when others, like Reynolds, used the expression "the world" when they were talking only about the upper ranks of society. But it was noticeable, she added, that no praise of any kind was ever "more welcome to Dr. Johnson than that which said he had the notions and manners of a gentleman."[19]

One amusing result of his self-struggle was that he had developed "many *rigid* maxims concerning the necessity of continued *softness* and compliance of disposition." Moreover, in his own self-conscious and sporadic pursuit of "good breeding," he would often go to a length that his more sophisticated friends thought hilarious in its contrast to the way he himself habitually looked and acted. Miss Reynolds gives some examples: his "emotion" one day at table (with complete oblivion to his own table manners) when he saw Frank Barber, who was waiting on them, put the salver under his arm; or his fastidious dislike of the way people who had to blow their noses thought nothing of using a handkerchief at the table, whereas he himself would ostentatiously get up from his chair "and go at some distance with his back to the company, performing the operation as silently as possible." He "piqued himself much upon knowledge of the rules of true politeness," and was especially "punctilious" in what he considered gallantry toward ladies. For example, he would never suffer a lady to walk from his house to her carriage, even during the daytime, without his own personal attendance. Yet, at the same time, he would have completely neglected his clothes, especially in the morning, to such an extent that

Miss Reynolds marveled "how a man in his senses could think of stepping outside his door in them, or even to be seen at home in them." As a result, crowds would immediately gather to stare at him wearing old shoes instead of slippers, and with the knees of his breeches hanging loose, his wig awry, and "his important air (that indeed cannot be described)."[20]

Another indirect result of his fascination with "the graces" ("Every man of any education," as he said one day to the surprise of the company, "would rather be called a rascal, than accused of deficiency in the *graces*") was a peculiarity that puzzled even Mrs. Thrale. Though Johnson was himself "at an immeasurable distance" from anything like contentment with "his own uncouth form and figure, he did not like another man much the less for being a coxcomb." Probably physical vanity was so remote from his own experience that he simply could not understand it, but, with overgenerous empathy, associated it with a kind of elegance he had wistfully admired at a distance ever since his boyhood visit to Cornelius at Stourbridge. And when Mrs. Thrale one day censured two friends of theirs "who were particularly fond of looking at themselves in a glass," "They do not surprise me at all by so doing (said Johnson): they see, reflected in that glass, men who have risen . . . who have merited their advancement . . . and I do not see why they should avoid the mirror."[21]

It was through his appeal to Johnson's ideal of good manners that Boswell engineered a feat no one else thought possible: getting Johnson to meet at dinner his old political enemy John Wilkes, whom he considered a scoundrel in every way—an encounter into which Boswell tricked him in order to see what would happen. The publishers Charles and Edward Dilly were giving a dinner to which Wilkes and Boswell, among others, were invited. Boswell at once sensed a dramatic opportunity. Would the Dilly brothers also invite Johnson? They were filled with horror at what could happen, but, at Boswell's pleading, left it in his hands. Approaching Johnson very indirectly, Boswell gave him the invitation to the Dillys'—which Johnson accepted—and then said that they would be happy to have him dine there provided the company they asked "is agreeable to you." Johnson, thus alerted to his own ideal of the social "graces," said that he would never dream of dictating to another "what company he is to have at his table." Then Boswell brought up the name of Wilkes—would even Wilkes be acceptable? Of course. It would be an insult to Johnson to think he could not meet any company. And everything did work out well, though at least as much because of the engaging charm of Wilkes sitting next to him as because Johnson had been put on his mettle.[22]

7

In his zeal to maintain that "all good humour and complaisance" can be "acquired," he could at times slip into violating the very ideal he was preaching. One day, at the home of Sir Joshua Reynolds, a clergyman who had greatly admired Johnson—Thomas Barnard, later Bishop of Limerick—innocently said that "after forty-five a man did not improve." This was a sentiment that Johnson in his gloomier moments shared, feeling that men like dogs tend to grow worse as they grew older. But now, struggling against the idea, he was aroused to strong antagonism: "I *differ* with you," he called out. "A man *may* improve, and," he hastily added, "you *yourself* have great room for improvement." (In fairness to Johnson, one must add that, when Miss Reynolds privately rebuked him for this, Johnson at once tried to make it up to Barnard. Going back to the drawing room, he sat on the sofa next to him, beseeching his pardon and "literally smoothing down his arms and knees—tokens of penitence, which were so graciously received . . . as to make Dr. Johnson very happy.") To the nice people, said Mrs. Thrale, who could not "bear to be waked at an unusual hour, or miss a stated meal," Johnson—in maintaining the need of "*being pleased*"—showed no mercy. And when Boswell, in the Highlands, had proposed carrying lemons so that Johnson would always have his lemonade instead of wine, Johnson became angry at the thought that he could not be "pleased" by the entertainment wherever he went: "I do not wish to be thought *that feeble man who cannot do without anything*. Sir, it is very bad manners to carry provisions to any man's house, as if he could not entertain you."[23]

There were also occasions when, exasperated by his own inner conflicts (his "loud explosions," as Boswell noted, were usually "guns of distress"), he was really impervious to the implications of what he had been saying. Once, said Miss Reynolds, Johnson spoke so roughly before a company to Mrs. Thrale that after the ladies withdrew, one of them expressed her indignation. But the patient Mrs. Thrale, knowing how Johnson was feeling, said only:

"Oh! Dear good man!" . . . [the other] Lady took the first opportunity of communicating it to him, repeating her own animadversion. . . . He seem'd much delighted with this intelligence, and sometime after, as he was lying back in his Chair, seeming to be half asleep, but more evidently musing on this pleasing incident, he repeated in a loud whisper, "Oh! Dear good man!"[24]

But this was an exception. In general, as Sir Joshua Reynolds said, he was "the first to seek after a reconciliation," and he would immediately say with shame, "I am sorry for it. I'll make it up to you twenty different ways as you please." Increasingly, the more testy of his quoted remarks usually have a context that is not remembered. An example is his reply to a foolish question of Mrs. Thrale's nephew, "Would you advise me to marry?" The immediate reply was: "I would advise no man to marry . . . who is not likely to propagate understanding." But when the quotation is given and justly laughed at, the sequel is rarely mentioned. Johnson, who had left the room, returned "and drawing up his chair among us," said Mrs. Thrale, "with altered looks and a softened voice . . . insensibly led the conversation to the subject of marriage," and talked in a way "so useful, so elegant, so founded on the true knowledge of human life . . . that no one ever recollected the offence, except to rejoice in its consequences." And there were at least moments now—at once touching and comic—when we find him able to relax from self-struggle into a happy satisfaction that he was at last attaining this quality of good nature that had so eluded him. One such moment occurred when he and Boswell were riding in a coach (he was now sixty-five), and he suddenly turned to Boswell and said:

"It is wonderful, Sir, how rare a quality good humour is in life. We meet with very few good humoured men." I mentioned four of our friends [Reynolds, Burke, Beauclerk, and Langton], none of whom he would allow to be good humoured. One was acid, another was muddy, and to the others he had objections which have escaped me. Then, shaking his head and stretching himself at his ease in the coach, and smiling with much complacency, he turned to me and said, "I look upon myself as a good humoured fellow."[25]

8

One of the ironies of his situation, in his later sixties, is that while he could at last afford to travel (for he could be content with simple accommodations), his health and age now made it impossible for him to travel alone for any long distance. Twenty years before, when he would not have needed companions so badly, it would have been easy to find them. Now it was almost impossible. Even his younger friends were now middle-aged and living settled lives. It was one thing for Boswell, who was more tied to his occupation and family responsibilities than we sometimes remember, to take off time for the very special trip they had made to the Hebrides in 1773. But anything of even comparable scale would be difficult for Boswell to repeat. Still less was he eager to take up Johnson's enthusiastic proposal that they now make a trip to the Baltic and the Scandinavian countries, and he tried politely, when he wrote to Johnson, to withdraw himself from any plan to go there.[26] Reynolds and Burke led busy professional lives, and the wealthy John Taylor had no curiosity about foreign parts. Only the Thrales were possible as traveling companions, and they had problems. Aside from the business, there were always the children, and Mrs. Thrale did not want to be absent from them for too long.

Meanwhile Johnson continued to speak wistfully of a long trip to India. At other times, lowering his sights, he would talk eagerly, said Tom Tyers, "of travelling into Poland, to observe the life of the Palatines." Above all, he wanted to see Italy. "The grand object of travelling;" he said (1776), "is to see the shores of the Mediterranean. On those shores were the four great Empires of the world; the Assyrian, the Persian, the Grecian, and the Roman.—All our religion, almost all our law, almost all our arts . . . come to us from the shores of the Mediterranean."[27] With so little else possible to him, he continued to make an almost annual circuit through Oxford to Lichfield and then to Ashbourne, where he would stay with John Taylor, listen to Taylor's remarks about his agricultural interests and his prize bull, and talk with local worthies at Taylor's dinner table. One of these trips lasted for more than two months, and another for more than three.*

There was, however, a two-month excursion with the Thrales to Paris in the autumn of 1775, during which they also saw French towns and cities on the way to and from Paris. This was not what he himself, in his heart, meant by "travel"—a combination of a boyish feeling of adventure in seeing distant places and inquiring into modes of life

---

* In 1775, May 29 to mid-August; in 1776, March 19 to 29 (cut short by Harry Thrale's death); in 1777, July 28 to November 6; in 1779, May 21 to the end of June. In addition, he made a trip to Bath (April 1776) and Essex (September 1778), and, though he disliked Brighton more than ever, would often spend some time there with the Thrales in the autumn (1775, 1776, 1777, 1780).

radically different. Moreover, travel with the Thrales, as he had learned on the Welsh trip, was not a foot-loose ramble but an organized undertaking, with a good deal of impedimenta, and was inevitably restricted to special levels of society. It was, in short, "tourism" as the affluent tend to conceive tourism. Still, he was glad to accept the invitation. It was the same group that had gone to Wales—Henry and Hester Thrale, the oldest girl, Queeney, now eleven, and Johnson, but with the addition this time of Giuseppe Baretti, Queeney's Italian tutor, who spoke French fluently and who acted as general guide and arranger of details. There were also a manservant and a couple of maids.

They arrived at Calais on Queeney's birthday (September 17), the day before Johnson's; and he spent a sleepless night on his own birthday trying to keep out of mind its implications—he was now sixty-six. They went through Arras, Amiens, and Rouen, where an old friend of Hester Thrale's—Mrs. Charles Strickland—joined their party. On the way Johnson made up a little rhyming distich for each place they stopped (for example, "A Calais/Trop de frais," "St. Omer/Tout est cher," or, for Arras, where the Thrales were appalled by the atrocious inn, "Arras/Helas!"). An accident occurred between Rouen and Paris. The postilion fell off his horse as they were going down a steep hill, the traces were broken, one of the horses was run over, and Mr. Thrale, leaping out of the carriage, hurt himself, though not seriously. Mrs. Strickland was indignant at the calm with which Johnson took the incident.[28] Though on setting out he had decided he would try to speak French as much as possible, he spoke Latin when he talked with French priests and learned men. In doing so, he was not, as is sometimes thought, showing a John Bull–like contempt of the French language. He simply felt that he should talk in the best way he could. Next to English, Latin was the language that allowed him to do so. Nor was there anything unusual or eccentric about this. Latin was still regarded and widely used by scholars as an international language.

October was spent in and around Paris, and was filled with sightseeing. They visited the École Militaire, the Chartreuse, the palaces, churches, and museums. They went out to Versailles, and at Fontainebleau were admitted with a large group (October 19) to watch the King and Queen eat dinner. Three days later Johnson ran a race in the rain with Baretti, who was ten years younger, and beat him. One day they visited the English Austin nuns at Notre Dame de Sion. It was probably here that he made his famous remark to the prioress:

"Madam, you are here, not for love of virtue, but the fear of vice"—to which she made the gentle reply that "she should remember this as long as she lived." Particularly interesting to Johnson were the Royal Menagerie, with its collection of unusual animals, like the rhinoceros, and places of manufacture—the porcelain works at Sèvres, the large brewery of A. J. Santerre, and the Gobelin tapestry factory. He also paid two visits to the Palais de Justice in order to hear the pleadings. Like Mrs. Thrale, he kept a journal of sorts, though only part of it survives. But unlike Mrs. Thrale's readable account, his own journal is written as a condensed series of factual details about what he saw (as contrasted with what he and the Thrales did otherwise)—details about things and places (chapels, churches, paintings), about manufactures, roads, libraries, and social conditions.[29]

9

On November 1 they left Paris and returned home by way of Chantilly, Douay, Lille, and Dunkirk. As he confessed a year later, there had really been no time for him to get to know France. What he had seen were only "the *visibilities* of Paris, and around it."[30]

But the Thrales were so pleased by their excursion that, to Johnson's delight, they now began to plan for next year the long trip to Italy that they and Johnson had so often discussed. They were assured by Baretti that they would need a full year, and Thrale agreed. But Hester wanted it confined to six months (April to October 1776) so that they would be home when their boy, Harry, entered Westminster School. Baretti again would be their guide, and he started to work out the itinerary.

As the following spring approached (they were due to leave on April 8), Johnson decided to pay a farewell visit in March to friends in Oxford, Lichfield, and Birmingham, and also to say good-bye to John Taylor at Ashbourne. Boswell, who had just come to London for a visit, set off with him (March 19). Johnson, he said, "seemed very happy" at the thought of going to Italy. But they had no sooner got to Lichfield than Johnson, while they were having breakfast with Lucy Porter, received word from John Perkins, the head clerk of the Thrale brewery, that the nine-year-old Harry Thrale, the only surviving son, had suddenly died two days before (March 23) after a short and violent illness—possibly a cerebral aneurysm. This had been a fearful blow to the family. Thrale took the news, said Baretti, "stiffly erect, and with such a ghastly smile, as was quite horrid to behold," while Mrs. Thrale collapsed into a series of fainting fits, emerging from one only to fall into another. Johnson, reading the news at Lucy Porter's house, startled Boswell by his remark—"One of the most dreadful things that has happened in my time"—which made Boswell assume he was talking of some dreadful public event, like the assassination of the King or a second great fire of London. "What is it?" they asked. "Mr. Thrale," he said, "has lost his only son. . . . This is a total extinction to their family, as much as if they were sold into captivity." When Boswell mentioned that Thrale had daughters, he replied, "Don't you know how you yourself think? Sir, he wishes to propagate his name."[31]

They cut their visit short, and hurried back to London. Johnson had hoped to console his friends, but just as they arrived they found Mrs. Thrale leaving with Queeney in the carriage for Bath. Her reason for going there, said Baretti, was to "avoid the sight of the funeral," which she felt she could not endure. Johnson did not offer to go with her since he felt that Mr. Thrale was especially in need of comfort. But Thrale had shut himself away from all company. He wished to see no one, even Johnson. A little hurt, but understanding the situation, Johnson went back to his own house. Thrale, a few days later (April 5), called on him, while Boswell was there. "He seemed to me," said Boswell, "to hesitate as to the intended Italian tour." But Johnson did not sense this. For when the subject came up, he spoke "with a tone of animation" of the places they would see, especially Rome, Naples, Florence, and Venice. But in another day or so, Thrale privately told him that the trip could not take place this year. Johnson not only accepted the decision with grace but stood up for it. "While grief is fresh," he said to Boswell, "every attempt to divert only irritates. You must wait till grief be *digested*, and then amusement will dissipate the remains of it." As for his own hopes to see Italy, "I am disappointed, to be sure; but it is not a great disappointment." Yet he probably took it for granted that the journey had not been merely deferred but that the Thrales now would never go to Italy. For he added that he might eventually "contrive to get to Italy some other way."[32]

10

The publication of Johnson's *Journey to the Western Islands of Scotland* (January 1775) brought with it one of the famous minor episodes in literary history—the angry response of James Macpherson, who resented what Johnson had said of his supposed translations of the Gaelic poet "Ossian," and Johnson's celebrated reply. Back in 1760, when Macpherson was twenty-four, he had brought out a book called *Fragments of Ancient Poetry Collected in the Highlands of Scotland*, which he said were translated from original Gaelic sources. When this book met with success, he claimed the next year that he had now discovered an "epic" about the Celtic hero Fingal, written in the third century by Fingal's poet son, Ossian. His first installment was published with the resounding title *Fingal, an Ancient Epic Poem, in Six Books, Together with Several Other Poems, Composed by Ossian, the Son of Fingal* (1761). A second installment appeared two years later: *Temora, an Ancient Epic Poem, in Eight Books, Together with Several Other Poems, Composed by Ossian . . .* (1763). He added an essay explaining how he had collected these poems and stressing their value as social history.

The style in which Macpherson wrote these supposed translations was a cadenced, half-chanting English prose, patterned after the Bible. His hope, in this style, was to combine an abrupt vigor—appropriate to a primitive bard—with a haunting suggestiveness, though a modern reader tends to find the style both stilted and jerky. The work was welcomed by many Scots, who were elated to think their poetic past extended so far back. It also caught the imagination of Europeans generally, who hungered for the "fresh" vigor and lost "sublime" of primitive, more "natural" societies. Herder and Goethe were among its admirers. Later, Napoleon carried an Italian translation of it on his campaigns, and sometimes modeled his military dispatches on its abrupt style. In addition, he had scenes from Ossian painted on the ceiling of his study.

Johnson, from the start, suspected that these works were not a true translation from a primitive poet. To his shrewd literary sense, there were too many things about it that proved it to be a modern work. Nor was he impressed by the quality of the result, which he described as "a mere unconnected rhapsody." When Hugh Blair, who had warmly championed the authenticity of the poems, asked him whether "any man of a modern age could have written such poems," Johnson jolted him by replying, "Yes, Sir, many men, many women, and many children," and later, talking with Reynolds, he said that "a man might write such stuff for ever, if he would *abandon* his mind to it." During his trip through the Highlands, he had made an effort to look into the matter more closely, and had concluded that the only "source" Macpherson could have had were some passages from old songs and some names and events that still lingered in popular stories. In his *Journey to the Western Islands,* he stated briefly his conviction that the works of Ossian "never existed in any other form than that we have seen"—that is, in no other form than Macpherson's supposed "translations." "The editor, or author could never show the original; nor can it be shown by any other. To revenge reasonable incredulity by refusing evidence is a degree of insolence with which the world is not yet acquainted; and stubborn audacity is the last refuge of guilt."[33] Getting wind of this while the book was still being printed, Macpherson tried to get the publisher, William Strahan, to cancel the passage, and, when this failed, to make Johnson publish an apology as an "Advertisement," which Macpherson obligingly wrote out in advance. This too failed. Then Macpherson wrote Johnson directly. The letter, which has not survived, was said by an anonymous friend of Macpherson's to inform Johnson that "his age and infirmities, alone, protected him," though, according to Baretti, the letter stated that "neither his age nor infirmities should protect him." There is some evidence that there were two letters, the second of which threatened physical violence.

Macpherson was a large, heavy man, noted for his thick legs, which he tried to hide by wearing high boots. In addition, he was twenty-seven years younger than Johnson. Johnson's reply, however familiar, can only be quoted again. For generations, the best-known version (there were three) was one that Boswell got Johnson to dictate. Finally the original letter turned up; for, incredible as it may seem, Macpherson—for whatever reason—kept the letter:

Mr James Macpherson—I received your foolish and impudent note. Whatever insult is offered me I will do my best to repel, and what I cannot do for myself the law will do for me. I will not desist from detecting what I think a cheat, from any fear of the menaces of a Ruffian.

You want me to retract. What shall I retract? I thought your book an imposture from the beginning, I think it upon yet surer reasons an imposture still. For this opinion I give the publick my reasons which I here dare you to refute.

But however I may despise you, I reverence truth and if you can prove the genuineness of the work I will confess it. Your rage I defy, your abilities since your Homer [a mediocre translation of the *Iliad* into "Ossianic" prose] are not so formidable, and what I have heard of your morals disposes me to pay regard not to what you shall say, but to what you can prove.

You may print this if you will.

Sam: Johnson

Johnson then provided himself with a weapon in case Macpherson lived up to his threats. It was a thick oak stick, says Hawkins, almost six feet high, with an immense knob at the top, the size of an orange, which he kept near his chair and his bed, within ready reach should Macpherson break in on him.[34]

11

Except for the *Journey to the Western Islands*, the publications of this period, until his seventieth year, were few and minor. All of them were short pieces written as favors to others—printed proposals for their works, or dedications, the best known of which are the Dedications for Charles Burney's *History of Music* (1776) and Reynolds's *Seven Discourses [on Art] Delivered in the Royal Academy* (1778).* For the monument to Goldsmith in Westminster Abbey, he wrote in Latin the fine epitaph that members of The Club petitioned him to rewrite in English as the language Goldsmith's own writings adorned. Johnson refused, saying he "would never consent to disgrace the walls of Westminster Abbey with an English inscription." The true reason is probably that he felt that the epitaph, as he had written it, had already phrased what he had to say in the best way he could do it, and he wanted to leave well enough alone. He also wrote a Prologue for a play he may never have read by a dead man he had never met. This was for Hugh Kelly, who had been a staymaker as well as a playwright of sorts. The proprietor of Covent Garden, Thomas Harris, put on a one-night performance of poor Kelly's *A Word to the Wise* (May 29, 1777) for the benefit of Kelly's widow and children, and got Johnson to write a Prologue that would conciliate the audience. But however generous in these ways, Johnson at times rebelled against one of the chronic penalties of literary eminence—the constant pestering by people with literary ambitions who tried to get him to read their

---

* Aside from the Dedications for Burney and Reynolds, publications included Proposals for the works of Charlotte Lennox (1775) and William Shaw's *Analysis of the Scotch Celtic Language* (1775); the Prologue for Hugh Kelly's play, *A Word to the Wise* (1777); a Preface for Baretti's *Easy Phraseology for the Use of Young Ladies . . . of the Italian Language* (1775); a Dedication for Zachary Pearce's *Four Evangelists and the Acts of the Apostles* (1777); an Advertisement for a new edition of work by his dead friend Dr. Robert James, *A Dissertation on Fevers* (1778); a Dedication for the *Poems* of Henry Lucas (1779), a Preface for the *Poems* of Thomas Maurice (1779), and an election address for Henry Thrale (September 5, 1780).

manuscripts. Aside from the time demanded for this privilege, there was the further fact, as he said, that no one was really satisfied with less than praise and, after that, one's influence with others in support of the work. "Praise," he once sighed to Hannah More, "is the tribute which every man is expected to pay for the grant of perusing a manuscript." One was being forced, in other words, either to be uncharitable or to lie. Asked once by Mrs. Thrale what he had said to the author of a tragedy that had been lying around his rooms for some time (it was a play by Arthur Murphy), "I told him," replied Johnson, "that there was too much *Tig* and *Tirry* in it." When she laughed, he explained: he had looked only at the list of characters, "and there was *Ti*granes and *Ti*ridates, or Teribazus, or such stuff. A man can tell but what he knows, and I never got any further than the first page."[35]

Among his charitable writings at this time, the most famous is the group of documents he wrote on behalf of the Reverend William Dodd, who had been convicted of forgery—then a capital crime—and sentenced on May 26, 1777, to be hanged.[36] Dodd, a man of forty-eight, had been for years one of the most popular preachers in London. Especially celebrated were the sermons he gave at Magdalen House—a charity for reformed prostitutes—where the audience would sob and wail as he spoke. The nobility often attended these sermons. Meanwhile, in the churches where he preached, there was often not even standing room. He also fancied himself an author, and turned out books easily, though their interest now is mainly as a curiosity.

Unfortunately Dodd had high social ambitions. Moreover, he was entranced by a naïve idea of luxury, typified by the long perfumed robe of silk and the large diamond ring that he wore as he preached. He acquired a country house, bought coaches and paintings (including some by Titian, Rembrandt, and Rubens), gave large parties, and was widely nicknamed "the macaroni parson." Living so extravagantly, he fell deeply into debt. In order to raise money, he forged the signature of the Earl of Chesterfield to a bond for £4,200, telling the broker that he had been secretly commissioned by Chesterfield to cash this bond for him in order to pay a private "debt of honour." This was not the famous Earl of Chesterfield but a young man of twenty-two—a cousin of the old Earl, who had died without issue four years before (1773). Dodd had been one of his tutors when he was a boy and, having always found him generous, assumed that he would not prosecute in case Dodd could not return the money in time. But the young Earl was unforgiving and appeared against him, and Dodd was convicted.

In his distress, Dodd thought of Johnson's compassionate nature and power of writing, though he had been in Johnson's company only once. There is some indication that the idea of asking Johnson came from a man of whom Johnson was very fond—Edmund Allen, the printer, who was Johnson's neighbor at Bolt Court and also his landlord. Allen then called on Johnson, carrying with him a letter from the Countess of Harrington, who had become interested in the matter, and who asked Johnson's help in securing a royal pardon. Johnson, said Allen, walked up and down his room for a while and "seemed much agitated." Finally he said, "I will do what I can." Here we may remind ourselves that the mysterious disgrace Johnson's brother, Nathaniel, had brought on himself—followed soon afterward by his death, possibly by suicide—was probably forgery.

Johnson threw himself into this effort, writing (as if from Dodd) letters to the Lord Chancellor, Henry Bathurst, and to Lord Mansfield, the Chief Justice; a petition from Dodd to the King and another from Mrs. Dodd to the Queen; a moving sermon preached by Dodd at the chapel in Newgate Prison (June 6) on the text "What must I do to be saved?" and published with the title "The Convict's Address to his Unhappy Brethren"; and several other pieces, including a letter sent under his own name (June 20) to Charles Jenkinson, the Secretary at War, who was close to the King—a letter that Jenkinson later claimed he had for some reason never received—stating:

He is, so far as I can recollect, the first clergyman of our church who has suffered publick execution for immorality; and I know not whether it would not be more for the interest of religion to bury such an offender in the obscurity of perpetual exile, than to expose him in a cart, and on the gallows, to all who for any reason are enemies to the clergy.

The supreme power has, in all ages, paid some attention to the voice of the people; and that voice does not least deserve to be heard, when it calls out for mercy. There is now a very general desire that Dodd's life should be spared. More is not wished; and, perhaps, this is not too much to be granted.

Meanwhile Earl Percy presented to the King a petition for mercy signed by twenty-three thousand people. All of these efforts proved fruitless. The petition, apparently on the advice of Lord Mansfield, was denied, and Dodd was executed on June 27. As Dodd mounted the scaffold with a faint smile, a Prussian traveler named Archenholtz turned to an acquaintance and said, "The English know how to die!"

Chapter 29

Lives of the Poets

Ironically it was during the very weeks when Johnson was trying to save the Reverend William Dodd from execution that one of the masterpieces in the history of both biography and literary criticism was being planned—the *Lives of the English Poets*. In his journal for this period, there is a single reference to it, on Saturday, March 29, the day before Easter, when he was thinking of many other things: "I treated with booksellers on a bargain, but the time was not long." A few weeks later (May 3) he described this new project in a letter to Boswell, who had seen an announcement of it by the publishers and wanted to know what it meant: "I am engaged to write little Lives, and little Prefaces, to a little edition of the English Poets."[1]

What lay behind this "bargain" was the sudden decision of thirty-six of the leading London booksellers or publishers to bring out an enormous collected edition of the works of the English poets. They felt prodded into taking this action because a Scottish firm—the Apollo Press, run by the Martin brothers, in Edinburgh—had already started printing a collection of this sort in small pocket-size volumes. The London publishers tried to dismiss this edition, and accused it of being cheaply and inaccurately printed. But in reality they were worried. For it was a sizable undertaking (when it was finished, the Apollo Press edition of *The British Poets* came to 109 of these small volumes). They were also alarmed because the Martins had, as their London agent, John Bell, a man of only thirty-two but already one of the most enterprising publishers in England; and they were afraid that the work, if widely distributed, might saturate the poetry-reading market in England itself. As a countermove to this "invasion," as Edward Dilly described it, "of what we call our Literary Property," he and the other publishers determined to blanket the Edinburgh edition with a really "elegant and accurate edition of all the English Poets of reputation from Chaucer to the present time"—a work that could easily extend to seventy or even one hundred full-size volumes. But they almost immediately decided that such a project was too large, and therefore limited the poets to the period from about 1660 to the present, excluding whatever poets were still alive. As it was, the number of poets they had in mind came to a total of forty-seven.[2]

As a crowning attraction, they hoped to get Johnson to write "a concise account of the life of each authour." By this, they were thinking of short biographical prefaces of perhaps no more than two to five pages. They appointed a committee of three men to call on Johnson about this—his old friends Tom Davies and William Strahan, and Thomas Cadell, who had shared in the publication of Johnson's *Journey to the Western Islands* and was currently one of the publishers of Gibbon's *Decline and Fall* (1776-88). They made their proposal to Johnson, and asked him to name his own terms. To their relief, he not only agreed, but, as terms, mentioned a mere two hundred guineas. Meanwhile, looking over the list of forty-seven poets that the publishers had decided to include, he suggested that they add the Scottish poet James Thomson, whom they had excluded—perhaps, since Thomson was a Scot, as a deliberate snub toward their rival, the Apollo Press, in Edinburgh. As time went on, he also suggested four minor poets (Richard Blackmore, Isaac Watts, John Pomfret, and Thomas Yalden) whom he thought equal to some of the other minor poets that the publishers were including. This brought the total to fifty-two. Boswell, when he next saw him, said he was disappointed to find this "was not an undertaking directed by him," but that he was to furnish a preface to any poet that booksellers chose. "I asked him if he would do this to any dunce's works, if they should ask him." "Yes, Sir," replied Johnson, "and *say* he was a dunce."[3]

2

The small amount Johnson asked—two hundred guineas—comes as a surprise from a man who was fond of saying that "nothing excites a man to write but necessity." He could have asked for fifteen hundred guineas, as Edmond Malone said, and the publishers would have at once agreed, even though they were assuming he would write only the short prefaces they were asking rather than the magnificent, richly distilled work of about 370,000 words that he ultimately gave them. (The historian William Robertson was paid £4,500 for his *History of Charles V*, and after Johnson's death, Arthur Murphy was paid £300 for his short *Essay on the Life and Genius of Johnson*.) It is true that Johnson—we have seen it repeatedly—needed some external incentive, whether of money or as an act of charity for others, in order to overcome his internal resistance to writing for "reputation." But a little money could go a long way. Moreover, much of his talk about money as an incentive ("No man but a blockhead ever wrote, except for money") came from his delight in puncturing the "cant" of people who pretended to more exalted motives when they plunged into the "epidemical conspiracy for the destruction of paper." He preferred aligning himself with the Grub Street writers who wrote (as he himself for so long had done) merely in order to stay alive, and who, he thought, were more honest about their motives. Otherwise, he was anything but mercenary, and Boswell is justified in saying that on the whole he gave "less attention to profit from his labours than any man to whom literature has been a profession"—that is, a means of livelihood. Later the publishers themselves added one hundred guineas to the original fee, and when another edition of the *Lives* appeared—as a separate publication apart from the works of the poets—they added a further one hundred.

When the work turned into something larger, Johnson continued to regard the modest sum he was paid as quite reasonable. The original intention, as he said when the *Lives* appeared, "was only to have allotted to every Poet an Advertisement, like those which we find in the French Miscellanies, containing a few dates and a general character; but I have been led beyond my intention, I hope, by the honest desire to give useful pleasure." This was his own decision, in other words, and he saw no reason why he should ask the publishers to give him more than they had originally agreed only because he himself had gone further than they had intended. "I have always said the booksellers were a generous set of men," he told John Nichols; "Nor, in the present instance, have I reason to complain. The fact is, not that they have paid me too little, but that I have written too much."[4]

527

3

What led him to write so much more than either he or the publishers had originally planned—and he started to do so with the very first life he took up (the *Life of Cowley*)—is that he now felt less of the inner resistance that had usually made writing an unwelcome chore.

His problem in the past was not that the idea of a major work intimidated him. But by arousing his old enemy—his own burden of self-demand—it also aroused another part of his divided self into mulish rebellion or resistance, so that the act of "composition" became more than ever an effort of "perseverance, to which the mind is dragged by necessity or resolution, and from which the attention is every moment starting to more delightful amusements." The chore of having to fight against both the self-demand and against the inner rebellion to that demand naturally fired his impatience, once he entered the arena against them, to dispatch a work quickly. On the other hand, these short lives on which he was embarking now—as contrasted, for example, with the edition of Shakespeare—were not conceived as a major work in which he had to fulfill unusually high expectations either from others or from himself. The subject, moreover, was congenial. "The biographical part of literature," as he had said years ago, "is what I love most." In addition, he already knew the works of most of these fifty-two poets fairly well, and some he knew superlatively well. Finally, the whole nature of the work was such that he would break his writing of it into separate units. He would write one of the longer lives or several of the shorter, and then stop and turn to other interests. (During one week in April 1780, he wrote four or five short lives; while, for the *Life of Milton*, he took six weeks.) After a pause he could easily turn to a new group of poets.[5]

For once, as Mrs. Thrale remarked, "he loved to be set at work, and was sorry when he came to the end of the business he was about." As always, he wrote rapidly during the hours he actually spent in writing. Yet this was more from old habit rather than from the desire to meet a deadline and get a work out of the way. But the speed with which he wrote—when he did write—mattered less now than it had ever done, even though he was often discussing writers at whom he had hardly looked for many years. His astonishing memory had retained them in solution. (When he handed the manuscript of the *Life of Rowe* to

John Nichols for printing, he "complacently observed," said Nichols, "that the criticism was tolerably well done, considering that he had not read one of Rowe's plays for thirty years.") A clergyman, the Reverend Mr. Parker, has left a picture of him writing one of the *Lives* at Lichfield, while visiting his old friend Elizabeth Aston. At her house on Stow Hill, he would sit writing at a table "by one of the windows . . . surrounded by five or six ladies engaged in work [needlework] or conversation."[6] Some of the *Lives* were written at Streatham, others at the Thrales' house in Southwark, where his room (the Round Tower) looked out into the busy courtyard of the brewery filled with workmen, horses, and wagons. Later, as difficulties began to descend on the Thrale family, he wrote several of the remaining *Lives* in his own house at Bolt Court, surrounded by the aging and quarreling inmates of his household.

Within a year after he had started, he was taking at least one part of the work—the major *Lives* (Cowley, Milton, Dryden, and Pope)—more seriously than he pretended. An amusing example appears in Boswell (May 12, 1778), who had come to London this spring and was now recording, from the times that he saw Johnson, one of the richest single collections of his talk. He was unaware that Johnson at this moment was deeply into his *Life of Dryden*, which was already, in Johnson's mind, to be one of the high points of the *Lives* as he was now conceiving them. Wishing to be of service, Boswell called on Lord Marchmont, who had known Alexander Pope, whose "life" would naturally be one of the most important of Johnson's *Lives*. At this point Johnson was not even thinking of Pope. Some time would elapse before he got to him. Even so, Boswell started to pump Lord Marchmont for information about Pope (intending to pass it on later to Johnson), and, in fact, in his attempt to ingratiate himself, went so far as to tell Marchmont that he "should revise" Johnson's future *Life of Pope*. The shrewd and kindly Marchmont shook his head, saying. "You would put me in a dangerous situation. You know how he knocked down Osborn the bookseller."

Boswell then officially—as though he were a sort of emissary from Johnson—made an appointment for Johnson to come and call on the Earl of Marchmont the very next day ("at one o'clock"), and bustled out to Streatham with the news. He waited until after dinner, so that Johnson would be in the best possible mood, and then, introducing the subject with the remark "I have been at work for you today," mentioned the appointment he had arranged. He was jolted by Johnson's reply:

"I shall not be in town to-morrow. I don't care to know about Pope." MRS. THRALE: (surprized as I was, and a little angry.) "I suppose, Sir, Mr. Boswell thought, that as you are to write Pope's Life, you would wish to know about him." JOHNSON. "Wish! why yes. If it *rained knowledge* I'd hold out my hand; but I would not give myself the trouble to go in quest of it." There was no arguing with him at the moment. Some time afterwards he said, "Lord Marchmont will call on me, and then I shall call on Lord Marchmont."

This could seem, of course, a kind of childlike pride; and in a way it was. But, as Boswell could have known, it was like the time, about fifty years before, when old Michael Johnson had angered his son by printing up his translation into Latin of Pope's *Messiah* and then sending it to Pope, whereas Johnson himself had been contemplating a more ceremonious and, as he thought, courteous approach. Later, when the first section of the *Lives of the Poets* was published, Johnson had a copy sent to Marchmont. Then, after Marchmont himself had paid a call on him, Johnson—completely mollified—called in return on Lord Marchmont (May 3, 1779) and learned from him everything he had to say about Pope. The interview was a pleasure to both of them, and Johnson confessed afterward to Boswell, "I would rather have given twenty pounds than not have come."[7]

4

The combined qualifications Johnson brought to the *Lives of the Poets* help to explain why, like the *Preface to Shakespeare*, the work is not merely a landmark in the history of criticism but a classic of world literature:

To begin with, there was his profound interest, both moral and psychological, in biography itself. Back in his thirties, when he was trudging the London streets, he had creatively felt his way into this form of writing that he had come to love so dearly—love because it could feed, like nothing else, his essentialism, his desire to find means that could be "put to use" by "helpless man." If he wrote lives of military and naval heroes, he was also searching his way—in his eagerness to discover what could be "put to use"—into those "quiet" lives, the lives of scholars, artists, and scientists, which seemed to so many people to lack startling events that would give them public and dramatic vividness. To look closely into these lives, as he has said in the *Rambler*, is of special value to frail human nature, struggling, in such time as any individual has, to achieve some goal, some purpose or ideal.

Now, thirty years later, as he turned to this panorama of fifty-two individuals—so many of whom were already being forgotten—we sense an instinctive desire to rescue them, if only briefly, from extinction in the sludge of time: to see them as part of the general drama of human effort, experience, risk, hope, and disappointment; to evaluate them as lives—as experiences in living. Of course, he was a little cavalier about dates and other details (he was, after all, covering fifty-two writers) in a way that could upset the modern scholar who may spend five years on only one of these figures and who can also draw on the accumulated research of other scholars as he proceeds. Nor was Johnson pretending to do "research" in the modern sense, though he turned up many interesting details and had the help of other scholars, including Isaac Reed and George Steevens.

But the fact remains that for the first time in the history of literature—as we noted in speaking of his early biographies—a mind of remarkable resources and range had turned to this form of writing, and now, in returning to it after thirty years of further thought about it, was creatively disclosing, as never before, the real possibilities for the biography of thinkers and writers. The most famous work of biographical art in the history of literature—Boswell's *Life of Johnson*—is one immediate result of what he opened up as a possibility. Boswell went to school, as it were, to Johnson. True, there are differences, above all the dramatic scenes that are the finest thing in Boswell; for Boswell was writing about one great man whom he was watching and recording, while Johnson was writing retrospectively, about writers in the past for whom few recorded conversations were available. Yet the principles and central interests were the same. Boswell learned them from Johnson.

Then we should add—since these are lives of writers—Johnson's more special qualifications in language and literature. His mastery of the English language, from Elizabethan times to his own age, had been shown years before by the *Dictionary*, with its thousands of quotations drawn from every form of writing. With his uncanny memory, he was constantly aware of literary influences and examples, classical and modern; and with his formidable analytic powers operating upon so ready and retentive a memory, he had an insight into poetic style that few "biographical" or "historical" critics of literature have ever begun to equal.

But even if others who have written about literature might be compared with him in all these ways, no one with a similar philosophical and literary breadth has also approached him in his direct knowledge of the *practical* sides of literature, which ranged from his forty years of experience in the world of publishing to aspects of the psychology of writing that the purely theoretical critic is always forgetting (including the hesitations and self-doubts of the writer in facing that most intimidating of objects—the blank page waiting to be filled—and the psychological pressures on him as he thinks of the array of famous writers, from Homer until yesterday, against whom he is forced to compete in order even to gain a hearing).[8]

A further dimension is given the *Lives* by Johnson's knowledge of the history of criticism itself. He even considered writing a "History of Criticism . . . from Aristotle to the present age"—a remarkably novel thought at this time, and something that no one tried to carry out until over a century after Johnson's death. It is partly because of his knowledge of the varied history of critical thought, and his long, unillusioned familiarity with "the cant of those who judge by principles rather than perception," that he is so difficult for us to label or to bracket neatly as a literary critic. No one of his time was more aware that in the arts and humanities—as distinct from works "raised upon principles demonstrative and scientific"—difference in opinion is inevitable simply because so many different considerations have to be taken into account, and that

as a question becomes more complicated and involved, and extends to a greater number of relations, disagreement of opinion will always be multiplied, not because we are irrational, but because we are finite beings, furnished with different kinds of knowledge, exerting different degrees of attention, one discovering consequences which escape another, none taking in the whole concatenation of causes and effects . . . each comparing what he observes with a different criterion, and each referring it to a different purpose.

As a result, Johnson—in his formal critical writing if not in his conversation—never forgets that "he who differs from us, does not always contradict us," and we "have less reason to be surprised or offended when we find others differ from us in opinion, because we very often differ from ourselves."[9]

Finally there is the perspective given by the range of Johnson's interests—intellectual, moral, and social. Accordingly we are always seeing literature, as well as the drama of individuals writing it, within larger contexts, through which and at times against which literature can be defined. We can sense this even in casual phrasing. A typical example is the close of the *Life of Gray*, when he turns to the famous *Elegy*: "I rejoice to concur with the common reader; for by the common sense of readers uncorrupted with literary prejudices . . . must be finally decided all claims to poetical honours." This is the kind of phrase—"uncorrupted by literary prejudices"—that only a critic of the mental stature of Goethe or Johnson can afford to make. It is so completely at odds with the critical approach of our own generation that it could almost seem a misprint for "corrupted by unliterary prejudices."

What we are dealing with is the rare ability, which was to become more rare within another generation, to look on literature as one example—one of several—of what mankind can do, and to prize and evaluate it accordingly. The sense of its value is further heightened by Johnson's inability to forget how precarious this, like all other human achievement, really is: how quickly it can be lost, how difficult it can be to reattain. Mankind is always seen by Johnson the moralist as a child learning or trying to learn, and often with immense odds against it. This was why he was so interested in the Renaissance, which represented for him one of the great moments in which "helpless man" was somehow able to pull himself up to something remarkable in mental and imaginative achievement. Such a perspective, in which literature is seen in proportion to the general human endeavor, is not reductive, but sustains the dignity of literature in a way that self-defeating attempts to isolate it—to fence it off as a special preserve—can never succeed in doing.

During the century after Johnson's death, "high culture," beginning with Romanticism, developed a life of its own—in a "pompous isolation," as Thomas Mann said in *Dr. Faustus*, "which was the fruit of the culture-emancipation, the elevation of culture as a substitute for religion," and where, he prophesied, it will soon be left "entirely alone, alone to die." What we think of as "high Modernism" in the twentieth century has been only superficially at odds with the nineteenth-century isolation of "culture," and its quarrels with the nineteenth century have proved to be only internecine ones. As the twentieth century draws to a close, we may be learning once again to take "high culture" less for granted, and to realize how thin the ice is on which we have been skating. If so, the kind of perspective Johnson provides, in his whole approach to literature, will help us to get our bearings. Some thought of this may have been in T. S. Eliot's mind during the Second World War when he wondered whether "the literary influence of Johnson," in the profounder sense of influence, "does not merely await a generation which has not yet been born to receive it."[10]

5

Typically, Johnson had no particular "theory" or "system" of literary biography in mind. Instead he brought so large an internal fund to these prefaces he had been asked to write, and wrote them so well, that in the process he created a new form of writing: "literary biography" in the genuine sense—that is, biography united with specific critical analysis of the writer's works and of the tone and character of his mind. Two generations were to pass before another critic of literature—Sainte-Beuve—could discuss a large number of writers with a combined biographical and critical penetration that compares with Johnson's; and Sainte-Beuve, though often psychologically subtler, cannot equal Johnson either in moral strength or insight into poetic form and style.

Even if we disregard the larger purpose of the *Lives*, and concentrate only on the critical discussions, the work continues to fascinate us. What the historian Robert Orme had said of the *Journey to the Western Islands* is even truer of the *Lives:* there are in it "great thoughts which had been rolled and rolled in his mind, as in the sea."[11] To an extent equaled only by the moral writing of his forties, we have here, at its finest and wisest, the dialectic and bisociative character of Johnson's mind. As a result, in the critical analyses, many of the issues that have divided literary criticism, from Aristotle to Johnson's day or even our own day, are constantly interplaying, each given justice, explored, and then usually, though not always, reconciled in a more dynamic and functional synthesis: imagination and judgment, uniformity and variety, the general and the particular, the "Ancients" and the "Moderns," tradition and originality, "elegance" and "refinement" versus imaginative vigor and range; imitation and reality (including several of the ancillary issues that go along with this, such as the whole

534

problem of imitation/reality versus the technical demands of poetic form; moral teaching versus truth to nature; or external reality versus the inner subjective life).[12]

Of special interest to us now, as we ourselves appear to be moving away from a period of exacting formalism comparable to the "high neoclassic mode" from 1660 to 1760, is the directness with which Johnson is always facing the issue of what he himself calls "human interest" (popular appeal, immediate pleasure, accessibility, and the virtues of "the familiar") versus concentrated power of thought, original invention, and technical brilliance. Never before or since, among the major critics of literature, has the "common reader" come so near to having a friend in court. We see it in every form, even in Johnson's refreshingly honest capacity—which seems so rare among professional critics—for boredom. "The first purpose of a writer," as he said, is to excite "him that reads his work to *read it through*." Prior's long poem *Solomon* lacks that quality "without which all others are of small avail. . . . *Tediousness* is the most fatal of all faults." Thomson's *Liberty*, "when it first appeared, I tried to read, and soon desisted. I have never tried again." Or, speaking of Congreve's early novel *Incognita*, which had once been praised by critics, "I would rather praise it than read it"; or, of Akenside's already forgotten odes: to examine them in detail is futile, "when once they are found to be generally dull . . . for to what use can the work be criticised that will not be read?" Yet, if Johnson remains one of the supreme spokesmen for the "common reader," he is constantly searching out whatever is new, or whatever is imaginatively creative even if neglected, or technically gifted even if overelaborate. His resurrection of the "metaphysical" poets is an example.[13]

On the other hand, his dialectic and bisociative habit of mind presents a continuing problem to the professional student of literature, who, as contrasted with the "common reader," is naturally tempted to try to classify critical approaches with firm labels and may feel confused by a form of criticism that moves back and forth, weighing virtues and faults. For example, everyone remembers the remark about *Paradise Lost*—"None ever wished it longer." And of course he puts his finger on what was to be at least a problem for Milton when he says:

The plan of *Paradise Lost* has this inconvenience, that it comprises neither human actions nor human manners. The man and woman who act and suffer, are in a state which no other man or woman can ever know. The reader finds no transaction in which he can be engaged; beholds no condition in which he can by any effort of imagination place himself; he has, therefore, little natural curiosity or sympathy. . . . The want of human interest is always felt.

But we should remember the way he concludes his discussion of the "defects" of the poem (something which "every work of man must have," and which it is naturally "the business of impartial criticism to discover"):

> Such are the faults of that wonderful performance *Paradise Lost;* which he who can put in balance with its beauties must be considered not as nice but as dull, as less to be censured for want of candour than pitied for want of sensibility.

The fact remains that it was Johnson who wrote the first major critique of the poem, most of which he knew by heart, and a few sentences may suggest the spirit of admiration that pervades it: the thoughts called forth in the progress of the poem

> are such as could only be produced by an imagination in the highest degree fervid and active, to which materials were supplied by incessant study and unlimited curiosity. The heat of Milton's mind might be said to sublimate his learning, to throw off into his work the spirit of science, unmingled with its grosser parts. . . .
> Whatever be his subject, he never fails to fill the imagination. . . . He was born for whatever is arduous; and his work is not the greatest of heroick poems, only because it is not the first.[14]

6

In the history of criticism, what has always stood up least well is not general theory—which rarely treads on the toes of anyone except rival theorists—but critical evaluations of particular writers and especially particular works. Goethe thought most of the younger writers of his own period "sickly," and Hazlitt's opinion was not much higher. Coleridge and Arnold dismissed most of the major poetry from 1660 to the 1790's; and at the height of the "metaphysical revival" from the 1920's to the 1940's, the nineteenth century was often condemned wholesale. But Johnson's critical evaluations—especially when we remember the large number of writers and particular poems he covers—

have proved remarkably sound. Because of the scores of literary histories that have gone over the subject since then and smoothed the way for us (though we often forget them and still read Johnson), any one of us can now give an opinion on a poet or poem of the time that is at least "safe" and with which later generations, if they bother to remember us, will not quarrel. But we should recall that the thinking about these poets had not been done in advance for Johnson. Moreover, he was still very close to them. The furthest away was no more remote than Tennyson is to us. "Considering all the temptations," said T. S. Eliot, "to which one is exposed in judging contemporary writing, all the prejudices which one is tempted to indulge in judging writers of the immediately preceding generation"—and Eliot may here be recalling his own earlier attacks on nineteenth-century poetry—"I view Johnson's *Lives of the Poets* as a masterpiece of the judicial bench." In fact, Johnson has been repeatedly paid one compliment in particular that no other critic has been paid to the same degree. Some of the poets he discusses are looked at now, especially by modern poets like Eliot, only because we are curious to see why Johnson spoke of them as he did.[15]

Of the half-hundred *Lives*, only three have ever been singled out for continued attack—the *Lives* of Milton, Swift, and Gray. There is certainly a vein of antagonism in Johnson to Milton the man as there is to Puritanism in general. At the root of it is Johnson's own heady conception of what he considers the rigidity and self-deception of the Puritan temperament—its self-deluding capacity (again as Johnson sees it) to disguise what he thinks is really an idolatry of self-will under a high and exacting moralism that will brook no compromise. This also applies to what he considers to be the tone and bias of Milton's political writings—a "surly republicanism" more interested in "levelling down" than in "levelling up." As a result, throughout the *Life of Milton*, we feel that Johnson is often sparring with him, and looking for a soft spot. But Milton's greatness as a poet is never in question; the *Life* itself is a richly complex work for its size; and leading Miltonists have long since made their peace with it. About Gray, we now feel less hotly defensive than the Victorians did, and Johnson's conception of him as both peevish and timid may seem uncharitable but by no means unreasonable. The *Life of Swift* justly strikes the modern reader as the only hopelessly biased *Life*. Here we can only try to remember Johnson's lifelong fear, especially after the breakdown in his fifties, of the powerful satiric bitterness of his own nature, and his dread—a dread with which he was constantly living—of falling into the anger and the sense of the emptiness about life that he associated with Swift.

If we look at his discussions of particular poems, remembering that well over a thousand poems are discussed, only the notorious paragraphs about Milton's "Lycidas" have really continued to rankle. This is not a bad record, when we think of major critics who have condemned entire poets and generations. The reason we forget this about other critics, and concentrate hypnotically on what Johnson said about "Lycidas," is that Johnson is so much more quotable than other critics. What he says really wounds the admirer of this great poem—certainly one of the greatest short poems in any language—leaving him incapable of either forgetting it or knowing how to answer an opinion that seems so hopelessly (I myself should say half-puckishly) perverse. All of us remember school texts—they still continue to appear—where, if "Lycidas" is included, Johnson is also quoted with shocked horror and then "answered" with nothing more than poor William Cowper's indignant response: "Oh! I could thresh his old jacket till I made his pension jingle in his pocket!" Needless to say, at a more sophisticated level, excuses or explanations are offered frequently for what Johnson said: (1) His love of "sincerity" in literature—actually a "Romantic" ideal—and his belief that the poem "is not to be considered as the effusion of real passion. . . . Passion plucks no berries from the myrtle and ivy, nor calls upon Arethuse and Mincius. . . . Where there is leisure for fiction, there is little grief." (2) His chronic impatience of the "pastoral" form generally as a worn-out convention and also as a completely "artificial" way of portraying life. (3) His related dislike—which we find him expressing constantly—of the modern use of "those mythological fictions," as he says of another poem, "which antiquity delivers ready to the hand; but which, like other things that lie open to every one's use, are of little value. The attention naturally retires from a new tale of Venus, Diana, and Minerva." He is incapable of granting that the use of classical mythology can have any genuine functional use for the modern reader. (4) Worst of all, the intermingling of these "outworn" and "trifling fictions" with "sacred truths, such as ought never to be polluted with such irreverent combinations." One can extend or nuance these attempts to defend what Johnson said. But they completely satisfy no one except apologists who—unlike Johnson himself—are determined that he can never make a slip, and who forget his dictum that "we must confess the faults of our favourite, to gain credit to our praise of his excellencies."[16]

7

We must look in more detail at a misconception about the *Lives* that has proved strangely persistent: the notion that the century of poets covered, from the 1660's to the 1760's, was selected by Johnson himself, or, even if not selected, agreed to; that therefore they represent his beau ideal of what poetry should be. "Where is Chaucer?" asks the writer of an Introduction to an edition of the *Lives of the Poets* still widely used—"Where are Spenser? Herrick? Lovelace? Campion? Crashaw? We soon find that poetry practically begins, in Johnson's judgment, with Waller, and reaches its consummation in Pope."[17]

The time span of the poets in this collection was fixed, as we already noted, by the publishers themselves. This edition was theirs, not Johnson's, and he was later, when they tried to capitalize on his name with the title *Johnson's Poets*, to remind them tartly that this was "*Your* Edition, which is very impudently called mine."[18] Given the scale on which they planned to publish (the total work ultimately reached sixty-eight volumes), they had dropped their original thought of beginning with Chaucer because they feared that so enormous a collection, already difficult enough to finance, could probably never sell enough to break even. (Similarly, the cut-off line at the other end—the exclusion of poets still alive—is not a symptom of Johnson's "antimodern" sentiments. It was a decision made by the publishers because they did not want to undercut the sales of living poets.)

But even when it is remembered that the selection was made by the publishers, there is a curious unwillingness to surrender the belief that this particular group of poets indicates the limits of what Johnson really appreciated in poetry. This applies not only to general historians of literature, eager to categorize Johnson quickly as a critic in order to get on to other matters, but also to many writers especially fond of Johnson himself. One of several arguments is that Johnson, given his prestige, could certainly have persuaded the booksellers to allow him to include poets if he had really wished to do so. It is forgotten that he was not simply writing a group of critical essays, which could have, of course, been expanded, but that what was involved was an enormous collection of the *Works of the English Poets*, which, if the beginning date were pushed back only to 1600, could have entailed the publication of another forty or fifty volumes. But the truth is that facts of this sort leave no lasting impression on the mind when there is a strong psychological need to believe otherwise. What we are really facing is a form of affection akin to that which sustains the cherished notion of Johnson as picturesque "Tory" and "Church of England" man: a form of love that needs to find faults or omissions in a "father image" in order to permit us to stand on our own feet, remedy or correct the defects of his "negative" side, and enjoy the pleasure of good-natured tolerance and affectionate condescension. As we have seen, no one has written more pointedly about this psychological need than Johnson himself in the moral essays.

There is a special irony in the notion that Johnson's literary sensibility and knowledge effectively begin at the point where the *Lives of the Poets* start. For no one of his time felt more deeply drawn to the period from the Renaissance to the end of the seventeenth century. One of his projected works was a life of Chaucer with a complete edition of his writings. Another was a "History of the Revival of Learning in Europe"—a comprehensive study of both the literary and intellectual history of the Renaissance. When I edited the *Rambler* for the Yale Edition of Johnson, one of the first peculiarities I especially noticed about it was his knowledge and use of the great Continental Humanists of the Renaissance—Bellarmine, Cardano, Castiglione, Cujacius, Erasmus, Fabricius, Gassendi, Grotius, Julius Libri, Lipsius, Politian, Pontanus, Quevedo, Sannazaro, the Scaligers, and Thuanus. They were a lifelong interest of Johnson's. The first major work to which he turned after leaving Oxford, and which failed only because he could not get subscriptions, was a scholarly edition of the Latin poems of Politian; and near the end of his life, according to John Nichols, he often spoke of making a translation of Thuanus.[19]

The same interest extended to the English writers from the Renaissance to the later seventeenth century. Typically, his citations of them in the *Rambler,* as we noticed earlier, occur more than twice as often as citations of eighteenth-century English writers. The *Dictionary* is studded with quotations from them in every field of writing. The "metaphysical poets" are an instance in point. Because he did not praise them with the unqualified enthusiasm shown in the "metaphysical revival" from the 1920's to the 1940's, it was assumed—and is still widely assumed—that he neither appreciated nor even knew them very well. Actually he had included over one thousand quotations from them (over four hundred from Donne alone) in the *Dictionary,* of which many were obviously quoted from memory.[20] True, he had strong reservations about the "metaphysical" mode, and, as T. S. Eliot granted when he tried to answer them, Johnson "is a dangerous person to disagree with." In particular he felt that the "metaphysical" style, with its premium on ingenuity, worked against two qualities he especially valued in poetry: (1) the "pathetic" (that is, what directly engages the heart or "moves the passions" of common humanity); and (2) the "sublime"—"that comprehension and expanse of thought which at once fills the whole mind, and of which the first effect is sudden astonishment, and the second rational admiration." But despite his reservations, he was strongly attracted to this form of poetry in which "nature and art are ransacked for illustrations . . . their learning instructs, and their subtlety surprises. . . . To write on their plan, it was at least necessary to read and think." This is a high tribute from Johnson, who, in the tamer neoclassic verse nearer his own period, so often found "no *thinking*." And in talking of Pope's power of "condensation," he once let slip the remark to Boswell, during the trip to the Hebrides, that "there is more *sense* in a line of Cowley, than in a page (or a sentence, or ten lines—I cannot be certain of the phrase) of Pope."[21]

Accordingly, he looked for a critical framework for judging the "metaphysicals" other than the body of critical values that had become orthodox since 1700. In the process he succeeded so effectively that T. S. Eliot and other defenders of the "metaphysical" style, a century and a half later, took over his premises and terminology as their starting point. He focuses on what most distinguishes them, the quality of "wit," and advances three definitions of "wit." (1) The conventional "neo-classic" equation of wit with "taste" and "Propriety" of language, typified by Pope's definition, "what oft was thought, but ne'er so well expressed." This Johnson rejects as degrading wit "from strength of thought to happiness of language." (2) In place of this he offers his own definition as that which is both "natural *and* new." Yet this is not a special distinction of the "metaphysicals," who tend to sacrifice the "natural" for the sake of the "new." (3) He then advances a third definition in which wit is "more rigorously and philosophically considered" (that is, considered psychologically, as an act of mind, and apart "from its effects upon the hearer"): "a kind of *discordia concors;* a combination of dissimilar images, or discovery of occult resemblances in things apparently unlike."[22]

In short, though he presents what is still the classical charge against the "metaphysicals," he also provides the basis for the classical defense of them. He was led to write at such length about them, as he told John Nichols, because they had never received any critical examination before and because he was interested in them. From his own point of view, he was trying to resurrect a group of poets almost completely forgotten, to discover a means by which they could be understood and evaluated, and also to see them in a balanced way. When he finished the *Life of Cowley* (October 11, 1777), he had devoted as much time to it as to any other life he was to write except the *Life of Pope*. It is because of the length and quality of this first *Life* that his whole conception of the project changed from the minor job he had at first expected it to be. He had set himself a standard for the rest of the work. But he never felt that he excelled his first *Life;* and, because of his discussion of the "metaphysicals," who had never received any critical examination before, he was always to think the *Life of Cowley* the best of the *Lives.*[23]

8

A few words should be added about the style. For Johnson, when he is at his best, writes one of the really great English prose styles; and in the *Lives*, written as he approaches and passes the age of seventy, he is at his very best.

By now his command of English vocabulary and syntax has been made more elastic and resilient through years of conversation. The language, especially when he is writing narrative, is more concrete, simple, and direct, and there is a new conversational ease. At the same time the more formal style of Johnson's middle years is still present in solution, especially his gift for tamped-down finality of statement through balance and antithesis. But it never becomes prominent until he leaves biographical narrative and turns to ideas or to poetic style or, above all, when he begins to sum up the intellectual character of a poet, as in the following passages from the *Life of Pope:*

He never passed a fault unamended
$$\text{by indifference,}$$
  nor quitted it
$$\text{by despair.}$$

He laboured his works
      first to gain reputation,
      and afterwards to keep it.

Of Pope's intellectual character, says Johnson, the principal quality was "good sense":

He saw immediately of his own conceptions
           what was to be chosen, and what was to be rejected;
   and, in the works of others,
           what was to be shunned, and what was to be copied.

And there is also the habit we noticed earlier of progressive assimilation within the body of the sentence—of stating a thing, then expanding or qualifying it, and then, after this is incorporated, returning and re-expanding or requalifying.* In addition to "good sense,"

Pope had likewise genius;
    a mind
       active
       ambitious
       adventurous,

    always investigating,
       always aspiring;

   in its widest searches
       still longing to go forward,
     in its highest flights
       still wishing to be higher;

    always imagining something greater than it knows,
    always endeavouring more than it can do.

Later, as he compares Dryden and Pope:

Of genius,
   that power which constitutes a poet;
   that quality without which
       judgment is cold
         and
       knowledge is inert;
   that energy which collects, combines, amplifies, and animates;

the superiority must, with some hesitation, be allowed to Dryden.

Or, as he sums up his discussion of the "metaphysical poets" in the *Life of Cowley:* in reading these poets,

* See above, pp. 399–400.

The mind is exercised
    either by recollection or inquiry;
    either something already learned is to be retrieved,
             or something new is to be examined.

If their greatness seldom elevates,
    their acuteness often surprises;
if the imagination is not always gratified,
    at least the powers of recollection and comparison are employed.

  , A distinctive peculiarity of Johnson's later style, which we also find in his conversation and letters, is his frequent use of short clauses. T. S. Eliot noticed this about Johnson in contrast to the other principal masters of formal style at this time. Whereas Burke and Gibbon, for example, use the long periodic sentences of the orator, Johnson, says Eliot, often seems to write like a man talking "in short breaths."[24] This is true, and we find it in both the relaxed narrative and reflective passages, and also—in a more taut, tensely braced form—in the islands of formal prose that are critical and philosophic rather than biographical or reminiscent. A good example of the former is the lovely passage, in the *Life of Edmund Smith*, where he pays a tribute to his old friend Gilbert Walmesley, who had long ago given him some of the information about Smith that he is using ("I knew him very early; he was one of the first friends that literature procured me. . . . He was of advanced age, and I was only not a boy; yet he never received my notions with contempt. . . . I honoured him, and he endured me").*

The use of short independent clauses permits another peculiarity of Johnson's later prose, especially in the more formal sections of the *Lives*. That is, the extraordinarily high number of verbs, which give his style the unusual strength and vigor that none of his imitators could ever capture. In the major English prose styles, verbs average about 10 percent to 14 percent of the total words. In Johnson's earlier work, the number is already fairly high (about 13 percent) and in the later work we find, for pages at a time, the highest sustained average in English— about 17 percent. An example of these short verbal clauses is the following passage from the *Life of Pope*, where the number of verbs rises to 23 percent, almost double the general average in English prose. He is speaking of Pope's poetic "prudence" or "good sense," and comparing him with Dryden:

---

* See above, p. 80.

But Dryden never desired to apply all the judgement that he had. He wrote, and professed to write, merely for the people; and when he pleased others, he contented himself. He spent no time in struggles to rouse latent powers; he never attempted to make that better which was already good, nor often to mend what he must have known to be faulty. He wrote, as he tells us, with very little consideration; when occasion or necessity called upon him, he poured out what the present moment happened to supply; and, when once it had passed the press, ejected it from his mind. . . .

Pope was not content to satisfy; he desired to excel, and therefore always endeavoured to do his best: he did not court the candour, but dared the judgement of his reader, and, expecting no indulgence from others, he showed none to himself. . . . Pope had perhaps the judgement of Dryden; but Dryden certainly wanted the diligence of Pope.[25]

9

In 1779, less than two years after he began, the first twenty-two *Lives* were published in four small volumes. The title of the work was *Prefaces, Biographical and Critical, to the Works of the English Poets.* (The conventional title we use now and have used for 150 years or more—the *Lives of the Poets*—is a shortened version of the title given later editions: *The Lives of the Most Eminent English Poets; with Critical Observations on their Works.*)

Just as he was finishing this first group of the *Lives*, he was shaken by the death of David Garrick (January 20, 1779). Garrick, who was only sixty-two, had suffered from kidney trouble for some time, and had retired early from the stage. Johnson, his old teacher at the little academy at Edial Hall, was naturally haunted now by the memory of the time they set out for London together forty-two years ago. His famous remark in the *Life of Edmund Smith*—that the death of Garrick has "eclipsed the gaiety of nations"—may seem to us cool and detached. But the words were carefully considered (he would not say "extinguish"), and Garrick's widow was eager to have them placed over her husband's grave. Meanwhile Richard Cumberland, who attended Garrick's funeral, never forgot the sight in Westminster Abbey of "old Samuel Johnson standing beside his grave, at the foot of Shakespeare's monument, and bathed in tears."[26]

When Johnson the following summer tried to turn to the last thirty *Lives*, he was distracted by anxieties to which we must turn in the next chapter. But in another fifteen months, only Swift and Pope, among the major lives, were yet to write, and that of Pope was fairly well along. Pope was the last really "great" life he had to do. He gave it special care, and in style, narrative, and critical amplitude it is the finest of all the *Lives*.

Finally, during the first week of March 1781, as he recorded in his journal, "I finished the lives of the Poets, which I wrote in my usual way, dilatorily and hastily, unwilling to work, and working with vigour, and haste."[27] Almost immediately these final thirty *Lives*—for he had been sending them to the press in installments as he went along—were published in six volumes. Within a month after he finished the *Lives*, his personal life—as he had possibly been fearing for some time—was to suffer a drastic and permanent change.

Chapter 30

Gathering Clouds; Death of
Henry Thrale

It had been almost four years since Johnson had signed up to write the *Lives*. This can be a considerable period in the life of anyone, during which fundamental changes for the worse can easily occur. "Circumstances," said Keats, "are like Clouds continually gathering and bursting—While we are laughing the seed of some trouble is put into the wide arable land of events . . . It sprouts, it grows, and suddenly bears a poison fruit which we must pluck." Moreover, Johnson had reached an age at which one is far more vulnerable to fundamental change. He had been approaching sixty-eight when he began the *Lives*, and he was now seventy-one and a half. The last year or so of this period had been haunted by an anxiety that he tried strongly to repress: the possible loss of what for fifteen years had been the nearest thing to a true "home" that he had—his home with the Thrale family. The entry in his journal that records his completion of the *Lives of the Poets* is immediately followed by another: "On Wednesday [April] 11, was buried my dear friend Thrale who died on Wednesday [April] 4, and with him were buried many of my hopes and pleasures."[1]

2

Within a year after Johnson began the *Lives,* problems in the Thrale household had started to thicken. Thrale, who was by then fifty

(1778), was again becoming hypnotized by the desire to outbrew his chief rivals, Whitbread and Calvert. As a result, he once more had an excess of beer on hand while finding himself short of capital. At the same time he was lavishly overspending on improvements at Streatham, and (though the family did not know about this) was also beginning to speculate with a union of quiet stubbornness and recklessness that naturally puzzled his friends. By July 1778 his financial affairs had reached another crisis, and Johnson, at the urging of Mrs. Thrale, tried to talk with him in detail about the brewery. Dropping his work on the *Lives of the Poets*, he drew up a scheme for Thrale to limit his brewing to eighty thousand barrels a year, for which Johnson figured out the profit. Thrale, who was in a state of depression, finally agreed with the scheme.[2]

The truth is that the taciturn Thrale was even more troubled than most people by the dissatisfactions with life that can deepen so rapidly in middle age, and he was reaching a point at which something stubbornly impulsive and self-destructive, in reaction to these dissatisfactions, was also beginning to emerge. Superficially Thrale had everything he could have desired at twenty-five or thirty. He had wealth; he had the sort of family many eighteenth-century men of means would want (though still there was no male heir); and through Johnson he was acquainted with some of the most notable men in the kingdom. But plainly these things were not enough to tide him over the reefs of his middle years.

In the midst of all this, he had become infatuated with a young woman, Sophia Streatfield. We should linger a little on this infatuation since it is important for understanding the reactions during the next few years of Mrs. Thrale—reactions that were in turn to have a significant effect on Johnson's personal life. Sophia Streatfeild, who was in her early twenties, had beautiful classic features and enjoyed the attention of older men. She had a remarkable knowledge of Greek, for she had been well tutored, and at the same time had developed arts of appeal—through coyness, exaggerated helplessness, and a readiness for gentle tears of sensibility—that many men, including Henry Thrale, found irresistible. Mrs. Thrale was understandably bitter, though she tried to be ironically debonair, comparing Sophy variously to a "white fricasse" or a piece of "pea green satin." She told herself the affair was "comical": "I will not fret about this Rival this S.S. no I won't." She found particularly obnoxious Sophy's ability to ensnare male hearts by suffusing her eyes with tears whenever she wished to suggest her capacity for tender emotion or whenever she had to say farewell. Sometimes at Streatham, in suppressed contempt, Mrs. Thrale would deliberately urge Sophy to display this ability to the company. Strangely enough, Sophy was usually ready to oblige. Fanny Burney records a typical example at Streatham one morning when she, Mrs. Thrale, and Sophy were having breakfast with Sir Philip Clerke and Dr. Delap:

> Sir Philip.— . . . I have heard so much of these tears, that I would give the universe to have a sight of them.
> Mrs. Thrale.—Well, she shall cry again if you like it.
> S. S.—No, pray, Mrs. Thrale.
> Sir Philip.—Oh, pray do! pray let me see a little of it.
> Mrs. Thrale.—Yes, *do* cry a little, Sophy (in a wheedling voice), pray do! Consider, now, you are going to-day, and it's very hard if you won't cry a little. . . .

Mrs. Thrale continued to coax her, as though she were "a nurse soothing a baby." Then suddenly, said Fanny, "two crystal tears came into the soft eyes of S. S., and rolled gently down her cheeks! . . . She was smiling all the time." Fanny thought it incredible that Sophy could be so oblivious to the way Mrs. Thrale viewed her, and assumed it was because Sophy was totally absorbed in her pleasure at "manifesting a tenderness of disposition that increased her beauty of countenance." But Sophy was no fool. She was quite aware of Mrs. Thrale's feelings and was secretly enjoying her triumph. (After Henry Thrale's death, Sophy made a point of "telling me," said Mrs. Thrale, "such tender passages of what pass'd between her and Mr. Thrale—that she half frights me somehow.")[3]

Johnson was, of course, partly aware of this. Yet the whole matter was too embarrassing for open discussion. To begin with, he could not let himself think that anything really serious could happen to the harmony of "his" family. Any trouble now was surely only temporary. Thrale had in the past had mistresses (though Sophy was by no means a mistress). Moreover, Johnson's loyalty to Thrale was complete, and all the more when a kind of deterioration seemed to be taking place in his rigid, calm, and taciturn friend. In any case, what could one say without sowing further dissension in the family? Mrs. Thrale understood this and respected it, though on one occasion she was so humiliated and hurt that she deeply resented Johnson's silence. Thirty years later she told the Reverend Edward Mangin about it. At a large dinner party at Streatham, when she was sitting at her usual place at the table, Thrale called across to her and asked her to change places with Sophy, "who was threatened with a sore throat, and might be injured by sitting near the door." Bursting into tears and saying that "perhaps ere long the lady might be at the head of Mr. T's table," she got up and left for the drawing room. After dinner Johnson and Burke joined her, and she at once asked whether, considering all that had happened, she was to blame for what she had said. Johnson replied:

"Why, possibly not; your feelings were outraged." I said, "Yes, greatly so; and I cannot help remarking with what blandness and composure you witnessed the outrage. Had this transaction been told of others, your anger would have known no bounds; but, towards a man who gives good dinners, & c, you were meekness itself." Johnson coloured, and Burke, I thought, looked foolish; but I had not a word of answer from either.[4]

3

Then suddenly—Johnson was at this time visiting John Taylor at Ashbourne and preparing to finish off the final thirty *Lives*—Henry Thrale, now fifty, had a stroke (June 8, 1779). On the day that this happened, Thrale was at the house of his sister, Mrs. Arnold Nesbitt, whose husband had recently died insolvent. Thrale had stood security for his brother-in-law for speculations that now, as he learned, could make him liable for £220,000. It was almost immediately after discovering this that Thrale, sitting down to the dinner table at his sister's, had his stroke.[5]

Thrale never completely recovered from this first stroke. The summer passed heavily for the whole family, though Johnson tried to keep the atmosphere at Streatham cheerful and gave Latin lessons to Queeney Thrale and Fanny Burney. Mrs. Thrale, who was far along in another pregnancy, had a miscarriage in August. At the same time troubles at the brewery became acute. Thrale was of no help. He simply wandered about there, said John Perkins, as though he were "planet-struck."[6]

For several weeks the brewery was run completely by Perkins, Mrs. Thrale, and Johnson, who dropped the *Lives of the Poets* to give time to the business. The deterioration of Thrale preyed on Johnson's mind more than he would allow himself to admit. Back when David Garrick was dying, said Mrs. Thrale, "no arguments, or recitals of such facts as I had heard, would persuade Mr. Johnson of his danger." This was not from indifference but from an anxiety too painful to be allowed into the open. It had to be denied, for the sake of one's own sanity, lest one's mind start to co-operate with the inevitable and draw one into despair. In fact, as Mrs. Thrale adds, "he had prepossessed himself with a notion, that to say a man was sick, was very near wishing him so," and few things more offended him than even mentioning the possible death of anyone he knew.[7] So in his reactions to Thrale now. Because he was frightened at bottom, he forgot what he knew of medicine, and, in complete subjectivity, began to fall back on arguments he was always having with himself—that most of our troubles are created by our own minds, and that what we need above all are "diversions" to get us out of ourselves. He thought it good for Thrale to have company about him, and encouraged him (though Thrale needed no encouragement) to go ahead with his large parties.

On February 21 Thrale had another stroke. It had been preceded by a large party two nights before at which Thrale, as his wife bitterly recorded, sat next to Sophy, "pressed her Hand to his Heart (as she told me herself) & said Sophy we shall not enjoy this long, & tonight I will not be cheated of my *Only Comfort*." A few days after his stroke, as he was becoming conscious, Sophy came to his bedside in order to sit with him. Looking up at her, the doting Thrale said to her, "Who would not suffer even all that I have endured, to be pitied by *you!*" In recording this, his distressed and humiliated wife naturally tried to hide her feelings: "His Sisters who had alternately sate up with him every Night & his Daughter, were offended; as they had never been treated with a kind Word from him; but *I*, who expect none, thought it rather good that he had *some* Sensibility for *some* human Being."[8]

Within a couple of weeks after this, Johnson's friend Topham Beauclerk, whom he had loved from the start as another Cornelius Ford, died at the age of only forty (March 11, 1780). In the death of those dear to us, for a long period of time, as Johnson now wrote to Dr. Lawrence after Lawrence lost his wife, "the *continuity of being is lacerated*"—whipped and cut through. He had known Beauclerk and prized him as a living Cornelius for over twenty years—as the only man, he said, that he really envied for his union of grace and brilliance. "His wit and his folly, his acuteness and maliciousness, his merriment and reasoning, are now over." Johnson is here writing to Boswell in Edinburgh, who was trying to get Johnson to send him a copy of the famous letter to Chesterfield and also hoping to draw him out on the subject of controlling melancholy. Johnson again disregarded the request for the Chesterfield letter. Nor was he in any mood, at this difficult time, to indulge Boswell's complaints about his own state of mind:

You are always complaining of melancholy, and I conclude from those complaints that you are fond of it. No man talks of that which he is desirous to conceal, and every man desires to conceal that of which he is ashamed. . . . Make it an invariable and obligatory law to yourself, never to mention your own mental diseases; If you are never to speak of them you will think on them but little, and if you think little of them, they will molest you rarely. When you talk of them, it is plain that you want either praise or pity; for praise there is no room, and pity will do you no good.[9]

4

While Johnson continued off and on to work on the *Lives*, Parliament was dissolved, and a new election was scheduled for the autumn. Thrale, despite his condition, was stubbornly determined to campaign for re-election. In the hope of getting him into better shape before he did so, Mrs. Thrale persuaded him to spend the summer in Brighton.

Johnson instinctively realized he should not obtrude too much on the Thrales at this time. By now he was thoroughly alarmed about Thrale's health (he had dropped all attempt to advise "diversion"); and he could sense that Mrs. Thrale, who was near the breaking point with anxiety, would not care to have another charge on her hands. He had already received a hint when she had taken Thrale to Bath, for a few weeks, before going to Brighton. She had told Johnson that, because they had Fanny Burney with them, they did not have an extra room for him. He could not help feeling a little hurt, and in one of his letters let slip a remark that was to express his thought increasingly during the next three years as he felt her attitude changing: "Do not let new friends supplant the old; they who first distinguished you have the best claim to your attention; those who flock about you now take your excellence upon credit, and may hope to gain upon the world by your countenance."

Feeling himself less welcome or needed than he had hoped, he spent the summer working on the *Lives* at his own house in Bolt Court, with his aging and quarreling pensioners, and by the end of the summer was at work on the *Life of Pope*. When Thrale returned in September to campaign, Johnson dropped the *Life of Pope* to help him with an election address and to write advertisements for the newspapers. But

Thrale was obviously an ill man, and in fact seemed to have another stroke, though mild, while trying to make an address. "His friends," said his wife, "now considered him as dying, his Enemies as dead." Thrale lost badly in the election, coming in a poor third, and, in sullen despair, bullheadedly plunged, against the advice of his physicians, into a round of pleasure and self-indulgence. The food at Streatham, when Thrale entertained, had always been famous. Now it had become almost gross in bulk and splendor, sometimes amounting to over forty different dishes. Samuel Crisp, a friend of the Burneys', describes a typical dinner at this time in a letter to his sister: "A vast deal of Company . . . Everything was most splendid and magnificent—two courses of 21 Dishes each, besides Removes; and after that . . . Pines and Fruits of all Sorts, Ices, Creams, &c., &c., &c., without end. . . . I never saw such at any Nobleman's."[10]

When winter came Thrale leased a house in Grosvenor Square. For years Mrs. Thrale had hoped they could move from the brewery in Southwark, which she had always loathed, to a more fashionable area. This time Thrale himself was willing to move. He had lost interest in his business; he grasped at the thought of the gaiety of a London social season; and his wife was glad to remind him that they would be nearer to his physicians if they were living in the West End. They moved to Grosvenor Square on January 30 (1781). Johnson, of course, was to have a room of his own there. He liked to believe that he was indifferent to "change of place." But the loss of his apartment in the Round Tower in Southwark, which was associated with so much of his past, was naturally a wrench; and it was also a poignant symbol of the general breakup of things that now seemed under way.

At the house in Grosvenor Square, Thrale continued to sink into apathy. But he had animated moments when he would talk of making their long-deferred trip to Italy and also spending some time at a German spa. Something of the way Mrs. Thrale had begun to feel about her husband is suggested by a remark at this time in her private journal: on this trip about which he now talks, "how shall we drag him hither? a Man who cannot keep awake four Hours at a Stroke, who can scarce retain his Faeces."[11]

5

Finally, at a dinner on April 2, two months after they had moved into their new house, Thrale ate so voraciously that his friends were appalled. Johnson spoke to him severely: "After the Denunciation of your Physicians this Morning, such eating is little better than suicide." Thrale, in sullen defiance, disregarded what they said. The next day he gorged himself again at dinner, while talking of plans for his next party. Later that afternoon Queeney went to look for him and found him on the floor. "What's the meaning of this?" she cried out. "I *chuse* it," replied Thrale, with bulldog stubbornness even in a semistupor. "I lie so o'*purpose*." The family immediately sent for Dr. Lucas Pepys, who found him suffering from a massive attack of apoplexy.[12]

During the night Johnson sat by his bed, while Mrs. Thrale, who could not bear to watch by the bedside, kept to her own room most of the time. Around five in the morning (April 4), Johnson felt the last flutter of Thrale's pulse and "looked for the last time upon the face that for fifteen years had never been turned upon me but with respect or benignity." Now and for weeks to come Johnson found himself "afraid of thinking what I have lost." He felt "like a man beginning a new course of life. I had interwoven myself with my dear friend." He made another remark to Mrs. Thrale that is of psychological interest, revealing once again that gratitude—rarely the strongest of emotions in the human heart—took precedence over every other affection in Johnson's desperate and loyal nature: "No death since that of my Wife"—and that had been almost thirty years before—"has ever oppressed me like this."[13] Tetty and Henry Thrale had one thing in common. Each, as Johnson saw it, had rescued him after a long period of profound despair. Whatever their failings, his moral nature placed gratitude and loyalty to them at the very forefront of what he cherished.

Mrs. Thrale, who always shrank from the presence of death, left at once for Streatham and then went to Brighton for two weeks, taking Queeney with her. Several people who had never really understood Johnson's relation with the family began to wonder whether Johnson and Mrs. Thrale would now get married. Boswell, who was currently in town, made up a "Song" of several stanzas the day after Thrale's funeral, which he proudly recited at several dinners—a sort of nuptial ode in which Johnson expresses his rapture in now being free to marry Mrs. Thrale. The verses, self-revelatory in more than one way of Boswell's divided character, are in appalling taste ("Desmullins may now go her ways," cries the ecstatic Johnson, "And poor blind Williams sing alone. . . . I with my arms encircle heaven." Release at last from the "lonely gloom" of his melancholy will come as "with de-

light/In the keen aphrodisian spasm/Shall we reciprocate all night/
. . . lip in rapture glewed to lip").[14]

While Mrs. Thrale was absent, her husband's will, made only a
couple of weeks before his death, was read. It provided that as long as
the brewery was in operation, his widow should receive £2,000 a year
plus an allowance for the maintenance of his five daughters (£150
yearly for each daughter under fifteen and £200 for each between
fifteen and twenty-one). If the brewery was sold, she was to receive
£30,000, with the rest held in trust for the daughters. Streatham was
left to her for her lifetime only, after which it was to pass to the
children. She was given outright the contents of both Streatham and
the Southwark house. There were also substantial separate bequests to
the daughters. Thrale appointed four executors besides his wife, one of
whom was Johnson. They were each left a token sum (£200).[15] Many
people thought that Thrale should have left more to Johnson. In this
they showed little knowledge of Johnson, who, as Thrale was quite
aware, would not have wished it. In fact, when Thrale made his will,
he may very well have talked with Johnson, whom he trusted completely. In this case, Johnson would have certainly excluded himself
from any special bequest. He did not need the money. He had always
resisted money as a gift. Thrale had done more than enough for him,
and what he left belonged entirely to his family.

Mrs. Thrale had no desire to keep the brewery. It had been a source
of worry to her for years and would, she knew, bring continual problems in the future. The executors arranged for its sale. Johnson was
particularly active in studying the resources of the brewery in order to
get a fair price, and at the same time helped John Perkins to manage it.
Boswell mentions hearing an account of Johnson hurrying around the
brewery "with an ink-pen in his button-hole, like an excise man; and
on being asked what he really considered to be the value of the property which was to be disposed of, answered, 'We are not here to sell a
parcel of boilers and vats, but the potentiality of growing rich, beyond
the dreams of avarice.' "[16]

Perkins would have loved to buy the brewery. But he could not
begin to afford the price, even though his brother-in-law, Sylvanus
Bevan, was willing to join him. But he was able to arouse the interest
of the well-known banker David Barclay, and on May 31, the brewery
was sold for £135,000 to David and Robert Barclay, Sylvanus Bevan,
and Perkins himself. The other partners would not have joined if they

had not been reassured by knowing that the brewery would be managed by the experienced Perkins. He did not have enough to pay his share at the start. But Mrs. Thrale, who was grateful for his loyalty over the years, took a bond for a loan to fill out his quarter. The firm of Barclay and Perkins remained in existence until 1955, when it merged with Courage, Ltd.[17]

6

During Thrale's last few months, Johnson seems to have realized that if Thrale died, his widow—still only forty-one—would have before her a different life that might not include, in any important way, an aging and ill man, thirty-one years older than she. He was partly able to repress this thought while he was working as an executor of Thrale's estate. But now, said Fanny Burney, he talked to her "incessantly" when they were alone, about Thrale and the sense of loss that he felt. On June 22 he wrote out a prayer asking for help to "remember with due thankfulness the comforts and advantages which I have enjoyed by the friendship with Henry Thrale." He stayed out at Streatham most of the summer, half feeling—though he seemed to have no particular reasons—that his days there were numbered. He made a special effort to be cheerful and to keep others amused and cheerful, and he continued to give Latin lessons to Queeney and Fanny Burney. But he was also trying to get his bearings. Finally, on August 9, in the afternoon, he retired to the little "summer house" at Streatham in order to think about his future. He was now almost seventy-two. So much that had made life endurable seemed to be leaving him now. Was there anything left except some kind of work to help get him out of himself? With this thought, he made a prayer followed, this time, by only one resolution: "To pass eight hours every day in some serious employment." The first project was to spend "the next six weeks upon the Italian language," possibly in preparation for the long-desired trip to Italy, though he was now growing feebler and though there was no one to go with him except—just possibly—Mrs. Thrale and her daughters.[18]

But Mrs. Thrale's own inner life was undergoing a more rapid change than Johnson may ever have expected, and certainly in a direction he could not have foreseen. If she had felt a few years earlier that life was beginning to slip away from her, she was now almost desperate not to let it slip completely away. For the past year she had felt a mild but growing interest in Queeney's Italian singing teacher, Gabriel Mario Piozzi. She now began to encourage this interest in herself as a means of filling a vacuum and perhaps making up for all she felt she had lacked. Piozzi, who was also forty-one, came from a middle-class family in Quinzano, which was part of the Venetian state. Since the family was large, he had to make his way by himself. After studying music and acquiring some local reputation as a singer, he went to London (1776). Very quickly Johnson's friend, Dr. Charles Burney—the historian of music, and father of Fanny Burney—became an unofficial sponsor to Piozzi, who was soon giving music lessons to children of wealthy families and also performing at concerts.

Mrs. Thrale's first meeting with the man who was to become her second husband was hardly auspicious. It had occurred more than three years before (in the winter of 1777–78) at an evening so richly comic—as Fanny Burney later described it[19]—that it inspired Virginia Woolf to retell it in one of her most delightful essays ("Dr. Burney's Evening Party"). Fulke Greville, a man very conscious of his impeccable lineage, had told Dr. Burney he would like to meet the famous Johnson, and so would his sharp-featured wife, known for her "Ode to Indifference," and their daughter, Mrs. Crewe, one of the most celebrated beauties in England. Burney therefore arranged a party at his house in St. Martin's Street, to which he invited the Grevilles and their daughter, the Thrales and Queeney, Johnson, of course, and Burney's protégé, Signor Piozzi. Also present were the four oldest of Burney's five daughters. It was to be a "brilliant encounter of wits," said Fanny, and Henry Thrale was especially looking forward to "the literary skirmishes" and "the sharp pointed repartees."

Johnson arrived neatly dressed, with clean linen and wearing his "company" wig, obviously prepared to enjoy an evening of good talk. Though the Thrales had seen to it that he looked his best, they apparently did not tell him that he was to be the lion of the party and was expected to perform. In any case, Dr. Burney was unaware that Johnson had been making a point for some time of never beginning a conversation but of waiting until someone else spoke to him directly. Johnson had come to associate this with "good manners." It was part of his renewed effort to acquire "good nature"—"easiness of approach," grace, and relaxation—and was an indication that he was not allowing himself to dominate the conversation and of his special care not to interrupt people when they were talking to each other. Mrs.

Thrale could have broken the ice. But it was not her party, and she felt she should keep in the background. Meanwhile the rest of the company, eagerly waiting for Johnson to talk, were afraid to start the conversation. This was particularly true of Fulke Greville. Ordinarily he would have felt he was the proper person to open the *conversazione*. But he had heard so much, from Topham Beauclerk and others, not only of Johnson's brilliance and knowledge but also of his overwhelming powers of ridicule that he was wary of making a start. In self-defense, therefore, he "planted himself," said Fanny, "immovable as a noble statue, upon the hearth, as if a stranger to the whole set," occasionally glancing at the company with what seemed to them a supercilious air of superiority. The minutes continued to pass while the company waited for Johnson to start and while he himself placidly sat in "good-natured" silence.

In an attempt to save the evening, Dr. Burney asked Piozzi to play and sing for them. Burney had complete faith in the power of music to unlock the heart and lift the spirit. But the effect this night was the opposite. By the time Piozzi had finished, Johnson—seeing the evening going in a different direction from what he expected, and assuming this was Burney's idea of entertainment—had lapsed into profound meditation. The Thrales and the Grevilles, who cared no more for music than Johnson did, remained silent, while Greville continued to stand on the hearth. Embarrassed, Dr. Burney then asked Piozzi to sing again. This time Mrs. Thrale, in a co-operative attempt to enliven things, rose from her chair, and stealing on tiptoe behind Piozzi, began to imitate his gestures as he sang and played, lifting her elbows "with ecstatic shrugs of the shoulders, and casting up her eyes, while languishingly reclining her head." Dr. Burney was shocked to see one of his guests mimicked in this way. He quietly went up to Mrs. Thrale and gently whispered to her that if she did not enjoy music herself, she might respect the feelings of those who did. Mrs. Thrale accepted the rebuke with grace, and returned to her chair, as she afterward told Fanny, "like a pretty little miss, for the remainder of one of the most humdrum evenings that she had ever passed." Johnson had not observed the little scene in which Mrs. Thrale mimicked Piozzi. He was sitting with his back to the harpsichord, staring at the fire—the view of which had been obstructed all this time by Greville's legs.

Finally Johnson came out of his reverie, looked up fixedly at Fulke Greville's face, and uttered his first remark of the evening: "If it were not for depriving the ladies of the fire," he said, "I should like to stand upon the hearth myself." While the others suppressed their impulse to giggle, Greville, with an uneasy smile, continued to stand on the hearth for a few more minutes, and then, with sudden firmness, rang the bell and asked for his carriage.

7

Mrs. Thrale did not see Piozzi again until the summer of 1780, when she took her ill husband to Brighton to get him in shape for the election campaign in September. One day in July she saw Piozzi outside a bookseller's shop, and impulsively asked him to give music lessons to her daughter Queeney. Piozzi, not knowing who she was, replied with aloof dignity that he was at Brighton to recover his voice. Later in the day, learning who she was, he immediately sought her out and expressed himself eager for the honor of teaching Queeney.

Recording the incident in her journal, Mrs. Thrale wrote, "He is amazingly like my Father." There was indeed some resemblance in the face. But Piozzi was otherwise far from being like John Salusbury, who had a firm if prickly Welsh integrity and could even be irascible. Piozzi, in contrast to John Salusbury, was quiet and controlled in temperament. The only two characteristics he shared with Mrs. Thrale's father were negative. Neither had much interest in business (though later Piozzi proved industrious and accurate in keeping his wife's accounts). Finally both Piozzi and John Salusbury, though in different ways, were radically unlike Henry Thrale.

It was the difference from Thrale that was to prove far more important than any superficial resemblance to her father. Piozzi—a foreigner, a musician, a Roman Catholic—was almost the diametrical opposite of her husband. Thrale was rich, stubborn, and taciturn. Piozzi was relatively poor, superficially docile, cheerful, and without the black moods to which Thrale had been inclined. Mrs. Thrale found it a relief that he was not absorbed in business. He also seemed less aggressively competitive. To some extent this was true. We tend to feel competitive, as Johnson had said long ago, mainly with people engaged in pursuits similar to our own rather than in those radically different. Any sense of competition Piozzi felt (he was quite jealous, for example, of the popular singer Gasparo Pacchierotti) was in a realm so unfamiliar to Mrs. Thrale that she would not have much noticed it or have been able to take it seriously if she did.

Finally there is the brute fact that Piozzi was a kind of "dependent," whereas Thrale was anything but a "dependent." This is not to say that Mrs. Thrale had the kind of ego that responded most warmly to an inferior or a dependent. Far from it. But ever since her mid-twenties she had been surrounded by "strong" personalities that were assertive as well as strong—her mother, Thrale himself, Johnson, the famous people she had met through Johnson, and now her daughter Queeney, who was in many ways like her father. She had become a kind of anvil against which firmly held hammers were always striking. Moreover, from the beginning, she had exerted herself to please them. This gallant effort, kept up for so long, had created a fatigue and desire for relief that a less generous person—who would never have made such an exertion—would probably not feel; and it was precisely such individuals who were the first to censure her later. It is a common mistake on the part of cooler, self-contained natures to assume that those who have a giving and ebullient character are what they are only because they cannot help it—that they are fed from a spring that will never stop rather than a reservoir that can be exhausted. Hence the feeling of stark disbelief or unpleasant shock on the part of others when the reservoir of effort and energy—for it turns out to be a reservoir—is almost gone.

Moreover, Hester Thrale was justified in thinking that her altruism, sympathetic ebullience, and affection had for years been passively accepted and taken for granted, and that the principal reward for those who give lavishly rather than meagerly is the expectation that they remain true to form and continue to give. Johnson was an exception. He knew the human heart too well. Moreover, in Johnson at least, if in no one else, there was genuine gratitude; and, as so often in him, gratitude had long since deepened into love. Even so, he had not been easy to live with, especially at the start, when he had been in so frightful a condition. After his death she wrote that the experience of those first years with him had been "terrifying," as well it might have been to a woman in her twenties who found on her hands a famous man so much older than herself, so different from anyone else she had met, and in a state he himself felt close to madness. And over the years, as he grew better and came to love her and Henry Thrale, the demand on her time and sympathy—while she was enduring one pregnancy after another and trying to maintain the kind of life Thrale wanted—could understandably begin to seem to her, as she said, almost like a "yoke."

But the rewards more than balanced this, as she knew perfectly well. The truth is that any fatigue or chafing of the spirit that she felt about Johnson and the world he brought to her (a world she welcomed and continued to value) was insignificant except as it was added to, or in her mind became coalesced with, her long complicated reaction to Thrale himself. Yet even with Thrale she had more than co-operated in this marriage which had been so far from a love match. She had accepted the fact that Thrale was considerably older, and that her principal function was to produce a family, year after year. Possibly, if Thrale had died in 1777 instead of 1781, her own later life would have been different. But her final three years with him, during his illness, had been very difficult for her.

In any case, Thrale was no longer there. She must begin to think of another future while she still had the chance; for she was now approaching menopause, and time had become an enemy. Piozzi in June had gone to Italy to visit his parents. She found herself thinking about him, and instinctively encouraged herself in doing so as a means of deepening a feeling that could give some new interest in life.

8

As if to begin to prepare himself in advance for some future change, Johnson meanwhile decided to take the only kind of trip he could now take alone—the familiar trip first to Oxford, then to Lichfield, then to John Taylor's at Ashbourne (October 15–December 11).

"The motives for my journey," he wrote in his diary, "I hardly know. I omitted it last year, and am not willing to miss it again." The people he wished to see at Lichfield—Lucy Porter, Mrs. Aston, Edmund Hector—were getting old. He had known Hector for over sixty years. "We have always loved one another. Perhaps we may be made better by some serious conversation." It was here, among these people, that his roots had been. He was instinctively turning to them now that he felt himself losing what had been so important in his later life. He also wished, he said, "to talk seriously with Taylor," who—impervious to so much of what troubled Johnson—had always tended, by the contagion of his bluff confidence, to steady him. But Johnson was not in good health before he set out. Only the month before, Fanny Burney had said she was "quite frightened about him; but he continues his strange discipline—starving, mercury, opium; and though for a time half demolished by its severity, he always, in the end, rises superior to both the disease and the remedy." At Lichfield, as he told Mrs. Thrale, he found Lucy Porter broken in health and very deaf. "I can scarcely make her understand me and she can hardly make me understand her." Old Mrs. Aston had become almost paralytic. "So here are merry doings." The trip, he said, was a case of "a sick man visiting the sick."[20]

Shortly before he returned, he wrote to Mrs. Thrale: "Do not neglect me, nor relinquish me. Nobody will ever love you better or honour you more." It was the only time thus far that he let himself come close to expressing a fear that had been haunting him for months. On his return Mrs. Thrale saw that his health had deteriorated, and wondered whether he was not in danger of a paralytic stroke. "There are really some Symptoms already discoverable, I think, about the Mouth particularly." She had been thinking that she might take a trip to Italy with the older girls and with Piozzi (who returned to England in November) as a guide. But "travelling with Mr. Johnson I cannot bear"—given his condition now—and "leaving him behind *he* could not bear." The problem was the graver since she was not thinking (at least within a few months she was not thinking) of an ordinary trip but of a really extended stay abroad, and beneath this was the growing attraction of the thought—if only still half-fanciful—of Piozzi as a possible husband: a thought of which Piozzi, however flattered by the interest of a woman of her position, seems thus far to have remained quite ignorant.[21]

9

Suddenly, on January 17 (1782), Johnson's friend of thirty-five years Robert Levet died of a heart attack at the age of seventy-seven. Only the night before, as Johnson told Bennet Langton, he had been thinking "with uncommon earnestness, that however I might alter my mode of life, or whithersoever I might remove, I would endeavour to retain Levett about me." The remark again shows how seriously he was taking the possibility that his life with the Thrales was almost over, and his need now to cling to those still left who were associated with the years before he had known the Thrales.[22]

In the weeks ahead, as he tried to come to terms with this further loss, he wrote a restrained poem, "On the Death of Dr. Robert Levet."

It is in the calm Horatian style he had come to love as a boy at Stourbridge. If it is a lament for this dutiful, awkward, and conscientious man, it is also a lament for life—for common humanity, and for the effort that human beings try to make, in this strange purgatory of our lives, to fulfill moral values and ideals. The situation of man is put at the outset in a short phrase, "Hope's delusive mine." We are like slaves condemned to dig in the mines. For we are working in the dark, forced to take our chance on what we may find; and the mine is "delusive" because it will never really yield what the heart had hoped. The image of a mine or cave has an archetypal richness: the cold, crowded cellars in the London slums into which Levet, with his sturdy trudge of several miles each day, would descend to minister to the sick poor ("In misery's darkest caverns known,/ His useful care was ever nigh"); the caverns of the human mind itself, in which hope haunts incentive and from which the sense of duty and responsibility emerges to help us march through life; and, finally, the grave into which this responsible man—"Of every friendless name the friend"—has now made his final descent:

> Yet still he fills affection's eye,
>> Obscurely wise, and coarsely kind;
> Nor, letter'd arrogance, deny
>> Thy praise to merit unrefin'd.

What is most striking about the poem, and the reason it is so often reprinted in anthologies, is the amount of thinking about life condensed and held in balance with a deep, dignified, and accurate feeling directly engaged with real and daily things. By "accurate" is meant that the writer is not pretending to feel more than he does. Because he is not overstating, there is a solidity and rightness about what he does say. (The care Levet brought to the helpless poor was "useful" care. So in the fine line "Obscurely wise"—covered up, not obvious—"and coarsely kind.") The conception of this ordinary man, now dead, becomes a paradigm for humanity. The grief is sublimated to a general statement in which moral virtue, humble or great, walks in the midst of life, fulfilling the parable of the talents that always haunted Johnson:

> His virtues walked their narrow round,
>> Nor made a pause, nor left a void;
> And sure the Eternal Master found
>> The single talent well employed.

10

Johnson was in poor condition to take the shock of Levet's death. Almost immediately afterward, a cold he had caught turned into a severe case of bronchitis, which was to last for several months. Joined with emphysema and with the congestive heart disease from which he was now beginning to suffer, it left him breathless and very weak. He was being bled constantly and, by March 21, fifty ounces of blood had been drawn from him.

Mrs. Thrale, who had rented a house in Harley Street, took him back for a while, finding him "very ill, ill indeed; & I do not see what ails him." Significantly there was no longer any special room in her house that could be considered exclusively his. This was the start of a series of strategic withdrawals on her part, though they may not at first have been wholly conscious. From here on he is increasingly put into a position in which he is forced to ask for even a fraction of what had been so freely offered him for sixteen years. The truth is that the innocent Johnson—in whatever plans or hopes she might have for the future—was simply in the way. His growing helplessness tugged at her conscience. She was at times close to desperation. What could she do about him? She could not talk to him frankly about Piozzi. With his stern moral principles and his immense powers of language, what would he say? In any case, was he really so ill? Was it not merely old age? "I do not see what ails him." Yet she was still inwardly divided; for she impulsively added, "If I lose *him* I am more than undone: Friend, Father, Guardian, Confidant." Nor did he stay with her long at Harley Street. He was soon back in his own house, which, with Levet dead and Miss Williams and Mrs. Desmoulins ill, was now a melancholy place. "My mind," he wrote in his journal (March 18), "has been for some time much disturbed."[23]

There may have been a slight quarrel between him and Mrs. Thrale —or rather hurt on his part and some annoyance on hers—for in late April he wrote her a short letter beginning, "I have been very much out of order since you sent me away; but why should I tell you, who do not care, nor desire to know?" Then, after mentioning people he has seen, he ends, "Do not let Mr. Piozzi nor any body else put me quite out of your head, and do not think that any body will love you like Your & c." At this, she took him out to Streatham. But in a few days he again returned to town for a week, pretending that he wished to see people there but really because he was trying to make still another effort, before it was too late, to live more alone. But he "got so very ill," said Mrs. Thrale (May 11), "that I thought I should never get him home alive—such Spasms on his Breath . . . & old Lawrence his Physician worse than he, dead on one Side [from a paralytic stroke]. Such a Scene!" Yet, within another week, he was again back in London, telling her he was better, though he quickly caught a fresh cold that reinforced his bronchitis.[24]

In order to breathe more easily, he tried sleeping all night in a chair. Hoping that a change of air would help him, he went to Oxford for a short visit (June 10–19). At a dinner given by Dr. Adams, he found Hannah More, whom he had always liked, and insisted on giving her a tour of Pembroke College. He seemed to her "very ill indeed—spiritless and wan. However, he made an effort to be cheerful." Then he returned to Streatham. Here he began to read the Bible regularly and occasionally made corrections for a new edition of the *Lives*, unaware that by October, shortly after he became seventy-three, he would be leaving Streatham forever.[25]

Chapter 31

Loss of the Thrale Family;
Failing Health

Because he seemed by August (1782) to be much better, Mrs. Thrale decided that this was the time to break the news to him of her future plans. "I mustered up resolution," she wrote in her journal (August 22), "to tell him the Necessity of changing a Way of Life I had long been displeased with." Moreover, she could not afford financially to keep up Streatham. She wanted to let it for three years. It would be cheaper, she thought, to go abroad and live for a while. At the same time, "to shew Italy to my Girls, and be shewed it by Piozzi, has long been my dearest wish." She emphasized that, because of Johnson's health, she had been reluctant to leave him. But now he appeared better. She had talked with Queeney about this, she added, and Queeney also liked the idea.

His reaction could have been predicted more easily than she now let herself think. For what could he say? He had for months been thinking with dread about the possibility of something like this happening. The least he could do now was to assent with grace and make things easier for her by trying to encourage her in a decision she had already made. Considering his condition, and how much his life had been interwoven with the Thrales, this selfless act was almost heroic. But of course Mrs. Thrale could not allow herself to see it for what it was. Summarizing their talk, she continues, "Mr. Johnson thought well of the project & wished me to put it early in Execution," and—she adds with transparent candor—"seemed even less concerned at parting with me than I wished him";

See the Importance of a Person to himself! I fancied Mr Johnson could not have existed without me forsooth, as we have now lived together above 18 Years, & I have so fondled and waited on him in Sickness & in Health—Not a bit on't! he feels nothing in parting with me, nothing in the least; but thinks it a prudent Scheme, & goes to his Book as usual. This is Philosophy & Truth; he always said he hated a Feeler.

It was not mere pique and vanity that led her to interpret him in this way. She knew him very well. Moreover, if he had begun to implore her not to leave, she would have resented it far more, as he himself knew, and—if it had temporarily deferred her departure—it would only have poisoned their relationship for whatever time was left. What was leading her to interpret his reaction in this way was deeper and more complex—the common human need, when we have injured others or are about to do so, to excuse and justify it with personal grievance, though our real motives have nothing to do with them personally. No grievance is more difficult to forgive or is quicker to harden into personal dislike than one that we manufacture, intensify, and hug for this purpose, since to drop that grievance is to leave us naked to a self-indictment greater than most of us are willing to endure.

To this need to reduce him as a claim on her affection and attention was added something else: a psychological "transference" to Johnson, as the symbol readiest to hand, of the resentment she was already feeling in advance of the way others generally would regard what she really hoped—and intended—to do. For it was not merely a prolonged stay in Italy that she had in mind. She was very close to deciding that Piozzi was to be her husband. She knew abstractly, but was not willing to give full emotional weight to it, what the general reaction would be. She would be especially censured since her children were so young. How were they to be brought up? And where were these young heiresses to be brought up—in Italy? What of their future? What sort of marriage could they look forward to there? Piozzi was not only a foreigner and a Catholic. His profession, though it demanded some abilities, was regarded with little respect. Moreover, he himself could seem a fortune hunter, though she herself knew better (and he was still, of course, innocent of her intentions). These intentions had not yet completely jelled. But they were at work in her mind. Naturally she felt frustrated at the possible hurdles. She could do nothing about them. Her annoyance and sense of frustration needed an object. Here was Johnson, still unaware of what was going on—so dependent, yet so moral and high-minded. His very ignorance of her plans and hopes had in a mysterious way intensified her resentment, her desire to detach him, as if stimulating her to take strong measures in advance. It is to Mrs. Thrale's credit that some of her generous feelings about Johnson ultimately returned—enough at least to allow her to print, without too much defensiveness, the anecdotes and accounts of him that she had been writing over the years. We must admit that this was after Johnson was no longer alive. Moreover, he was very famous, and her acquaintance with him was her own principal passport to fame. Yet it would have been very easy for her to be more defensive and less generous, and on the whole she refrained from being so.

But now, feeling so guilty at what she was doing to him, she was desperate to vindicate herself. And the mere presence of the man she was injuring only because he seemed to be in the way—the man she had only a few months before called "Friend, Father, Guardian, Confidant"—was becoming daily more unpleasant to her as a rebuke to her conscience and a symbol of problems she might face later. After describing their talk this August, she added, as a footnote to her journal, the ugliest and least honest remark she was ever to make about Johnson.

I begin to see (now every thing shews it) that Johnson's Connection with me is merely an interested one—he *loved* Mr Thrale I believe, but only wish'd to find in me a careful Nurse and humble Friend for his sick and his lounging hours: yet I really thought he could not have existed without *my Conversation* forsooth. He cares more for my roast Beef & plumb Pudden which he now devours too dirtily for endurance: and since he is glad to get rid of me, I'm sure I have good Cause to desire the getting Rid of *him*.[1]

Eager to get Streatham off her hands, Mrs. Thrale quickly arranged to lease the house and its contents to Lord Shelburne for three years. She planned to spend the autumn at Brighton, and then rent a house in London for the winter during which she would make arrangements with Piozzi for their departure to Italy. Johnson, who in past years had been so ready to express himself about the family's plans, kept quiet. But to Fanny Burney he almost broke down as he accompanied her in the coach to London one day. Lifting a shaking hand toward the house as they left it, he said in a tremulous voice, "That house is lost to me—forever!"[2] The family, he knew, would never return to Streatham in his lifetime, if at all.

2

On Sunday, October 6 (1782), Johnson attended the little church at Streatham for what he knew was the last time. He had written for the occasion a special prayer on leaving what had been his home more than any other place. He wanted to express gratitude for all that Streatham and the Thrale family had meant to him. But his special purpose was to bless the remaining family in the uncertain future they faced: "To thy fatherly protection, O Lord, I commend this family. Bless, guide, and defend them."

So breathless was he now that he had to rest several times as he walked the short distance to the church. He was apparently alone when he walked there, and certainly no one was looking as he left the building. Rather bashfully he put in Latin, in his journal, what he now did: "I bade the church farewell with a kiss" (*"Templo valedixi cum osculo"*).

Early the next morning—for once far earlier than anyone else in the family—he arose. "I packed up my bundles," he said. There was not much to pack, and he was soon finished. He had always traveled lightly through life; and even here, where he had felt so much at home for sixteen years, he had allowed himself to collect few possessions. Then, since the others were still not up, he went into the library, where the walls were hung with the portraits Thrale had commissioned Reynolds to paint, including portraits of Garrick, Goldsmith, and Thrale himself, all dead. As his "parting use of the library," Johnson read some passages of the Bible.[3]

3

Mrs. Thrale naturally asked him if he wished to accompany them to Brighton. Ordinarily he might not have done so except for a short visit. The place typified all that he disliked about fashionable "resorts." But now the situation was different. There would be no Streatham to which he could return later. To say good-bye to the remaining Thrales at the very moment that he was leaving Streatham permanently was too much like bidding a permanent good-bye to them as well. He had always had a "secret horrour of the last," and especially in anything that had to do with people he loved. Who knew—given the rapidly shifting circumstances, and his own age and frailty—whether life with them would be even the shadow of what it had been if the thread of "continuity of being" were suddenly snapped or even loosened at this important time? He could not say good-bye to them now and go back to his own bleak dwelling in Bolt Court, with Levet dead and Miss Williams querulous and ailing. The whole past year had "battered" him, he wrote to Boswell, though he did not go into details. He had no choice but to go to Brighton. Perhaps a home of sorts could be re-established somewhere in other places where the Thrale family lived if only he were with them at the time.

But during the weeks at Brighton (October 7 to November 20), his state of mind was one of constant pain. Where was his own philosophy? True, one of the lessons in *Rasselas*, written so long ago, was that the philosopher who discoursed so bravely about death and loss proved to be as vulnerable as others. Nor was the philosopher to be laughed at for that reason. He was showing himself to be a human being. Still, as Dr. Adams had told Johnson when he was working on the *Dictionary*, he was a proud man—as proud in his own way as Lord Chesterfield. He should now be able to face what was left of his life both with personal fortitude and also with compassionate understanding toward those he loved.

Yet fortitude can conflict with tenderness to others. For example, he was deeply hurt. When Mrs. Thrale's mind was not on the consuming passion she had encouraged in herself for Piozzi, she was distracted only by the thought of the problems created by her own daughters. "My Head," she confided to her journal (November 4), "is full of nothing but my Children—my Heart of my beloved Piozzi!"[4] Johnson was kept ignorant of what was really happening, and not only by Mrs. Thrale but by Fanny Burney and Queeney, who were now entirely aware of the situation. Accordingly, it could not have occurred to him that, as a responsibility, he was as much in the way as Mrs. Thrale's imagination now regarded him. But he could tell that, for some reason he did not understand, he had suddenly become unwanted, and that, whatever else was awry, the problem had to do partly with him being a burden—the burden he had always feared he might be to those he loved. His stubborn loyalty suggested to him that Mrs. Thrale might not be well. In any case, because he was hurt was no reason why he should withdraw from this family which now seemed to him helplessly adrift and to which he owed all the tenderness of which he was capable. "The shepherd in Virgil"—as he had said long ago in the letter to Chesterfield—"grew at last acquainted with Love, and found him a native of the rocks." His life was completely "interwoven" with this family, as he had said of Henry Thrale himself when Thrale died. Of course he could not leave them. And in addition to their need of him, there was his need of them.

Torn by self-conflict, unable as a young man might have been to cut or loosen his moorings and start another life, if only as a supplement or active alternative, Johnson hung on at Brighton. In trying to hold down and control what really distressed him, his tongue could at times become bitter or caustic when he talked with strangers. He was not this way constantly. But in the kind of society that frequented Brighton, a very little sharp language from a man of Johnson's powers could go a long way. Soon, as Fanny wrote to her father, Johnson was "omitted in all cards of invitation sent to the rest of us." Being left alone naturally made him feel worse. Moreover, others were becoming afraid to call at the house. William Pepys, hitherto a frequent visitor and a friend of the family, fell into an argument with him one night at a party in which "Johnson was certainly right with respect to the argument and to reason; but his opposition was so warm, and his wit so satirical" that Fanny "grieved to see how unamiable he appeared, and how greatly he made himself dreaded." Poor Pepys "was so torn to pieces . . . that he suddenly seized his hat, and abruptly walked out of the room in the middle of the discourse. . . . Dr. Delap confesses himself afraid of coming as usual to the house."[5]

Added to his feeling of distress was his sense of growing physical helplessness. In walking even from the inn to the Thrale house, he had to stop and rest four times, and almost every night, after being in bed for a couple of hours, he had to sit up for a while in order to breathe more easily. To occupy his mind, he had resumed the study of Dutch. Within a few weeks he was reading it fluently. But its appeal as a distraction was limited. What he needed was companionship. One evening he insisted on going to a foolish ball with Fanny, Mrs. Thrale, and Queeney, "to the universal amazement of all who saw him there," said Fanny. She pressed him to know why he went. "It cannot," he answered, "be worse than being alone." Luckily he ran into a good friend of Joshua Reynolds's, named Philip Metcalfe, and they got along so well that he prevailed on Metcalfe to make a trip with him to Chichester to see the cathedral there and surrounding sights, although the puzzled Metcalfe confessed to Fanny that why Johnson desired this "I cannot imagine, for how shall a blind man see a cathedral?" Fanny assured Metcalfe Johnson was not really "blind," and the two men took an excursion (November 8–10), during which Johnson took notes of the places they saw.[6]

4

When they returned to London (November 20), where Mrs. Thrale had rented a house in Argyll Street, she threw herself into an active social life and also confided her feelings even more openly to Piozzi ("dear generous, prudent, noble-minded Creature"). Piozzi naturally sensed that new doors were opening to him. Meanwhile Johnson kept to his own house most of the time waiting to be asked to come and stay at Argyll Street—a pathetically inadequate substitute for Streatham, or the Round Tower in Southwark. He tried to keep up a correspondence, and wrote her frequent notes. One, written the day after Christmas, mentions some visitors who had called on him and gently adds, "But I have not seen those of whom I once hoped never to have lost sight." Mrs. Thrale at last took the hint, and asked him over, and Fanny the next day found him "comic and good-humoured." Yet in a few more days (January 4, 1783) she learned how ill he was. He could hardly speak as he sat by her at dinner, unable to eat, except to repeat to her, "You little know how ill I am." But throughout the evening "he was excessively kind to me, in spite of all his pain."[7]

Meanwhile, unknown to Johnson, a crisis was arising in the Thrale family. Queeney's reaction to her mother's attachment to Piozzi—and by now she knew all about it—was one of cold scorn. Even when Queeney was younger, Mrs. Thrale had been half afraid of her eldest daughter, who reminded her of Henry Thrale in his prime. Though Queeney was still only eighteen, she was older than her years and accustomed to taking long views. Aside from her personal disgust at her mother's infatuation, she was frankly embarrassed at the spectacle of a woman of her position pursuing a foreign music teacher of Piozzi's modest abilities. It was already arousing gossip in London society. Her conduct, thought Queeney, would be remembered and would affect any future chances the Thrale daughters might have to make good marriages. Queeney lined up the younger girls, who stood beside her during a showdown with their mother. Even Fanny Burney, Hester Thrale's trusted confidante, went over to Queeney's side. Moreover, one of the executors, Jeremiah Crutchley, was strongly opposed to her plan to go to Italy. Except for Queeney, the daughters were still quite young. The plan struck him as irresponsible. Nor did he much like Mrs. Thrale anyway. In order to prevent the Italian journey, he now proposed making the Thrale children "wards in Chancery"—something which Thrale had actually requested in his will but which had thus far not been executed.

Faced with such opposition, Hester Thrale surrendered. Piozzi was summoned (January 27) and told that this was the end. He then thought he would talk privately to Queeney, who proved more formidable than he had expected. She bluntly told him, as Mrs. Thrale learned immediately afterward, that what was happening was degrading to her mother's good name and that "our Connection would be the ruin of their Family." Finding the whole situation beyond him, Piozzi went back to his place in Wigmore Street, "brought all my Letters Promises of Marriage & c," said Mrs. Thrale, "put them into *her* hand," and—his English getting a little uncertain in his excitement—cried out to Queeney dramatically, "Take your Mama—and make it of her a Countess—It shall kill *me* never mind—but it shall *kill her too!*"[8]

While Piozzi prepared to return to Italy in the spring, Mrs. Thrale decided to go to Bath to recover her health and spirits. But at this point the two youngest girls became ill—Cecilia, who was six, with whooping cough, and little four-year-old Harriet with measles. Mrs. Thrale, who had never had whooping cough, lived in dread of catching it, and in fact once hurried out of a church in the middle of a service when she thought she heard "the fatal Sound." Hence she arranged to have the girls looked after, and, as soon as they seemed better, set off for Bath with Queeney, Susanna, and Sophia. On April 5, the day before she left, she said good-bye to Johnson. (They were not to meet again until a year later, and then only briefly.) Within a few days she learned that Harriet had died. She immediately hurried back to bury Harriet in St. Leonard's Church at Streatham next to the others, and, before returning to Bath, tried to see Piozzi again, who was on the point of leaving for Italy. Understandably bruised at the way things had worked out, he refused to see her. He simply wanted to go home. But she did not wish him to forget her, and sent, as a farewell message, some embarrassingly bad verses ("Fondly to bless my wandering Lover/ And make him dote on dirty Dover").[9]

Meanwhile Boswell, after an absence of almost two years, had arrived in London (March 20) for a visit of several weeks. Calling on

Johnson the next day, he found him pale and "distressed with a difficulty of breathing." "I am glad you are come," said Johnson; "I am very ill." But the conversation soon began to lift Johnson's spirits, and he said gratefully, "You must be as much with me as you can. You have done me good. You cannot think how much better I am since you came in." The compliment, which Boswell naturally treasured, came from the heart. Johnson was not only ill but very lonely, and he was touched that Boswell, the very morning after he arrived, should at once seek him out. As his spirits rose, a touch of his old humor reappeared:

BOSWELL. "Pray, Sir, can you trace the cause of your antipathy to the Scotch?" JOHNSON. "I can not, Sir." BOSWELL. "Old Mr. Sheridan says, it was because they sold Charles the First." JOHNSON. "Then, Sir, old Mr. Sheridan has found out a very good reason."[10]

Boswell, though he was now settling into middle age (forty-two), was still young enough, still curious and spontaneous enough, to draw out Johnson in a way that few people any longer were able to do. In stepping into the breach, he brought back memories of their tour to the Hebrides. During the next few weeks Boswell records some fine scenes. On Good Friday (April 15), he found Johnson at breakfast "drinking tea without milk, and eating a cross-bun to prevent faintness." They went to St. Clement's and, when they came back, Johnson sat placidly on a stone seat at the door of his little garden in Bolt Court. As he looked at his tiny estate, he began to muse what he would do if he were a country gentleman. Being so lonely, his first thought had to do with the company he would have. But he would probably be considered inhospitable. For he would not, like many country gentlemen, have "crowds" of visitors at a time. "Sir Alexander Dick," said Boswell, "tells me, that he remembers having a thousand people in a year to dine at his house." Johnson, almost like his old self, replied, "That, Sir, is about three a day." Boswell: "How your statement lessens the idea." That, said Johnson, "is the good of counting. It brings everything to a certainty, which before floated in the mind indefinitely." Boswell then drew him out on chemistry, gardens, and fruit-growing; and, when a couple of other friends stopped by, the conversation shifted to elocution, oratory, and the origin of language.* Another

* This also was the weekend (Easter Day, April 20) when Boswell snatched the chance to interview Mrs. Desmoulins on the subject he labeled "Extraordinary Johnsoniana—*Tacenda*" (above, pp. 263–64).

time, at breakfast, while Mrs. Desmoulins made tea, she and Boswell, intending to flatter him, began to talk with each other about "his not complaining of the world, because he was not called to some great office, nor had attained to great wealth." He became strangely heated at this, as though they were trying to encourage a spirit of ingratitude and complaint. He had never "sought the world," he said. Why should the world have showered gifts on him? "It is rather wonderful that so much has been done for me. All the complaints which are made of the world are unjust. I never knew a man of merit neglected: it was generally by his own fault that he failed of success."

The day before Boswell left for Scotland, he paid a final call (May 29). Johnson "embraced me, and gave me his blessing. . . . I walked from his door today, with a fearful apprehension of what might happen before I returned."[11]

5

Suddenly, early in the morning of June 17 (1783), Johnson awoke to find he was suffering a paralytic stroke. As he described it later to Mrs. Thrale, "I was alarmed, and prayed God, that however he might afflict my body, he would spare my understanding. This prayer, that I might try the integrity of my faculties, I made in Latin verse. The lines were not very good, but I knew them not to be very good." As the dawn approached, he was able with some difficulty—for his hand kept making the wrong letters—to send a note to his neighbor Edmund Allen:

DEAR SIR,

It has pleased GOD, this morning, to deprive me of the powers of speech; and as I do not know but that it may be his further good pleasure to deprive me soon of my senses, I request you will on the receipt of this note, come to me, and act for me, as the exigencies of my case may require.

I am,
Sincerely yours,
SAM. JOHNSON[12]

The next day Tom Davies wrote to Mrs. Thrale at Bath, giving her a strong hint that her help would mean a great deal to Johnson at this time. "He is really much to be pitied. He has no female friend in his House that can do him any service on this occasion." Mrs. Desmoulins, apparently after a quarrel with Miss Williams, had left a month before, and Miss Williams—blind, and rapidly declining in health—was naturally of no help. Then, on June 19, Johnson himself wrote Mrs. Thrale an account of what had happened. He was trying to understand what it meant, to see it in some perspective, and he was also instinctively turning to the one person left among those he had most trusted when confronted with personal distress. True, she had changed; and he was both defensive and diffident as he asked her help. Perhaps she will now read what he is writing with an indifference unimaginable before:

> For this diminution of regard however, I know not whether I ought to blame You, who may have reasons which I cannot know, and I do not blame myself who have for a great part of human life done You what good I could, and have never done you evil.
>
> I have loved you with virtuous affection, I have honoured You with sincere Esteem. Let not all our endearment be forgotten, but let me have in this great distress your pity and your prayers. You see I yet turn to You with my complaints as a settled and unalienable friend, do not, do not drive me from You, for I have not deserved either neglect or hatred.[13]

At one time she would have hurried to London. Now she simply made a vague offer to come, but in such a way that he would be forced to request it as something really necessary. Naturally he could not bring himself to do this. He simply thanked her for the offer, and said, "I will lay it up for future use." She not only failed to go to London but did not even ask him to come to Bath when he recovered. Though he kept it to himself, he was deeply hurt. The whole thing seemed incredible to him. What had he done? But the truth is that she was preoccupied with only one interest. Because she had given in to Queeney, she had lost what had increasingly become a symbol of freedom—freedom to make a fresh start, and in a way in which she would never again fail to have the reins in her hand, as she had not had with Thrale. Why had she given in this way to Queeney? Had she not devoted enough of her life to pleasing others? She had become ill with anger and frustration. Overriding every other concern was her determination to find some means to defy, or circumvent, Queeney and the others, and to "shorten the Absence that destroys my Health, consumes my Soul, and keeps me to mourn *his* Distance to whom only I wish to be near." Johnson's presence, if he were seriously ill, might shake her in that single-minded resolution. She easily convinced herself that he was not in such bad shape after all, and in her journal (June 24) speaks of him with condescending benevolence as though he were a mere acquaintance:

A Stroke of Palsy has robbed Johnson of his Speech I hear, dreadful Event! & I at a Distance—poor Fellow! a Letter from himself in his usual Style [which was something that had cost him great effort] convinces me that none other of his Faculties have fail'd him, & his Physicians say that all present Danger is over.
I sincerely wish the Continuance of a Health so valuable.[14]

6

He quickly regained the ability to speak, though not at first too distinctly nor for very long at a time. Resolved to keep active, he then paid a visit to Bennet Langton at Rochester for a couple of weeks (July 10–23), and while there made some short excursions.

During this time he was beginning to feel some pain from an ailment he had been treating lightly. Back in the winter of 1781–82, a year and a half before, a swelling had started in his left testicle. He had disregarded it, but the swelling had increased during the last six months. It was obviously, he thought, a hydrocele, and he therefore assumed it could be punctured and drained "as soon as more formidable disorders gave me leisure." It was a minor operation. Even so, in the days before anesthetics, it was naturally painful.

But the prospect of the operation did not bother him much. He had more serious problems that made something like a hydrocele or an operation for it seem like a trifle. Aside from the state of mind in which the events of the past two years had left him, there were the "more formidable disorders" of physical health that he mentions. His resistance had been severely shaken by the past two years. By this summer (1783) no less than four chronic diseases were simultaneously converging on him in a more acute form:

1. There was the general circulatory disease of which the stroke was the first dramatic symptom.

2. For years, as we have been noticing, he had been troubled with chronic bronchitis; and, as so often with chronic bronchitis in its advanced stage, it had been gradually accompanied by emphysema. Hence his growing breathlessness. The autopsy was to reveal so extreme a case of emphysema ("The lungs," it states, "did not collapse as they usually do when air is admitted, but remained distended, as if they

had lost the power of contraction")[15] that we can infer the disease was already severe by the summer of 1783.

3. The strain this produced on the heart was unquestionably the principal cause of the next difficulty: congestive heart failure, of which edema (dropsy) was such a prominent symptom before the widespread use of digitalis. The preceding April, in writing an account of himself to Robert Chambers, now in India, he mentioned that "my legs have begun to swell."[16] By the following autumn this condition was to become far graver. The "asthma" mentioned in his letters and journal refers to a twofold difficulty in breathing—that produced by the bronchitis and emphysema, and that produced by congestive heart failure (cardiac asthma). It is the latter that led him so often to try to sleep in a chair at night, since the excess of fluid, which during the day tends to gravitate to the legs, begins to overload the lungs when one is lying in bed.

4. The progressive rheumatoid arthritis that afflicted him, though hardly in the same class of seriousness with the other diseases, added greatly to his discomfort. It is this to which Johnson generally refers when he speaks of his struggles with "gout." The term was loosely applied in the eighteenth century to rheumatoid diseases of the joints and connective tissue as well as to the much rarer disease that we now mean by "gout." In fact, Johnson's principal definition of it in the *Dictionary* equates it with "arthritis." (There is no evidence that he had true "gout" in the modern sense. His diet alone would have safeguarded him. For some time he had been eating sparingly—a roll or some milk at breakfast, and otherwise one meal a day; and of course he drank little or no alcohol.) For Johnson, the worst result of arthritis was the extent to which it was to cut down—especially in combination with emphysema and dropsy—on his ability to get around. Ever since the breakdown after he left Oxford, when he would walk to Birmingham and back, he would try to deal with mental despair—if no friend were present to help him—by some form of physical activity. He had long since learned in the hardest way "how much happiness is gained," or, to put it more accurately, "how much misery escaped, by frequent and violent agitation of the body."[17] But even this desperate means of partial escape was being closed off to him now.

Chapter 32

Iam Moriturus

The stroke on June 17 was a clear warning that time was running out, especially since he was becoming seriously ill in other ways. Yet, physical ills, however grave, were not the principal problem. What preyed on him most was loneliness.

"Happiness," he had said long ago, "is not found in self-contemplation; it is perceived only when it is reflected from another." Nor was it simply a matter of finding "happiness" but of avoiding outright misery. Throughout his life it was loneliness more than anything else that released the self-condemnation that was his worst enemy. This in turn led to the radical inner conflict—the battle for survival against merciless self-demand—that made companionship, empathy, humor, activity with and through others, not only a supreme pleasure but a means of survival. Otherwise he was in the pit of the arena, like the condemned Roman gladiators, supported only by stoical fortitude. In one of his finest passages, Boswell compares Johnson's mind to the Colosseum. In the center stood his judgment, forced constantly to combat "those apprehensions that, like the wild beasts of the *Arena*, were . . . ready to be let out upon him. After a conflict, he drove them back into their dens; but not killing them, they were still assailing him."[1]

He was especially vulnerable now, and not only because of his age. He was also having to pay a high price (though he never doubted it had been worth it) for having surrendered so much of his life to the Thrales. His older friends had long since become accustomed to seeing

579

less of him. There was no diminution of regard. But when they saw him now, it was on a more formal basis. Their own lives had been developing independently, and habit had confirmed them in other claims and interests that naturally usurped their time. Younger people, whom he had got to know more recently, were in general too respectful to drop in on him casually and to talk with the affectionate and open ease he so prized in the young. In any case, they and the remaining older friends whom he saw were, as he said, "visitors." They were no substitute for "familiar and domestick companions," without which one has "no middle state between general conversation and self-tormenting solitude." As he wrote to Mrs. Thrale (not that he was expecting her to do anything; he was writing frankly out of old habit): "When I arise my breakfast is solitary, the black dog waits to share it, from breakfast to dinner he continues barking. . . . Dinner with a sick woman [Miss Williams] you may venture to suppose not much better than solitary. After Dinner what remains but to count the clock, and hope for that sleep which I can scarce expect?"[2]

He could hardly trust himself to respond graciously to his friend John Ryland, who in a letter enclosed some verses he had written expressing—as was so common in poetry of the time—the joys of solitude and retirement. In his reply Johnson did not mention the verses. Ryland wrote again and pressed him for an opinion. Johnson, not wishing to hurt Ryland's feelings, avoided speaking of the poetic quality of the lines. He had "not read them critically." But he could not help saying that they "favour solitude too much." Retirement and solitude may be justified if one has reached "a state of imbecillity." And there may be times when a truly religious man may need solitude in order to meditate. But we should "meditate for the sake of acting." Otherwise, "retreat from the world is flight rather than conquest, and in those who have any power of benefiting others, may be considered as a kind of *moral suicide*."[3]

2

By sheer luck a gifted young man of twenty-eight who had seen him only occasionally before—William Bowles, the son of the canon of Salisbury—got up courage to ask Johnson to come for a visit to their country house at Heale, near Salisbury. Though he knew of Johnson's stroke, he fortunately did not know how ill Johnson was in other ways or he might have been more diffident.

Bowles had in some way sensed that Johnson was more alone than the young usually imagine the old and famous to be. Johnson was deeply touched by the invitation, which seemed to be coming to him now from a world he had forever lost. But it tells us something about his state of mind and his feeling of helplessness that the invitation inspired not only gratitude but a new anxiety. What if he disappointed Bowles? He was no longer sure of himself. He was only half joking, and concealing his anxiety under apparent humor, when Fanny Burney told him that "Mr. Bowles was very much *delighted* with the expectation of seeing him." To her surprise, Johnson said, "He is so delighted, that it is shocking!—it is *really shocking* to see how high are his expectations." She still could not understand why the famous Johnson should feel this way, and when she pressed him, he said, "If any man is expected to take a leap of twenty yards, and does actually take one of ten, everybody will be disappointed."[4]

Yes, he must not disappoint his young friend. Unfortunately, in addition to all the other problems of health, the hydrocele—as he still thought it to be—was suddenly getting worse. He must have it taken care of first. A quick puncture revealed that it was a flesh tumor—a sarcocele, as it used to be called. The short delay led to some correspondence with Bowles ("I am ashamed to write so often about a visit, as if I thought my presence or absence of importance. Surely life and experience have taught me better"). Meanwhile, in his eagerness to make this visit, he was reflecting back on the way in which he had always dismissed the idea that "change of place" could make so much difference to human happiness when the true source of happiness or misery is within ourselves. Once again he was proving to be like the philosopher in *Rasselas* who discoursed so eloquently and then found he was very human. It is true, as he now said, that "no man can run away from himself." But to stay in a sickroom or in places associated only with "pain" is to court thoughts of "useless uneasiness." After all, that famous passage "The mind is its own place, and in itself / Can make a heaven of hell, a hell of heaven" was spoken by Satan in *Paradise Lost*. It was "the boast of a fallen angel, that had learned to lie. External locality has great effects, at least upon all embodied Beings."[5]

The visit with Bowles (August 28 to September 18) did him a great deal of good. They talked about everything—religion, literature, chemistry, human nature, and occasionally even Johnson himself. It was to Bowles that he mentioned his burlesque project—"a work to shew how small a quantity of REAL FICTION there is in the world; and that the same images, with very little variation, have served all the authours who have ever written." More personally, he confessed how often he had been misinterpreted because so much of what he said was "in jest." And it was to Bowles—himself a kind of Cornelius Ford, though more high-minded—that he made the famous remark, which Cornelius himself could have made, but that had come to Johnson in so hard-earned a way: "As I know more of mankind I expect less of them, and am ready now to call a man *a good man*, upon easier terms than I was formerly." Naturally the young Bowles wrote down notes of what Johnson said. But he was not looking for immortality in doing so. When he sent them to Boswell, after Johnson's death, he asked to remain anonymous.[6]

On one matter Johnson did not speak readily at all. Mrs. Thrale was currently at Weymouth, which was an easy visit. Thinking to please him, Bowles suggested they call on her for a few days. But Johnson, without pursuing the matter, made it plain that "he had no great mind to see Mrs. Thrale." Though he still continued to write to her not only frequently but with affection and frankness, he knew their relationship was in a precarious state. But he was afraid lest his presence should upset it further.

3

While he was visiting Bowles, Miss Williams died (September 6) at the age of seventy-seven. She had simply wasted away, as Dr. Brocklesby wrote him. Though her death had been expected at any time during the past year, there was now a terrible sense of finality for Johnson. Like Mr. Levet, she had been a "domestick companion" for thirty years. As long as she was alive, Johnson never had to feel that he was returning, as he now would be, "to a habitation vacant and desolate." During all that time, until she became terminally ill, she would be sitting up for him; and, with a more delicate courtesy than others ever thought him capable of, he would drink the tea she would serve him, and they would talk until he felt he could sleep.

Less than ever did he now want to go back to his house. But the pain of the sarcocele became so bad that he finally did so, since Dr. Percival Pott had insisted that an operation was necessary if the tumor increased. Before Pott could do the operation, the sarcocele, which had been punctured by the earlier operation to see whether it was a hydrocele, suddenly burst, and the inflammation subsided. But while this was happening, his arthritis flared up to such a degree that, as he wrote to Queeney, he could not raise himself from bed without help, "nor without much pain and difficulty by the help of two sticks convey himself to a chair." Annoyed that, on top of everything else, he should suddenly have an abscessed tooth, he sent for a dentist and had it pulled out. A new friend, John Philip Kemble, the actor, began to call on him, and one day brought his sister—the famous tragic actress Mrs. Siddons—to see him. He won her heart immediately as she entered. For, there being at the moment no extra chair, he said, "Madam, you who so often occasion a want of seats for other people, will the more easily excuse the want of one yourself." And as soon as a chair was brought, he placed himself next to her, and with "great good humour," said Kemble, talked with her about acting and her favorite roles. She promised to perform for him Queen Catherine in *Henry VIII*, and, when she did so, he assured her he "will once more hobble out to the theatre myself." Meanwhile his friend William Gerard Hamilton, for whom twenty years before he had written up notes for Hamilton's work in Parliament, delicately inquired of one of Johnson's physicians whether his illness was costing him so much in medical fees as to be a problem. If so, Hamilton wanted to help. Johnson was so touched that he immediately told others of this, while at the same time reassuring Hamilton that his physicians were generously insisting on charging him very little.[7]

As November passed he was determined to battle the domestic solitude in which he was now living by new efforts, however helpless he felt. Frank Barber had by now moved back into the house, after having for years lived next door because of Miss Williams's antagonism. But Frank was not used to being on call at all hours. He was a married man, and, unlike Miss Williams, was in bed long before Johnson was able to get to sleep. At some time during this winter, Mrs. Desmoulins returned, but was herself so ill that she offered little companionship. Nor was her complaining nature such that she had ever been a substitute for Miss Williams or Mr. Levet. While trying to think what to do, Johnson got the surviving members of the old Ivy Lane Club to meet again at the Queen's Arms Tavern near St. Paul's. Only four showed up (December 3)—Hawkins, John Ryland, John Payne, and Johnson himself. At 10:00 P.M., said Hawkins, the other old members left to go to bed. Johnson, prepared for an all-night session, sighed, said Hawkins, "with a sigh that seemed to come from his heart," saying he was left to retire "to solitude and chearless meditation."[8]

Almost immediately he resolved to found a new club—and one that would meet not occasionally, or even once a week, but three times a week (every Monday, Thursday, and Saturday). He would have made it seven days a week if he thought the others would agree. Eager to touch base in as many ways as he could with his earlier life, he fixed on a little tavern in Essex Street called the Essex Head, which was now kept by a former footman of Henry Thrale's named Samuel Greaves. He tried to get Sir Joshua Reynolds to join. But Reynolds, however fond of Johnson himself, was a man of many social obligations; and this little group did not attract him. Arthur Murphy joined at once, and John Nichols, Dr. Brocklesby, and a few others. Later members, when they were in town, were William Bowles and Boswell. With great eagerness Johnson attended the first meetings (starting Monday, December 8).

But within another week, soon after he got to the Essex Head Club, he had an attack of what was almost certainly a coronary thrombosis. Dr. Brocklesby at once brought him home, where he was confined for over four months. Meanwhile the dropsy from congestive heart failure had so increased, said Arthur Murphy, that "he was swelled from head to foot." On Christmas and New Year's a large number of visitors dropped in on him, bringing presents of game. Doubtless Mrs. Thrale—he says to her in a letter—will wonder why, with so many visitors, he speaks of solitude. But the real balm of friendship comes from those who are always near: "Such society I had with Levet and Williams; such as I had where—I am never likely to have it more." Incapacitated though he was, he continued to hold small dinner parties at his house, including at least two for the old Ivy Lane Club. By early February his dropsy had become extreme. He was keeping track of the discharge of urine, as dropsical patients were asked to do. Then suddenly, on Friday, February 20, he experienced an astonishing relief. Within a few hours he discharged twenty pints of urine and the dropsical swellings subsided. Only the day before he had decided in desperation to shut himself up and spend the whole of Friday in prayer and religious devotion. So dramatic was the relief that began as the day advanced that he wondered to himself whether it was not a sign of divine grace. He was reluctant to say so. But when he mentioned the circumstances to Sir John Hawkins the next day, Hawkins told him "it would be little less than criminal, to ascribe his late relief to causes merely natural." Johnson, he added, "seemed to acquiesce in all that I said in this important subject, and, several times, while I was discoursing with him, cried out, 'It is wonderful, very wonderful!' "[9]

On March 10, though his physicians still insisted that he remain in the house, he started to dress in his ordinary street clothes. This was something of an event for him. He had been for weeks wearing "sick clothes." These consisted of loose flannel clothes and a robe rather similar to what one wears in a hospital now, permitting easy examination by the physicians and allowing them to put blisters on his chest to relieve his heart "spasms" and his breathing. Around this time (March 1) his two principal physicians, Dr. Brocklesby and Dr. Heberden, decided to give him, for his congestive heart failure and dropsy, the digitalislike drug made from squills, a Mediterranean plant that had been known since the time of Hippocrates. It seems strange that this had not been done before. Until William Withering published his celebrated work on digitalis extracted from the foxglove (1785), the use of squills for congestive heart failure was well known. On the other hand, the powder made from squills often produced bad side effects (as does digitalis itself, unless it is carefully controlled), leading to nausea and diarrhea. In fact, it so upset Johnson's digestion that his physicians, after a few days' trial, decided to stop it. But within a short time they had him resume taking squills, and it thereafter became a regular medicine for him, however unpleasant the side effects continued to be.[10]

A note at this point should be added about his use of opium, for the word now calls up vivid associations of Chinese opium dens, Coleridge's long struggle against his addiction to it, and the prevalence of one of its derivatives, heroin, since the 1960's. That is why we often find remarks being made, with alarmed relish and the implication that a fearsome secret has been discovered, that Johnson "used opium." But we should remember that from the middle of the eighteenth century to the beginning of the twentieth, the moderate use of opium—as a powder taken with water or as laudanum (mixed with some alcohol)—was the most common single medical treatment for calming the nervous system, in everything from heart palpitation and troubles in breathing to digestive spasm. As we have noticed, Johnson had for some years been taking very small doses of it for his bronchitis and for what was now becoming "cardiac asthma"—about as much as two or three teaspoons of paregoric would contain. His physicians were soon prescribing considerably more: three grains a day (this would be three grains of unrefined opium, far milder than an equivalent weight of one of the modern derivations of opium). Little was known about addiction to opiates until Sir Astley Cooper's discussion of it many years later (1824). Even so, Johnson disliked the use of them. "I dread their effects upon the mind more than those of wine or distilled spirits." Despite his physicians, he cut the prescribed dose to a sixth—from three grains to a half grain—and, in addition, did not even take that amount daily but confined it to two or three times a week.[11]

4

He had counted every day of this long confinement until April 21— 129 days—"more than the third part of a year, and no inconsiderable part of human life." Since his middle years he had been haunted by the text put on his watch: "The night cometh. . . ." Now more than ever he was thinking how close the night was.

A mere three days after his confinement ended, he insisted on attending a dinner celebrating the exhibition of pictures at the Royal Academy (April 24). The dinner was held on the top floor, and he virtually raced Dr. Brocklesby, who was thirteen years younger, up the stairs "without stopping to rest or to breathe, 'In all the madness of superfluous health.' " Then, on May 5, Boswell arrived from Scotland for a London visit of a couple of months, and for what was to prove his last chance to see Johnson. He noticed the effort Johnson was making to dine out as much as he could—in what "fine spirits" he was and how, in every company, he appeared "to relish society as much as the youngest man."[12]

During the period he had been confined to his house, he one day urged his friend Bennet Langton to tell him frankly in what ways his life had been "faulty." Langton thought he would proceed delicately, asked for time, and showed up later with several texts from the Bible (*e.g.*, "Blessed are the meek . . ."; "with long-suffering, forbearing one another in love . . ."; "Charity suffereth long . . . is not easily provoked"). All that Langton had in mind was Johnson's impatience— the chronic inner uneasiness that led him to contradict or to speak roughly at times. But the various texts could also seem to imply a lack of "Christian charity." The result, as Reynolds said, "was a scene for a comedy." For Johnson first thanked his friend earnestly and began reading the texts. Then, said Langton, he suddenly shouted in an angry tone, "What is your drift, Sir?" As Johnson told the story to Boswell a few weeks later (May 19)—for the matter had lain uneasily on his conscience:

"When I questioned him what occasion I had given . . . all that he could say amounted to this,—that I sometimes contradicted people in conversation. Now what harm does it do to any man to be contradicted?" BOSWELL. "I suppose he meant the manner of doing it; roughly,—and harshly." JOHNSON. "And who is the worse for that?" BOSWELL. "It hurts people of weak nerves." JOHNSON. "I know no such weak-nerved people." Mr. Burke, to whom I related this conference, said, "It is well, if when a man comes to die, he has nothing heavier upon his conscience than having been a little rough in conversation."[13]

Of course he knew what Langton had meant. How many times, "with tears in his eyes," as Hawkins said, Johnson would apologize "to those whom he had offended by contradiction or roughness of behaviour." What he was really trying to find out now was not whether such a fault existed but how bad a fault it actually seemed to other people. And Hawkins says that, after Johnson's death, he found among his papers an "anonymous letter" (Hawkins may simply have preferred not to say who wrote it) by someone who knew him very well. It went into detail about his habits of contradiction, his lack of deference to the opinions of others, and his temptation to talk for victory. The letter was written

in a spirit of charity, and with a due acknowledgment of those great talents with which he was endowed, but contained in it several home truths. In short, it was such a letter as many a one, on the receipt of it, would have destroyed. On the contrary, Johnson preserved it, and placed it in his bureau, in a situation so obvious, that, whenever he opened that repository of his papers, it might look him in the face.[14]

5

As his first trip after his long illness, he was eager to visit Dr. Adams at Oxford for a couple of weeks. Boswell went along (June 3), and there were also two American ladies in the coach, Mrs. Richard Beresford and her daughter. Johnson, who had looked forward to the trip, spoke so fluently and without reserve that the two women, who knew who he was, were delighted. "How he does talk!" whispered Miss Beresford to Boswell. "Every sentence is an essay." Nor was she disconcerted when he suddenly stared at her while she was knotting, and said almost absent-mindedly, "Next to mere idleness I think knotting is to be reckoned in the scale of insignificance; though I once attempted to learn knotting. Dempster's sister," he added, turning to Boswell, "endeavoured to teach me it; but I made no progress."

He seemed to feel more elated as they approached Oxford, and, when they reached Dr. Adams's house at Pembroke, quickly "dispatched the inquiries which were made about his illness and recovery, by a short and distinct narrative," quoted the lines of Swift, "Nor think on our approaching ills,/ And talk of spectacles and pills," and plunged at once into general conversation. The talk during the next few days ranged from Thomas Newton's *Dissertations on the Prophecies*, Milton's sonnets, Catholicism, the forms of prayer, and law as a profession, to vaccination, the use of quinine, marriage, the attraction women feel to licentious men, politics, and when, if at all, it is morally justifiable to lie. Miss Adams, the middle-aged daughter of Dr. Adams, had never heard conversation of this quality, even at Oxford, carried on with such imagination and good nature. Simply as a person—however ill others told her he was—she thought him "infinitely agreeable and entertaining."

The momentum of effort continued when he returned to London, and, though the other members thought he looked very unwell, he showed up at the Literary Club (June 22)—it proved to be the last time he ever attended it—and "exerted himself to be as entertaining as his indisposition allowed him." And when he said farewell to Boswell (July 1), who was returning to Scotland, he sprang away from the carriage in a way unlike him—"With a kind of pathetick briskness, if I may use that expression, which seemed to indicate a struggle to conceal uneasiness, and impressed me with a foreboding."[15]

6

We must turn to what had meanwhile been happening to Mrs. Thrale, but only briefly now, since her life during the past year—and certainly from this point on—becomes a separate story.

Throughout the summer and early autumn of 1783, she had shut herself off from society at Bath, brooding on her situation and on the means by which she might get Piozzi back. By November she had worked herself into a condition that seemed—to herself, her physicians, and even her daughters—to be close to nervous collapse. Queeney, who had suspected all along that her mother's "seizures" were put on for effect, finally capitulated and allowed Piozzi to be summoned back from Italy. At this point her mother's health began rapidly to improve.

On the other hand, Piozzi seemed in no hurry to return. He had been burned once. Who knew what the formidable Queeney would next decide to do? He needed reassurance. It was better to wait for a while and see whether the invitation was not an impulse of the moment. He pleaded the necessity of delay. The Alps were hazardous to cross in the winter. Repeated letters kept assuring him all would turn out well for him and Mrs. Thrale. It was not until May that he was ready to leave. Mrs. Thrale's health during all this time had remained good, either because she was confident all along that he would return or else because her illness of the previous autumn had accomplished its purpose—to get Queeney to relent. In middle May she went to London for a week in order to make plans for Piozzi's arrival and to arrange to have the children cared for after she left with him for Italy (the executors were not allowing her to bring up her daughters in Italy in what would now be a Catholic home). While in London she stayed with Fanny Burney, and, fearing Johnson would hear of her visit anyway, appears to have seen him very briefly. She naturally made no mention of her plans. Though he had been hearing gossip for some time, he could not quite believe what he had heard, nor had he the heart to distress both her and himself by inquiring more specifically.

The letter she sent him on June 30 therefore came as a shock. She sent a form letter to all the executors of her intention to marry Piozzi on his return. But for Johnson she also enclosed a special note, begging his pardon "for concealing from you a Connection which you must have heard of by many People, but I suppose never believed. Indeed, my dear Sir, it was concealed only to spare us both needless pain." She is telling him now only "because all is *irretrievably settled*" (the implication being she was already married, though the marriage did not take place till July 23). Completely taken off guard, he wrote her a reply in which all the pain of the last year and a half suddenly expresses itself:

Madam

If I interpret your letter right, you are ignominiously married, if it is yet undone, let us once talk together. If you have abandoned your children and your religion, God forgive your wickedness; if you have forfeited your Fame, and your country, may your folly do no further mischief.

If the last act is yet to do, I, who have loved you, esteemed you, reverenced you, and served you, I who long thought you the first of human kind,

entreat that before your fate is irrevocable, I may once more see you. I was,
I once was,

Madam, most truly yours,
Sam: Johnson.

July 2, 1784
I will come down if you permit it.[16]

Of course, he had no sooner sent the letter than he was filled with
remorse. And when she wrote him a calm, dignified reply (though
adding that she thought their correspondence should now end "till you
have changed your Opinion of Mr. Piozzi"), he wrote a very different
letter:

Dear Madam

What you have done, however I may lament it, I have no pretence to
resent, as it has not been injurious to me. I therefore breathe out one sigh
more of tenderness perhaps useless, but at least sincere.

I wish that God may grant you every blessing, that you may be happy in
this world for its short continuance, and eternally happy in a better state.
And whatever I can contribute to your happiness, I am very ready to repay
for that kindness which soothed twenty years of a life radically wretched.

Do not think slightly of the advice which I now presume to offer. Prevail
upon Mr. Piozzi to settle in England. You may live here with more dignity
than in Italy, and with more security. Your rank will be higher, and your
fortune more under your own eye. I desire not to detail all my reasons; but
every argument of prudence and interest is for England, and only some
phantoms of imagination seduce you to Italy.

I am afraid, however, that my counsel is vain, yet I have eased my heart
by giving it.

When Queen Mary took the resolution of sheltering herself in England,
the Archbishop of St. Andrew's attempting to dissuade her, attended on
her journey and when they came to the irremeable stream that separated the
two kingdoms, walked by her side into the water, in the middle of which
he seized her bridle, and with earnestness proportioned to her danger and
his own affection, pressed her to return. The Queen went forward.—If the
parallel reaches thus far; may it go no further. The tears stand in my eyes.

I am going into Derbyshire, and hope to be followed by your good wishes,
for I am with great affection

Your most humble servant,

London July 8. 1784   Sam: Johnson
Any letters that come for me hither, will be sent me.[17]

But inevitably their friendship—or what was left of it—was at an end.
This caused no pain to Hester Thrale. Her interests lay elsewhere, and

a very different stage of her life had now begun. But for Johnson, whose own life was coming to an end—a life in which the Thrales had been so important—a desperate effort had to be made, not only now but until the end, to "drive her" and all she had meant "wholly from my mind." Whenever he came across one of her old letters, he burned it.

7

Shortly before Boswell returned to Edinburgh (July 1), he and some other friends of Johnson's, while dining at General Paoli's house, had talked about his lifelong desire to see Italy and the benefit to him of a milder climate. Surely, they thought, the government could defray the modest expenses involved for "the first literary character of a great nation," who in addition had written a *Dictionary* that matched or excelled those of national Academies. Boswell offered to approach the Lord Chancellor, Edward Thurlow, and ask him to use his influence with the King or with the Prime Minister, who was now the Younger Pitt. Thurlow had long admired Johnson, and wrote at once to say he would do what he could.

When Johnson was told of the matter somewhat later, at Sir Joshua Reynolds's house, he was naturally moved. Trying to control his voice, he said, "This is taking prodigious pains about a man." When Boswell then added, "Your friends would do everything for you," he sat in silence growing "more and more agitated,—till tears started into his eyes." "God bless you all," he said, and then rose suddenly and left the room "quite melted in tenderness." Nothing came of Thurlow's efforts. No one has ever learned who was responsible. Possibly it was Pitt himself, as Macaulay implied. Certainly this rather frightening and single-minded man of twenty-five could lapse into penny-pinching moods on anything about which he was not concentrating. More probably Pitt was not involved, and the King, preoccupied with other anxieties, simply neglected to follow up the request. In any case, Lord Thurlow was embarrassed, and, through Sir Joshua Reynolds, let Johnson know (this was on September 9, three months later) that he could draw personally on him for £500 or £600. This was put in such a tactful way as to imply that Johnson would be under no "obligation" (it was to be a kind of "mortgage" on his future pension, but of such a kind that would never apply in Johnson's lifetime). When this happened, Johnson wrote him a letter at once grateful and delicate:

After a long and attentive observation of Mankind, the generosity of your Lordship's offer, excites in me no less wonder than gratitude. Bounty, so liberally bestowed if my condition made it necessary, I should gladly receive, for to such a Mind who would [not] be proud to own his obligations? But it has pleased God to restore me such a measure of health, that if I should now appropriate so much of a fortune destined to do good I should not escape from myself the charge of advancing a false claim. . . .

Your Lordship was Solicited without my knowledge, but when I was told that you were pleased to honour me with your patronage, I did not expect to hear of a refusal. Yet as I had little time to form hopes, and have not rioted in imaginary opulence, this cold reception has been scarce a disappointment; and from your Lordship's kindness I have received a benefit which only Men like You can bestow, I shall live *mihi carior* ["more valuable to myself"—an echo of Ovid] with a higher opinion of my own merit.[18]

8

Meanwhile he once again took the familiar trip to Lichfield and then to John Taylor's at Ashbourne (July 13 to November 16). There was no one at Lichfield that he knew well who was either young or happy. Both Lucy Porter and Elizabeth Aston were ill. They also were coming to the end of their lives, and within another two years both would be dead. After five days at Lichfield Johnson hurried on to John Taylor's house. Of course, there was nothing to do there, and no one with whom he could talk. Taylor and he had known each other for over sixty years, and Taylor, who was not much interested in intellectual subjects, doubtless felt they had long since said to each other everything they had to say. Moreover, on days when Taylor was well, he was out in the fields looking after his crops or checking on his prize bulls, and at night he was in bed by nine. When he felt ill, as he increasingly did, he was even less inclined to talk about ideas.

But Johnson was in no hurry to return to his almost empty house in London. Though he could not care less about the subjects that interested Taylor, especially the prize bulls, he drew out his stay at Ashbourne. Taylor was linked to his past in a way that hardly anyone else was who was still alive. It was Taylor with whom, when he left Oxford fifty-five years before, "having hid his toes in a pair of large boots," he had walked to the highway in order to get the coach that would take him back to Lichfield, to old Michael and Sarah, to the bookshop and the parchment factory. During the weeks at Ashbourne he read a good deal, and he wrote letters to friends. It was cold and rainy much of the time. He laughed at himself for the way he had always dismissed talk of the weather as proofs of an empty head, whereas now, as he wrote to Dr. Burney, he was "reduced to think, and am at last content to talk of the weather. Pride must have a fall." He passed his seventy-fifth birthday at Ashbourne (September 18), and then a few days later (September 27) went back to Lichfield. Lucy Porter and Elizabeth Aston seemed now in better health. Though autumn was hurrying forward, he lingered as long as he could. He really did not want to return to London.

Throughout these months at Ashbourne and Lichfield, he was continuing to try to learn to live day by day. This is what he himself had always prized as a moral ideal. Fortitude, as he had said for years, is not to be found primarily in meeting rare and great occasions. And this was true not only of fortitude but of all the other virtues, including "good-nature." The real test is in what we do in our daily life, and happiness—such happiness as exists—lies primarily in what we can do with the daily texture of our lives. This lesson, of which he had always reminded himself, had become more urgent than ever before. "Life," as he said now, "is very short and very uncertain; let us spend it as well as we can."[19]

Long ago he had been struck by a remark that Sir William Temple made of the Dutch. Melancholy, said Temple, was "a Disease too refined for this Country and People, who are well, when they are not ill; and pleas'd when they are not troubled." This came back to Johnson's mind now, as something of a motto for the way to face what remained of life. And when Boswell wrote complaining about melancholy, he repeated it, both underlining it and putting it in quotation marks: *"Be well when you are not ill, and pleased when you are not angry."*[20]

9

Because he was so susceptible to symbols, his impulse had always been to deny their power over the imagination and to try to put them at arm's length. The dignity of human nature required this if one was to remain a "free agent." Typical was the way he would dismiss the effect on us of the seasons ("imagination operating on luxury"). But now, in many ways, he was changing—not changing in his character but in what he said or admitted.

As November came to Lichfield, which he could reasonably doubt that he would ever see again, he felt the poignance of autumn as never before. One of Horace's odes especially (IV, ivii) haunted him—. the one in which the large revolving changes of nature, destroying and re-creating, are contrasted with the hopes and destiny of short-lived man. Before Johnson left Lichfield he translated it into English verse. The snows of winter—the ode begins—are melting as spring returns. The fields and woods are again green. But the human being, after entering his own winter, will not return. He will be like those millions of others who have entered the night—"ashes and a shade." The ode, in its clear-eyed existential honesty and mellow acceptance, typifies what Johnson had prized in Horace when he was a boy at Stourbridge—a union of qualities he had associated with Cornelius, who had seemed to the half-blind, half-deaf, awkward youth such a model of grace and classical acceptance of fact. Of the many translations of this famous ode, none catches the spirit of Horace more closely. At moments it is even more condensed than Horace. "Each revolving year," says Horace, "each hour that snatches the day, bids us not to hope for immortal life." Johnson wrote, "The changing year's successive plan / Proclaims mortality to man." Yet this is balanced by a flourish of stoic gaiety that goes beyond Horace. "Who knows whether the gods," asks Horace, "will add tomorrow's time to the sum of today?" In Johnson this becomes: "Who knows if Jove who counts our score/ *Will toss us in one morning more?*"

10

After leaving Lichfield on November 10, he spent a couple of days at Birmingham with his old childhood friend Edmund Hector. They talked of their early years. Suddenly Johnson asked Hector whether, during their early days in Birmingham, Hector "had observed in him a tendency to be disordered in his mind." Hector said he had; and the subject was then dropped.[21]

On his way home he stopped at Oxford for a few days (November 12–16) to visit Dr. Adams. Back in June, when he had gone to Oxford after his long confinement at home, he had made an enormous effort to dismiss all thought of illness, in his own mind and those of others, and to be as entertaining and as interested in subjects as he could. But one dreadful moment had occurred that shows how demanding the standard was by which he measured his own sincerity. They were talking about the forms of prayer. Dr. Adams casually suggested that Johnson compose some family prayers. Johnson, with curious reluctance to pursue the subject, said he had thought of collecting prayers already written, perhaps adding a few, and then prefixing to them a discussion of prayer in general. At this, said Boswell, who was there, everyone gathered around him, and started to urge him to go ahead with this plan. Then suddenly, to the surprise of the company, Johnson

in great agitation called out, "Do not talk thus of what is so awful. I know not what time GOD will allow me in this world. There are many things which I wish to do." Some of us persisted, and Dr. Adams said, "I never was more serious about any thing in my life." JOHNSON. "*Let me alone, let me alone; I am overpowered.*" And then he put his hands before his face, and reclined for some time upon the table.

Of course, the subject was immediately dropped. But the thought lingered in his conscience. While at Ashbourne (August 1), he wrote in his journal a short list of resolutions: "To work as I can. / To attempt a book of prayers. / To do good as occasion offers itself. / To review former resolutions." Now, in seeing Dr. Adams again, he said he was finally "in a right frame of mind" to do this.[22]

11

When he returned to London, he was in "a worse state of health," said Hawkins, "than I had ever seen him in." He had, in fact, less than a month to live. The astonishing thing was that he should have been so active during the last half year. Most others in his condition would have long since taken to their beds. He refused to lead the life of an invalid now, though he admitted he was "very weak."

Hawkins for months had been trying to get him to make a will, and before Johnson left for the country had even made a draft of one for him. Johnson's principal concern was to leave a substantial annuity to Frank Barber. This was partly because of the obligation he felt to Barber himself, whom he had raised since childhood, and whom he felt he had not adequately trained to make his own way, despite the money lavished—to Miss Williams's annoyance—on his education. But that obligation was as strong as it was because Barber from the start was associated with the man Johnson seems to have loved more than any other. This, of course, was Richard Bathurst, who had come to him in his middle years when he was beginning once again to feel lost. Bathurst was all that Cornelius had been, in humor, intelligence, grace, and good nature, except for the addition of something Cornelius did not have—moral rectitude and high-mindedness. When Bathurst prematurely died at Havana, something of the pent-up affection Johnson felt toward him had carried over to the helpless Negro boy from Jamaica. Barber was the only symbol left of this man to whom, as he once told Mrs. Thrale, he had completely opened his heart. Hawkins, for his part, was appalled at the size of the bequest Johnson wanted to give Barber, describing it as "ill-directed benevolence" and "ostentatious bounty."

In the draft of the will Hawkins prepared, he put in the legacy to Barber, and then left blanks in which Johnson could insert the names of other legatees and the executors. But he found him "exceedingly averse" to doing anything more about the will, though Johnson had been willing enough a few years before to urge Henry Thrale to make a will ("Do not let those fears prevail which you know to be unreasonable; a will brings the end of life no nearer"). While Johnson was in the country, Hawkins officiously wrote him once in a while asking him to complete the will. Johnson paid no attention. When Johnson returned to London, Hawkins immediately began to bother him again about the will. Hoping to have done with the subject, Johnson quickly signed and sealed the draft Hawkins had prepared months before. When Hawkins reminded him that the draft he had signed was full of blanks, Johnson replied, "You should have filled them up yourself!" At last he gave in to Hawkins and dictated a will on the spot.[23]

Meanwhile (around December 1) he began to burn large masses of his personal papers. These included some letters he had kept that had been written to him by his mother long ago, and he burst into tears as he gently laid them in the fire. Among the papers and records he destroyed were the famous two quarto volumes with their detailed account of his own life. A couple of other small books of private meditations and reflections were picked up at this time (December 5) by Hawkins, who explains that a man connected with the newspapers was lurking outside the house looking for private information about Johnson's life. Johnson, ill as he was, noticed what Hawkins had done and asked that he return what he had taken. He also tried to make a joke, saying that if he had not known what had happened to the books, he would have roared for them "as Othello did for his handkerchief." The next day Hawkins wrote him an apology (he was trying, he said, to keep these private notes out of the hands of less scrupulous persons). Johnson, hardly able to write, sent a verbal reply by Bennet Langton, which, said Hawkins, "were I to repeat it, would render me suspected of inexcusable vanity; it concluded with these words. 'If I was not satisfied with this, I must be a savage.'" With a sense that time had almost run out, Johnson also took action on a matter he had long deferred. He arranged with Richard Green at Lichfield to have stones placed over the graves of his parents and his brother, Nathaniel, in St. Michael's Church, and sent epitaphs to be engraved on them (December 2). He also got hold of his old friend John Nichols. He wanted to borrow some of the early volumes of the *Gentleman's Magazine*. The *Parliamentary Debates* lay on his conscience. When he had spun them largely out of his head, he "had no conception he was imposing upon the world." Since they were now widely accepted as genuine, he wanted to point out the pieces he had written. The books now lay on the table, and he started to turn down the leaves of these pages.[24]

A few days before this, he had decided he would try to reform his household and, according to John Hoole, was planning to take into it his final waif—Martha Hall, the widowed sister of John Wesley. She was now seventy-seven. Her unhappy marriage had not improved her as a companion—she was described as "lean, lank, and preaching"—but Johnson thought her a virtuous woman according to her lights, and, equally important, she was in need. He intended to give her Miss Williams's old room. But this would take time to arrange. Worried at how helpless he had become, his friends in the meantime insisted on employing a man from the neighborhood to sit up with him at night in order to help him when necessary. Johnson found the man useless and "as sleepy as a dormouse," but otherwise did not object, assuming that the man needed the money (he was paid half a crown a night). Johnson, who was sitting upright much of the night in order to breathe, slept lightly. During wakeful hours he would occasionally occupy the time by translating epigrams from the Greek Anthology into Latin verse.[25]

During the day he made an effort to be up and around. "I will be *conquered*," he said. "I will not capitulate." However great the effort of will needed, he would find "new topicks of merriment, or new incitements to curiosity." "The first talk of the sick," he had said a few months before, "is commonly of themselves." He would try to resist this now. When John Hoole called on him on November 27, he learned Johnson was now so breathless that he was "scarce able to speak," and had gone in a carriage to Mr. Strahan's out in Islington, where the air was better. There, as he got his breath, he talked "cheerfully." On the way back in the coach, he "told stories" to entertain the friends with him, and, when they reached his house, had tea served for them, though for once he could not drink it himself.

A few days later (December 5), he composed a prayer: "Almighty and most merciful Father . . . forgive and accept my late conversion, enforce and accept my imperfect repentance. . . . Bless my Friends, have mercy upon all men." Soon afterward he asked Sir John Hawkins where the executors would bury him. "Doubtless," said Hawkins, "in Westminster Abbey." The answer did not come as a surprise. For some years he had been reluctant to enter the Abbey. Once, when Lady Knight had arranged for a party to visit the Abbey, she asked him to join them. "No," he replied, "not while I can keep out."[26]

12

As he entered his final week, he at last lay helpless. Once, when Dr. Brocklesby called on him, Johnson looked up at him and quoted the passage from *Macbeth* beginning "Canst thou not minister to a mind diseas'd; / Pluck from the memory a rooted sorrow; / Raze out the written troubles of the brain?" To which Brocklesby replied with the doctor's own reply from *Macbeth*. "Therein the patient / Must minister to himself." Johnson agreed. And he was through with taking opiates. He asked Brocklesby to tell him plainly whether he could recover. Brocklesby, after asking him whether he could bear the whole truth, told him that without a miracle he could not recover. If that was the case, replied Johnson, he saw no point in taking further medicine of any kind. Least of all would he "meet God in a state of idiocy, or with opium in his head." He began even to refuse food, perhaps with the thought of keeping his mind clearer. But by December 12, said John Hoole, he was becoming "somewhat delirious."[27]

By now the dropsy had spread from his breast to his feet. Johnson asked the surgeon William Cruikshank to make further cuts in his leg to drain the fluid. Cruikshank was afraid mortification might set in, and only gently lanced the surface. Johnson cried out. "Deeper, deeper; I want length of life, and you are afraid of giving me pain, which I do not value." When Cruikshank was gone, Johnson told Frank to get him a lancet so that Johnson himself could cut his legs, but as he started to do this the man who sat up with him interfered. Later, when no one was looking, Johnson managed to get hold of a pair of scissors in a drawer near the bed, and plunged them deeply into the calves of each leg. The only result was a large effusion of blood, and Mr. Cruikshank had to be called to dress the wounds. This was on December 12.

On Monday, December 13, a young lady—a Miss Morris—insisted on seeing him in order to ask his blessing. He managed to say "God bless you!" Several of his friends remained in the house during this final day. Among his last words, either on December 12 or 13, were those spoken to the Italian teacher Francesco Sastres, who had become a friend of Johnson's and a member of the little Essex Head Club. As Sastres entered the room, Johnson stretched his hand toward him and called out, *"Iam Moriturus"*—"I who am about to die." Spoken in delirium, the words echo the ancient Roman salutation of the dying gladiators to Caesar.[28]

That evening he died quietly at about seven. The next day John Hoole and William Seward called at the house to learn how he was. What they found instead was something they never forgot: "the most awful sight of Dr. Johnson *laid out on his bed, without life!*" The same sense of incredulity was shared by everyone who had known him. This was especially true of those who knew something of his early life— Johnson walking the wet road to the school at Market Bosworth, leaving for London with David Garrick, writing the parliamentary debates in a garret room, trudging the street all night with Richard Savage—as well as the Johnson who wrote the *Dictionary, The Vanity of Human Wishes,* the *Rambler,* and struggled against despair to bring out the edition of Shakespeare; who looked after waifs and strays, ran the race with tiny John Payne, imitated the kangaroo, rolled down hills, wrote the *Lives of the Poets,* and became the greatest talker in the history of the English language. As Boswell said of himself, when he heard the news in Edinburgh, "My feeling was just one large expanse of Stupor. . . . I could not believe it. My imagination was not convinced." William Gerard Hamilton put it best: "He has made a chasm, which not only nothing can fill up, but which *nothing has a tendency to fill up.*—Johnson is dead.—Let us go to the next best: There is nobody;—*no man can be said to put you in mind of Johnson.*"[29] Though most of them would have found it hard to explain, Johnson had touched home to them and even changed their lives in some profound way that no one else had ever done. He had given them the most precious of all the gifts one can give another, and that is hope. With all the odds against him, he had proved that it was possible to get through this strange adventure of life, and to do it in a way that is a tribute to human nature.

Short Titles

A   Hester Lynch Piozzi, *Anecdotes of the Late Samuel Johnson, LL. D.,* in G. B. Hill, ed., *Johnsonian Miscellanies,* Vol. I (Oxford, 1897).

BNB   *Boswell's Note Book 1776–1777,* R. W. Chapman, ed. (London, 1925).

BP   *The Private Papers of James Boswell from Malahide Castle,* Geoffrey Scott and Frederick A. Pottle, eds., 19 Vols. (privately printed, 1928–37).

H   Sir John Hawkins, *The Life of Samuel Johnson, LL. D.* (London, 1787).

JG   Aleyn Lyell Reade, *Johnsonian Gleanings,* 11 Vols. (privately printed, 1909–52).

JM   *Johnsonian Miscellanies,* G. B. Hill, ed., 2 Vols. (Oxford, 1897).

L   *Boswell's Life of Johnson,* 6 Vols., G. B. Hill, ed., revised and enlarged by L. F. Powell (Oxford, 1934-50).

R   Samuel Johnson, *The Rambler,* in Yale Edition (Y, below, Vols. III–V), W. J. Bate and Albrecht B. Strauss, eds. (New Haven, 1969).

T   *Thraliana: The Diary of Mrs. Hester Lynch Thrale . . . 1776–1809,* Katherine C. Balderston, ed., 2 Vols. (Oxford, 1942; reprinted, 1951).

W   *Correspondence and Other Papers of James Boswell Relating to the Making of the Life of Johnson,* Marshall Waingrow, ed. (New York, 1969).

Y   *Yale Edition of the Works of Samuel Johnson,* now in process, 10 Vols. to date (New Haven, 1958–   ).

Bloom   Edward A. Bloom, *Samuel Johnson in Grub Street* (Providence, R.I., 1957).

Clifford   James L. Clifford, *Young Sam Johnson* (New York, 1955).

Clifford, *Piozzi*	James L. Clifford, *Hester Lynch Piozzi (Mrs. Thrale)* (Oxford, 1941).
D'Arblay	*Diary and Letters of Mme. d'Arblay,* Austin Dobson, ed., 6 Vols. (London, 1904–5).
Diaries	Samuel Johnson, *Diaries, Prayers and Annals,* in Yale Edition (Y, above, Vol. I), E. L. McAdam, with Donald and Mary Hyde, eds. (New Haven, 1958).
Greene	Donald J. Greene, *The Politics of Samuel Johnson* (New Haven, 1960).
Hazen	Allen T. Hazen, *Samuel Johnson's Prefaces and Dedications* (New Haven, 1937).
Hebrides	*Boswell's Journal of a Tour to the Hebrides,* F. A. Pottle and C. H. Bennett, eds. (New York, 1936).
Hyde	Mary Hyde, *The Impossible Friendship: Boswell and Mrs. Thrale* (Cambridge, Mass., 1972).
Hyde (II)	Mary Hyde, *The Thrales of Streatham Park* (to be published September 1977, Cambridge, Mass. Entries are cited by date).
Letters	*The Letters of Samuel Johnson,* R. W. Chapman, ed., 3 Vols. (Oxford, 1952).
Lives	*Lives of the English Poets by Samuel Johnson,* G. B. Hill, ed., 3 Vols. (Oxford, 1905).
Poems	Samuel Johnson, *Poems,* in Yale Edition (Y, above, Vol. VI), E. L. McAdam, with George Milne, eds. (New Haven, 1964).
Shaw	William Shaw, *Memoirs of the Life and Writings of the Late Dr. Samuel Johnson* (London, 1785).
Sledd and Kolb	James H. Sledd and Gwin J. Kolb, *Dr. Johnson's Dictionary* (Chicago, 1955).
Works (1825)	*The Works of Samuel Johnson, LL.D.,* 11 Vols. (Oxford, 1825).

Notes *

PART I

Chapter 1

1. The date was September 7 according to the Julian calendar, which was replaced by the Gregorian calendar in England in 1752.
2. Reference to the *Annals,* here and below, are to JM, I, 129–32, and to *Diaries,* pp. 3–23.
3. JG, X, 22.
4. BNB, p. 12; cf. JG, III, 78. Boswell got the story partly from Bishop Percy and partly from Johnson, who had been told it by his mother but himself "had no recollection of it."
5. JM, I, 360.
6. L, v, 496.
7. *Letters,* No. 886; A, p. 267; H, p. 396; *Idler,* No. 11.
8. A, p. 149; L, II, 299.
9. JG, III, 9–10; X, 6.
10. A, p. 148.
11. Ford endowed Sarah with £230, and agreed to give another £200 to the trustees within nine months of the marriage, at which time Michael was to add £100. For details, including the provision Michael was to make for children, see JG, III, 41–42, 48–49; IV, 5–8.
12. JG, X, 16–17; and *TLS,* July 27, 1940, pp. 363, 365.
13. *Diaries,* p. 7.
14. *Diaries,* p. 10.
15. *Diaries,* pp. 8–9; T, I, 160; Clifford, pp. 11–12; JG, III, 61–65.
16. L, I, 38. It could be argued that Miss Adye did not say Sacheverell actually *preached.* The boy could have been taken to the cathedral simply to see him, or hear him read the service. The age of nine months still presents a problem. For a full account, see JG, III, 68–71; cf. Clifford, p. 22.
17. *Diaries,* p. 10.
18. A, p. 159.

* Place of publication is mentioned only if it is not London.

603

Chapter 2

1. A, pp. 152–53; L, V, 307–8. For various versions of the duck poem, see JG, III, 72–73.
2. A, pp. 153–54.
3. A, pp. 150, 159–63.
4. BNB, p. 3.
5. L, I, 40; A, pp. 156–57.
6. "Addison," *Lives*, II, 79; L, I, 50; JG, III, 78–80; X, 29.
7. Clifford, p. 46; *Diaries*, p. 17; JG, X, 34.
8. JG, III, 84; H, pp. 6–7.
9. *Diaries*, pp. 112–13.
10. The passage (*Diaries*, p. 15) makes better sense if it is recognized that the word "not" has been omitted, either by Johnson when he wrote it or by Richard Wright in his transcription (the original manuscript does not survive).
11. L, I, 49.
12. L, I, 49; A, p. 158.

Chapter 3

1. For discussion of Jane Hackett's remark on Hunter, see JG, III, 34.
2. This and following quotations about the trip to Birmingham are from *Diaries*, pp. 14–21.
3. JG, III, 108–9.
4. L, I, 45–46; John Campbell, *Lives of the Chief Justices* (1849–57), II, 280; H, p. 7.
5. JM, I, 414; L, I, 44–46; A, p. 159; Shaw, pp. 11–12; Thomas Davies, *Memoirs of the Life of David Garrick* (1784), I, 3–4.
6. *Diaries*, p. 14. The passage is the "Moral" added by Charles Hoole to the ninth fable of the version of Aesop they used.
7. L, I, 47–48; BNB, p. 4.
8. A, pp. 178, 160; H, pp. 7–8 (cf. W, pp. 49–50).
9. L, II, 226; A, p. 332; Bowles to Boswell (November 4, 1787), W, p. 251; L, I, 71.
10. L, II, 339; A, p. 266.
11. JM, II, 42; W, pp. 99–100; *Letters*, No. 461; L, II, 463.
12. *Poems*, pp. 342–43; A, p. 224; JM, II, 4 (cf. L, II, 299).
13. A, p. 149; Reed, in *Johnsoniana*, J. W. Croker, ed. (Philadelphia, 1842), p. 437; Parker, JM, II, 415.
14. L, I, 67–68.
15. A, pp. 157–58.
16. JG, III, 49, 89–94, 119–20; Clifford, pp. 71–73.

Chapter 4

1. JG, III, 148–52; X, 55.
2. Probably by his friend John Henley, in *The Hyp-Doctor*, August 24–31, 1731; reprinted in JG, IX, 1–15. See also James Osborn, *TLS*, April 16, 1938, p. 262.
3. Quoted by Arthur Murphy, and given in another version by Jonathan Richardson, JM, I, 359.
4. H, p. 8.
5. A, p. 155; T, I, 171.
6. *Lives*, III, 75.
7. A, p. 155; L, I, 441.
8. JM, II, 208.
9. *Diaries*, p. 24.
10. JG, III, 154–55; L, I, 50.
11. JG, III, 157.
12. JG, X, 55.
13. A, p. 159; *Percy Letters* (Baton Rouge, 1944), p. 43 (cf. W, p. 206).
14. L, I, 50.
15. W, p. 245.
16. BP, IX, 257.
17. JM, II, 52; A, p. 211.
18. L, I, 92. Though Boswell states this was while Johnson was "at Stourbridge school," Hector, from whom he learned about Olivia Lloyd, had said simply that it happened while Johnson was "at Stourbridge" (W, p. 88). Johnson could very well have met Olivia while he was living at Cornelius's house before he attended the school.
19. L, II, 459–60.
20. JG, III, 159–60; Samuel Lloyd, *The Lloyds of Birmingham*, 3d ed. (Birmingham, 1909), pp. 106–19; J. Hill and R. K. Dent, *Memorials of the Old Square* (Birmingham, 1897), p. 26.
21. L, III, 78; *The Lloyds of Birmingham*, pp. 115–18, reprints her own version of one of the notable disputes recorded by Boswell.

Chapter 5

1. W, p. 48; L, I, 377n.
2. Hector's phrasing is somewhat ambiguous (see W, pp. 48–49).
3. *Letters*, No. 233; "Rowe," *Lives*, II, 267; BNB, p. 19.
4. BNB, p. 19.
5. Printed and discussed by Greene, p. 259.
6. Partly an imitation of the pseudo-Homeric *Batrachomyomachia*, or "Battle of the Frogs and Mice."

7. In *Essays in Criticism*, XVI (1966), 281–89; cf. the discussion in Donald Davie, *Purity of Diction in English Verse* (1952), Chap. III.

Chapter 6

1. W, p. 51.
2. That of Adam Littleton. The book is in the Johnson birthplace at Lichfield.
3. Shaw, pp. 14–15.
4. L, I, 56–57, 445–46, and n. 3; BNB, pp. 20–21.
5. R, No. 110.
6. L, IV, 427–28.
7. JG, X, 64; H, pp. 6–7; letter from Henry White, March 19, 1794, in John Nichols, *Illustrations of the Literary History of the Eighteenth Century* (1848), VII, 362; L, I, 82.
8. *Lives*, II, 20–21.
9. JG, III, 171–74; Clifford, pp. 98–104.
10. *Poetical Works* (1810), I, xix.
11. Thomas Davies, *Memoir of the Life of David Garrick*, 4th ed. (1784), I, 4–6. (The suggestion of the north drawing room is made by Clifford, pp. 102–3.) Johnson did, however, write an Epilogue about this time to Ambrose Philips's *The Distrest Mother*, for "some young ladies at Lichfield." But they apparently did not use it (*Poems*, p. 83).
12. W, pp. 78–79; JM, II, 227–28.
13. L, III, 309–10.
14. Clifford, pp. 100, 104; *Hebrides*, p. 378.

Chapter 7

1. JG, III, 180; *Diaries*, p. 6.
2. JG, V, 3–4, 119–23; W, p. 103; H, p. 9; JG, V, 4–5.
3. For a list of the books, see JG, V, 213–29.
4. L, I, 43; F. D. Mackinnon, *Cornhill Magazine*, new ser., LXI (1926), 444–45; Clifford, p. 111.
5. W, p. 102.
6. W, p. 23; L, I, 59.
7. L, I, 60–61, 272; H, p. 9.
8. "Milton," *Lives*, I, 162; L, I, 60, 71; A, p. 165; William Windham, *Diary* (1866), p. 17.
9. H, p. 13.
10. "Addison," *Lives*, II, 82; W, p. 57. For the other Latin exercises, in particular a translation of Dryden's epigram on Milton, see *Poems*, pp. 27–29.

11. H, p. 13; W, p. 104; A, pp. 164, 166.
12. JG, V, 12.
13. JG, V, 12; L, IV, 94.
14. JG, V, 30; Clifford, pp. 125–26; L, I, 70.
15. H, p. 12.
16. L, I, 86, 128 (citing James Northcote's *Reynolds* [1819], I, 236).
17. L, I, 61; A, p. 170; H, p. 9; JG, X, 71.
18. W, p. 103; cf. L, I, 76–77.
19. L, I, 74 (cf. W, p. 207).
20. L, II, 52; JG, V, 139–42; L, I, 271–74.
21. H, pp. 12–13.
22. R, Nos. 41, 2.
23. A, p. 263; L, I, 73 (cf. BNB, 7–8).
24. Clifford, p. 113; L, II, 444 (cf. BNB, p. 8); JG, V, 129–39 (who reproduces the picture of Jones, p. 131).
25. L, III, 302–7; on Edwards, see JG, V, 143–50.
26. L, III, 291–93; T, I, 184; A, pp. 207, 268.
27. L, I, 68.
28. For an authoritative discussion of Law's influence on Johnson, see Katharine C. Balderston, *PMLA*, LXXV (1960), 382–94.
29. W, p. 57; L, I, 73–74. Boswell, misreading his own original note, transcribed it in the *Life* as "mad and violent" instead of "rude and violent."
30. H, pp. 11, 18.
31. L, I, 76–77; JG, V, 21–22, and *TLS*, February 10, 1921, p. 92; W, pp. 103–4.
32. *Diaries*, p. 26. The writers he lists are Lucretius, Cicero (*Letters*), and the historians Velleius Paterculus and Justinus.
33. JG, V, 124–25.
34. L, I, 79; BNB, pp. 8, 21–22 (Boswell in the *Life*, I, 57, phrases Adams's remark as "the best qualified for the University that he had ever known come there").
35. JG, V, 56–57; *Diaries*, p. 27.
36. W, p. 49, n. 9.
37. R, Nos. 93, 183.

PART II

Chapter 8

1. W, p. 104.
2. A. L. Reade, *London Mercury*, XXI (1930), 247–49; cf. W, p. 468.

3. W, p. 50; T, I, 384.
4. W, pp. xxix–xli.
5. H, p. 288; L, I, 64.
6. R 85.
7. *Diaries,* pp. 38, 50, 56, 63, 69, 71, 78, 82, 92–93, 121, 133, 162, 225, 303. My italics.
8. A, p. 148; *Hebrides,* p. 174.
9. L, I, 144–45; Murphy, JM, I, 409; *Idler* 84.
10. L, II, 15.
11. *Letters,* No. 772.
12. L, I, 146–47, 143; cf. W, pp. 121–22.
13. Suggested as a result of prolonged anoxia (lack of oxygen) at birth by Peter Chase, *Yale Journal of Biology and Medicine,* XLVI (1951), 370–79, especially pp. 370, 376.
14. A, p. 318.
15. Clifford, pp. 131 and 338, n. 8 (Percy Laithwaite, *History of the Lichfield Conduit Lands Trust* [Lichfield, 1947], p. 69).
16. Clifford, pp. 133–34.
17. JG, V, 64–67; Clifford, pp. 134–35; *Diaries,* p. 28.
18. A, p. 151; L, II, 43; JG, V, 68, 74.
19. Richard Warner, *Tour through the Northern Counties* (Bath, 1802), I, 105 (reprinted in JM, II, 426–27). Boswell uses the somewhat briefer account by the Reverend Henry White (L, IV, 372–73). For the date, see Clifford, pp. 135 and 339, n. 17.

Chapter 9

1. Clifford, p. 137; S. Hopewell, *The Book of Bosworth School* (Leicester, 1950), p. 53; L, I, 84.
2. BNB, p. 10; W, pp. 170–71; Clifford, pp. 136–37; Hopewell (n. 1, above), p. 52 (in another version, by Mrs. Thrale, the interview is with the Queen; see Abraham Hayward, *Autobiography of Mrs. Piozzi* [1861], II, 103–4).
3. JG, V, 88–90.
4. W, p. 88.
5. Clifford, pp. 143–44; JG, V, 92–97; W, p. 87; L, I, 85.
6. W, pp. 88–91; Clifford, pp. 142–43.
7. W, pp. 90–91; Joseph Hill, *Bookmakers of Old Birmingham* (Birmingham, 1907), pp. 41–46; JG, V, 99.
8. L, I, 86–87; W, pp. 87–88; H. W. Liebert, *Yale University Library Gazette,* XXV (1950), 23–28.
9. L, I, 88–89; III, 7.
10. Greene, pp. 66–72. The paragraph in the text briefly summarizes Mr.

Greene's discussion, and is also indebted to Joel J. Gold, "Johnson's Translation of Lobo," *PMLA*, 80 (1965), 51–61. The Dedication (L, I, 89) was addressed to William Warren, presumably a relative of Thomas Warren's (JG, V, 107–8).

11. H, pp. 26–27, 445; L, I, 90; JG, V, 100–101.
12. H, p. 163; *Diaries*, pp. xv–xvi.
13. L, I, 91–92; *Letters*, I, 3–4; H, p. 29.

Chapter 10

1. JG, VI, 1–21.
2. L, I, 94–95.
3. W, p. 80.
4. Shaw, pp. 28–29.
5. JG, VI, 23–26; Anna Seward, *Letters* (Edinburgh, 1811), I, 44; Shaw (pp. 25–26) says that it was the widow's brother who made this offer; but it is plain that he is speaking of Harry Porter's brother (JG, VI, 32).
6. L, I, 96; A, p. 249.
7. JG, VI, 130; V, 108–13; Stebbing Shaw, *History and Antiquities of Staffordshire* (1798–1801), I, 235.
8. Taylor, when he left Oxford (1730), turned the books over to a fellow student, John Spicer, who was still there in 1735. The friend whom Johnson asked to get them from Spicer was Gilbert Repington (JG, V, 27–28; *Letters*, I, 4–5).
9. H, p. 327; L, III, 306; II, 56–57, 128, 165, 461.
10. L, I, 99.
11. H, p. 313.
12. Shaw, pp. 25–26, 111; A, p. 248.
13. *Letters*, I, 6.
14. JG, X, 114; VI, 29–30; Clifford, p. 159.
15. JG, VI, 35–42; Clifford, pp. 160, 341, n. 22.
16. Percy Fitzgerald, in his edition of L, I, 54, n. 1. Cf. JG, VI, 42. H. F. Cary, *Lives of English Poets* (1856), p. 9, states simply that an "old countryman" made the remark, which, in his version, was "that Johnson was not much of a scholar to look at, but that master Garrick was a strange one for leaping over a stile." Clifford (p. 163) follows Reade in attributing the remark to Bird, but uses Cary's version in which it is Garrick who is remembered leaping over the stiles.
17. L, IV, 458; JG, II, 85.
18. JG, VI, 44–45; H, pp. 35–38; Clifford, pp. 160–61. Boswell's account of the curriculum (I, 99–100) mistakenly combines with it part of a letter of advice from Johnson to his cousin Samuel Ford, who had

written asking him for help in preparing to enter Oxford (JG, VI, 52–54; *Letters*, I, 7–8).

19. L, I, 98.
20. A, p. 248; L, I, 531; Joseph Cradock, *Literary . . . Memoirs* (1828), IV, 244; "Tacenda" Ms., Yale Boswell Papers; Clifford, pp. 162–63.
21. B. H. Bronson, in *Johnson Agonistes and Other Essays* (Cambridge, 1946), pp. 100–156; Greene, pp. 72–80, for the political implications especially (cf. also his *Samuel Johnson* [New York, 1970], pp. 65–67); and M. Waingrow, in *From Sensibility to Romanticism*, F. W. Hilles and H. Bloom, eds. (New Haven, 1965), pp. 79–92.
22. John Disney, *Memoirs of . . . A. A. Sykes* (1785), p. 200 (Nichols, *Literary Anecdotes*, IX, 778, and Clifford, p. 169); cf. L, I, 101, 572. For the possibility that the story is apocryphal, see Donald Greene, *TLS*, October 13, 1961, p. 683.
23. L, II, 464–65; H, p. 439; L, II, 299; T, p. 189.
24. R. L. Chambers, *Transactions, Johnson Society* (Lichfield, 1969), p. 38.
25. For the text of the letter (in the Birthplace Museum), see JG, I, 1–2.
26. *Letters*, II, 389, 407; *Diaries*, p. 67. For other discussion of Nathaniel, see JG, VI, 58–61, and Clifford, pp. 165–68, 171–72.
27. John Nichols, *Gentleman's Magazine*, LV (1785), 3; JG, VI, 46–48; L, I, 445–46.
28. JG, VI, 48, 55–56, 150–53.
29. So we can infer from a second letter of Walmesley's (March 2) to his friend Colson, where he now says Johnson has just left with Garrick "to try his fate with a tragedy, and to see to get himself employed in some translation, either from the Latin or the French" (L, I, 102).

Chapter 11

1. H, p. 43; Murphy, JM, I, 380.
2. *Diaries*, pp. 39–40.
3. L, I, 103–5.
4. L, I, 106; V, 483–84.
5. Lucy Porter said that Walmesley gave him a letter of introduction to his bookseller, Henry Lintot, and that "Johnson wrote some things for him" (L, I, 103). But no one has yet succeeded in tracing them.
6. L, I, 110.
7. BNB, p. 11.
8. L, IV, 409; H, pp. 46–48; Clifford, pp. 184–86.
9. "Pope," *Lives*, III, 176.
10. The poem was written sixteen months before Savage left London. Savage, however, could have been talking long before about leaving for

Wales. Since Johnson said he did not know Savage at the time he wrote *London*, the likeliest explanation is Clifford's (pp. 207–8): that while writing the poem, he had heard of Savage's intention to leave for Wales and incorporated it in his conception of "Thales."

11. Bloom, pp. 29–31.

12. Clifford, pp. 202–5; Bloom, pp. 31–36.

13. Hawkins said "while he was in a lodging at Fleet-street, she was harboured by a friend near the Tower" (p. 89). If true, she was back again in Castle Street when Johnson wrote her in January 1740.

14. L, I, 135; JG, VI, 85.

15. Richard Cumberland, *Memoirs* (1807), I, 355–56.

16. H, p. 53; L, I, 163–64; Murphy, JM, II, 371.

17. *Johnsoniana*, J. W. Croker, ed. (Philadelphia, 1842), p. 418; "Savage," *Lives*, II, 431.

18. L, I, 164; H, p. 54; Clifford, p. 211. But cf. F. A. Pottle, *New Light on Dr. Johnson*, F. W. Hilles, ed. (New Haven, 1959), pp. 153–62.

19. L, I, 133–34; W, pp. 58, 160 (on the application to Adams); and, for detailed discussion of the Appleby matter, JG, VI, 96–114.

20. *Letters*, II, 103.

21. A, p. 255.

22. JG, VI, 176–77.

23. L, IV, 15; III, 281, 148–49; A, p. 256; on the Meynells generally, JG, VI, 125–26, 163–66, and Clifford, pp. 225–27.

24. JG, VI, 122.

Chapter 12

1. *Letters*, No. 12.

2. B. H. Bronson, *Johnson Agonistes and Other Essays* (Cambridge, 1946), and Donald J. Greene, *The Politics of Samuel Johnson* (New Haven, 1960). In what I say of Johnson's politics, I partly summarize or paraphrase what is said in these works. See also the detailed commentary in Mr. Greene's volume of the political writings in the Yale Edition (Vol. X), which is currently being published.

3. Cf. Greene, p. 53.

4. P. 7. For a concise statement of what constituted the Tory party, see Greene's introductory chapter in *The Politics* (pp. 1–21).

5. L, III, 200–5; cf. II, 476–77.

6. Greene, p. 259.

7. *Hebrides*, p. 170; Hester Chapone, *Posthumous Works* (1807), I, 73.

8. L, II, 170.

9. L, IV, 117.

10. Murphy, JM, I, 371.

11. Greene, p. 105; for discussion of both these pamphlets, see pp. 96–108.
12. H, p. 123. For authoritative discussion of the debates see especially B. B. Hoover, *Samuel Johnson's Parliamentary Reporting* (Berkeley, 1953), and Greene, pp. 112–40.
13. Murphy, JM, I, 378–79. It has been said Johnson was not living in Exeter Street at the time. But we are not certain. He was moving around a great deal in the 1740's.
14. Nichols, JM, II, 412; L, IV, 408–9; Hoover, *Parliamentary Reporting*, pp. 55–130, 160.
15. Greene, pp. 122–29; JM, II, 309; cf. H, pp. 514–15.
16. L, IV, 409; John Nichols, *Rise and Progress of the Gentleman's Magazine* (1821), p. xxxi; H, p. 99.
17. L, II, 138–39.

Chapter 13

1. L, I, 163, n. 1.
2. On their residences, see L, III, 405, 535; on the mortgage, see JG, IV, 8–11, Clifford, pp. 279–80, and *Letters*, Nos. 19, 20–22, 40.
3. Shaw, p. 112.
4. T, I, 177–78; A, pp. 247–49.
5. L, IV, 187.
6. For the most complete account of him, see Frederic J. Foley, S.J., *The Great Formosan Imposter* (New York, 1968).
7. L, III, 314.
8. Shiels's "Boyse," in Theophilus Cibber, *Lives* (1753), V, 169–70; A, p. 228; cf. Nichols, in JM, II, 411–12, and H, pp. 158–60.
9. JG, V, 94; Clifford, pp. 241–42, 349, n. 10; Steevens, JM, II, 325.
10. JM, II, 80–82; Jeremy Bentham, *Works* (1843), X, 51; D'Arblay, I, 58–59. The authoritative biography of Hawkins is Bertram H. Davis, *A Proof of Eminence* (Bloomington, Ind., 1973).
11. L, III, 184.
12. L, III, 311, 264, 371, n. 1.
13. *Hebrides*, p. 207, n. 3.
14. R 60, and *Idler* 84.
15. *Hebrides*, p. 55.
16. Allen Hazen, *Bulletin of the Institute of the History of Medicine*, IV, (1936), 455–65; L. C. McHenry, *Journal of the History of Medicine and Allied Sciences*, XIV, (1967), 298–310.
17. *Letters*, No. 23.
18. *Letters*, No. 15; Greene, pp. 147–48, 313–14.
19. JM, II, 343.
20. L, I, 165.

21. W. Y. Fletcher, *English Book Collectors* (1902), pp. 150–56. Cf. also Edward Edwards, *Lives of the Founders of the British Museum* (1870), pp. 241–42, who estimates the pamphlets as nearer 400,000.

22. For general discussion of Oldys, see Lawrence Lipking, *Philological Quarterly*, XLVI (1967), 385–407. On his life, see James Yeowell's memoir, *A Literary Antiquary* (1862).

23. H, pp. 133–49.

24. Yeowell (above, n. 23), p. xxviii.

25. H, p. 150; L, I, 154, 534; JM, II, 34; A, p. 304.

26. James M. Osborn, *TLS*, October 9, 1953, p. 652.

27. L. F. Powell, in L, V, 483–84; cf. Clifford, pp. 285–87.

28. L, I, 318, 545; Clifford, p. 353, n. 38.

29. L, I, 176. On the copyright, see JM, I, 382, n. 1.

PART III

Chapter 14

1. *Garrick Correspondence* (1831), I, 44–45.

2. W, pp. 59, 161. Boswell dates this in 1738 (I, 134). But Smallbrooke did not receive his degree and begin practice in Doctors' Commons until 1745 (JG, VI, 116). By April 1746 Johnson was started on the *Dictionary*. We can therefore date the episode as late 1745 or early 1746.

3. R 2.

4. T, I, 178; L, I, 99.

5. H, pp. 313–14.

6. John Burnett, *A History of the Cost of Living* (1969), p. 172.

Chapter 15

1. L, I, 182; III, 405. In this chapter I am especially indebted to the authoritative work on the *Dictionary* by Sledd and Kolb (1955), and also to suggestions in W. K. Wimsatt's essay in *New Light on Dr. Johnson*, F. W. Hilles, ed. (New Haven, 1959), pp. 65–90.

2. L, III, 405.

3. In the Hyde Collection.

4. L, I, 328, n. 1; JM, II, 259.

5. L, I, 536; II, 379; *Letters*, No. 467.

6. D'Arblay, I, 112; L, III, 37.

7. L, III, 29–31, especially 31n.; publisher's agreement with Cibber in the Hyde Collection..

8. L, I, 183.

9. W, pp. 105–6.

10. L, I, 256–57.

11. Sledd and Kolb, p. 161.

12. *Ibid.*, p. 32 (and Chap. I, *passim*); L, I, 186.

13. L, I, 188; JM, II, 213–14. For discussion of the amanuenses, see Eugene Thomas, *Transactions, Johnson Society* (Lichfield, 1974), pp. 20–30.

14. Wimsatt (above, n. 1), pp. 69, 81; H, p. 175.

15. Sledd and Kolb, pp. 37–40.

16. H. B. Wheatley, *Antiquary*, XI (1885), 11–12.

17. L, I, 293, 378. The largest collection of "curiosity" definitions is George A. Stringer, *Leisure Moments in Gough Square* (Buffalo, 1886).

18. See especially David Littlejohn, *Dr. Johnson and Noah Webster* (1971). When Johnson, on the other hand, uses Bailey's *Dictionary* for definitions, he acknowledges them (as "Bailey" or "Dict.," which is understood to refer to Bailey).

19. *Plan, Works*, V, II; *Lives*, I, 2.

20. Sledd and Kolb, p. 107; *Hebrides*, p. 29.

21. L, I, 326.

22. L, I, 192, and esp. 537.

23. L, I, 228–31; Hazen, pp. 77–84; Donald Greene, *PMLA*, LXXIV (1959), 83–84; J. L. Clifford, *Philological Quarterly*, 54 (1975), 342–56.

24. L, I, 532.

25. See especially Arthur Sherbo, *Journal of English and Germanic Philology*, LII (1953), 543–48, and *Johnsonian Studies*, M. Wahba, ed. (1962), pp. 133–59; Donald Greene, *PMLA*, LXXIV (1959), 75–85; Gwin Kolb, *Studies in English Literature*, I (1961), 77–95.

26. Sledd and Kolb, pp. 107–10, 227–30; L, I, 287.

27. L, I, 271–83.

28. L, I, 262, n. 1.

29. L, I, 261–65; W, pp. 21–22, 62.

30. Sledd and Kolb, pp. 100–104.

31. L, I, 260; IV, 128 (cf. W, p. 25); Sledd and Kolb, pp. 102–3.

32. R 39.

33. Sledd and Kolb, p. 110. On the editions, see pp. 105–33.

Chapter 16

1. John Burnett, *A History of the Cost of Living* (1969), p. 176.

2. L, I, 238.

3. A. L. Reade, *London Mercury*, XXI (1930), 248.
4. *Letters*, Nos. 157–59, 161, 165.
5. It was so unusual for her to appear in public that everyone who knew Johnson would have remarked on her presence had she been there.
6. W, pp. 22, 106.
7. L, I, 196–98, 200; JM, I, 286.
8. Said by Thomas Birch in a letter of August 6 (British Museum, Add. MS. 35, 397, f. 140).
9. H, pp. 219–20, 252–53, 258.
10. H, pp. 220–22, 232–33.
11. JM, II, 396; H, 222–32, 252–53; L, IV, 11, n. 1; I, 253, n. 1.
12. A, p. 158; T, I, 205, 601.
13. JG, II, 1–11; L, I, 190, 242; H, pp. 234–35.
14. *Diaries*, pp. 79, 92, 150, 156.
15. The best discussion of her is Miriam Small, *Charlotte Ramsay Lennox* (New Haven, 1935).
16. H, pp. 286–87.
17. L, I, 243; *Gentleman's Magazine*, LV, i (1785), 101–2.
18. H, p. 435; L, I, 417.
19. JM, II, 171–76; H, pp. 321–25. On her poems, see Hazen, pp. 213–16.
20. Lady Knight (who got the account from Miss Williams), JM, II, 173–74.
21. D'Arblay, II, 270.
22. *Diaries*, p. 46; L, I, 238.
23. JM, I, 476; H, pp. 316, 320; Shaw, pp. 112–13.
24. *Diaries*, pp. 46, 50, 61, 71, 79, 127, 319.
25. L, III, 306; Mary Hyde, Presidential Address, *Transactions, Johnson Society* (Lichfield, 1957), pp. 44–45.
26. A, p. 332.

Chapter 17

1. JM, II, 313–14.
2. L, I, 193.
3. Sir Walter Scott, *Miscellaneous Prose Works* (1827), III, 288.
4. Hazlitt, "On Gusto," *Works*, P. P. Howe, ed. (1930–34), IV, 79–80.
5. Of the 208 numbers, he wrote 201. Friends contributed 4: Nos. 30 (Catherine Talbot), 97 (Samuel Richardson), 44 and 100 (Elizabeth Carter); parts of three others were written by Hester Mulso, later Mrs. Chapone (10), Garrick (15), and Joseph Simpson (107). Several of the details in the following discussion of the *Rambler* are presented at more length in my general Introduction to it for the Yale Edition

(Vol. III), from which I have incorporated some passages. For other discussion, see especially Leopold Damrosch, *ELH* (*Journal of English Literary History*), XL (1973), 70–89.

6. Tyers and Murphy, JM, II, 350; I, 391; L, I, 202.
7. A, p. 178; L, I, 215.
8. L, III, 194; JM, II, 302, 229.
9. Y, II, 333–35.
10. *Diaries*, p. 43; *Correspondence of Samuel Richardson*, A. L. Barbauld, ed. (1804), I, 164–70.
11. Y, III, xxx–xxxiv.
12. W. K. Wimsatt, *Philosophic Words* (New Haven, 1948).

Chapter 18

1. *Rasselas*, Chap. 32; R 41 (Y, III, 221); T, I, 179. Italics mine. The first part of this chapter condenses material presented in more detail in my book *The Achievement of Samuel Johnson* (New York, 1955), Chaps. 2–4 (pp. 63–147). For other discussions of Johnson's moral thought, see especially Robert Voitle, *Samuel Johnson the Moralist* (Cambridge, Mass., 1961); Paul Alkon, *Samuel Johnson and Moral Discipline* (Evanston, Ill., 1967); Arieh Sachs, *Passionate Intelligence* (Baltimore, 1967); Leopold Damrosch, *Samuel Johnson and the Tragic Sense* (Princeton, 1972).
2. *Biographia Literaria*, Shawcross, ed. (Oxford, 1907), I, 167.
3. L, I, 441; II, 79; R 202 (Y, V, 289–90), 58 (Y, III, 310).
4. R 45 (Y, III, 243–47).
5. R 6 (Y, III, 32–35).
6. R 146 (Y, V, 13–17), 2 (Y, III, 13); cf. R 21.
7. R 2 (Y, III, 11); *Idler* 58 (Y, II, 182).
8. R 54 (Y, III, 290), 159 (Y, V, 84), 146 (Y, V, 13–14).
9. A, p. 199.
10. See especially Kathleen Grange, *Journal of Nervous and Mental Diseases*, CXXXV (1962), 93–98.
11. R 76 (Y, IV, 34–37).
12. R 183 (Y, V, 198–99); cf. R 205, 206.
13. *Adventurer* 45 (Y, II, 360–61); R 93 (Y, IV, 134).
14. *Rasselas*, Chap. 9.
15. R 183 (Y, V, 199–200).
16. *Idler* 32 (Y, II, 99–100).
17. *Rasselas*, Chap. 11.
18. L, I, 539 (*Letters*, No. 116).
19. R 60 (Y, III, 318–19).
20. A, p. 201; L, I, 471; *Rasselas*, Chap. 11.

Chapter 19

1. L, I, 274–75, n. 2.
2. *Diaries*, pp. 52–53.
3. The subject is authoritatively discussed in Donald and Mary Hyde, *Dr. Johnson's Second Wife* (1953), revised and reprinted in F. W. Hilles, ed., *New Light on Dr. Johnson* (New Haven, 1959), pp. 133–51.
4. *Letters*, Nos. 78–82.
5. A, p. 257.
6. Johnson implied the club broke up around 1751–53, while Hawkins said 1756 (L, I, 191, n. 5). G. B. Hill thought there was a sort of rump continuation to 1756 (*Letters*, 1892, II, 364, n. 5).
7. A, pp. 306–7; L, I, 356; Murphy, JM, I, 407–8.
8. H. D. Best, JM, II, 390; L, I, 247–48, 320, 476; III, 304.
9. Boswell assumed Johnson and Reynolds met in 1752. But F. W. Hilles has shown that it was not before 1755 and more probably in 1756, at which time Reynolds became thirty-three. See F. W. Hilles, *Literary Career of Sir Joshua Reynolds* (New Haven, 1936), pp. 12–13.
10. Frances Reynolds, JM, II, 261; L, I, 246 and n. 2.
11. JG, II, 12–24, 27–28; L, I, 348. W, pp. 164–65; H, pp. 327–28.
12. D. J. Greene, *Review of English Studies*, new ser., VII (1956), 367–92. See also Hazen, pp. 125–28, and Bloom, pp. 88–112. For general discussion of Johnson and the Seven Years' War, see D. J. Greene, *English Writers of the Eighteenth Century*, J. H. Middendorf, ed. (New York, 1971), pp. 37–65; and J. L. Clifford, *Lex et Scientia*, II (1975), 72–88.
13. On Rolt, see L, I, 139; Hazen, 198–200. On the Dedications, see Hazen, pp. 12–13, 146–51, 110–16 (the Sully *Memoirs*, though dated 1756, were actually published in November 1755). On the *Universal Visiter*, see Bloom, pp. 117–35.
14. Y, VII, xvi–xix; Arthur Sherbo, *Shakespeare Quarterly*, IX (1958), 426–28.
15. *Diaries*, p. 14.
16. H, p. 363.
17. Murphy, JM, I, 414; *Letters*, Nos. 112–13; L, I, 324 n., 329. For the Tonson loans, see the article by David Fleeman, *Studies in the Book Trade in Honor of Graham Pollard* (Oxford Bibliographical Society, Oxford, 1975), p. 214. I regret that I saw this valuable article on Johnsons' earnings too late to make more general use of it.
18. Of the twelve *Idler*s written by others, three were by Reynolds (76, 79, 82), three by Thomas Warton (33, 93, 96), one each by Langton (67), Bonnell Thornton (15), and William Emerson (98), and three (9, 42, 54) by people whose names Johnson later forgot. For information generally on the background of the *Idler*, see my Introduction to Y, II, xv–xxviii.

19. *Letters*, Nos. 118–27; L, I, 340–41; R. W. Chapman, Introduction to his edition of *Rasselas* (1927). The title page lists as publishers only the Dodsley brothers and William Johnston, Strahan apparently deciding to serve as a "silent partner." For details, see Gwin Kolb, *Studies in Bibliography*, XV (1962), 256–59.

20. L, I, 341, n. 2 (Malone); IV, 119. In saying he had "never since read it over," he meant since the second edition, which soon followed (June 26), and which has several verbal changes.

21. On the Ethiopian and Biblical backgrounds, see D. M. Lockhart, *PMLA*, 78 (1963), 516–28, and T. R. Preston, *PMLA*, 84 (1969), 274–81.

22. See especially Gwin Kolb, *PMLA*, LXVI (1951), 698–717; F. W. Hilles, in *Johnson, Boswell and their Circle: Essays . . . L. F. Powell* (Oxford, 1965), pp. 111–21; *RES*, new ser., xviii (1967), 387–401; E. Jones, M. Wahba, *Bicentenary Essays on Rasselas* (1959).

Chapter 20

1. *Letters*, No. 130; L, III, 535 (App. F).
2. L, IV, 122–23; *Diaries*, p. 68.
3. *Diaries*, pp. 63–89.
4. For his rooms in Inner Temple Lane, the customary rent was about £16 (L, I, 546); but these chambers were sublet to Johnson, presumably at a reduced rate. Since Staple Inn was considered an unattractive place, and Johnson moved from it as soon as he could, the rent was certainly less than for Inner Temple Lane (perhaps £10 to £12).
5. L, I, 347–48; III, 245.
6. L, I, 347–48, and 347, n. 2.
7. L, II, 299; I, 331.
8. L, I, 249–51.
9. Hazen, pp. 6–8, 41–42, 62–66, 74–77, 84–89, 91–94, 98–102.
10. Greene, *Samuel Johnson* (New York, 1970), pp. 84–85.
11. L, I, 464, 550–52; R. W. Chapman, *Review of English Studies*, V (1929), 69–70.
12. *Diaries*, pp. 71, 77.
13. JM, II, 257, n. 2.
14. Murphy, JM, I, 416–17; L, II, 125, 406.
15. JM, I, 416; *Letters*, No. 142.
16. JM, II, 259; L, I, 350, n. 3, 366, n. 1.
17. L, I, 416.
18. H, p. 383; L, II, 118–19; JM, II, 401; L, I, 421.
19. Humphry, JM, II, 400–401; L, I, 435–36.
20. *The Ghost*, III, 801–6. See Douglas Grant, *The Cock Lane Ghost*

(1965) and Grant's edition of Churchill's *Poetical Works* (Oxford, 1956), pp. 482–85, 490, 497–98.

21. JM, I, 417–19; L, I, 372–79.
22. J. L. Clifford, "Johnson's Trip to Devon in 1762," in *Eighteenth-Century Studies in Honor of Donald F. Hyde*, W. H. Bond, ed. (New York, 1970), pp. 3–28, which I follow here. For the remarks quoted above and immediately below from Reynolds and his sister, see L, I, 145, and JM, II, 275, 279.
23. May 2, 1769. See L, IV, 77, 484.
24. Clifford (see n. 22), p. 17.
25. *Letters*, No. 146; L, I, 378–79; Clifford (n. 22 above), pp. 18–20.
26. JM, II, 278.
27. Geoffrey Scott, ed. (Vols. 1–6) and Frederick A. Pottle, ed. (Vols. 7–18). Of the standard biography, Vol. 1 has appeared: F. A. Pottle, *James Boswell, the Earlier Years, 1740–1769* (New York, 1966). For a history of the papers, see David Buchanan, *The Treasure of Auchinleck* (New York, 1974). For the account of the meeting with Johnson, see L, I, 390–95.
28. *London Journal*, F. A. Pottle, ed. (New York, 1950), p. 62; BP, I, 151–52; *Boswell in Holland*, F. A. Pottle, ed. (New York, 1952), p. 80; BP, VII, 72, 103; IX, 156; X, 91; XVIII, 71. My italics.
29. Pottle, *James Boswell* (n. 27 above), p. 119; L, I, 457–72.
30. P. A. W. Collins, *Notes and Queries* (April 1956), 163–66.
31. H, p. 446; L, II, 332, n. 1.
32. Best, JM, II, 390–91.

PART IV

Chapter 21

1. *Diaries*, pp. 73–74; L, IV, 406; *Diaries*, pp. 77–81, 92, 105–7. My italics.
2. W, pp. 24, 161, where it is dated 1766. For Boswell's modified version (which he now dates 1764), see L, I, 483.
3. *Works* (1825), VI, 64–65.
4. A, pp. 199, 207.
5. See especially *Civilization and Its Discontents*, J. Strachey, trans. (New York, 1961), p. 27.
6. H, p. 435.
7. *Diaries*, pp. 70, 82, 99, 105, 108.

8. A, pp. 300–2.
9. The most detailed account of this and other compulsive gestures is Miss Reynolds's in JM, II, 273–75; cf. L, I, 484–86, IV, 322–23.
10. L, IV, 322–23.
11. Printed in *Poetical Calendar*, F. Fawkes and W. Woty, eds., XII (December 1763); reprinted *Gentleman's Magazine* (January 1764), 24.
12. *Rasselas*, Chap. 46; *Diaries*, pp. 78–79, 93.
13. T, I, 384–85.
14. *Civilization and Its Discontents* (n. 5, above), pp. 70–81.
15. Tyers, JM, II, 338–39; T II, 625 and n. 4.
16. A, p. 199.

Chapter 22

1. Y, VII, xxii. For the chronology and details generally, see Bertrand Bronson's and Arthur Sherbo's Introduction and notes to Y, VII, and Sherbo's *Samuel Johnson, Editor of Shakespeare* (Urbana, Ill., 1956).
2. *Letters*, Nos. 142–43.
3. L, IV, 111.
4. L, I, 49, 486, 553–54; II, 136, n. 4; Steevens, JM, II, 314–15.
5. For Steevens, see especially J. Nichols, *Literary Anecdotes* (1812–15, II, 650–63), and *Literary History* (1828), V, 427–43; JM, II, 328; Sherbo (n. 1, above), p. 10.
6. Y, VII, 93, 55; R. E. Scholes, *Shakespeare Quarterly*, XI (1960), 163–71.
7. L, II, 192; Steevens, JM, II, 316.
8. Sir Walter Raleigh, *Johnson on Shakespeare* (Oxford, 1908), p. xvi.
9. L, I, 496, n. 4; IV, 499 (from Malone's Preface to his edition of Shakespeare [1790], I, lxviii).
10. T. S. Eliot, "Shakespearian Criticism: I. From Dryden to Coleridge," *Companion to Shakespeare Studies*, H. Granville-Barker and G. B. Harrison, eds. (New York, 1960), p. 300; Y. VII, 61.
11. JM, II, 362.
12. Y, VII, 66–67.
13. Printed as "A Project for the Employment of Authors," *Works* (1825), V, 355–56.

Chapter 23

1. A, p. 234; Murphy, JM, I, 423.
2. British Museum, Add. MS. 35,4000 (*Diaries*, p. 98).
3. *Diaries*, pp. 96–98; W. G. Hamilton, *Parliamentary Logick* (1808), pp. ix, 239–53; Greene, pp. 197–99.
4. *Diaries*, p. 106; L, II, 8.

5. *Diaries*, pp. 102–3.
6. Knight, JM, II, 172–73; Hazen, pp. 213–16.
7. T, I, 206; *A Series of Letters . . . Carter . . . Talbot*, M. Pennington, ed. (1809), III, 135.
8. A, pp. 253–54.
9. A, pp. 233, 240; G. Kearsley, JM, II, 169.
10. A, pp. 232–33; Clifford, *Piozzi*, pp. 57–58.
11. A, p. 200.
12. A, p. 235; Clifford, *Piozzi*, p. 67, n. 2. The tradition that Johnson's eyes were gray is based on a remark by Mrs. Thrale in A, p. 344. Descriptions in the earlier *Thraliana* are generally more precise. Presumably his eyes were of a light grayish-blue.
13. A, p. 339; A. Hayward, *Autobiography . . . of Mrs. Piozzi* (1861), I, 16.
14. A, p. 205; Clifford, *Piozzi*, p. 68.
15. E. L. McAdam, *Dr. Johnson and the English Law* (Syracuse, 1951), pp. 65–122.
16. L, II, 7–8.
17. *Letters*, Nos. 187.1–187.3.
18. McAdam (see above, n. 15), pp. 81–120, prints most of these, omitting some that Johnson may simply have revised. For comparison of the styles, see pp. 71–73.
19. *Diaries*, p. 112.
20. L, II, 33–42.
21. *Letters*, Nos. 191–92; *Diaries*, p. 115.
22. *Diaries*, pp. 116–17; edition of L, with marginal comments by Mrs. Thrale, E. G. Fletcher, ed. (1938), I, 389.
23. Hyde, p. 12; Clifford, *Piozzi*, p. 77.
24. *Diaries*, pp. 122–23; Clifford, *Piozzi*, 75–76.
25. L, II, 67–68.

Chapter 24

1. *Diaries*, p. 123; A, pp. 150, 288; JM, II, 405.
2. L, II, 68–69; *Boswell in Search of a Wife*, F. Brady and F. A. Pottle, eds. (New York, 1956), pp. 269–83.
3. Benjamin Victor, *History of the Theatres* (1771), III, 204–32; Percy Fitzgerald, *Garrick* (1899), pp. 328–38; Martha England, *Garrick's Jubilee* (New York, 1964), pp. 3–65.
4. L, II, 73–75, 80–83.
5. H. W. Liebert, *A Constellation of Genius* (New Haven, 1958) prints the complete trial.
6. L, II, 78–79.

7. L, II, 100–1.
8. *Hebrides,* p. 62; L, V, 87; A, p. 287.
9. Clifford, *Piozzi,* pp. 90–91.
10. A, pp. 180, 196; T, I, 415.
11. *Autobiography,* A. Hayward, ed. (1861), II, 25–26. Clifford, *Piozzi,* pp. 92–99; BP, VI, 92.
12. *Letters,* No. 311.1; Hyde, p. 20.
13. *Letters,* No. 307.1.
14. *Letters,* No. 311.1a.
15. *Diaries,* p. 157.

Chapter 25

1. Clifford, *Piozzi,* p. 74, n. 2.
2. *Samuel Johnson,* p. 165. For detailed consideration, see Greene, pp. 204–19, and his discussions in the latest volume of the Yale Edition of Johnson (Vol. X).
3. A, p. 173.
4. *Works* (1825), X, 27.
5. L, IV, 324–25.
6. *Works* (1825), X, 60.
7. J. P. Sullivan, trans., in *Samuel Johnson . . . Poems,* J. D. Fleeman, ed. (1971), pp. 146–49.
8. *Diaries,* pp. 142, 146.
9. L, I, 405; III, 299.
10. *Sermons on Different Subjects, Left for Publication by John Taylor* (1789). The sermons have been brilliantly interpreted and discussed by James Gray, *Johnson's Sermons* (Oxford, 1972), who, with Jean Hagstrum, is currently editing them for the Yale Edition of Johnson.
11. A, pp. 241–44; L, III, 188; IV, 298. For a succinct discussion of Johnson and the problem of evil, see especially Leopold Damrosch, *Samuel Johnson and the Tragic Sense* (Princeton, 1972), pp. 78–90.
12. *Idler* 89; *Adventurer* 120; A, p. 330; L, II, 298.
13. L, IV, 299; III, 295–96; JM, I, 439; for Wesley's remark, see Damrosch (n. 11, above), p. 71.
14. *Diaries,* p. 269.
15. L, II, 126; "Milton," *Lives,* I, 155.
16. L, II, 214; *Diaries,* p. 153; JM, II, 285; L, III, 352; H, p. 452.
17. *Diaries,* p. 153; L, II, 173; JM, II, 319.
18. On the Augustinian element in Johnson generally, see especially D. J. Greene, in *Johnsonian Studies,* M. Wahba, ed. (Cairo, 1962), pp. 61–92.
19. *Works* (1825), IX, 421–22.
20. A, p. 219.

Chapter 26

1. L, IV, 27–28; A, p. 273; L, III, 269, 459; *Letters*, 417.
2. L, I, 450; V, 392, n. 6.
3. *Hebrides*, pp. 11–32; L, II, 269, n. 1.
4. *Hebrides*, pp. 8, 309, 33–34.
5. *Hebrides*, pp. 53–58, 189.
6. *Hebrides*, p. 98, n. 6.
7. *Hebrides*, p. 110.
8. *Hebrides*, pp. 113, 192, 304, 121, 242.
9. *Letters*, No. 326.
10. *Hebrides*, pp. 342, 39 (cf. L, I, 392), 45, 390, 122, 231, 122.
11. *Hebrides*, pp. 297, 363–64, 133, 143, 176–77.
12. BP, X, 148.
13. *Journey to the Western Islands*, Y, IX, 163–64.
14. *Hebrides*, pp. 246–52, 309, 313.
15. *Hebrides*, pp. 312–13, 336; *Journey*, Y, IX, 148.
16. *Hebrides*, pp. 353–69, 390–91.
17. *Hebrides*, pp. 369–77; L, V, 382, n. 2; G. B. Hill, *Footsteps of Dr. Johnson* (1890), pp. 278–79.
18. *Diaries*, p. 162.
19. L, II, 270–71; A, p. 184.
20. Campbell, JM, II, 46.
21. *Dr. Johnson and Mrs. Thrale*, A. M. Broadley, ed. (1910), pp. 158–219; *Diaries*, pp. 163–222.
22. D'Arblay, I, 130.
23. Broadley (n. 21, above), p. 219; cf. T, I, 316.
24. *Letters*, No. 360.1.
25. *Diaries*, p. 191; JM, II, 397.

Chapter 27

1. Sigmund Freud, *Der Witz und seine Beziehung zum Unbewussten* (Leipzig, 1905), *passim*, especially VII, 7–8, and the later paper, "Humor," (1928), *Collected Papers* (New York, 1950), V, 215–21.
2. Arthur Koestler, *The Act of Creation* (New York, 1964), p. 96.
3. A, pp. 345, 269, 287; JM, I, 452; H, p. 257; Boswell, *London Journal*, p. 260; T, I, 329–30.
4. JM, II, 366, 19.
5. L, II, 363; II, 463; II, 187; IV, 193; A, p. 289; *Hebrides*, p. 147; A, pp. 286, 207; JM, II, 268.
6. R 194; L, III, 191–92, 410; IV, 286; II, 88–89; IV, 73.
7. A, p. 287; JM, II, 164; *Hebrides*, p. 121; H, p. 257.

8. *Hebrides*, p. 357; D'Arblay, I, 211; JM, II, 396.
9. *Hebrides*, p. 226.
10. A, p. 345; L, II, 231.
11. L, II, 260–62.
12. A, p. 260.
13. *Hebrides*, pp. 211–12.
14. William Hazlitt, "Conversations with Northcote," *Works*, P. P. Howe, ed. (1930–34), XI, 265 (for Johnson's remark to Opie); D'Arblay, I, 101–2.
15. A, p. 335.
16. Hester M. Chapone, *Posthumous Works* (1807), I, 73; *Hebrides*, p. 170.
17. The present section of this chapter summarizes examples discussed at more length in an article, "Johnson and Satire *Manqué*," that I wrote for *Eighteenth-Century Studies: In Honor of Donald F. Hyde*, W. H. Bond, ed. (New York, 1970), pp. 145–60.
18. *Lives*, II, 379. My italics.
19. R 72.
20. R 72; A, p. 318.
21. "Swift," *Lives*, III, 61.
22. JM, II, 256.

Chapter 28

1. A, pp. 204–5; Cooke, JM, II, 393; F. Reynolds, JM, II, 251; A, p. 218.
2. T, I, 185.
3. L, III, 222.
4. L, IV, 321–22; T, I, 532; *Letters*, Nos. 292.1, 293.1, 343.1.
5. *Letters*, No. 591; H, p. 404; D'Arblay, I, 113.
6. JG, II, 22–23, 32, 86–98. Reade guesses that the second child was a son, but Hawkins (p. 586 n.) states that the first two children were daughters.
7. T, I, 532; L, IV, 197; A, p. 318.
8. J. W. Croker's edition of *Life* (1833), I, 533–34 (App. III).
9. L, III, 327–29.
10. L, III, 271–73.
11. L, II, 331–33.
12. *Hebrides*, pp. 175, 91, 208–9. For the legal statements, see L, II, 183–85, 196–201, 242–46, 372–74; III, 59–62, 201–3; IV, 74, 129–31, and *Boswell, Johnson, and the Petition of James Wilson*, W. H. Bond, ed. (1971).
13. L, II, 139, n. 1 (Johnson's remark that his speeches there did not succeed should not be taken literally); John L. Abbott, *Journal of the Royal Society of Arts*, CXV (1967), 395–400, 486–91; John Brown and

J. de L. Mann, *Modern Language Review*, XLI (1946), 16–23, 410–11; Steevens, JM, II, 325; L, III, 337.

14. L, IV, 26–27.
15. *Diaries*, pp. 264, 291–92, 295–96. My italics.
16. L, II, 359; *Hebrides*, p. 169; L, III, 335.
17. L, II, 440.
18. A, p. 221; L, III, 272; R 80; *Hebrides*, p. 393; L, III, 57; A, p. 328; L, III, 398; H, p. 531; L, IV, 360, n. 2.
19. A, pp. 253–54.
20. A, p. 246; JM, II, 276, 260; L, II, 405–6.
21. L, II, 54; A, p. 349.
22. L, III, 64–79.
23. JM, II, 262–65; L, IV, 431–33; A, p. 328; *Hebrides*, p. 50.
24. JM, II, 273.
25. JM, II, 223; A, pp. 213–14; L, II, 362–63.
26. *Letters*, No. 545; L, III, 456.
27. Tyers, JM, II, 367; L, III, 36.
28. *French Journals of Mrs. Thrale and Dr. Johnson*, M. Tyson and H. Guppy, eds. (1932), pp. 79, 88–89.
29. *Diaries*, pp. 228–56.
30. L, II, 401.
31. Clifford, *Piozzi*, pp. 136–37; L, II, 468–69. For the probable diagnosis of Harry Thrale's illness, I am indebted to Mary Hyde. An alternative, she states, would be a case of pneumonia, which in a child at that time could prove quickly fatal. The old diagnosis of a ruptured appendix is ruled out since it would take three days for peritonitis.
32. L, III, 6, n. 1, 19, 27–28.
33. L, I, 396; IV, 183; *Journey*, Y, IX, 118. On Macpherson generally, see the biography by Bailey Saunders (1898; reprinted 1968).
34. *Letters*, No. 373 (cf. L, II, 298); H, p. 491.
35. L, III, 81–85, 113–14; JM, II, 192; A, p. 332.
36. Boswell's account (III, 139–48), should be supplemented by Percy Fitzgerald, *A Famous Forgery* (London, 1865) and more recently by J. H. Warner, *Queen's Quarterly*, 53 (1946), 41–53, and E. E. Willoughby, *Essays by Divers Hands* (Royal Society of Literature), 29 (1958), 124–43.

Chapter 29

1. *Diaries*, p. 264; L, III, 109.
2. L. III, 100–1.
3. L, III, 137.
4. *Lives*, I, xxvi; Nichols, *Literary Anecdotes*, VIII, 16.

5. *Adventurer* 138; L, I, 425; *Letters*, No. 658; *Gentleman's Magazine*, LV (1785), 9, n. 1.

6. A, p. 298; L, IV, 36, n. 3; JM, II, 401, 414.

7. L, III, 344–45, 392.

8. W. J. Bate, *The Burden of the Past* (Cambridge, Mass., 1970), *passim*.

9. L, IV, 381, n. 1; *Adventurer* 107 (Y, II, 441–42, 445).

10. Thomas Mann, *Dr. Faustus*, H. T. Lowe-Porter, trans. (New York, 1948), p. 322; T. S. Eliot, *On Poetry and Poets* (New York, 1957), p. 185.

11. BP, X, 198; cf. the version in L, II, 300.

12. For a comprehensive treatment of his criticism generally, including the *Lives*, see especially Jean Hagstrum, *Samuel Johnson's Literary Criticism* (Minneapolis, 1952).

13. *Preface to Shakespeare*, Y, VII, 83; *Lives*, II, 206, 214; III, 301, 419–20. For discussion of "Johnson on Novelty and Originality," see the article by James Engell forthcoming in *Modern Philology*.

14. *Lives*, I, 180–83, 177–78, 194.

15. T. S. Eliot, *The Use of Poetry and the Use of Criticism* (New York, 1934), p. 64, and *On Poetry and Poets* (see above, n. 10), p. 185.

16. *Lives*, I, 163–65; II, 283; L, I, 500.

17. Arthur Waugh, in World Classics edition of *Lives of the Poets* (1964), I, xii.

18. *Letters*, No. 670; cf. L, IV, 35, n. 3.

19. Y, III, xxxi–xxxiv.

20. David Perkins, *Journal of English Literary History*, XX (New York, 1953), 210–11.

21. T. S. Eliot, "Metaphysical Poets," *Selected Essays* (1932), p. 250; *Lives*, I, 20; L, I, 421; *Hebrides*, p. 348; W. J. Bate, *Achievement of Samuel Johnson* (New York, 1955), pp. 189–90, 212–16.

22. *Lives*, I, 19–22.

23. L, IV, 38.

24. *Use of Poetry* (n. 15, above), p. 65.

25. Passages in the above section on style are from *Lives*, I, 22; III, 216–18, 220–22.

26. Richard Cumberland, *Memoirs* (1807), II, 210.

27. *Diaries*, pp. 303–4.

Chapter 30

1. John Keats, *Letters*, H. E. Rollins, ed. (Cambridge, Mass., 1958), II, 79; *Diaries*, p. 304.

2. Hyde (II), July 18, 1778.

3. Hyde (II), December 1778; Clifford, *Piozzi*, p. 173; D'Arblay, I, 238–40; T, I, 493.
4. Edward Mangin, *Piozziana* (1833), pp. 22–23.
5. Hyde (II), June 1779.
6. T, I, 393, 401, n. 2.
7. A, pp. 276–77.
8. T, I, 432; Hyde (II), February 1780.
9. *Letters,* Nos. 650, 655.
10. *Letters,* No. 654; Clifford, *Piozzi*, p. 190; W. H. Hutton, *Burford Papers* (1905), p. 49.
11. T, I, 487.
12. T, I, 488–89 (my italics).
13. *Diaries,* p. 304; *Letters,* Nos. 719, 721, 717.
14. For the full text, see Hyde, pp. 173–74; cf. BP, XIV, 196, 198.
15. Clifford, *Piozzi*, p. 200, n. 2.
16. L, IV, 87.
17. Hyde (II), May 1781.
18. *Diaries,* pp. 307–8.
19. For her account, see her *Memoirs of Dr. Burney* (1832), II, 101–13; cf. *Early Diary of Frances Burney*, A. R. Ellis, ed. (1889), II, 284–85.
20. *Diaries,* p. 310; D'Arblay, II, 52.
21. *Letters,* No. 753; T, I, 521, 525, n. 2.
22. *Letters,* No. 770.
23. T, I, 528; *Diaries,* p. 314.
24. *Letters,* No. 778; T, I, 535.
25. H. More, JM, II, 198–99.

Chapter 31

1. T, I, 540–41 and n. 1.
2. Fanny Burney, *Memoirs of Dr. Burney* (1832), II, 252.
3. *Diaries,* p. 337–39.
4. T, I, 548.
5. D'Arblay, II, 122; Constance Hill, *The House in St. Martin's Street* (1907), pp. 343–44.
6. D'Arblay, II, 105, 118; *Diaries,* pp. 348–49.
7. T, I, 551; *Letters,* No. 819.1; D'Arblay, II, 171.
8. Clifford, *Piozzi*, p. 218; T, I, 557–60.
9. Clifford, *Piozzi*, pp. 220–21; T, I, 565.
10. L, IV, 168–69.
11. L, IV, 203–8, 171–72, 226.
12. L, IV, 228–30 (*Letters,* No. 847).
13. L, IV, 522; *Letters,* No. 850.

14. *Letters*, No. 854; T, I, 568.
15. The autopsy, made by James Wilson, is printed in Russell Brain, "A Post-Mortem on Dr. Johnson," *Some Reflections on Genius* (1960), pp. 99–100. For a detailed discussion of his emphysema and a drawing of the lungs as they looked at the autopsy, see L. C. McHenry, *Archives of Internal Medicine*, CXIX (1967), 98–105.
16. *Letters*, No. 835.1.
17. R 85.

Chapter 32

1. L, II, 106.
2. *Letters*, No. 857.
3. *Letters*, No. 871.1.
4. L, IV, 235, n. 2.
5. *Letters*, Nos. 871.2, 871.3, 873.2, 877.
6. L, IV, 236–39.
7. L, IV, 242, 245.
8. H, p. 563.
9. Russell Brain, *Some Reflections on Genius* (1960), p. 28 (on the coronary thrombosis); JM, I, 440; *Letters*, No. 921; L, IV, 272; H, pp. 565–66; cf. Donald Greene's article, n. 26 below.
10. *Letters*, No. 937.
11. *Letters*, Nos. 929.2, 1003.1.
12. *Letters*, No. 956; L, IV, 273, 275.
13. L, IV, 280–81 and n. 1.
14. H, pp. 409, 601.
15. L, IV, 284, 326, 339.
16. *Letters*, No. 970.
17. *Letters*, No. 972.
18. L, IV, 327–28, 348–50, 367–68, 542–43 (*Letters*, No. 1008).
19. *Letters*, Nos. 984, 982.
20. *Letters*, No. 982.1.
21. W, p. 91.
22. L, IV, 293–94 (my italics), 376; *Diaries*, p. 378.
23. H, pp. 566–82, 605. For the will and codicil, see L, IV, 402–5, n. 2.
24. H, pp. 586–87; L, IV, 393–94, 405 n. 1, 408–9; JM, I, 446.
25. JM, II, 147–48; L, IV, 92–93; H, p. 589; L, IV, 410; H, pp. 579–80.
26. L, IV, 374; JM, II, 126, 149, 151; Donald Greene, *Johnsonian Studies*, M. Wahba, ed. (Cairo, 1962), pp. 61–92; H, p. 589; JM, II, 175.
27. L, IV, 400; H, p. 577.
28. JM, I, 447–48; H, p. 590–91; JM, II, 159.
29. JM, II, 160; L, IV, 553–54, 420–21.

Index

Aberdeen, J visits, 464–5
Abyssinia, see Lobo, Father Jerome
Accademia della Crusca, dictionary by, 247–8, 258
Adams, George, 412
Adams, Sarah, 588
Adams, William, on J's learning, 76; on J at Oxford, 89–90, 97, 103, 106–7; tries to get law degree for J, 232–3; on J's remark about *Dictionary*, 248; on J's idea of literary digest, 327; J's state of mind in 1760's, 372–3, 389; discusses faith with J, 450–1; J's last visit to, 594–5. Other refs., 99, 255, 411, 484, 565, 570, 587–8
Addenbrooke, John 147–8
Addison, Joseph, 22, 92, 241, 361; "Cranes and Pigmies," J's transl. of, 65, 68–70; *Tatler* and *Spectator*, 289, 294; J emulates style in *Idler*, 335
Adye, Mary, 16
Aesop, 25
Akenside, Mark, J on odes of, 535
Aldrich, Stephen, 353
Alexander, Earl, 473
Alexander the Great, and drink, 311
Alkon, Paul, 616
Allen, Edmund, 524; J writes him after stroke, 575
Alnwick Castle, 505–6
Amanuenses, for *Dictionary*, 243–5, 265–6
Anacreon, 76
Anne, Queen, 14–5, 224
Appleby Grammar School, 182
Arbuthnot, Charles, 92
Argyll, Duke and Duchess of, 473

Aristotle, 403, 481, 532, 534
Arkwright, Sir Richard, 213, 508
Arnold, Matthew, 536
Arne, Thomas, 429
Ashbourne, 37, 131, 184–5, 200, 319; later visits to, 435, 447, 476, 550, 561, 592, 594–5
Ashburton, Lord, 504
Ashmole, Elias, 22
Aston, Catherine, 166, 183
Aston, Elizabeth, J visits, 529, 561–2, 592–3
Aston, Magdalen, 155, 166, 183, 226
Aston, Molly, *183–4;* 150, 186, 200, 226, 476
Attwood, Dr. Thomas, 14, 87
Auchinleck, Alexander Boswell, Lord, 360; J visits, 474
Augustine, St., 455, 458
Augustus, J on court of, 328

Bacon, Sir Francis, and J's style, 292, 295; 340
Bailey, Nathan, dictionary by, 241, 249
Balderston, Katharine, on J's melancholy, 385–6; 607
Baltic, J wishes to visit, 516
Bankes, John, 357
Banks, Sir Joseph, 466, 504
Baratier, J.P., J's life of, 219
Barber, Betsey, 503
Barber, Francis, *325–7, 503–4;* A. Williams on expense of his schooling, 327; marriage, 503; 360, 408, 512, 583, 595, 596
Barber, Samuel, 504
Barclay, David and Robert, 555

629